Revolutionizing Financial Services and Markets Through FinTech and Blockchain

Kiran Mehta
Chitkara Business School, Chitkara University, India

Renuka Sharma
Chitkara Business School, Chitkara University, India

Poshan Yu
Soochow University, China & Australian Studies Centre, Shanghai University, China

IGI Global
PUBLISHER of TIMELY KNOWLEDGE

A volume in the Advances in Finance, Accounting, and Economics (AFAE) Book Series

Published in the United States of America by
IGI Global
Business Science Reference (an imprint of IGI Global)
701 E. Chocolate Avenue
Hershey PA, USA 17033
Tel: 717-533-8845
Fax: 717-533-8661
E-mail: cust@igi-global.com
Web site: http://www.igi-global.com

Library of Congress Cataloging-in-Publication Data

Names: Mehta, Kiran, 1980- editor. | Sharma, Renuka, 1980- editor. | Yu, Poshan, editor.
Title: Revolutionizing financial services and markets through fintech and blockchain / Kiran Mehta, Renuka Sharma, Poshan Yu.
Description: Hershey, PA : Business Science Reference, [2023] | Includes bibliographical references and index. | Summary: "The use of information and communication technology (ICT) in the business processes and operations of the financial services industry has undergone significant transformations during the last decade. Because of the growing number of customers who use mobile phones, laptops and the internet, the financial industry has begun to provide services based on ICT. Consequently, all types of financial services, such as stock trading and banking, are now accessible electronically or digitally over the internet. Most financial organisations have realised the importance of an IT department and identified cost-saving and efficiency-boosting solutions. Furthermore, improved financial services have enhanced client satisfaction and demand. Since the concept of blockchain was first conceived, the financial sector has been widely regarded as its primary use case. After Bitcoin's base notion in 2009, the idea became widely known. Because of its unique qualities, blockchain technology has the potential to benefit the financial sector greatly. Major stock exchanges are studying blockchain for its capacity to provide nearinstant settlements and automate compliance via smart contracts while providing improved security and transparency. Therefore, the current project's prime objective is to describe the application of blockchain technology to financial services and financial markets"-- Provided by publisher.
Identifiers: LCCN 2023010059 (print) | LCCN 2023010060 (ebook) | ISBN 9781668486245 (hardcover) | ISBN 9781668486252 (paperback) | ISBN 9781668486269 (ebook)
Subjects: LCSH: Financial services industry--Technological innovations. | Banks and banking--Automation. | Banks and banking--Technological innovations.
Classification: LCC HG1709 .R486 2023 (print) | LCC HG1709 (ebook) | DDC 332.1068--dc23/eng/20230322
LC record available at https://lccn.loc.gov/2023010059
LC ebook record available at https://lccn.loc.gov/2023010060

This book is published in the IGI Global book series Advances in Finance, Accounting, and Economics (AFAE) (ISSN: 2327-5677; eISSN: 2327-5685)

British Cataloguing in Publication Data
A Cataloguing in Publication record for this book is available from the British Library.

Advances in Finance, Accounting, and Economics (AFAE) Book Series

Ahmed Driouchi
Al Akhawayn University, Morocco

ISSN:2327-5677
EISSN:2327-5685

Mission

In our changing economic and business environment, it is important to consider the financial changes occurring internationally as well as within individual organizations and business environments. Understanding these changes as well as the factors that influence them is crucial in preparing for our financial future and ensuring economic sustainability and growth.

The **Advances in Finance, Accounting, and Economics (AFAE)** book series aims to publish comprehensive and informative titles in all areas of economics and economic theory, finance, and accounting to assist in advancing the available knowledge and providing for further research development in these dynamic fields.

Coverage

- Microeconomics
- Macroeconomics
- Interest Rates and Annuities
- Finance and Accounting in SMEs
- Banking
- Field Research
- Economics of Migration and Spatial Mobility
- Applied Accounting
- Microfinance
- Development Economics

IGI Global is currently accepting manuscripts for publication within this series. To submit a proposal for a volume in this series, please contact our Acquisition Editors at Acquisitions@igi-global.com or visit: http://www.igi-global.com/publish/.

The Advances in Finance, Accounting, and Economics (AFAE) Book Series (ISSN 2327-5677) is published by IGI Global, 701 E. Chocolate Avenue, Hershey, PA 17033-1240, USA, www.igi-global.com. This series is composed of titles available for purchase individually; each title is edited to be contextually exclusive from any other title within the series. For pricing and ordering information please visit http://www.igi-global.com/book-series/advances-finance-accounting-economics/73685. Postmaster: Send all address changes to above address.

Titles in this Series

For a list of additional titles in this series, please visit: http://www.igi-global.com/book-series/advances-finance-accounting-economics/73685

The Past, Present, and Future of Accountancy Education and Professions
Nina T. Dorata (St. John's University, USA) Richard C. Jones (Hofstra University, USA) Jennifer Mensche (St. Joseph's University, USA) and Mark M. Ulrich (CUNY Queensborough Community College, USA)
Business Science Reference • © 2023 • 240pp • H/C (ISBN: 9781668454831) • US $215.00

Changing World Economic Order in the Post-Pandemic Period
Sushanta Kumar Mahapatra (The ICFAI Foundation for Higher Education (IFHE) (Deemed), Hyderabad, India) and Vishal Sarin (Lovely Professional University, India)
Business Science Reference • © 2023 • 305pp • H/C (ISBN: 9781799868965) • US $260.00

Principles of Financial Control in the Public Sector
Plamena Georgieva Nedyalkova (University of Economics, Bulgaria)
Information Science Reference • © 2023 • 190pp • H/C (ISBN: 9781668488836) • US $185.00

Accounting and Financial Reporting Challenges for Government, Non-Profits, and the Private Sector
Fábio Albuquerque (Instituto Politécnico de Lisboa, Portugal) and Paula Gomes dos Santos (Instituto Politécnico de Lisboa, Portugal)
Business Science Reference • © 2023 • 322pp • H/C (ISBN: 9781668472934) • US $240.00

Perspectives on Blockchain Technology and Responsible Investing
Sonal Trivedi (Chitkara Business School, Chitkara University, India) Rashmi Aggarwal (Chitkara Business School, Chitkara University, India) and Gurmeet Singh (The University of the South Pacific, Fiji)
Business Science Reference • © 2023 • 317pp • H/C (ISBN: 9781668483619) • US $250.00

Mainstreaming Cryptocurrency and the Future of Digital Finance
Hamed Taherdoost (University Canada West, Canada)
Business Science Reference • © 2023 • 330pp • H/C (ISBN: 9781668483688) • US $250.00

Handbook of Research on Designing Sustainable Supply Chains to Achieve a Circular Economy
Yanamandra Ramakrishna (Skyline University College, UAE) and Siti Norida Wahab (Universiti Teknologi MARA, Malaysia)
Business Science Reference • © 2023 • 697pp • H/C (ISBN: 9781668476642) • US $295.00

IGI Global
PUBLISHER of TIMELY KNOWLEDGE

701 East Chocolate Avenue, Hershey, PA 17033, USA
Tel: 717-533-8845 x100 • Fax: 717-533-8661
E-Mail: cust@igi-global.com • www.igi-global.com

EDITORIAL ADVISORY BOARD

Table of Contents

Detailed Table of Contents

Financial institutions' digital advancements are vital for sustainability, with blockchain having transformative potential. Banking pursues digital transformation due to fintech competition and cybersecurity worries, driven by technology advancements and customer expectations. FinTech start-ups prompt innovation from big banks. Industry 4.0 integrates blockchain, AI, and technology platforms that align with SDG8 and SDG9, promoting transparency, cost reduction, and company expansion. Therefore, the present research seeks to answer: What drives banks to adopt blockchain technology? It aims to identify factors influencing bankers' intention to adopt blockchain for digital transformation in Indian banks. A standardized scale with the addition of two more constructs (sustainability agenda and psychological framework) was used to achieve the objective of the study. The findings of the research enhance understanding of banks' technology usage and blockchain adoption. Findings validate nine factors influencing bankers' blockchain adoption.

Several of the inefficiencies and risks that afflict traditional stock market infrastructure have been addressed by blockchain technology. Blockchain, due to its decentralized and transparent nature, can provide a safe and efficient platform for investors and issuers to exchange assets without the need for middlemen. This chapter investigates the influence of blockchain technology on the stock market, examining the possible benefits and hazards connected with its implementation. The authors contend that blockchain has the potential to transform the stock market by lowering transaction costs, increasing liquidity, and improving transparency. Nevertheless, there are problems and hazards connected with integrating blockchain technology into the stock market, including regulatory and legal hurdles, interoperability concerns, and the possibility of market disruption. As blockchain technology evolves, market players must carefully assess the consequences of its adoption and work together toward its ethical and sustainable integration.

a trade-off might arise among policy objectives if the eNaira cannot achieve multiple policy objectives at the same time.

Technological innovation in the financial sector has brought significant development in the list of baskets of financial products available and convenience in delivery of financial services. This is reflected in terms of payment services, lending activities, management of assets, third party administrators, etc., among others that form the new business models and strategic management in financial sectors. FinTech or digital innovations in the financial sector has emerged as one of the qualitative changes in the financial markets across the globe with its associated potential specifically with regard to efficiency and performance of financial institutions. However, the financial innovations and its services are no exception to different form of risks for the customers in particular and to financial institutions at large. In this connection, this chapter attempts to give a critical review of the risks and uncertainties that may arise in the access and uses of FinTech-based platform in delivering digital financial products across the globe.

This chapter explores the barriers and potential of blockchain technology in the FinTech sector. It begins by highlighting the fundamental characteristics of blockchains, emphasizing their ability to securely store and transfer data without the involvement of intermediaries. The transparency provided by blockchain's transaction visibility is contrasted with traditional banking systems. The decentralized nature of blockchain is discussed, along with its applicability in various industries such as cryptocurrencies, financial services, risk management, IoT, and public and social services. The chapter acknowledges the extensive research conducted to analyze blockchain technology and its applications, leading to a need for a comprehensive examination. It addresses blockchain taxonomy, consensus techniques, applications, technological challenges, and recent developments, offering insights into the future possibilities of this technology. By identifying both the barriers and potential, this chapter aims to contribute to the understanding of blockchain technology's role in the FinTech industry.

With the aid of fintech, this study seeks to undertake a systematic review of peer-to-peer lending literature. In this chapter, the authors learn how fintech has aided peer-to-peer lending and how it has facilitated the provision of services like simple credit, the recording of borrower information, etc. Additionally, they examine the development of fintech, and the findings of this study demonstrate that COVID-19 has significantly altered the primary determinants of P2P lending. According to the findings, P2P fintech financing is now the most practical alternative credit option available to borrowers. Because they highlight the value of P2P lending platforms, their potential advantages, and the causes of defaults that do occur, the findings are significant and are likely to be of interest to investors, practitioners, academics, and legislators. The authors also learn about the evolution of the traditional lending system.

With the unprecedented growth of technological development and digitalization across the globe, cryptocurrency has emerged to attract investors. It all started in the year 2013 when there were large fluctuations in the financial market. The novelty of this emerging asset class has led researchers to devise anomalous trade patterns and behavioral fallacies in the crypto market. This chapter will help researchers, academicians, and investors in understanding the importance of cognitive and emotional biases in the cryptocurrency market concerning investment decision-making. Moreover, the reader will be able to gain an understanding of the existing market and the challenges of cryptocurrency and financial technologies.

Literature reviews are used by practitioners and researchers to combine numerous bodies of knowledge. There are various SotA papers on blockchain applications. The authors looked at 100 articles about the use of blockchain in financial services that were published between 2013 and 2023. The data sources used for the same are Science Direct and Google Scholar. The three phases for conducting SotA reviews are provided in this chapter. In the 100 articles looked at for SotA in title, 69 were tagged as SotA reviews, and the rest were either tagged as 'literature review' or 'systematic literature review'. The summary of 69 articles is presented in the literature review section of the study. An interpretive synthesis of SotA reviews in the current study describes where we are presently in the field of application of blockchain in finance. The chapter also presents the changes brought by application of blockchain in the value chain of the banking sector and future scope of study in the field.

Modern technology is influencing our daily lives, from using a remote to control equipment to utilizing voice notes to give orders. Because of its properties of decentralization, enforceability, and sharing, blockchain technology is frequently used in banking, digital asset trade, and other sectors. Blockchain has emerged as a popular issue in fintech research, influencing the evolution of traditional financial forms. It is regarded as the foundation of the digital economy. Blockchain technology may be defined as a data structure that keeps transactional records and, by ensuring security, transparency, and decentralization, eliminates the possibility of fraudulent behaviour or transaction repetition without the use of a third party. This study examines the characteristics and challenges of blockchain technology, the impact of blockchain technology on the operation and administration of the banking and financial sector and the possibilities for blockchain technology implementation in banking and financial sector in India.

Kumar Shalender, Chitkara University, India
Babita Singla, Chitkara University, India
Sandhir Sharma, Chitkara University, India

Blockchain technology can be easily considered one of the most revolutionary innovations of our times. The open ledger has proved enormously beneficial for the financial sector, and thanks to its characteristics like decentralized structure, high safety, and immutable traceability, its adoption has witnessed unprecedented growth in the financial sector. That said, there are many challenges that blockchain adoption in the financial domain faces, and this research takes a close look at all these issues that can potentially hamper its adoption in the sector. The research found that primary inhibitors in the growth of blockchain include cost factors, lack of regulations, rigid work culture, and inadequate infrastructure and offer solutions to tackle these issues. Further, the study also develops a conceptual model involving important stakeholders and interaction variables between them to facilitate the adoption of an open ledger in the sector.

Gurpreet Kaur, Chitkara Business School, Chitkara University, India

Blockchain is one of the revolutionary tools that has proven to be effective in resolving various problems in the banking industry. Blockchain technology has diversified applications over varied sectors as it facilitates the systematic recording of transactions in an effective, cheap, and safe manner. Blockchain technology offers various services to the banking industry which have improved the scalability and security of the banks. Thus in order to captivate the interest of researchers, academicians and bankers, the chapter presents a comprehensive review of the impact of blockchain on the banking industry. Moreover there is an urgent need to conduct extensive research into several aspects of banking with blockchain so as to overcome hindrances in the adoption of blockchain. The study provides a holistic framework highlighting the present status and future prospects of the adoption of blockchain technology in banks. Further, it describes how the adoption of blockchain can make the banking industry more secure and facilitate faster transaction recording.

Preface

In the modern era, the financial services industry has been undergoing a significant transformation fueled by technological advancements. The emergence of Financial Technology, or FinTech, and the revolutionary potential of blockchain technology have revolutionized the way financial services are delivered and conducted. From traditional banking to investment management, payment systems to insurance, these disruptive technologies have the power to reshape the entire financial landscape. The current project explores the transformative impact of FinTech and blockchain on financial services and markets, highlighting the key innovations, benefits, and challenges associated with these technologies. FinTech, a term coined by combining "financial" and "technology," refers to the use of cutting-edge digital technologies to enhance and streamline financial services. It encompasses a wide range of innovations, including mobile banking applications, digital payment platforms, robo-advisors, crowdfunding platforms, and peer-to-peer lending platforms. FinTech companies leverage technology to improve efficiency, accessibility, and customer experience, challenging the traditional banking and financial services model dominated by established institutions.

One of the most disruptive technologies in the FinTech space is blockchain. Originally developed as the underlying technology for the digital currency Bitcoin, blockchain has far-reaching applications beyond cryptocurrencies. At its core, blockchain is a decentralized and immutable ledger that securely records and verifies transactions across multiple participants. Its distributed nature eliminates the need for intermediaries, reduces transaction costs, enhances transparency, and strengthens security. Blockchain has the potential to revolutionize various sectors of the financial industry, including payment systems, trade finance, identity verification, and smart contracts. The impact of FinTech and blockchain on financial services and markets has been substantial. One of the key benefits is the increased accessibility to financial services for underserved populations. With the proliferation of mobile devices and internet connectivity, FinTech solutions have enabled individuals in remote areas to access banking services, make payments, and manage their finances through mobile applications. This inclusivity promotes financial empowerment and drives economic growth. Moreover, FinTech has revolutionized the payments industry, simplifying transactions and reducing reliance on traditional banking systems. The convenience, speed, and cost-effectiveness of these solutions have disrupted the traditional payment infrastructure, challenging the dominance of traditional banks and opening doors for new entrants in the financial market.

In investment management, FinTech has introduced robo-advisors, which provide algorithm-based automated investment advice. These platforms use machine learning and artificial intelligence to analyze financial data, create personalized investment portfolios, and offer low-cost investment options. Robo-advisors democratize access to investment services, making it more affordable for individuals with limited capital. They also provide greater transparency and reduce human bias, potentially delivering higher returns to investors.

The integration of blockchain technology in financial services has brought transparency, efficiency, and security to various areas. Blockchain-based smart contracts have the potential to automate and streamline complex contractual agreements, reducing paperwork and minimizing the risk of fraud. Trade finance, which traditionally involves a complex web of documentation and intermediaries, can benefit from blockchain's ability to provide secure and tamper-proof records of transactions, reducing costs and enhancing efficiency.

Despite the numerous benefits, the implementation of FinTech and blockchain also presents challenges and risks. One of the primary concerns is cybersecurity. With increased reliance on digital systems and the potential for large-scale data breaches, protecting sensitive financial information becomes paramount. Financial institutions and FinTech companies are investing in robust security measures to safeguard customer data and maintain trust in the digital ecosystem.

Furthermore, regulatory frameworks and compliance requirements need to adapt to the rapidly evolving FinTech and blockchain landscape. Regulators face the challenge of balancing innovation and consumer protection, ensuring that these technologies are used responsibly and in line with legal and ethical standards. Collaborative efforts between regulatory bodies, industry players, and technology providers are crucial to establish appropriate regulatory frameworks that foster innovation while mitigating risks.

In conclusion, the rise of FinTech and blockchain technologies has ushered in a new era in the financial services industry. From providing inclusive financial services to transforming payment systems, investment management, and identity verification, these technologies offer immense potential for efficiency, transparency, and security. However, their widespread adoption requires addressing challenges such as cybersecurity and regulatory compliance. As FinTech and blockchain continue to evolve, financial institutions, policymakers, and technology providers must collaborate to navigate this dynamic landscape and leverage the transformative power of technology to revolutionize financial services and markets.

This book aims to comprehensively explore the transformative impact of FinTech and blockchain on the financial landscape. It delves into the key innovations, challenges, and opportunities that these technologies bring to the table, offering readers a deeper understanding of their potential to reshape how we access and interact with financial services. The chapters of this book are meticulously crafted to guide you through various aspects of the FinTech and blockchain revolution. We begin by introducing the concept of FinTech and its diverse applications across different financial industry sectors. From mobile banking applications to peer-to-peer lending platforms, we delve into how FinTech democratises financial services, making them more accessible, efficient, and customer-centric.

The eRupee or digital currency issued by the Reserve Bank of India is the subject of Chapter 1 titled "Central Bank Digital Currency in India: The Case for a Digital Rupee," which examines its advantages and disadvantages. People in India who searched for 'cryptocurrency' were also interested in 'central bank digital currency,' according to the report. The research also revealed that there might be advantages to implementing CBDC, such as less reliance on cash, more seigniorage owing to decreased transaction costs, and lower settlement risk.

Chapter 2 titled "Mobile Payments in the FinTech Era: Disrupting the Banking System Through Blockchain Applications" investigates blockchain's influence on the fintech age and how it is altering the financial industry. The paper goes into the benefits of adopting blockchain for mobile payments, such as greater security, transparency, and efficiency. It also looks at the constraints and limits of blockchain technology in mobile payments, such as regulatory issues and scalability concerns.

Chapter 3 titled "Extending UTAUT2 Model With Sustainability and Psychological Factors in Adoption of Blockchain Technology for Digital Transformation of Banks in India" sets out to solve is what motivates financial institutions to use blockchain. The study's goal is to determine what characteristics lead Indian lenders to consider using blockchain technology as part of their digital transformation initiatives. The researchers accomplished their goal by adapting a conventional scale to include two additional components (sustainable agenda and psychological framework). The results of this study provide new light on the ways in which banks use and adapt new technologies, such as blockchain.

Chapter 4 titled "Impact of Blockchain Technology in Stock Market" examines the impact of blockchain technology on the stock market, exploring the potential advantages and risks associated with its deployment. The study believes that blockchain has the potential to revolutionize the stock market by cutting transaction costs, enhancing liquidity, and increasing transparency. Nonetheless, there are issues and risks associated with incorporating blockchain technology into the stock market, such as regulatory and legal challenges, interoperability difficulties, and the risk of market disruption.

In recent years, academics and investors have paid close attention to digital currencies, also known as cybercash, digital money, and electronic money. Cryptocurrency arose as a consequence of advances in financial technology, presenting a unique opportunity for study in the sector. However, projecting cryptocurrency values is difficult owing to their dynamic and unpredictable character. The purpose of Chapter 5 titled "Predicting Cryptocurrency Prices Model Using a Stacked Sparse Autoencoder and Bayesian Optimization" is to overcome this issue by developing a novel prediction model called Bayesian Optimization with Stacked Sparse Autoencoder based Cryptocurrency Price Prediction (BOSSAE-CPP). The primary goal of this model is to accurately anticipate cryptocurrency values.

Chapter 6 titled "Digitalization of Financial Sector New Opportunities and Challenges During the COVID-19 Crisis" highlighted the emergence and growth of digital finance in the context of technology and finance integration, emphasizing the opportunities it presents as well as the need for regulatory measures. This research also underscores the opportunities and facilities created by intelligent digital finance, while acknowledging the challenges and risks associated with the digitalization process.

Chapter 7 titled "Blockchain Technology Adoption in Financial Services: Opportunities and Challenges" provides a thorough framework for examining the relationship between "Industry 4.0" and blockchain technology, as well as its potential and adoption problems in the financial services sector. The chapter is divided into three main sections: i) The Fourth Industrial Revolution and Blockchain, ii) the impact of technology on the financial industry and related services. iii) Future challenges and difficulties with technology.

Chapter 8 titled "The Green Revolution of Smart Contracts: How Innovative Architecture Is Driving Performance, Pollution Reduction, and Energy Conservation" analyzes the problems that might arise while using smart contracts. The study suggests a method that may solve all the existing problems with smart contracts. The research also suggests a different design for blockchain and smart contracts. The author recognizes the issues, analyzes them, and proposes a solution that improves the efficiency and scalability of smart contracts while also fostering a more sustainable society via less pollution and increased energy efficiency.

Sustainable finance, a cutting-edge growth trend in the financial sector, has gained global significance due to its relevance in addressing climate change and its environmental impacts while supporting adaptation. Chapter 9 titled "A Bibliometric Analysis of Green Finance: Present State and Future Directions" conducts a comprehensive review of existing knowledge on green finance, utilizing bibliometric methods.

The study also employs visual depictions and network analysis. By consolidating research in this field, the study contributes to a deeper understanding of green finance and its implications for sustainable finance.

Chapter 10 titled "Using eNaira CBDC to Solve Economic Problems in Nigeria" explains how the eNaira central bank digital currency (CBDC) may address various Nigerian economic issues. The eNaira is a payment alternative, monetary policy instrument, and financial stability tool for Nigeria's economic issues. The study demonstrates that the eNaira can help solve fiscal revenue issues, inflation, foreign exchange accretion, exchange rate management, food insecurity, financial stability hazards, poverty, and recession recovery.

Digital financial innovations have emerged as one of the qualitative shifts in global financial markets, with associated potential in terms of efficiency and performance of financial institutions. However, financial innovations and their services are not immune to many types of dangers for clients in particular and financial institutions in general. In this regard, the Chapter 11 titled "Innovations in Finance and the Future of Finance: A Critical Review" aims to provide a critical assessment of the risks and uncertainties that may occur in the access and usage of FinTech-based platforms in the delivery of digital financial goods throughout the world.

Chapter 12 titled "Barriers and Potential of Blockchain Technology in FinTech" highlights the fundamental characteristics of blockchains, including secure data storage and transfer without intermediaries. It discusses blockchain's decentralization and its applications in various industries. The paper recognizes extensive research on blockchain and the need for comprehensive examination. By identifying barriers and potential, this paper contributes to understanding blockchain's role in FinTech.

SotA papers on blockchain applications are many. Chapter 13 titled "Convention of Blockchain in Financial Services: A State-of-the-Art Literature Review" analyzed papers published between 2013-2023 that discussed the use of blockchain technology to the financial services industry. The study details the three stages involved in carrying out a SotA review and provides synopses of 69 separate pieces of research. Using an interpretative synthesis of SotA evaluations, the current research summarizes the current state of blockchain's financial applications. The study discusses the impact of blockchain technology and its potential future applications in the financial services industry's value chain.

The relevance of cognitive and emotional biases in the cryptocurrency market with regards to investing decision-making is discussed in Chapter 14 titled "Behavioral Finance and Cryptocurrency Market," which will be useful for researchers, academics, and investors. In addition, the reader will learn about the current market and the difficulties associated with bitcoin and financial innovations.

Chapter 15 titled "Evolution of the P2P Lending System in FinTech: A Systematic Review of Literature" examine the ways in which fintech has simplified the provision of P2P lending services such as easy credit and the recording of borrower data. The results of this research show that the COVID-19 has modified the most important factors in P2P lending. In light of these results, peer-to-peer (P2P) FinTech financing has emerged as borrowers' most viable alternative credit choice. Significant and certainly of interest to investors, practitioners, researchers, and lawmakers, the results illustrate the usefulness of P2P lending platforms, their potential benefits, and the reasons of defaults that do occur.

Chapter 16 titled "A Study on Application of Blockchain Technology in Banking and Financial Sector in India" examines what blockchain technology is, what it's not, how it may change the way banks and other financial institutions are run, and whether or not it's feasible to adopt blockchain technology in India's banking and financial industry.

Next Chapter 17 titled "Blockchain Adoption in Financial Sector: Challenges, Solutions, and Implementation Framework" delves deeply into the various obstacles that stand in the way of widespread use of blockchain technology in the banking industry. The study identifies financial considerations, a lack of rules, a restrictive work culture, and insufficient infrastructure as significant barriers to blockchain's expansion and proposes strategies to overcome them. The research goes further by creating a conceptual model for the adoption of an open ledger in the industry, which includes key players and their interaction factors.

Chapter 18 titled "Blockchain Technology: Perspective From Banking Sector" provides an in-depth examination of the influence of blockchain on the banking sector. The paper presents a comprehensive framework outlining the current state and future possibilities of blockchain technology adoption in banks. It also outlines how blockchain adoption may make the banking sector more secure and allow for speedier transaction recording.

Chapter 19 titled "Consumers' Preferences Towards Digital Payments While Online and Offline Shopping Post COVID-19" evaluates consumer preferences in the digital age for online payments when shopping at omni channel retail. The analysis in this study employed a demographic and descriptive research technique to explore client preferences toward digital payment. Furthermore, based on the themes stated, the researcher conducted a personally administered survey with the permission of the retail mall and store managers in terms of good or negative omni-channel attitudes application users.

Overall, the book *Revolutionizing Financial Services and Markets Through FinTech and Blockchain* provides an in-depth look at the revolutionary possibilities of FinTech and blockchain technology in the financial services industry. In this book, we explore the game-changing technologies that have revolutionized banking and investing to create a system that is more accessible, efficient, and safe for all participants. Our goal is to encourage readers to take advantage of the possibilities offered by FinTech and blockchain by discussing the most recent developments, problems, and practical applications. Our long-term objective is to have a positive impact on the global financial services industry and the lives of people, companies, and economies everywhere. As we set out on this adventure, let us imagine a world where innovation in technology takes the financial sector to uncharted heights of development and wealth.

Kiran Mehta
Chitkara Business School, Chitkara University, India

Renuka Sharma
Chitkara Business School, Chitkara University, India

Poshan Yu
Soochow University, China & Australian Studies Centre, Shanghai University, China

Acknowledgment

In this very moment, our hearts overflow with an overwhelming sense of pride and accomplishment, encapsulating the culmination of arduous endeavours. The triumph of this remarkable work stands as a testament to the collective collaboration that has been woven into its very fabric, and we find ourselves deeply indebted to the vast array of individuals who have graciously bestowed upon us their unwavering support, both on a professional and personal level.

It is with profound gratitude that we acknowledge the reviewers, whose incisive scrutiny of the chapters, detailed feedback, and adept improvisations have enriched the intellectual tapestry of this work. Their profound contributions have played an instrumental role in refining its substance, ensuring its resonance and scholarly merit.

The true strength and essence of this book derive from the tireless efforts of the researchers, subject experts, intellectuals, and practitioners who have poured their knowledge, expertise, and rich experiences into the tapestry of its chapters. It is through their contributions that this work has flourished, embracing a multidimensional tapestry of insights, expertise, and practical wisdom that will undoubtedly inspire and propel its readers.

We would like to extend our utmost appreciation to the esteemed members of the Editorial Board and the dedicated publishing staff at IGI Global. Their unwavering commitment, relentless work ethic, and unwavering focus on excellence have played a pivotal role in ensuring the success and impact of this publication. Their steadfast dedication, meticulous attention to detail, and fervent support have been indispensable in bringing this labour of love to fruition, enabling its dissemination to a global audience.

Amidst our expressions of gratitude, we humbly acknowledge the divine providence that has guided us throughout this intellectual odyssey. The benevolent presence of the almighty GOD has served as a constant source of inspiration, illuminating our paths and providing the strength and resilience necessary to overcome challenges along the way.

Last but certainly not least, we wish to convey our most profound appreciation to our beloved parents. Their unwavering love, guidance, and blessings have been a wellspring of steadfast support throughout our journey, empowering us to embark on this ambitious endeavour and traverse its intricate pathways with unwavering resolve.

In closing, we stand humbled and grateful, cherishing the collaborative spirit that has propelled this work to fruition. May its impact transcend boundaries, ignite intellectual curiosity, and contribute to the betterment of knowledge and society as a whole.

Chapter 1
Central Bank Digital Currency in India: The Case for a Digital Rupee

Peterson K. Ozili
Central Bank of Nigeria, Nigeria

ABSTRACT

This chapter explores the benefits and issues surrounding the digital Rupee, also known as the eRupee or the central bank digital currency in India. The study found that Indian people who were interested in 'cryptocurrency' information were also interested in 'central bank digital currency' information. The study also showed that the introduction of CBDC has potential benefits such as reduced dependency on cash, higher seigniorage due to lower transaction costs, and reduced settlement risk. However, the India CBDC has associated risks that need to be carefully evaluated against the potential benefits. The introduction of a digital Rupee or CBDC in India will require legal and regulatory changes to make the phased CBDC implementation possible.

INTRODUCTION

The objective of this study is to explore the benefits and issues surrounding the digital Rupee, also known as the eRupee or the central bank digital currency in India.

A central bank digital currency (CBDC) is money in digital form and a legal tender issued by a central bank. A CBDC is the same as fiat currency and can be exchanged at a rate of one-to-one with the fiat paper currency or cash (Bordo, 2021; Chaum, Grothoff and Moser, 2021). The only difference is that a CBDC is money in digital form (Inozemtsev and Nektov, 2022; Kahn, Singh and Alwazir, 2022). Most CBDCs can be held in an account-based wallet or token-based wallet (Xu, 2022).

In August 2022, the Reserve Bank of India (RBI) announced that a digital rupee — a central bank digital currency — will be introduced in phases beginning with wholesale businesses in the 2022 to 2023 financial year. The India CBDC is being developed for both retail and wholesale use simultaneously. However, the Reserve Bank of India may roll out the digital currency for wholesale businesses

DOI: 10.4018/978-1-6684-8624-5.ch001

first. There are four main motivations for issuing a CBDC in India, namely, (i) the Reserve Bank of India (RBI)'s desire to join other central banks that have issued a CBDC, (ii) the significant growth in digital transactions in India, (iii) the threat posed by private digital currencies, and (iii) the presence of a well-functioning and developed payment system in India.

Prior to the announcement of a phased CBDC implementation in India, the Reserve Bank of India had repeatedly opposed private digital currencies. It is widely believed that the emergence of private digital currencies, especially bitcoin, inspired the Reserve Bank of India to begin plans to launch a CBDC digital Rupee. The Reserve Bank of India also proposed amendments to the Reserve Bank of India Act of 1934 which would enable it to launch a digital rupee CBDC. The government also plans to prohibit all private digital currencies in India with certain exceptions. The RBI's argument for prohibiting private digital currencies is that private digital currencies encourage money laundering, terror financing and tax evasion. The Reserve Bank of India also noted that the number of Unified Payments Interface (UPI) transactions in India grew by 427 percent from March 2020 to August 2022 while the number of UPI QR code enabled payment acceptance points increased by 86 percent year-on-year at end of July 2022. The Reserve Bank of India suggests that these developments in the digital payment space reflect the growing acceptance and preference for digital contactless payments in India and indicates that India is ready to embrace a central bank digital currency. This development also inspired the Reserve Bank of India to initiate a phased CBDC implementation strategy. The Reserve Bank of India will also examine the appropriate use case of the India CBDC and issue a CBDC that is non-disruptive.

Meanwhile, in the literature, many studies focus on the best use case of CBDC such as Fegatelli (2022), Michel (2022), Agur et al (2022), Zhang and Huang (2022), Davoodalhosseini (2022), Minesso et al (2022), Auer et al (2022) and Chen and Siklos (2022). Only few studies focus on country specific CBDC such as Xu (2022) and Ozili (2022b). But no study has examined the case of India.

The discussion about the India CBDC contributes to the growing academic and policy literature on central bank digital currency. Existing studies have examined CBDC design issues such as account-based CBDC versus token-based CBDC, one-tiered CBDC or two-tiered CBDC, distributed ledger CBDC or centralized CBDC (e.g., Agur, Ari and Dell'Ariccia, 2022; Ozili, 2023; Kolozsi, Lehmann and Szalai, 2022; Frankó, Oláh, Sass, Hegedüs and Varga, 2022; Dinh and Dinh, 2022). Some studies have also examined the implications of CBDC for the financial stability and monetary policy objectives of the central bank (e.g., Bhowmik, 2022; Cova, Notarpietro, Pagano and Pisani, 2022; Davoodalhosseini, 2022; Kim and Kwon, 2019; Vallet, Kappes and Rochon, 2022; Wang and Hausken, 2022; Hamza and Jedidia, 2020). Other studies have examined how CBDC can improve financial inclusion for unbanked segments of the population (e.g., Ozili, 2022a). Existing studies have also examined country specific CBDC use cases in the US, Canada, China and Nigeria (e.g., García, Lands, Liu and Slive, 2020; Ricks, Crawford and Menand, 2020; Ozili, 2022b; Vodrážka, Bízek and Vojta, 2022; Coulter, 2022; Liu, Wang, Wu and Zhang, 2022; Slawotsky, 2022; Huang, 2022). But such studies do not exist for India. There is a need to explore the India CBDC, its benefits and issues. This study also contributes to the Indian CBDC literature. This paper focus on the Indian context. It provides early insight into the possible design, benefits and issues of the India CBDC.

The rest of the paper is structured as follows. Section 2 presents the literature review. Section 3 presents the data analysis. Section 4 presents the benefits of the India CBDC. Section 5 presents the possible operational CBDC design. Section 6 highlights some considerations for India. Section 7 highlights the risks to watch out for. Section 8 presents the conclusion.

LITERATURE REVIEW

Hayashi and Toh (2022) showed that although central banks in several emerging markets and developing economies have implemented or plan to implement a general-purpose or retail CBDC to promote financial inclusion and improve their payment systems, central banks in many advanced economies have not yet found a compelling case to issue a retail CBDC. Ozili (2023), reviewed the CBDC literature, and found that many central banks are researching the potential to issue a CBDC due to its many benefits but some studies have called for caution against over-optimism about the potential benefits of CBDC due to the limiting nature of CBDC design and its inability to meet multiple competing goals. Bolt et al (2022) argued that public and private money need to coexist, and there should be effective regulation of private digital money such as cryptocurrency and stablecoins.

Some studies examine country specific CBDC issuance and adoption. Adalid et al (2022) considered the case of a digital euro CBDC. They conducted some analytical exercises about the consequence of a digital euro CBDC on bank intermediation in the euro area. They find that the effect of a digital euro CBDC on bank intermediation will vary across credit institutions in normal times, and the effect would be potentially larger in stressed times. They also find that the digital euro's capacity to alter system-wide bank run dynamics depends on the CBDC remuneration and CBDC usage limits. Ozili (2022b) showed that Nigeria launched the eNaira CBDC. The proposed benefits of the Nigeria CBDC include efficient payments and increased financial inclusion while the risks include digital illiteracy, increased propensity for cyber-attacks, data theft and the changing role of banks in a full-fledged CBDC economy. Xu (2022) examined the case of China CBDC. The author showed that Internet and technology companies may join commercial banks in distributing the China CBDC. The author also showed that the China CBDC will help improve domestic financial monitoring and policy implementation. Also, the China CBDC will play a role in the RMB's internationalization or even the international monetary system's evolution. Fegatelli (2022) examined the conditions under which a digital euro could be introduced on a large scale without leading to bank disintermediation or a credit crunch. The author argued that the central bank would require proper mechanisms to manage the volume and the user cost of CBDC in circulation. The central bank should continue to facilitate access to its long-term lending facilities, to provide banks with a funding source alternative to client deposits at an equivalent cost. The author also argued that a digital euro could improve bank profitability and competitiveness by absorbing large amounts of idle (and expensive) excess reserves without penalizing lending while incentivizing bank digitalization. Awang Abu Bakar et al (2023) examined the case of Malaysia and show that Malaysia's Central Bank has no intention to issue a CBDC for Malaysia; however, Malaysia's Central Bank continues to study the CBDC potential especially in the digital assets and payments space. Michel (2022) examined the issuance of a digital dollar CBDC in the United States. Michel (2022) argued that while Americans have long held money predominantly in digital form, a CBDC would differ from existing digital money available to the general public because a CBDC would be a liability of the Federal Reserve, not of a commercial bank. This feature is central to why Congress should make sure that the Federal Reserve never issues a retail CBDC. The problem is that the federal government, not privately owned commercial banks, would be responsible for issuing deposits. This would be a major problem for the free society as it will give government too much control over people's money.

Regarding the design of a CBDC, Agur et al (2022) analyzed the optimal design of a CBDC in an environment where agents sort into cash, CBDC, and bank deposits according to their preferences over anonymity and security. They showed that a CBDC can be designed with attributes similar to cash or deposits and can be interest-bearing. They argued that the optimal CBDC design is one that trades off bank intermediation against the social value of maintaining diverse payment instruments. Zhang and Huang (2022) analyzed both the functional and non-functional requirements of CBDC design. They find that permissioned blockchain is more suitable for CBDC than permissionless blockchain. They also show that there are some challenges in blockchain-based CBDC, such as performance, scalability and cross-chain interoperability.

Regarding the challenge and consequence of CBDC, Davoodalhosseini (2022) studied the optimal monetary policy when only cash, only CBDC or both cash and CBDC are available to agents in Canada. The author showed that if the cost of using CBDC is not too high, more efficient allocations can be implemented by using CBDC than with cash. Also, having both cash and CBDC available may result in lower welfare than in cases where only cash or only CBDC is available in Canada. Minesso et al (2022) examined the open-economy implications of the introduction of a central bank digital currency. They show that the presence of a CBDC amplifies the international spillovers of shocks to a significant extent, thereby increasing international linkages; but the magnitude of these effects depends crucially on CBDC design and can be significantly dampened if the CBDC possesses specific technical features. Auer et al (2022) showed that CBDCs should be considered in the full context of the digital economy and the centrality of data, however, CBDCs could raise concerns around competition, payment system integrity and privacy. Chen and Siklos (2022) explored the hypothetical impact of CBDC on inflation and financial stability, and showed that CBDC may not lead to high inflation but it could increase financial instability risks. Ozili (2022c) showed that the emergence of CBDC presents many implications for cryptocurrency. It might lead to calls to regulate cryptocurrency and may lead to the acceptance of stablecoins even though the benefits of stablecoins do not outweigh the benefits of issuing a CBDC. Nevertheless, the general benefits of CBDC for society appear to outweigh the risks, thereby, making CBDC more attractive than cryptocurrency. Whited et al (2022) examined how introducing a central bank digital currency can affect the banking system. They showed that CBDC may not reduce bank lending unless frictions and synergies bind deposits and lending together. They showed that a CBDC can replace a significant fraction of bank deposits especially when it pays interest. They also showed that CBDC has a much smaller impact on bank lending because banks can replace a large fraction of any lost deposits with wholesale funding. Keister and Monnet (2022) showed that banks will do less maturity transformation when depositors have access to CBDC, which leaves them less exposed to runs. They also showed that monitoring the flow of funds into CBDC allows policymakers to identify and resolve weak banks sooner, which also decreases depositors' incentive to initiate a run on banks. They conclude that a well-designed CBDC may decrease financial fragility.

DATA ANALYSIS

Methodology

Internet search data for India were collected from Google Trends database. Data were collected from January 2022 to September 2022. The data were collected for three variables: (i) the 'cryptocurrency' search term, (ii) the 'CBDC' search term and (iii) the 'central bank digital currency' search term. The last two variables are similar. Data were collected for the last two variables to take into account the fact that internet users in India may use the term 'CBDC' and 'central bank digital currency' interchangeably when searching for internet information about central bank digital currency.

Correlation Between Interest in 'CBDC' and 'Cryptocurrency' as Search Terms on the Internet

This section analyses the correlation between local interest in internet information about 'cryptocurrency' as a search term on the internet and local interest in internet information about 'CBDC' as a search term on the internet. The Pearson correlation analysis reports a 0.59 correlation between local interest in internet information about 'cryptocurrency' and 'CBDC'. The correlation is positive and significant at the 1 percent level. This indicates that there is a significant positive correlation between interest in internet search for information about 'cryptocurrency' and 'CBDC' in India. This implies that Indian people who were interested in 'cryptocurrency' information were also interested in 'CBDC' information.

Correlation Between Interest in 'Cryptocurrency' and 'Central Bank Digital Currency' as Search Terms on the Internet

This section analyses the correlation between local interest in internet information about 'cryptocurrency' as a search term on the internet and local interest in internet information about 'central bank digital currency' as a search term on the internet. The Pearson correlation analysis reports a 0.38 correlation between local interest in internet information about 'cryptocurrency' and 'central bank digital currency'. The correlation is low, positive and significant at the 1 percent level. This indicates that there is a significant positive correlation between interest in internet search for information about 'cryptocurrency' and 'central bank digital currency' in India. This implies that Indian people who were interested in 'cryptocurrency' information were also interested in 'central bank digital currency' information.

Table 1. Correlation analysis for India

Search Term on the Internet	Cryptocurrency	CBDC	Central Bank Digital Currency
Cryptocurrency	1.000		

CBDC	0.592***	1.000	
	(0.00)	-----	
Central bank digital currency	0.386***	0.318***	1.000
	(0.00)	(0.00)	-----
P-value is reported in parenthesis. *** represents statistical significance at the 1% level.			

Source: Google Trends and author's computation

Regional Interest in 'Central Bank Digital Currency' as a Search Term by Internet Users in India

Figure 1 shows the regional distribution of interest in internet information about 'central bank digital currency' in India. Figure 1 is derived from the Google Trends data obtained from Section 2.1. Figure 1 shows that interest in internet information about 'central bank digital currency' was very high in Delhi followed by Karnataka, Kerala, Uttar Pradesh, Tamil Nadu and Maharashtra. Interest in online information about 'central bank digital currency' exceeded the 50-point mark in each of these regions in India. In contrast, interest in internet information about 'central bank digital currency' was much lower in West Bengal, Telangana and Gujarat. Interest in online information about 'central bank digital currency' was below the 50-point mark in each of the three regions in India.

Figure 1. Local interest in internet information about 'central bank digital currency'
Source: Google Trends

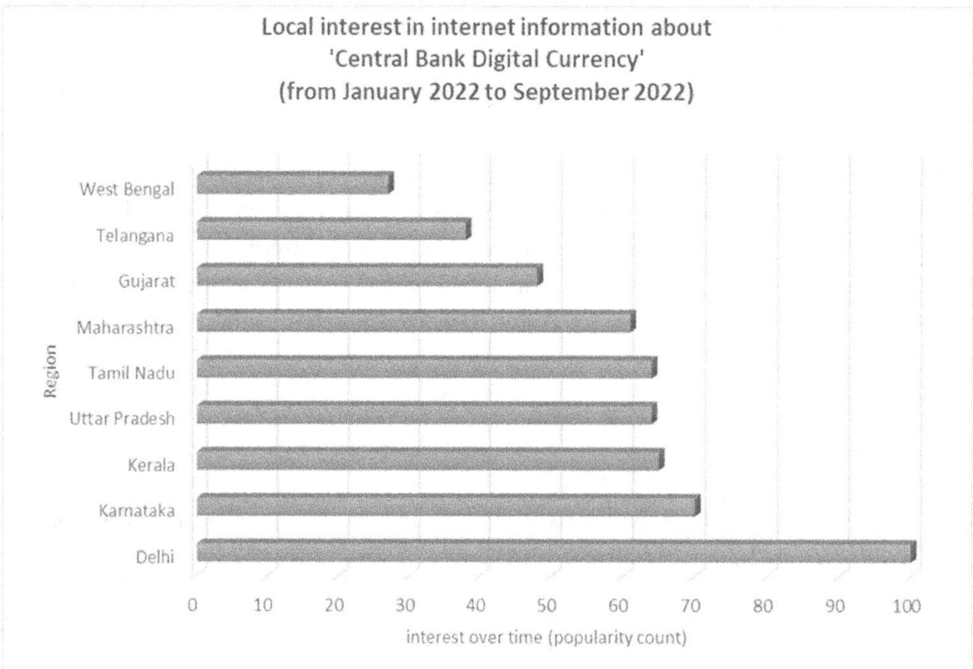

Regional Interest in 'CBDC' as a Search Term by Internet Users in India

Figure 2 shows the regional distribution of interest in internet information about 'CBDC' in India. Figure 2 is derived from the Google Trends data obtained from Section 2.1. Figure 2 shows that interest in internet information about 'CBDC' was very high in Delhi followed by Karnataka, Maharashtra and Odisha. Interest in online information about 'CBDC' exceeded the 50-point mark in each of these regions in India. In contrast, interest in internet information about 'CBDC' was much lower in Kerala and Uttarakhand. Interest in online information about 'CBDC' was below the 50-point mark in the two regions in India.

Figure 2. Local interest in internet information about 'CBDC'

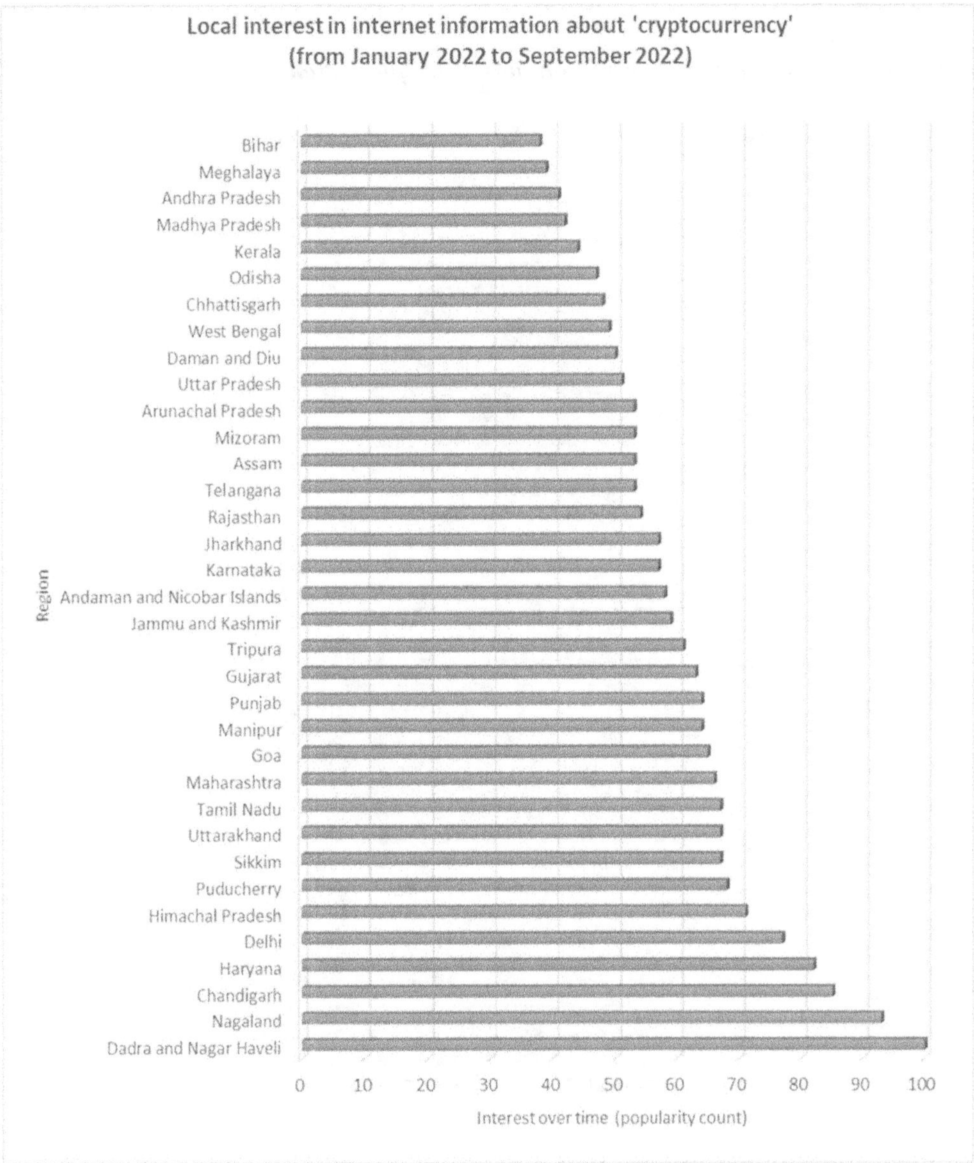

Regional Interest in 'Cryptocurrency' as a Search Term by Internet Users in India

Figure 3 shows the regional distribution of interest in internet information about 'cryptocurrency' in India. Figure 3 is derived from the Google Trends data obtained from Section 2.1. Figure 3 shows that interest in internet information about 'cryptocurrency' was very high in Dadra and Nagar Haveli followed by Nagaland, Chandigarh, Haryana and Delhi. Interest in online information about 'cryptocurrency' exceeded the 50-point mark in each of these regions in India. In contrast, interest in internet information about 'cryptocurrency' was much lower in Bihar, Meghalaya and Andra Pradesh. Interest in online information about 'cryptocurrency' was below the 50-point mark in the three regions in India.

Figure 3. Local interest in internet information about 'cryptocurrency'

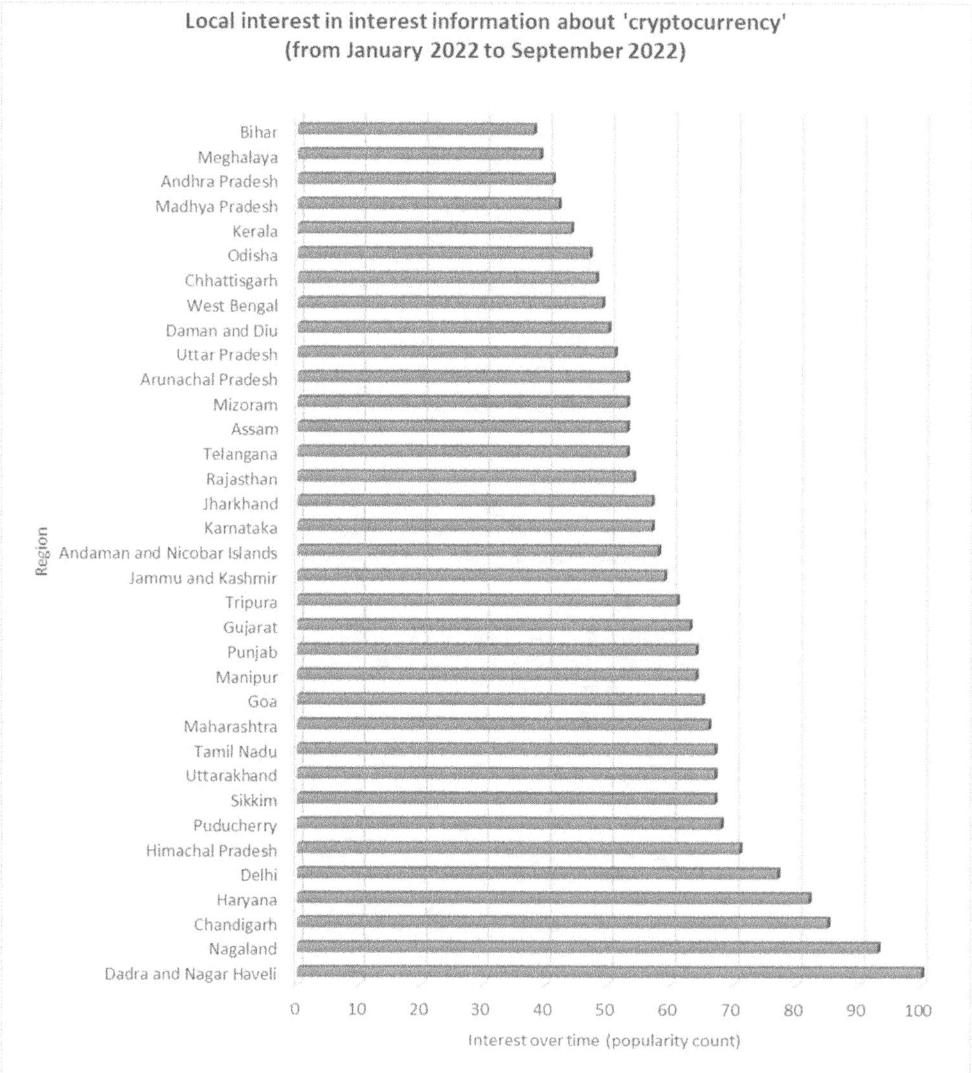

Benefits on India Digital Rupee CBDC

The introduction of a central bank digital currency (CBDC) in India offers some benefits. They include:

- **Cheaper Currency Management System:** The India CBDC will reduce the burden of handling cash, printing cash and the logistics of cash management in India. It will help to reduce dependence on cash and lead to higher seigniorage due to lower transaction costs
- **Eliminate Payment Risk:** The India CBDC will eliminate payment risk through reduced settlement risk, efficient payments, trusted payment option, reducing time and cost of cross-border transactions.
- **Boost the Digital Economy:** The introduction of a central bank digital currency in India will give a big boost to the digital economy in India especially when the India CBDC is launched in partnership with Fintech providers.
- **Increase Financial Inclusion:** By making people use CBDC, India can bring more unbanked adults into the formal financial system.
- **Curbing Illegal Financial Activities:** The India CBDC can help to implement anti-money laundering (AML) and combating financial terrorism (CFT) measures by acting as a highly secure way for cross-border transactions.

Possible Operational Design

- **Traceability:** The RBI will make all CBDC transactions traceable. This means that there will be no scope of anonymous transaction.
- **Non-Disruptive:** The RBI will ensure that the phased introduction of CBDC will be gradual so that there is no disruption in the banking system.
- **Conformity With Central Bank Objectives:** The design of the India CBDC will be in conformity with the RBI's stated objectives of monetary policy, financial stability, price stability and efficient operations of currency and payment systems.

Considerations for the India CBDC

- **The CBDC Should Be Non-Disruptive:** The India CBDC should be non-disruptive. It should not interfere with the RBI's ability to carry out its core mandate and it should not interfere with the public policy objective of the government.
- **The Need for Co-Existence:** The CBDC should coexist and complement other existing forms of money including cash and settlement accounts. The CBDC should not lead to the immediate replacement of existing payment alternatives such as cash especially when there is still high demand for cash in India.
- **Use CBDC as a Tool for Innovation and Competition:** The government should encourage people to use CBDC together with other payment instruments. This will increase competition and encourage process improvement across all the existing payment channels including CBDC (Shen and Hou, 2021; Piazzesi and Schneider, 2020).
- **Scope of the India CBDC:** The RBI should determine whether the India CBDC will be used for retail payments or wholesale payments.

- **The Underlying Technology:** The RBI should determine whether the CBDC will be delivered on a distributed ledger or a centralized ledger. The RBI should also determine whether the choice of technology will vary according to use cases.
- **The Validation Mechanism:** The RBI need to decide whether the validation mechanism for the CBDC should be token-based or account-based.
- **Direct or Indirect Issuance or Distribution:** The RBI need to decide whether the CBDC will be issued directly by the RBI to the end-user or issued to the end-user through public banks or private banks.

Risks to Watch Out For

- **Risk of Increased Financial Exclusion:** More than 540 million people in India still use non-smart phones. The implication is that people using non-smart phones may not be able to use CBDC for payment transactions. This can increase digital financial exclusion for non-smart phone users. The RBI should ensure that the India CBDC is designed in a way that cater for both users of smart phones and non-smart phone users within the country. Another challenge is that over 800 million people have smartphones in India, but many still do not use mobile banking or digital payments in their daily lives. This can also increase the risk of digital financial exclusion when CBDC is adopted as a mainstream payment option.
- **Privacy Risk:** With CBDC, payment transaction privacy will not be guaranteed. The transactions of people and businesses will not be completely anonymous. As a result, many people who want to conduct private digital transactions may not use the India CBDC. This issue makes it important for the authorities to strike a balance between pursuing its anti-money laundering objectives and maintaining the confidentiality of transactions for users.
- **Cyber Security Risk:** CBDC may face threats such as hacking which might lead to server blockages, timeouts or service declines. The CBDC can also be exposed to other cyber threats such as distributed denial-of-service (DDoS) attacks that disrupt services.
- **Digital and Financial Illiteracy:** There are literacy barriers to widespread CBDC adoption in India. A large segment of the population is living on wages, and they are not equipped with financial literacy or digital literacy that would enable them to seamlessly embrace CBDC in India. This can delay the widespread acceptance of CBDC in India.
- **Resistance in the Informal Economy:** The size of India's informal economy is estimated to be 52.4% which represents approximately $4,858 billion in 2021. The introduction of CBDC might face strong resistance in the informal economy especially when people do not want their transaction to be monitored by the government. This means that CBDCs might not be welcomed or well perceived in the informal economy.

CONCLUSION

This paper explored CBDC adoption and issues in India. It was found that Indian people who were interested in 'cryptocurrency' information were also interested in 'central bank digital currency' information.

The study also showed that the introduction of CBDC has potential benefits such as reduced dependency on cash, higher seigniorage due to lower transaction costs and reduced settlement risk. However, CBDC has associated risks that need to be carefully evaluated against the potential benefits. The implication is that the India CBDC will be a powerful tool in the RBI's monetary policy tools but the introduction of CBDC in India will require legal and regulatory changes. For this reason, the transition to a CBDC-led digital economy in India will not be easy. But it is a necessary step to support the evolution of society and the monetary system in India. Future studies can examine how CBDC can be used to support growth in specific sectors of the Indian economy. Other studies can explore the pertinent issues surrounding the best design and use-case for India CBDC.

REFERENCES

Adalid, R., Álvarez-Blázquez, Á., Assenmacher, K., Burlon, L., Dimou, M., López-Quiles, C., Fuentes, N. M., Meller, B., Muñoz, M., Radulova, P., & d'Acri, C. R. (2022). *Central bank digital currency and bank intermediation.* ECB Occasional Paper, No. 293.

Agur, I., Ari, A., & Dell'Ariccia, G. (2022). Designing central bank digital currencies. *Journal of Monetary Economics, 125*, 62–79. doi:10.1016/j.jmoneco.2021.05.002

Auer, R., Frost, J., Gambacorta, L., Monnet, C., Rice, T., & Shin, H. S. (2022). Central bank digital currencies: Motives, economic implications, and the research frontier. *Annual Review of Economics, 14*(1), 697–721. doi:10.1146/annurev-economics-051420-020324

Awang Abu Bakar, N. S., Yahya, N., Khairuddin, I. E., Zainal Abidin, A. F., Mohamad Zain, J., Idris, N. B., & Engku Ali, E. R. A. (2023). The Central Bank Digital Currency in Malaysia: A Literature Review. In *International Conference on Business and Technology* (pp. 307-317). Springer. 10.1007/978-3-031-08090-6_18

Bhowmik, D. (2022). Monetary policy implications of central bank digital currency with special reference to India. *Asia-Pacific Journal of Management and Technology, 2*(3), 1–8.

Bolt, W., Lubbersen, V., & Wierts, P. (2022). Getting the balance right: Crypto, stablecoin and central bank digital currency. *Journal of Payments Strategy & Systems, 16*(1), 39–50.

Bordo, M. D. (2021). Central Bank Digital Currency in Historical Perspective: Another Crossroad in Monetary History (No. w29171). National Bureau of Economic Research.

Chaum, D., Grothoff, C., & Moser, T. (2021). *How to issue a central bank digital currency.* arXiv preprint arXiv:2103.00254.

Chen, H., & Siklos, P. L. (2022). Central bank digital currency: A review and some macro-financial implications. *Journal of Financial Stability, 60*, 100985. doi:10.1016/j.jfs.2022.100985

Chorzempa, M. (2021). China, the United States, and central bank digital currencies: How important is it to be first? *China Economic Journal, 14*(1), 102–115. doi:10.1080/17538963.2020.1870278

Coulter, K. A. (2022). *'Stop Creating Private Money!': Should the Bank of England Introduce a Central Bank Digital Currency to Compete with Cryptocurrency? A Review of the UK Bank of England's Proposed Retail CBDC.* A Review of the UK Bank of England's Proposed Retail CBDC.

Cova, P., Notarpietro, A., Pagano, P., & Pisani, M. (2022). *Monetary policy in the open economy with digital currencies.* Bank of Italy Temi di Discussione (Working Paper) No, 1366.

Davoodalhosseini, S. M. (2022). Central bank digital currency and monetary policy. *Journal of Economic Dynamics & Control, 142*, 104150. doi:10.1016/j.jedc.2021.104150

Dinh, H. T. L., & Dinh, T. C. (2022, August). Verification of the Impact of Central Bank Digital Currency (CBDC) Issuance on Net Interest Income of Vietnamese Commercial Banks. In *2022 IEEE/ACIS 7th International Conference on Big Data, Cloud Computing, and Data Science (BCD)* (pp. 301-305). IEEE.

Fegatelli, P. (2022). A central bank digital currency in a heterogeneous monetary union: Managing the effects on the bank lending channel. *Journal of Macroeconomics, 71*, 103392. doi:10.1016/j.jmacro.2021.103392

Frankó, A., Oláh, B., Sass, Z., Hegedüs, C., & Varga, P. (2022, May). Towards CBDC-supported Smart Contracts for Industrial Stakeholders. In *2022 IEEE 5th International Conference on Industrial Cyber-Physical Systems (ICPS)* (pp. 1-6). IEEE. 10.1109/ICPS51978.2022.9816857

García, A., Lands, B., Liu, X., & Slive, J. (2020). *The potential effect of a central bank digital currency on deposit funding in Canada (No. 15).* Bank of Canada.

Hamza, H., & Jedidia, K. B. (2020). Central Bank Digital Currency and Financial Stability in a Dual Banking System. In Impact of Financial Technology (FinTech) on Islamic Finance and Financial Stability (pp. 233-252). IGI Global. doi:10.4018/978-1-7998-0039-2.ch012

Hayashi, F., & Toh, Y. L. (2022). *Assessing the Case for Retail CBDCs: Central Banks' Considerations.* Payments System Research Briefing.

Huang, Y. (2022). Virtual Currencies, ICOs and Central Bank Digital Currencies in China. In *Law and Practice of Crowdfunding and Peer-to-Peer Lending in Australia, China and Japan* (pp. 125–141). Springer. doi:10.1007/978-981-19-3834-4_7

Inozemtsev, M. I., & Nektov, A. V. (2022). Digital Platforms for Cross-Border Settlement of CBDC. In The Platform Economy (pp. 131-145). Palgrave Macmillan. doi:10.1007/978-981-19-3242-7_9

Kahn, M. C. M., Singh, M. M., & Alwazir, J. (2022). *Digital money and central bank operations.* International Monetary Fund. doi:10.5089/9798400206955.001

Keister, T., & Monnet, C. (2022). Central bank digital currency: Stability and information. *Journal of Economic Dynamics & Control, 142*, 104501. doi:10.1016/j.jedc.2022.104501

Kim, Y. S., & Kwon, O. (2019). *Central bank digital currency and financial stability.* Bank of Korea Working Paper, No. 6.

Kolozsi, P. P., Lehmann, K., & Szalai, Z. (2022). Is CBDC strengthening the monetary transmission mechanism? In Central Banking, Monetary Policy and the Future of Money (pp. 94-119). Edward Elgar Publishing. doi:10.4337/9781800376403.00011

Liu, X., Wang, Q., Wu, G., & Zhang, C. (2022). Determinants of individuals' intentions to use central bank digital currency: Evidence from China. *Technology Analysis and Strategic Management*, 1–15. doi:10.1080/09537325.2022.2131517

Michel, N. (2022). *Central Bank Digital Currencies Are about Control—They Should Be Stopped. Center for Monetary and Financial Alternatives*. Cato Institute.

Minesso, M. F., Mehl, A., & Stracca, L. (2022). Central bank digital currency in an open economy. *Journal of Monetary Economics*, *127*, 54–68. doi:10.1016/j.jmoneco.2022.02.001

Ozili, P. K. (2022a). Can central bank digital currency increase financial inclusion? Arguments for and against. In *Big Data Analytics in the Insurance Market* (pp. 241–249). Emerald Publishing Limited. doi:10.1108/978-1-80262-637-720221013

Ozili, P. K. (2022b). Central bank digital currency in Nigeria: opportunities and risks. In The New Digital Era: Digitalisation, Emerging Risks and Opportunities (Vol. 109, pp. 125-133). Emerald Publishing Limited. doi:10.1108/S1569-37592022000109A008

Ozili, P. K. (2022c). Global Central Bank Digital Currency Research and Developments: Implication for Cryptocurrency. Cryptocurrency. *Concepts, Technology, and Issues*.

Ozili, P. K. (2023). Central bank digital currency research around the World: A review of literature. *Journal of Money Laundering Control*, *26*(2), 215–226. doi:10.1108/JMLC-11-2021-0126

Piazzesi, M., & Schneider, M. (2020). *Credit lines, bank deposits or CBDC? competition and efficiency in modern payment systems*. Unpublished, Stanford University.

Ricks, M., Crawford, J., & Menand, L. (2020). *FedAccounts: digital dollars*. Vanderbilt Law Research Paper, 18-33.

Shen, W., & Hou, L. (2021). China's central bank digital currency and its impacts on monetary policy and payment competition: Game changer or regulatory toolkit? *Computer Law & Security Report*, *41*, 105577. doi:10.1016/j.clsr.2021.105577

Slawotsky, J. (2022). Digital currencies and great power rivalry: China as a disseminator in the digital age. *Asia Pacific Law Review*, *30*(2), 242–264. doi:10.1080/10192557.2022.2085412

Vallet, G., Kappes, S., & Rochon, L. P. (Eds.). (2022). *Central Banking, Monetary Policy and the Future of Money*. Edward Elgar Publishing. doi:10.4337/9781800376403

Vodrážka, M., Bízek, T., & Vojta, M. (2022). Are there relevant reasons to introduce a retail CBDC in the Czech Republic from the perspective of the payment system? *BIS Papers*, 65.

Wang, G., & Hausken, K. (2022). A game between central banks and households involving central bank digital currencies, other digital currencies and negative interest rates. *Cogent Economics & Finance*, *10*(1), 2114178. doi:10.1080/23322039.2022.2114178

WhitedT. M.WuY.XiaoK. (2022). Central Bank Digital Currency and Banks. Available at SSRN 4112644.

Xu, J. (2022). Developments and implications of central bank digital currency: The case of China e-CNY. *Asian Economic Policy Review*, *17*(2), 235–250. doi:10.1111/aepr.12396

Zhang, T., & Huang, Z. (2022). Blockchain and central bank digital currency. *ICT Express*, *8*(2), 264–270. doi:10.1016/j.icte.2021.09.014

Chapter 2
Mobile Payments in the FinTech Era:
Disrupting the Banking System Through Blockchain Applications

Nicola Del Sarto
University of Florence, Italy

ABSTRACT

Mobile payments have become increasingly popular as consumers prefer to pay for goods and services using their mobile phones. FinTech companies are disrupting the traditional banking system by providing innovative payment solutions that are faster, cheaper, and more convenient. Blockchain technology is at the forefront of this disruption, with its applications enabling secure and efficient mobile payments. This chapter examines the impact of blockchain on the fintech era and how it is disrupting the banking system. The chapter discusses the advantages of using blockchain for mobile payments, including increased security, transparency, and efficiency. It also explores the challenges and limitations of blockchain technology in mobile payments, such as regulatory hurdles and scalability issues. The chapter concludes that blockchain's applications have the potential to revolutionize mobile payments and disrupt the traditional banking system.

INTRODUCTION

The purpose of this paper is to examine the impact of these technologies on the payments industry, specifically focusing on the three main vectors of digital payments: instant payment, cryptocurrency, and mobile payment.

In recent years, the global banking industry has been undergoing a significant transformation due to the emergence of FinTech, which is reshaping its structure and operations. FinTech encompasses seven macro-areas that cover most of the services provided by traditional financial institutions (Thakor, 2020). The most prominent among these areas is digital payments, which are revolutionizing the payments industry by gradually replacing traditional payment methods such as checks and cash. The shift towards

DOI: 10.4018/978-1-6684-8624-5.ch002

digital payments is driven by three main factors: the increasing use of digital tools such as smartphones and tablets, the policies of governments to incentivize digital payment systems to combat money laundering and the underground economy, and the COVID-19 pandemic and the associated health risks of using cash (Jonker, Van der Cuijsen, Bijlsma, & Bolt, 2020).

The growing importance of FinTech and digital payments has prompted regulators in Europe and Italy to introduce regulations to govern the sector, such as the Payment Services Directive (PSD2) and the General Data Protection Regulation (GDPR). However, there is still a need for more comprehensive regulation. Despite the overall decline in global investment in the FinTech sector in 2020 due to the pandemic, venture capitalists invested $42.3 billion, the second-highest amount ever recorded (Capgemini, 2018). A survey of 60 CFOs of large financial companies operating in 23 different markets confirmed that digital payments and e-wallets have been the most impacted segment since the rise of FinTech (Capgemini, 2018).

Therefore, it is crucial to analyze the potential and limitations of FinTech and digital payments.

BACKGROUND

Digital Payments Systems

Payment refers to the act of transferring money or goods from a payer to a payee to settle an obligation between them (Boel, 2019). Payment systems encompass procedures, rules, and technologies designed to facilitate the exchange of money or other goods between two or more parties within an economic system (Widayani et al., 2022). These systems are evolving due to the advent of financial technology (FinTech), which is transforming the entire financial and banking industry. Payment systems can be broadly divided into two categories based on transaction size: wholesale payment systems and retail payment systems (Bech & Hancock, 2020).

Wholesale payment systems facilitate transactions involving large sums of money and are utilized by banking institutions and large commercial enterprises. The Real-Time Gross Settlement (RTGS) system is a notable example of a wholesale payment system that facilitates high-unit-amount transactions without bundling or clearing. RTGS payments occur in real-time, increasing security by reducing the exposure to cyber attacks (Bech & Hancock, 2020). The Eurosystem introduced the TARGET2 system in 2008, which replaced the previous TARGET system and enables cross-border transactions in diverse currencies, including the Eurozone countries and other EU member states (Banca D'Italia, n.d.; European Central Bank, 2019).

Retail payment systems are utilized by individuals and businesses for transactions with amounts of 500,000€ or less. Retail payment systems include cash, debit cards, credit cards, prepaid cards, wire transfers, checks, innovative payments (mobile payments, instant payments, and wearable payments), and cryptocurrencies. The retail payment industry is rapidly transforming due to digital and FinTech, introducing new players and increasing competition, resulting in greater consumer focus (Bech & Hancock, 2020).

In conclusion, payment systems are critical to the functioning of the global economy, and their evolution is driven by technological advancements. Wholesale payment systems are used for high-unit-amount transactions, while retail payment systems cater to daily transactions (Fratini Passi, 2022). The payment industry is constantly changing, and new payment methods are being introduced regularly. Understanding the characteristics of these payment systems and their evolution is crucial for policymakers, financial institutions, and consumers alike.

The Impact of Blockchain in Banking System

To comprehend the potential impact of blockchain on the traditional banking system, it is essential to examine the revenue and cost generation process. Banks generate revenue primarily through two sources, net interest income and non-interest income. The combination of these two areas constitutes the total revenue, with net interest income accounting for an average of 56% and non-interest income accounting for 44% (Cetorelli & Goldberg, 2012). Lending activities primarily generate net interest income, wherein banks use the funds collected from direct fundraising to offer loans and generate interest income. On the other hand, non-interest income is derived through commissions and fees for banking services, mainly from indirect fundraising, such as commissions on assets under management.

Credit risk is the primary challenge banks face when issuing credit. It refers to the possibility that borrowers may not fully repay the debt or default on it. To mitigate this risk, banks typically require collateral, insurance, and grant loans based on the credit scores of the counterparties. This process involves multiple actors, leading to inefficiencies and costs related to their interactions, and increasing the time required to grant loans (Allen & Carletti, 2019).

Blockchain technology presents an innovative solution to these challenges, promising faster and more precise payment processing, reduced transaction costs and errors, faster settlement times, and opportunities for new revenue streams. To implement distributed ledger technology, banks often opt for private and permissioned blockchain networks, as they offer numerous benefits (Crosby et al., 2016).

Individuals and businesses often open bank accounts to access financial services and save money. Bank accounts provide a safer option than holding cash, which can be lost, stolen, or destroyed. Moreover, bank accounts earn interest and are less susceptible to inflation than cash. However, opening a bank account requires a minimum deposit and entails various fees such as maintenance, withdrawal, and account statement copy fees (Swan, 2015).

With the emergence of blockchain technology, traditional bank accounts may become obsolete. Blockchain enables users to store cryptocurrency directly on a distributed ledger, which records the transaction rather than the physical currency itself. Each transaction generates a unique public key and corresponding private key, and the private key associated with the owner's public key tracks the transaction and proves ownership and availability of the cryptocurrency Kshetri, N. (2018).

To maintain a record of transactions, a corresponding number of private keys need to be stored. Crypto-currency wallets are software programs that store private and public keys and interact with blockchain to facilitate digital currency transactions and track balances. These wallets come in different types, including online, mobile, desktop, hardware, and paper wallets. While both digital wallets and bank accounts store and protect value, digital wallets pose a lower risk of fraud due to the private key only being known to the owner. Although there is a risk of fake e-wallets stealing private keys, the security benefits of digital wallets still exist, making them a potentially more secure option than traditional bank accounts (Li et al., 2019).

Blockchain technology eliminates the need for trust and trusted intermediaries like banks, which could reduce costs and fees and enable micropayments. This could have significant social impact, such as providing financial services to unbanked individuals in developing countries. Furthermore, distributed ledger technology can transform lending, including identity verification and credit score determination, making loan approval quicker and more transparent. Peer-to-peer lending through blockchain technology has the potential to disrupt traditional banking, enabling borrowers to access credit and investors to achieve higher returns without intermediaries. P2P lending platforms also reduce financial risks, such as fraud, and dissolve geographical barriers and interest rate differences, increasing competition and lowering interest rates.

Overall, distributed ledger technology and P2P lending have the potential to increase efficiency in lending and benefit consumers by lowering fees and increasing transparency.

Payment Systems in the FinTech Era

In recent years, financial technology (Fintech) has drastically changed the way we engage with financial services. One of the most significant changes has been the shift towards digital payments, which has introduced new payment methods and disrupted traditional payment systems. This section of the paper aims to examine the impact of Fintech on payment systems by analyzing its effects on transaction costs, security, and access to financial services.

The emergence of new digital payment systems is revolutionizing the entire payment sector. This transformation is expected to impact traditional payment methods such as cash and checks, with the latter facing the possibility of becoming obsolete, while also redefining the role of credit and debit cards and bank transfers. This transformation can be attributed to three primary trends that are redefining the payment sector in different ways. The first trend is that of mobile payments, which is the most developed trend. The second trend is instant payments, which facilitates quick and seamless transactions. Finally, the third trend is cryptocurrencies, which operate on blockchain technology and offer a decentralized payment system.

Research has shown that Fintech has significantly impacted payment systems by reducing transaction costs and increasing access to financial services. According to a report by the World Bank, digital payments can reduce transaction costs by up to 90% compared to traditional payment methods (World Bank, 2016). Fintech has also made payment systems more secure through the implementation of advanced encryption techniques, biometric authentication, and tokenization (Foster & Gupta, 2020). Additionally, Fintech has made financial services more accessible by providing digital payment options to those who are unbanked or underbanked, thus promoting financial inclusion (Gomez, Paniagua, & Santos, 2019).

In conclusion, Fintech has brought about a significant transformation in payment systems through the introduction of new payment methods and the disruption of traditional payment systems. This transformation has been driven by three primary trends: mobile payments, instant payments, and cryptocurrencies. Fintech has also impacted payment systems by reducing transaction costs, increasing security, and promoting financial inclusion. As a result, payment systems are becoming more efficient and accessible to a wider population.

Mobile Payments

The payment sector is undergoing a revolution due to the emergence of new digital payment systems. This transformation is set to have a significant impact on traditional payment methods such as cash and checks, as well as on digital payment systems. Mobile payment is a term that refers to payments made using a device, including digital wallets, e-commerce payment providers, and digital remittances (Ramos de Luna, Liébana-Cabanillas, Sánchez-Fernández, & Muñoz-Leiva, 2019; Iman, 2018A). E-wallets and digital commerce are the two areas of mobile payment that have had the greatest impact on the payment market, with a business volume of $910 billion recorded in the United States in 2020 alone. This value is estimated to cross the $1 trillion mark in 2021, while globally, transactions worth $4.9 trillion were recorded in 2020, with an estimated value of $8.2 trillion projected for 2024 (Statista, 2020).

E-Wallets

Digital wallets, or e-wallets, have revolutionized the way we conduct financial transactions, allowing users to easily transfer funds in peer-to-peer mode or make payments in physical shops through their smartphones. One of the first e-wallets to gain popularity was M-Pesa, which was launched in Kenya in 2007 by mobile operators Safaricom and Vodafone. M-Pesa operates through a system of SMS-based movements that store monetary value on the user's phone credit (Ferrari, 2016). The user can load funds onto their M-Pesa account through affiliated points of sale and then use it to transfer funds to other M-Pesa users, make purchases, or withdraw cash from agreed points. By 2009, M-Pesa had already been adopted by 38% of Kenya's adult population, greatly increasing financial inclusion in Kenya and other countries in Africa and Asia (Jack & Suri, 2011).

In contrast to M-Pesa, e-wallets that are based on smartphones require an internet connection and an app to function. Credit can be loaded onto the app through a variety of methods, such as by linking credit or debit cards or depositing funds from a current account. The advantage of e-wallets is that users can always have access to their funds through their smartphones, making payments without needing to carry a physical wallet. E-wallets can be categorized based on the frontend and backend processes used for transactions (Iman, 2018B).

Digital Commerce

The digital payment landscape is evolving rapidly, with new technologies and platforms revolutionizing the sector. One such technology is e-wallets, which enable users to transfer funds in P2P mode or make payments in physical shops through their smartphones. M-Pesa, the first mobile money service, was launched in Kenya in 2007, and it allowed users to store monetary value on their mobile phones and carry out transactions via SMS. Within just two years, M-Pesa was being used by 38% of Kenya's adult population, which highlighted its potential to promote financial inclusion (Jack & Suri, 2011). Unlike M-Pesa, e-wallets require an internet connection and an app to function. Loading credit into the e-wallet can be done in different ways, such as loading the data of credit or debit cards or depositing funds from a current account. One of the advantages of e-wallets is that they allow users to carry a universal payment instrument with them and make payments without the need for a physical wallet. E-wallets can be classified based on their frontend and backend processes. Another important digital payment system is digital commerce, which facilitates payments made online or via apps. Digital commerce systems act as intermediaries, and the underlying processes can be either open or closed loop. PayPal, Amazon Pay, Stripe, and AliPay are among the most widely used digital commerce platforms in the West. In 2020, PayPal recorded a total transaction volume of 936 billion dollars, a growth of 31% compared to 2019, which highlights the growth potential of the digital payments sector (PayPal, 2021). It is worth noting that larger companies, such as Apple, Google, or PayPal, offer both e-wallet and digital commerce services in a single app, providing users with a seamless and universal payment experience. Digital commerce payments are gaining more prominence due to the growth of e-commerce and online commerce, which require convenient payment solutions for their customers.

Instant Payment

Instant Payment, Real-Time Payment, and Faster Payment all refer to the same concept: instant payment systems in the retail payments market. In contrast to the traditional delayed settlement model, instant payments allow for immediate monetary transfers from the buyer's account to the merchant's account, taking less than 10 seconds to complete. This results in reduced waiting times, improved liquidity management, and potentially greater market efficiency. Furthermore, instant payment services operate 24/7, providing a continuous service that is not restricted by bank hours or working weeks. The immediate confirmation of the transaction reduces uncertainty and minimizes credit risk. However, the introduction of instant payment services also requires appropriate implementation, monitoring, and fraud management to ensure their successful integration (Bank for International Settlements, 2016).

Instant payment systems build upon real-time gross settlement (RTGS) systems, which allow for instantaneous large-sum transfers in the wholesale payments market. However, these systems were not suitable for the high volume of smaller transactions that are typical in retail payments (Bech & Hancock, 2020). Instant payment systems were developed to address this limitation, enabling the trade-off between speed and number of transactions to be overcome.

Despite the potential benefits of instant payment systems, fraud management remains a significant challenge. As transactions cannot be cancelled, any errors or fraudulent activities could result in significant inconvenience for the parties involved. Therefore, effective fraud management is essential to ensure the success of instant payment services.

Cryptocurrencies

As mentioned earlier, Bitcoin was the first cryptocurrency to be introduced in the world. Cryptocurrencies are digital currencies that operate independently of a central authority, unlike traditional currencies whose issuance is controlled by a central bank. Instead, cryptocurrencies rely on algorithms to regulate their issuance (Narayanan et al., 2016). This is why the most significant innovation that cryptocurrencies have brought about is not the creation of a new means of exchange, but rather the technology underlying them - blockchain. Since Bitcoin's inception in 2009, the cryptocurrency and blockchain world has undergone significant evolution. In addition to the traditional cryptocurrencies that rely solely on blockchain technology, stablecoins and Central Bank Digital Currencies (CBDCs) are also being developed. To analyze the vast and diverse world of cryptocurrencies, it is important to start by understanding the underlying blockchain technology, followed by an examination of the different types of cryptocurrencies currently available.

RESEARCH METHOD

This paper uses a case study approach to examine four payment systems: Google Pay, Bitcoin, Square, and Klarna. The case study approach is a qualitative research method that allows for an in-depth analysis of a particular phenomenon (Yin, 2017). The method involves collecting data from multiple sources to gain a comprehensive understanding of the cases being studied (Flyvbjerg, 2006). Secondary data was collected from various sources, including academic journals, industry reports, news articles, and company websites. The data was analyzed using a thematic analysis approach, which involves identifying common patterns and themes within the data (Braun & Clarke, 2006). This allowed for a comparison of the different payment systems in terms of their features, benefits, and limitations. The four cases were selected based on their popularity and relevance in the payments industry. Google Pay is a digital wallet that allows users to make payments using their mobile devices, Bitcoin is a decentralized cryptocurrency that operates on a blockchain, Square is a mobile payment system that enables merchants to accept card payments using a smartphone or tablet, and Klarna is a buy-now-pay-later payment service that allows customers to make purchases without upfront payment. Limitations of the study include the potential for biases in the secondary data sources and the inability to directly observe the payment systems in action. However, efforts were made to use a variety of sources and to critically evaluate the reliability of the data.

Overall, the case study approach provides a detailed and nuanced analysis of the four payment systems, which can inform future research and decision-making in the payments industry.

GOOGLE PAY AND ANTI-MONEY LAUNDERING

Anti-money laundering (AML) refers to a set of activities and regulations aimed at preventing money laundering, which involves transforming proceeds of illegal activities into legitimate money in order to conceal their origin (Whisker & Eshwar Lokanan, 2019). To accomplish this, money laundering often uses shell companies to pass through the illicit funds, making them appear to be legitimate cash in the eyes of the state. Money laundering is illegal and subject to criminal penalties in many countries, including Italy. Governments around the world have implemented regulations to curb this phenomenon, which often involves the use of cash due to its lack of traceability. In response, many states have integrated their anti-money laundering and anti-corruption regulations with rules aimed at limiting the use of cash, thereby promoting more traceable instruments, such as digital payments.

Google Pay is a popular digital wallet service that emerged from the merger of two pre-existing services, Android Pay and Google Wallets, in 2018. It is a leading digital wallet globally and the leading e-wallet for smartphones running the Android operating system, operating in 75 countries with a range of services offered depending on the country (Vlcek, 2011). However, Google Pay has been subject to legal scrutiny in Italy due to its potential use for illicit activities, such as the recent case of bribes paid through Google Pay by managers of the Italian company Trans Part to officials of the Leonardo company (Reuters, 2021). Google Pay was used to return capital from off-shore companies abroad to Italy, making it a suspect in the investigation for international money laundering.

The use of mobile payment services, such as Google Pay, raises concerns about their potential role in facilitating illicit activities, including money laundering and corruption (Whisker & Eshwar Lokanan, 2019). One challenge is the lack of transparency in the internal management of transactions, due to the anonymity these services provide to their users. Another concern is the verification of the identity of users, which is critical to complying with anti-money laundering regulations, such as the Know Your Customer (KYC) requirement. In the absence of adequate KYC, digital payment systems are susceptible to being used for illicit activities. While digital payments can be effective in combatting illicit activities, governments need to update their anti-money laundering regulations to create more restrictive rules for companies that offer digital payment services to ensure anonymity while maintaining traceability.

BITCOIN: SPECULATIVE ASSET OR DIGITAL CURRENCY

Bitcoin, the first cryptocurrency created in 2009 by anonymous developers under the pseudonym Satoshi Nakamoto, holds the top spot in the global cryptocurrency market, with a current market capitalization of approximately 1,180 billion dollars. Like most cryptocurrencies, it operates without a centralized governing authority, and its transactions are validated and recorded on its blockchain by its users. The blockchain is designed to handle both transactions and monetary policy, with a block being validated every 10 minutes, and 12.5 Bitcoin issued as a reward to the miners who validate the block. On average, the Bitcoin blockchain validates 300,000 transactions daily, issuing approximately 1,800 Bitcoins per day or 54,000 Bitcoins monthly. Bitcoin's monetary policy is implemented through the halving of issued Bitcoin every four years, which is due to the protocol's limit of 21 million Bitcoins. As of March 2021, 18.67 million Bitcoins had been issued.

Recently, large international companies such as PayPal and Tesla announced their acceptance of Bitcoin as a payment method, sparking renewed discussion on its potential as a trading currency. However, there remains a debate over Bitcoin's true nature, whether it is a currency for commercial transactions or simply a speculative asset. To qualify as a currency, an asset must have three main characteristics: a unit of account, a store of value, and a means of exchange. Currently, Bitcoin lacks the first two characteristics and has a market trend characterized by volatility.

Two additional factors undermine Bitcoin's status as a currency of exchange. First, its energy-intensive mining process has significant environmental impacts, making it incompatible with global efforts to limit energy consumption. Second, although Bitcoin is the first and most well-known cryptocurrency, it has significant limitations due to its first-mover status.

AN EASY WAY TO PAY: SQUARE

Square Inc. is a fintech company based in San Francisco, California, that is transforming the payment system. Founded in 2009 by Jack Dorsey and Jim McKelvey, Square has grown to become one of the most successful fintech companies in the world, offering a range of financial services, including payment processing, payroll processing, small business loans, and other financial services (Suen, 2019). The company's main product, Square Reader, is a small device that can be plugged into a smartphone or tablet to process credit and debit card payments. One of the ways Square is impacting the payment system is by making it easier for small businesses to accept payments. Traditionally, small businesses had to rely on traditional payment processors, which could be expensive and difficult to set up. With Square, small businesses can easily accept credit and debit card payments, and they don't need to worry about setting up a complex payment processing system. Additionally, Square is making the payment system more accessible to consumers with its Cash App. Consumers can easily send and receive money from friends and family members, as well as pay for goods and services at participating merchants. This has made it easier for consumers to make payments without having to carry cash or cards. Overall, Square is a great example of a fintech company that is making a significant impact on the payment system (Zhang & He, 2020).

KLARNA: BUY NOW AND PAY LATER

Klarna, a Swedish fintech company established in 2005, has rapidly grown to become one of the most successful fintech startups globally, valued at $45.6 billion as of September 2021 (CB Insights, 2021). This company has disrupted the traditional payment system by offering innovative payment solutions to both merchants and consumers (Johansson & Hellström, 2021). Klarna provides alternative payment methods that are more convenient and flexible than traditional payment systems. Customers can choose to pay for their purchases later, split their payments into several installments, or pay for their items in full upfront. This has made it easier for people to purchase products and services without having to worry about the immediate financial burden (Johansson & Hellström, 2021).

Moreover, Klarna has streamlined the checkout process for both merchants and customers. With Klarna's "buy now, pay later" option, customers can make purchases with just a few clicks, without having to enter their payment details each time they shop. Merchants can also benefit from Klarna's streamlined checkout process by reducing shopping cart abandonment rates and increasing conversion rates (McKinsey & Company, 2020). Additionally, Klarna offers instant loans to consumers, allowing them to finance their purchases at the point of sale. This has disrupted the traditional loan system, which typically requires customers to go through a lengthy application process before receiving funding. Klarna's instant loan service has made it easier for people to access credit and has allowed merchants to sell more expensive items (Johansson & Hellström, 2021).

Klarna's success is largely attributed to its ability to leverage data and analytics to improve its services (Johansson & Hellström, 2021). By analyzing customer behavior and transaction data, Klarna can offer personalized payment options and tailored recommendations to customers. This has helped Klarna build a loyal customer base and has made it a popular payment option for millennials and Gen Z shoppers (CB Insights, 2021).

In conclusion, Klarna has revolutionized the payment system by offering alternative payment options, streamlining the checkout process, offering instant loans, and leveraging data to improve its services. Its success has inspired other fintech startups to follow suit, and it has forced traditional payment providers to adapt to changing customer preferences (Johansson & Hellström, 2021).

CONCLUSION

In conclusion, the adoption of new technologies, such as blockchain, has had a significant impact on the payment system. Our study examined several empirical cases of firms that have disrupted the payment system using blockchain technology, highlighting the benefits of decentralization, security, and efficiency.

Firstly, we found that blockchain technology enables fast and secure payment transactions without the need for intermediaries. This has significant cost-saving implications for businesses, reducing transaction fees and other associated costs. Secondly, blockchain technology can enhance the transparency and trust in payment systems, by providing an immutable record of transactions that can be accessed by all parties involved. This can lead to increased confidence in payment systems, which is especially important for businesses operating in international markets.

Our study also highlighted some of the challenges associated with the adoption of blockchain technology in payment systems. These include issues around scalability, interoperability, and regulatory compliance. However, we found that these challenges can be overcome through collaboration between businesses and regulators, as well as through the development of new technological solutions.

Overall, our findings suggest that blockchain technology has the potential to significantly disrupt the payment system, creating new opportunities for businesses and consumers alike. While challenges remain, the benefits of blockchain technology for payment systems are clear, and we expect to see continued growth and innovation in this area in the coming years.

As with all research, this paper presents some limitations which may be useful for future scholars.

In particular, the study examined several empirical cases of firms that have disrupted the payment system using blockchain technology, but the number of firms examined may not be representative of the entire population of businesses using blockchain technology in the payment system. Moreover the empirical cases examined in the study may not represent a diverse range of industries or geographies, limiting the generalizability of the findings. Finally the study may have focused on the short-term impact of blockchain technology on the payment system, but the long-term implications are yet to be fully understood.

ACKNOWLEDGMENT

This research received no specific grant from any funding agency in the public, commercial, or not-for-profit sectors.

REFERENCES

Allen, F., & Carletti, E. (2019). The Global Financial Crisis: Lessons and Opportunities. *Journal of Financial Stability*, *42*, 1–6. doi:10.1016/j.jfs.2019.05.005

Banca D'Italia. (n.d.). *TARGET2*. Retrieved from https://www.bancaditalia.it/compiti/sistemi-pagamenti/target2/index.html?com.dotmarketing.htmlpage.language=1

Bank for International Settlements. (2016). *Committee on Payment and Market Infrastructures. Fast payments–Enhancing the speed and availability of retail payments*. Bank for International Settlements.

Bech, M. L., & Hancock, D. (2020). *The evolution ofpayment systems: an overview*. BIS Quarterly Review.

Bech, M. L., & Hancock, D. (2020). The evolution of payment systems: Lessons learned from the crisis and beyond. *Journal of Financial Market Infrastructures*, *8*(3), 1–26.

Boel, M. (2019). Payment systems. In The Oxford Handbook of Banking and Financial History. OUP.

Boot, A., Hoffmann, P., Laeven, L., & Ratnov, L. (2021). Fintech: What's old, what's new? *Journal of Financial Stability*, 1–13.

Braun, V., & Clarke, V. (2006). Using thematic analysis in psychology. *Qualitative Research in Psychology*, *3*(2), 77–101. doi:10.1191/1478088706qp063oa

Carstens, A. (2019). *The future of money and the payment system: what role for central banks?* Bank for International Settlements.

Cetorelli, N., & Goldberg, L. (2012). Banking Globalization and Monetary Transmission. *The Journal of Finance*, *67*(5), 1811–1843. doi:10.1111/j.1540-6261.2012.01773.x

Crosby, M., Pattanayak, P., Verma, S., & Kalyanaraman, V. (2016). Blockchain Technology: Beyond Bitcoin. *Applied Innovation*, *2*(6-10), 71–81. doi:10.1016/j.apin.2016.01.001

European Central Bank. (2019). *TARGET2 - Frequently Asked Questions*. Retrieved from https://www.ecb.europa.eu/paym/target/target2/html/index.en.html

Ferrari, A. (2016). Mobile payments: The Kenyan experience. *Journal of Payments Strategy & Systems*, *10*(1), 59–71.

Flyvbjerg, B. (2006). Five misunderstandings about case-study research. *Qualitative Inquiry*, *12*(2), 219–245. doi:10.1177/1077800405284363

Foster, S., & Gupta, A. (2020). Fintech and digital payments: A global review of trends and challenges. *International Journal of Advanced Research in Engineering and Technology*, *11*(4), 1–18.

Fratini Passi, L. (2022). Open banking and digital transformation in Italy: The current situation and the challenges ahead. *Journal of Payments Strategy & Systems*, *16*(4), 358–368.

Gomez, J. C., Paniagua, J., & Santos, L. (2019). Fintech and financial inclusion: A review. *Sustainability*, *11*(1), 1–20.

Iman, R. (2018A). Digital remittances: An examination of the impact of fintech on remittances. *Journal of Money Laundering Control*, *21*(3), 369–378. doi:10.1108/JMLC-10-2017-0066

Iman, S. (2018B). A Review on E-wallets: A Payment Instrument in Digital World. *International Journal of Advanced Science and Technology*, *117*, 29–38.

Insights, C. B. (2021). *Fintech 250: The Top Fintech Companies Of 2021*. Retrieved from https://www.cbinsights.com/research/fintech-250-startups-companies-to-watch/

Jack, W., & Suri, T. (2011). Mobile money: The economics of M-PESA. National Bureau of Economic Research.

Johansson, M., & Hellström, D. (2021). The impact of fintech on traditional banking services. *Journal of Financial Services Marketing*, *26*(3), 136–148.

Jonker, N., Van der Cuijsen, C., Bijlsma, M., & Bolt, W. (2020). *Pandemic payment patterns*. DeNederlandscheBank.

Kher, V., Terjesen, S., & Liu, C. (2019). The cryptocurrency revolution: The rise of bitcoin. *Journal of International Management*, *25*(2), 107–118.

Kshetri, N. (2018). Blockchain's roles in meeting key supply chain management objectives. *International Journal of Information Management*, *39*, 80–89. doi:10.1016/j.ijinfomgt.2017.12.005

Li, Y., Du, X., Liu, J., & Qiao, C. (2019). Blockchain and Internet of Things-based credit scoring system for P2P lending. *Computer Networks*, *149*, 90–99. doi:10.1016/j.comnet.2018.11.036

McKinsey & Company. (2020). *Buy now, pay later: A fresh approach to lending*. Retrieved from https://www.mckinsey.com/business-functions/risk/our-insights/buy-now-pay-later-a-fresh-approach-to-lending

Narayanan, A., Bonneau, J., Felten, E., Miller, A., & Goldfeder, S. (2016). *Bitcoin and Cryptocurrency Technologies: A Comprehensive Introduction*. Princeton University Press.

PayPal. (2021). *PayPal Holdings, Inc. Reports Fourth Quarter and Full Year 2020 Results*. https://investor.paypal-corp.com/news-releases/news-release-details/paypal-holdings-inc-reports-fourth-quarter-and-full-year-2020/

Ramos de Luna, I., Liébana-Cabanillas, F., Sánchez-Fernández, J., & Muñoz-Leiva, F. (2019). What drives mobile payment adoption? A meta-analysis. *Computers in Human Behavior*, *99*, 182–198. doi:10.1016/j.chb.2019.04.008

Ramos de Lunaa, I., Liébana-Cabanillas, F., Sánchez-Fernández, J., & Muñoz-Leiva, F. (2019). Mobile payment is not all the same: The adoption of mobile payment systems depending on the technology applied. *Technological Forecasting and Social Change*, *146*, 931–944. doi:10.1016/j.techfore.2018.09.018

Reuters. (2021). *Google Pay under scrutiny in Italy over alleged privacy abuse*. Reuters. https://www.reuters.com/article/us-alphabet-italy-google-pay-idUSKBN29I2SO

Statista. (2020). *Mobile payment transaction value worldwide from 2015 to 2019 and forecasted till 2024*. Retrieved from https://www.statista.com/statistics/226530/mobile-payment-transaction-value-worldwide/

Suen, R. (2019). Jack Dorsey's Square transformed the payment industry by making it cheap and easy for small businesses to accept credit cards. *Business Insider*. https://www.businessinsider.com/how-square-transformed-the-payment-industry-2019-8

Swan, M. (2015). *Blockchain: blueprint for a new economy*. O'Reilly Media, Inc.

Thakor, A. V. (2020). Fintech and banking: What do we know? *Journal of Financial Intermediation*.

Truby, J. (2018). Decarbonizing Bitcoin: Law and policy choices for reducing the energy consumption of Blockchain technologies and digital currencies. *Energy Research & Social Science*, *44*, 399–410. doi:10.1016/j.erss.2018.06.009

Vlcek, B. (2011). Mobile payments and anti-money laundering regulations. *Journal of Money Laundering Control*, *14*(4), 352–361. doi:10.1108/13685201111170839

Whisker, R., & Eshwar Lokanan, M. (2019). Cryptocurrencies and anti-money laundering regulations: The need for KYC. *International Journal of Financial Research*, *10*(4), 45–57. doi:10.5430/ijfr.v10n4p45

Widayani, A., Fiernaningsih, N., & Herijanto, P. (2022). Barriers to digital payment adoption: Micro, small and medium enterprises. *Management & Marketing*, *17*(4), 528–542. doi:10.2478/mmcks-2022-0029

World Bank. (2016). *The Global Findex Database 2014: Measuring financial inclusion around the world*. World Bank.

Yin, R. K. (2017). *Case study research and applications: Design and methods*. Sage publications.

Zhang, Z., & He, W. (2020). Disruptive innovation and firm value: The impact of fintech on the payment industry. *Technological Forecasting and Social Change*, *160*, 120237. doi:10.1016/j.techfore.2020.120237

Chapter 3
Extending UTAUT2 Model With Sustainability and Psychological Factors in Adoption of Blockchain Technology for the Digital Transformation of Banks in India

Renuka Sharma
https://orcid.org/0000-0002-6514-3411
Chitkara Business School, Chitkara University, India

Navpreet Sidhu
https://orcid.org/0000-0003-3963-6623
Chitkara Business School, Chitkara University, India

Kiran Mehta
Chitkara Business School, Chitkara University, India

Vishal Vyas
Atal Bihari Vajpayee-Indian Institute of Information Technology and Management, India

ABSTRACT

Financial institutions' digital advancements are vital for sustainability, with blockchain having transformative potential. Banking pursues digital transformation due to fintech competition and cybersecurity worries, driven by technology advancements and customer expectations. FinTech start-ups prompt innovation from big banks. Industry 4.0 integrates blockchain, AI, and technology platforms that align with SDG8 and SDG9, promoting transparency, cost reduction, and company expansion. Therefore, the present research seeks to answer: What drives banks to adopt blockchain technology? It aims to identify factors influencing bankers' intention to adopt blockchain for digital transformation in Indian banks. A standardized scale with the addition of two more constructs (sustainability agenda and psychological framework) was used to achieve the objective of the study. The findings of the research enhance understanding of banks' technology usage and blockchain adoption. Findings validate nine factors influencing bankers' blockchain adoption.

DOI: 10.4018/978-1-6684-8624-5.ch003

INTRODUCTION

Climate issues are still relevant amid the pandemic, and it is now more important than ever to prevent environmental degradation (Huynh, 2020; Huynh et al., 2022; Kovilage, 2020; Liu et al., 2021; Vyas et al. 2023). Most ecological problems are caused by greenhouse gas emissions, primarily from fossil fuels and non-renewable energy sources. One way to promote green banking is to emphasize how crucial it is to link the desire to use online banking with the desire to protect the environment and be happy. Banking is going through a technological revolution because fin-tech companies are getting increasingly competitive and want to offer green banking and sustainable financial services (Mehta et al., 2022). The service sector is a significant part of most developed countries' GDP today (Borghi, 2019). Fin-tech start-ups that use technology to give customers different banking and other financial services have made the big banks have to develop new ideas to stay competitive. Intelligent decision models used data mining in the 1990s to improve the way standard bank functions worked for insurance (Anand, Patrick, Hughes, and Bell, 1998). "Industry 4.0" is a new wave of disruptive technologies that have recently appeared in our society and spread to several industries (Hou et al., 2020; Chang et al., 2019). Industry 4.0 includes a wide range of technologies, such as artificial intelligence (AI), blockchain, and the internet of things (IoT), as well as cloud computing, 3D printing, and cyber-physical systems (CPS) (Chang et al., 2020). ATMs have replaced human tellers for repetitive cash withdrawals and deposits, reducing the need for human help. (Huang & Rust, 2018). Modelling with neural networks showed that the perceived ease of use is essential for online banking to be accepted in developing countries like India.

Artificial intelligence has recently helped Indian banks cut down on technical inefficiency by up to 11%, and when combined with big data, it makes smart marketing possible. (Kushwaha, Kar & Dwivedi, 2021; Verma, Sharma, Deb & Maitra, 2021; Mor & Gupta, 2021;). Banks have the potential to leverage the vast quantities of data they handle to greatly improve decision-making across a broad spectrum of activities. By incorporating artificial intelligence (AI) into their operations, banks can enhance their ability to make more informed and effective choices in areas including back-office operations, customer experience, marketing strategies, product delivery, risk management, and compliance. AI-driven systems can analyze and interpret data on a massive scale, enabling banks to optimize processes, personalize customer interactions, target marketing efforts, streamline product delivery, mitigate risks, and ensure regulatory compliance. Artificial intelligence would change banks by emphasizing the amount of data more than the size of their assets. Instead of making things for many people, banks would now want to give their customers unique experiences. Banks will now be able to pay more attention to their customers and keep them by giving them big reasons to stay instead of making them pay big fees to switch (Khanna & Sharma, 2017). Banks would no longer depend only on human innovation to improve their services. Instead, skill and technology would work together to improve performance. According to the WEF report "The New Physics of Financial Services," the use of AI in banking and financial services will make it possible for growth in those fields. These options are spread across capital markets, deposits, loans, payments, investment management, and market infrastructure.

Over the past century, the amount of greenhouse gases (GHG) has steadily gone up. About 584 Gt of CO2 from fossil fuels, changes in land use, and industrial activity are a big reason why the global temperature has increased by 0.9 °C since 1960. The top GHG-emitting countries globally include the USA, China, Japan, Germany, and India, which have been the major ecological footprint hotspots since 2019. The banking industry has adopted many platforms that are based on technology. It helps with operational transparency and reduces the bank's overall cost. It has also helped the business grow by letting them use working capital to grow and hire more people (SDG 8 and SDG 9). Blockchain could eliminate intermediaries by automating, simplifying, and improving how banks do business now. It would make transactions more transparent and easier to track. Gartner says, "Blockchain is an ever-growing list of cryptographically signed, irreversible transaction records that everyone in a network shares." Each record has a timestamp and links to transactions that have already happened. Those with the proper permissions and access can use this information to track the history of transactions. (Drosatos & Kaldoudi, 2019; Andoni et al., 2019; Beck et al., 2017). In order to better serve their customers, several well-known Indian banks, including the RBI, SBI, Axis and Yes Bank, are considering implementing blockchain technology (Yoo, 2017; Andoni et al., 2019; Sharma, 2018). Blockchain technology could be beneficial for the whole system of investing and banking. (Oh and Shong, 2017; Hassani et al., 2018; Beck, 2017). Third-party facilitation can raise the cost of sending money from 2 to 3% to as much as 20% in a typical banking system. It is especially true for cross-border payments.

It is worthwhile to investigate how bankers intend to use blockchain. This study examines the undisclosed reasons why a bank might want to use blockchain technology. With a complete understanding of the factors that drive adoption, changes that could make the drivers better have also been explored. Instead of re-testing an existing framework or getting the factors from secondary data and testing them in the real world to make a theoretical framework, our study wants to find out what factors affect bankers' intention to adopt blockchain technology for the digital transformation of banks. This research will look at how banks in India use blockchain technology since there is not much research in this area. This research is meant to answer the following questions:

What are the enablers/drivers/factors that are making banks intention to adopt blockchain technology?

The present research contributes to the existing body of knowledge on both banks' technology utilization and the specific domain of blockchain technology in several significant ways. Primarily, we extend the literature by adopting and validating a conceptual model for the adoption of blockchain technology, drawing upon the well-established framework of the Unified Theory of Acceptance and Use of Technology (UTAUT2) developed by Venkatesh et al. in 2012. Our approach combines qualitative interviews to identify additional factors that are not accounted for in the UTAUT2 model, and a quantitative survey to empirically test the relevance and impact of these factors in real-world scenarios. Through this mixed methodology, we enhance the understanding of the complex dynamics involved in the adoption of blockchain technology within the banking industry. The framework supports and verifies nine factors that affect bankers' intention to adopt blockchain: performance expectations, effort expectations, habits, enabling conditions, price value, hedonic motivation, social influence, psychological framework, and sustainability agenda. The following section has critically examined the extant literature on technology adoption in general and the application of the UTAUT2 model and use of blockchain technology more specifically.

REVIEW OF LITERATURE

Some financial institutions struggle to remain relevant and valuable in the digital age and an ever-changing market. The digital era has witnessed a multitude of technological advancements, opening up avenues for fresh entrants, including individuals outside the traditional realms of banking and finance (Wamba-Taguimdje et al., 2020; Alkhowaiter, 2020; Stamoulis et al., 2002;). Even though the UTAUT2 model was first launched in 2012, it has already gotten over 6000 citations from the IS field and other domains, demonstrating its predictive potential. Accordingly, researchers may utilise UTAUT2 as a theoretical lens to evaluate technology adoption-related difficulties in various contexts, either alone or in combination with other theories or by adding external factors. For example, clients were lured to digital banking due to social pressure, cost concerns, regular tasks, and banks' customer service methods. Customer service and the unified model (UTAUT-2) were chosen as the theoretical lenses to examine the determining factors, which include both the positive and negative sides of the adoption of digital banking and the development of technology in the banking industry for sustainability.

The rapid advancement of ICT has prompted banks and fintech enterprises to adapt by establishing versatile multi-channel distribution systems. These systems enable them to cater to diverse customer demands effectively. Keeping up with the evolving landscape, this transformation allows for enhanced accessibility and convenience in accessing financial services. This phenomenon has been extensively discussed by Alkhowaiter (2020), Shankar and Jebarajakirthy (2019), and Stamoulis et al. (2002) in their respective studies. However, according to the studies, banks are often reluctant to embrace technology because the expenses would force them to fail, shut down, or be acquired, even though global banking has been robust (Deloitte, 2019).

The most recent white papers in the banking sector highlight three areas where artificial intelligence (AI) has great promise: 1) pricing, 2) the creation of new products and services, and 3) sales of goods and services. However, only some studies have used text mining to improve the delivery of service-oriented organizations. (Kumar et al., 2021). For example, the Wells Fargo mobile chatbot software utilizes Facebook Messenger and artificial intelligence to reply to clients' natural language interactions, determine how much money is in their bank accounts, and identify the nearest ATM (Arjun et al., 2021). By visualizing business helpers in financial transactions, applications for virtual advisers facilitate the connection between customers and banks. Additionally, the organization is adapting several technologies to meet evolving consumer requirements. Consequently, digital banking products may boost a company's profitability and a salesperson's capacity to satisfy client expectations. The current emphasis of banks is on relationship banking. Nearly 33,000 banking customers from 18 nations participated in worldwide research conducted by Accenture Financial Services. Participants said that customer service increases their loyalty by 49%.

Globally, digital technologies are incorporated into several aspects of everyday life. Individuals, organizations, and the government are seeing an expansion of options, an improvement in efficiency, and the introduction of new communication channels due to technological advancements. The global microfinance market is swiftly embracing technological advancements seen in the banking industry. One such innovation is the M-Wallet, a digital wallet that functions like a physical wallet, allowing individuals and businesses to send and receive money through a mobile app and make payments on various e-commerce platforms. The primary objective of the M-Wallet is to leverage cutting-edge digital technologies, reducing banking costs while enhancing customer service (Singh & Sinha, 2020; Leong et al., 2020; Singh et al., 2020). Furthermore, leveraging the internet as a distribution channel empowers financial institutions and fintech firms to offer clients superior services, reliable information, and strategic partnerships, thereby fostering customer loyalty (Nazaritehrani and Mashali, 2020; Shankar and Jebarajakirthy, 2019; Stamoulis et al., 2002; Nso, 2018).

Nations such as Africa have been able to create cutting-edge technologies, such as mobile money, to enhance the financial inclusion of citizens by leveraging existing infrastructures (Lashitew et al., 2019; Germain, 2019; N'Dri & Kakinaka, 2020). The "Afriland First Bank" created the "SARA by Afriland" M-Banking application so that its clients and non-customers may have a mobile wallet or account. "SARA"

Money, a sort of electronic wallet, provides services to users without bank accounts, whilst "SARA" Banking provides services to customers with bank accounts (Aloys in 2020, Bive'e in 2020, Yannick in 2019 and Fonchamnyo in 2013). Incorporating connected technologies into their services, banks have introduced a distinctive payment mechanism, notably the QR code. This innovative feature allows for seamless transfers between bank accounts and digital wallets, as well as peer-to-peer transactions, all without the need for a password. Users simply scan the QR code to initiate secure and convenient transactions, eliminating the hassle of password inputs. This streamlined approach to payments demonstrates the transformative power of connected technologies within the banking sector. The "SARA" M-Banking app has the potential to increase financial inclusion in Cameroon dramatically, and this technology may be considered a catalyst for this transformation. (Bive'e, 2020; Valence, 2017). The UTAUT model was created after a comprehensive literature review of the traditional models commonly used to explain IS/IT usage behaviour. It seeks to explain user intentions and subsequent behaviour while interacting with an information system. According to (Baabdullah et al., 2019) examination of UTAUT2, the usage of M-Banking by Saudi Arabian customers is impacted by characteristics such as performance anticipation, enabling circumstances, and hedonic motivation. Investigate the variables influencing Jordanian bank customers' adoption of mobile banking by expanding UTAUT2 with a trust construct (Alalwan et al., 2017). To utilise this approach to emphasise the importance of habit while assessing the popularity of mobile online gaming (Ramirez-Correa et al., 2019).

Several studies have explored the factors influencing the adoption of mobile-based technologies, specifically Mobile Wallet/Money (Banking), and have found that these factors vary depending on the study setting. Malaquias and Hwang (2019) conducted a study in developed nations, such as the United States, and highlighted the significant role of social influence in determining technology usage. Conversely, in emerging economies like Brazil, perceived ease of use emerged as the most crucial factor in technology adoption. In India, the desire to embrace, adapt, and advocate for mobile wallet services is driven by multiple factors, including ease of use, usefulness, perceived risk, and overall attitude. These findings emphasize the contextual nature of technology adoption and the importance of considering specific factors relevant to each setting. In contrast, user happiness and recommendation of the mobile wallet are influenced by stress. Banks and telecom providers are simplifying their procedures and making it simpler for consumers to do business with them.

Through blockchain and bitcoin, information on multiple loans previously stored as difficult-to-find database data is now readily accessible. It also benefited the banking industry in keeping track of information on prospective borrowers who needed loans but could not receive them owing to a lack of trust resulting from incorrectly inaccessible documents. In addition to wasting time and money, the industry employs unreliable agents. Consequently, awarding loans would be onerous and hard to oversee. As a solution to this issue, blockchain technology has been proposed and has also assisted in implementing measures for the financial sector's sustainable functioning.

ICT utilizes computers, microelectronics, and telecommunications to facilitate the reliable, swift, and cost-effective production, storage, and transmission of information in various forms—be it pictures, words, or numbers. Hardware and software form integral components of this technology. In the modern era, the financial sector has witnessed profound transformations due to the impact of telecommunications and information technology (Beck et al.). Among these advancements, blockchain stands out as a trustless technology that ensures privacy and security. By leveraging blockchain, a framework can provide enhanced security, trust, and privacy while reducing fraud and boosting efficiency within the financial sector. A recent study highlighted that implementing a blockchain-based framework for microfinance outreach to farmers would enable microfinance organizations to dynamically tailor loans based on farmers' actions, mitigating the risk of severe debt and improving agricultural practices. This, in turn, would increase farm outputs, income, and overall financial stability. Preliminary findings suggest that blockchain technology has the potential to address various social, political, and economic challenges. Trust concerns hinder NGO's and borrowers in the microcredit system. More publications are addressing the combination of microfinance with technology, which opens up new opportunities for the advancement of the underprivileged and encourages lenders to employ this technology for long-term viability. Using blockchain technology will avoid any transaction defaults. On their invested capital, lenders may earn larger interest rates than banks. Borrowers might profit from lower interest rates on borrowed funds than banks. Blockchain will precisely give rapid output, benefiting not just the conventional banking industry but also linked companies since banks take time to implement changes.

Self-sovereign identification is a sort of identity provided by blockchain technology that cannot be altered in any way. It provides more security than conventional identification systems. Users can validate their identities using the self-sovereign ID, eliminating the need for passwords. This self-sovereign identity was designed with the notion that each individual should control how their identity is used. Users may use this identification to manage their identities, access information, and change it. Users can choose which data they want to keep private. In addition, users have the opportunity to delete their identities if required. This strategy will give users control over their data instead of giving it to large organisations (Sharma et al., 2022). Typically, each organisation or platform has its authentication procedure. With self-sovereign identification, on the other hand, we only need to confirm our identity once in any organisation. Due to this identification, official processes to verify identity are no longer required. Due to its desirable characteristics of cheap cost, high speed, transparency, and security, blockchain-based transactions have attracted the interest of several solution providers, who have subsequently developed blockchain-based payment systems (Sharma & Sharma, 2022). It was incorporated in the UTAUT2 model and demonstrates that the overall user experience of the technology is equally important to consumer adoption as internal beliefs and the technology's corresponding value (Alalwan et al., 2017; Venkatesh et al.,2012).

Existing research has shown the significance of technology adoption throughout the evolution of new technologies, and the same holds true for blockchain technology. With the introduction of new technologies, more empirical proof is necessary. The purpose of the present study is to delve further into the use of the UTAUT2 model in Indian banks for the adoption of blockchain technology. The theory's conceptual model is a seven-factor UTAUT2 model to which two more elements were added after experts in the banking industry were consulted.

DATA INPUTS AND RESEARCH METHODOLOGY

The current study is based on primary data gathered through surveying and in-person interviews. To develop the research instrument, a combination of constructs was utilized, incorporating a standardized scale provided by Venkatesh et al. (2012), as well as newly constructed elements derived from the personal interview method. This comprehensive approach ensured a robust and well-rounded assessment of the research variables. Seven constructs which are used as independent factors and behavioural intention as dependent factor were provided via the study's standardized scale, and two more were discovered through one-on-one interviews with bankers in strategic positions. These two more constructs

Table 1. Profile of respondents

Profile of Respondents		No. of Respondents	% of Respondents
Gender			
	Male	193	61.46
	Female	121	38.54
	Total	**314**	**100.00**
Department	Legal Department	12	3.82
	Human Resource Management	18	5.73
	Information Technology/Information security	63	20.06
	Central operations	88	28.03
	Customer service related	133	42.36
	Total	**314**	**100.00**
Experience			0.00
	Less than 3 years	106	33.76
	3-8 years	57	18.15
	8-14years	81	25.80
	More than 14 years	70	22.29
	Total	**314**	**100.00**

were discovered after a thorough examination of interview snippets. The newly created measurement scale was then employed as a survey instrument for bankers at managerial levels. A final sample of 314 respondents was considered for further analysis. The analysis began with exploratory factor analysis to extract the total number of constructs, and two newly identified constructs were named *sustainability agenda* and *psychological framework*. First, the newly identified scale was checked for reliability and validity. Next, the factors influencing bankers' intentions to adopt blockchain technology for banks' digital transformation were discovered using structural equation modelling. Finally, the profile of bank managers was employed as a moderating variable to understand the results. Three moderating variables were used in the current study to account for the bank managers' experience, gender, and department. The profile of respondents is given in Table 1.

Figure 1. Integrated model of the study

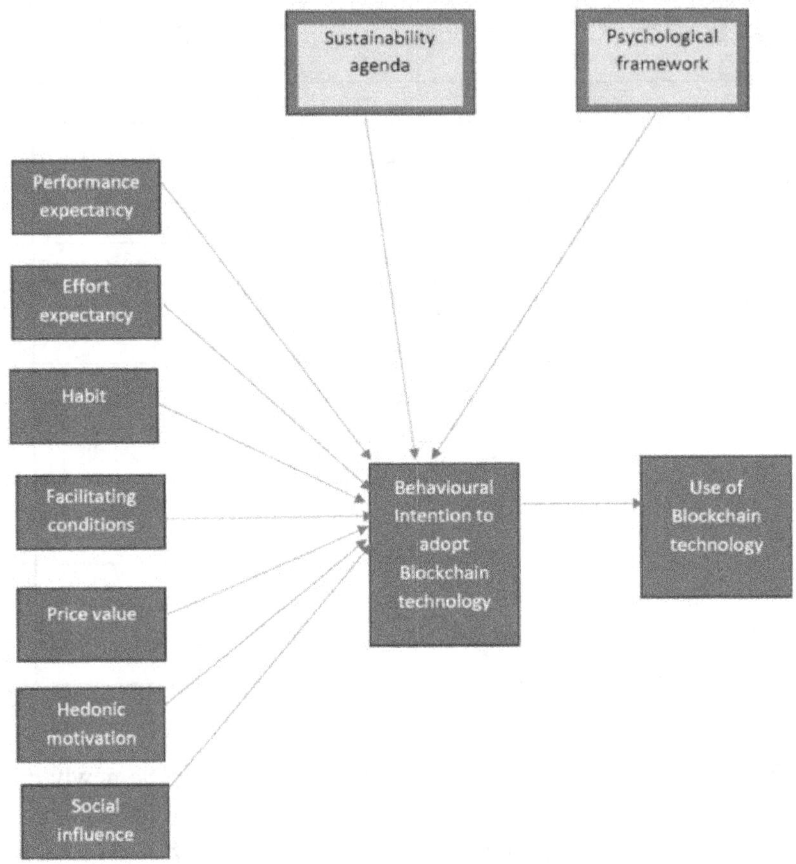

RESULTS AND INTERPRETATION

The findings of the study are explained in the following sections. The data collected were first analyzed using exploratory factor analysis (EFA) followed by confirmatory factor analysis (CFA). After that, the structural equation modelling was used to study the causal effect of independent factors on dependent factor. Finally, the results are further elaborated using different moderating variables mentioned in the above section.

RESULTS OF EFA

In order to examine the association between variables, exploratory factor analysis (EFA) is employed to determine the number of constructs. This technique condenses the study's variables into fewer, more meaningful interrelated dimensions (Kinnear & Gray, 2010; Hair et al., 2010). Before conducting EFA, two tests are conducted to ensure the suitability of the data for factor analysis. The first is the Kaiser-Meyer-Olkin (KMO) test, which measures the adequacy of the sample for factor analysis, with coefficients ranging from 0 to 1. Additionally, Bartlett's Test of Sphericity examines the hypothesis that the

Table 2. KMO and Bartlett's test

Kaiser-Meyer-Olkin Measure of Sampling Adequacy.		0.874
Bartlett's Test of Sphericity	Approx. Chi-Square	4163.248
	df	528
	Sig.	0.000

study's variables are unrelated, and the correlation matrix is an identity matrix. The results of both tests confirm that the data is appropriate for factor analysis. The KMO coefficient is 0.874, and Bartlett's test is significant, refuting the hypothesis (see Table 2). All items in the study have a factor loading of more than 0.4, except for two items, which are therefore excluded from further analysis (Hair et al., 1998). Varimax rotation and principal component analysis (PCA) are utilized to identify the study's constructs. The factor analysis results reveal ten primary constructs, with eigenvalues greater than 1, collectively explaining 67.995% of the total variation (see Table 3). These factors exhibit no cross-loading and fall within an acceptable range of factor loading. Subsequently, these constructs are subjected to reliability and validity testing.

Table 3. Total variance explained

Component	Initial Eigenvalues			Extraction Sums of Squared Loadings			Rotation Sums of Squared Loadings		
	Total	% of Variance	Cumulative %	Total	% of Variance	Cumulative %	Total	% of Variance	Cumulative %
1	8.962	27.157	27.157	8.962	27.157	27.157	2.708	8.207	8.207
2	2.464	7.467	34.624	2.464	7.467	34.624	2.597	7.870	16.077
3	1.746	5.292	39.916	1.746	5.292	39.916	2.552	7.735	23.812
4	1.677	5.082	44.998	1.677	5.082	44.998	2.397	7.264	31.076
5	1.453	4.403	49.401	1.453	4.403	49.401	2.395	7.259	38.335
6	1.375	4.168	53.569	1.375	4.168	53.569	2.101	6.366	44.701
7	1.341	4.064	57.633	1.341	4.064	57.633	2.079	6.300	51.001
8	1.269	3.847	61.479	1.269	3.847	61.479	2.054	6.225	57.226
9	1.136	3.443	64.922	1.136	3.443	64.922	1.922	5.825	63.051
10	1.014	3.073	67.995	1.014	3.073	67.995	1.632	4.944	67.995

DISCRIMINANT VALIDITY OF THE CONSTRUCTS

To assess discriminant validity in the present research, various methods were employed, including the use of the Average Variance Extracted (AVE) measure as suggested by Hair et al. (1998). The findings of the study, as presented in Table 3, indicate that all the constructs demonstrate satisfactory discriminant validity. This indicates that each construct measures a distinct and unique aspect, further strengthening the robustness of the research outcomes.

Table 4. Construct matrix showing discriminant validity: Dependent variable behavioral

AVE		AdopFactrs	BeInt
0.532992	AdopFactrs	0.532992	
0.5726	BeInt	0.295936	0.5726

Diagonal values are SQRT of AVE and off-diagonal values are interconstruct correlations
Source: Authors' compilation

MEASUREMENT MODEL AND SUMMARY OF MODEL FIT INDICES

The measurement model of the study is depicted in Figure 2, and an evaluation of the model fit has been conducted, with all indices meeting the threshold criteria (refer to Figure 1). The summary of the model fit for the measurement model can be observed in Figure 2. The default model satisfied all the criteria for a good measurement model. To assess the fit of both the measurement and structural models, the authors employed several key indices, including normed chi-square (CMIN/Df), Comparative Fit Index (CFI), Tucker Lewis Index (TLI), Goodness of Fit index (GFI), Adjusted Goodness of Fit index (AGFI), and Root Mean Square Error of Approximation (RMSEA). The study's findings indicate that all model components and constructs meet acceptable limits. The minimal discrepancy, as indicated by CMIN/Df, is the initial criterion for assessing the quality of fit, with a suggested range of 2 to 5 (Wheaton et al., 1977; Ullman, 2001). GFI/AGFI ratios of 1.00 imply an excellent match, while values of .95 indicate a good fit, and .90 suggest an acceptable fit (Jöreskog & Sörbom, 1981). An NFI and TLI score of .9 or above is considered excellent, according to Hu and Bentler (1999). The current research's measurement model satisfies these indicators.

Figure 2. Measurement model of the study

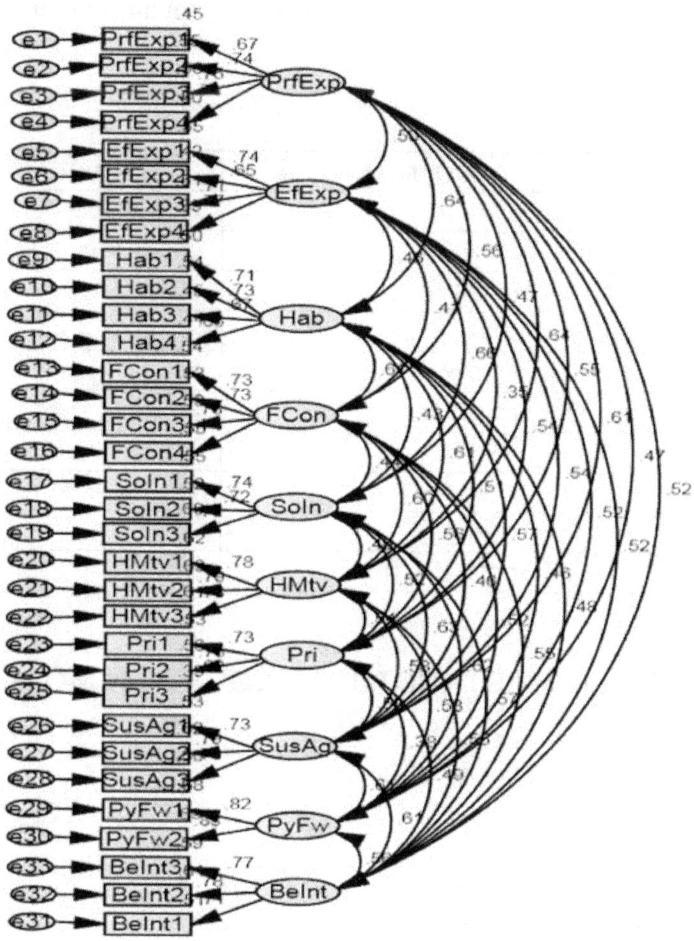

RESULTS OF RELIABILITY AND VALIDITY OF CONSTRUCTS

The table given below presents the measures of composite construct reliability and average variance extracted for different constructs examined in the study. Composite construct reliability assesses the internal consistency and reliability of each construct, while average variance extracted reflects the extent to which the construct captures variance in relation to measurement errors.

Based on the table, most constructs demonstrate acceptable composite construct reliability, with values ranging from 0.672 to 0.738. The constructs have good internal consistency and reliability in measuring the underlying concepts. Similarly, the average variance extracted values range from 0.482 to 0.683, indicating that the constructs account for substantial variance in their respective constructs beyond the measurement errors.

The findings presented in Table 5 illustrate the Average Variance Extracted (AVE) and Composite Construct Reliability (CCR) results, which are utilized to assess the convergent and discriminant validity of the constructs. The coefficients for both AVE and CCR were found to meet the recommended thresholds of 0.5 and 0.6, respectively, as suggested by Bagozzi and Yi (1988), Fornell and Larcker (1981), and Hair et al. (1998). These results confirm the validity of all constructs examined in the study.

Table 5. Composite construct reliability and average variance extracted

	Composite Construct Reliability	Average Variance Extracted
PrfExp	0.701	0.514
EfExp	0.737	0.518
Hab	0.672	0.482
FCon	0.734	0.536
SoIn	0.686	0.556
HMtv	0.700	0.617
BeInt	0.695	0.573
Pri	0.629	0.492
SusAg	0.710	0.547
PyFw	0.738	0.683

RESULTS OBTAINED FROM STRUCTURAL EQUATION MODELLING

Figure 3. Structural equation model of the study

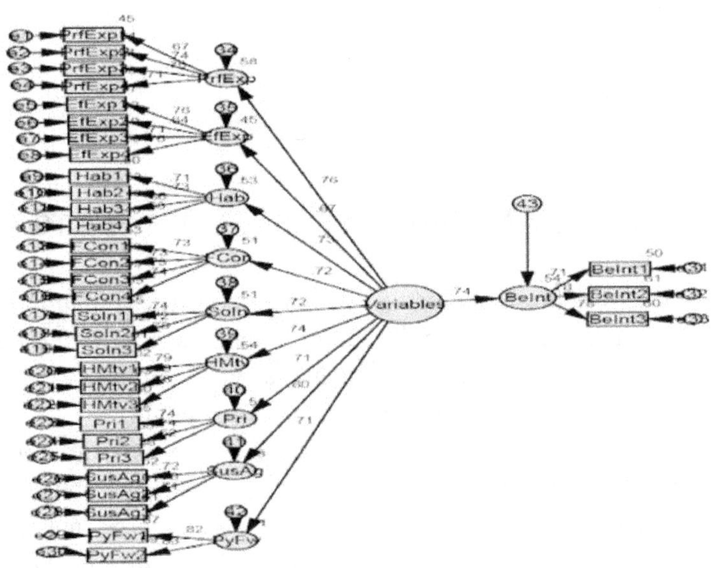

Table 6 presents the results obtained from a structural equation model (SEM). The table displays the standardized regression weights and their corresponding standard errors (S.E.) between two variables, specifically between "BeInt" (bankers' intention to adopt) and "AdopFactrs" (adoption factors). The standardized regression weight of 0.738 indicates the strength and direction of the relationship between "BeInt" and "AdopFactrs." This weight suggests a positive and significant association between bankers' intention to adopt (BeInt) and the nine adoption factors represented by "AdopFactrs". Furthermore, the note below the table indicates that the adoption factors are found to be significant at the 0.05 level of significance, suggesting that these factors have a significant impact on bankers' intention to adopt. Finally, it is important to note that the adoption factors are defined by the nine variables represented by "Adopfactrs." Overall, the table provides information on the strength of the relationship and the significance of the adoption factors concerning bankers' intention to adopt blockchain technology.

Table 6. Results obtained from structural equation model

			Standardized Regression Weights	S.E.
BeInt	<---	AdopFactrs	0.738	1.124

***The adoption factors are found significant at 0.05 level of significance.** *Variable is defined by nine factors (Adopfactrs)*

CONCLUSION AND IMPLICATION OF THE STUDY

This research contributes to the existing body of knowledge on both banks' technology usage and blockchain technology in several significant ways. Firstly, it adopts and validates a conceptual model of blockchain technology adoption based on the Unified Theory of Acceptance and Use of Technology (UTAUT2 by Venkatesh et al., 2012). The research employs a mixed methodology approach, combining qualitative interviews to identify factors not included in the UTAUT2 model and a quantitative survey to test these factors in real-world settings. The findings support and validate nine factors influencing bankers' intention to adopt blockchain technology: performance expectations, effort expectations, habits, enabling conditions, price value, hedonic motivation, social influence, psychological framework, and sustainability agenda. Additionally, the study critically examines the existing literature on technology adoption in general and specifically explores the application of the UTAUT2 model and the use of blockchain technology.

The study has made several significant contributions. Firstly, it has advanced the existing technology adoption theory by identifying two additional constructs: the sustainability agenda and the psychological framework. Furthermore, these constructs have been thoroughly examined for their reliability and validity, enhancing our understanding of this field.

Additionally, the study has provided valuable managerial insights, including the following:

1. The study's findings highlight various moderating variables and offer valuable assistance to bankers in their decision-making processes.
2. The study's exploration of the significance levels of technology adoption factors across different profiles of bankers and functional areas within a bank can provide important insights for developing technology adoption strategies in the current dynamic scenario.
3. Bankers, strategic managers, and board members can refer to these findings to develop effective technology adoption and implementation mechanisms within their respective banks.

4. The findings also hold significance for technology solution providers, as they offer insights from bankers' perspectives, enabling them to better understand their customers' needs and preferences.
5. Given the ever-evolving nature of technology, technology adoption will continue to be an area of ongoing research. Thus, researchers can utilize these findings as a valuable resource for future studies.

The study's contributions extend theoretical knowledge and practical applications, making it a valuable resource for various stakeholders in technology adoption.

LIMITATIONS AND SCOPE OF THE STUDY

The study findings are based on a limited sample collected in a narrow geographical area. The two new constructs identified in the study have extended the existing UTAUT2 model. This model needs to be validated through new sample surveys covering a broader population across different countries. In the future, researchers can explore these possibilities with more empirical evidence.

REFERENCES

Alalwan, A. A., Dwivedi, Y. K., & Rana, N. P. (2017). Factors influencing adoption of mobile banking by Jordanian bank customers: Extending UTAUT2 with trust. *International Journal of Information Management*, *37*(3), 99–110. doi:10.1016/j.ijinfomgt.2017.01.002

Alkhowaiter, W. A. (2020). Digital payment and banking adoption research in Gulf countries: A systematic literature review. *International Journal of Information Management*, *53*, 102102. doi:10.1016/j.ijinfomgt.2020.102102

Arjun, R., Kuanr, A., & Suprabha, K. R. (2021). Developing banking intelligence in emerging markets: Systematic review and agenda. *International Journal of Information Management Data Insights*, *1*(2), 100026.

Baabdullah, A. M., Alalwan, A. A., Rana, N. P., Kizgin, H., & Patil, P. (2019). Consumer use of mobile banking (M-Banking) in Saudi Arabia: Towards an integrated model. *International Journal of Information Management*, *44*, 38–52. doi:10.1016/j.ijinfomgt.2018.09.002

Baabdullah, A. M., Alalwan, A. A., Rana, N. P., Patil, P., & Dwivedi, Y. K. (2019). An integrated model for m-banking adoption in Saudi Arabia. *International Journal of Bank Marketing*, *37*(2), 452–478. doi:10.1108/IJBM-07-2018-0183

Baabdullah, A. M., Rana, N. P., Alalwan, A. A., Islam, R., Patil, P., & Dwivedi, Y. K. (2019). Consumer adoption of self-service technologies in the context of the Jordanian banking industry: Examining the moderating role of channel types. *Information Systems Management*, *36*(4), 286–305. doi:10.1080/10580530.2019.1651107

Dwivedi, Y. K., Hughes, L., Ismagilova, E., Aarts, G., Coombs, C., Crick, T., Duan, Y., Dwivedi, R., Edwards, J., Eirug, A., Galanos, V., Ilavarasan, P. V., Janssen, M., Jones, P., Kar, A. K., Kizgin, H., Kronemann, B., Lal, B., Lucini, B., ... Williams, M. D. (2021). Artificial Intelligence (AI): Multidisciplinary perspectives on emerging challenges, opportunities, and agenda for research, practice and policy. *International Journal of Information Management*, *57*, 101994. doi:10.1016/j.ijinfomgt.2019.08.002

Farrell, L., Fry, T. R., & Risse, L. (2016). The significance of financial self-efficacy in explaining women's personal finance behaviour. *Journal of Economic Psychology*, *54*, 85–99. doi:10.1016/j.joep.2015.07.001

Farrell, L., Fry, T. R., & Risse, L. (2016). The significance of financial self-efficacy in explaining women's personal finance behaviour. *Journal of Economic Psychology*, *54*, 85–99. doi:10.1016/j.joep.2015.07.001

Fonchamnyo, D. C. (2013). Customers' perception of e-banking adoption in Cameroon: An empirical assessment of an extended TAM. *International Journal of Economics and Finance*, *5*(1), 166–176.

Gourisaria, M. K., Agrawal, R., Singh, V., Rautaray, S. S., & Pandey, M. (2022). AI and IoT Enabled Smart Hospital Management Systems. In *Data Science in Societal Applications* (pp. 77–106). Springer. doi:10.1007/978-981-19-5154-1_6

Hair, J., Black, W., Babin, B., & Anderson, R. (2010). Multivariate data analysis (7th ed.). Prentice Hall Inc.

Hair, J. F., Anderson, R. E., Tatham, R. L., & William, C. (1998). *Multivariate data analysis*. Academic Press.

Jebarajakirthy, C., & Shankar, A. (2021). Impact of online convenience on mobile banking adoption intention: A moderated mediation approach. *Journal of Retailing and Consumer Services*, *58*, 102323. doi:10.1016/j.jretconser.2020.102323

Kamdjoug, J. R. K., Wamba-Taguimdje, S. L., Wamba, S. F., & Kake, I. B. E. (2021). Determining factors and impacts of the intention to adopt mobile banking app in Cameroon: Case of SARA by afriland First Bank. *Journal of Retailing and Consumer Services*, *61*, 102509. doi:10.1016/j.jretconser.2021.102509

Khanna, V., & Sharma, R. (2017). Customer Switching Behavior in Retail Banking in India. *International Journal of Applied Business and Economic Research*, *15*(9), 427–441.

Malaquias, R. F., & Hwang, Y. (2019). Mobile banking use: A comparative study with Brazilian and US participants. *International Journal of Information Management*, *44*, 132–140. doi:10.1016/j.ijinfomgt.2018.10.004

Mehta, K., Sharma, R., Vyas, V., & Kuckreja, J. S. (2022). Exit strategy decision by venture capital firms in India using fuzzy AHP. *Journal of Entrepreneurship in Emerging Economies*, *14*(4), 643–669. doi:10.1108/JEEE-05-2020-0146

Nazaritehrani, A., & Mashali, B. (2020). Development of E-banking channels and market share in developing countries. *Financial Innovation*, *6*(1), 1–19. doi:10.118640854-020-0171-z

Nso, M. A. (2018). The role of e-banking as a marketing tool. *Innovative Marketing*, *14*(4), 56–65. doi:10.21511/im.14(4).2018.05

Ozturk, A. B., Bilgihan, A., Salehi-Esfahani, S., & Hua, N. (2017). Understanding the mobile payment technology acceptance based on valence theory: A case of restaurant transactions. *International Journal of Contemporary Hospitality Management, 29*(8), 2027–2049. doi:10.1108/IJCHM-04-2016-0192

Ramírez-Correa, P., Rondán-Cataluña, F. J., Arenas-Gaitán, J., & Martín-Velicia, F. (2019). Analysing the acceptation of online games in mobile devices: An application of UTAUT2. *Journal of Retailing and Consumer Services, 50*, 85–93. doi:10.1016/j.jretconser.2019.04.018

Sai, B. D. S., Nikhil, R., Prasad, S., & Naik, N. S. (2023). A decentralised KYC based approach for microfinance using blockchain technology. *Cyber Security and Applications, 1*, 100009. doi:10.1016/j.csa.2022.100009

Shankar, A., & Jebarajakirthy, C. (2019). The influence of e-banking service quality on customer loyalty: A moderated mediation approach. *International Journal of Bank Marketing, 37*(5), 1119–1142. doi:10.1108/IJBM-03-2018-0063

Sharma, A., & Sharma, R. (2022). Exploring Tax Decision Factors: A Perspective from North Indian Tax Practitioners. *Journal of Tax Reform, 8*(3), 285–297. doi:10.15826/jtr.2022.8.3.122

Sharma, R., Mehta, K., & Goel, A. (2022). Non-linear relationship between board size and performance of Indian companies. *The Journal of Management and Governance*. Advance online publication. doi:10.100710997-022-09651-8

Singh, N., Sinha, N., & Liébana-Cabanillas, F. J. (2020). Determining factors in the adoption and recommendation of mobile wallet services in India: Analysis of the effect of innovativeness, stress to use and social influence. *International Journal of Information Management, 50*, 191–205. doi:10.1016/j.ijinfomgt.2019.05.022

Stamoulis, D., Kanellis, P., & Martakos, D. (2002). An approach and model for assessing the business value of e-banking distribution channels: Evaluation as communication. *International Journal of Information Management, 22*(4), 247–261. doi:10.1016/S0268-4012(02)00011-7

Tamilmani, K., Rana, N. P., Wamba, S. F., & Dwivedi, R. (2021). The extended Unified Theory of Acceptance and Use of Technology (UTAUT2): A systematic literature review and theory evaluation. *International Journal of Information Management, 57*, 102269. doi:10.1016/j.ijinfomgt.2020.102269

Venkatesh, V., Thong, J. Y., & Xu, X. (2012). Consumer acceptance and use of information technology: Extending the unified theory of acceptance and use of technology. *Management Information Systems Quarterly, 36*(1), 157–178. doi:10.2307/41410412

Vyas, V., Mehta, K., & Sharma, R. (2023). The nexus between toxic-air pollution, health expenditure, and economic growth: An empirical study using ARDL. *International Review of Economics & Finance, 2023*(84), 154–166. doi:10.1016/j.iref.2022.11.017

Wamba-Taguimdje, S. L., Wamba, S. F., Kamdjoug, J. R. K., & Wanko, C. E. T. (2020). Influence of artificial intelligence (AI) on firm performance: The business value of AI-based transformation projects. *Business Process Management Journal, 26*(7), 1893–1924. doi:10.1108/BPMJ-10-2019-0411

Wamba-Taguimdje, S. L., Wamba, S. F., Kamdjoug, J. R. K., & Wanko, C. E. T. (2020). Impact of Artificial Intelligence on Firm Performance: Exploring the Mediating Effect of Process-Oriented Dynamic Capabilities. In *Digital Business Transformation* (pp. 3–18). Springer. doi:10.1007/978-3-030-47355-6_1

Chapter 4
Impact of Blockchain Technology on the Stock Market

C. V. Suresh Babu
https://orcid.org/0000-0002-8474-2882
Hindustan Institute of Technology and Science, India

Sanjai Das
https://orcid.org/0009-0005-9902-6378
Hindustan Institute of Technology and Science, India

ABSTRACT

Several of the inefficiencies and risks that afflict traditional stock market infrastructure have been addressed by blockchain technology. Blockchain, due to its decentralized and transparent nature, can provide a safe and efficient platform for investors and issuers to exchange assets without the need for middlemen. This chapter investigates the influence of blockchain technology on the stock market, examining the possible benefits and hazards connected with its implementation. The authors contend that blockchain has the potential to transform the stock market by lowering transaction costs, increasing liquidity, and improving transparency. Nevertheless, there are problems and hazards connected with integrating blockchain technology into the stock market, including regulatory and legal hurdles, interoperability concerns, and the possibility of market disruption. As blockchain technology evolves, market players must carefully assess the consequences of its adoption and work together toward its ethical and sustainable integration.

INTRODUCTION

The stock market is a complicated and dynamic system that is vital to the global economy. It provides a platform for businesses to obtain funds and for investors to buy stock in those businesses, supporting economic growth and development. Yet, the stock market is prone to fraudulent operations, inefficient processes, and high transaction costs, which can undermine investor confidence and impair the market's capacity to perform successfully. The rise of Blockchain technology offers a viable solution to these problems.

DOI: 10.4018/978-1-6684-8624-5.ch004

Blockchain technology is projected to play an important role in future stock markets. It allows for the construction of immutable transaction records that are visible to all network members. Many blocks are "chained" together to build a Blockchain database by making references to the one before it in each block.

Each block consists of one or more events, which are effectively changes to the assets' stated owners. Members of the Blockchain network use a consensus process to validate transactions before adding new blocks to the chain.

The breakthrough allows for the creation of a network that is "completely peer-to-peer, with no trusted third party," such as a government agency or financial institution. The findings of this proposal will provide light on the role of Blockchain technology in changing the stock market, as well as providing insights for policymakers, investors, and market participants.

RELATED WORK

Problem Identified

The present stock market infrastructure is built on a centralized system with several intermediaries, such as brokers, custodians, and clearinghouses. With high transaction fees, extended settlement timeframes, and a lack of transparency, this system is complicated and costly. It also carries considerable dangers, including counterparty risk and the possibility of fraudulent activity.

Blockchain technology has emerged as a viable replacement for existing stock market infrastructure in recent years. Blockchain is a distributed ledger system that enables safe, transparent, and immutable transaction record-keeping. It ensures the integrity and secrecy of data using cryptographic techniques, and it eliminates the need for middlemen by offering a decentralized and trustless system.

Numerous Blockchain-based efforts have been undertaken to disrupt the stock market. For example, tZero, a Blockchain-based trading platform, intends to cut settlement time, boost transparency, and lower transaction costs. Similarly, NASDAQ has introduced Linq, a Blockchain-based platform that allows private firms to issue and exchange shares on a Blockchain-based platform.

Literature Survey

Satoshi Nakamoto wrote Bitcoin: A Peer-to-Peer Electronic Currency System in 2008, in which he suggested the basic concept of the first cryptocurrency, Bitcoin and this is where it all begins. Use of Blockchain technology in a completely different level (Nakamoto, 2008).

The Blockchain, as a distributed ledger, is a chain structure linked in timestamp order by cryptography. The peer-to-peer network topology, for example, uses a consensual method to chain or verify trade events. This enables the Blockchain to include transactions between parties while being an immutable, secure, and trustless platform (Chang & Chen, 2020).

Data is copied among various participants, Blockchain does not enable privacy by design. Many techniques for preserving privacy in Blockchain have been presented, which may be divided into two categories: I data distortion and (ii) data encryption-based approaches (Li & Wang, 2018).

The stock market is a system comprised of financial and governmental institutions that exchange shares, bonds, or other securities in a trading (Bhandarkar et al., 2019).

We choose Blockchain technology to overcome the limits and inadequacies of the traditional stock exchange platform. Blockchain is defined as a "network of computers that must all agree that a transaction has occurred before it is stored in a 'chain' of computer code." The transfer details are stored on a public ledger that anybody on the network may access (Ahram et al., 2017).

It is made up of blocks, each of which contains a hash of the preceding block and confirmed transaction data secured by hash signatures (Chen, Chen, & Lin, 2018; Lundqvist et al., 2017; Samaniego et al., 2016).

Transactions are broadcast over the network and validated by a process known is mining, which is performed out by nodes in the network known as mining nodes (Ahram et al., 2017).

Chapron emphasizes the issues associated with legislative debasement in natural supportability. He makes a case for Blockchain's unique record powers in enabling the "4 successes" of cryptogovernance: ownership, accountability, motivational factors, and policy. Crypto innovations have a particularly strong potential for verifying ownership for "from the a birth certificate to a salmon or a woodland" (2017).

It looks that they will only be able to find 41 participant publications published by 2015. Among the most intriguing things they point out is the fact that 80 percent of the articles they identified were on the use of network for Bitcoin - a digital money.

While it was apparent that focusing just on digital money was a strong possibility in this field of study, researchers chose to focus on specialised difficulties with Blockchain - security, execution, adaptability, and so on. They also discovered that the analysis was somewhat focused on Blockchain security and identifying constraints Yli-Huumo et al., (2016).

Argue that Blockchain represents the most crucial technology for university education going forward. They provide warnings about what will likely happen if such technology is not used, but they also push us to research the wide possibilities for how Blockchain may enhance the situation of higher education. They highlight four areas for higher education innovators to work on: student records, pedagogy, prices, and instructional models.

The idea of value is central to their argument, and the internet is severely constrained in this regard. We may distribute data via the World Wide Web, but when we communicate papers and files, we are exchanging copies rather than the originals. They emphasise that the Blockchain may be utilised to store data Tapscott & Tapscott, (2016).

The producers start by applying a bank, for example, and all assets that are really wasted because of putting away and representing all trades themselves claim that fewer assets used, whether hard drives to store their data or the additional power required to keep operating in, not only cost banks more money than a record produced from a Blockchain, but also result in less assets being used. As a result, reduced technological trash and vitality use would benefit the environment. Furthermore, the cost of a Blockchain exchange has become less expensive as the average of intensity utilisation per exchange has decreased Cocco et al., (2017).

Advantages

1. **Transparency:** Because Blockchain technology offers transparent record-keeping, it has the potential to reduce fraud and boost investor confidence.
2. **Security and Efficiency:** Blockchain technology provides a very secure platform for storing financial data and processing transactions, potentially lowering the danger of cyberattacks and hacking. The

implementation of Blockchain technology might speed the settlement process, lowering transaction costs and the time required to execute trades.

3. **Accessibility:** Blockchain technology has the potential to make the stock market more available to investors, particularly those in developing nations where entry is now restricted.
4. **Increased Accuracy:** Because Blockchain technology produces an accurate and tamper-proof record of all transactions, it has the potential to eliminate errors and improve financial reporting accuracy.
5. **Automated Compliance:** Blockchain technology can be used to automate compliance with regulatory standards, lowering the risk of non-compliance and the accompanying penalties.
6. **Decentralization:** Blockchain technology enables decentralized control, which has the potential to lessen the power of huge financial institutions and foster a more democratic stock market.
7. **Traceability:** Blockchain technology provides a clear and visible record of ownership and transaction history, which may lower the risk of fraudulent behavior and increase security tracking.

Disadvantages

1. **Technical Complexity:** Because Blockchain technology demands specialized technical knowledge, it may be out of reach for smaller businesses and investors.
2. **Scaling Issues:** The current Blockchain network may not be able to manage the enormous number of transactions required by the stock market, resulting in slower processing times and greater costs.
3. **Costly and Time-Consuming:** Developing and executing games and simulations may be time-consuming and resource-intensive, necessitating large investments in technology and skills.
4. **Lack of Standardization:** There is presently no industry-wide standard for Blockchain technology, which may cause interoperability challenges and stymie adoption.
5. **Energy Consumption:** The amount of energy required for Blockchain technology could be a substantial obstacle to adoption, particularly as worries about climate change and sustainability develop.

A Comparison of The Impact of Blockchain Technology in Past Years

In 2017, the notion of Blockchain technology was still relatively new to the stock market, with many companies researching its potential but few using it. There were other important pilot projects and initiatives, such as Nasdaq's Linq platform, which employed Blockchain technology for private market securities, and Overstock.com's tZero platform, which attempted to provide a Blockchain-based alternative to traditional stock exchanges. Overall, the influence of Blockchain technology on the stock market in 2017 remained minimal, with most companies still in the exploring phase.

In 2018: The impact of Blockchain technology on the stock market began to be felt more strongly in 2018, with the debut of many high-profile initiatives and projects. One of the most notable developments was the creation of the Bakkt platform, a joint venture between the Intercontinental Exchange and many other organizations that attempted to build a regulated exchange and clearinghouse for digital assets. Another major development was the introduction of the Security Token Offering model, which used Blockchain technology to issue and trade securities, as well as the use of Blockchain technology for proxy voting and shareholder participation. Overall, Blockchain technology had a significant impact on the stock market in 2018, with several key efforts and projects launched. phase.

In 2019, with several key advances and partnerships announced, the impact of Blockchain technology on the stock market has grown. One of the most notable was the collaboration between Nasdaq and Symbiont to develop a Blockchain-based platform for maintaining and trading private company shares. Another major development was the introduction of Blockchain-based exchange-traded funds (ETFs), as well as the growing usage of Blockchain technology for proxy voting and shareholder engagement. Nevertheless, Blockchain technology's impact on the stock market remained considerable in 2019, with an increasing number of initiatives and collaborations targeted at incorporating the technology into current systems.

In 2020, the stock market's perception of Blockchain technology was influenced by the COVID-19 outbreak, which created considerable disruption and confusion. Despite this, several important advancements occurred, including the debut of the Blockchain-based trading platform INX and the growing use of Blockchain technology for proxy voting and shareholder engagement. Due to the consequences of the pandemic, the overall influence of Blockchain technology on the stock market in 2020 was considerably muted compared to prior years.

In 2021, With several important efforts and partnerships announced, the impact of Blockchain technology on the stock market has grown. The creation of Canada's first Blockchain-based exchange-traded fund, which employed Blockchain technology to manage and trade assets, was one of the most significant breakthroughs. Other important developments include the expanding use of Blockchain technology for proxy voting and shareholder participation, as well as an increased interest in decentralized finance and non-fungible tokens. Nevertheless, the impact of Blockchain technology on the stock market remained considerable in 2021, with an increasing number of initiatives and collaborations targeted at incorporating the technology into current systems.

Challenges of Implementation of Blockchain in Stock Market

Scaling issues regularly plague Blockchain networks such as Bitcoin and Ethereum. Many public Blockchain presently have limited activity production capability, which may not be sufficient to fulfil the high transaction volume and speed requirements of stock exchanges. Scaling difficulties are being investigated using approaches like as decentralised consensus and off-chain protocols. The present regulatory structure for traditional stock markets don't always completely handle the usage of Blockchain technology. Clear norms and regulations are required to handle the distinct qualities and possible hazards connected with Blockchain use in stock markets. This encompasses ownership, property, data, and proper record.

Interoperability: Stock markets are ecologically important with many players, including traders, buyers, authorities, and clearinghouses. It is critical for smooth integration to ensure compatibility between existing systems and Blockchain-based solutions. To allow effective communication and data interchange across diverse platforms, standardizing initiatives and the creation of endpoints are essential.

While Blockchain technology provides intrinsic stability though the cryptography algorithms, there are still issues about the personal rights of sensitive trading data. As stock market transactions involve private information that must be protected, balancing the need for transparency and privacy is critical. Creating secrecy strategies that do not compromise the benefits of openness is an existing research topic.

Administration and Agreement Procedures: To validate transactions and ensure system integrity, Blockchain networks require governance models and consensus procedures. It is essential to create and carry out effective governance systems that would provide equality, diversity, and accountability. Agreement among several participants in a remote context may be difficult, and the quest for optimal consensus algorithms is an important topic of study.

Acceptance and User Friendliness: To promote widespread use of Blockchain technology in the stock market, user-friendly interfaces and seamless connectivity with existing trading platforms are required. User experience and education are critical in getting market adoption from players who are unfamiliar with Blockchain principles. Increasing accessibility, lowering complexity, and offering strong technical support are all important elements in promoting adoption.

Information Accuracy and Reliability: Because stock market transactions contain crucial financial information, it is critical to keep reliable and precise records. Blockchain systems must maintain the integrity and integrity of data throughout the network. Resolving data quality, validation, and synchronizing challenges is critical to establishing trust and confidence in the Blockchain-based stock market architecture.

Why Blockchain in the Stock Market?

The stock market, in instance, has seen Blockchain technology emerge as a possible answer. Its influence on the stock market has the potential to be huge and disruptive. One of the most significant advantages of Blockchain technology in the stock market is increased transparency. Blockchain enables all players to have real-time knowledge of the same data by providing a transparent and immutable ledger for recording transactions. Even though transactions can be easily verified by all stakeholders, this disclosure minimizes the chance of forgery and exploitation.

Through complement to transparency, Blockchain boosts stock market efficiency. Customary stock market operations can include many brokers and formal verification, resulting in delays and expensive transaction costs. By automating settlement and removing the need for intermediates, Blockchain technology can simplify these procedures. Actual settling and minimized processing save time and money for investors as well as market participants.

A critical consideration is security. The distributed and encrypted Blockchain protocol provides a strong security foundation for the stock market. Transactions on the Blockchain are tamper-proof and secured by powerful encryption methods. This makes it more difficult for hackers or hostile actors to falsify or modify transaction data, which enhances the overall protection of the share price ecosystem.

Furthermore, Blockchain technology has the potential to improve stock market accessibility. Blockchain-based systems enable fractional ownership and exchange of formerly illiquid assets. This creates financial options for those who may not have the money to invest in full stocks or accumulate losses.

Another significant benefit of Blockchain is the data integrity it provides. The Block chain's transaction records are permanent and auditable, making it a dependable source of information for audits and regulatory reasons. This increases confidence and lowers the need for human record validation and confirmation. Distributed ledger technology makes way for stock market transformation. It allows for the development of fresh financial goods such as tokenized assets and digital securities that may be transacted on distributed exchanges. These gadgets are able to equalize capital access to the market while also raising market stability.

Finally, the use of Blockchain technology in the stock market can enhance transparency, effectiveness, assurance, connectivity, regulation, integrity of information, and advancement significantly. While there are challenges and considerations to be addressed, the long term benefits make Blockchain a captivating new tech for the stock economy's future.

Why CTR Model

Access Control Optimisation: CTR encryption may be coupled with access control techniques to guarantee that only permitted parties have access to particular data within the Blockchain. Access privileges may be carefully controlled by encrypting data at the granular level and controlling encryption keys, prevent unauthorised parties from reading critical information.

Increased Data Integrity: CTR encryption offers a way for verifying the integrity of Blockchain data. Any unlawful alterations to the encrypted data can be discovered by encrypting the data and computing cryptographic hash functions. This guarantees that the stock market's transaction history is lie and get away and that the industry's data stay accurate.

Argument Definition

Blockchain technology can transform the stock market by delivering a new level of transparency, security, and efficiency. With Blockchain, investors may exchange assets simply and securely without the need for middlemen, lowering transaction costs and enhancing liquidity.

Moreover, Blockchain can provide a tamper-proof record of all trades and ownership transfers, minimizing the chance of fraud and enhancing investor trust. Yet, there are hurdles and hazards connected with the use of Blockchain technology in the stock market, such as regulatory concerns and the potential for market disruption.

As a result, before using Blockchain technology on a broad scale, it is critical to thoroughly weigh the benefits and hazards of Blockchain technology in the stock market.

METHODOLOGY

Classic Stock Market

According to one definition of the stock market, it is "an average of buying and offering bids for an item" Bhandarkar et al., (2019). Bonds, stocks, or other market assets might be the asset. To trade stocks, investors or traders must first create a brokerage account only with National Securities Depository, which manages clients' brokerage accounts and personal information. Due to market regulations, investors cannot put orders directly into the system and must instead go via a 3rd party, typically a broker.

Overseas traders use a financial institution known as a custodian to make orders on the local market. The matching engine for the tried to enter purchase and sale orders is hosted by the Stock Exchange. The Central Bank settles financial transactions between dealers and custodians.

All member authorities and investment firms must adhere to the norms and guidelines established by the Global Financial Authorities. It is also in charge of regularly monitoring and analanalyzing the stock exchange platform.

Outline of Trade

The classic stock market is a controlled system with a distinct design and a distinct series of action that occur when a new buyer enters the market. To begin, the investor must open an investment account with CSD and get a National Investment Number.

The buyer must then open a trades with a intermediate and supply the necessary NIN number. When the investor's information has been confirmed, he or she can use the associated broker facilities, such as the mobile app or website, to make purchases to buy or sell shares Suresh Babu, (2023).

The broker is in the position to transmit the investment's order through its Order Management System. Following the completion of a beneficial deal for that.

Figure 1. Outline of trade

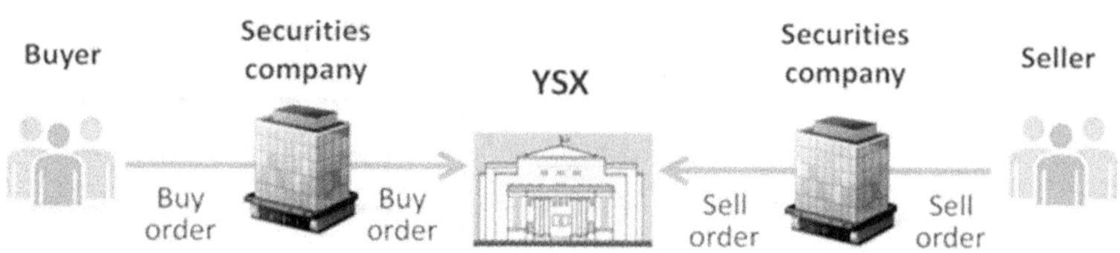

Order Types

Buyers can place a variety of transactions to buy or sell shares Pop et al., (2018). Several types of orders are detailed below to show how an acceptable match between purchasing and selling transactions occurs since certain orders allow the company to establish conditions that, if met, cause the transaction to be performed and hence create trades:

Buy/Sell Order: The purchaser wants to purchase the stock at its present price on the market. The vendor is in the same boat. This order type doesn't really apply provide the most financial profit from the transaction, but it does guarantee that order is performed as soon it has been placed.

Pending Order: The buyer indicates the highest price costumer is accepting to pay for a certain share. Any offer to sell that is similar to or lower than this threshold is accepted. The seller's limit is going to be the lowest price at which he or she is willing to sell. A purchase order is executed with such a price more than or equal for the fixed threshold.

Validity Defined Order: A limitation or a limit order can be combined with the transaction. The order will be valid for one day or until the specified date. If no legitimate date is supplied, most exchanges cancel the transaction after around 6 months.

FOK Order: FOK – Fill or Kill both carry out all the entire transaction (sell or buy all of the stated shares) or terminate the order.

Accept Order: The order is completed as soon as possible, and the unfilled amount is terminated.

Blockchain Overview

We picked Blockchain technology to solve the limits and inadequacies of the classic stock market system. A "Blockchain" is defined as "a distributed computer system in which all participants must agree that a deal occurred before it is stored in a "series" of computer code." The transfer data is saved in an official information that anyone who uses the internet may access.

It is made up of blocks, each of which includes a hash reference to the previous block as well as confirmed purchase history protected by hash signatures.

Trades on the Blockchain are spread all through the network and authenticated through mining, which is executed by network nodes known as mining nodes.

Figure 2. Overview of blockchain

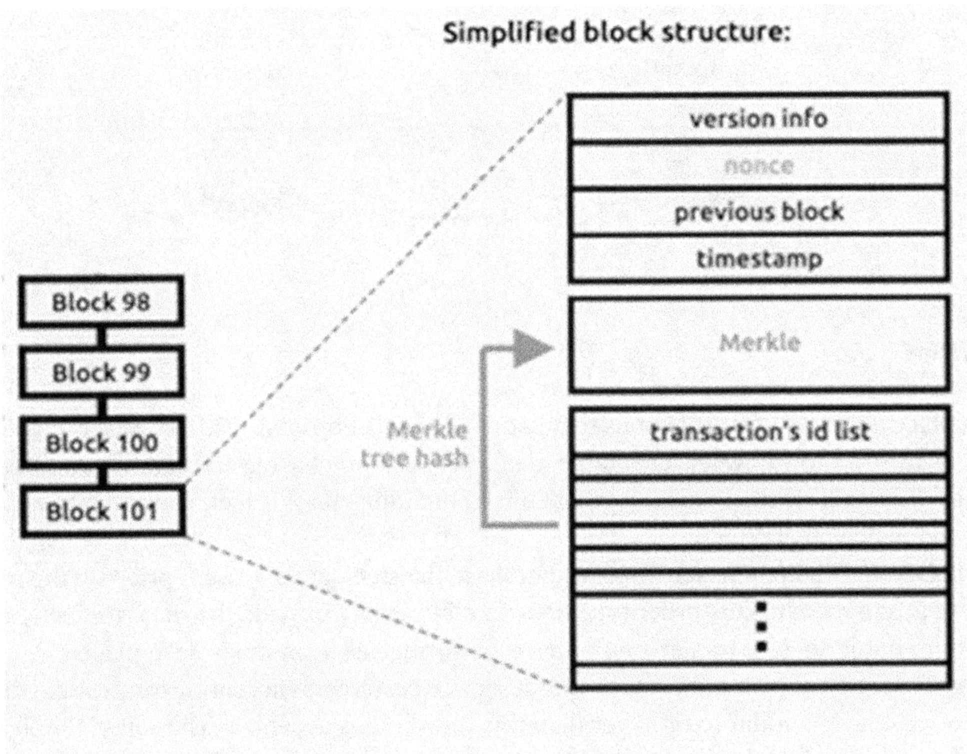

Types of Blockchain Implementation

Since nodes in a p2p network like a Blockchain do not respect each other, all nodes must reach an acceptance or cooperation regarding the next block to be added to the chain. Yet, depending on the kind of application and Blockchain technology used, multiple consensus techniques can be applied. There are two ways to implement a Blockchain network: both private and public.

1) Public permissionless Blockchain

Every user can become a node in a current Blockchain system and link to the infrastructure across the internet. The system leverages the P2p network concept, which employs a distributed architecture without a client functioning as an administrator. A flat topology links all clients on the network, with each peer having the same liberties and freedoms as their counterparts, as well as access to the same assets Ahram et al., (2017).

2) Public permissioned Blockchain

A public permissioned Blockchain is a sort of Blockchain network in which anybody may join and participate, but only authorized parties can validate transactions or blocks. This implies that, while the network is open to anyone, the ability to validate transactions is restricted to a small number of participants who have been granted authorization by network administrators.

3) Private Blockchain

Private Blockchain networks, unlike public Blockchain nodes, are identifiable and authenticated. In certain systems, an organization is in charge of looking after the roles and duties of a node and allowing them access to the information as needed.

Applying the CTR In the Stock Market

CTR Encryption

It also known as Counter encryption mode is a symmetric key encryption technique used to encrypt data in electronic communication, particularly stock market transactions. In this encryption method, a unique counter value is coupled with a symmetric encryption key to encrypt each block of data, ensuring the data's secrecy and integrity.

Since it is quick, efficient, and simple to deploy, CTR encryption has grown in favor of the stock market. It can instantly encrypt massive volumes of data, making it ideal for high-speed trading operations. Moreover, CTR encryption offers excellent security assurances and is immune to a wide range of conventional cryptographic attacks.

To encrypt each block of data, CTR encryption combines a unique counter value with a symmetric encryption key. This implies that even if an attacker intercepts the data, decrypting it will be difficult. CTR encryption is a very efficient and speedy choice for the financial industry, particularly the stock market.

Use of CTR in the Stock Market

CTR encryption, when applied in the stock market, can assist in protecting the privacy and security of sensitive financial information, including trading orders and account balances. Encrypting this data makes it far more difficult for attackers to intercept or alter the information in transit, aiding in the prevention of fraud and other sorts of cybercrime. Ultimately, CTR encryption is a significant tool for safeguarding electronic communication in the stock market and other industries, and its use is anticipated to rise as the demand for secure, high-speed data transfer grows.

Figure 3. CTR (counter mode encryption)

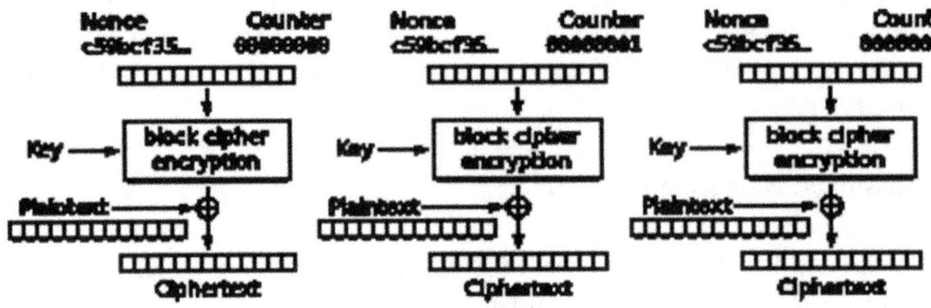

Counter Mode Encryption (CTR) is a symmetric key block cipher operating mode that has grown in popularity in the realm of electronic communication and financial transactions. Because the stock market relies extensively on electronic communication and financial transactions, effective security measures are required to safeguard sensitive financial data from illegal access or manipulation. CTR encryption is a powerful instrument that can assist in meeting this need by providing robust security and privacy for electronic communication and transactions.

CTR encryption can be used in the stock market to safeguard sensitive financial data such as trading orders, account balances, and other secret information. CTR encryption can assist prevent illegal access, alteration, or interception of data in transit by encrypting it. This contributes to data integrity and confidentiality, lowering the danger of fraud, insider trading, and other destructive behaviors, when paired with Blockchain technology, can give an extra degree of security and anonymity to stock market transactions. Blockchain is a decentralized, tamper-proof ledger that securely and transparently records all transactions. By encrypting the data before adding it to the Blockchain via CTR encryption, the data is safeguarded from illegal access or tampering, maintaining the data's integrity and validity.

Moreover, CTR encryption may be used to protect smart contracts, which are self-executing agreements between parties recorded on the Blockchain. These smart contracts can execute complicated financial operations like trading without the use of middlemen. The use of CTR encryption to safeguard the data in these smart contracts ensures the confidentiality and privacy of the transactions while reducing the danger of fraud or cyber-attacks.

CTR encryption also has the benefit of being immune to several typical cryptographic attacks, such as the plaintext attack and the selected plaintext attack. As a result, it is a very secure alternative for safeguarding financial data and transactions. It is crucial to remember, however, that while CTR encryption is extremely effective, it is not a cure-all for all security issues. To acquire access to encrypted data, attackers might still attempt to exploit flaws in the underlying systems or steal passwords or keys. To secure the greatest degree of security for financial data and transactions in the stock market, it is critical to adopt many levels of protection, such as strong passwords, multi-factor authentication, and frequent security assessments.

RESULT

Effectiveness of CTR in Economics

The speed and efficiency of CTR encryption are its main advantages. CTR encryption encrypts each block of data by mixing a unique counter value with a symmetric encryption key. This makes it more efficient and quicker than conventional encryption techniques, which need extensive computations for each block of data. When used with Blockchain technology, CTR encryption can provide a quick and effective method of securing financial transactions.

Because Blockchain technology is decentralized and tamper-resistant, it may provide a safe and transparent record of financial transactions without the use of middlemen. By encrypting the data before adding it to the Blockchain via CTR encryption, the data is safeguarded from illegal access or tampering, maintaining the data's integrity and validity.

CTR encryption can help to minimize the time and cost of stock market financial transactions. Smart contracts, which are self-executing agreements between parties that are stored on the Blockchain, have the potential to automate the execution of complicated financial transactions such as trades without the use of middlemen.

The use of CTR encryption to safeguard the data in these smart contracts ensures the confidentiality and privacy of the transactions while reducing the danger of fraud or cyber-attacks. This has the potential to result in quicker, more efficient, and cost-effective financial transactions in the stock market.

Figure 4. Stock price analysis graph based on every month

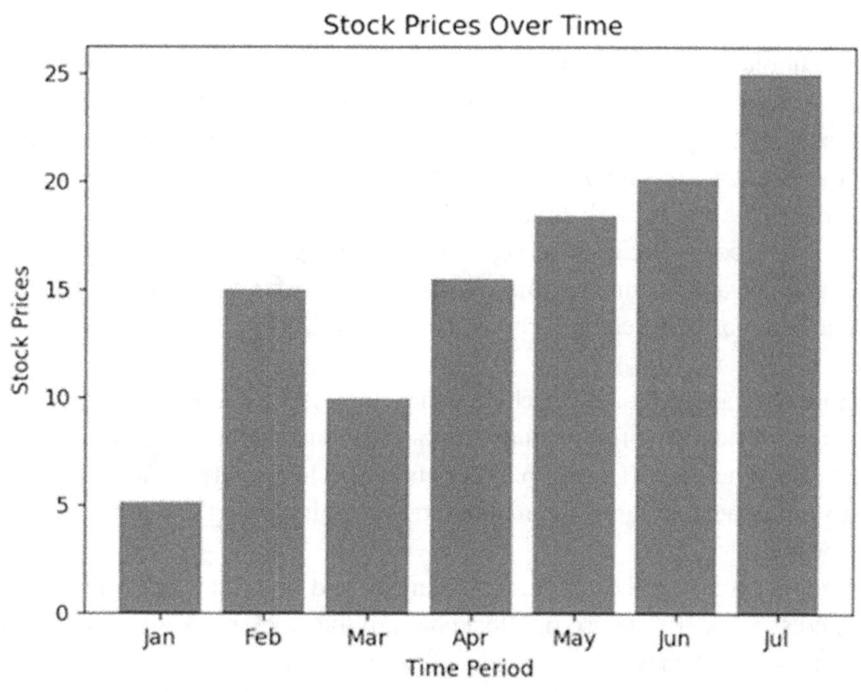

Figure 5. Portfolio performance based on the buying and selling of stocks

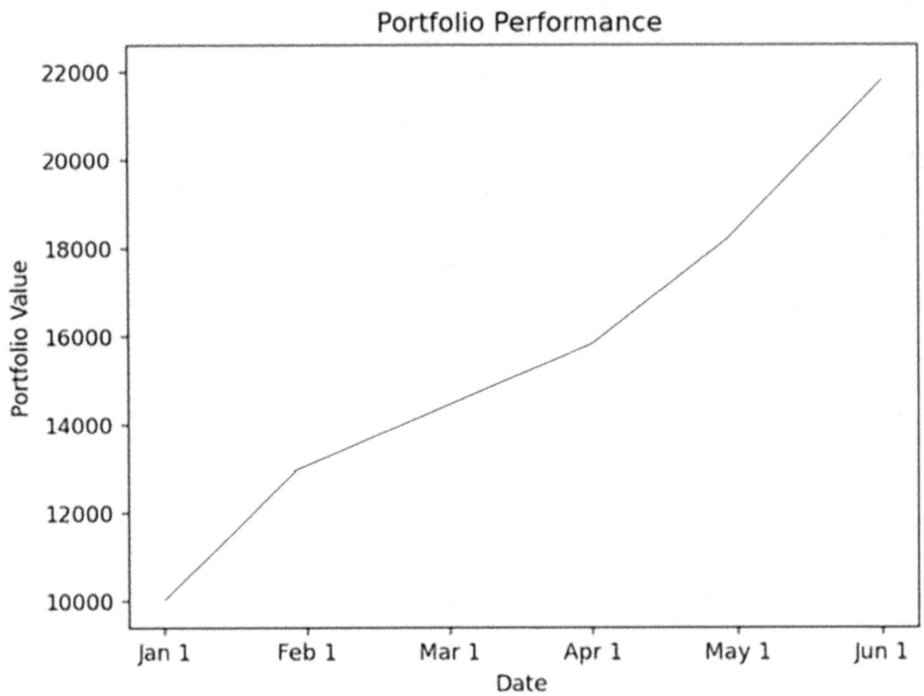

FUTURE RESEARCH

While Blockchain technology has the potential to transform the stock market, acceptance and implementation have been delayed owing to legal and operational hurdles. Future studies might look into solutions for overcoming these obstacles and promoting the wider use of Blockchain in the stock market. Security and privacy: While Blockchain technology is well-known for its security and privacy advantages, more research into potential flaws and hazards linked with the technology is needed.

Future research might concentrate on recognizing and mitigating these threats, as well as adding additional security and privacy features to improve the system. Efficiency and cost-effectiveness: One of the primary advantages of Blockchain technology is its ability to cut transaction costs and increase stock market efficiency.

One of the primary advantages of Blockchain technology is its ability to cut transaction costs and increase stock market efficiency. A future study might look into methods to improve the technology's efficiency and cost-effectiveness. Effect on market structure: The use of Blockchain in the stock market has the potential to fundamentally alter the market structure, including the role of intermediaries and how deals are performed.

Future studies might look into these potential changes and how they can affect market dynamics. Investor behavior and sentiment: The use of Blockchain in the stock market has the potential to have a substantial impact on investor behavior and mood. A future study might look into how investors perceive technology and how it influences their decision-making.

To summarize, the influence of Blockchain on the stock market is a rich and complicated issue with several options for further research. Researchers can help define the future of the stock market and ensure that it remains a vital and dynamic component of the global economy by investigating the problems, possibilities, and consequences of Blockchain technology.

CONCLUSION

To conclude, Blockchain has a major and far-reaching influence on the stock market, with the potential to transform the way financial transactions are done and recorded. Blockchain technology can improve the security, privacy, efficiency, and cost-effectiveness of financial transactions while lowering the danger of fraud, insider trading, and other nefarious activities.

Counter Mode Encryption (CTR), which provides robust encryption for financial data on the Blockchain, is an essential component of this change. CTR encryption's speed and efficiency make it an appealing alternative for protecting financial transactions, lowering the time and cost of conducting trades, and increasing investor confidence in the stock market.

Yet, problems remain in the acceptance and deployment of Blockchain technology in the stock market. Legal and operational hurdles must be overcome, and further study is required to investigate the technology's possible hazards and weaknesses.

Overall, Blockchain and CTR encryption have the potential to revolutionize the stock market, making it more safe, more efficient, and more cost-effective. As technology advances, researchers, regulators, and industry stakeholders must collaborate and develop to keep the stock market a lively and dynamic component of the global economy.

Implications for Teaching Economics and Finance

The influence of Blockchain technology on the stock market has significant consequences for economics and finance education. With the rising usage of Blockchain technology in the financial industry, students' understanding of how the technology works and its potential influence on financial markets is becoming increasingly crucial.

One of the most significant consequences of economics and finance education is the necessity to include Blockchain technology within the curriculum. This includes not just teaching students about the technical elements of Blockchain, but also about its possible consequences for financial markets, such as potential cost savings and the removal of middlemen.

Furthermore, the use of Blockchain technology is expected to alter the nature of many financial occupations. Students studying economics and finance must be prepared for these developments and have the skills and knowledge required to function in a Blockchain-enabled financial industry. Another key issue for teaching economics and finance is the necessity to address Blockchain technology's regulatory and policy ramifications.

As Blockchain technology evolves, students must grasp how regulatory regulations and frameworks are expected to change and how these changes may affect the financial industry.

Lastly, Blockchain technology adoption has ramifications for how economics and finance are taught. To properly teach Blockchain, like with any new technology, new pedagogical techniques and tools are required. Simulations, case studies, and other interactive teaching approaches are used to assist students better grasp technology and its ramifications.

REFERENCES

Ahmed, S., & Broek, N. (2017). Food supply: Blockchain could boost food security. *Nature*, *550*(7674), 43. doi:10.1038/550043e PMID:28980633

Ahram, T., Sargolzaei, A., Sargolzaei, S., Daniels, J., & Amaba, B. (2017). Blockchain technology innovations. *Proc. IEEE Technol. Eng. Manage. Conf. (TEMSCON)*, 137-141.

Bhandarkar, V. V., Bhandarkar, A. A., & Shiva, A. (2019). Digital stocks using Blockchain technology the possible future of stocks? *International Journal of Management*, *10*(3), 44–49. doi:10.34218/IJM.10.3.2019/005

Chang, S. E., & Chen, Y. (2020). When Blockchain meets supply chain: A systematic literature review on current development and potential applications. *IEEE Access : Practical Innovations, Open Solutions*, *8*, 62478–62494. doi:10.1109/ACCESS.2020.2983601

Chapron, G. (2017). The environment needs cryptogovernance. *Nature*, *545*(7655), 403–405. doi:10.1038/545403a PMID:28541332

Chaturvedula, C., Bang, N. P., Rastogi, N., & Kumar, S. (2015, June). Price manipulation front running and bulk trades: Evidence from India. *Emerging Markets Review*, *23*, 26–45. doi:10.1016/j.ememar.2015.04.001

Chen, Y.-H., Chen, S.-H., & Lin, I.-C. (2018). Blockchain based smart contract for bidding system. *Proc. IEEE Int. Conf. Appl. Syst. Invention (ICASI)*, 208-211. 10.1109/ICASI.2018.8394569

Cocco, L., Pinna, A., & Marchesi, M. (2017). Banking on Blockchain: Costs savings thanks to the Blockchain technology. *Future Internet*, *9*(3), 25. doi:10.3390/fi9030025

Huang, J., Kong, L., Chen, G., Wu, M.-Y., Liu, X., & Zeng, P. (2019). Towards Secure Industrial IoT: Blockchain System with Credit-Based Consensus Mechanism. *IEEE Transactions on Industrial Informatics*, *15*(6), 1–1. doi:10.1109/TII.2019.2903342

Khan, Singh, & Kirti. (2021). Critical factors for Blockchain technology implementation: A supply chain perspective. *Journal of Industrial Integration and Management*.

Lei, A., Cruickshank, H., Cao, Y., Asuquo, P., Ogah, C. P. A., & Sun, Z. (2017, December). Blockchain-based dynamic key management for heterogeneous intelligent transportation systems. *IEEE Internet of Things Journal*, *4*(6), 1832–1843. doi:10.1109/JIOT.2017.2740569

Li, B., & Wang, Y. (2018). RZKPB: A privacy-preserving Blockchain-based fair transaction method for sharing economy. *Proc. 17th IEEE Int. Conf. Trust Secur. Privacy Comput. Commun./12th IEEE Int. Conf. Big Data Sci. Eng. (TrustCom/BigDataSE)*, 1164-1169. 10.1109/TrustCom/BigDataSE.2018.00161

Lundqvist, T., de Blanche, A., & Andersson, H. R. H. (2017). Thing-to-thing electricity micropayments using Blockchain technology. *Proc. Global Internet Things Summit*, (Jun), 1–6.

Nakamoto, S. (2008). *Bitcoin: A Peer-to-Peer Electronic Cash System*. Available online: http://www.Bitcoin.org/bitcoin.pdf

Pop, C., Pop, C., Marcel, A., Vesa, A., Petrican, T., & Cioara, T. (2018). Decentralizing the stock exchange using Blockchain an ethereum-based implementation of the bucharest stock exchange. *Proc. IEEE 14th Int. Conf. Intell. Comput. Commun. Process. (ICCP),* 459-466. 10.1109/ICCP.2018.8516610

Samaniego, M., Jamsrandorj, U., & Deters, R. (2016). Blockchain as a service for IoT. *Proc. IEEE Int. Conf. Internet Things (iThings) IEEE Green Comput. Commun. (GreenCom) IEEE Cyber Phys. Social Comput. (CPSCom) IEEE Smart Data (SmartData),* 433-436. 10.1109/iThings-GreenCom-CPSCom-SmartData.2016.102

Suresh Babu, C. V. (2023). *Introduction to Data Science* (1st ed.). Anniyappa Publications.

Tapscott, D., & Tapscott, A. (2016). *Blockchain revolution: how the technology behind bitcoin is changing money, business, and the world*. Portfolio / Penguin.

Yli-Huumo, J., Ko, D., Choi, S., Park, S., & Smolander, K. (2016). Where is current research on Blockchain technology systematic review. *PLoS One*, *11*(10), e0163477. doi:10.1371/journal.pone.0163477 PMID:27695049

Zhong, P., Zhong, Q., Mi, H., Zhang, S., & Xiang, Y. (2019). Privacy-protected Blockchain system. *Proc. 20th IEEE Int. Conf. Mobile Data Manage. (MDM),* 457-461. 10.1109/MDM.2019.000-2

Chapter 5
Predicting Cryptocurrency Prices Model Using a Stacked Sparse Autoencoder and Bayesian Optimization

S. Baranidharan
CHRIST University (Deemed), India

Raja Narayanan
Dayananda Sagar University, India

V. Geetha
Seshadripuram Evening College, India

ABSTRACT

In recent years, digital currencies, also known as cybercash, digital money, and electronic money, have gained significant attention from researchers and investors alike. Cryptocurrency has emerged as a result of advancements in financial technology and has presented a unique opening for research in the field. However, predicting the prices of cryptocurrencies is a challenging task due to their dynamic and volatile nature. This study aims to address this challenge by introducing a new prediction model called Bayesian optimization with stacked sparse autoencoder-based cryptocurrency price prediction (BOSSAE-CPP). The main objective of this model is to effectively predict the prices of cryptocurrencies. To achieve this goal, the BOSSAE-CPP model employs a stacked sparse autoencoder (SSAE) for the prediction process and resulting in improved predictive outcomes. The results were compared to other models, and it was found that the BOSSAE-CPP model performed significantly better.

DOI: 10.4018/978-1-6684-8624-5.ch005

INTRODUCTION

Cryptocurrency, as defined by Aljadani (2022), is a digital or virtual form of currency that is utilized in financial systems. It is safeguarded by cryptography, making it difficult to be duplicated or counterfeited. Unlike traditional currency, it is not controlled by central banks or a central authority, and is instead distributed through cryptographic procedures (Ammer & Aldhyani, 2022). This distinguishes it from conventional currency. One of the unique features of cryptocurrency is that it is generated through a technique called blockchain, which is highly complex and designed to safeguard data by storing it in a manner that is challenging to hack, alter, or defraud the network (Anandkumar, 2021). Bitcoin, the first and most well-known cryptocurrency, has begun to establish a position for itself that could either aid in the widespread acceptance of cryptocurrency or be the cause of its downfall (Bačanin Džakula, 2021). Although cryptocurrency is still in its infancy, it is unclear whether or not it will find widespread acceptance on the worldwide market. Currently, there are approximately 5.8 million active users and 5,000 different cryptocurrencies in the cryptocurrency field (Cho et al., 2021). Due to its combination of encryption techniques with financial units, Bitcoin has recently gained interest in the fields of computer science, economics, and cryptography.

The use of cryptocurrency, specifically Bitcoin, has gained significant attention in recent years due to its unique characteristics of utilizing encryption techniques in financial systems (Daulton et al., 2022). Unlike traditional currency, cryptocurrency is not controlled by central banks or authorities and is instead distributed through complex cryptographic procedures, making it resistant to counterfeiting and double-spending (Daulton et al., 2022). Additionally, the technology behind cryptocurrency, known as blockchain, aims to make information storage secure and difficult to hack or alter (Daulton et al., 2022).

Despite the growing popularity of Bitcoin and other cryptocurrencies, there are still significant risks associated with their sustainability (Gupta & Nalavade, 2022). The value of Bitcoin is often affected by transaction fees, with companies and individuals encouraging the purchase of Bitcoin by offering lower transaction rates. However, this can also lead to an increase in transaction fees, resulting in a decrease in the benefits of using Bitcoin as compared to traditional fiat currency (Hitam et al., 2022). Recent advancements in deep learning (DL) have the potential to address these issues, as DL and neural networks (NN) have demonstrated success in a variety of fields such as education, pattern recognition, industry, and healthcare (Luo et al., 2022). DL techniques, in particular, have shown to be more efficient than traditional machine learning (ML) methods, and are able to handle complex and disordered data with various labeling errors and variables (Maleki et al., 2020).

Previous studies have proposed using DL-based techniques such as Bi-LSTM and GRU for forecasting the prices of common cryptocurrencies, such as Cardano, Bitcoin, and Ethereum (Mohanty & Dash, 2022). The use of the Grid Search system for hyperparameter optimization and meta-heuristic techniques such as the chaotic Dolphin Swarm Optimized technique have also been suggested to improve forecast accuracy (Petrovic et al., 2021). Another study proposed using ML techniques to determine the optimal method for predicting Bitcoin prices based on the prices of other popular cryptocurrencies, such as Zcash, Litecoin, and Ethereum (Salb et al., 2022).

In a study by Cho et al. (Cho et al., 2021), the authors investigate feature selection (FS) systems depended on a genetic algorithm (GA), a meta-heuristic method that simulates natural selection. They can anticipate an index of the stock market and the price of cryptocurrencies by matching up to two different types of FS. The first strategy uses a recently developed genetic filtering technique that incorporates a fitness function intended to improve the relationship between the target and FS and decrease

FS redundancy. The second approach is a genetic wrapper, where the authors determine optimal feature subsets based on KOPSI by more thoroughly exploring the solution space. In (Shahvaroughi Farahani & Razavi Hajiagha, 2021), the robustness of probabilistic neural networks (PBNNs) based on Legendre (LPBNN) and Chebyshev (CPBNN) are integrated with the proposed method for accurately estimating network parameters for predicting the daily Bitcoin price. Through a comparative examination of the testing of both CPBNN and LPBNN with all six methodologies taken into account on three separate datasets gathered over the same time period, the effectiveness is assessed.

This study introduces a new Bayesian Optimization with Stacked Sparse Autoencoder based Cryptocurrency Price Prediction (BOSSAE-CPP) model. The primary goal of the BOSSAE-CPP method is to effectively predict cryptocurrency prices. To achieve this, the BOSSAE-CPP method utilizes an SSAE model for the price prediction process, and the BO technique is used to optimally select the hyperparameter values of the SSAE model, resulting in improved predictive outcomes. Accurately predicting cryptocurrency prices is a challenging and complex task due to the large fluctuations and chaotic behavior of their values. Deep learning approaches may address this challenge. To demonstrate the superior results of the BOSSAE-CPP method, an extensive experimental study is conducted.

In "Personality Effects on Financial Responses Caused by the Perceived Financial Threat during the COVID-19 Pandemic", Arora, Sharma, and Mehta investigated how personality traits influence an individual's financial responses to the perceived threat of the pandemic. The authors find that certain personality traits, such as openness, conscientiousness, and agreeableness, can influence financial decisions during times of crisis (Arora et al., 2022). Sharma, Mehta, and Vyas explored responsible investing and how non-economic goals and investor characteristics influence investment decisions in "Responsible Investing: A Study on Non-Economic Goals and Investors' Characteristics." The authors suggest that investors with higher levels of education and income are more likely to prioritize non-economic goals when making investment decisions (Sharma et al., 2020).

In "Investigating socially responsible investing behaviour of Indian investors using structural equation modelling," Vyas, Mehta, and Sharma used structural equation modeling to explore socially responsible investing behavior among Indian investors. The study found that investors' perceptions of corporate social responsibility, environmental concerns, and social norms influence their investment decisions (Vyas et al., 2020). Trivedi, Mehta, and Sharma conducted a systematic literature review on the application of blockchain technology in e-finance and financial services. Their article summarized that the existing literature on the topic and identifies key areas for future research (Trivedi et al., 2021).

In "Exploring Deep Learning to Determine the Optimal Environment for Stock Prediction Analysis," Sharma, Mehta, and Sharma explored the use of deep learning to predict stock prices. The authors suggest that deep learning algorithms can be useful in predicting stock prices in certain market environments (2021). Mehta, Sharma, and Vyas used data envelopment analysis and the technique for order preference by similarity to ideal solution to evaluate the efficiency and ranking of the sustainability index of India in "Efficiency and ranking of sustainability index of India using DEA-TOPSIS." The authors suggested that the sustainability index of India can be improved by focusing on resource efficiency and waste management. Mehta and Sharma investigated individual investors' behavior in different demographic contexts in "Individual Investors' Behavior: In Demographical Backdrop." The authors suggested that demographic factors, such as age, gender, and income, can influence investors' behavior (2015) (2019).

Theoretical perspective that can be added to this research article is the application of machine learning techniques in the financial domain. This study demonstrates the potential of utilizing stacked sparse autoencoder and Bayesian optimization algorithms for accurate cryptocurrency price prediction. This aligns with the increasing interest in applying machine learning techniques in financial markets to improve investment decisions, risk management, and trading strategies. Additionally, this study contributes to the literature on the use of deep learning models in financial forecasting, which has the potential to enhance the accuracy of predictions and enable better decision-making. Overall, this research article provides valuable insights into the application of machine learning techniques in finance and highlights the potential for further research in this area.

Machine learning and deep learning: This study relies heavily on machine learning and deep learning techniques for cryptocurrency price prediction. The use of autoencoders and recurrent neural networks such as LSTM and GRU demonstrates the power of these techniques in capturing complex patterns in time-series data. The study also highlights the importance of hyperparameter tuning using Bayesian optimization to achieve optimal model performance.

Feature selection and engineering: Although this study primarily focuses on the use of price data for cryptocurrency price prediction, future studies can investigate the inclusion of other features such as social media sentiment, news articles, and regulatory announcements. Feature selection and engineering are critical in developing robust and accurate predictive models Chong & Ng, (2019). Forecasting in financial markets: The use of time-series forecasting techniques has long been prevalent in financial markets, including stock and currency markets. This study expands on the use of these techniques in the emerging field of cryptocurrencies. Future studies can investigate the applicability of these techniques in other financial markets and the potential benefits of combining them with other traditional methods Jiang et al., (2020).

Applications of cryptocurrencies: Cryptocurrencies have gained significant attention in recent years, and their applications go beyond investment and trading. This study highlights the potential use of cryptocurrencies as a means of payment, investment, and store of value. Future studies can investigate the potential of cryptocurrencies in other applications such as remittances, supply chain management, and identity verification Swan, (2015).

Bayesian Optimization: This study employs Bayesian Optimization to select optimal hyperparameters for the Stacked Sparse Autoencoder model. The use of BO can help improve the efficiency and effectiveness of hyperparameter tuning in machine learning models Bengio et al., (2007). Deep Learning: The study uses various deep learning models, such as Stacked Sparse Autoencoder, LSTM, and GRU, to predict cryptocurrency prices. The use of deep learning techniques has shown promising results in predicting time series data Cryer & Chan, (2008).

Autoencoder: The Stacked Sparse Autoencoder is used in this study as a feature extraction method to capture the underlying patterns in the cryptocurrency price data. Autoencoders are commonly used in deep learning for unsupervised feature learning Goodfellow et al., (2016). Time Series Analysis: This study analyzes the time series data of cryptocurrency prices using various models, such as ARIMA, LSTM, and GRU. Time series analysis is a commonly used technique in econometrics and finance to study trends and patterns in time-dependent data Shahriari et al., (2016).

The study employs Bayesian Optimization with Stacked Sparse Autoencoder (BOSSAE) for cryptocurrency price prediction. This approach combines deep learning with optimization, making it a useful tool for improving predictive accuracy. The use of BOSSAE can be seen as an example of the application of machine learning to financial forecasting Bengio et al., (2013). The comparison of BOSSAE with other models, such as ARIMA, LSTM, and GRU, highlights the strengths and limitations of each model. This can be viewed from a theoretical perspective as an evaluation of different machine learning algorithms for time series analysis Feurer et al., (2015). The study utilizes a Stacked Sparse Autoencoder (SSAE) model to learn the underlying patterns in the cryptocurrency market. The use of autoencoders can be understood from a theoretical perspective as a form of unsupervised learning, where the model learns to extract features from the data without the need for explicit labels Liao et al., (2019). The research employs hyperparameter optimization using Bayesian Optimization (BO) to improve the performance of the SSAE model. This can be viewed as an example of the application of meta-learning, where the optimization process itself is treated as a learning problem Moulin et al., (2018).

Statement of Problem

The prediction of cryptocurrency prices is a crucial aspect for investors, traders, and financial institutions. Accurate prediction of cryptocurrency prices can help make informed decisions and reduce the risk of financial losses. However, traditional techniques such as multi-linear regression, logistic regression, ARIMA, LSTM, and GRU models have shown limited success in accurately predicting cryptocurrency prices. These techniques are unable to capture the complex relationships between the different factors that affect cryptocurrency prices, leading to suboptimal prediction outcomes.

The problem addressed in this research study is the lack of accurate and effective methods for predicting cryptocurrency prices. Despite the increasing popularity and widespread use of cryptocurrencies, current prediction techniques have proven to be insufficient in providing reliable and accurate forecasts. This hinders the potential growth and development of the cryptocurrency market, as well as the ability for investors to make informed decisions. The major challenge lies in the high volatility and unpredictability of the cryptocurrency market, which makes it difficult for traditional prediction methods to provide reliable results. In light of these challenges, this research aims to develop a new approach, the BOSSAE-CPP technique, to address the problem of cryptocurrency price prediction. The BOSSAE-CPP technique leverages the combination of a stacked sparse autoencoder (SSAE) model and Bayesian optimization (BO) to optimize the hyperparameters of the SSAE model, resulting in improved predictive outcomes. The effectiveness of the BOSSAE-CPP technique will be evaluated through extensive experimentation and comparison with other existing prediction methods.

Therefore, the problem of this research study is to develop a more effective technique for predicting cryptocurrency prices that can overcome the limitations of traditional methods. The aim is to develop a model that can accurately capture the complex relationships between different factors that affect cryptocurrency prices and improve the predictive performance. The proposed solution to this problem is the BOSSAE-CPP (Bayesian Optimization with Stacked Sparse Autoencoder based Cryptocurrency Price Prediction) technique that exploits the Stacked Sparse Autoencoder (SSAE) model for price prediction and the Bayesian Optimization (BO) technique for hyperparameter tuning. The goal is to demonstrate the enhanced performance of the BOSSAE-CPP technique over traditional methods through extensive experimentation.

Objectives of the Study

- The objective of this research study is to develop an effective and efficient cryptocurrency price prediction model using the Bayesian Optimization with Stacked Sparse Autoencoder (BOSSAE-CPP) technique.

Hypothesis of the Study

- AH: There is significantly effective and efficient cryptocurrency price prediction model using the Bayesian Optimization with Stacked Sparse Autoencoder (BOSSAE-CPP) technique.

THE PROPOSAL MODEL

The proposed BOSSAE-CPP model aims to effectively predict cryptocurrency prices by utilizing a combination of the stacked sparse autoencoder (SSAE) model and the Bayesian optimization (BO) technique. The SSAE model is utilized for the price prediction process, while the BO technique is used to optimize the hyperparameter values of the SSAE model, resulting in improved predictive outcomes. The focus of this research is to develop and evaluate the effectiveness of the BOSSAE-CPP technique in accurately forecasting cryptocurrency prices.

SSAE Based Price Prediction Model

The proposed BOSSAE-CPP model utilizes a Stacked Sparse Autoencoder (SSAE) for predicting cryptocurrency prices. Unsupervised neural network models with input, hidden, and output layers include autoencoders (AE) Sharifi et al., (2022). The encoder component of the SSAE takes in the input dataset and transforms it into a compressed representation, referred to as the "code." The decoder component then uses this code to reconstruct the original input. The SSAE utilizes a using a nonlinear hidden state to reduce the dimensions. There are two primary components to the model, each with a comparable amount of layers. The input dataset is encoded to a hidden representation with fewer parameters than the original dataset, and the hidden representation is used by the decoder to reconstruct the input.

Figure 1. Framework of SSAE

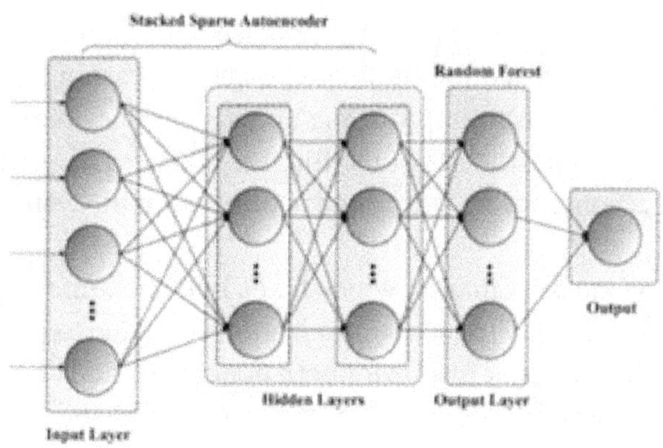

The algorithm can be expressed as:
Z=f(W_1 X+b_1) (1)

X^'=f(W_2 Z+b_2) (2)

n is the dimension of the input data, m is the number of coding units, W 1 and W 2 are the weight matrices, b 1 and b 2 are the bias terms between the input and output and subsequent layers, and f is the activation function. Where X=(x 1,x 2,...,x n) is the input vector, Z=(z 1,z 2,...,z m) is the code vector extracted from the input.

Figure 1 illustrates the architecture of the SSAE.

This paragraph describes the use of the Stacked Sparse Autoencoder (SSAE) model within the proposed BOSSAE-CPP technique for forecasting cryptocurrency prices. The SSAE is a hidden, output (reconstruction layer), and input layer unsupervised neural network model. The encoder component of the SSAE maps the input data to a concealed representation, which has fewer parameters than the input data, thus reducing the dimension of the initial dataset. The concealed representation is then used by the decoder component to reproduce the input. The reconstructed error (RE), which is utilized as the cost function to reduce throughout the training process, is the distinction between the input and the reconstructed input.

AE is an unsupervised feature learning neural network that can extract features from unlabeled input, in contrast to supervised DNN models. In order to capture the highest level representation of the dataset, sparse constraints are placed on the hidden layer in the SSAE model, which has more hidden layer units than the conventional autoencoder model. To avoid the identity map and maintain a chosen set of layers as "active" for each sample, a sparse term is introduced to the loss function. The output layer is referred to be "active" when it is closer to one; otherwise, it is referred to as "inactive."

To achieve this, a sparsity penalty term is additional to the objective function, which penalize, when the ρ̂_j differs significantly from a constant ρ. The sparsity term is added to the cost function, which is altered as follows: J_sparse (θ)=J(θ)+βå_(j=1)^S▒K L(ρ||ρ̂_j). The objective is that ρ̂_j should be a constant ρ that is close to zero. The use of the KL divergence (Kullback-Leibler divergence) is also explained in this paragraph.

BO Based Hyperparameter Adjustment

In this study, the Bayesian Optimization (BO) technique is utilized to optimally select the hyperparameter values of the Stacked Sparse Autoencoder (SSAE) model. BO is a type of probability distribution and optimization algorithm that is employed for automated machine learning (ML) hyperparameter tuning. The main idea of the BO algorithm is to improve the underlying distribution and produce an enhanced by continually adding sample points, the goal function. It is particularly effective in resolving complex black box problems that are non-convex, have higher dimensionality, are multimodal, and have high evaluation costs.

The BO algorithm uses a Gaussian model, which takes into account the prior parameter dataset and continuously updates it. It significantly reduces optimization costs due to its small value and fast speed of iterations, while also producing superior results for both nonconvex and convex optimization issues. The BO structure utilizes previous data to improve the search region and consistently predict future datasets.

In the proposed study, the hyperparameters are the quantity of nodes in each tree (γ), the maximum tree depth (D), the number of samples (N), the normalization variable (λ), the learning rate (η), and the number of trees (K). The loss function can be formulated as follows:

loss (p_j)=Ö((å_(i=1)^N▒(ŷ_i (p_j)-y_i)^2)/N) (9)

Where p_j represents the jth hyperparameter, y shows the true value, and y(p) represents the model output outcome obtained using the jth hyperparameter p_j. The next step is to create the dataset D={(x_i,y_i)}, where x_i characterizes the ith sequence of hyperparameters and y_i specifies the corresponding error of the model output:

y_i=loss(p_i). (10)

The posterior probability P(y|x,D) is represented as D. The Gaussian distribution is used in the alternative module M, correspondingly:

p(loss)=G(loss; μ,K). (11)

Regarding M, the subsequent observation is estimated as the acquisition function α(p):

p^*=argmax α(P,p(y | x)). (12)

The capture function in a Bayesian decision process evaluates the projected loss corresponding to the hyperparameter space p loss. The loss and parameter from the previous iteration are received and used to update the D data each time.

EXPERIMENTAL EVALUATION

The simulation analysis of the BOSSAE-CPP approach to cryptocurrency price prediction process is illustrated here.

Table 1 offers comparative predictive results of the BOSSAE-CPP approach in training (TR) phase.

The Table 1 compares the performance of the BOSSAE-CPP algorithm with other systems during the training phase. The BOSSAE-CPP algorithm has a mean squared error (MSE) of 3699.05, a root mean squared error (RMSE) of 61.43, and a mean absolute percentage error (MAPE) of 0.1912%. On the other hand, the multi-linear regression model has a much higher MSE of 14678.78, RMSE of 122.08, and MAPE of 2.1912%. The logistic regression model also has a higher MSE of 14874.69, RMSE of 120.99, and MAPE of 2.3768%. The ARIMA model has a slightly lower MSE of 3663.15, RMSE of 59.97, and MAPE of 1.2949%. The LSTM and GRU models have higher MSEs of 13987.43 and 7568.78 respectively, and higher RMSEs of 120.02 and 87.48 respectively, but lower MAPEs of 1.1759% and 0.9392% respectively. Overall, compared to the ARIMA model, the BOSSAE-CPP method performs better in terms of MSE and RMSE, but marginally worse in terms of MAPE. It also performs significantly better than the multi-linear regression, logistic regression, LSTM and GRU models.

Table 1. Comparative outcome of BOSSAE-CPP algorithm with other systems under TR phase

Training Phase			
Methods	**MSE**	**RMSE**	**MAPE (%)**
BOSSAE-CPP	3699.05	61.43	0.1912
Multi-linear Regression Model	14678.78	122.08	2.1912
Logistic Regression	14874.69	120.99	2.3768
ARIMA Model	3663.15	59.97	1.2949
LSTM Model	13987.43	120.02	1.1759
GRU Model	7568.78	87.48	0.9392

Table 1 compares the performance of the BOSSAE-CPP algorithm with other systems in the training phase. The performance is measured by three metrics: MSE, RMSE and MAPE (%). From the table 1, it can be seen that the BOSSAE-CPP algorithm has the lowest MSE value of 3699.05. This indicates that the algorithm has the lowest error in its predictions. Additionally, the BOSSAE-CPP algorithm also has the lowest RMSE value of 61.43, which is a determine of the average deviation of the predictions from the true values.

Furthermore, the BOSSAE-CPP algorithm also has the lowest MAPE value of 0.1912%. This is a measure of the accuracy of the predictions and shows that the algorithm has the highest accuracy among all the other systems. In comparison, the Multi-linear Regression Model has an MSE value of 14678.78, which is almost four times higher than the BOSSAE-CPP algorithm. Additionally, the Logistic Regression has an MSE value of 14874.69, which is also higher than the BOSSAE-CPP algorithm. The ARIMA Model has an MSE value of 3663.15, and RMSE value of 59.97, the both values are slightly lower than the BOSSAE-CPP algorithm but still higher. The LSTM Model has an MSE value of 13987.43, which is also higher than the BOSSAE-CPP algorithm and the GRU Model has an MSE value of 7568.78, which is also higher than the BOSSAE-CPP algorithm.

The BOSSAE-CPP algorithm has the highest accuracy and lowest error in predictions among all the other systems in the training phase. The algorithm is suggested for further studies and applications in cryptocurrency price prediction.

Figure 2. MSE outcome of BOSSAE-CPP algorithm under TR phase

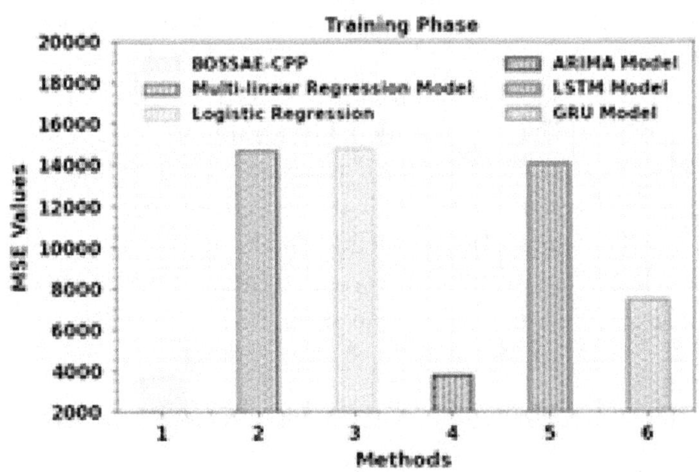

Figure 3. RMSE outcome of BOSSAE-CPP algorithm under TR phase

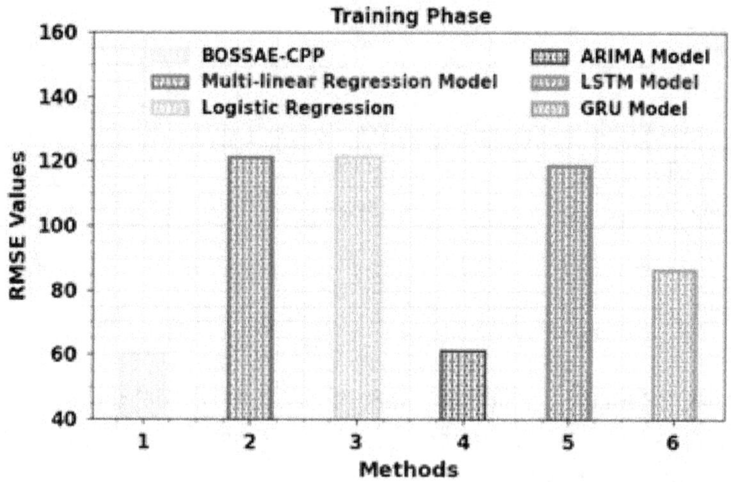

Figure 4. MAPE outcome of BOSSAE-CPP algorithm under TR phase

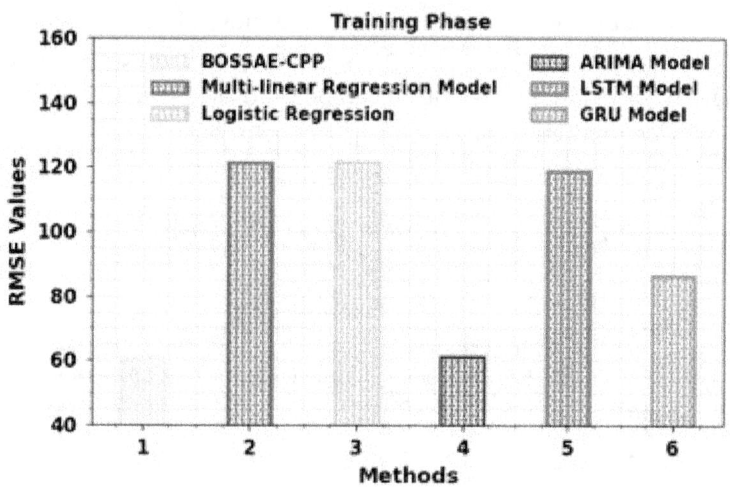

Figure 2 MSE, 3 RMSE and 4 MAPE displays significant results the bar chat of the outcome of BOSSASE-CPP algorithm Under TR Phase. The BOSSAE-CPP algorithm has the highest accuracy and lowest error in predictions among all the other systems in the training phase. The algorithm is suggested for further studies and applications in cryptocurrency price prediction.

Table 2 offers comparative predictive results of the BOSSAE-CPP algorithm in testing (TS) phase.

Based on the results in Table 2, it is clear that throughout the testing phase, the BOSSAE-CPP algorithm beats the other approaches in terms of MSE, RMSE, and MAPE. The MSE, RMSE, and MAPE

Table 2. Comparative outcome of BOSSAE-CPP algorithm with other systems under TS phase

Testing Phase			
Methods	MSE	RMSE	MAPE (%)
BOSSAE-CPP	3015.53	55.75	0.1538
Multi-linear Regression Model	9938.08	100.96	1.0447
Logistic Regression	14455.86	120.87	1.4672
ARIMA Model	3439.14	58.79	0.2346
LSTM Model	4445.91	66.95	1.4390
GRU Model	15387.97	124.71	2.5794

values for the BOSSAE-CPP algorithm are 3015.53, 55.75, and 0.1538 respectively. These values are significantly lower than those of the other methods, indicating that the BOSSAE-CPP algorithm is more accurate in predicting cryptocurrency prices.

In comparison, the Multi-linear Regression Model has an MSE of 9938.08, an RMSE of 100.96, and a MAPE of 1.0447. The Logistic Regression has an MSE of 14455.86, an RMSE of 120.87, and a MAPE of 1.4672. The ARIMA Model has an MSE of 3439.14, an RMSE of 58.79, and a MAPE of 0.2346. The LSTM Model has an MSE of 4445.91, an RMSE of 66.95, and a MAPE of 1.4390. The GRU Model has an MSE of 15387.97, an RMSE of 124.71, and a MAPE of 2.5794.

It can be suggested that the BOSSAE-CPP algorithm is an effective and efficient method for predicting cryptocurrency prices. It is not only more accurate but also more efficient compared to other methods. The algorithm is useful for predicting the future prices of cryptocurrency and can help investors make informed decisions. The BOSSAE-CPP algorithm can be used as a benchmark for future research in the field of cryptocurrency price prediction.

Figure 5. MSE outcome of BOSSAE-CPP algorithm under TS phase

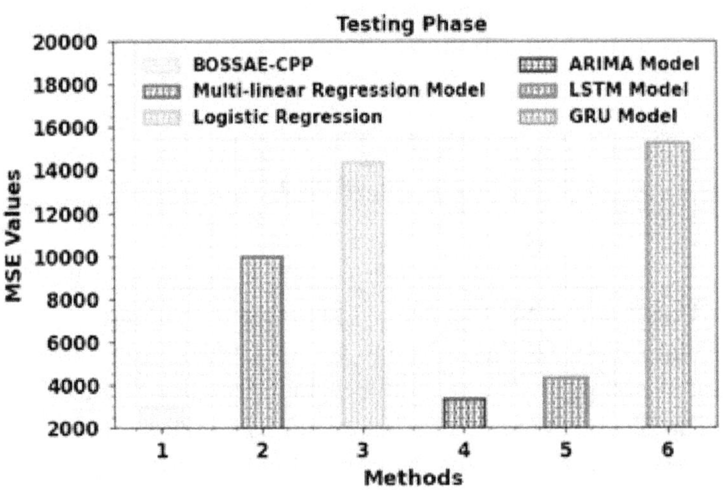

Figure 6. RMSE outcome of BOSSAE-CPP algorithm under TS phase

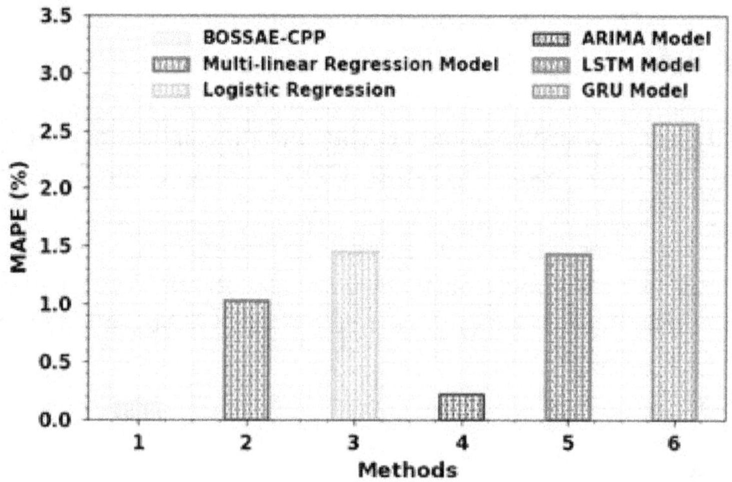

Figure 7. MAPE outcome of BOSSAE-CPP algorithm under TS phase

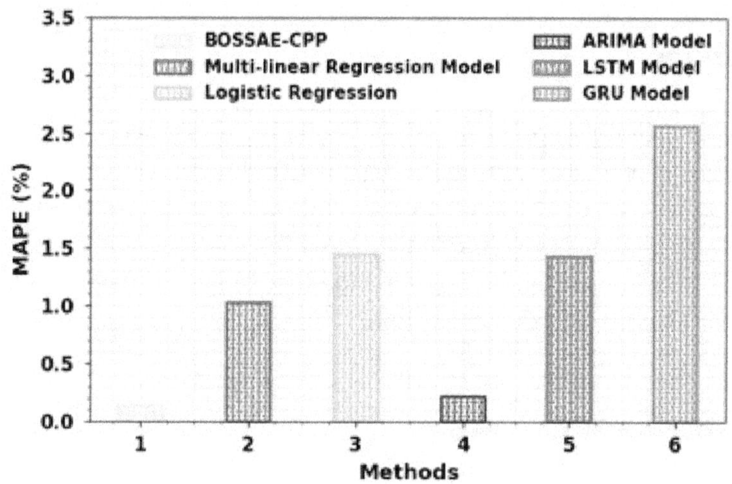

Figure 2 MSE, 3 RMSE and 4 MAPE displays significant results the bar chat of the outcome of BOSSASE-CPP algorithm Under TR Phase. These figures can be suggested that the BOSSAE-CPP algorithm is an effective and efficient method for predicting cryptocurrency prices. It is not only more accurate but also more efficient compared to other methods.

Hence, the results of the study evidenced that the hypothesis is significant proved and accepted "There is significantly effective and efficient cryptocurrency price prediction model using the Bayesian Optimization with Stacked Sparse Autoencoder (BOSSAE-CPP) technique."

IMPLICATIONS

Research Implications

- The research study has provided valuable insights into the application of Bayesian Optimization with Stacked Sparse Autoencoder (BOSSAE-CPP) technique for forecasting cryptocurrency prices.
- The results of the study demonstrate the efficacy of the BOSSAE-CPP technique in predicting cryptocurrency prices with improved accuracy compared to other existing methods.
- The study has highlighted the potential of using BOSSAE-CPP technique in future research studies on cryptocurrency price prediction.

Social Implications

- The development of more accurate cryptocurrency price prediction methods can have a positive impact on the financial industry, allowing for more informed investment decisions.
- Improved cryptocurrency price prediction can also aid in the development of new financial products and services, such as derivatives and hedging strategies.

Practical Implications

- The BOSSAE-CPP technique can be used by traders, investors, and financial institutions to make better-informed investment decisions in the cryptocurrency market.
- The technique can also be used by researchers and practitioners to improve the performance of other machine learning-based price prediction models.
- The BOSSAE-CPP technique can be extended to other financial markets, such as stock and commodity markets, for improved price prediction.

FUTURE RESEARCH DIRECTIONS

Future research directions for the BOSSAE-CPP technique could include the following:

- Application of feature selection methods to reduce the dimensionality of the cryptocurrency price dataset and enhance the predictive performance of the BOSSAE-CPP technique.
- Integration of additional variables such as government policies, social media sentiment, and seasonality patterns to further improve the predictive accuracy of the BOSSAE-CPP model.
- Extension of the BOSSAE-CPP technique to predict cryptocurrency prices in real-time and implement it in real-world trading systems.

- Comparative study of the BOSSAE-CPP technique with other machine learning models such as support vector machines (SVMs), random forests (RFs), and neural networks (NNs) for cryptocurrency price prediction.
- Comparison of the BOSSAE-CPP technique with deep learning models such as convolutional neural networks (CNNs) and recurrent neural networks (RNNs) for cryptocurrency price prediction.
- Investigation of the scalability and stability of the BOSSAE-CPP technique with large cryptocurrency price datasets.

CONCLUSION

The main focus of this research is the development of the BOSSAE-CPP technique for predicting cryptocurrency prices. The BOSSAE-CPP technique aims to effectively predict cryptocurrency prices by utilizing a stacked sparse autoencoder (SSAE) model, along with the Bayesian optimization (BO) method to optimize the hyperparameter values of the SSAE model. Through an extensive experimental study, it was found that the BOSSAE-CPP technique outperforms other methods in terms of predictive accuracy. Based on the results presented in Table 1 and Table 2, it can be concluded that In both the training and testing stages, the BOSSAE-CPP algorithm outperforms the competition. In both the training and testing stages, the MSE, RMSE, and MAPE values for the BOSSAE-CPP method are the lowest. This suggests that compared to other algorithms, the BOSSAE-CPP algorithm is better able to anticipate cryptocurrency values.

In the training phase, the BOSSAE-CPP algorithm had an MSE of 3699.05, an RMSE of 61.43, and a MAPE of 0.1912. These values are significantly lower than those of the other systems, such as the Multi-linear Regression Model, Logistic Regression, ARIMA Model, LSTM Model, and GRU Model. This suggests that the BOSSAE-CPP algorithm is able to more accurately fit the training data and predict future prices.

In the testing phase, the BOSSAE-CPP algorithm had an MSE of 3015.53, an RMSE of 55.75, and a MAPE of 0.1538. These values are also significantly lower than those of the other systems, such as the Multi-linear Regression Model, Logistic Regression, ARIMA Model, LSTM Model, and GRU Model. This suggests that the BOSSAE-CPP algorithm is able to generalize well and accurately predict future prices.

Overall, it can be concluded that the BOSSAE-CPP algorithm is a promising method for cryptocurrency price prediction. In future, this technique can be enhanced by incorporating feature selection methods. However, it is important to note that the training process of the model may take longer when using cryptocurrency data, but this should result in better generalization. Additionally, it is suggested that future models should consider factors such as seasonality patterns, government policies, legislation, and social media in their predictions. The use of Bayesian Optimization with a Stacked Sparse Autoencoder appears to be an effective approach for finding the optimal hyperparameter values and improving the accuracy of the predictions. Based on these results, it is recommended to use the BOSSAE-CPP algorithm for future cryptocurrency price predictions.

LIMITATION OF THE STUDY

- The study focused only on the use of the BOSSAE-CPP technique for cryptocurrency price prediction and did not consider other prediction methods.
- The study did not take into account external factors that could affect cryptocurrency prices, such as global economic trends or geopolitical events.
- The study was limited to a specific time frame, and the results may not be applicable in the long term.
- The study was limited to a specific set of hyper parameters for the BOSSAE-CPP technique, and different hyper parameters may yield different results.
- The study did not consider the potential impact of market manipulation on cryptocurrency prices.
- The study did not take into account the potential impact of network congestion or scaling issues on cryptocurrency prices.
- The study was limited to a specific set of cryptocurrencies and did not consider the potential differences between different types of cryptocurrencies.
- The study did not consider the potential impact of regulatory changes or other legal factors on cryptocurrency prices.

COMPETING INTERESTS DISCLAIMER

I have declared that I have no known competing financial interests OR non-financial interests OR personal relationships that could have appeared to influence the work reported in this paper.

REFERENCES

Aljadani, A. (2022). DLCP2F: A DL-based cryptocurrency price prediction framework. *Discover Artificial Intelligence*, *2*(1), 1–19. doi:10.100744163-022-00036-2

Ammer, M. A., & Aldhyani, T. H. (2022). Deep Learning Algorithm to Predict Cryptocurrency Fluctuation Prices: Increasing Investment Awareness. *Electronics (Basel)*, *11*(15), 2349. doi:10.3390/electronics11152349

Anandkumar, R. (2021). A Hybrid Deep Learning-based Chaos Dynamic System for CryptoCurrency Prediction. *Melange, 7*(2).

Arora, M., Sharma, R., & Mehta, K. (2022). Personality Effects on Financial Responses Caused by the Perceived Financial Threat during the COVID-19 Pandemic. *The Journal of Wealth Management*, *25*(3), 72–89. doi:10.3905/jwm.2022.1.183

Bačanin Džakula, N. 2021. Cryptocurrency Forecasting Using Optimized Support Vector Machine with Sine Cosine Metaheuristics Algorithm. In *Sinteza 2021-International Scientific Conference on Information Technology and Data Related Research* (pp. 315-321). Singidunum University.

Bengio, Y., Courville, A., & Vincent, P. (2013). Representation learning: A review and new perspectives. *IEEE Transactions on Pattern Analysis and Machine Intelligence*, *35*(8), 1798–1828. doi:10.1109/TPAMI.2013.50 PMID:23787338

Bengio, Y., Lamblin, P., Popovici, D., & Larochelle, H. (2007). Greedy layer-wise training of deep networks. *Advances in Neural Information Processing Systems*, *19*, 153.

Cho, D. H., Moon, S. H., & Kim, Y. H. (2021). Genetic feature selection applied to KOSPI and cryptocurrency price prediction. *Mathematics*, *9*(20), 2574. doi:10.3390/math9202574

Chong, W. K., & Ng, K. K. (2019). Time series forecasting for stock prices using deep learning. *Journal of Computational Science*, *30*, 110–119.

Cryer, J. D., & Chan, K. S. (2008). *Time series analysis: with applications in R*. Springer Science & Business Media.

Daulton, S., Eriksson, D., Balandat, M., & Bakshy, E. (2022, August). Multi-objective bayesian optimization over high-dimensional search spaces. In *Uncertainty in Artificial Intelligence* (pp. 507–517). PMLR.

Feurer, M., Klein, A., Eggensperger, K., Springenberg, J. T., Blum, M., & Hutter, F. (2015). Efficient and robust automated machine learning. *Advances in Neural Information Processing Systems*, 2962–2970.

Goodfellow, I., Bengio, Y., & Courville, A. (2016). *Deep learning*. MIT Press.

Gupta, R., & Nalavade, J. E. (2022). Metaheuristic Assisted Hybrid Classifier for Bitcoin Price Prediction. *Cybernetics and Systems*, 1–25. doi:10.1080/01969722.2022.2129376

Hitam, N. A., Ismail, A. R., Samsudin, R., & Alkhammash, E. H. (2022). The Effect of Kernel Functions on Cryptocurrency Prediction Using Support Vector Machines. In *International Conference of Reliable Information and Communication Technology* (pp. 319-332). Springer. 10.1007/978-3-030-98741-1_27

Jiang, X., Li, X., Yang, J., & Li, J. (2020). Feature selection and engineering for time series forecasting: A review. *Expert Systems with Applications*, *144*, 113–138.

Liao, W., Zheng, Y., Xu, Q., & Zhang, Y. (2019). Deep learning models for stock price prediction: A survey. *Frontiers in Neuroinformatics*, *13*, 23.

Luo, C., Pan, L., Chen, B., & Xu, H. (2022). Bitcoin Price Forecasting: An Integrated Approach Using Hybrid LSTM-ELM Models. *Mathematical Problems in Engineering*. doi:10.1155/2022/2126518

Maleki, N., Nikoubin, A., Rabbani, M., & Zeinali, Y. (2020). Bitcoin price prediction based on other cryptocurrencies using machine learning and time series analysis. *Scientia Iranica*, *0*(0), 0. doi:10.24200ci.2020.55034.4040

Mehta, K., & Sharma, R. (2015). Individual Investors' Behavior: In Demographical Backdrop. SCMS Journal of Indian Management, 12(3), 25-36.

Mehta, K., Sharma, R., & Vyas, V. (2019, June 17). Efficiency and ranking of sustainability index of India using DEA-TOPSIS. *Journal of Indian Business Research*, *11*(2), 179–199. doi:10.1108/JIBR-02-2018-0057

Mohanty, S., & Dash, R. (2022). Neural Network-Based Bitcoin Pricing Using a New Mutated Climb Monkey Algorithm with TOPSIS Analysis for Sustainable Development. *Mathematics*, *10*(22), 4370. doi:10.3390/math10224370

Moulin, F., Tomasini, M., & Zanetti, M. (2018). Bayesian optimization for financial risk management. *Journal of Risk and Financial Management*, *11*(2), 22.

Petrovic, A., Strumberger, I., Bezdan, T., Jassim, H. S., & Nassor, S. S. (2021, November). Cryptocurrency Price Prediction by Using Hybrid Machine Learning and Beetle Antennae Search Approach. In *2021 29th Telecommunications Forum (TELFOR)* (pp. 1-4). IEEE. 10.1109/TELFOR52709.2021.9653305

Salb, M., Zivkovic, M., Bacanin, N., Chhabra, A., & Suresh, M. (2022). Support vector machine performance improvements for cryptocurrency value forecasting by enhanced sine cosine algorithm. In *Computer Vision and Robotics* (pp. 527–536). Springer. doi:10.1007/978-981-16-8225-4_40

Shahriari, B., Swersky, K., Wang, Z., Adams, R. P., & De Freitas, N. (2016). Taking the human out of the loop: A review of Bayesian optimization. *Proceedings of the IEEE*, *104*(1), 148–175. doi:10.1109/JPROC.2015.2494218

Shahvaroughi Farahani, M., & Farrokhi-Asl, H. (2022). Improved market prediction using meta-heuristic algorithms and time series model and testing market efficiency. *Iran Journal of Computer Science*, 1–33.

Shahvaroughi Farahani, M., & Razavi Hajiagha, S. H. (2021). Forecasting stock price using integrated artificial neural network and metaheuristic algorithms compared to time series models. *Soft Computing*, *25*(13), 8483–8513. doi:10.100700500-021-05775-5 PMID:33935586

Sharifi, A.M., Khalili Damghani, K., Abdi, F., & Sardar, S. (2022). A hybrid model for predicting bitcoin price using machine learning and metaheuristic algorithms. *Journal of Applied Research on Industrial Engineering, 9*(1), 134-150.

Sharma, R., Mehta, K., & Sharma, O. (2021). Exploring Deep Learning to Determine the Optimal Environment for Stock Prediction Analysis. *International Conference on Computational Performance Evaluation,* ComPE 2021, 148–152. 10.1109/ComPE53109.2021.9752138

Sharma, R., Mehta, K., & Vyas, V. (2020). Responsible Investing: A Study on Non-Economic Goals and Investors' Characteristics. Applied Finance Letters, 9(SI), 63-78. https://doi.org/ doi:10.24135/afl.v9i2

Swan, M. (2015). *Blockchain: blueprint for a new economy*. O'Reilly Media, Inc.

Trivedi, S., Mehta, K., & Sharma, R. (2021). Systematic Literature Review on Application of Blockchain Technology in E-Finance and Financial Services. *Journal of Technology Management & Innovation*, *16*(3), 90–102. doi:10.4067/S0718-27242021000300089

Vyas, V., Mehta, K., & Sharma, R. (2020). Investigating socially responsible investing behaviour of Indian investors using structural equation modelling. *Journal of Sustainable Finance & Investment*, 1–23. doi:10.1080/20430795.2020.1790958

Wang, S. H., Zhang, X., & Zhang, Y. D. (2021). DSSAE: Deep stacked sparse autoencoder analytical model for COVID-19 diagnosis by fractional Fourier entropy. *ACM Transactions on Management Information Systems*, *13*(1), 1–20. doi:10.1145/3451357

KEY TERMS AND DEFINITIONS

AE Learning Neural Network: AE (Autoencoder) learning neural network refers to a type of machine learning model that aims to recreate the input data in an unsupervised manner through a series of hidden layers. The objective of an AE learning neural network is to learn the underlying patterns in the data by reconstructing the input data with high accuracy.

ARIMA, LSTM, and GRU Models: ARIMA stands for Autoregressive Integrated Moving Average, LSTM stands for Long Short-Term Memory, and GRU stands for Gated Recurrent Unit. ARIMA, LSTM, and GRU models are popular time series prediction algorithms commonly used in the field of machine learning for forecasting future values based on historical data.

Bayesian Optimization (BO): Bayesian Optimization (BO) is a probabilistic model-based approach to optimization problems, where the objective function is unknown but can be evaluated at any given point.

Cryptocurrency: Cryptocurrency is a digital or virtual currency that uses cryptography for security and operates independently.

DNN Models: DNN stands for Deep Neural Network models, which are a type of artificial neural network with multiple hidden layers used for complex data analysis and predictions.

Hyperparameter Values: Hyperparameter values refer to the adjustable settings in a machine learning model that are set before training the model and have a direct impact on its performance.

Machine Learning (ML): Machine learning is a subfield of artificial intelligence that focuses on the development of algorithms and models that enable computers to learn and make predictions or decisions based on data.

Operates Independently: It refers to an action or system that functions without outside influence or control.

Price Prediction: Price prediction refers to the forecasting or estimation of the future price of a particular asset, commodity, or currency, based on various factors such as market trends, demand, and supply.

Reconstructed Error (RE): The Reconstructed Error (RE) is a measure of the difference between the actual value and the predicted value in a machine learning model, often used as a metric for evaluating the performance of autoencoder models.

Stacked Sparse Autoencoder (SSAE): Stacked Sparse Autoencoder (SSAE) is a deep learning architecture that consists of multiple autoencoder layers, each layer being trained to learn representations of the input data in a compact and sparse format.

Chapter 6
Digitalization of the Financial Sector:
New Opportunities and Challenges During the COVID-19 Crisis

Karima Toumi Sayari
Al Zahra College for Women, Oman

ABSTRACT

Digital finance emerges and grows along with the environment of the unlimited integration of information technology and finance. This led to a shift from the traditional way of performing finance in different areas to another digital one. With the ongoing evolution of technology, financial innovation has made new inventions. More intelligent digital finance has emerged, which creates new opportunities and facilities. The COVID-19 pandemic has accelerated global digital transformation by altering businesses' and consumers' relationships with digital technologies in months. Digital finance becomes a necessity and offers previously unseen opportunities. The digitalization process also poses new challenges and risks which require a continuous update of regulations set by supreme committees and institutions to safeguard national security. Strict legal law is needed to strengthen trust and confidence in using e-services. Progress in three key areas will boost the prospects for broader adoption of digital finance, crypto, and decentralized finance (DeFi) markets.

INTRODUCTION

The shifting of financial activities to a digitally connected world is known as the digitalization of the economy, and it is be associated with a considerable changes and updates in many areas, notably the finance sector. The International Finance Corporation's strategy for promoting private sector growth in any country includes two key objectives: stimulating the digital economy and increasing financial inclusion.

In the domain of finance, technological advancement is nothing new, but digital revolution has greatly enhanced system connection, processing power and cost, and newly created and usable data. The manu-

DOI: 10.4018/978-1-6684-8624-5.ch006

facturing of financial services could be broken down as a result of the greater information exchange and decreased transaction costs by technology.

The idea of a "technological revolution" has the benefit of marking people's minds, but it also runs the risk of making those minds insensitive to subtleties. It appears that the financial sector has always been guided by technological advancements, and from this perspective, the age of "digitalization" of financial activities fits into a continuity rather than a breakdown. The way businesses are conducted has changed as a result of digital transformation and the incorporation of new technologies. The mechanisms used to deliver banking and financial services and products are increasingly more secure and open. The huge, rapidly expanding pool of acquired data is the most beneficial byproduct of digitization. Big data analytics are now possible thanks to advanced computing. Application program interface (API) and social media, mobile, analytics, and cloud (SMAC) technologies have made it possible for various data streams to communicate with one another very effectively. Currently, businesses of all sizes, from start-ups to multinational organizations, utilize financial technologies. The new Digital ecosystem develops new business models that offer new services, new assets, new opportunities, new types of risk and performance data, new job functions, and ultimately a new vocabulary are all part of this.

This chapter looks at the scope and importance of digital finance development, by developing a multi-covered framework to explore the embedded architecture and the diverse digital finance areas. It explains, further, the benefits and new challenges faced by digital finance under different aspects. Moreover, the increase in digital finance during the COVID-19 crisis will be analyzed. Finally, we will deal with the efforts made by regulatory bodies to minimize risks and insecurities generated by digital finance.

SCOPE AND EVOLUTION OF DIGITAL FINANCE

As a disruptive force in the financial industry, digital finance has the potential to increase economic development, efficiency, and financial inclusion. However, structural ruptures may have had a substantial impact on the trajectory of acceptance of digital banking because the adoption and dissemination of digital finance have not been consistent across different nations and regions.

A structural change is a substantial change to the basic framework of an economic or financial system, such as one brought about by adjustments to market conditions, laws, rules, or technology. Depending on how they influence the incentives, possibilities, and risks faced by individuals, organizations, and politicians, these breaks may facilitate or impede the adoption and expansion of digital finance.

The adoption and expansion of digital money can also be determined by the government's actions. Governments may, for instance, set up regulatory frameworks that promote innovation and competition while safeguarding consumer interests from possible harm. To increase access and raise awareness of digital money among disadvantaged individuals, they can also invest in infrastructure and digital literacy programs.

Technological developments as a new potential for the adoption of digital finance have been opened by technological developments in fields like mobile banking, e-payments, and blockchain. Digital finance may be more widely adopted and used in economies with a high level of technological proficiency and digital infrastructure deployment. Financial services are changing due to digital innovation. The globe has witnessed the arrival of recent financial technology innovations like mobile money, peer-to-peer (P2P) or marketplace financing, Robo-advice, assurance technology (insurtech), and crypto-assets. Dif-

Figure 1. Major global drivers supporting the growth of fintech sector

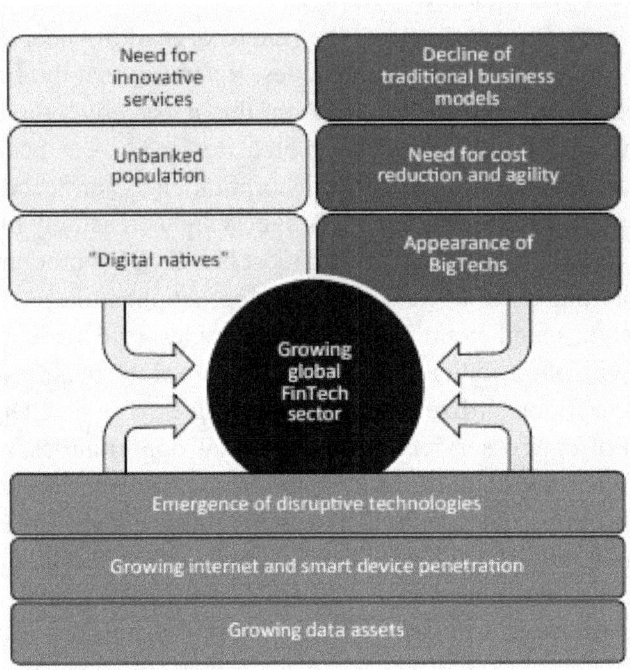

ferent terminologies are used but almost similar in meaning: Internet Finance, Financial Technology, and Digital Finance services.

These terms are used interchangeably in literature. At this point, the term Digital finance is used in the sense of the comprehensive understanding to refer to the digitalization of different aspects of the financial system with technology-enabled. New digital technologies are disrupting established financial service providers and bringing new goods and players to the financial market. Financial services are being delivered in fundamentally different ways and by different parties. This transformation process is referred to as "digital finance" (Digital finance: areas of action, 2022).

The financial sector has been undergoing a digital disruption that alters the ultimate prospects and behaviors in a culture, market, industry, or process and is brought on by or expressed through digital capabilities, channels, or assets. The financial sector has been experiencing this (Gartner, 2020).

The FinTech industry is expanding rapidly in terms of its user base, product and service offerings, funding, and market valuation, and this development is further aided by unique supply, demand, and technology variables. Specific demand, supply, and technology aspects help the fintech sector grows. Some noticeable driving variables that are perceptible on a worldwide scale and support the expansion of the FinTech sector assist the dynamic explosion of innovative financial services (FinTech and Digitalization report, 2020). The following figure precise these variables from the demand and supply side as well.

On the demand side, there is a growing demand for innovative financial services that can be used quickly and comfortably when taking into account the demand side and consumer behaviors. Additionally, the young "digital native" generation, which mostly conducts its finances online, gives the good market potential for innovative businesses. Additionally, traditional financial service providers' business and operational models are under pressure. Existing players also want more agile, flexible, and cost-

Figure 2. Financial system components

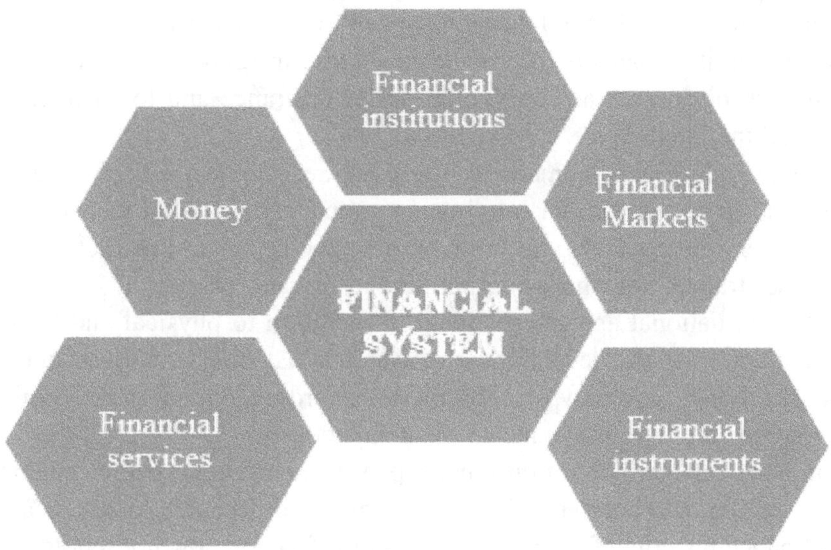

effective operations. Their old business models are under a lot of pressure as a result of the migration of services to the digital arena. They also face new challenges as BigTech companies with far larger customer bases and technological capabilities enter the market for financial services. Besides, technological advancement plays an important role to accelerate the growth of the fintech industry. It is important to indicate also that greater collaboration between service providers could lead to sustainable growth. While the competition between incumbents and FinTechs first appeared to be intensifying, establishing and enhancing cooperation became increasingly crucial for both parties once the opportunities provided by the synergies were recognized.

The graph summarizes the components of the financial system. These components have been subject to the digital transformation of different segments of the financial system. There have been quick growth of revolutions touching all these components. It encompasses a range of items that have changed the way that banking and financial services are typically provided, including products, apps, procedures, and business models. The first segment is financial institutions. Traditional Banks are replaced by innovative ones, technology-powered banks with full-service, "built-for-digital" banking systems, such as challengers banks or financial instituitions established by big tech corporations. Several technology-enabled innovation periods have already been experienced by banks. Traditional banks continue to fight with bringing their legacy-based infrastructure into the digital age. To develop investment strategies that can be offered successfully with their current infrastructure, banks adopt innovative technology. Banks are developing sophisticated abilities for maintaining a value-added remote client connection while preserving transactions, reducing fraud, and using new technologies like biometry, video, and chatbots. Many inventions aim to establish simple but reliable consumer identification systems. The appearance of Neo-banks is essentially a subset of Fintech. Neo-banks seek to duplicate existing banks' capabilities while introducing novel services and solutions.

Insurance companies, as non-bank financial institutions, starts also a digitalization stage. Although less developed than digital payments and lending, digital insurance products including auto, travel, and health insurance are provided on demand through apps or marketplaces have appeared. Initial advances focused on exploiting digital channels to provide low-value insurance products to balance costs and revenues. Some fintech businesses are providing digital insurance and loans to farmers by utilizing satellite data and machine intelligence.

The second component is Financial markets. These markets connect lenders-savers with excess cash through borrowers and investors who wish to borrow money. New digital technologies are disrupting established financial service providers and bringing new goods. Several markets are depending on the type of financial asset traded, encompassing public and private, primary and secondary, money and capital, spot and future, national and international, in addition to physical and virtual (Narcisa et al 2019). Digitalization results in the development of systems that shape, appraise, and process financial items including stocks, bonds, currency, and contracts. According to modern economists, Fintech refers the use of technology to automate and enhance financial activity.

With its exceptional characteristics of minimal expense, extensive exposure, and high-level efficacy, digital finance has significantly accelerated the advancement of financial products and services (Ye et al. 2022). Digital finance may therefore have a variety of effects on how household financial assets are allocated. First, family investment is made more convenient in terms of time and space thanks to digital banking, especially in distant places where traditional financial activities are geographically constrained. In addition, the diffusion of digital finance generates more investment opportunities. For investors looking to make a wise investment allocation, the coexistence of cryptocurrencies with various technology creates a highly varied market that is challenging to realize and control. The cryptocurrency market has rapidly expanded into a sizable new market.

Financial instruments are an essential component in the financial system which is in perpetual development as a result of financial innovation and digitalization. Crypto assets are example of private digital assets, those that rely heavily on distributed ledger technology and cryptography (Financial Stability Board 2020). Central bank digital currencies, Bitcoin, and other crypto products are new financial instruments generated by the digitalization of the financial sector.

Regarding Financial services, digital transformation changes the way how they are provided to individuals inside and outside of their business. Further, the growth of digital finance has increased public admission to digital financial facilities. With a modernized and digitalized relationship model, neo-banks aim to gain a presence in the banking industry by shifting away from the branch-centered client connection model. There are also more sophisticated services added to the DFS eco-system as economies transition from cash-based to a digital one (Figure 3).

The fifth segment is money. As an intermediate of exchange, money is used in payment transactions on a national and international level and is in direct relation to other components of the financial system. The influence of digitalization manifests through a new type of money which includes electronic payment systems that function as substitutes for traditional financial exchanges, such as cryptocurrencies and blockchains. Also, Central Bank Digital Currencies (CBDC) is a project started by some countries which have fully launched a digital currency (China, Russia, Thailand, Malaysia, South Korea, and the United Arabs). The following figure shows a digital Finance overview.

Figure 3. Digital finance summary

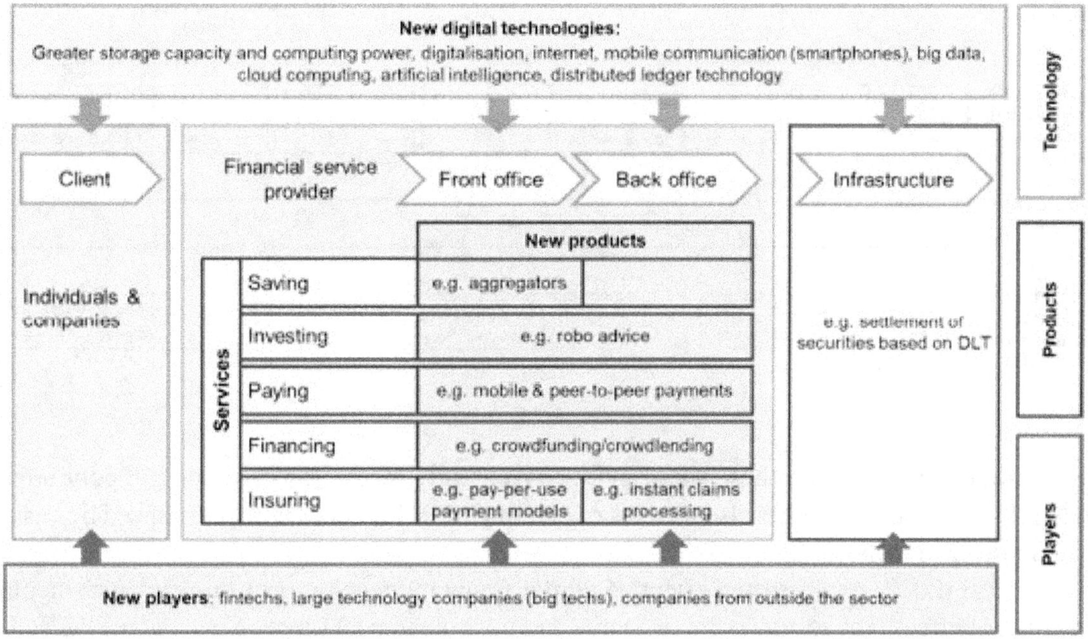

LITERATURE REVIEW: ADVANTAGES OF DIGITAL FINANCE

This section looks at the effects of digital finance on financial enclosure and financial system constancy. By focusing on digital finance and investigating some of its benefits in different areas.

The advancement of digital finance has favorable effects on allocating resources more efficiently and creating a modern financial system that is extremely adaptable, competitive, and inclusive.

According to the World Bank, it has been clear for some time that extensive use of digital financial services promotes economic growth and poverty reduction. The work with developing nations around the world has shown that more developed financial systems are associated with more dynamic growth, faster reductions in poverty rates, and faster progress toward income equality.

As the world tackles the COVID-19 virus crisis, the requirement for these digital services in enabling citizens and governments to use safe, affordable, non-contact financial tools becomes even more ostensible. The improved access to basic services like accounts payable, credit, insurance, and savings products let the poor increase their incomes and become more resilient. The ability to send and obtain money, save money, and obtain credit to expand one's business might be particularly important for women.

The academic basis for the connection between digital finance and financial inclusion is the assumption that a large proportion of the prohibited population owns (or has access to) a computer,

and mobile phone, as well as the provision of financial services via mobile phone. Mobile phones and similar devices can facilitate access to financial support for the excluded population (World Bank, 2014). The benefits of digital finance for financial inclusion vary. When applied to the lives of low-income and poor people, greater digital finance can improve their access to basic services, leading to greater financial inclusion in rural areas.

Figure 4. Constraints to financial inclusion and the development of digital financial services

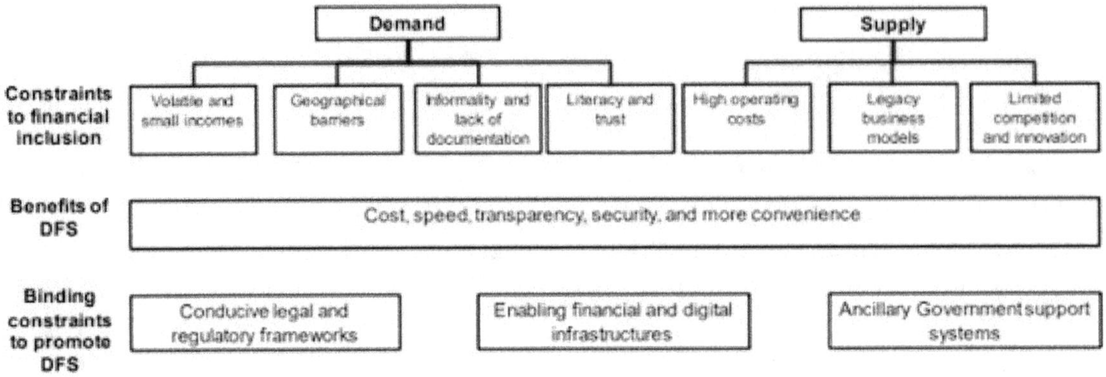

DFS facilitate the access for those who cannot conveniently access banks because of poor infrastructure networks or others. It reduces also the cost of opening more branches and time wasted by customers' presence in these branches.

Wang and Ji (2022) explored the effect of digital financial development on residents' income and the networks of effect. The results point to a large and positive impact on people's income caused by the expansion of digital financial services. They demonstrated that the benefits of digital financial development go to rural communities, low-skilled employees, and people employed in basic sectors.

Hasan et al. (2020) developed a theoretical Background for Encouraging inclusiveness through Digital Financial Services (DFS). They investigated the connections between traditional financial services and promoted inclusive finance. The theoretical framework explains how DFS affects financial inclusion. By providing DFSs, the digitalization of financial systems and the subsequent development of ICT have aided in the achievement of the main objectives of inclusive finance.

Today, financial inclusivity purposes to make a broader range of facilities, trough technological innovations and expand access to insurance, micro-loans, and money-transfer services to those who are currently excluded.

Pazarbasioglu et al. (2020) summarizes the constraints to financial inclusion and how they are alleviated through the digitalization of financial services.

As the figure clarifies, there are different constraints to financial inclusion from the demand and supply sides as well. On the demand side, constraints consist of low income. The poor need affordable, low-value financial services that enable them to cope with their volatile and low income. DFS can solve this problem and lowers the cost of these financial services through pre-paid e-money products. Approximately two-thirds of adults without access to financial services in developing economies say that they don't have enough money to open an account (Demirgüç et al., 2018). These authors specified that the majority of people in Latin America and the Caribbean who lack access to financial services complain that accounts are too costly, according to their estimates.

DFS can be offered more affordably with lower marginal and fixed expenses. the barrier to account ownership is another constraint to financial inclusion. Using retail agents and mobile devices, DFS enables the disadvantaged to send money or convert digital balances to cash. DFS can help the undocumented poor, which reduces costs, by using digital techniques for transaction start and authentication. Informality and lack of documentation present also impediments to financial inclusion because of the difficulty to own an account. But, DFS can help the undocumented poor by using digital techniques for transaction initiation and authentication, which decreases costs. Regarding the supply side, constraint consists, firstly, of high costs of operation. Many officials have historically retained old and obsolete technologies and relied on expensive and time-consuming manual and paper processes. Small-value transactions are now commercially viable thanks to DFS's ability to be automated, customized to the needs of the consumer, and given distantly at a cheaper cost. Legacy business models are a second offer-side constraint. But those with unstable incomes who are disadvantaged may require more latitude to spread out payments or to pay back when they have the money, which may be the same day they took out the loan. DFS can meet the needs of the underprivileged at a lower cost.

Limited competition and innovation are moreover, a constraint to financial inclusion. In fact, due to entry difficulties created by prohibitive rules and a fragile startup ecosystem, executives have enjoyed significant market influence in many developing economies. Due to this, these financial institutions were unrestrained in their capacity to impose high fees and margins and were under less of a need to participate in and implement new technology to penetrate underserved and unexplored market niches. New competitors are now given the option to offer bank-like services that successfully compete on both price and quality thanks to DFS business models.

Nimble incumbents that engage in digital transformation or work with startups can also stimulate competition and encourage innovation.

Figure 4 also emphasizes the requirement for an effective collection of qualifying comportments to provide the consumer protection, financial integrity, financial stability, and competition required to develop robust and trustworthy markets that will attract investment and consumer adoption. Modern, strong, accessible, and interoperable digital and financial infrastructures, as well as auxiliary government support mechanisms, all contribute to the growth of the DFS. These frameworks enable responsible DFS innovation.

Within the context of the benefits of Digital finance to financial markets, Yun et al. (2022) found that the use of digital finance greatly encourages family participation in speculative financial marketplaces. Also, household engagement in digital finance is impacted by three factors: enhancing family access to financial information, improving investment channels, and raising a potential appetite for risk among households. As a consequence, the emergence of digital finance efficiently lessens the restrictive impact of capital and intellectual barriers on household involvement in uncertain financial markets.

The rapid expansion of the numerical economy is being driven by a new generation of digital technologies characterized by blockchain, and cryptographic techniques, and speeding the change of the digital economy has gained the support of the entire society. Cryptographic techniques are at the center of the implementation of cryptocurrencies, which are virtual digital money. Cryptocurrencies are a subset of digital currencies, according to the World Bank, which defines them as digital representations of value that are denominated in their unit of account. This is in contrast to e-money, which is merely a digital payment system that represents and is denominated in fiat money.

The creation of the first cryptocurrency, bitcoin, in 2009, is credited with the emergence of cryptocurrencies as they are well known today. After that, cryptocurrency experiences began in 2011 with the introduction of Solid Coin, IXcoin, Namecoin, and other coins. As of August 1, 2018, there are more than 1,737 distinct cryptocurrencies available (Narcisa et al., 2019).

Gkillasa and Longinb (2019) examined the advantages of using bitcoin at times when the financial markets are incredibly volatile. They found that bitcoin can play an important role in asset management by providing diversification benefits in periods of extreme price volatility in financial markets. This

Table 1. Main benefits to financial stability

Potential benefit	Link to financial stability
Decentralisation and diversification	Decentralisation and diversification in the financial system can dampen the effects of financial shocks in some circumstances.[29] Failure of a single (or type of) institution is less likely to shut down a market as there would be other (types of) providers of financial services.
Efficiency	Efficiency in operations, including through incentives created by contestability,[30] supports stable business models of financial institutions and contributes to overall efficiency gains in the financial system and the real economy.
Transparency	Transparency reduces information asymmetries and enables risks to be more accurately assessed and better priced.[31] It can further foster the creation of financial instruments with exposure to specific risks, completing markets and improving market participants' ability to manage risk.
Access to, and convenience of, financial services	Access to, and convenience of, financial services affects the financial inclusion of households and businesses, including SMEs. This is important for supporting sustainable economic growth and providing a diversification of exposure to investment risk.

suggests that in times of financial market instability, both assets, gold, and bitcoin, may be beneficial when used in combination. Bitcoin might also be practical for asset management, as the addition of bitcoin and gold significantly enhances the risk-return characteristics of stock holdings. So, bitcoin can be considered the new digital gold.

The launch of Central Bank Digital Currencies (CBDCs) signaled the start of a new financial age. Unlike Bitcoin and other early-stage crypto products, central bank digital currencies are centralized and governed by governments, just like conventional currencies. CBDC, a virtual form of a country's fiat currency issued by the central bank, was originally named a Digital Fiat Currency (DFC), This is inspired by well-known crypto assets like Bitcoin.

Financial Stability Board (2017) states that Digital finance supports financial stability and contributes to economic development and financial stability in a variety of ways, as shown in the following table:

DIGITAL FINANCE DURING THE COVID-19 CRISIS

In this section, the role that digitalization in the financial system has played during COVID-19, as well as post-pandemic, is addressed. The implementation of digital resources to avoid and better deal with the effects of the pandemic has been significant, highlighting the link between the health crisis and technological advancement.

In this time of social rupture, the decline in demand, reduction in provisioning, and tightening of credit terms, the COVID-19 Pandemic is highlighting the urgent need to turn to dematerialized services to preserve the operation of financial systems and people's safety. Financial technology, or "fintech," assists governments in transferring monetary transfers and other types of financial support quickly and securely, as well as in providing urgent liquidity to businesses. It enables people to send money, including to other countries, and to make purchases from home at a market or store without making a physical connection.

Governments and society are being forced by the pandemic to rely on digital technology to address the problem. Governments are being forced to embrace an open government strategy and use digital communication channels to offer accurate information on regional and global COVID-19 developments (United Nations, 2021).

Certainly, digital technologies have been critical in addressing the health and economic crisis and assisting flexibility. The challenges faced in tackling digital solutions to cope with the pandemic are discussed, and lessons to be learned from policy responses are highlighted.

The COVID-19 shock has accelerated the digitalization of public and private sector activities in many countries. This crisis is limiting people and goods movement; modes of the transaction have shifted dramatically. While digital financial inclusion was a development priority before the COVID19 pandemic, it has now turn into necessary. Governments are being urged to implement efficient digital technologies to contain the outbreak due to the widespread implementation of lockdowns and other social isolation measures as well as the growing reliance of people on the internet for information and guidance (United Nations, 2021).

Figure 5. E-commerce and digital economy related measures in selected developing countries (percentage)

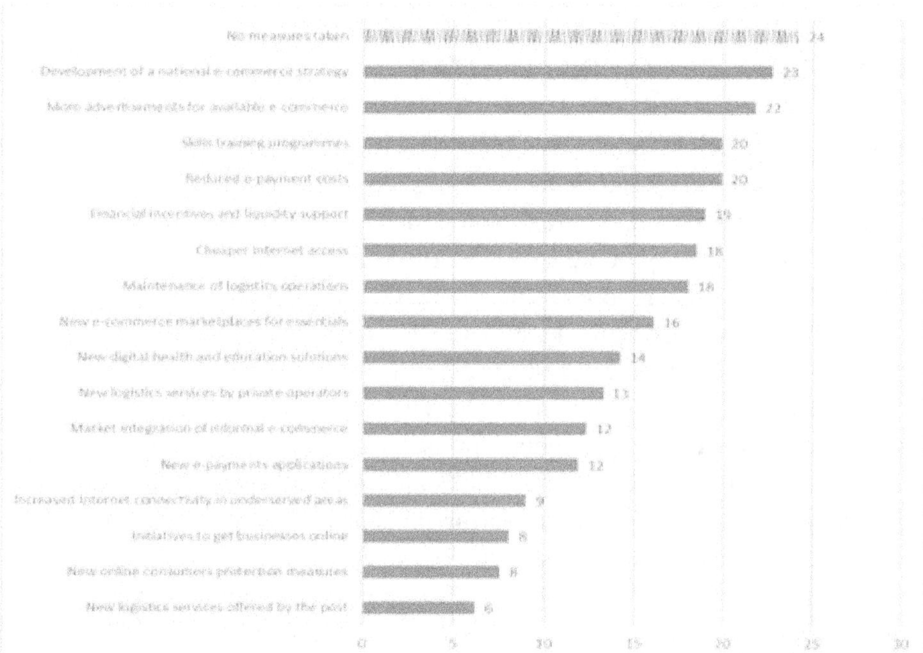

The brief advises policymakers to take advantage of the COVID-19 crisis to create custom digital government tools, strategies, and partnerships for the future. The crisis has shown that society cannot ignore technological improvements because they are constantly altering business structures and people's daily lives. Governments should seize the opportunities presented by these technological and policy advancements to assist the long-term sustainable growth of their nations.

The expanding application of DFS has transformed the crisis into an occasion, allowing formerly unbanked individuals and small businesses to enter the financial system. Regulations have evolved to keep pace with technology, but specific policies are required to ensure that no one falls behind. The pandemic of COVID-19 has augmented the digital revolution.

Digital connectivity will become increasingly important as physical connections between customers and suppliers and in the provision of financial services are replaced. Navigating the pandemic and the post-COVID-19 world as economies, financial service providers, companies, and people.

A change in consumer behavior brought on by the coronavirus pandemic made Africa the region with the fastest growth in the adoption of digital technology in the banking sector in 2020. As a result of the COVID-19 crisis, the use of electronic payment methods has increased significantly. This is because many small businesses have been forced to undergo their digital transformation, while banks and fintech companies like Pay stack have been quick to offer solutions to businesses that had previously only accepted cash as a form of payment (Africa CEO Forum, 2022).

According to a McKinsey & Company report, between June 2019 and June 2020, the availability of digital banking services increased by 20% annually in Africa, far outpacing growth in all other parts of the world. The adoption of digital technology has nearly multiplied by five in some countries, such as the South African region, where there was little digital banking activity before 2019.

BANKS ARE RAPIDLY BECOMING DIGITAL

The digitalization of the financial sector is accelerated by the health crisis. Since the turn of the century, the relationship between consumers and financial actors has undergone a significant transformation due to a rise in the usage of digital tools. However, the foundation of these relationships was up to that point rather stable. Most often, an agency or advisor is involved in the subscription of banking or insurance products. This kind of relationship is about to blow out. The advanced nations gradually conform to the pattern followed by the less heavily banked nations.

The COVID-19 crisis represents a catalyst for digitalization. Indeed, the dematerialization of monetary interactions is accelerated by the health crisis. The Economist claims that because of the global healthcare crisis, the percentage of non-monetary transactions has reached the levels they had predicted would be reached in the next two to five years. Banks are rapidly becoming digital.

With a long history of extensive digital transformation, banks are now moving faster than ever thanks to the global health crisis, which has increased internal telecommuting and customer use of remote financial services. Niemand et al. (2021) noted that in this era of rapid technological growth, banks which are characterized by innovation and a willingness to take risks, should have a clear understanding for automation revolution. Also, Anvarovich (2022) states that the banking industry should develop digital transformation through a rigorous examination of customer needs, an analysis of available opportunities, and the creation of a fresh, cutting-edge approach that is centered on the interests of the client.

These people are the ones who use banking services, and by expressing their demands, they help create the demand for contemporary banking products and services.

Figure 6 shows the growth and acceleration of fintechs in recent years, mainly, during the COVID 19 crisis, and the rise of assets in decentralized finance, driving coins in stablecoins.

Figure 6. Growth of digital assets

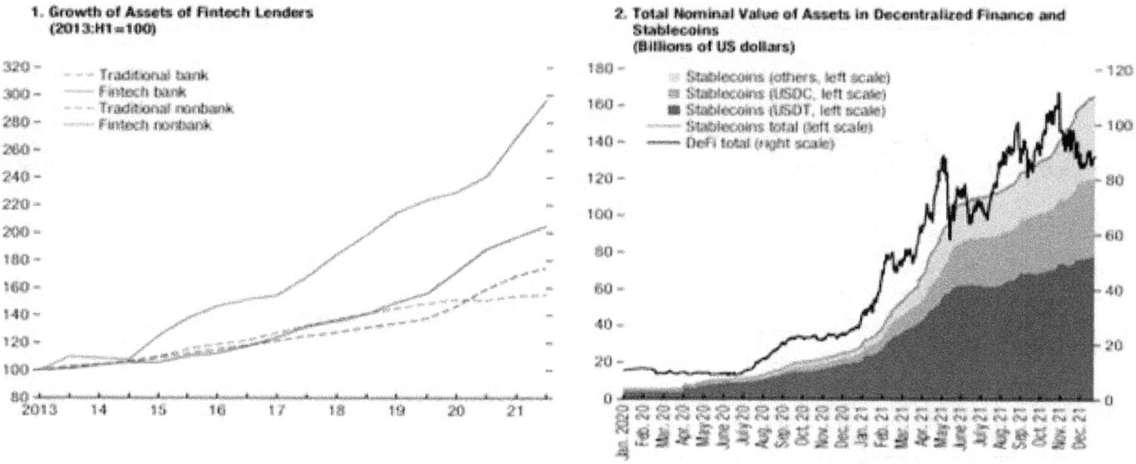

The major target of banks' digital transformation remains a better understanding to the needs of their clients. Since clients and businesses prefer to engage with banks quickly, easily, and affordably in the digital economy, the banking industry must be prepared to provide the most cutting-edge services.

The COVID-19 crisis has brought to light the numerous advantages of digital financial services as well as their essential role in reaching the Sustainable Development Goals. However, for their deployment to be accelerated, the following levers must act:

- Investing in the necessary infrastructure for the development of digital financial services;
- Developing digital identity systems, particularly biometric devices;
- Expansion of open application programming interfaces, which provide developers with a way to access proprietary software and enable communication and interaction between new apps;
- Legal and regulatory frameworks that allow the majority of people to take advantage of digital financial services and maintain a competitive ecosystem; and
- Facilitating access to platforms for government data.

Beyond these efforts to promote the development of digital finance, risk management is crucial. As a result, the user may be exposed through the data files created by digital systems to unauthorized disclosure, improper use of their personal information, or even discrimination.

THE DIGITALIZATION OF THE FINANCIAL SECTOR POSES NEW CHALLENGES

Digitalization can open up new opportunities for individuals and economies to grow and prosper. Utilizing new technology might make it easier for market manipulation, but it also has the ability—probably more certainly—to increase risk, insecurity, and exposure to cyberattacks. Which also makes it harder to stop money laundering and terrorism financing.

Table 2. List of risks and opportunities emanating from financial technologies and innovations

	Risks	Opportunities
Impact on consumer sector	A. Data privacy B. Data security C. Discontinuity of banking services D. Inappropriate marketing practices	A. Financial inclusion B. Better and more tailored banking services C. Lower transaction costs and faster banking services
Impact on banks and banking system	A. Strategic and profitability risks B. Increased interconnectedness between financial parties C. High operational risk – systemic D. High operational risk – idiosyncratic E. Third-party/vendor management risk F. Compliance risk including failure to protect consumers and data protection regulation G. Money laundering – terrorism financing risk H. Liquidity risk and volatility of bank funding sources	A. Improved and more efficient banking processes B. Innovative use of data for marketing and risk management purposes c. Potential positive impact on financial stability due to increased competitions D. Regtech

From a security point of view, IT risk, or Cyber risk is an issue related to the ongoing digital transformation of the financial system. The importance of data is expanding, which prompts urgent concerns regarding the security and management of personal data. Client protection continues to be a difficult task. The financial system's actors' exposure and vulnerability to cyber risk have increased dramatically as a result of digital change. This is due in large part to the actors' internal transformation, which is motivated by the growth of information systems built as open platforms and the rising usage of outsourcing, notably in cloud computing. The extensive usage of new collaborative tools and software has corresponded with the widespread adoption of teleworking. The sector as a whole is more vulnerable now that new labor organizations and third-party technologies have been implemented, sometimes in a rushed manner.

Due to the ongoing evolution and sophistication of the cyber-attack danger, this rise in the exhibition surface requires even greater caution. Technically, the availability of hacking tools, and the overall improvement in computer skills all contribute to this growth.

This increase in the exhibition surface calls for more attention as the threat of cyber attacks is constantly evolving and becoming more sophisticated. From a technical point of view, the distribution of hacking tools and the general increase in computer skills explain part of this evolution. From an economic point of view, the remunerative nature of these attacks explains the multiplication of hacking candidates.

Cyber risk has evolved in dimension as a result of this dual evolution: It is a significant operational risk for the entire organization, and it is now a systemic danger for the entire financial system.

The application of Distributed Ledger Technology (DLT)-based technologies, as a digital innovation, has the potential to enhance the performance of market infrastructures and payment methods, notably in terms of transaction speed, the number of intermediaries, and transaction costs. Finally, financial sector innovation creates additional concerns regarding monetary stability and sovereignty, particularly with the rise of BigTech and the development of new settlement assets in the form of crypto-assets.

Significant losses have resulted from the current market downturn and the ensuing failure of some projects and crypto assets. These events have also revealed peculiar risks and vulnerabilities in protocols, brought to light systemic issues in the crypto landscape and made politicians more aware of the need to regulate the crypto and decentralized finance (DeFi) ecosystem.

Effective regulation and oversight are hampered by the absence of centralized bodies overseeing DeFi. Regulation should concentrate on centralized exchanges and stable coin issuers, two components of the crypto ecosystem that facilitate DeFi. Authorities should promote strong governance of DeFi platforms as well as programs, including self-regulatory bodies and industry codes. These organizations could deliver an efficient channel for regulatory control.

THE CHALLENGES OF REGULATING CRYPTO

The market for crypto-assets has expanded quickly in recent years. Although banks' exposure to crypto assets is still limited and the crypto assets market is still modest in absolute terms compared to the size of the global financial system, its absolute size is significant, and advancements are still happening quickly. The expansion of crypto assets and related services has the potential to increase bank risks and cause worries about financial stability.

Policymakers will have to deal with a challenging macroeconomic and geopolitical environment as well as some particular characteristics of this developing ecosystem.

After the global financial crisis of 2007–2009, regulators have shown they are ready and able to put coordinated, all-encompassing, and successful measures in place to lower risks in the international financial system. According to the Financial Stability Board's statement published on July 11, 2022, this ecosystem "must be subject to appropriate regulation and inspection proportional to the risks they entail, both at the local and international level." But when it comes to governing this novel world of crypto and DeFi, the saying in the stock market that "past performance does not guarantee future results" may be applicable. Regional standard-setters and supervisors will face several challenging issues. The following figure summarizes these challenges.

Figure 7. The challenges of regulating crypto

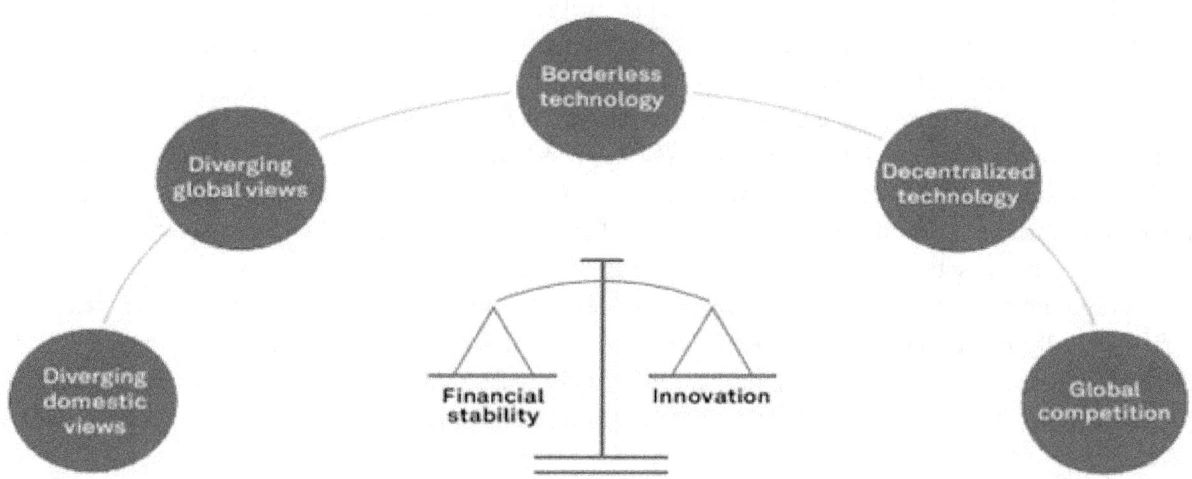

- **Diverging Domestic Views:** Cryptocurrency and DeFi are diverging topics in domestic political contexts. Politicians, central bankers, and regulatory agencies' perspectives on these issues can therefore be very diverse.
- **Diverging Global Views:** The policy perspective will probably continue to be inconsistent amongst jurisdictions which may result in conflicting (geo)political goals. Additionally, there are regional differences in institutional trust, financial access for the general populace, and attitudes toward privacy.
- **Borderless Technology:** The fact that using numerous protocols simply requires internet access is one of the technology's main draws. Developers can work virtually from anywhere thanks to the blockchain technology at its core, and protocols can be instantly made available across boundaries.
- **Decentralized Technology:** The question of who should be regulated when power is dispersed is a crucial one raised by blockchain technology.
- **Global Competition:** In this rapidly changing environment, the adjustment of domestic regulations may present a chance for jurisdictions to become the cores of a developing international market.

HOW TO MEET DIGITALIZATION CHALLENGES?

In the wake of the massive expansion of digital connections throughout the epidemic, cautions realized include the significance of preserving personal and commercial information and data secure. Cybersecurity has become a primary focus.

Accelerating regulatory actions doesn't always shield established players in traditional finance. Creating a strong regulatory framework for digital assets and DeFi may legitimize and speed up sector growth by attracting new clients and encouraging new entrants who pose a threat to established players in traditional finance's operating methods. Regulations may ultimately enable more absorbency between the traditional finance (TradFi) and digital finance (DeFi) worlds.

The first axe comes from the knowledge that security strongly depends on a regulatory environment that promotes financial innovation and ensures economic stability, both of which can improve user experience and system performance.

In this light, as part of its digital finance strategy, the European Commission unveiled a proposal for a regulation on Markets in Crypto-Assets (MiCA) and Digital Operational Resilience Act (DORA) regulatory projects, both of which were unveiled in September 2020. With the release of the MiCA project, the European Union was the first G20 legal entity to respond to the urgent need to regulate the market for crypto-assets (Deloitte Tax & Consuling,2022).

The regulatory framework's single adaptation does not, however, address all of the challenges posed by financial digitalization. Being an innovator is also important to assure system performance.

The integration into the European innovation ecosystem first manifests as a commitment to facilitate and support initiatives that may help ensure the diversity and convergence of effective solutions that are tailored to the needs of users.

The active support for financial innovation has also taken the form of an ambitious program to test a CBDC. To maintain the function of central bank money's issuance in the digital age, numerous central banks have seriously begun working on the production of a CBDC. This is a significant issue given cur-

Table 3. Practical instances of PSMOR applied to fintech

	PSMOR	Practical implementation for fintech developments
Fundamental principles of operational risk management		
1	Ensuring a strong risk culture	Ensuring integrated risk culture shared throughout the supply chain.
2	Risk management framework	Capturing fintech-driven new risks and risk profile changes.
Governance		
3	Effectively implementing risk policies, processes and systems	Building up framework to capture and control fintech-driven new risks.
4	Setting and reviewing risk appetite and risk tolerance	Setting appropriate risk appetite and tolerance with effective thresholds to trigger prompt remedial action.
5	Implementing the policies, processes and systems. to control risks	Ensuring prompt reporting, assessment and early risk mitigation for fintech-driven risks.
Risk management environment		
6	Identifying/assessing risks in all processes and systems	Enhancing capacity to identify, assess and mitigate risks arising from extended processes and systems in fintech migrations.
7	Assessing risks in the launch of every product, activity, process and system	Ensuring the timely and overarching identification, assessment of risks in the launch and delivery of fintech-driven processes and systems.
8	Appropriate risk monitoring and proactive risk management	Updating the frequency of monitoring and reporting with appropriate escalation according to the size and nature of the risks.
9	Strong risk control environment	Affording appropriate capacities and resources allocated to promptly and effectively control fintech-driven risks.
Business resiliency and continuity		
10	Business resiliency and continuity plans for severe business disruption	Incorporating business continuity and disaster recovery plan with business disruption scenarios in fintech-driven processes and systems.
Role of disclosure		
11	Public disclosure of risk management	–

rent trends toward the digitization of financial markets and payment systems, as well as the rise of new non-bank actors in the field of financial intermediation.

The development of fintech makes banks subject to different risks such as strategic, operational, cyber, and consistency threats. These dangers were noted for both current banks and fintech players in the financial sector. Banks should guarantee that they have efficient governance structures and risk management procedures in place to identify, manage, and monitor risks related to the use of enabling technologies, the emergence of new business models, and the entry of new players into the banking system brought about by fintech developments. According to Basel Committee on Banking Supervision (2017), these structures should contain:

- Strong strategic and business planning procedures that let banks change their revenue and profitability projections in light of the potential effects of new technology and market entrants;
- Adjustment of managing procedures to effectively address changes in company processes as well as in technology;
- Adoption of the Basel Committee's principles for sound management of operational risk (PSMOR), taking into account advancements in fintech; and

- When launching new products, services, or channels, it is important to monitor and review accordance with appropriate governing guidelines, particularly those relating to consumer protection, data protection, and AML/CFT. Table 3 includes Practical examples of PSMOR useful to fintech.

To be innovative in delivering financial products and services, banks and fintech companies are progressively adopting and utilizing modern technology. Application programming interfaces (APIs), cloud computing, distributed ledger technology (DLT), artificial intelligence (AI), machine learning (ML), and advanced data analytics all offer opportunities but also come with inherent risks. To meet these risks, banks need to make sure they have efficient IT and other risk management procedures that handle the threats posed by pioneering technology and put in place the proficient control frameworks required to effectively support major advances (Committee on Banking Supervision, 2017).

PRUDENTIAL MANAGEMENT OF BANKS' CRYPTO-ASSET EXPOSURES

The fundamental principles for international banking rule and risk management are being developed by the Basel Committee on Banking Supervision (BCBS). The Committee thinks that many consultations would likely be necessary when developing policy for exposures to crypto assets because of this asset class's fast evolution.

In 2021, the committee issued its initial consultation paper on the prudential treatment of crypto asset exposures. According to the document, banks with exposure to digital assets ought to hold $1 in capital for every $1 of these assets they own. This first document was followed by a second revised one in 2022.

The initial consultation's proposal's basic framework called for categorizing crypto assets continuously into two groups: crypto assets in group 1 are those which fully satisfy a set of classification requirements. They would be subject to at least equivalent risk-based capital requirements based on the risk weights of underlying exposures as specified in the current Basel capital framework. These assets include tokenized traditional assets and crypto assets with effective stabilization mechanisms. Crypto assets from group 2 are those which do not satisfy any of the classification requirements. They, therefore, present more risks than Group 1 crypto assets, and as a result, would be subject to the newly recommended conservative capital treatment. In 2022, the committee made amendments to the categorization requirements and clarify the Basel framework that should be applied in respect of banks' exposures to crypto assets. Also, the committee set a minimum capital requirement for each group of crypto assets, for credit, operational risk, market risk, and other requirements.

The following diagram highlights major new features compared to the first proposal and shows the structure of the proposed risk-based capital requirements as laid out in the second consultative paper.

In light of recent market volatility in digital assets, BCBS emphasized the urgency of these restrictions. The body aims to complete the framework for banks to treat digital assets prudentially by the end of 2022. As mentioned in the above figure, the new elements are highlighted in dashed/dotted boxes.

Figure 8. Structure of the proposed risk-based capital requirements

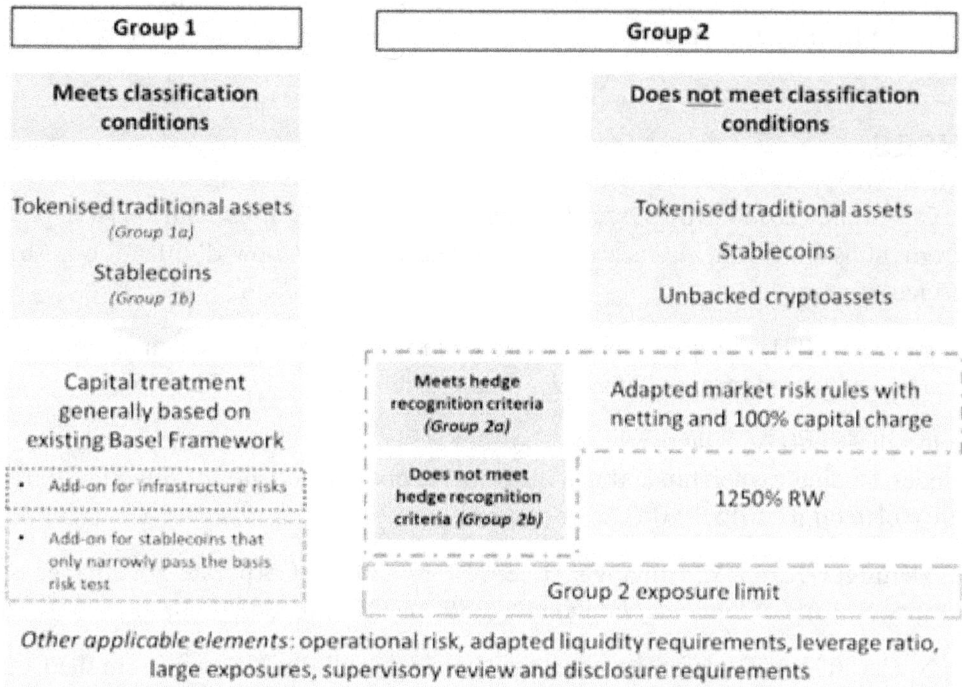

CONCLUSION

For the past 30 years, the finance industry has focused on computerizing transaction processing and digital transformation. Regarding its benefits, all players in this sector are exploring investments in digital finance.

The COVID-19 outbreak has intensified the necessity for fintech to keep financial institutions working and keep people protected during this period of societal distancing, diminishing demand, decreased input supply, stricter lending conditions, and rising uncertainty.

However, to avoid these new technologies from worsening the issues brought on by this crisis, related risks must be properly addressed, especially for the poor and disadvantaged. Other required expenditures are important for the development of digital financial services. They include the expansion of digital identity, mobile broadband infrastructure (even in distant areas), and open application programming interfaces. To ensure a competitive environment and enable the majority of customers to use digital financial services, these investments should be supplemented by the necessary legislative and regulatory frameworks.

Digital Finance still is a specialized market with some dangers, but it also has motivating properties in terms of efficiency, transparency, accessibility, and composability. As such, DeFi may potentially contribute to a more robust and transparent financial infrastructure.

The BCBS is working to update the regulatory framework for different aspects of digital finance.

In anticipation of additional development, Central Bank Digital Currency is currently beyond the framework's preview. As was already mentioned, it is anticipated that once in circulation, it will be treated much more favorably, similar to maintaining reserve accounts with central banks or actual currency.

REFERENCES

Africa C. E. O. Forum. (2021). *How Digitalization is strengthening Financial services post – COVID.* Retrieved from https://www.theafricaceoforum.com/en/ressources/how-digitization-is-strengthening-financial-services-post-covid/

Al, A., & Ahmed, A. (2021). Cryptography in financial markets: Potential channels for future financial stability. *Academy of Accounting and Financial Studies Journal, 25*(4), 1528–2635.

Allen, F., Demirguc-Kunt, A., Klapper, L., & Martinez Peria, M. S. (2016). The foundations of financial inclusion: Understanding ownership and use of formal accounts. *Journal of Financial Intermediation, 27*, 1–30. doi:10.1016/j.jfi.2015.12.003

Anginer, D., Demirguc-Kunt, A., Huizinga, H., & Ma, K. (2018). Corporate governance of banks and financial stability. *Journal of Financial Economics, 130*(2), 327–346. doi:10.1016/j.jfineco.2018.06.011

Anvarovich, N. E. (2022a). Transformation of the Banking Sector in Uzbekistan in the Context of Co-vid-19 Coronavirus Pandemia. *Academic Journal of Digital Economics and Stability, 13*, 76–85.

Arner, D. W., Barberis, J. N., & Buckley, R. P. (2015). The Evolution of Fintech: A New Post-Crisis Paradigm? SSRN *Electronic Journal*. https://doi.org/ doi:10.2139/SSRN.2676553

Arun, T., & Kamath, R. (2015). Financial inclusion: Policies and practices. *IIMB Management Review, 27*(4), 267–287. doi:10.1016/j.iimb.2015.09.004

Barbesino, P., Camerani, R., & Gaudino, A. (2005). Digital finance in Europe: Competitive dynamics and online behavior. *Journal of Financial Services Marketing, 9*(4), 329–343. doi:10.1057/palgrave.fsm.4770164

Barde, S. (2022). Blockchain and Cryptocurrencies. *Emerging Computing Paradigms*, 235-246. doi:10.1002/9781119813439.ch13

Bernards, N., & Campbell-Verduyn, M. (2019). Understanding technological change in global finance through infrastructures: Introduction to Review of International Political Economy Special Issue 'The Changing Technological Infrastructures of Global Finance'. *Review of International Political Economy, 26*(5), 773–789. doi:10.1080/09692290.2019.1625420

Christiaens, T. (2016). *Digital subjectivation and financial markets: Criticizing Social Studies of Finance with Lazzarato.* https://doi.org/ doi:10.1177/2053951716662897

Corbet, S., Larkin, C., & Lucey, B. (2020). The contagion effects of the COVID-19 pandemic: Evidence from gold and cryptocurrencies. *Finance Research Letters, 35*, 101554. Advance online publication. doi:10.1016/j.frl.2020.101554

Deloitte Tax & Consulting. (2022). *Digital Finance: European Parliament adopts MiCA Regulation, paving the way for innovation-friendly crypto regulation*. Retrieved from:https://www2.deloitte.com/content/dam/Deloitte/lu/Documents/financial-services/lu-rna-digital-finance-mica-regulation.pdf

Demirgüç-Kunt, A., & Klapper, L. (2013). Measuring financial inclusion: Explaining variation in the use of financial services across and within countries. *Brookings Papers on Economic Activity*, 279-321. doi:10.1353/eca.2013.0002

Gkillas, K., & Longin, F. (2019a). Is Bitcoin the New Digital Gold? Evidence From Extreme Price Movements in Financial Markets. SSRN *Electronic Journal*. https://doi.org/ doi:10.2139/SSRN.3245571

Gomber, P., Koch, J. A., & Siering, M. (2017). Digital Finance and FinTech: Current research and future research directions. *Journal of Business Economics*, *87*(5), 537–580. doi:10.100711573-017-0852-x

Hasan, M. M., Yajuan, L., & Khan, S. (2020). *Promoting China's Inclusive Finance Through Digital Financial Services*. https://doi.org/ doi:10.1177/0972150919895348

Hu, A. S., Parlour, C. A., & Rajan, U. (2019). Cryptocurrencies: Stylized facts on a new investible instrument. *Financial Management*, *48*(4), 1049–1068. doi:10.1111/fima.12300

Katsiampa, P. (2019a). An empirical investigation of volatility dynamics in the cryptocurrency market. *Research in International Business and Finance*, *50*, 322–335. doi:10.1016/j.ribaf.2019.06.004

Kim, Y. S., & Kwon, O. (2022a). Central Bank Digital Currency, Credit Supply, and Financial Stability. *Journal of Money, Credit and Banking*. Advance online publication. doi:10.1111/jmcb.12913

Kirkby, R. (2018a). Cryptocurrencies and Digital Fiat Currencies. *The Australian Economic Review*, *51*(4), 527–539. doi:10.1111/1467-8462.12307

Liu, G., Huang, Y., & Huang, Z. (2021). Determinants and mechanisms of digital financial inclusion development: Based on urban-rural differences. *Agronomy (Basel)*, *11*(9), 1833. Advance online publication. doi:10.3390/agronomy11091833

Lorenzo, L., & Arroyo, J. (2022). Analysis of the cryptocurrency market using different prototype-based clustering techniques. *Financial Innovation*, *8*(1), 1–46. doi:10.118640854-021-00310-9

Niemand, T., Rigtering, J. P. C., Kallmünzer, A., Kraus, S., & Maalaoui, A. (2021). Digitalization in the financial industry: A contingency approach of entrepreneurial orientation and strategic vision on digitalization. *European Management Journal*, *39*(3), 317–326. doi:10.1016/j.emj.2020.04.008

Ozili, P. K. (2018). Impact of digital finance on financial inclusion and stability. *Borsa Istanbul Review*, *18*(4), 329–340. doi:10.1016/j.bir.2017.12.003

Pazarbasioglu, C., Mora, A. G., Uttamchandani, M., Natarajan, H., Feyen, E., & Saal, M. (2020). *Digital Financial Services*. Academic Press.

Roxana, N., Aue, M., Uae, R., & Moşteanu, N. R. (2019). International Financial Markets face to face with Artificial Intelligence and Digital Era. *Theoretical and Applied Economics*, *26*(3), 123–134.

Wang, T., & Ji, C. (2022). How Does Digital Finance Affect People's Income: Evidence from China. *Security and Communication Networks*, *2022*, 1–15. doi:10.1155/2022/8288855

Wang, Y., Lucey, B. M., Vigne, S. A., & Yarovaya, L. (2022a). The Effects of Central Bank Digital Currencies News on Financial Markets. *Technological Forecasting and Social Change*, *180*, 121715. Advance online publication. doi:10.1016/j.techfore.2022.121715

Ye Id, Y., Pu, Y., & Xiong, A. (2022). *The impact of digital finance on household participation in risky financial markets: Evidence-based study from China*. Academic Press.

Chapter 7
Blockchain Technology Adoption in Financial Services: Opportunities and Challenges

Jeevesh Sharma
Manipal University Jaipur, India

ABSTRACT

FinTech has been widely coined to distinguish the substantial use of technology in the field of finance because technology has transformed the industrial age into the silicon age. One such potent technology that has accompanied Industry 4.0 is blockchain. Blockchain is a decentralized database made up of blocks that store data and enable the network's nodes to track any data transfer. Blockchain is a network of decentralized and distributed blocks that store information with digital signatures. Blockchain properties such as decentralization, consistency, accountability, and transparency make transactions more reliable and safer. Blockchain technology has been implemented in various areas other than bitcoin, such as financial services, risk management, and healthcare facilities. The purpose of this research is to describe the various advantages and disadvantages of implementing blockchain technology in the financial services business. This study also contributes to the development of a comprehensive framework that have highlighted the opportunities and challenges of blockchain in the financial services sector. There are three primary divisions within the chapter: 1) Industry 4.0 and blockchain, 2) influence of technology in the financial sector along with financial services, and 3) upcoming technological problems and obstacles.

INTRODUCTION

Industry 4.0's meet the unique requirements of each client, which has an impact on business administration, research and development, manufacturing, supply, product use, and recycling (Neugebauer et al., 2016). The Internet of Things, cloud computing, industrial integration, corporate architecture, service-oriented architecture, handling business processes, and other fields are all covered by these technologies (Xu et al., 2018). Due to the industrial revolution, technological advancements have resultant to higher industrial efficiency. The steam engine provided factory power in the nineteenth century, electrification

DOI: 10.4018/978-1-6684-8624-5.ch007

enabled mass output in the early twentieth century, and industry's mechanization began in the 1970s. However, compared to the innovations that revolutionized IT, mobile communications, and e-commerce, industrial technology gains in the following decades were rather modest (Rubmann et al., 2015). The underlying digital transformation and the 4th industrial revolution, usually known as Industry 4.0, are both growing rapidly. Digitalization has drastically changed people's lives and jobs, yet people are nevertheless optimistic about the potential for sustainability that Industry 4.0 may offer (Ghobakhloo, 2020).

With the emergence of various technologies in Industry 4.0, blockchain technology is one among them. Digital transformation of the business has risen the efficiency of business operations through less waste, cutting cost and time, efficient management of data through cloud storage, etc. Blockchain is an advanced feature to keep records and information because it can overcome several obstacles. Mainly four attributes of blockchain technology are decentralization, reliability, confidentiality, and tracking. Blockchain can considerably save expenses and boost efficiency due to these features. Due to its decentralized, peer-to-peer transactions, and immutable characteristics, blockchain technology has been increasingly popular in recent years. It is a public digital ledger that is accessible to every user connected to the network. This concept can be used in a variety of fields, including the logistics industry, healthcare, and the Internet of Things (IoT).

The study analyses the adoption of blockchain in the financial service sector. This study emphasises how a new destructive system built on Blockchain is bringing in a new financial era for the finance industry. Earlier financial industry plans for goods and services were observed to be expensive and ineffective. The financial markets could become more efficient and secure due to blockchain technology. Therefore, the present investigation seeks to determine a connection between blockchain technology and the financial sector as well as Industry 4.0. The study gives an outline of the ideas and their shared characteristics in order to deal with the obstacles to their acceptance.

The chapter is categorized into seven sections. Section second explains the evolution of technology in the industry from industry 1.0 to 4.0, addition to it highlights the concept of industry 4.0. Section three explains the association industry 4.0 with the development of blockchain technology and its structure and key features, whereas fourth section delas with the implication and influence of blockchain in financial sector, financial services, and the working of blockchain technology. The adoption of blockchain various areas of financial services is described in the section fifth, section sixth presents the scenario of blockchain technology in Indian financial sector and seventh section presents the opportunities and challenges associated with blockchain.

INDUSTRY 4.0

Industry 4.0 is not a new term, the digital formation in the organization is known as Industry 4.0 (Soni & Naik, 2020). The phrase "ubiquitous computing" was first used in 1991 by Mark Weiser to describe a vision of the intelligent environment. Manufacturing-related problems are approached using this method (Erro-Garces, 2019). The terms "Industry 4.0," "smart factory," and "real-time factory" refer to emerging tendencies in the manufacturing industries. Industry 4.0 was initially implemented in 2011 by a federal government project in Germany that involved academic institutions and for-profit businesses. In order to increase the productivity and efficiency of the national industry, it was a conscious decision to establish cutting-edge manufacturing (Kagermann et al., 2013). For this future industrial stage, where all value

Figure 1. Progression of industry technology
Source: Author's compilation

chain working activities will be carried out using an intelligent strategy, the socio-technical evolution of the human function in production systems is necessary (Stock et al., 2018).

Managers are currently working to deploy automated industrial processes to boost efficiency, and several associations are being formed to establish new platforms for emerging industrial technology. Even industry 4.0 standards for sustainability and the circular economy are important factors. The phrase " The term "industry 4.0" refers to the fourth industrial revolution, which places a greater emphasis on serving the demands of more specialised clients and offers a new level of organisation and command across the entire supply chain at each stage of product development (Vaidya et al., 2018; Frank et al., 2019). Conventional machines must evolve into self-aware, self-learning machines in order to increase their overall performance and maintenance management while incorporating their environment (or "industry 4.0" machines). Building an open, intelligent manufacturing platform for industrial networks of information is the vision of Industry 4.0 (Lee et al., 2014).

The primary requirements of Industry 4.0 are real-time data monitoring, tracking of product status and positions, and holding of instructions to regulate manufacturing processes. There is a progression and revolution of technologies in the industry recognized as Industry 1.0, Industry 2.0, Industry 3.0, and Industry 4.0. Each revolution scenario has its different features. Industry 1.0 symbolizes that there was the mechanism of steam and water engines, Industry 2.0 deals with the electrification in the production line, and mass production/globalization, whereas Industry 3.0 shows the emergence of computers and automated production, and Industry 4.0 represents the current environment that is digital transformation in the business operations along with the development of various advanced technologies like machine learning, artificial intelligence, cybersecurity, and autonomous system. Therefore, the fourth industrial revolution is regarded as a key step toward the combination and modernization of several industries using new technology (Bhatnagar et al., 2021). Figure 1 shows the timeline of the revolution in Industry.

The four main drivers underlying Industry 4.0, which support the transition of the production process into an entirely automated and cognitive one, are the Internet of Things (IoT), Industrial Internet of Things (IIoT), Cloud-based manufacturing, and smart manufacturing (Erol et al., 2018). Industry 4.0 is the first significant transition that has gone from a technologically oriented to a sophisticated one and that would depend on various pillars, including the openness of knowledge, help, and linkages (Javaid et al., 2021). Due to this, traditional production linkages between producers, vendors, and customers as well as between people and machines evolved and become more effective (Rubmann et al., 2015; Bai et al., 2020).

The main element of Industry 4.0 is the creation of cyber-physical systems (CPS), which is based on the merging of heterogeneous data and knowledge (Zanero, 2017). To meet the production's flexibility and dynamic requirements, CPS plays a significant role. Additionally, they must work to increase the

Table 1. Nine technologies revolution in Industry 4.0

S.no.	Technologies	Description
1.	Autonomous Robot	To handle complex situations, also flexible, easy to use, and interactive and work safely with humans.
2.	Simulation	business effectively analyses and improves the business products and industrial system.
3.	Industrial Internet of things (IIoT)	Smooth and quick response to customer preferences and designing products accordingly also provides real-time data regarding the business performance
4.	Cloud computing	The emergence of AI and ML technologies to IoT. Organize data in cyber-physical mode.
5.	Augmented reality	Nascent stage but in the future will provide real-time information on the improvement of decision-making and work procedures.
6.	Big data and analytics	Comprehensive evaluation and collection of data from various sources like production equipment, system, and organization
7.	Additive Manufacturing	Promote digitalization in business which results in reducing prototype time and cost and producing less waste and scraps.
8.	Cyber security	To protect from various cyber-attacks, secure communication is a must in the industry.
9.	System Integration	Organizations, clients, and suppliers are connected to one another which makes task completion very efficient.

Source: Rubmann et al. (2015) and Bai et al. (2020)

organization's overall efficacy and efficiency. Internet of Things (IoT), Internet of Services (IoS), cloud-based manufacturing, radio frequency identification (RFID), and enterprise resource planning (ERP) are just a few of the technologies that form Industry 4.0 (Soni & Naik, 2020). Therefore, Multiple advantages come with Industry 4.0, such as lower labor costs, simpler corporate procedures, fewer inventory errors, and increased logistics process transparency (distribution cost, dispatching time, carriage delay). Changes in the quantity of a shipment that is delayed; inventory reduction; indemnity; frequency of service; accurate predictions; trustworthiness; agility; applications, and so on (Mohamed, 2018).

BLOCKCHAIN TECHNOLOGY

The launch of Bitcoin in 2009 is seen as the commencement of the blockchain. A new decentralized peer-to-peer electronic payment system that relies on BLOCKS that are CHANGED with one other to convey the movement of information in real-time (Nakamoto, 2008). Physical and digital technology can be categorized under Industry 4.0. In general, "physical technologies" refers to equipment used in production, such as additive manufacturing, sensors, and drones. Contemporary communication and information technologies including cloud storage, blockchain, big data analytics, and modelling are referred to as "digital technologies" across the scenario (Bai et al., 2020). Blockchain is one of the new digital technologies that are being introduced as part of Industry 4.0. The core technology that underpins bitcoin, blockchain, is currently employed across industries and is not limited to the financial sector (Sheth & Dattani, 2019; Zheng et al., 2017; Mohanta et al., 2019). Both small and large businesses can benefit from the integration of blockchain to increase security, privacy, and data openness.

Table 2. Type of blockchain technology

S. No.	Technology Type	Description
1.	Public Blockchain	Open ledger, no central authority, transparent, anyone can participate.
2.	Private Blockchain	Closed ledger, one organization, efficiently handling data, closed network, faster transaction, more scalable
3.	Hybrid Blockchain	Combination of public and private, scalable,
4.	Consortium Blockchain	More secure and have better scalability, well-defined governance structures, and access controls.

Source: Author's compilation

Industry 4.0 is a collection of modern production methods that expedites company goal-achieving (Javaid et al., 2021). Blockchain is a decentralized network that supports smart contracts, enabling documentation, distribution network automation, payment applications, and other business interactions (Sheth & Dattani, 2019; Golosova & Romanovs, 2018). Blockchain offers an immutable record that is duplicated in almost real-time between a network of business partners (Zheng et al., 2017; Yaga et al., 2019; Seth et al., 2019). Accessibility and numerous versions of the events are two key benefits of blockchain technology, because of this blockchain technology is irreversible and non-destructive (Golosova & Romanovs, 2018). In 2021, it is expected that global spending on blockchain-related items would amount to $6.6 billion. Forecasts indicate that during the following few years, spending on blockchain solutions would rise, reaching over 19 billion dollars by 2024[1]. Table 2 presents the description of four types of blockchain technology. Afterward, the following section explains the working and major features of blockchain technology.

Architecture of Blockchain

The encrypted ledger is kept in a publicly accessible distributed database. Blockchain is a piece of technology that anyone with an internet connection may use to access a worldwide database. With a vast network watching over it, it becomes nearly hard to manipulate the system by fabricating documents, transactions, and other details. In a network of nodes, a blockchain stores data indefinitely. This disseminates the data as well as decentralizes it. The Blockchain network can be stored locally on each node that is connected to the network, and it is upgraded often to maintain consistency between all nodes. A blockchain is a platform for distributed computation and information sharing that allows different nodes who do not trust one another to participate in decision-making. Figure 2 presents that each block is connected to one another, so any modification or addition will be updated accordingly with other blocks also.

Figure 2. Architecture of blockchain
Source: Author's presentation

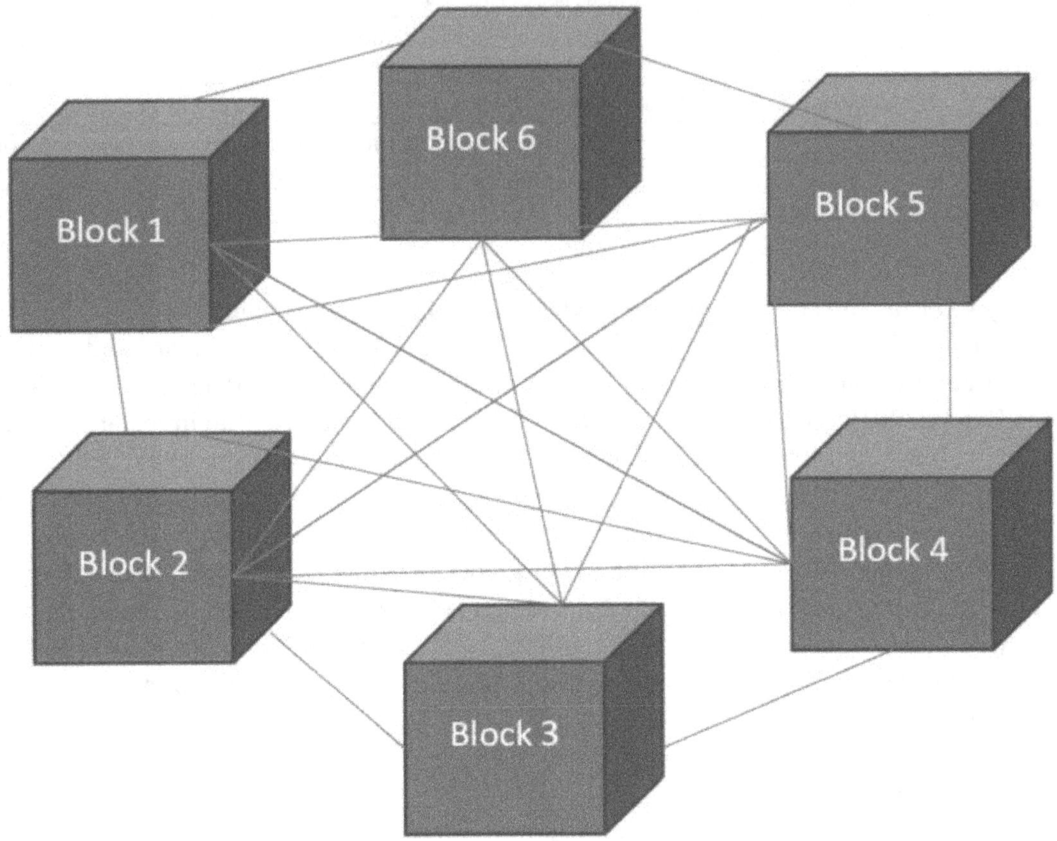

Characteristics of Blockchain

The following are the key characteristics of blockchain technology.

1. **Decentralized:** Contrary to conventional centralized transaction systems, which mandate that each transaction be approved by a single reliable third party (such as the central bank), blockchain-based systems do not require this. This eliminates the cost and performance inefficiencies associated with central servers. Blockchain does away with the need for middlemen, in contrast to the centralized model. Distributed ledger technology used consensus techniques to ensure data consistency across diverse networks.
2. **Privacy/Security:** As each piece of information from the entry to the approval of it is required to be passed through multiple nodes. The information on the blockchain is more secured comparative to conventional systems.
3. **Quick Settlement:** Fast verification of every event ensures that serious miners won't accept any transactions that aren't valid. Removing or undoing a transaction after it has been added to the

blockchain is exceedingly challenging. Blocks with the wrong number of transactions in them may be immediately identified.

4. **Anonymous:** Everyone may interact with the blockchain using a randomly generated address that conceals their identity. The clients are either anonymous or pseudonymous.
5. **Immutable:** The development of immutable ledgers is one of Blockchain's fundamental concepts. Any centralised database is susceptible to fraud and hacking since it takes confidence for a third party middleman to keep the database secure.
6. **Traceability:** Once the information is stored in the blocks, it can be easily traceable.

Figure 3. Characteristics of blockchain technology
Source: Author's compilation

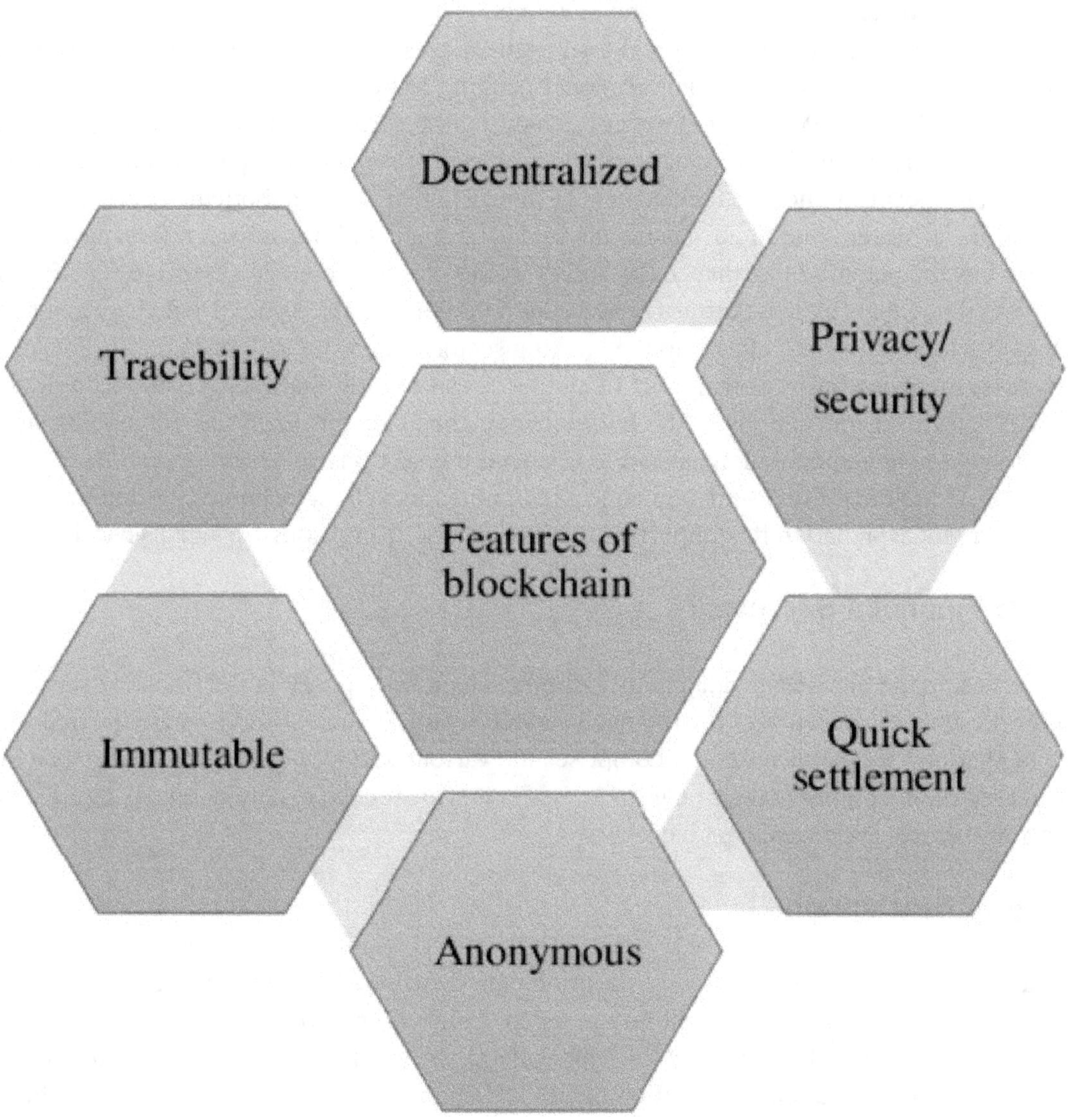

BLOCKCHAIN AND FINANCIAL SECTOR

The financial sector may benefit from innovative and more cost-effective products because of the digitization of many financial processes, including credit, portfolio management, investment advisory, and funds transfer (Vives, 2017). When blockchain technology was used to power the digital currency Bitcoin in 2009, it garnered considerable media interest. Blockchain's distinctive features have the ability to significantly benefit the finance sector. The traditional financial industry has been impacted by fintech. The environment of the financial sector has changed as a result of increasing financial reform and improvements in financial innovation during the 2008 Financial Crisis. In fintech, there are three primary areas of development. Mobile payments come first. The second is a "smart contract"-based system. Another practice recognized as being within the smart contract category is peer-to-peer lending. The third one is known as the Blockchain and is one of the most popular (Chang et al., 2020). The fundamental differentiating characteristics of these three fintech businesses' three key pillars are instant communication, live data, credit ratings, and updating.

The blockchain technologies model had a substantial adverse effect on commercial banking, conventional financial operations, and the traditional banking sector is about to undergo reform. Due to consumer demand and market competitiveness, traditional banking platforms have begun conducting financial transactions online, but the outcomes have not been promising. It is also encouraging traditional banks to seek for novel solutions. Blockchain may significantly transform both the FinTech industry and the existing fiscal system due to advancements in data storage and transmission (Chang et al., 2020). Blockchain has the potential to enhance the ability of the present financial system to transfer assets or to strengthen the global financial infrastructure, claim (Trivedi et al., 2021). Blockchain can save costs and bring about long overdue reforms to the banking sector, according to studies on its effects.

Therefore, by reviewing various pieces of studies it can be said that blockchain technologies have given birth to various innovations in the traditional financial sector. With the burgeoning use of the internet among the huge population had made financial transactions very easy and reduced the burden of cost and time. As the present study aimed to explain the blockchain technology adoption in financial services before its explanation it is important to know what encompasses financial services.

What Are Financial Services?

Before discussing the blockchain adaptability of blockchain technology in the financial service sector, the author presents an overview of the financial service sector. Financial services are the major component of any nation's financial system, it comprises the various services offered by the finance industry. Financial services encompass a wide range of activities that are related to commercial banking, insurance company, brokerage, and investment banks.

Working of Blockchain

Blockchain technology works on five basic principles distributed ledger, peer-to-peer transmission, transparency & pseudonymity, irreversibility in records, and computational logic (Tapscott & Tapscott, 2017). Figure 4 presents the process of the blockchain works. There are six key steps in this cycle starting with a new transaction, the creation of a block against the transaction entered, and the block is transmitted to all the nodes of a network, after these steps all nodes of the network validate the block

Figure 4. Working of blockchain
Source: Author's compilation

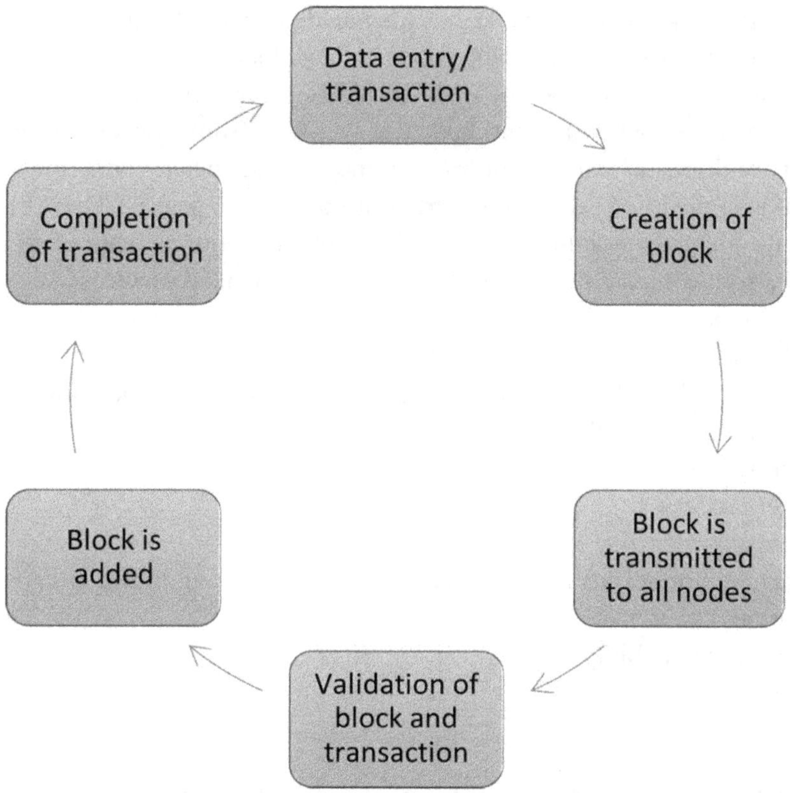

& transaction, after validation the block is added to the existing chain of blocks, lastly the transaction is verified and completed.

Blockchain and Financial Services

The ever-growing digitization is affecting virtually every aspect of human life. We can now utilize digital tools to easily execute a variety of chores, such as buying tickets and commodities and carrying out financial transactions, because of the convenience that technology has offered. Initially, blockchain impacted the back-office processing of transactions, which exists in financial services. The documenting of the transaction when a financial institution deals with a syndicated loan or derivatives and this process takes time and requires onerous back-office procedures. To complete the transaction, these procedures rely on contracts that have been drafted with several related lawyers and communication between the parties (Fanning & Centers, 2016). A lot of benefits that blockchain in financial services can offer could contribute to changing the financial sector. According to KPMG, blockchain technology may increase productivity by 40%, reduce capital expenditure by up to 75%, and reduce errors by up to 95%. An interesting concept that has the potential to completely transform the financial industry is blockchain in banking. According to Statista (2020), the blockchain market will have grown significantly over the past few years internationally, reaching a value of 39 billion dollars by 2025. The characteristics of blockchain, including its multi-stakeholder platform, electronic payments, trust, and visibility, are what is driving its rapid growth (Trivedi et al., 2021).

Blockchain application in financial services has also made decentralized finance, more technically known as DeFi, viable. DeFi, a form of financing supported by blockchain technology, aims to eliminate middlemen from the financial services sector with the aid of smart contracts. Consumers, the current banking system, and society as a whole are anticipated to gain a lot from blockchain technology. Beyond the effects on security and greater transaction transparency for all stakeholders, including institutions and customers, it can also positively effect on market pricing and expenses. Thus, blockchain and its key attributes had played a major role in the successful implementation and adoption of blockchain in financial services. The following are the uses of blockchain in financial services:

- Helps in recording and verifying a transaction.
- Help in trade finance, blockchain can help international trading documentation become more efficient while lowering the possibility of fraud.
- Help in syndicating loans.
- Automating other processes
- Help in tracing assets.
- It provides authentication services like a smart contract, validating transactions etc.
- Enhancing customer experience
- Transparency and accountability
- Faster settlement

ADOPTION OF TECHNOLOGIES IN VARIOUS DOMAINS

The emergence of fintech has been a game-changer for the financial services industry. Fintech is the intersection of finance and technology. Blockchain technology was developed in the Bitcoin cryptocurrency afterward this technology has been adopted in various domains of the financial service sector (Fanning et al., 2016).

The following sections describe the adoption of technology in banking services, healthcare, insurance, and stock market.

(i) Banking services

For the banking sector, blockchain technology offers a number of benefits, such as higher transparency, quicker transactions, increased traceability, lower costs, the ability to track secure payment histories, and a reduced chance of fraud (Trivedi et al., 2021). In addition, the use of blockchain and smart contracts in banking operations will reduce the need for KYC, speed up transactions, reduce expenses, and improve security for both customers and banks (Jena, 2022).

Each block in a blockchain-based ledger comprises transactional data and a unique hash that points to the block before it. Each network member also receives a copy of the transactions. Because to these features, blockchain technology is resistant to fraud, decentralised denial-of-service assaults, and data breaches (Toufaily et al., 2021). Moreover, fintech has the potential to increase financial inclusion, particularly in emerging markets. It has been found that fintech can provide low-cost and accessible financial services to people who are traditionally underserved by traditional banks. This can include services such as mobile banking, microfinance, and digital payments. By increasing financial inclusion, fintech can benefit consumers and the industry. It can also provide new opportunities for growth and innovation, particularly in developing countries where traditional banking infrastructure may be lacking. Additionally, fintech companies cut other costs than conventional banks, which allows them to offer low fees and increased the interest of customers (Gupta & Gupta, 2018). This has led many consumers to switch from traditional banks to fintech companies for their banking needs.

By giving real-time records of all transactions taking place within an organization, blockchain increases transparency. It accomplishes this by chaining together a number of blocks, each of which contains details about the ones before it and links them together (Kalil et al., 2021). A distributed ledger with restricted access to its data is known as a permission blockchain. The user can only carry out the tasks for which they have been given authorization (by the ledger administrator), and they must authenticate themselves in order to approve such changes.

(ii) Healthcare

The healthcare sector is exploring opportunities offered by various technologies to address some of these major issues. As a result, there is a great need for new technologies that could make the transition to patient-centred interoperability easier. Blockchain technology has the potential to significantly improve healthcare accessibility and assist put patients at the centre of the ecosystem (Odeh et al., 2022). Using cutting-edge technologies is necessary for the healthcare industry because patients, physicians, and the drug department must all work together to improve services to end users. One of the most crucial issues in the healthcare business that needs to be addressed is privacy. The characteristics of blockchains demonstrate how to solve problems (Balasubramanian et al., 2021). A digital database can be shared among users while protecting anonymity using blockchain. In the healthcare sector, the distributed ledger technology (DLT) of blockchain helps to record the medical history of patients which incorporates personal information, drug information, and other treatment particulars (Elangovan et al., 2022).

The healthcare and life sciences sectors already had serious problems with interoperability, privacy, and supply chain traceability preceding COVID-19. The use of private electronic health record systems is a significant obstacle (Attaran, 2022). As the disease spreads, healthcare and the life sciences must modify supply chains to deliver protective equipment and keep up with the rapid innovation of cures, testing, and vaccinations. By encouraging trust and cooperation, blockchain technology has already shown its worth in the healthcare and life sciences sectors.

(iii) Insurance

Blockchain technology is bolstering the insurance industry by automating claim classification and processing thanks to the security feature of smart contracts. Any kind of claim settlement entails several procedures, including cross-industry data accessibility, an easy technique for assessing customer transactional history, and a centralised pool of client authentication. All these procedures are advancing and helping to make the claim settlement process fraud-free. A manual claim settlement involves extensive contact between numerous parties, including the customer, broker, insurer, and bank. As a result, it is a consumes more time and costly procedure (Oberoi & Kansra, 2022). These exchanges also involve task duplication, information cross-checking, and confirmation. With blockchain, these clients are associated to one another via pooled, safe network and work together in a way that cuts down on waste and rationalizes the complete end-to-end process. As a result, it facilitates more productive and efficient collaboration between businesses.

(iv) Stock Market

Stock markets require robust cybersecurity protection due to their high level of volatility in order to ensure seamless transaction flow. In order to ensure security, a number of significant stock exchanges are looking at the potential applications of blockchain technology. The fundamental idea is to reduce transaction time and operational costs to enable almost immediate stock settlements. This system uses smart contracts to increase transparency and safety while automating compliance. As an example, the NASDAQ uses blockchain technology to issue and disseminate private securities. Another example is the London Stock Exchange, which is looking at how blockchain technology can change how assets are exchanged in Europe with the help of businesses from other industries. The modern stock market uses a number of organisations, including brokers, regulators, and the stock exchange, all of which increase system costs. A decentralised stock exchange administration system would be very effective. Blockchain can eliminate the need for third-party regulators since smart contracts can be used to create regulations.

(v) Digital Payments

Mobile payments, for example, have become increasingly popular in recent years, with consumers seeking convenience and ease of use. Fintech companies such as PayPal, Square, and Stripe have made significant strides in this area, with mobile payments accounting for a significant portion of their revenue. In contrast, traditional banks have been slow to adopt mobile payments, with many still relying on outdated technology. Blockchain technology is recognized for enhancing payment traceability, efficiency, trust, and security (Khalil et al., 2021). Also, it is well known to reduce expenses for both consumers and financial service providers. Before, transferring money between banks may occupy to a week to process, but now, thanks to the blockchain, money can be moved instantly. In addition to it, the adoption of distributed ledger technology and digital notes has provided an opportunity for consumers to make transactions more promptly, securely, and conveniently. As a result, blockchain facilitates significant time, money, and resource savings for all stakeholders (Gupta & Gupta, 2018).

The demand for middle-office and back-office staff has also diminished as a result of the instantaneous settlement of payments. With the aid of a synchronised blockchain process and optimised operations, the distributed ledger can become the ideal technique for facilitating quicker and cheaper payments. Because banks charge fees for each transaction, sending money or goods across borders becomes expensive and time-consuming. Anyone can send and receive money using blockchain technology with little assistance from outside parties. Blockchain payment solutions made possible by blockchain networks like Stellar and Ripple can also quickly and cheaply handle cross-border transactions (Garg et al., 2021).

(vi) Asset Management

One of the industries with the quickest rate of growth is asset management, which is expected to increase by USD 150 trillion by 2025. The everyday expansion of international trade and commerce is to blame for this rise. The asset management and supply chain network today places a strong focus on a centralised digital system that offers real-time visibility of assets within your systems. Using current technology for centralised data management, a network of distributed ledger systems is being built. The use of time-consuming and challenging tasks is made possible by blockchain technology. The distributed ledger concept enables direct cross-border trading and settlements and contributes to cost reduction, data accuracy enhancement, and processing speed improvements. When parties trade assets, it exposes you to errors, fraud, and misunderstandings. The blockchain-powered Funds DLT platform is a prime illustration of how blockchain technology is affecting the asset management industry.

BLOCKCHAIN IN THE FINANCIAL SECTOR IN INDIAN SCENARIO

The RBI wrote a piece titled "Distributed Ledger Technology, Blockchain and Central Banks" and it was released in February 2020. It describes the application of DLT and blockchain technology, the most recent advancements in blockchain technology, and its use by central banks in India and other countries around the world.

In response to the RBI's initiatives, several public and private banks have begun to collaborate and engage in the fintech industry in order to take advantage of DLT and blockchain's advantages. For example, the SBI and JP Morgan collaborated to use blockchain technology, while Axis, ICICI, and Yes Bank associated with JP Morgan-founded Interbank Information Network. To provide DLT solutions to the financial sector, Indian Banks' Blockchain Infrastructure Co Pvt Ltd raised equity shares from HDFC Bank, SBI, IDFC First Bank, South Indian Bank, and ICICI Bank. This investment sent shockwaves through the digital lending space.

Global investment in blockchain solution was 4.5 billion US$ in 2020 and it is estimated to reach 19 billion US$ by 2024. Almost 60% of respondents who were global company executives in the poll who indicated having intentions to invest in blockchain for their companies said they had set aside at least $1 million USD for the distributed ledger technology[2].

OPPORTUNITIES AND CHALLENGES

Accreditation is another significant issue. Since blockchain technology is still in its infancy, there is no universally applicable solution. It will be necessary for each bank to create its own system, which can take time and money. One of the primary acceptances challenges that banks will need some time to get over before they can start implementing blockchain technology and also there is a lack of proficiency and skepticism in the technology as well as uncertainties regarding laws, cost savings, and security. A lot of benefits of DLT-based blockchain technology had provided many opportunities to financial institutions, stakeholders, and the economy. The following are the opportunities:

- **Blockchain Testing:** Before the implementation of blockchain in industry or in other aspects it should be testes and standardized. There are two phases of blockchain testing *standardization and testing phase*. Based on a set of precise criteria, the standardization phase will evaluate the creators' proposals on their blockchain applications. The testing phase is used to evaluate how well the blockchain-based solution works.

- **Big Data Analytics and Blockchain:** Blockchain and big data may complement each other well. Data management and data analytics are the two broad categories into which the combination has been separated in this case. In terms of handling information, as blockchain is secure and decentralized, it might be used to store important data. Blockchain may also ensure the data's uniqueness. For contrast, if a patient's medical data is stored on a blockchain, the data cannot be changed, therefore it is challenging to steal such sensitive information.
- **Artificial Intelligence (AI):** Technology advancement in the blockchain is providing a new potential for applications of AI. Several blockchain difficulties may be helped by AI technology. For example, an oracle is always in charge of determining if the contract requirement has been satisfied. This oracle is frequently a trustworthy external source. Artificial intelligence may be used to develop an intelligent oracle.
- The technological components essential to the blockchain system include network security and smart contracts. The organization may be self-sufficient thanks to the smart contract's automatic code execution. The main element of this function is network security, which gives users confidence in the system for commercial transactions.

Despite the opportunities in the application of blockchain in the financial sector there is still some challenges in adopting blockchain in the financial sector or financial services that need to be addressed in the future time:

- If blockchains are to produce the best benefits, widespread adoption is necessary. This is especially true in the financial services industry, where there are plenty of interconnected organizations that need a standard method for conducting transactions. For a straightforward example, before money can be moved via blockchain, each bank involved in the transfer must have acknowledged it.
- The prior challenge is made more challenging by the many blockchains' lack of interoperability, which precludes them from interacting with one another.
- Considering the dearth of competent blockchain engineers, switching to blockchain technology can be expensive and time-consuming. Some financial institutions, particularly smaller ones, could be reluctant to make the investment necessary to update current systems.
- A blockchain prevents data changes. This is a benefit of using blockchain, but financial companies that constantly need to modify stored data may find it difficult to use. For these companies to use blockchain, their business processes would need to change.
- Since blockchain technology is still at nascent stage and expanding so quickly, regulators have not yet caught up with it. Governments will most likely pass laws that affect blockchain and the companies that use it.
- The transition to blockchain technology is a time- and money-consuming process. It's because there aren't enough qualified blockchain developers available. Because of this, smaller financial institutions can decide against making investments in addition to existing system renovations.
- Scalability is also a major concern in it. The daily increase in transactions causes the blockchain to expand in size. To confirm a transaction on the blockchain and identify whether the source of the current transaction has been spent or not, each node is required to preserve a record of every transaction.

Solution of Challenges of Blockchain Technology in The Financial Sector

Blockchain technology has been touted as a potential game-changer in the financial sector due to its ability to provide a secure, transparent, and immutable ledger for financial transactions. However, like any new technology, it also faces several challenges that need to be addressed before it can be widely adopted. Here are some of the major challenges of blockchain technology in the financial sector and possible solutions:

- **Scalability:** One of the biggest challenges of blockchain technology is scalability, which refers to the ability of the blockchain network to handle a large number of transactions simultaneously. As more users join the network and more transactions are made, the network can become congested, leading to slower transaction times and higher fees. To address this challenge, several solutions have been proposed, including:
- **Lightning Network:** A second-layer solution that enables off-chain transactions between users, reducing the load on the blockchain network.
- **Sharding:** A technique that involves partitioning the blockchain into smaller, more manageable pieces, each of which can handle a subset of the transactions.
- **Interoperability:** Another challenge of blockchain technology is interoperability, which refers to the ability of different blockchain networks to communicate with each other. With hundreds of different blockchain networks in existence, each with its own set of protocols and standards, achieving interoperability can be a daunting task. To address this challenge, several initiatives have been launched, including:
- **Atomic Swaps:** A technique that allows users to exchange cryptocurrencies between different blockchains without the need for a centralized exchange.
- **Cross-Chain Bridges:** Bridges that connect two different blockchains together and allow them to exchange information and assets.
- **Regulatory Compliance:** Blockchain technology operates in a largely unregulated space, which presents a challenge for financial institutions that need to comply with strict regulations. To address this challenge, several solutions have been proposed, including:
- **Smart Contracts:** Digital contracts that can self-execute when certain conditions are met, reducing the need for intermediaries and increasing transparency.
- **Know-Your-Customer (KYC) and Anti-Money Laundering (AML) Compliance:** These regulations can be built into the blockchain network itself, making it easier for financial institutions to comply with them.
- **Permissioned Blockchains:** Blockchains that are restricted to a specific group of users or organizations, making it easier to enforce regulatory compliance.

In conclusion, while blockchain technology has the potential to revolutionize the financial sector, it still faces several challenges that need to be addressed before it can be widely adopted. Scalability, interoperability, and regulatory compliance are just a few of the challenges that need to be overcome, but with the right solutions, blockchain technology could transform the financial industry and make it more secure, transparent, and efficient.

CONCLUSION

"Industry 4.0" describes an innovative era in industrial development where various developing technologies are blended to offer digital solutions. Nevertheless, little is known about how companies use this technology. Hence, one of our objectives is to understand how Industry 4.0 technologies are being used in the financial services industry. A metaphor for the beginning of the fourth industrial revolution might be "industry 4.0." It represents the company's current preference for automation technologies. It addresses technological advancements including cloud computing, IoT, and CPS (Soni & Naik, 2020). Blockchain innovation has changed every aspect of banking institutions' traditional payment processes. from bank operations to participants in transactions, including those tasked with streamlining a variety of financial services processes. Blockchain technology has the potential to methodically address the whole financial supply chain. Millions of transactions worth trillions of dollars occur daily in the financial services sector, where privacy, visibility, and cost-effectiveness are top priorities. Cybercrime affects 45% of financial organisations every year, including payment networks, stock exchanges, and money transfer services. Blockchain technology has become widely used because of its inherent ability to manage transactions in a secure, practical, and cost-effective way.

REFERENCES

Attaran, M. (2022). Blockchain technology in healthcare: Challenges and opportunities. *International Journal of Healthcare Management*, *15*(1), 70–83. doi:10.1080/20479700.2020.1843887

Bai, C., Dallasega, P., Orzes, G., & Sarkis, J. (2020). Industry 4.0 technologies assessment: A sustainability perspective. *International Journal of Production Economics*, *229*, 107776. doi:10.1016/j.ijpe.2020.107776

Balasubramanian, S., Shukla, V., Sethi, J. S., Islam, N., & Saloum, R. (2021). A readiness assessment framework for Blockchain adoption: A healthcare case study. *Technological Forecasting and Social Change*, *165*, 120536. doi:10.1016/j.techfore.2020.120536

Bhatnagar, S., Sharma, D., & Agrawal, S. (2021). Can Industry 4.0 revolutionize the Wave of green finance adoption: A bibliometric analysis. In *Recent Advances in Smart Manufacturing and Materials: Select Proceedings of ICEM 2020* (pp. 515-525). Springer Singapore.

Chang, V., Baudier, P., Zhang, H., Xu, Q., Zhang, J., & Arami, M. (2020). How Blockchain can impact financial services–The overview, challenges and recommendations from expert interviewees. *Technological Forecasting and Social Change*, *158*, 120166. doi:10.1016/j.techfore.2020.120166 PMID:32834134

Elangovan, D., Long, C. S., Bakrin, F. S., Tan, C. S., Goh, K. W., Yeoh, S. F., Loy, M. J., Hussain, Z., Lee, K. S., Idris, A. C., & Ming, L. C. (2022). The use of blockchain technology in the health care sector: Systematic review. *JMIR Medical Informatics*, *10*(1), e17278. doi:10.2196/17278 PMID:35049516

Erol, S., Jäger, A., Hold, P., Ott, K., & Sihn, W. (2016). Tangible Industry 4.0: A scenario-based approach to learning for the future of production. *Procedia CIRP*, *54*, 13–18. doi:10.1016/j.procir.2016.03.162

Erro-Garcés, A. (2019). Industry 4.0: Defining the research agenda. *Benchmarking*, *28*(5), 1858–1882. doi:10.1108/BIJ-12-2018-0444

Fanning, K., & Centers, D. P. (2016). Blockchain and its coming impact on financial services. *Journal of Corporate Accounting & Finance*, *27*(5), 53–57. doi:10.1002/jcaf.22179

Frank, A. G., Dalenogare, L. S., & Ayala, N. F. (2019). Industry 4.0 technologies: Implementation patterns in manufacturing companies. *International Journal of Production Economics*, *210*, 15–26. doi:10.1016/j.ijpe.2019.01.004

Garg, P., Gupta, B., Chauhan, A. K., Sivarajah, U., Gupta, S., & Modgil, S. (2021). Measuring the perceived benefits of implementing blockchain technology in the banking sector. *Technological Forecasting and Social Change*, *163*, 120407. doi:10.1016/j.techfore.2020.120407

Ghobakhloo, M. (2020). Industry 4.0, digitization, and opportunities for sustainability. *Journal of Cleaner Production*, *252*, 119869. doi:10.1016/j.jclepro.2019.119869

Golosova, J., & Romanovs, A. (2018, October). Overview of the blockchain technology cases. In *2018 59th International Scientific Conference on Information Technology and Management Science of Riga Technical University (ITMS)* (pp. 1-6). IEEE. 10.1109/ITMS.2018.8552978

Gupta, A., & Gupta, S. (2018). blockchain technology application in Indian banking sector. *Delhi Business Review*, *19*(2), 75-84. https://www.sciencedirect.com/science/article/abs/pii/S0959652619347390

Javaid, M., Haleem, A., Singh, R. P., Khan, S., & Suman, R. (2021). Blockchain technology applications for Industry 4.0: A literature-based review. *Blockchain: Research and Applications*, *2*(4), 100027.

Jena, R. K. (2022). Examining the factors affecting the adoption of blockchain technology in the banking sector: An extended UTAUT model. *International Journal of Financial Studies*, *10*(4), 90. doi:10.3390/ijfs10040090

Kagermann, H., Wahlster, W., & Helbig, J. (2013). *Recommendations for Implementing the Strategic Initiative Industrie 4.0: Securing the Future of German Manufacturing Industry. Final Report of the Industrie 4.0 Working Group*. Acatech, Forschungsunion.

Khalil, M., Khawaja, K. F., & Sarfraz, M. (2021). The adoption of blockchain technology in the financial sector during the era of fourth industrial revolution: A moderated mediated model. *Quality & Quantity*, 1–18.

Lee, J., Kao, H. A., & Yang, S. (2014). Service innovation and smart analytics for industry 4.0 and big data environment. *Procedia CIRP*, *16*, 3–8. doi:10.1016/j.procir.2014.02.001

Mohamed, M. (2018). Challenges and benefits of industry 4.0: An overview. *International Journal of Supply and Operations Management*, *5*(3), 256–265.

Mohanta, B. K., Jena, D., Panda, S. S., & Sobhanayak, S. (2019). Blockchain technology: A survey on applications and security privacy challenges. *Internet of Things*, *8*, 100107. doi:10.1016/j.iot.2019.100107

Nakamoto, S. (2008). Bitcoin: A peer-to-peer electronic cash system. *Decentralized Business Review*, 21260.

Neugebauer, R., Hippmann, S., Leis, M., & Landherr, M. (2016). Industrie 4.0-From the perspective of applied research. *Procedia CIRP*, *57*, 2–7. doi:10.1016/j.procir.2016.11.002

Oberoi, S., & Kansra, P. (2022). Blockchain Technology in the Insurance Industry. In Applications, Challenges, and Opportunities of Blockchain Technology in Banking and Insurance (pp. 160-172). IGI Global. doi:10.4018/978-1-6684-4133-6.ch009

Odeh, A., Keshta, I., & Al-Haija, Q. A. (2022). Analysis of Blockchain in the Healthcare Sector: Application and Issues. *Symmetry*, *14*(9), 1760. doi:10.3390ym14091760

Rubmann, M., Lorenz, M., Gerbert, P., Waldner, M., Justus, J., Engel, P., & Harnisch, M. (2015). Industry 4.0: The future of productivity and growth in manufacturing industries. *Boston Consulting Group, 9*(1), 54-89.

Sheth, H., & Dattani, J. (2019). Overview of blockchain technology. *Asian Journal for Convergence in Technology*.

Sony, M., & Naik, S. (2020). Key ingredients for evaluating Industry 4.0 readiness for organizations: A literature review. *Benchmarking*, *27*(7), 2213–2232. doi:10.1108/BIJ-09-2018-0284

Stock, T., Obenaus, M., Kunz, S., & Kohl, H. (2018). Industry 4.0 as enabler for a sustainable development: A qualitative assessment of its ecological and social potential. *Process Safety and Environmental Protection*, *118*, 254–267. doi:10.1016/j.psep.2018.06.026

Tapscott, A., & Tapscott, D. (2017). How blockchain is changing finance. *Harvard Business Review*, *1*(9), 2–5.

Toufaily, E., Zalan, T., & Dhaou, S. B. (2021). A framework of blockchain technology adoption: An investigation of challenges and expected value. *Information & Management*, *58*(3), 103444. doi:10.1016/j.im.2021.103444

Trivedi, S., Mehta, K., & Sharma, R. (2021). Systematic literature review on application of blockchain technology in E-finance and financial services. *Journal of Technology Management & Innovation*, *16*(3), 89–102. doi:10.4067/S0718-27242021000300089

Vaidya, S., Ambad, P., & Bhosle, S. (2018). Industry 4.0–a glimpse. *Procedia Manufacturing*, *20*, 233–238. doi:10.1016/j.promfg.2018.02.034

Vives, X. (2017). The impact of FinTech on banking. *European Economy*, (2), 97–105.

Xu, L. D., Xu, E. L., & Li, L. (2018). Industry 4.0: State of the art and future trends. *International Journal of Production Research*, *56*(8), 2941–2962. doi:10.1080/00207543.2018.1444806

Zanero, S. (2017). Cyber-physical systems. *Computer*, *50*(4), 14–16. doi:10.1109/MC.2017.105

Zheng, Z., Xie, S., Dai, H., Chen, X., & Wang, H. (2017, June). *An overview of blockchain technology: Architecture, consensus, and future trends. In 2017 IEEE international congress on big data (BigData congress)*. IEEE.

Zheng, Z., Xie, S., Dai, H. N., Chen, X., & Wang, H. (2018). Blockchain challenges and opportunities: A survey. *International Journal of Web and Grid Services*, *14*(4), 352–375. doi:10.1504/IJWGS.2018.095647

ENDNOTES

1. https://www.statista.com/statistics/800426/worldwide-blockchain-solutions-spending/
2. https://www.statista.com/topics/5122/blockchain/#topicOverview

Chapter 8
The Green Revolution of Smart Contracts:
How Innovative Architecture Is Driving Performance, Pollution Reduction, and Energy Conservation

Rinat Galiautdinov
Independent Researcher, Italy

ABSTRACT

The focus of this study is to examine the challenges associated with smart contracts and their overall concept. The research proposes a solution that can effectively address all the current issues related to smart contracts. Furthermore, the study recommends a new architecture for smart contracts and blockchain. The author identifies the problems, conducts an analysis, and presents a solution that will enhance the performance of smart contracts, increase their extensibility, and promote an eco-friendly environment by reducing pollution and conserving energy.

INTRODUCTION

For more than ten years, blockchain has been recognized as a technology that functions as a distributed database (Bernstein & Lange, 2016). It is utilized to track financial transactions involving various types of cryptocurrencies (Brown, 2016) like BTC, ETH, and others. Transactions are processed through a peer-to-peer network, which decentralizes the network participants and grants them equal privileges. This network architecture differs from the traditional client-server architecture, where clients are dependent on the server. If the server is down, no client can connect and perform transactions (Heuvel, 2014).

Blockchain technology (see Figure 1) also introduced the concept of smart contracts, which was first proposed by Nick Szabo in the 1990s (Szabo, 1997). The idea is straightforward: a smart contract is a computer program that verifies various conditions and decides which function(s) to execute to perform the smart contract.

DOI: 10.4018/978-1-6684-8624-5.ch008

Figure 1. Illustrates a typical blockchain schema

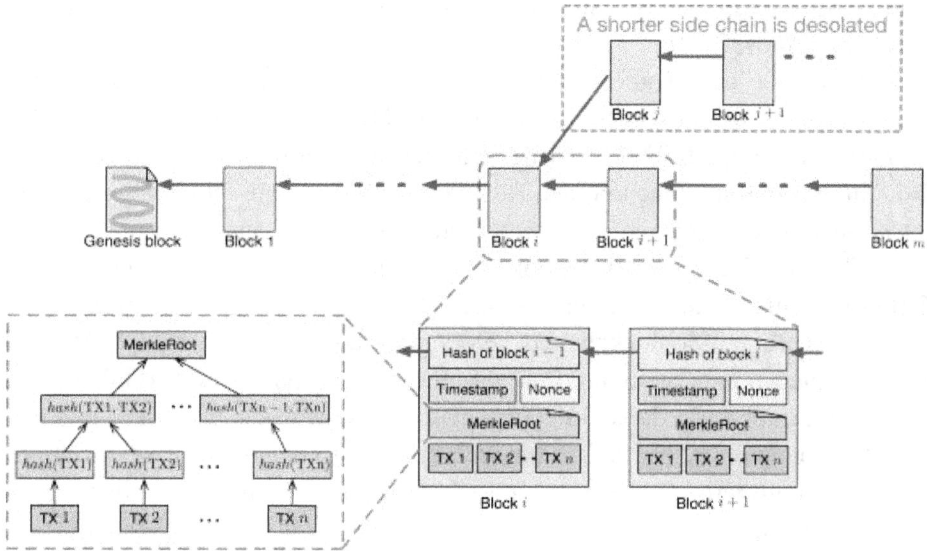

Bitcoin is widely recognized as the first cryptocurrency that gained global popularity, although an earlier version had appeared in the early 1990s (Li et al., 2017). Bitcoin's blockchain primarily focuses on financial transactions, and it doesn't contain any other data. Ethereum is the second well-known cryptocurrency that introduced the concept of smart contracts into the blockchain world (Nguyen, 2019; Nguyen et al., 2019; Atzei et al., 2017). Smart contracts are small programs that run on the blockchain when triggered by a request, allowing users to add more logic to the blockchain beyond financial transactions, including creating simple games. From a technical perspective, a smart contract is treated as a user that can send and receive transactions and has a record of different states, or variables, which can be changed or read on the blockchain (Szabo, 1997; Pearce, 2021).

Blockchain technology has revolutionized the way we conduct transactions and store data. Smart contracts, in particular, have gained immense popularity due to their ability to automate and execute agreements without the need for intermediaries. However, the current architecture of smart contracts has several limitations that hinder their full potential. The current approach is too slow and limited, consuming too much electricity, and has scalability issues. These limitations make it difficult for blockchain technology to reach its full potential and make it less attractive to businesses and developers. Furthermore, security vulnerabilities and lack of interoperability between different blockchain networks pose serious threats to the integrity of the technology. Inflexibility in the current architecture of smart contracts also makes it difficult to modify and upgrade the contracts when needed (Galiautdinov & Mkrttchian, 2019a, 2019b; Galiautdinov, 2020a). Changing the architecture of smart contracts can address these limitations and provide more flexibility, adaptability, and scalability to blockchain technology. It can also enable interoperability between different blockchain networks, allowing for seamless transactions and communication between them. A new architecture can also make smart contracts more secure and less prone to hacks, ensuring the safety and integrity of the transactions. In addition, a new architecture can attract more developers and businesses to adopt blockchain technology, leading to increased innovation and growth in the industry. The current architecture of smart contracts has limited adoption as it doesn't provide enough benefits to attract more developers and businesses (Zhang et al., 2019). A new architecture can provide more benefits, such as faster transaction times, lower fees, and more efficient use of energy (Galiautdinov, 2020b).

The implementation of Elliptic Curve Cryptography (ECC) in blockchain architecture has been widely adopted due to its efficiency and security. According to Daniel R. L. Brown's SECG SEC 1: Elliptic Curve Cryptography, Version 2.0, ECC provides a higher level of security with smaller key sizes compared to traditional cryptography techniques. However, as blockchain technology continues to evolve, it is essential to re-evaluate the current architecture and make necessary changes to ensure the highest level of security. The adoption of newer versions of ECC, such as the Edwards-curve Digital Signature Algorithm (EdDSA), could potentially enhance the security of blockchain systems and prevent potential attacks. Therefore, it is crucial for blockchain developers to stay up-to-date with the latest advancements in cryptography and incorporate them into their systems for optimal security (Galiautdinov, 2023).

Thus, studying and improving the architecture of smart contracts is necessary to advance the capabilities of blockchain technology and make it more attractive to businesses and developers. It can lead to increased innovation, growth, and security in the industry. Changing the architecture can address the limitations of the current approach, leading to a more scalable, secure, and efficient blockchain network.

Despite the numerous benefits of blockchain technology, such as decentralization, transparency, and security (Tasca, 2019), there are still some challenges, one of which is the slow speed of reading data from the blockchain. There are various reasons why reading data from a blockchain can be slow. One of them is the size of the blockchain, as the amount of data that needs to be processed and verified increases as the blockchain grows, which can result in longer transaction times and slower data retrieval.

Moreover, the consensus mechanism used by the blockchain can also affect the speed of data retrieval. For instance, some consensus mechanisms, such as proof-of-work, require complex mathematical calculations to be performed by the nodes in the network, which can take a lot of time and slow down the overall performance of the blockchain.

Additionally, changing variables or states in a smart contract can be expensive due to the amount of time and funds required for transaction processing and building a transaction block. Every state change consumes funds, also known as gas in the Ether world, and it requires making a transaction, processing the transaction, and building a transaction block that contains a new value for a smart contract (Zhang Rong, 2020). Before the hard fork in the Ether world, the time for building a new block was 21 seconds, and even after the hard fork, it still takes 12.5 seconds, which is a considerable amount of time in the world of IT (Mkrttchian et al., 2019).

Different cryptocurrencies use different approaches to process transactions (Chen, 2017; Saleh Fahad, 2021), as shown in Table 1. Efforts are ongoing to improve the scalability and speed of blockchain technology, including the implementation of sharding and other scaling solutions. In conclusion, blockchain technology has significant potential to revolutionize many industries, but there are still challenges that need to be addressed to improve its efficiency and usability.

We can use the example of a smart contract between a buyer and a supplier to illustrate how blockchain technology and smart contracts can streamline business processes. As shown in Figure 2, the supplier sends a product catalog to the buyer through the blockchain network, including all relevant details related to shipping and payment terms. The catalog is stored and distributed in the blockchain, allowing the buyer to verify the authenticity and reputation of the supplier.

Table 1. Demonstrates different crypto-currencies use different approaches to process the transactions

Cryptocurrency	Consensus Mechanism	Approach to Transaction Processing
Bitcoin	Proof of Work (PoW)	Miners compete to solve cryptographic puzzles to validate transactions and add blocks to the chain.
Ethereum	Proof of Stake (PoS)	Validators hold and stake tokens to earn transaction fees and validate transactions.
Ripple	Federated Byzantine Agreement (FBA)	Validators are chosen by Ripple to approve transactions through consensus.
Stellar	Federated Byzantine Agreement (FBA)	Validators are chosen by Stellar to approve transactions through consensus.
Cardano	Proof of Stake (PoS)	Validators hold and stake tokens to earn transaction fees and validate transactions.
Polkadot	Nominated Proof of Stake (NPoS)	Validators are nominated by token holders to validate transactions and add blocks to the chain.
Solana	Proof of History (PoH) + Proof of Stake (PoS)	Transactions are first timestamped through PoH, then validators holding and staking tokens validate the transactions through PoS.
Binance Coin	Delegated Proof of Stake (DPoS)	Validators are elected by token holders to validate transactions and add blocks to the chain.
Dogecoin	Proof of Work (PoW)	Miners compete to solve cryptographic puzzles to validate transactions and add blocks to the chain.

Once the buyer confirms the order with the specified quantity and payment date via the blockchain, a purchase contract (Contract 1) is formed, enclosed in the blue box in Figure 2. The entire process is completed between the buyer and supplier without the intervention of a third party.

Smart contracts are becoming increasingly popular due to several reasons, such as risk optimization, cutting down administration and service costs, improving business process efficiency, ensuring transparency, managing transactions, and minimizing paperwork. With conditional immutability of blockchains, smart contracts cannot be arbitrarily altered once they are issued, and all transactions are traceable and auditable, making it difficult for malicious actors to engage in financial fraud. Smart contracts eliminate the need for intermediaries, reducing administration and service costs and improving efficiency. They ensure transparency by monitoring transactions between parties, manage transactions with simple logic, and require less paperwork, reducing time and costs.

After *Contract 1* is done, the supplier will search for a carrier in the blockchain to complete the shipping phase. Like *Contract 1*, the carrier also publishes the shipping description (such as transportation fees, source, destination, capacity and shipping time) as well as shipping conditions and terms in the blockchain. If the supplier accepts the contract issued by the carrier, the products will be delivered to the carrier who will finally dispatch the products to the buyer. This whole procedure constructs *Contract 2* (enclosed in the pink box) as shown in Figure 2. Similarly, the whole procedure of *Contract 2* is also conducted without the intervention of a third party.

In addition to automatic execution of *Contract 1* and *Contract 2*, the payment procedures (including the payment from the supplier to the carrier and that from the buyer to the supplier) are also completed automatically. For example, once the buyer confirms the reception of the products, the payment between the buyer and the supplier will be automatically triggered as the predefined condition is met. The financial settlement from the buyer to the supplier is conducted via crypto currencies (*e.g.*, Bitcoin or

Figure 2. Demonstrates an interaction between a buyer and a supplier via a smart contract usage

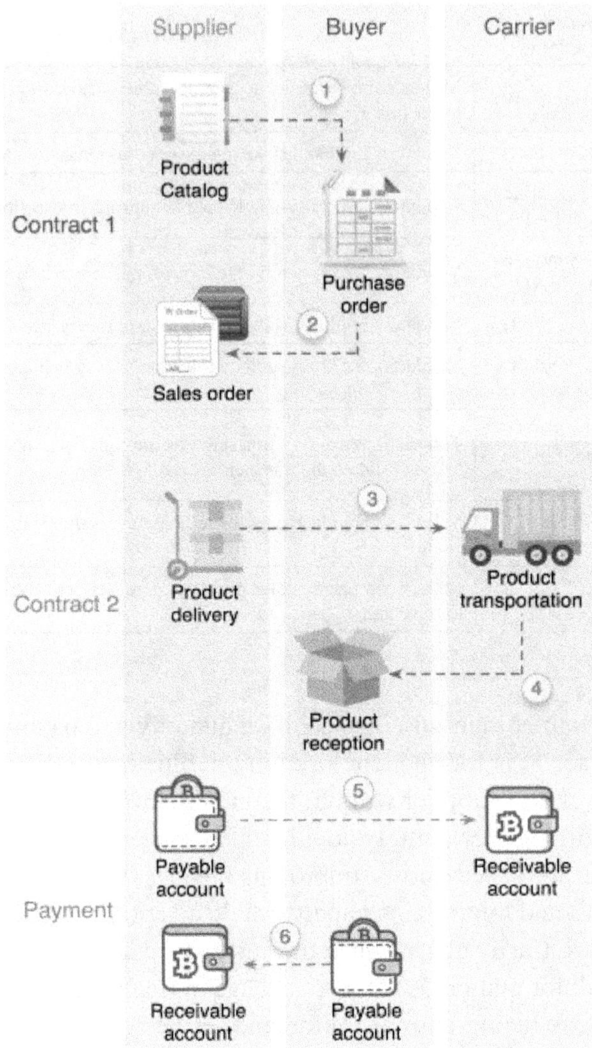

Ether.1). In contrast to conventional transactions, the whole process is done in a peer-to-peer manner without the intervention of third parties like banks. As a result, the turnaround time and transactional cost can be greatly saved.

Figure 3. Shows the number of smart contracts created in Ethereum blockchain

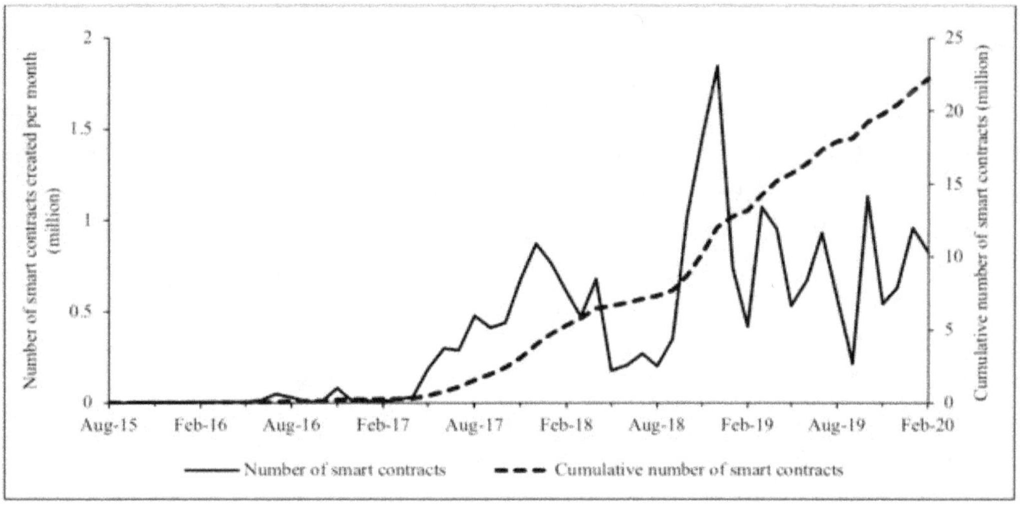

Table 2. Comparison of smart contract platforms

Platform	Description	Consensus Mechanism	Language	Mainnet Launch Year
Ethereum	A decentralized platform for building dApps	PoW (soon to be PoS)	Solidity	2015
Binance Smart Chain	A blockchain for creating dApps and tokens	PoSA	Solidity	2020
Polkadot	A multi-chain platform for building dApps	Nominated Proof-of-Stake (NPoS)	Ink, Rust, C++	2020
Cardano	A decentralized platform for building dApps	Proof-of-Stake (PoS)	Plutus, Marlowe	2017
Algorand	A blockchain for creating and deploying dApps	Pure Proof-of-Stake (PPoS)	TEAL	2019
EOS	A blockchain for creating and deploying dApps	Delegated Proof-of-Stake (DPoS)	C++	2018

Smart contracts, like any other technology, are vulnerable to attacks. In fact, in 2016, the Decentralized Autonomous Organization (DAO) smart contract was manipulated to steal approximately 2 Million ETH, which was equivalent to 50 Million USD at the time, due to its re-entrancy vulnerability. This event serves as a reminder that smart contracts must be carefully designed and thoroughly audited to prevent such security breaches from happening (Tasca Paolo, 2019).

Apart from security vulnerabilities, smart contracts also face other challenges such as privacy, legal, and performance issues. It is important for developers to take into account these challenges and address them appropriately to ensure that smart contracts can be effectively utilized in various applications.

One example of a re-entrancy attack on a smart contract is provided below:

```
#![allow(dead_code)]use std::collections::HashMap;#[derive(Default)]struct Auction {    bidders: HashMap<String, u128>,    locked: bool,}impl Auction {    fn bid(&mut self, sender: String, value: u128) {        self.bidders.entry(sender).and_modify(|v| *v += value).or_insert(value);    }    fn refund(&mut self, sender: String) -> Result<(), String> {        let refund_amount = self.bidders.get(&sender).unwrap_or(&0).clone();        if refund_amount > 0 {            let result = sender.parse::<address>().unwrap().call(            "",            refund_amount.into(),            0,            gas_left(),            0,            0,            );            match result {                Ok(_) => {                    self.bidders.insert(sender, 0);                    Ok(())                }                Err(_) => Err("failed!".to_string()),            }        } else {            Err("No refund amount".to_string())        }    }    fn current_balance(&self) -> u128 {        address().balance.into()    }}
```

Upon initial inspection of the smart contract, it appears that the refund method should retrieve the user's funds and send them back to the user with the following line of code:

```
let mut success = false;if let Some(sender) = msg.sender {    if let Ok(mut sender_balance) = sender.balance() {        if sender_balance >= refund_amount {            success = sender.transfer(refund_amount).is_ok();        }    }}
```

Below is an example of a smart contract that carries out a re-entrancy attack on the Auction contract:

```
contract AuctionAttack {    const BID_AMOUNT: u128 = 1 ether;    let auction: AuctionHacked;    fn new(_auction: address) -> Self {        Self {            auction: AuctionHacked::new(_auction),        }    }    fn proxy_bid(&mut self) {        assert_eq!(msg.value, BID_AMOUNT, "incorrect");        self.auction.bid(msg.value);    }    fn attack(&mut self) {        self.auction.refund();    }    fn receive(&mut self) {        if self.auction.current_balance() >= BID_AMOUNT {            self.auction.refund();        }    }    fn current_balance(&self) -> u128 {        self.address().balance()    }}
```

What happens here is: an intruder first calls for a *proxy_bid()* function to send some funds to the Action contract. Then the Action contract will receive this money and will make a record that a new user made a bid equal to some amount of the money. But then intruder calls for a *attack()* function which automatically calls a *refund()* function of the Action smart contract. The Action smart contract checks whether the user has the funds (yes) and tries to send them. However in the world of smart contract of Etherium instead of making an update on the user's record making it 0, it will run the *receive()* function of an intruder which contains another request for the Action smart contract:*refund()* and as a result, the intruder will get all the money possessed by Auction smart contract.

This attack can be avoided if we make some changes in the Action smart contract:

```
contract Auction {     let bidders: HashMap<address, u128>;     let locked: bool
= false;     fn refund(&mut self) no_reentrancy {         let refund_amount:
u128 = self.bidders.get(&msg.sender).copied().unwrap_or(0);         if refund_
amount > 0 {             self.bidders.insert(msg.sender, 0);             let
result = msg.sender.send(refund_amount);             assert!(result.is_ok(),
"failed!");         }     }     fn no_reentrancy(&mut self, f: impl FnOnce(&mut
Self)) {         assert!(!self.locked, "no reentrancy!");         self.locked =
true;         f(self);         self.locked = false;     }}
```

For developers who are new to the world of smart contracts and come from other areas of software development, understanding the intricacies of smart contract platforms may not be immediately apparent.

Smart contract platforms face a range of functional challenges that need to be addressed. Some of the representative challenges include: (1) Re-entrancy, which refers to the ability to safely call a function that was interrupted. This vulnerability can be exploited by malicious users to steal digital currency, as noted in Li et al. (2017). (2) Block randomness, which is important for smart contract applications such as lotteries and betting pools that require random outcomes. However, malicious miners may manipulate the block generation process to alter the outcome of the pseudo-random generator, as demonstrated in Bonneau et al. (2015). (3) Overcharging, which occurs when smart contracts are not optimized properly and can lead to patterns such as dead code and expensive operations in loops that involve repeated computations, as shown in recent work by Chen et al. (2017).

There have been several advances in addressing these functional issues in smart contract platforms.

Smart contracts are self-executing programs that operate based on the rules encoded within them. However, there are several functional issues that have been identified in smart contract platforms, including re-entrancy, block randomness, overcharging, and others. These issues can lead to serious security vulnerabilities and inefficiencies in the execution of smart contracts.

One of the most commonly discussed functional issues in smart contracts is re-entrancy. Re-entrancy occurs when a malicious actor is able to repeatedly execute a function within a smart contract, causing it to malfunction and potentially allowing the attacker to steal digital currency or other assets. This vulnerability was famously exploited in the 2016 attack on the DAO, which resulted in the loss of around 2 million ETH (50 million USD at the time). To address this issue, developers have implemented various mechanisms to prevent re-entrancy attacks, such as using the "pull over push" method, where funds are only transferred when requested by the recipient, and using mutex locks to prevent concurrent calls to the same function.

Another functional issue in smart contracts is block randomness. Some smart contract applications, such as lotteries and betting pools, require randomness in the generation of blocks. However, the block generation process is deterministic, so generating true randomness is difficult. Malicious miners can also manipulate the generation of blocks, resulting in biased or predictable outcomes. To address this issue, developers have implemented various solutions, such as using cryptographic hashes of block information as a source of randomness and using verifiable random functions (VRFs) to generate random numbers. Based on above propositions a multi-round protocol to verify delay functions using a refereed delegation model. It reduces the cost of verifying the output from \$30 to \$0.4 (Tessaro, 2016).

Overcharging is another functional issue in smart contracts. Overcharging occurs when the execution of a smart contract requires more computational resources than necessary, resulting in higher transaction fees and slower transaction processing times. This can be caused by inefficient or redundant code, poorly optimized loops, and other factors. To address this issue, developers have developed various optimization techniques, such as using gas-efficient data structures, minimizing the use of loops, and using compiler optimizations to generate more efficient code. Besides from caring the efficiency of their programs, developers of smart contract also need to pay attention to their execution costs. It's noticed that over 90% of real smart contracts suffer from gas-costly patterns in Ethereum (Zhang et al., 2019). A researcher proposed GasReducer, a tool used to detect gas-costly patterns. GasReducer can replace under-optimized byte code with efficient byte code.

In addition to these functional issues, smart contracts also face other challenges, such as privacy, legal compliance, and performance issues. Developers are constantly working to address these challenges and improve the functionality and security of smart contracts.

Certainly, here's an elaboration on the issues surrounding smart contracts and their limitations:

While smart contracts have the potential to revolutionize the way we handle transactions and interact with decentralized applications, they are not without their limitations. One major issue is the various types of attacks that can be executed on smart contracts, such as re-entrancy attacks or block timestamp manipulation.

However, these attacks are not the only problems that smart contracts face. There are also issues with their design and architecture that can hinder their potential. For example, in many cases, smart contracts are treated as part of the payment system, which is a fundamentally flawed approach. The logic for processing financial transactions should not be tied to the blockchain where data is stored. This can lead to problems such as pollution, high transaction costs, and excessive energy consumption.

To address these issues, it is important to consider new approaches to smart contract design and architecture. One potential solution is to separate the payment processing logic from the blockchain itself, so that the blockchain can be used purely as a data storage and management system. This can help to reduce the pollution and energy consumption associated with smart contracts, while also lowering transaction costs and improving their overall efficiency.

Another potential solution is to explore alternative blockchain architectures that are specifically designed for smart contract execution. For example, some blockchains are built using a virtual machine architecture, which can make it easier to develop and execute complex smart contracts. These approaches can help to mitigate many of the limitations and challenges associated with smart contracts, and pave the way for a more robust and efficient blockchain ecosystem.

In conclusion, while smart contracts have the potential to revolutionize many aspects of our digital lives, they are not without their limitations and challenges. By addressing these issues head-on and exploring new approaches to smart contract design and architecture, we can unlock the full potential of this exciting technology and create a more efficient and sustainable blockchain ecosystem.

LITERATURE REVIEW

The literature on smart contracts has explored various aspects of this emerging technology, including their potential benefits, limitations, and challenges (Delmolino et al., 2016; Yang et al., 2019; Yao et al., 2019). One of the main advantages of smart contracts is their ability to reduce transaction costs, increase efficiency, and reduce the potential for fraud. By automating the execution of contracts and eliminating the need for intermediaries, smart contracts can streamline various business processes and enhance trust among parties. However, the literature also points out several limitations of smart contracts. For instance, smart contracts may not be suitable for complex contracts that involve multiple variables and require human interpretation and discretion. Moreover, smart contracts may be vulnerable to hacking or programming errors, which could lead to significant losses for parties involved in the contract. Therefore, organizations need to carefully consider the potential benefits and drawbacks of smart contracts before implementing them. In addition to the benefits and limitations of smart contracts, the literature also emphasizes the importance of legal and regulatory frameworks to support their use. Smart contracts require a legal framework that recognizes and enforces their validity and enforceability. Furthermore, organizations need to consider dispute resolution mechanisms that are compatible with smart contracts and ensure that their use does not violate any existing regulations or laws. The literature suggests that organizations should invest in technology infrastructure and expertise to ensure that smart contracts are implemented correctly and securely (Chen & Wang, 2019; Gervais et al., 2016). With the right approach and precautions, smart contracts have the potential to transform the way business is conducted, but their adoption requires careful consideration and planning.

Smart contracts have been a topic of discussion in the business world for several years. Proponents tout their potential benefits, while critics point out their limitations. Smart contracts are self-executing contracts with the terms of the agreement between buyer and seller being directly written into lines of code (Chakraborty & Sural, 2018). They have the potential to reduce transaction costs, increase efficiency, and reduce the potential for fraud. However, they may not be suitable for complex contracts that require human interpretation and discretion, and they may be vulnerable to hacking or programming errors.

Several articles have discussed the potential benefits and drawbacks of smart contracts (Nikolic et al., 2018). A Harvard Business Review article suggests that smart contracts are best suited for simple, standardized agreements, such as those used in supply chain management. The article notes that smart contracts may require significant investment in technology infrastructure and expertise, which could limit their widespread adoption. The article also emphasizes the importance of legal and regulatory frameworks to support the use of smart contracts, particularly in areas such as contract enforcement and dispute resolution.

A TechRadar article provides a more detailed analysis of the potential benefits and drawbacks of smart contracts. The article notes that smart contracts have the potential to reduce transaction costs and increase efficiency by eliminating the need for intermediaries. However, the article also points out that smart contracts may be vulnerable to hacking or programming errors, which could lead to significant losses for parties involved in the contract. The article concludes that organizations should carefully consider the potential benefits and drawbacks of smart contracts before implementing them.

Similarly, a CIO Dive article also emphasizes the limitations of smart contracts. The article suggests that smart contracts may not be suitable for all types of contracts, particularly those that require human interpretation and discretion. The article notes that smart contracts may be vulnerable to hacking or programming errors, which could lead to significant losses for parties involved in the contract. The article suggests that organizations should carefully consider the potential benefits and drawbacks of smart contracts before implementing them.

Overall, the literature suggests that while smart contracts have the potential to offer significant benefits, they may not be suitable for all types of contracts. Organizations should carefully consider the potential benefits and drawbacks of smart contracts before implementing them, and should ensure that legal and regulatory frameworks are in place to support their use. Additionally, organizations should invest in technology infrastructure and expertise to ensure that smart contracts are implemented correctly and securely. With the right approach and precautions, smart contracts have the potential to transform the way business is conducted (Liu et al., 2019; Li et al., 2019; Tikhomirov & Yakovlev, 2019).

PROBLEM

The current approach to the architecture of smart contracts has several disadvantages, including:

- Slow speed
- Inability to horizontally scale
- Limited runtime environments for running smart contracts
- SOLID
- Inability to use external services or databases
- High cost of running a smart contract
- Limited number of operations inside a contract
- Limited types of smart contracts

These limitations can make it difficult for developers to build and deploy effective smart contracts. Additionally, the advantages of sand-boxing, which specify that smart contracts cannot be modified, are not always true. For example, the situation with Luna, ETH, BTC blockchain suggests that modifications can be made. Furthermore, developers often use a programming pattern that allows them to switch between different versions of smart contracts (Galiautdinov, 2020b).

To address these limitations, new approaches to smart contract architecture are being developed, such as sharding and off-chain computing. These approaches aim to improve the scalability and speed of smart contracts, while also enabling more complex and flexible applications. As the technology continues to evolve, it will be important for businesses and developers to stay up-to-date with the latest advances in smart contract architecture in order to take full advantage of their potential benefits.

```
```ruststruct Proxy {     implementation: Address,     x: u32,}impl Proxy
{     fn set_implementation(&mut self, imp: Address) {          self.imple-
mentation = imp;     }     fn _delegate(&self, imp: Address) {          let
mut data = Vec::new();          data.extend_from_slice(&msg::calldata().un-
wrap());          let result = imp.delegate(&data);          match result {
Ok(output) => {               msg::sender().transfer(output);               }
Err(_) => {               msg::revert();               }          }     }}#[no_man-
gle]pub extern "C" fn receive() {}#[no_mangle]pub extern "C" fn fallback()
{     let proxy = Proxy {          implementation: Address::default(),          x:
0,     };     proxy._delegate(proxy.implementation);} struct V1 {     imple-
mentation: Address,     x: u32,}impl V1 {     fn new() -> Self {          V1
{               implementation: Address::default(),               x: 0,          }
}     fn inc(&mut self) {          self.x += 1;     }     fn enc(&self) -> Vec<u8>
{          abi::encode_function_selector("inc()", &[])     }     fn enc_x(&self)
-> Vec<u8> {          abi::encode_function_selector("x()", &[])     }}struct V2 {
implementation: Address,     x: u32,}impl V2 {     fn new() -> Self {          V2
```
```

```
{            implementation: Address::default(),            x: 0,         }
}     fn inc(&mut self) {          self.x += 10;     }     fn dec(&mut self) {
self.x -= 1;     }     fn enc1(&self) -> Vec<u8> {          abi::encode_function_
selector("inc()", &[])     }}```
```

Is there any other advantage of placing smart contracts on the blockchain? It is highly unlikely. On the other hand, the list of disadvantages is quite extensive.

Firstly, smart contracts have slow speed as they run on a miner's machine which is limited by the speed of the computer (Galiautdnov, 2023).

Secondly, smart contracts cannot be horizontally scaled, which means a miner's machine cannot create multiple instances of a smart contract to speed up its work and accept multiple incoming requests. Additionally, smart contracts cannot be stateless (if they are doing something meaningful), and they also create additional issues because currently there is no way to split data from logic.

Thirdly, a smart contract does not support a situation where multiple smart contracts run in their own isolated runtime environments. They also do not support the creation of separate processes and threads, which negatively affect their performance.

Fourthly, the SOLID paradigm, which stands for Single Responsibility, is a well-known principle in software development that suggests that each service should only be responsible for its own business entity. However, this approach should not be applied to the cryptocurrency sphere as smart contracts should never be a part of the blockchain.

Fifthly, smart contracts cannot use any external services, databases, or any other resources which dramatically limits their abilities.

Sixthly, running a smart contract can be quite expensive as the consumer of a smart contract has to pay for every operation, leading to a limitation on the complexity of the smart contracts.

Seventhly, smart contracts have a very limited number of operations, cycles, and allowed types, which limits their overall abilities.

All these issues clearly demonstrate the poor side of smart contracts and the lack of progress in this direction.

SOLUTION

To address the issues related to smart contracts, it is necessary to split them into two parts: data and services. This approach is commonly used in software development design patterns, such as the Visitor pattern. However, splitting smart contracts is only the first step towards a complete solution. The next step is to remove smart contract logic from the blockchain and store it on cloud platforms like AWS or Azure.

To implement this solution, we can introduce two new types of smart contracts: Data Contracts and Service Contracts. Service Contracts should be stateless, meaning that they should not store any state, which will allow them to be horizontally scaled to process multiple requests simultaneously. This approach will resolve several issues related to smart contracts, including slow speed, inability to scale horizontally, limited runtime environments, and more.

Additionally, by storing smart contract logic in the cloud, developers can easily use external databases and apply big data to blockchain. This will make running a smart contract cheaper and more efficient, and will allow for the introduction of new types of smart contracts that were previously not possible.

One potential concern with this approach is that it makes smart contracts more changeable, and there is no guarantee that the logic was not changed. However, the author of the article proposes a pattern used by smart contract developers that allows for different logic depending on the version of the smart contract, making it a non-issue. The blockchain will only contain Data related to Data Contracts and the version number of a Service Contract used to process the data. The Service Contract will be located on a Cloud Platform, have its own version, and work on the principals of Proof-of-Stake.

Proof-of-stake is a cryptocurrency consensus mechanism that secures the blockchain by validating entries into a distributed database. This approach will make blockchain and financial systems more logical and stable, while also reducing the negative impact on the natural environment and saving energy.

Regarding the benefits of Proof-of-Stake (PoS), cryptocurrency owners validate block transactions based on the number of staked coins, which is an alternative to the original consensus mechanism, Proof-of-Work (PoW). While PoW requires miners to solve cryptographic puzzles, PoS requires validators to hold and stake tokens for the privilege of earning transaction fees. Compared to PoW, PoS is seen as less risky because it structures compensation in a way that makes an attack less advantageous. Additionally, the next block writer on the blockchain is selected randomly, with higher odds being assigned to nodes with larger stake positions.

Furthermore, PoS is a more energy-efficient alternative to PoW, which is essential in today's world where reducing pollution is critical. PoS reduces the amount of processing power needed to validate block information and transactions, which in turn lowers network congestion and removes rewards-based incentives that PoW blockchains have. While both consensus mechanisms have pros and cons, they have different approaches. Under PoS, block creators are called validators, while under PoW, block creators are miners. Validators check transactions, verify activity, vote on outcomes, and maintain records, while miners work to solve for the hash, a cryptographic number, to verify transactions. To become a block creator under PoS, you only need to own enough coins or tokens to become a validator, while under PoW, miners must invest in processing equipment and incur hefty energy charges to power the machines attempting to solve the computations.

Table 3.

Proof of Stake	Proof of Work
Block creators are called validators	Block creators are called miners
Participants must own coins or tokens to become a validator	Participants must buy equipment and energy to become a miner
Energy efficient	Not energy efficient
Security through community control	Robust security due to expensive upfront requirement
Validators receive transactions fees as rewards	Miners receive block rewards

Despite the potential benefits of crypto-currencies, there are still several weaknesses and concerns that need to be addressed. One such issue is the possibility of collisions in the hash functions that form the foundation of the crypto-currency system. While collisions are rare, they can occur over time, creating potential vulnerabilities.

Another concern is the self-destruct mechanism present in many crypto-currencies, including Bitcoin. This mechanism is triggered by a specific command or programming instruction, and can lead to the permanent destruction of the currency. While this feature may be intended to prevent fraud or misuse, it also poses a significant risk to investors and the wider market.

Furthermore, the lack of a publicly published theorem proving the concept of hash functions used in crypto-currencies leaves room for doubt and uncertainty. This raises questions about the reliability and security of the entire crypto-currency system, as well as the potential for manipulation or exploitation.

Despite these concerns, the popularity and use of crypto-currencies continue to grow, and efforts are being made to address these weaknesses and strengthen the security and stability of the system. It remains to be seen whether these efforts will be enough to ensure the long-term viability and success of crypto-currencies.

CONCLUSION

The article delves into the current limitations of smart contracts and blockchain technology, highlighting the shortcomings that have been hindering their full adoption and effectiveness. The author conducted extensive research and proposed a groundbreaking solution that has the potential to revolutionize the way smart contracts work and the architecture that underpins them.

The author identifies several well-known issues related to smart contracts, including their lack of scalability and flexibility, their inability to handle real-world scenarios, and the fact that they are often unable to interact with external systems. These limitations have been a major barrier to the widespread adoption of smart contracts and have prevented them from fulfilling their potential as a transformative technology.

To address these challenges, the author presents a novel solution that completely changes the architecture used in smart contracts and blockchain. The proposed solution has the potential to not only resolve the current limitations of smart contracts but also positively impact the environment by reducing pollution and saving energy.

The solution is based on a new architecture that leverages advanced machine learning algorithms and other cutting-edge technologies to enable smart contracts to interact with real-world data and systems in a seamless and secure manner. This new architecture is designed to be highly scalable, enabling smart contracts to handle large volumes of data and complex scenarios.

Moreover, the proposed solution has the potential to significantly reduce the energy consumption and carbon footprint of blockchain and smart contract systems. This is achieved by using innovative approaches to optimize energy usage and reduce the computational resources required for smart contract execution.

Overall, the proposed solution represents a significant step forward in the evolution of smart contract technology, offering a powerful and innovative approach to addressing the current limitations of the field. If successful, it could pave the way for a new era of smart contract adoption and bring about significant positive impact on both the performance of smart contracts and the environment.

REFERENCES

Atzei, N., Bartoletti, M., & Cimoli, T. (2017). A survey of attacks on Ethereum smart contracts. *Lecture Notes in Computer Science*, *7*(2), 109–123. doi:10.1007/978-3-662-54455-6_8

Bernstein, D. J., & Lange, T. (2016). *SafeCurves: Choosing safe curves for elliptic-curve cryptography.* https://safecurves.cr.yp.to/

Bonneau, J., Clark, J., & Goldfeder, S. (2015). On bitcoin as a public randomness source. IACR Cryptol. ePrint Archive, p. 1015.

Chakraborty, S., & Sural, S. (2018). Smart Contract Architecture for IoT Applications. In *Proceedings of the 2nd International Conference on Inventive Communication and Computational Technologies* (pp. 295-299). ACM. https://doi.org/10.1145/3157967.3157980

Chen, T., Li, X., Luo, X., & Zhang, X. (2017), Under-optimized smart contracts devour your money. *Proceedings of 24th International Conference on Software Analysis, Evolution and Reengineering, SANER,* 442–446. 10.1109/SANER.2017.7884650

Chen, Y., & Wang, Q. (2019). A smart contract-based incentive mechanism for crowd sensing. *IEEE Transactions on Mobile Computing, 18*(11), 2548–2561. doi:10.1109/TMC.2019.2909559

Daniel, R. L. B. (2016). *SECG SEC 1: Elliptic Curve Cryptography* (Version 2.0). https://www.secg.org/sec1-v2.pdf

Delmolino, K., Arnett, M., Kosba, A., Miller, A., & Shi, E. (2016). Step by step towards creating a safe smart contract: Lessons and insights from a cryptocurrency lab. *Proceedings of the 22nd ACM SIGSAC Conference on Computer and Communications Security,* 79-91. 10.1007/978-3-662-53357-4_6

Galiautdinov R., (2020a). Brain machine interface: the accurate interpretation of neurotransmitters' signals targeting the muscles. *International Journal of Applied Research in Bioinformatics.* DOI: doi:10.4018/IJARB.20200102

Galiautdinov, R., (2020b). MicroService Oriented Architecture in distributed Artificial Intelligence systems and the language of AI in bio-neural systems. *International Journal of Applied Research in Bioinformatics.* doi:10.4018/IJARB.2020070103

Galiautdinov, R. (2023). Nonlinear Filtering Methods in Conditions of Uncertainty. In E. Oyekanlu (Ed.), *Applied AI and Multimedia Technologies for Smart Manufacturing and CPS Applications.* doi:10.4018/978-1-7998-7852-0.ch010

Galiautdinov, R., & Mkrttchian, V. (2019a). Math model of neuron and nervous system research, based on AI constructor creating virtual neural circuits: Theoretical and Methodological Aspects. In V. Mkrttchian, E. Aleshina, & L. Gamidullaeva (Eds.), *Avatar-Based Control, Estimation, Communications, and Development of Neuron Multi-Functional Technology Platforms* (pp. 320–344). IGI Global. doi:10.4018/978-1-7998-1581-5.ch015

Galiautdinov, R., & Mkrttchian, V. (2019b). Brain machine interface – for Avatar Control & Estimation in Educational purposes Based on Neural AI plugs: Theoretical and Methodological Aspects. In V. Mkrttchian, E. Aleshina, & L. Gamidullaeva (Eds.), *Avatar-Based Control, Estimation, Communications, and Development of Neuron Multi-Functional Technology Platforms* (pp. 345–360). IGI Global. doi:10.4018/978-1-7998-1581-5.ch016

Gervais, A., Karame, G. O., Wüst, K., Glykantzis, V., Ritzdorf, H., & Capkun, S. (2016). On the security and performance of proof of work blockchains. *Proceedings of the 2016 ACM SIGSAC Conference on Computer and Communications Security*, 3-16. 10.1145/2976749.2978341

Heuvel, S. (2014). *The demand for short-term, safe assets and financial stability: Some evidence and implications for central bank policies.* Academic Press.

Li, L., Yu, Y., Li, Z., & Li, X. (2019). Smart contract-based secure data sharing scheme for cloud storage. *Future Generation Computer Systems*, *100*, 968–980. doi:10.1016/j.future.2019.05.003

Li, W., Andreina, S., Bohli, J.-M., & Karame, G. (2017). Securing Proof-of-Stake Blockchain Protocols. In J. Garcia-Alfaro, G. Navarro-Arribas, H. Hartenstein, & J. Herrera-Joancomartí (Eds.), *Data Privacy Management, Cryptocurrencies and Blockchain Technology* (pp. 297–315). Lecture Notes in Computer Science. Springer International Publishing. doi:10.1007/978-3-319-67816-0_17

Li, X., Jiang, P., Chen, T., Luo, X., & Wen, Q. (2017). A survey on the security of blockchain systems. *Future Generation Computer Systems*.

Liu, Y., Zhang, Y., Yang, X., Wang, J., & Zhang, L. (2019). A smart contract-based approach to secure data storage in cloud computing. *IEEE Transactions on Cloud Computing*, *7*(3), 759–770. doi:10.1109/TCC.2018.2847744

Mkrttchian, V., Gamidullaeva, L., & Galiautdinov, R. (2019). *Design of Nano-scale Electrodes and Development of Avatar-Based Control System for Energy-Efficient Power Engineering: Application of an Internet of Things and People (IOTAP) Research Center. International Journal of Applied Nanotechnology Research.* doi:10.4018/IJANR.2019010104

Nguyen, C. T., Hoang, D. T., Nguyen, D. N., Niyato, D., Nguyen, H. T., & Dutkiewicz, E. (2019). Proof-of-Stake Consensus Mechanisms for Future Blockchain Networks: Fundamentals, Applications and Opportunities. *IEEE Access : Practical Innovations, Open Solutions*, *7*, 85727–85745. doi:10.1109/ACCESS.2019.2925010

Nikolic, I., Kolluri, A., Sergey, I., Saxena, P., & Hobor, A. (2018). Finding the greedy, prodigal, and suicidal contracts at scale. *Proceedings of the 27th USENIX Security Symposium*, 811-828. https://www.usenix.org/system/files/conference/usenixsecurity18/sec18-nikolic.pdf

Pearce, S. (2021). *Smart contracts: The good, the bad and the ugly*. TechRadar. https://www.techradar.com/news/smart-contracts-the-good-the-bad-and-the-ugly

Saleh, F. (2021). Blockchain without Waste: Proof-of-Stake. *The Review of Financial Studies, 34*(3), 1156–1190. doi:10.1093/rfs/hhaa075

Staff, H. B. R. (2021). Smart Contracts: Hype vs. Reality. *Harvard Business Review*. https://hbr.org/2021/07/smart-contracts-hype-vs-reality

Szabo, N. (1997). *The idea of smart contracts*. Nick Szabo's Papers and Concise Tutorials.

Tasca, P., & Tessone, C. J. (2019). A Taxonomy of Blockchain Technologies: Principles of Identification and Classification. *Ledger, 4*. doi:10.5195/ledger.2019.140

Tessaro, S. (2016). Sloth: A Lightweight Delay Function for ASIC-Resistant Proof-of-Work Based on Nakamoto's Consensus Algorithm. *Journal of Cryptology*, *29*(2), 613–638.

Tikhomirov, S., & Yakovlev, A. (2019). Formal verification of smart contracts: Short survey. *Proceedings of the 3rd International Conference on Cryptography, Security and Privacy*, 278-283. https://doi.org/10.1145/3312446.3312456

Vogel, P. S. (2021, May). *Why smart contracts may not be smart after all.* CIO Dive. https://www.ciodive.com/news/smart-contracts-limitations/599279/

Yang, Y., Yao, D., Liu, S., & Wang, X. (2019). A smart contract-based access control model for secure data sharing in cloud storage. *Journal of Network and Computer Applications*, *140*, 34–44. doi:10.1016/j.jnca.2019.03.013

Yao, D., Liu, S., Yang, Y., & Wang, X. (2019). A smart contract-based approach for secure data sharing in cloud storage. *Future Generation Computer Systems*, *97*, 736–745. doi:10.1016/j.future.2019.02.018

Zhang, R., & Chan, W. K. (2020). Evaluation of Energy Consumption in Block-Chains with Proof of Work and Proof of Stake. *Journal of Physics: Conference Series, 1584*(1), 012023. doi:10.1088/1742-6596/1584/1/012023

Zhang, Y., Sun, Y., Chen, J., & Liu, J. (2019). GasReducer: Detecting and Mitigating Gas-Costly Patterns in Ethereum Smart Contracts. *IEEE Transactions on Dependable and Secure Computing*, *17*(2), 405–419. doi:10.1109/TDSC.2018.2863135

Chapter 9
A Bibliometric Analysis of Green Finance:
Present State and Future Directions

Renuka Sharma
Chitkara Business School, Chitkara University, India

Kiran Mehta
Chitkara Business School, Chitkara University, India

Shivam Ahuja
Chitkara Business School, Chitkara University, India

ABSTRACT

Sustainable finance is one of the most cutting-edge growth trends in the financial sector, thanks to its growing worldwide significance. Climate finance/green finance/carbon finance has developed in recent years as a potential tool for tackling climate change and its environmental implications while also funding adaptation. Green financing, a novel kind of financial support, aims to support green development while simultaneously reducing carbon emissions. It's an emerging concept that is often explored in the context of preparing for and reducing climate-related environmental degradation. The present study aims to give a detailed review of existing knowledge on the subject of green finance. This chapter used bibliometric methods to analyse 349 articles related to sustainable finance published between 2000 and 2022. The study examined the number of publications, nations, journals, keywords, topic areas, and organisations, as well as highly cited individuals and articles. The study also aims to effectively communicate its findings by using visual depictions and network analysis.

DOI: 10.4018/978-1-6684-8624-5.ch009

INTRODUCTION

The notion of "Green Finance" (GF) has developed through time in line with economic expectations. Growing worldwide concern about protection of environment, tackling climate change, and resilience has drawn academic, scholars and politicians' attention to green finance, that is an endeavor of nations to transfer to new and sustainable financial systems (Vyas et al., 2023). The world has been paying close attention to the issues of sustainability and climate change. At the 2015 UN Climate Change Conference (COP 21 or Conference of the Parties), a total of 195 countries signed the Paris Agreement on climate change mitigation, with the aim of ensuring that the increase in global temperature does not exceed 2 °C. Numerous nations have worked to encourage the growth of green production and green innovation in order to meet these long-term climate goals (Acemoglu et al., 2016; Li et al., 2018). In recent times, the expression "green finance" has grown in prevalence as a result of the international agreement to take action on climate change, refers to investments and loans that support environmentally sustainable development (GFSG, 2016). The area of finance known as "green finance" is relatively new. There has been no agreement between international organizations and economists on a precise definition. However, numerous scholars, associations, and governments have created useful descriptions for the public (Labatt, S.; White, R.R., 2003). Green finance is the term used to describe the actions taken by financial organizations to support the financing of initiatives that focus on environmental protection and the conservation of energy. It aids in shifting the industrial processes and boosting faster economic growth. Green Finance contributes to the environmental regulatory enforcements and also distribute funds from industries that produce pollution and are energy driven to those who have green technologies and innovative solutions (Wang et al., 2021).

Green finance aims to increase the worth of fiscal resources that originate from investments, banking, and insurance to be utilized for sustainable development programs in the public, private, and non-profit realms (United Nations Environment Programme, 2020; Mehta et al., 2019). Green finance is frequently referred to as "sustainable finance," "environmental finance," "climate finance," as well as "green investment." Research on sustainable finance may be broken down into seven primary categories, including socially responsible investment, green financing, climate finance, carbon finance, energy finance, impact investing, and the regulation/governance of sustainable investing and financing (Sharma et al., 2020; Vyas et al., 2020). During the eleventh G-20 meeting in Hangzhou, China in 2016, there was a noticeable increase in attention and discussion on the subject of green finance (Liu et al., 2019; Schäfer, 2018). Considering the "green" nature of green finance, it is essential to direct financial resources to all economic areas that are associated with social integration, renewable energy, green construction, climate alteration, and corporate administration (Yuan & Gallagher, 2018). Green finance is the provision of funds to support investments that are beneficial for the environment through the goal of creating a win scenario between economic growth and enhanced environmental quality (International Finance Corporation). Green finance is a financial approach which is designed to optimize both economic and ecological advantages. (Wang & Zhi, 2016). One of the strategies employed to address the challenges brought about by global warming and the transition to a carbon-free economy is the use of green finance as part of a self-sufficient financial system. Green finance is a type of financial investment that is employed in ventures such as formulating policies, providing insurance or risk management, issuing bonds, and/or other forms of commercial operations that have a lesser negative effect on the environment, or make a positive contribution to it (Cai & Guo, 2021). The utilization of the funds allotted for environmental conservation through detailed plans and proposals for returns on investment is taken into consideration from a financial perspective in green finance. By considering environmental risk management techniques and the feasibility of plans, it highlights the benefits of environmental protection (Jeucken, 2010).

The emphasis may be placed on making existing infrastructure costs more eco-friendly or initiating new investment into essential industries such as renewable power sources, conservation of biological diversity, monitoring of natural resources, ecosystem preservation, sustainable travel, and the prevention and regulation of pollution. To meet the rising requirements, the finance industry is coming up with different types of financial products including green bonds and carbon market instruments and also establishing new financial entities like green banks and green funds.

The combination of products and institutions is what makes up green financing. Changes in the regulatory frameworks of countries could be one way to encourage green financing, as could the harmonisation of public monetary incentives, an increase in the provision of financial support from different industries, governmental organizations aligning their financial decisions that is consistent with the environmental aspect of the SDGs, an expansion in the investment of clean and environmentally friendly technologies, financing for eco-friendly economies based on natural resources and those based on climate change, and an increase in the utilization of green assets.

Going beyond climate finance, green finance encompasses a broad range of activities. These activities involve financing green investments from both the public and private sectors, facilitating the funding of government policies that promote the implementation of approaches to prevent environmental damage, and featuring components of the financial sector that specialize in green investments, such as green bonds, together with the legal and policy structure terms that govern them (Lindenberg, 2014). With a view to cutting back on greenhouse gas emissions and the damage they can cause to human health and secure a sustainable environment, green financing is indispensable for the funding of green and renewable energy advancements, as well as for creating climate-resilient infrastructure in cities. Many SDGs are linked either directly or indirectly with boosting climate finance, green finance, carbon free and clean energy activities (Sachs et al., 2019). To realize the objectives of sustainable development that factor in environmental development, investing in green finance is imperative. Therefore, the concept of equitable green development can be realized through inclusive green financing, as it necessitates financial institutions to offer green services in savings, loans, insurance, remittances, and modern digital methods to support people dealing with an unpredictable climate. (Desalegn & Tangl, 2022).

The banking sector has placed significant emphasis on green finance in light of various initiatives to safeguard banks as well as society as a whole against unforeseeable potential economic difficulties posed by social unrest, corporate scandals, and unanticipated global financial happenings (Ziolo et al., 2019). Globally significant central banks and participants in the banking industry made commitments to assist the promotion of environmentally friendly financial products at the Paris "One Planet Summit" in December 2017 (Kim, 2017). In the corporate sector, green finance is becoming more and more common. To ensure compliance with the many environmental requirements and industry best practices, firms from diverse industries are embracing sustainability. For instance, the adoption of renewable energy sources by industrial enterprises is a result of the majority of global regulations requiring less use of fossil fuels. Furthermore, financial lenders are willing to extend aid to these companies in exchange for the addition of hazard assessment and return on eco-friendly investment in their annual financial statements (Al-Sheryani & Nobanee, 2020).

Green finance aims to bring about a green economy where the industries that receive funding are expected to reduce their carbon output significantly. The green economy offers three advantages. First, the expansion of green finance brings to the forefront the importance of corporate governance factors.

Second, by encouraging producers and consumers to switch to green energy, the green economy raises environmental consciousness and guarantees environmental protection. Third, green financial development may effectively reduce overcapacity in traditional industries, optimize the supply structure of production elements, and foster economic change (Bergset, 2015). To deliver a range of financial products and services that generate an attractive return and are in line with the environment, green finance needs to tap into traditional capital markets (Sharma et al., 2021). This has led to the emergence of new financial tools, such as green bonds and carbon market instruments, along with new financial entities, for example green banks and green funds, to meet the growing need for green finance (Lee, 2020).

Due to the substantial initial capital expenditure and lengthy return on investment timeline, the environmental protection industry should have a distinct funding avenue. Therefore, in order to effectively address the funding crunch that the government faces, the relevant policies must first identify sources of funding that align with the term structures of projects; second, the pertinent subjects can issue financial derivatives to alter the term structures of projects; and finally, the pertinent policies should improve the activity of the green finance market by establishing ecological finance, building a market for climate derivatives, and creating other secondary financial markets (Wang & Zhi, 2016). In order to reduce the uncertainty connected to green finance, the implementation of green credit guarantee systems can be beneficial, as the government will be responsible for some of the potential risks. Profiting from large-scale green energy initiatives can be made more feasible for investors through the provision of some of the tax gains generated by the indirect economic benefits of supplying renewable power. The introduction of greater visibility and reviewability through a combination of the Hometown Investment Trust Fund (HIT) and Distributed Ledger Technologies (DLT) could potentially expand the pool of investors and, thereby, decrease the risk involved with investing in smaller-scale green initiatives. (Taghizadeh-Hesary & Yoshino, 2019).

Green finance serves to strengthen organizations and initiatives that are beneficial to the environment, thus improving the environmental conditions. For instance, the idea of green credit has been included into banks' loan approval processes, which has greatly decreased the ability of high-pollution firms to obtain finance (Liu et al., 2019). Green bond issuance benefits shareholders, which will encourage companies to participate in green initiatives and meet their carbon reduction goals (Tang & Zhang, 2018). Due to the government's encouraging green finance regulations, expenditure in renewable energy sector could increase (Romano et al., 2017). Central banks have a great deal of authority over money, credit, and the financial sector, which gives them the power to foster the growth of green finance models and urge financial establishments to properly consider environmental and carbon risks when pricing. It is of the utmost importance to consider the means through which central banks and other associated financial regulatory entities can oversee environmental risk and promote sustainable finance by way of financial governance regulations (Dikau & Volz, 2018).

RESEARCH METHODOLOGY

The use of bibliometric analysis by the researchers enabled them to achieve the study's aim. Pritchard (1969) was the first person to utilise it, and since then, it has garnered widespread appeal as a tool to assist quantitative analysis in better comprehending the literature. Previous research (Cobo et al., 2011; Ansari and Kant, 2017) has regularly used this analytic technique to illustrate and highlight key characteristics (country, institutes/institutions, researchers/authors, publications, etc.) in a variety of academic themes. The bibliometric process is broken down into the following phases, which are followed by this research (Capobianco-Uriarte et al., 2019). These processes include establishing the scope of the research, choosing a database, choosing a search phrase, applying codes to the chosen material, and finally, analysing the data that has been gathered up to this point. When evaluating the academic output of an author, a number of other metrics may be used; nonetheless, the total number of papers published, and the overall number of articles published over a certain time period are the ones that are used the most often. There are measures that may be used to evaluate the volume of publications that are published. It takes into account the overall number of citations, the average number of citations per piece of work, as well as the influence of the journals in which the publications are published. When doing a bibliometric analysis of the manuscripts, all of these factors should be taken into consideration. Some of the most important studies include types of research like bibliographic coupling, co-citation, and the co-occurrence of important phrases. After that, a comprehensive discussion has been had on each of the subsequent topics (Boyack & Klavans, 2010; Zupic & Ater, 2015; Merigó et al., 2018): The term "bibliographic coupling" pertains to "a common reference between two papers." For illustration, the fact that document A is referenced in papers B and C is evidence that the publications are coupled/connected bibliographically. Another research found Kessler (1963) discovered that the strength of this relationship increased proportionately with the number of common references that were included. A "co-citation" occurs when a single piece of writing makes reference to more than one other article. Co-citation is the term used to describe situations such as when papers A and C are both referenced in the same paper (Small, 1973). Co-authorship is a word referring to articles that contain more than one author, which allows for the recognition of scientific collaboration (Merigó et al., 2018). Co-authorship is a term that refers to papers that include more than one author. The researchers conducted bibliometric analysis based on a variety of criteria, including topics, authors, countries or regions, institutions, and more (Bonilla et al., 2015; Liao et al., 2018; Cancino et al., 2018). Before going into the intricacies, we'd like to display how we got our search started. We built on studies after developing the parameters of green/sustainable finance based on key research. We began our analysis by using the phrases "green finance" and "sustainability," which are pre-defined keywords obtained from the titles, abstracts, and keywords of papers published between 2000 and 2022. Because there is no clear conceptual definition of green finance, we focus on keywords: green finance, climate finance, carbon finance and sustainability. We also include a variety of terms to improve the coverage of relevant material, green investment/green bond are used in addition to the above three terms. We retrieve three eighty-two documents from the database after entering this keyword. Then we chose 'articles,' 'English language,' from the SCOPUS. Finally, we omitted conference proceedings and other materials from our study. To filter out unsuitable articles, we go over each one's title and abstract by manually. In the end, we decided to do more research on 349 of the articles. The material that is specific to these articles is obtained in text format and then downloaded to be connected to the VOSviewer in order to undergo further analysis based on a variety of parameters (Eck and Waltman, 2017) discussed in earlier section. The VOSviewer is an advanced programme that may be used to describe, envision, and find diverse research maps. Furthermore, in order to help analysis and interpretation, diagrams that illustrate the connections between countries, organisations, journals, authors, and terms are also presented (Castillo-Vergara et al., 2018).

Figure 1. Outline of research

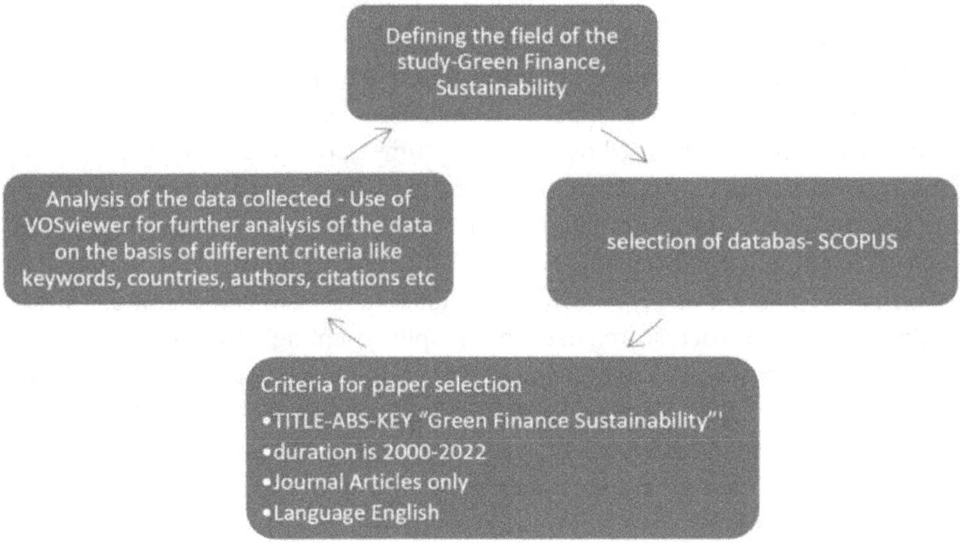

RESULTS AND INTERPRETATIONS

Our bibliometric investigation will concentrate on major areas like, Which journals have these papers been published in? What is the country of origin of the writers? What are the primary interests of these research (as determined by keyword analysis)? In what ways are these papers referenced in the literature?

NUMBER OF PUBLICATIONS EVERY YEAR

Figure 2 shows the number of papers published between 2000 and 2022. Results from Figure 1 show an increasing rate of publications over the study period, indicating that academics are becoming more interested in the research topic. From 2015, a significant rise in the number of publications has been observed, and this is due to the Paris Agreement. Green finance became a popular area of research, and studies on it started flourishing. According to an analysis of the amount of published works, 2022 is the most efficient year, with 147 papers, followed by 2021 with 71 papers and 2020 with 37 papers. With one paper in 2000 to 147 papers in 2022, the research in this area has grown enormously.

Figure 2. Publications on green finance

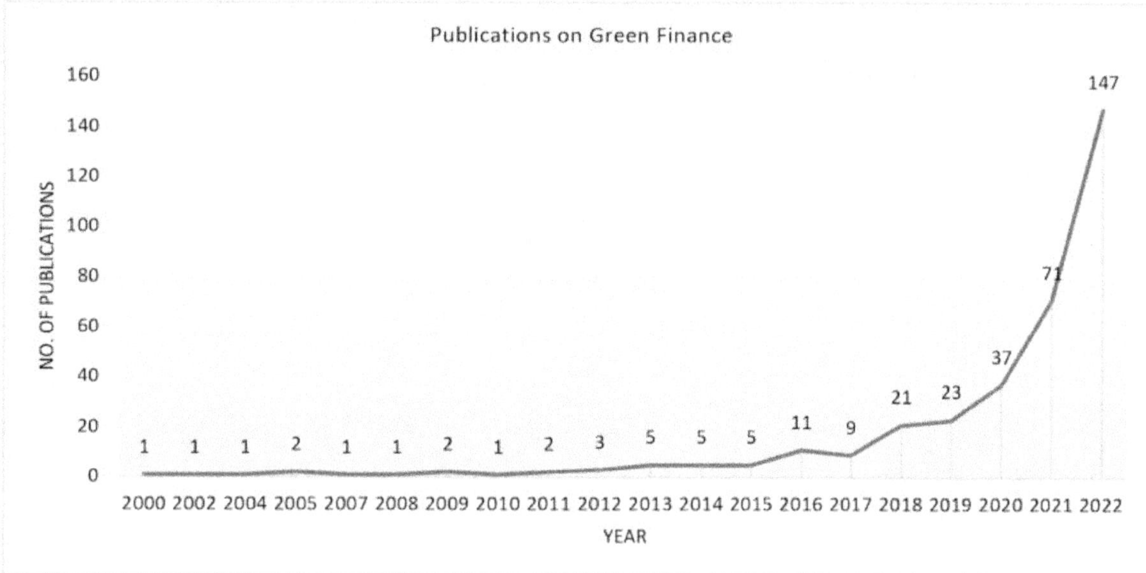

TOP LEADING JOURNALS CONTRIBUTING TO GREEN FINANCE RESEARCH

The allocation of journals that published more green finance research is an important part of the analysis. Table 1 lists the journals that publish research on green finance, and journals with up to five or more published papers are selected as samples. Sustainability Switzerland is the leading journal in the field of green finance research, with 37 papers published. This also indicates that Sustainability Switzerland is the author's favored journal for publishing their articles on green finance. The Journal of Cleaner Production is second, with 18 papers, and Environmental Science and Pollution Research is third, with

Table 1. Top leading journals contributing to green finance researches

Source Title	Number of Published Papers	Citations
Sustainability Switzerland	37	364
Journal Of Cleaner Production	18	810
Environmental Science And Pollution Research	14	212
Energy Economics	9	86
Resources Policy	9	72
Journal Of Sustainable Finance And Investment	8	90
Frontiers In Environmental Science	7	41
Climate Policy	6	52
Economic Research Ekonomska Istrazivanja	6	22
Energies	5	8
Energy Policy	5	386
Environment Development And Sustainability	5	21
International Journal Of Environmental Research And Public Health	5	61
Journal Of Environmental Management	5	233
Renewable Energy	5	29
Technological Forecasting And Social Change	5	131

Figure 3. Visualization of citation analysis of top journals

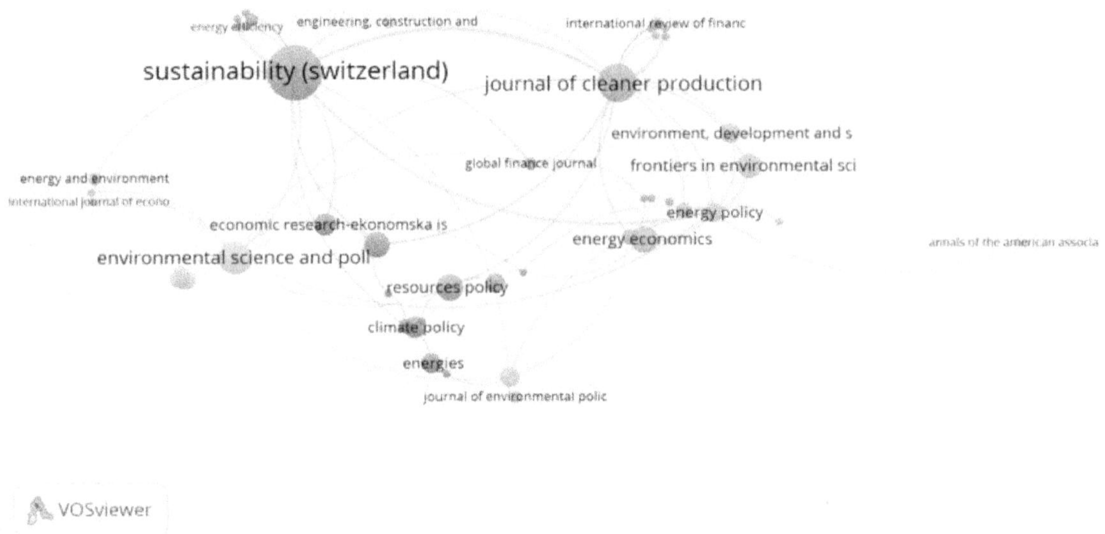

14 articles. When compared to other journals, the top 3 journals published more than 10 publications on green finance. The Journal of Cleaner Production has published 18 papers, but it has received 810 citations, meaning that the quality of the papers produced in this journal is significantly higher than that of Sustainability Switzerland. Several journals publishing research on Energy, Climate, and the Environment reached the list.

Figure 3 depicts the citation analysis of the top journals that publish papers on green finance. The results are obtained from a total of 187 sources in the database, with only 77 documents showing a citation relationship. The analysis shows that Sustainability Switzerland, Journal of Cleaner Production, and Environmental Science and Pollution Research are the three leading journals with effective citation networks.

PARTICIPATION OF COUNTRIES IN RESEARCH ON GREEN FINANCE

The participation of countries in green finance initiatives is particularly valuable in examining the regional division of green finance research. Examining a nation's involvement in green finance can indicate the state of progress in green finance in the nation's financial systems. Various nations contribute to green finance, which is why Figure 3 represents the top ten countries where substantial green finance research is published across the sample period between 2000 and 2022. Figure 4 indicates that China is the most involved nation, with 110 publications, indicating that China places a high priority on green finance research. The United Kingdom ranks second with 44 journals, while the United States ranks third with 34 journals. Over half of all publications come from the top three nations. Pakistan and Italy are two more countries that have made significant contributions to green finance research. India also reached the top 10 with 13 publications. Asian countries such as China, Pakistan, India, and Malaysia lead major studies on green finance from a continental perspective. European countries such as the United Kingdom,

Figure 4. Participation of countries in research on green finance

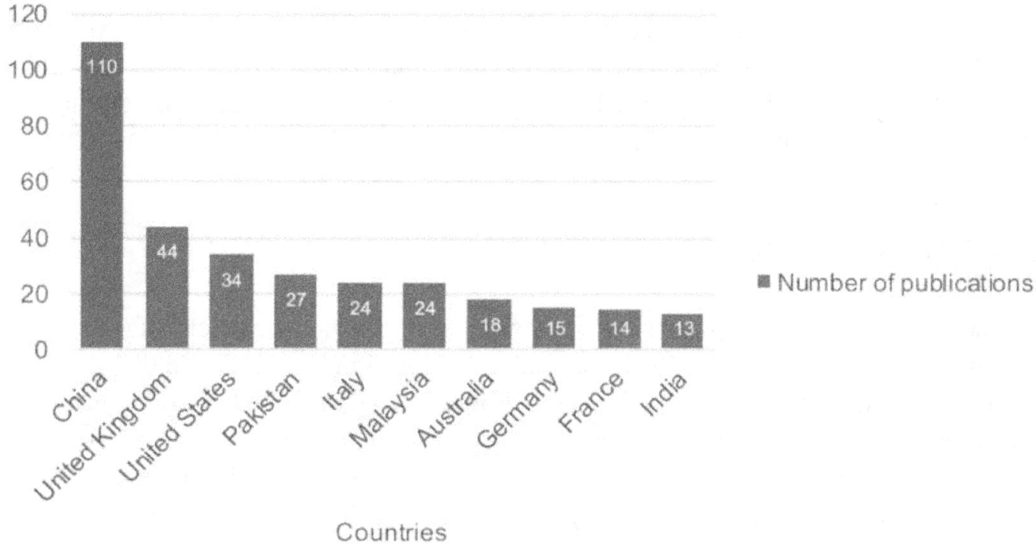

Italy, France, and Germany are ranked second, while African countries such as Zimbabwe, Kenya, and Nigeria published only a few documents and contributed very little.

It is intriguing to discover how the authors of various countries that are involved in green finance research are connected. The co-authorship analysis reveals a network of collaboration between authors from various countries to advance green finance research. Figure 5 shows the co-authorship connection

Figure 5. Co-authorship between countries

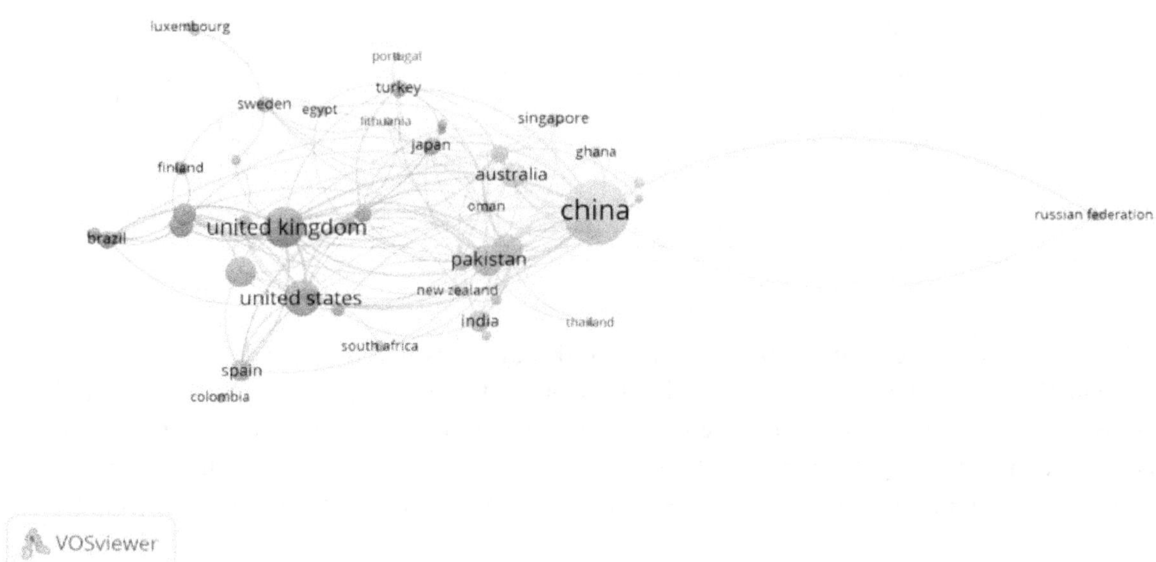

among the authors from various countries. The criteria for a country's minimum number of documents are considered to be two, and a total of 50 countries are connected in terms of co-authorship. The findings demonstrate the interconnections between authors from diverse nations, displayed in a range of different colours. China stands out for its extensive collaborations when it comes to co-authorship with other nations like the United Kingdom, the United States, Brazil, France, and Italy. Authors from India and Pakistan are also actively participating.

ANALYSIS OF KEYWORDS

Keyword analysis assists in the detailed understanding of green finance by describing the key terms most commonly used in research. Keyword analysis can be used to find similarities in the literature. The top 10 keywords and their frequencies are displayed in Table 2. The top three keywords that are frequently used in the journals are Sustainability, Sustainable Development, and Finance, which expressly indicate "green finance" as the acquisition of finance for sustainable development. Furthermore, China is ranked fifth, indicating that it is a leading country in green finance and has published numerous studies on the subject. The keywords, such as Investments, Climate Change, and Green Economy, reveal that in order to tackle the challenges posed by climate change, green finance necessitates both substantial expenditure and a transition to a green economy.

Table 2. Top 10 keywords

Keywords	Number of Occurencies
Sustainability	161
Sustainable Development	119
Finance	102
Green Finance	77
China	47
Environmental Economics	42
Investments	40
Climate Change	39
Green Economy	37
Sustainable Finance	32

Figure 6 depicts a graphical representation of all keywords found in the data set. For the purpose of conducting the analysis, it is established to have at least 10 occurrences of a given keyword, and 52 keywords out of 2249 met the requirement. The analysis reveals that, in addition to the major keywords displayed in Table 2, keywords like banking and green bonds shown in Figure 5 highlight the fact that several studies on the contribution of banks to the development of green finance have been done.

Figure 6. Visualization of co-occurrence analysis including all keywords

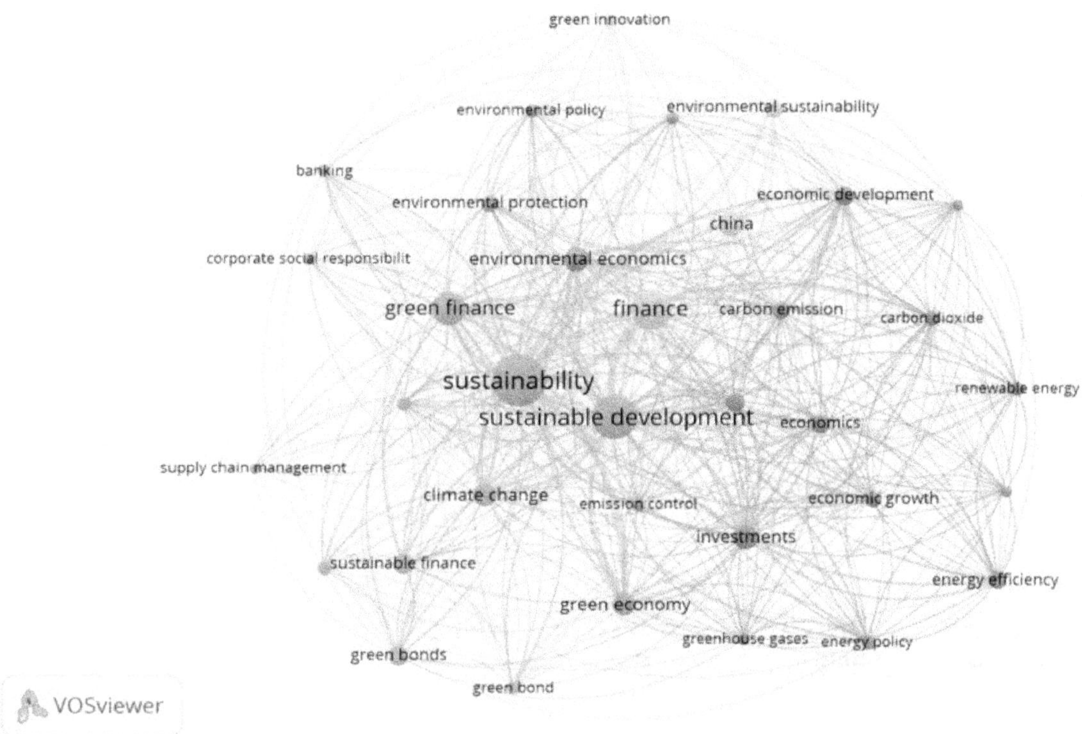

MAIN SUBJECT AREAS INVOLVED IN GREEN FINANCE PUBLICATION

Figure 7 depicts the subject areas that frequently publish papers on green finance. The top three subject areas constantly contributing research on green finance are Environmental Science, Social Sciences, and Energy. It portrays the role that energy, social science, and the environment play in green finance. Other subject areas, such as economics and finance, as well as business management and accounting, are collaborating on green finance studies from an economic, managerial, and business standpoint.

Figure 7. Main subject areas involved in green finance publication

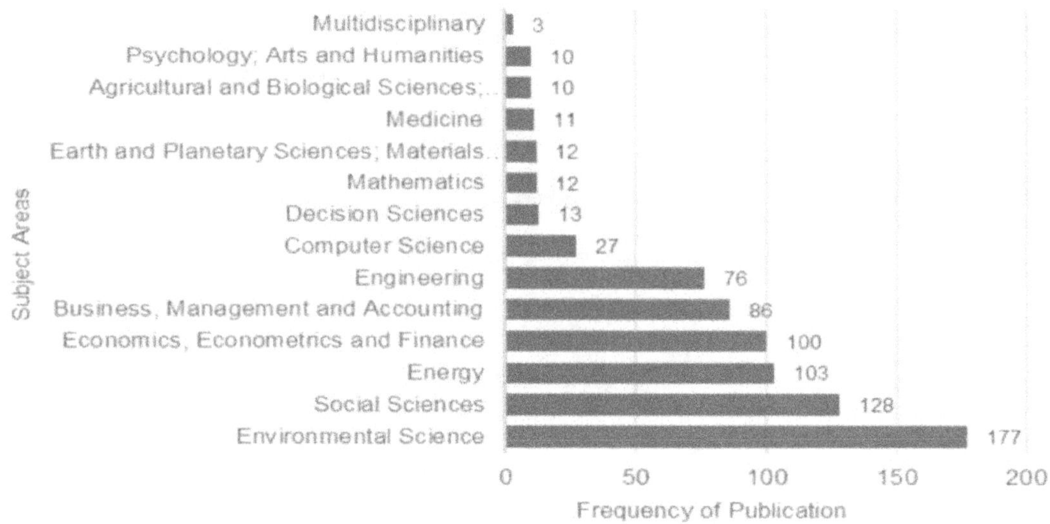

TOP ORGANIZATIONS THAT HAVE PUBLISHED RESEARCH ON GREEN FINANCE

Table 3 shows the top 20 organizations with at least ten citations in the specified research area over the years. According to the analysis, Capital University of Economics and Business in China is a top-ranked institution with two documents and 231 citations. The University of Wah of Pakistan ranks second with three documents and 170 citations, and King Saud University of Saudi Arabia ranks third with two documents and 127 citations. Capital University of Economics and Business obtained a much higher citation than the University of Wah. This shows that the research conducted by the institution has been frequently cited, indicating their influence in the domain of green finance. The findings indicate that Asian institutions predominate in the domain of green finance research, with institutes from China and Pakistan playing a leading role.

Table 3. Top organizations that have published research on green finance

Organization	Documents	Citations
School of Economics, Capital University of Economics and Business, Beijing, 100070, China	2	231
Department of Economics, University of Wah, Quaid Avenue, Wah Cantt, Pakistan	3	170
Department of Management, College of Business Administration, King Saud University, Riyadh, Saudi Arabia	2	127
Transportation Engineering College, Dalian Maritime University, Dalian, China	3	76
School of Economics and Management, University of Chinese Academy of Sciences, Haidian District, Beijing, 100190, China	2	55
Faculty of Business, Sohar University, Sohar, Oman	2	49
School of Management and Economics, Beijing Institute of Technology, Beijing, 100081, China	2	42
Stockholm Environment Institute, Stockholm, Sweden	2	37
Stockholm Sustainable Finance Centre, Stockholm, Sweden	2	37
Kubeac, University of Management & Technology, Sialkot Campus, Pakistan	2	35
Faculty of Business, Yasar University, Turkey	2	28
German Development Institute, Bonn, Germany	2	28
School of Economics and Management, Shaanxi University of Science and Technology (sust), Weiyang University Park, Weiyang District, Shaanxi, Xi'an, 7100	2	23
School of Management, Forman Christian College (A Chartered University), Lahore, Pakistan	2	22
School of Finance and Accounting, Fuzhou University of International Studies and Trade, Fujian, China	2	13
School of Finance and Trade, Wenzhou Business College, Wenzhou, 325035, China	2	13
Department of Marketing and Supply Chain Management, University of Cape Coast, Cape Coast, Ghana	2	12
School of Management, Shenyang University of Technology, Shenyang, China	2	11
Unisa Business, University of South Australia, Adelaide, Australia	2	11
School of Economics, Qingdao University, China	2	10

CITATION ANALYSIS OF THE HIGHLY CITED ARTICLES AND THE MOST ACTIVE AUTHORS

Citation analysis is a helpful technique to evaluate the value and reliability of a particular article and its writer by taking into account the amount of times the paper or author has been mentioned in other works. A higher number of citations implies that the research is extremely reliable. We used citation analysis on documents and authors to assess the influence of certain articles and authors on green finance research. The top 10 articles and authors in our sample with the most citations are listed in Table 4. The results indicate that 192 studies cited a paper titled "Public spending and green economic growth in BRI region: Mediating role of green financing." The findings reinforce the importance of public spending on green energy as a means of advancing green finance. The majority of the articles have more than 50 citations, indicating that papers in green finance are frequently cited. We also identified the authors who are most actively contributing to the studies using the VOS-viewer software. Figure 7 depicts the mapping of the most cited authors.

Table 4. Highly cited articles and authors

Author	Article Title	Citations
Zhang D., Mohsin M., Rasheed A.K., Chang Y., Taghizadeh-Hesary F.	Public spending and green economic growth in BRI region: Mediating role of green finance	192
Flammer C.	Corporate green bonds	139
Gianfrate G., Peri M.	The green advantage: Exploring the convenience of issuing green bonds	123
Nassani A.A., Aldakhil A.M., Qazi Abro M.M., Zaman K.	Environmental Kuznets curve among BRICS countries: Spot lightening finance, transport, energy and growth factors	114
Lenferink S., Tillema T., Arts J.	Towards sustainable infrastructure development through integrated contracts: Experiences with inclusiveness in Dutch infrastructure projects	100
Criscuolo C., Menon C.	Environmental policies and risk finance in the green sector: Cross-country evidence	91
Singal M.	The Link between Firm Financial Performance and Investment in Sustainability Initiatives	89
Newton P., Meyer D.	Exploring the attitudes-action gap in household resource consumption: Does "Environmental Lifestyle" segmentation align with consumer behaviour?	79
Tolliver C., Keeley A.R., Managi S.	Drivers of green bond market growth: The importance of Nationally Determined Contributions to the Paris Agreement and implications for sustainability	72
Ng T.H., Tao J.Y.	Bond financing for renewable energy in Asia	71
Falcone P.M., Morone P., Sica E.	Greening of the financial system and fuelling a sustainability transition: A discursive approach to assess landscape pressures on the Italian financial system	70

From the total of 349 documents in the database, 77 documents have a citation relationship. According to Figure 7, Zhang (2021a), Flammer (2021), and Gianfrate (2019) are the top three authors with the highest number of citations. Zhang (2021a) is the author with the most citations. The document set in this analysis has been divided into fourteen clusters of varying colors. The most cited authors are grouped and divided into clusters, and each cluster is linked with the others. The authors with the most citations dominate each cluster due to their strong networking connections with the other authors. The clusters reflect the interconnections between the most cited authors who have contributed to the area of green finance.

Figure 8. Mapping of most cited authors

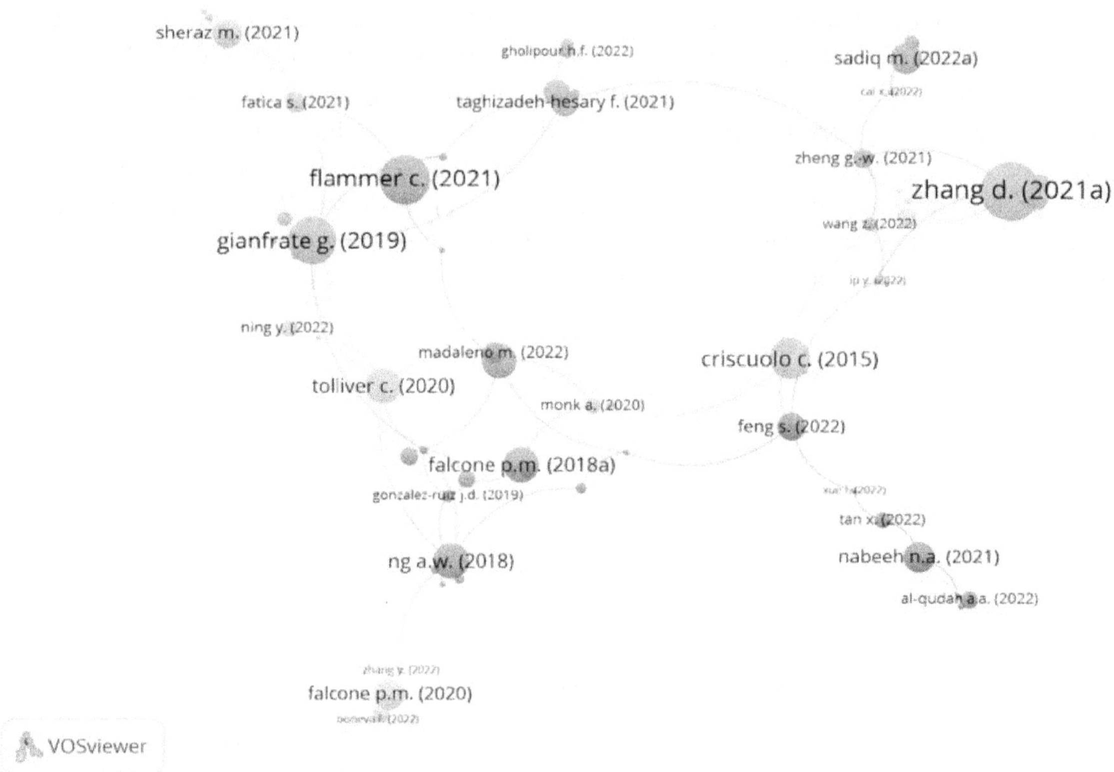

CLUSTER ANALYSIS

1. **Responsible Investment:** It looks into the strategies of investing that consider the impressions of a company's ESG elements. It helps in comprehending the correlation between the intentions of ESG and the decisions of investors when selecting portfolios. Moreover, it assesses if a company's ESG performance is conducive to steady growth.
2. **Green Bond:** An exhaustive evaluation of green bond initiatives that are designed to decrease greenhouse gas emissions and better the environment is being conducted. The risk-return assessment of green bond investments is essential for investors. Additionally, examination of the regulatory framework for green bonds and its effect on the growth of financial markets is also being undertaken.
3. **Low-Carbon Transition:** The emergence of the clean energy sector is playing an instrumental role in reducing the reliance on fossil fuels, while encouraging the adoption of more ecological sources of energy. The study looked into the effects of curtailing the subsidies for fossil fuels on

the uptake of low-carbon practices. The development of a low-carbon index has been formulated to minimize the use of fossil fuels and incentivize both domestic and international investments.

4. **Vulnerable Countries:** It evaluated climate financing commitments in nations that are particularly exposed to risk, making use of burden-sharing strategies. It gauged the variables that make it easier or more complicated for countries to secure and gain access to international bilateral adaptation assistance. It also determined the extent to which adaptation aid was customized to meet the requirements of the countries receiving it.
5. **Low-Carbon Investment:** It involves a series of studies to strengthen the reliability of investing in low-carbon solutions and evaluating the influence of these investments on the economy and society. It provides investors with a better comprehension of low-carbon investment prospects and encourages them to make educated choices. By utilizing a macroeconomic structure, studies evaluated the social and economic effects of transitioning to low-carbon investment opportunities.
6. **Business Model:** Research is conducted to evaluate if the strategies used by different organizations engaging in sustainable financial practices align with the accepted principles of a green business model.
7. **Financial Development:** It delves into the tie between financial growth and carbon dioxide emissions, particularly as it relates to accomplishing goals of sustainable development. The study evaluates the consequences of globalization, financial progression, and energy utilization on carbon dioxide emissions in Asian countries. The ambition is to comprehend the interdependence of economic, financial, and energy issues and their effects on carbon emissions.
8. **Supply Chain:** The subject of sustainability in the supply chain industry is explored. The research looked at the impact of green credit and trade credit financing on carbon emissions in the supply chain, as well as their effects on sustainable investments in various supply chain structures. Analysis was also conducted regarding the implications of low-carbon investment on the supply chain.
9. **Sustainable Financing:** An in-depth study into various approaches to financing with the purpose of achieving sustainability and shrinking inequality has been undertaken. The research into sustainable economic practices has gone through an extensive examination, as well as the challenges that come with its implementation.
10. **Environmental Investment:** This includes the connection between several elements and the amount of money invested in environmental efforts. It further looks into the effect of innovation on Chinese listed businesses environmental investments and how such investments affect financial performance.
11. **Green Credit Policy:** The study investigates the consequence of China's green credit policy on numerous aspects of the economy, such as investment and financing options, emissions of pollutants, and the green technology of different enterprises. Furthermore, the research assesses how this policy has an effect on the environmental quality of provinces.

CONCLUSION AND IMPLICATIONS

Over the course of the last several years, there has been a steady increase in the global impact of sustainable finance. The United Nations, the European Union, the United States of America, the United Kingdom, and a large number of other developed countries have, one after the other, released policies and initiatives to encourage the development of a sustainable society. Companies and investors are under increasing pressure to adopt more sustainable practises, and now is the moment to take advantage of this trend. There will be increasing pressure to adopt more environmentally friendly methods as the public becomes more concerned about the implications of climate change. The primary issues will be the same, that more private capital is corresponding to the requirements of developing countries and have the potential to create growth. These issues are pertinent to both private and public investments. This research paper used a bibliometric technique to give an outline of the existing situation of green finance literature. The study concludes that "Socially responsible investments, climate change, corporate social responsibility, green finance, carbon credits, and renewable energy" are some of the major topics today. Between the years 2000 and 2022, a noteworthy contribution to the academic basis of sustainable finance took place with numerous papers published on socially responsible investing. The study provided useful research insights by analyzing data on publications, countries, journals, keywords, subject areas, and organizations, as well as highly cited authors and papers. Visual illustrations have been used to explain the findings clearly and efficiently. Over the last few years, there has been a steady surge in the number of papers published in the field, displaying an intensified fascination with the subject. The majority of research in this field is primarily focused on a few main countries, with China, the United States, and the United Kingdom being the top contributors. The majority of articles can be found in the field's most prestigious journals, such as Sustainability Switzerland, The Journal of Cleaner Production, and Environmental Science and Pollution Research. The research also discovered that environmental science, social sciences, and energy are the most relevant subject areas for green finance. The analysis of keywords found that the most frequently used terms in the literature are "Sustainability," "Sustainable Development," and "Finance." The study also revealed that the most active organizations in green finance research are the University of Wah, the University of Science and Technology, and Dalian Maritime University. Further, the paper also identified a number of highly cited authors and articles on the subject, including authors such as Zhang d., Flammer c., and Gianfrate g., and papers such as "Public spending and green economic growth in BRI region". The most cited authors and articles found in this study are a useful resource for researchers interested in green finance.

Overall, this research paper offered a comprehensive analysis of the literature on green finance. The study's findings have meaningful implications for practitioners and academics working in this area, as well as for those wishing to learn more about the latest studies in this field. This research provides a more detailed understanding of the major countries and institutions contributing to green finance research, which could be useful for networking and collaboration. This study can provide useful insight into the current discrepancies in the domain of green finance and serve to uncover potential areas of exploration. By identifying these gaps, the researchers may focus their efforts on filling them to enhance our knowledge of green finance. By highlighting the key areas, authors, and papers that have been most impactful in shaping the current understanding of green finance, this research paper has presented a complete overview of the trends in the field of green finance.

FUTURE RESEARCH RECOMMENDATIONS

Further research on green finance can be conducted by evaluating the effectiveness of various policy instruments needed to promote green finance. During the study period, the hot research topics were responsible investment, green bonds, low-carbon transition, vulnerable countries, low-carbon investment, business model, financial development, supply chain, conventional investment dilemma, sustainable financing, environmental investment, and green credit policy. Green bonds, green finance, socially responsible mutual funds, and ESG investor preferences were the research topics of the publications with the biggest transformative potential. Further research can be done on these many fields to have more insights on the green finance.

Similarly, the impact of various regulations, tax incentives, and subsidies on the growth of green finance should be analyzed. Further research could be done to examine the performance of innovative financial instruments like green bonds and green funds in allocating capital towards environmentally sustainable developments. It is possible to leverage green bonds to take care of the extensive financial requirements for green and environment-friendly investments associated with the transformation of the real economy. Green bonds should be studied in terms of multiple markets (fiscal, carbon, renewable energy, eco-friendly stocks) and macroeconomic steadiness in different nations. To study Green Bonds, research by Boukhatem et al (2021) help in quantifying the parameters.

Enhance Company/corporate level green financing. Green finance injects financial resources into initiatives to protect the environment through various strategies such as borrowing, issuing bonds, investing, and releasing stocks. Company-led green environmental protection projects are increasing. Green innovation improves resource efficiency, business reputation, and financial success, Vasileiou et al. (2022), but corporate governance influences sustainability and environmental choices (Farza et. al. (2022). Thus, further research could be done to investigate how corporate governance affects green finance and how financial companies funded by the group promote it.

Subsequent studies in the area of green finance should focus on gauging the ecological effects of financial investments through the use of modern data analytics and machine learning techniques. Research could be carried out to identify potential obstacles that could impede the progression of green finance, such as insufficient knowledge or understanding among investors or a lack of information on a company's environmental performance. Further research can include comparisons of green finance trends and advancements across different nations.

LIMITATIONS OF THE STUDY

The scope of this study is restricted to the bibliometric data obtained from the Scopus database. The study relied on a limited data set because it excluded papers published outside of the Scopus database. This could imply that the study is missing crucial contributions from academics who may have published their work in other databases. Also, the study only looked at articles published between 2000 and 2022 and excluded studies published before that date. This could imply that the study ignored valuable ideas and perspectives from earlier research on green finance because it only focused on a specific time period.

REFERENCES

Akomea-Frimpong, I., Adeabah, D., Ofosu, D., & Tenakwah, E. J. (2021). A review of studies on green finance of banks, research gaps and future directions. *Journal of Sustainable Finance & Investment*, 1–24.

Al-SheryaniK.NobaneeH. (2020). Green Finance: A Mini-Review. Available at SSRN 3538696.

Ansari, Z., & Kant, R. (2016). A state-of-art literature review reflecting 15 years of focus on sustainable supply chain management. *Journal of Cleaner Production*, *142*, 2524–2543. Advance online publication. doi:10.1016/j.jclepro.2016.11.023

Ansari, Z. N., & Kant, R. (2017). Exploring the framework development status for sustainability in supply chain management: A systematic literature synthesis and future research directions. *Business Strategy and the Environment*, *26*(7), 873–892. Advance online publication. doi:10.1002/bse.1945

Bonilla, C. A., Merigó, J. M., & Torres-Abad, C. (2015). Economics in Latin America: A bibliometric analysis. *Scientometrics*, *105*(2), 1239–1252. doi:10.100711192-015-1747-7

Boukhatem, J., Ftiti, Z., & Sahut, J.-M. (2021). Bond market and macroeconomic stability in East Asia: A nonlinear causality analysis. *Annals of Operations Research*, *297*(1-2), 53–76. Advance online publication. doi:10.100710479-020-03519-6

Boyack, K. W., & Klavans, R. (2010). Co-Citation Analysis, Bibliographic Coupling, and Direct Citation: Which Citation Approach Represents the Research Front Most Accurately? *Journal of the American Society for Information Science and Technology*, *12*(61), 2389–2404. doi:10.1002/asi.21419

Cai, R., & Guo, J. (2021). Finance for the environment: A scientometrics analysis of green finance. *Mathematics*, *9*(13), 1537. doi:10.3390/math9131537

Cancino, C. A., Merigó, J. M., Torres, J. P., & Diaz, D. (2018). A bibliometric analysis of venture capital research. *Journal of Economics, Finance and Administrative Science*, *23*(45), 182–195. doi:10.1108/JEFAS-01-2018-0016

Capobianco-Uriarte, M. de las M., Casado-Belmonte, M. del P., Marín-Carrillo, G. M., & Terán-Yépez, E. (2019). A Bibliometric Analysis of International Competitiveness (1983–2017). *Sustainability (Basel)*, *11*(7), 1877. doi:10.3390u11071877

Castillo-Vergara, M., Alvarez-Marin, A., & Placencio-Hidalgo, D. (2018). A bibliometric analysis of creativity in the field of business economics. *Journal of Business Research*, *85*, 1–9. doi:10.1016/j.jbusres.2017.12.011

Cobo, M. J., López-Herrera, A. G., Herrera-Viedma, E., & Herrera, F. (2011). Science mapping software tools: Review, analysis, and cooperative study among tools. *Journal of the American Society for Information Science and Technology*, *62*(7), 1382–1402. doi:10.1002/asi.21525

Desalegn, G., & Tangl, A. (2022). Enhancing green finance for inclusive green growth: A systematic approach. *Sustainability (Basel)*, *14*(12), 7416. doi:10.3390u14127416

Falcone, P. M. (2020). Environmental regulation and green investments: The role of green finance. *International Journal of Green Economics*, *14*(2), 159–173. doi:10.1504/IJGE.2020.109735

Farza, K., Ftiti, Z., Hlioui, Z., Louhichi, W., & Omri, A. (2021). Does it pay to go green? The environmental innovation effect on corporate financial performance. *Journal of Environmental Management*, *300*, 113695. doi:10.1016/j.jenvman.2021.113695 PMID:34649325

Farza, K., Ftiti, Z., Hlioui, Z., Louhichi, W., & Omri, A. (2022). The Effect of Corporate Board Characteristics on Environmental Innovation. *Environmental Modeling and Assessment*, *27*(6), 1021–1042. doi:10.100710666-022-09836-3

Kessler, M. M. (1963). Bibliographic coupling between scientific articles. *American Documentation*, *24*, 123–131.

Lee, J. W. (2020). Green finance and sustainable development goals: The case of China. *Journal of Asian Finance Economics and Business*, *7*(7), 577–586. doi:10.13106/jafeb.2020.vol7.no7.577

Liao, H., Tang, M., Luo, L., Li, C., Chiclana, F., & Zeng, X. J. (2018). A bibliometric analysis and visualization of medical big data research. *Sustainability (Basel)*, *10*(1), 1–18. doi:10.3390u10010166

Liu, X., Zhan, F. B., Hong, S., Niu, B., & Liu, Y. (2012). A bibliometric study of earthquake research: 1900–2010. *Scientometrics*, *92*(3), 747–765. doi:10.100711192-011-0599-z

Mehta, K., Sharma, R., & Vyas, V. (2019). Efficiency and ranking of sustainability index of India using DEA-TOPSIS. *Journal of Indian Business Research*, *11*(2), 179–199. doi:10.1108/JIBR-02-2018-0057

Merigó, J. M., Pedrycz, W., Weber, R., & de la Sotta, C. (2018). Fifty years of Information Sciences: A bibliometric overview. *Information Sciences*, *432*, 245–268. doi:10.1016/j.ins.2017.11.054

Pritchard, A. (1969). Statistical Bibliography or Bibliometrics? *The Journal of Documentation*, *25*, 348–349.

Sachs, J. D., Woo, W. T., Yoshino, N., & Taghizadeh-Hesary, F. (2019). Importance of green finance for achieving sustainable development goals and energy security. In *Handbook of Green Finance* (pp. 3–12). Springer. doi:10.1007/978-981-13-0227-5_13

Sharma, R., Mehta, K., & Sharma, O. (2021). Exploring Deep Learning to Determine the Optimal Environment for Stock Prediction Analysis. *2021 International Conference on Computational Performance Evaluation,* ComPE 2021, 148–152. 10.1109/ComPE53109.2021.9752138

Sharma, R., Mehta, K., & Vyas, V. (2020). Responsible Investing: A Study on Non-Economic Goals and Investors' Characteristics. *Applied Finance Letters, 9*(SI), 63-78. doi:10.24135/afl.v9i2.245

Small, H. (1973). Co-citation in the scientific literature: A new measure of the relationship between two documents. *Journal of the American Society for Information Science*, *24*(4), 265–269. doi:10.1002/asi.4630240406

Taghizadeh-Hesary, F., & Yoshino, N. (2019). The way to induce private participation in green finance and investment. *Finance Research Letters*, *31*, 98–103. doi:10.1016/j.frl.2019.04.016

Van Eck, N. J., & Waltman, L. (2010). Software survey: VOSviewer, a computer program for bibliometric mapping. *Scientometrics*, *84*(2), 523–538. doi:10.100711192-009-0146-3 PMID:20585380

van Eck, N. J., & Waltman, L. (2017). Citation-based clustering of publications using CitNetExplorer and VOSviewer. *Scientometrics*, *111*(2), 1053–1070. doi:10.100711192-017-2300-7 PMID:28490825

Vasileiou, E., Georgantzis, N., Attanasi, G., & Llerena, P. (2022). Green innovation and financial performance: A study on Italian firms. *Research Policy*, *51*(6), 104530. doi:10.1016/j.respol.2022.104530

Vyas, V., Mehta, K., & Sharma, R. (2020). Investigating socially responsible investing behaviour of Indian investors using structural equation modelling. *Journal of Sustainable Finance & Investment*, •••, 1–23. doi:10.1080/20430795.2020.1790958

Vyas, V., Mehta, K., & Sharma, R. (2023). The nexus between toxic-air pollution, health expenditure, and economic growth: An empirical study using ARDL. *International Review of Economics & Finance*, *84*, 154–166. doi:10.1016/j.iref.2022.11.017

Wang, M., Li, X., & Wang, S. (2021). Discovering research trends and opportunities of green finance and energy policy: A data-driven scientometric analysis. *Energy Policy*, *154*, 112295. doi:10.1016/j.enpol.2021.112295

Wang, Y., & Zhi, Q. (2016). The role of green finance in environmental protection: Two aspects of market mechanism and policies. *Energy Procedia*, *104*, 311–316. doi:10.1016/j.egypro.2016.12.053

Yu, C. H., Wu, X., Zhang, D., Chen, S., & Zhao, J. (2021). Demand for green finance: Resolving financing constraints on green innovation in China. *Energy Policy*, *153*, 112255. doi:10.1016/j.enpol.2021.112255

Zhang, D., Zhang, Z., & Managi, S. (2019). A bibliometric analysis on green finance: Current status, development, and future directions. *Finance Research Letters*, *29*, 425–430. doi:10.1016/j.frl.2019.02.003

Zhou, X., Tang, X., & Zhang, R. (2020). Impact of green finance on economic development and environmental quality: A study based on provincial panel data from China. *Environmental Science and Pollution Research International*, *27*(16), 19915–19932. doi:10.100711356-020-08383-2 PMID:32232752

Zupic, I., & Čater, T. (2015). Bibliometric methods in management and organization. *Organizational Research Methods*, *18*(3), 429–472. doi:10.1177/1094428114562629

Chapter 10
Using eNaira CBDC to Solve Economic Problems in Nigeria

Peterson K. Ozili
https://orcid.org/0000-0001-6292-1161
Central Bank of Nigeria, Nigeria

ABSTRACT

This chapter discusses how the eNaira central bank digital currency (CBDC) might be used to solve some economic problems in Nigeria. It presents the eNaira as a payment option, a monetary policy tool, and a financial stability tool to solve some economic problems in Nigeria. The author shows that the eNaira can be instrumental in solving fiscal revenue challenges, controlling inflation, increasing foreign exchange accretion, managing exchange rate, addressing food insecurity, reducing financial stability risks, reducing poverty level, and recovering from a recession. The implication is that the eNaira can support the monetary, fiscal, and regulatory authorities in preserving macroeconomic stability. However, a trade-off might arise among policy objectives if the eNaira cannot achieve multiple policy objectives at the same time.

INTRODUCTION

This paper discusses how the eNaira central bank digital currency (CBDC) might be used to solve some economic problems in Nigeria.

The recent COVID-19 pandemic plunged many countries into a recession including Nigeria. The pandemic led to growing interest in private digital currencies which many individuals used as safe haven assets during the pandemic. This trend led central banks around the world to monitor the developments in private digital currencies and study their economic implications.

Many central banks have recently gained some interest in a digital currency that is issued by the central bank, commonly known as a central bank digital currency (CBDC). A CBDC is the digital equivalent of physical money and is a liability of the central bank. A CBDC has the potential to enlarge access to central bank reserves so that both commercial banks and the general public would be able to use central bank money to transact and save (Minesso, et al, 2022). A BIS survey suggests that 80 percent of central

DOI: 10.4018/978-1-6684-8624-5.ch010

banks around the world are working on a CBDC (Barontini and Holden, 2019). Only few countries have issued a CBDC, such as Nigeria and the Bahamas, while other countries are still researching CBDCs to determine the economic benefits, risks and the best use case of a CBDC.

The motivations for the growing interest in CBDC are due to the need to ensure adequate central bank money for the public; preserve central bank seigniorage revenue; reduce the lower bound on interest rates; support unconventional monetary policy; reduce financial stability risks; increase contestability in payments; promote financial inclusion; inhibit criminal activity associated with physical cash; and to counteract the growing influence of private digital currencies in the domestic economy (Engert and Fung, 2017; Barontini and Holden, 2019; Obiora, 2022).

These motivations, although relevant to most countries, are not enough reasons for a central bank to issue a CBDC in a country. Each central bank need to identify the domestic macroeconomic and financial implications of issuing a CBDC, and also identify a pressing economic need or problem which a CBDC can help to solve. Therefore, an important question that arises for central banks in developing countries and poor countries is whether a CBDC can assist in solving their most pressing economic challenges.

In this article, I focus on Nigeria, and discuss how the eNaira can be used to solve some economic problems in Nigeria. The discussion in the article contribute to the monetary economics literature that examine the economic implications of a CBDC. This discussion paper contributes to existing studies that examine the monetary and financial implications of issuing a CBDC such as Bindseil (2019), Kumhof and Noone (2021), Davoodalhosseini (2022), and Agur, Ari and Dell'Ariccia (2022). This study also contributes to on-going policy debates about country-specific CBDC design and implementation, and how it affects the economy.

The rest of the paper is organised as follows. Section 2 presents the literature review. Section 3 describes how the eNaira can solve a number of economic problems such as the fiscal revenue challenges, inflation, economic recession, foreign exchange accretion, food insecurity, financial instability, and rising poverty. Section 4 presents the conclusion of the study.

LITERATURE REVIEW

Several studies examine how central bank digital currencies can be used to solve some economic problems. But these studies have not analysed how the eNaira CBDC can be used to solve economic problems in Nigeria. Bordo and Levin (2017) show that a central bank digital currency (CBDC) can transform the monetary system and facilitate the transparent conduct of monetary policy by serving as a practically costless medium of exchange, secure store of value, and stable unit of account. They emphasize that, to achieve these benefits, the CBDC should be account-based and interest-bearing in order for CBDCs to bring price stability benefits. Kwon, Lee and Park (2022) show that a CBDC can significantly reduce tax evasion which is carried out in cash transactions. CBDCs will improve welfare by discouraging tax evasion and rewarding tax payments, but this beneficial effect of the CBDC depends on whether the central bank is permitted to perform a fiscal role in the economy. Ozili (2023a) shows that the Nigeria CBDC can increase financial inclusion by (i) offering an easy account opening process for greater financial inclusion, (ii) enabling digital access to diverse financial services in the financial system, (iii) offering lower cost of financial products and services, (iv) eliminating excessive bank charges that causes banked adults to exit the formal financial sector, and (v) attracting people who have lost confidence in banks. Ozili (2023b) shows that CBDCs have the potential to preserve financial stability because central banks will not issue a CBDC if it limits central banks' ability to achieve their core mandate which includes monetary stability, financial stability and price stability; therefore, the issuance of a CBDC by a central bank would promote financial stability or, at least, the CBDC will not pose any material risks to financial stability.

SOLVING NIGERIA'S ECONOMIC PROBLEMS USING THE ENAIRA

Below are some economic problems that the eNaira can assist in solving.

Fiscal Revenue Challenges

Nigeria's Revenue Problem

Nigeria has a significant revenue problem, not a debt problem. Nigeria's revenue is far smaller than its true potentials. The tax-to-GDP ratio in Nigeria has been decreasing in the last 10 years. The tax-to-GDP ratio in Nigeria was 7.3 percent in 2010 and further decreased to 6.3 percent in 2020, making Nigeria's revenue-GDP ratio one of the lowest in the world.

Nigeria's revenue is low because of many self-inflicted wounds ranging from highly organized oil theft to significant vandalism. As a result, Nigeria's crude oil production fell from about 2.4 million metric tons in 2012 to less than 1.5 million metric tons in 2021. This has meant that Nigeria's share of crude oil exports decreased from 5.68 percent of global crude oil exports in 2012 to 4.68 percent in 2020. Whilst Nigeria earned US$89.8 billion from crude oil sales in 2012, it only earned US$30 billion in 2020. Keeping in mind that crude oil sales accounts for a vast majority of Nigeria's revenues, it is easy to see how devastating a 67 percent decline (from US$89.8 bn to US$30 bn) in oil revenues can be to the fiscal health of Nigeria.

Although tax collection has doubled, and tax administration has improved in the last couple of years, some improvements are still very much needed. For example, Nigeria's VAT rate at 7.5 percent is still amongst the lowest in the world. Nigeria's VAT rate is less than half of the average VAT rate in the World at 15.3 percent and in the Africa region at 15.4 percent. Yet, efforts to increase Nigeria's VAT rate to a double-digit rate has received fierce resistance by many.

There is a need to find alternative ways to generate more revenue for Nigeria which can be collected using the eNaira to avoid revenue leakages. The fiscal authorities can take advantage of the eNaira to rebuild Nigeria's fiscal buffers and change Nigeria's fiscal fortunes.

For example, Nigeria can increase revenue by introducing a hotel surcharge that should be paid to the government via the eNaira. The government can generate huge sums from imposing a surcharge for hotel accommodations that will be paid to the government through the eNaira. Assuming there are 500 hotels with an average of 40 rooms each in Abuja, and a room rate of N60,000 per night with an occupancy rate of 70 percent per annum, it means that the government can generate over N15 billion annually from this surcharge alone through CBDC payment. Note too that this idea does not affect the poor and vulnerable in Nigeria, given the fact that most people who stay in hotels are well-off and rich people.

The government can also introduce Federal property taxes in the FCT and collect the taxes using the eNaira. The government can achieve this by segregating the city into towns and exempt places where the median income is low. For example, property taxes can only be collectible in Wuse, Maitama, Gwarinpa,

Maitama, Asokoro, Central Area, and the likes, whereas Kubwa, Kuje, Lugbe, Maraba and the likes can be exempted. In doing so, the government only tax those who can afford it and exempt the poor. Given the penchant for hiding the identity of home owners in Abuja, the government can simply give buildings unique identities/code, and allow CBDC payments to be done using the building code despite the concealed ownership. At this stage, all that the government want is revenue payment through CBDC payment. The government can deal with ownership later.

Tax Administration and Collection Using CBDC

The low tax revenue in Nigeria is also caused by poor tax administration and tax evasion which deprives the Federal Government of the tax revenue it needs to fund the Federal Budget (Gurama et al, 2015). Many research studies have associated tax revenue problems to the physical properties of cash (Chodorow-Reich et al, 2020; Chan et al, 2022). Existing research also show evidence that tax evasion and tax fraud are easier to carry out in a cash-based economy like Nigeria, and these practices are more rampant with informal taxes which are often collected in the form of cash (Otusanya, 2011; Onyeka and Nwankwo, 2016).

There is a need to devise an alternative way to collect and administer taxes in Nigeria. A possible alternative is to use the eNaira to collect taxes in a more efficient manner. A central bank digital currency has a digital recordkeeping technology that can help the tax authorities to better monitor taxpayers' transactions to combat tax evasion and fraud with a view to increase tax revenue. When the eNaira is deployed for tax collection purposes, eNaira payments made for a certain amount will be recorded on an electronic medium known as the blockchain. The eNaira payments will be visible and traceable for onward remittance to the tax authorities. The traceability of payments will compel agents to report their income truthfully for tax purposes.

Paying taxes using eNaira allows tax payers to be able to observe their revenues, expenses and payable taxes in real time, and it helps taxpayers to keep a track of their taxes both paid and due so that they are not shocked by extensive taxes at the end of the year. Introducing tax policies that encourage the use of the eNaira for the digital payment of taxes can improve tax administration and collection in Nigeria.

However, the use of the eNaira to assist in tax collection and administration efforts should be supported with strong internal control, whistle-blower protection, corruption auditing, increasing collaboration between government and taxpayers, improving access to public services, and greater tax transparency.

Controlling Inflation

Nigeria's double-digit inflation rate has remained a persistent in the last 7 years. The annual inflation rate in Nigeria was 15.7 percent in 2015, 12.1 percent in 2018, 13.2 percent in 2020 and 17 percent in 2021. Common causes of the double digit inflation in Nigeria include excess liquidity in the banking sector as well as other factors such as the high cost of doing business, insecurity, herder-farmer clashes, logistics bottlenecks in food supply and other external shocks, etc.

The eNaira can reduce the level of inflation in two ways. First, the widespread use of the eNaira in Nigeria, alongside a limited use of cash, would reduce the amount of cash outside the banking sector. This will reduce the hoarding of physical currency notes which are often used to engage in speculative activities that are inflationary in nature. When there is widespread eNaira adoption, physical currency notes will no longer be available for hoarding as they will be replaced with a central bank digital currency, thereby starving speculators of the currency notes they use to engage in speculative activities that are inflationary.

Another way in which the eNaira can be used to control inflation is if the eNaira is interest-bearing. The CBDC is a potent monetary policy tool for controlling rising inflation levels especially when the CBDC is interest-bearing and when there is limited use of cash in society (Minesso et al, 2022). In Nigeria, the Central Bank can use an interest-bearing eNaira to reduce the inflation rate. The Central Bank can achieve this by raising the interest rate paid on eNaira deposits above the interest rate paid on bank deposits. This will lead to a flow of funds from banks to the Central Bank in the form of eNaira deposits as depositors will migrate a portion of their bank deposits to eNaira deposits to benefit from the high eNaira deposit rate. This will reduce liquidity in the banking sector and reduce inflation that is caused by excess liquidity in the banking sector (Keister and Sanches, 2019; Bhowmik, 2022).

Moreover, if the eNaira is interest-bearing, the eNaira deposit rate would constitute the floor for the monetary policy rate because banks would not lend below the eNaira deposit rate, rather they will lend above the eNaira deposit rate. In this way, increasing the eNaira deposit rate will help to control inflation as it will compel banks to reprice their loans by increasing the interest rate on new loans which would reduce credit supply and reduce inflation that is caused by excessive bank lending.

Economic Recession

An economic recession often refers to a period of temporary economic decline during which consumption, investment, production and trade activities are reduced, thereby leading to a fall in economic output (Abberger and Nierhaus, 2008; Kambil, 2008). An economic recession is often characterized by a fall in GDP in two successive quarters. The recent economic recessions in Nigeria, particularly the 2016 and 2020 recessions, were caused by a sustained fall in oil prices and the COVID-19 pandemic which transmitted adverse shocks to the Nigerian economy. It led to a significant fall in foreign exchange revenue, rising debt levels, rising fiscal deficit, rising unemployment and a sustained decrease in economic output for two consecutive quarters. In times like this, the Central Bank of Nigeria can use the eNaira as a monetary policy tool or fiscal policy tool to support recovery from an economic recession.

A non-interest-bearing eNaira can be used as a fiscal policy tool to facilitate recovery from a recession through the provision of eNaira-based fiscal stimulus to households and small businesses during a severe economic recession, in order to increase aggregate demand towards recovery from the recession. The Central Bank and the fiscal authorities can use eNaira to roll out a number of interventions to alleviate the economic hardship faced by Nigerian households and SMEs during a recession. The Central Bank can also roll out a CBDC-based targeted credit facility to support large corporations whose economic activities have been significantly affected by the recession.

An interest-bearing eNaira can also be used to facilitate a recovery from a recession. Using the interest rate paid on eNaira deposit as a monetary policy tool, alongside a reduction in cash holdings, would eliminate the interest rate effective-lower-bound as a constraint on monetary policy. This will allow the interest rate on eNaira deposit to go as negative as needed to offset a major negative shock to aggregate demand and exit a recession caused by prolonged low aggregate demand. The low interest rate, or negative interest rate, on eNaira deposit will stimulate aggregate spending towards economic recovery, and could lead to a much quicker recovery from the recession.

Foreign Exchange Reserves Accretion and Exchange Rate

The Central bank can use the eNaira to increase foreign exchange reserves accretion in a more efficient way. Presently, Nigeria has inadequate foreign exchange supply which has put constant pressure on the exchange rate. There are four major sources of foreign exchange inflow into Nigeria. They include (i) foreign exchange from the proceeds of oil exports, (ii) foreign exchange from proceeds of non-oil exports, (iii) foreign exchange from diaspora remittances, and (vi) foreign exchange from foreign direct/portfolio investments. All these sources were adversely affected by the COVID-19 pandemic. In addition, most of them are unreliable sources that are perennially prone to exogenous vicissitudes of global economic developments such as the COVID-19 pandemic, unfavourable fall in oil prices, geopolitical conflicts and trade wars.

The foreign exchange from the proceeds of oil exports accounts for over 90 per cent of Nigeria's foreign exchange inflows. However, the proceeds from oil revenue has fallen since the start of the COVID-19 pandemic in 2020, and fell to an all-time low in early 2022 despite Nigeria's economic recovery from the 2020 recession during the pandemic. This led to shortage of foreign exchange amid rising demand for foreign exchange. The low foreign exchange supply and rising demand for foreign exchange increased pressure on the exchange rate which led the Central Bank to depreciate the Naira in order to ease the pressure on the Naira against the Dollar. The Central Bank's efforts to control the demand for foreign exchange has to be accompanied by a corresponding increase in foreign exchange supply.

The eNaira can facilitate increase in foreign exchange flows to Nigeria. The eNaira would increase foreign exchange inflow from remittances into Nigeria by removing third party intermediaries and reducing regulatory barriers, which would encourage increased remittance flow and increase foreign exchange inflow to Nigeria. The eNaira can also be used to enhance the effectiveness of the Central Bank's Naira-4-Dollar Scheme in order to boost remittances from the current US$6 million per week to over US$150 million per week. The eNaira can also be used to achieve the goals of the RT200 FX programme which aim to raise US$200 billion in foreign exchange earnings over the next 3-5 years from non-oil proceeds.

Furthermore, widespread eNaira adoption in Nigeria would enable the CBN to reduce the amount of physical currency notes in circulation, some of which are hoarded by currency speculators and used to speculate against the Naira, which adds further pressure on the Naira and leads to currency depreciation. The widespread adoption of the eNaira, along with the limited use of cash, would ultimately strengthen the Naira because currency speculation would be difficult to achieve using the eNaira.

Food Insecurity

Food insecurity in Nigeria is caused by recurrent floods, herder-farmer clashes, insecurity, rising prices of imported food ingredients, and disruptions in supply chain logistics. Over the last 7 years, the CBN has rolled out several development finance interventions in the agricultural sector to increase food security in Nigeria. The eNaira can be used to channel intervention funds to smallholder farmers and corporations in the agricultural value chain who are valuable stakeholders in the effort to increase food security. The eNaira can act as an efficient and effective payment tool for channelling intervention funds to the agricultural sector of the economy to increase food production and food security.

For example, the eNaira can be used to facilitate payments to support the Anchor Borrowers' Programme (ABP) and Commodity Development Initiative (CDI) which together are aimed at strengthening key agricultural commodities' value chains and repositioning Nigeria to become a self-sufficient food and industry raw material producer. The eNaira can be used as a payment tool for lending to smallholder farmers and for stimulating investments across the agriculture value chains.

The eNaira can also facilitate the payment of intervention funds to rice millers to ramp up the production of paddy rice for processing under the Paddy Aggregation Scheme (PAS), and to provide working capital facility to rice millers to ensure all year round activities. The eNaira can also facilitate the payment of intervention funds to more than 53,000 maize farmers cultivating 62,910 hectares, with an expected yield of 188,730 million metric tonnes across 30 States of the Federation. The eNaira can also facilitate the efficient payment of intervention funds under the Commercial Agriculture Credit Scheme (CACS) scheme which has financed more than 610 commercial agricultural projects across the country.

Financial System Instability

The last major financial crisis in Nigeria occurred in 2010, and was caused by poor lending practices, poor corporate governance and weak risk management practices. Since then, the Nigerian financial system has been largely stable in recent times. The eNaira can be used as a potent tool to assist the Central Bank in achieving its goal of preserving financial stability. The eNaira can be used to avert a financial crisis in Nigeria and it can also be designed to incorporate safeguards that mitigate financial stability risks caused by eNaira activity. But the eNaira's ability to offer these solutions depend on whether the eNaira is interest-bearing or non-interest-bearing.

When there is widespread eNaira adoption, an interest-bearing eNaira can be used to quell a liquidity crisis that makes the banking sector unstable (assuming the liquidity crisis is not caused by eNaira activity or bank-to-eNaira disintermediation). In such times, the Central Bank could reduce the eNaira deposit rate below the rate on consumer deposit in banks. The Central Bank could reduce the eNaira deposit rate to 'zero' or a negative rate to encourage and incentivize individuals to move their eNaira holdings to bank deposits. The resulting eNaira-to-bank deposit migration will give banks access to cheap funding and liquidity, which can be used to quell an ongoing liquidity crisis in the banking sector.

An interest-bearing eNaira can also be used to put an end to excessive risk-taking which often manifests in the form of excessive and risky lending. Excessive risk-taking by banks can lead to risky lending which can increase systemic risk in the banking sector and propagate financial stability risks. In times of excessive-risky lending, the Central Bank could significantly raise the eNaira deposit rate above the rate on consumer deposit to encourage and incentivize bank customers to move their customer deposits to eNaira holdings. The resulting bank-to-eNaira deposit migration will reduce banks' ability to lend from cheap customer deposits as the amount of customer deposits at the disposal of banks will be reduced. This will reduce bank lending, decrease risk-taking and reduce systemic risk in the financial system.

Furthermore, there are financial stability risks associated with widespread CBDC usage. The most important risk is financial stability risk arising from disorderly and structural bank disintermediation. It arises mainly from the absence of regulatory limits to individual CBDC holdings which could lead to higher volatility in customer deposits and/or a significant reduction in customer deposits in the banking sector. Any significant reduction in customer deposit funding would require banks to either (i) increase competition for market-based funding, (ii) obtain costly market-based funding, (iii) reduce their assets; (iv) increase risk-taking to offset expected margin shortfall, and (v) increase interest rates. These actions by banks could affect bank profitability, lending, the provision of financial services and increase banks' susceptibility to a bank run (Keister and Sanches, 2019; Fernandez-Villaverde et al, 2020). To mitigate CBDC-induced financial stability risks, the eNaira has been designed to have a regulatory threshold for individual CBDC holdings. This will limit the movement of customer deposits from banks to the eNaira wallet, thereby mitigating the risk of bank disintermediation. Other safeguards that may be considered include: (i) a further reduction in the amount of eNaira that can be held by individuals, and (ii) paying uncompetitive interest rates on eNaira holdings to discourage and disincentivise large bank-to-eNaira deposit migration.

Finally, the Central Bank's issuance of a non-interest-bearing eNaira has some positive benefits for financial system stability. One, a non-interest-bearing eNaira would encourage Nigerians to use their eNaira holdings primarily for payments rather than as a safe haven asset. This would reduce the incentive for large-scale bank-to-eNaira deposit migration which would occur if the eNaira bears interest and is considered to be a safe haven asset. Two, the introduction of a non-interest-bearing eNaira is unlikely to affect bank profitability and lending, as banks will not need to raise their own deposit rates to match the eNaira deposit rate. This will further preserve financial system stability. Three, the introduction of a non-interest-bearing eNaira will allow Nigerian banks to retain their market power in the market for customer deposits. This helps to ensure that banks are not pressured to raise their deposit rates to match the eNaira deposit rate which would compel banks to increase the interest rates charged on lending, and might lead to a decrease in the demand for loans. More importantly, the introduction of a non-interest-bearing eNaira might not have a large impact on individual bank runs because it is already possible to digitally and instantly transfer money between a weak and a strong bank, or from the Central Bank to a failing bank through the eNaira.

Rising Poverty

Nigeria is among the countries with the highest number of people living in poverty in the world. Nigeria was ranked 103 of 121 countries in the World Bank's 2022 *Poverty and Prosperity Report*. Despite having a booming digital economy (ICT) sector which contributed almost 18 per cent to Nigeria's GDP growth in the second quarter of 2021, Nigeria contributed three million people to global extreme poverty and is considered to be home to a large share of the global extreme poor in 2021 and 2022. This devastating statistic shows that there is a need to ensure that the eNaira has features that caters for the needs of people living in extreme poverty in Nigeria.

Rural and remotes communities in Nigeria can be lifted from hardship and poverty by deploying eNaira possibilities to those communities despite the challenges in these communities such as digital and physical connectivity problems, limited Internet penetration, lack of secure Internet servers and limited access to financial systems.

The eNaira can be used to offer financial services to poor people living in rural and remote communities where there are poor digital infrastructure and poor internet connectivity. The eNaira has both online and offline capabilities which ensures that poor people can be on-boarded at any time even without internet connectivity. Poor people in such communities can use the eNaira to safely receive stipends and upkeep allowances from family, friends and relatives and donors. They can also use the eNaira to make low-cost payments and to receive income for services rendered which will enable them to earn income and rise above poverty.

The eNaira also offers low transaction cost or zero transaction cost. In the past year, there were no transaction cost or fees for eNaira payments. If the zero transaction cost on eNaira is sustained, it will benefit poor people who mostly perform low-value digital transactions using the eNaira. This can encourage poor people to use eNaira digital payments.

The eNaira also offer solutions that cater for the large number of poor people that use non-smart phones. The Central Bank has taken steps to ensure that non-smart phone users have the capability to perform eNaira transactions seamlessly, and to avoid digital discrimination between smart phone users and non-smart phone users. The Central Bank introduced the *997# eNaira USSD code which enables poor people without a non-smart phone to perform eNaira transactions using their non-smart phones. They can use the eNaira USSD capability to access a range of financial services that meet their needs.

The eNaira can also be used to channel investment in human capital development, financial development and social protections activities and projects that expand economic opportunities for the poor. This will create jobs and increase financial access for poor women and poor young people in rural communities.

eNaira payment solutions can also be used to support the development of a robust and well-funded technical and vocational education system and training programmes for millions of Nigerians outside the formal school system, or who possess only a primary education. eNaira Payments made for this purpose can be tracked, monitored and audited to ensure that the funds are sent to the intended beneficiaries who are poor (Obiora, 2022).

The eNaira can also be used to broaden access to microfinance to reduce poverty in Nigeria. The eNaira can be used to increase financial inclusion of the poor, and enable the Nigerian government to better plan and provide microfinance services that cater for the needs of the poorest of the poor. Also, when poor people are financially included, the eNaira can provide a more reliable, faster, cheaper and more auditable platform for the Nigerian government to send direct payments to poor citizens who are eligible for social welfare benefits.

CONCLUSION

This paper discussed the ways in which the eNaira might be used to solve some economic problems in Nigeria. It was shown that the eNaira can be instrumental in solving fiscal revenue challenges, controlling inflation, increasing foreign exchange accretion and managing exchange rate, addressing food insecurity, reducing financial stability risks, reducing poverty level, and recovering from an economic recession. The implication of the findings is that the eNaira can assist in solving some economic problem either as a payment platform or as a monetary policy tool or as a financial stability tool. Whichever is the case, the Central Bank should ensure that the eNaira incorporate features that help to achieve some pressing economic objectives or central bank objectives.

Although the eNaira will evolve with time and its possibilities are endless, the Central Bank should not allow endless changes to the eNaira just for the sake of it. Rather, the Central Bank should ensure that the reasons and implications of new changes to eNaira design and other technical changes are well understood so that new eNaira innovations can assist in preserving macroeconomic stability for businesses, for citizens and for society as a whole.

REFERENCES

Abberger, K., & Nierhaus, W. (2008). How to define a recession*? CESifo Forum*, *9*(4), 74–76.

Agur, I., Ari, A., & Dell'Ariccia, G. (2022). Designing central bank digital currencies. *Journal of Monetary Economics*, *125*, 62–79. doi:10.1016/j.jmoneco.2021.05.002

Barontini, C., & Holden, H. (2019). *Proceeding with caution-a survey on central bank digital currency. Proceeding with Caution-A Survey on Central Bank Digital Currency.* BIS Paper, No. 101.

Bhowmik, D. (2022). Monetary policy implications of central bank digital currency with special reference to india. *Asia-Pacific Journal of Management and Technology*, *2*(3), 1–8.

Bindseil, U. (2019). Central bank digital currency: Financial system implications and control. *International Journal of Political Economy*, *48*(4), 303–335. doi:10.1080/08911916.2019.1693160

Bordo, M. D., & Levin, A. T. (2017). *Central bank digital currency and the future of monetary policy (No. w23711).* National Bureau of Economic Research. doi:10.3386/w23711

Chan, H. F., Dulleck, U., Fooken, J., Moy, N., & Torgler, B. (2022). Cash and the hidden economy: Experimental evidence on fighting tax evasion in small business transactions. *Journal of Business Ethics*, 1–26.

Chodorow-Reich, G., Gopinath, G., Mishra, P., & Narayanan, A. (2020). Cash and the economy: Evidence from India's demonetization. *The Quarterly Journal of Economics*, *135*(1), 57–103. doi:10.1093/qje/qjz027

Davoodalhosseini, S. M. (2022). Central bank digital currency and monetary policy. *Journal of Economic Dynamics & Control*, *142*, 104150. doi:10.1016/j.jedc.2021.104150

Engert, W., & Fung, B. S. C. (2017). *Central bank digital currency: Motivations and implications* (No. 2017-16). Bank of Canada Staff Discussion Paper.

Fernández-Villaverde, J., Sanches, D., Schilling, L., & Uhlig, H. (2020). *Central bank digital currency: central banking for all?* NBER Working Paper Series, No 26753.

Gurama, Z. U., Mansor, M., & Pantamee, A. A. (2015). Tax evasion and Nigeria tax system: An overview. *Research Journal of Finance and Accounting*, *6*(8), 202–211.

Kambil, A. (2008). What is your recession playbook? *The Journal of Business Strategy*, *29*(5), 50–52. doi:10.1108/02756660810902341

Keister, T., & Sanches, D. (2019). *Should Central Banks Issue Digital Currency?* Federal Reserve Bank of Philadelphia Working Paper.

Kumhof, M., & Noone, C. (2021). Central bank digital currencies—Design principles for financial stability. *Economic Analysis and Policy*, *71*, 553–572. doi:10.1016/j.eap.2021.06.012

Kwon, O., Lee, S., & Park, J. (2022). Central bank digital currency, tax evasion, and inflation tax. *Economic Inquiry*, *60*(4), 1497–1519. doi:10.1111/ecin.13091

Minesso, M. F., Mehl, A., & Stracca, L. (2022). Central bank digital currency in an open economy. *Journal of Monetary Economics*, *127*, 54–68. doi:10.1016/j.jmoneco.2022.02.001

Obiora, K.I. (2022). *Special Remarks at the IMF CBDC Seminar in Frankfurt Germany, June*. Academic Press.

Onyeka, V. N., & Nwankwo, C. (2016). The effect of tax evasion and avoidance on Nigeria's economic growth. *European Journal of Business and Management*, *8*(24), 158–166.

Otusanya, O. J. (2011). The role of multinational companies in tax evasion and tax avoidance: The case of Nigeria. *Critical Perspectives on Accounting*, *22*(3), 316–332. doi:10.1016/j.cpa.2010.10.005

Ozili, P. K. (2023a). eNaira central bank digital currency (CBDC) for financial inclusion in Nigeria. In Digital Economy, Energy and Sustainability: Opportunities and Challenges (pp. 41-54). Cham: Springer International Publishing.

Ozili, P. K. (2023b). CBDC, Fintech and cryptocurrency for financial Inclusion and financial stability. *Digital Policy. Regulation & Governance*, *25*(1), 40–57. doi:10.1108/DPRG-04-2022-0033

Chapter 11
Innovations in Finance and the Future of Finance: A Critical Review

Sofia Devi Shamurailatpam
The Maharaja Sayajirao University of Baroda, India

ABSTRACT

Technological innovation in the financial sector has brought significant development in the list of baskets of financial products available and convenience in delivery of financial services. This is reflected in terms of payment services, lending activities, management of assets, third party administrators, etc., among others that form the new business models and strategic management in financial sectors. FinTech or digital innovations in the financial sector has emerged as one of the qualitative changes in the financial markets across the globe with its associated potential specifically with regard to efficiency and performance of financial institutions. However, the financial innovations and its services are no exception to different form of risks for the customers in particular and to financial institutions at large. In this connection, this chapter attempts to give a critical review of the risks and uncertainties that may arise in the access and uses of FinTech-based platform in delivering digital financial products across the globe.

INTRODUCTION

Globally, over the last decade the landscape of financial system has experienced significant changes, thereby interrupting the traditional bank business model through the emergence of digital bank model and neo-bank models. These new business models captured a substantial share of the market with its technological innovations in terms of new digitized financial products design and services. The traditional banking system, on the other hand, are confined with the conventional business models with its structural characteristics of high operating costs, cumbersome processes in delivery of products, complex processing of data, static organizational designs & marketing, etc. in the functioning of the financial system. Countries across the globe have come up with new technological innovations, enforcement of technological laws, stringent regulatory framework to incorporate technology along with the functioning

DOI: 10.4018/978-1-6684-8624-5.ch011

of traditional business models for faster delivery, convenience, universally accessibility and inclusion of financial system to all. Technological innovation in the financial sector has impacted considerably the landscape of financial products and services across the globe, thereby resulting to new business models and applications along with regulatory sandboxes subject to certain safeguards and oversight. A regulatory sandbox is a framework that allows live or virtual testing of new products or services, in a (controlled) testing environment, with or without any 'regulatory relief' (RBI, 2021b). These technological start-ups emerged with an array of services in the form of crowd funding platforms, mobile and online payment solution, international remittances, peer to peer lending, block chain technology, distributed ledgers technology, smart contracts, etc. to mention a few that challenges the traditional banking system and financial players. The financial industry is on the approach of new financial age and one of the new disruptive structure is the block-chain technology, that has potential to enhance efficiency and security of financial markets (Trivedi et al., 2021).To say, the term 'FinTech' is used to describe the companies that operates in the financial technology sector, relating to small start-up companies that develop innovative technological solutions in online and mobile payments, big data, alternative finance and financial management (Statista, 2022a). According to Financial Stability Board of the Bank for International Settlement (BIS), "FinTech is technologically enabled financial innovation that could result in new business models, application, processes, or products with an associated material effect on financial markets and institutions and the provision of financial services." Globally, in the last decades there are significant transformation in the functioning and operation of the traditional banking system particularly in payments system, mode of lending, management of financial resources & wealth, provision of retail assets & liabilities products along with no exception to increase in the number of start-ups FinTech companies. A significant impact in retail segment of banking businesses with the advent of FinTech is the rise in global competition and hence banks are forced to look at the trade-off between customer retention and customer acquisition, thereby leading banks in formulating strategies to increase customer satisfaction and customer loyalty (Mehta et al., 2023). Banks and financial institutions are tilting towards delivery of qualitative services with stringent competitions among the peers as these firms are of oligopolistic in nature, producing more or less similar products, the only way to switch more number of customers is through adding value additions in terms and conditions to the existing conventional products and services. In another study by Khanna and Sharma (2017), price, reputation, responses to service failure, customer satisfaction, service quality, service products, competition, customer commitment and involuntary switching have their significant effect on customers' switching behaviour. These calls for the business orientation for qualitative and more responsible investment towards sustainable finance from the perspectives of social, economic and environmental dimensions in particular. We can say that, large information technology companies and e-Commerce platforms plays a significant role to leverage out the expansion and outreach of these services given the challenges in technological innovations. In other words, these FinTech firms have potential benefits in terms of convenience, accessibility, operational efficiency, digitization and greater scope for financial inclusion specifically to developing and emerging countries of the world. However, despite these significant advantages of FinTech, key challenges in the form of risks in regulating and supervising the evolving technology with its different facets of uncertainties are major concerns. This chapter gives a brief overview of the recent technological innovations in the financial services industries and the challenges of unanticipated risks arising from applications of financial technology specifically in developing and emerging economies.

The chapter is divided into seven sections. Section II gives a brief overview of global FinTech scenario. Section III reports the fundamental features of FinTech firms. In the next section, financial innovation in

India is presented. Section V discusses critical reviews on FinTech start-up firms. Section VI highlighted the various challenges and policy. The last section concludes.

GLOBAL SCENARIO OF FINTECH FIRMS

According to the Fintech Statistics, the sector attracted $128 billion in investment globally in 2018 to $310 billion in 2022, with an annual compound growth rate of the industry at 25 percent. Indeed, the nature of FinTech industries revealed the growing dominance of the industry in financial sector, its market shares by regions, consumer adoptions and blockchain statistics, thereby maximizing the insights for businesses in the financial sector. The total value of investments into FinTech companies globally has increased from 9 billion US dollar in 2010 to 215.1 billion US dollar in 2019 to 226.5 billion US dollar in 2021 (Table 1). The region that attracts the most major portion of the investments in FinTech is United States with 10,755 start-ups in 2021, followed by 9,323 in EMEA (Europe, Middle East, Africa) and 6,268 in APAC (Asia-Pacific) respectively, though the Asian countries lead FinTech companies by revenue.

Table 1. Global FinTech investments during 2010 to 2021

Year	2010	2015	2019	2021
Amount (in billion)	$9	$67.1	$215.1	$226.5

Source: Statista (2022a)

Table 2. Number of FinTech start-ups by region between 2018 and 2021

Year	Americas	EMEA	APAC
2018	5,686	3,581	2,864
2019	5,779	3,583	2,849
2020	8,775	7,385	4,765
2021	10,755	9,323	6,268

Source: Statista (2022b)

Table 3 reports global top ten fund raising FinTech companies according to the Global Financial Hub Report of 2018. Majority of the fund raising FinTech companies are confined in China and United States. Among the top fund raising companies to mention a few are Ant Financial ($20B) in Hangzhou; JD Finance (RMB34B) in Beijing; Social Finance ($1.9B) in San Francisco, each dealing with the general business. Other companies listed in top 10 start-ups specialized in marketplace lending, consumer finance and online insurance. FinTech companies that are headquartered in United States and China ranked top in market capitalization globally as on 2021 with almost 478 billion US dollars by Visa (United States), followed by MasterCard (China) with market capitalization share of 368 billion US dollars. Other com-

Table 3. Global top ten fund raising FinTech companies, 2018

Sr. No.	Name of FinTech Firms	City	Country	Business	Total Fund Raised (Approx.)
1	Ant Financial	Hangzhou	China	General	$20B
2	JD Finance	Beijing	China	General	RMB34B
3	Social Finance	San Francisco	USA	General	$2B
4	Du Xiaoman Financial	Beijing	China	General	$1.9B
5	Avant	Chicago	USA	Marketplace Lending	$1.8B
6	Suning Finance	Nanjing	China	General	RMB12B
7	Lufax	Shanghai	China	Marketplace Lending	$2.3B
8	ZhongAn	Shanghai	China	Online Insurance	$2.8B
9	Qudian	Beijing	China	Consumer Finance	$1.8B
10	Kabbage	Atlanta	USA	Marketplace Lending	$1.6B

Source: Global FinTech Hub Report (2018)

panies that follows amongst the top ten FinTech companies in 2021 are - Ant Financial, Tencent, Intuit, PayPal, Stripe, Fiserv, Adyen and Square (Table 4).

FinTech offers central banks the scope to explore new products/services, digital/virtual currency, cost reduction in minting currencies and digital financial inclusion. It has become a major enabler and competitive financial markets, and bringing more number of underserved consumers to access and use of financial products/services. However, FinTech is not exception to risks to consumers/investors/entrepreneurs and the regulators at the macro economy. In the following sections, the critical views and the comments on the FinTech products/services are discussed.

Table 4. Market capitalization of largest FinTech companies worldwide in 2021

Ranking	Company	Countries	Market Shares (in Billion US Dollars)
1	Visa	United States	477.95
2	MasterCard	United States	367.84
3	Ant Financial	China	312.00
4	Tencent	China	238.12
5	Intuit	United States	156.94
6	Paypal	United States	140.10
7	Stripe	Ireland	95.00
8	Fiserv	United States	65.72
9	Adyen	Netherlands	65.21
10	Square	United States	58.78

Source: Statista (2022c)

FINTECH: FEATURES, ENABLERS, AND ADVANTAGES

FinTech innovations have emerged as a transformative drive in the global financial markets through digital innovations and delivering financial services in path-breaking ways. As such, the financial markets are opened to new business models, financial products and services, as well as challenges towards risk profiles of the banks/financial institutions. A lot of attention has been given by regulators and authorities to promote and facilitate innovations through initiatives like –regulatory sandboxes, innovation hub centres, innovation accelerators to actively monitor FinTech developments. To say, countries have passed new Regulatory Sandbox (RS) to review the regulatory framework and with constant attention can respond to the changing dimensions of rapidly gaining FinTech environment. For example, the Reserve Bank of India has released in 2018 the Regulatory Sandbox framework, in order to live test new products or services in a controlled/test regulatory environment to conduct evidence on the benefits and risks of new financial innovations, while carefully monitoring and containing their risks (RBI, 2021a). Given the strong institutional and regulatory framework, these start-ups firms need to focus on good governance, regulatory compliance, mitigation of risks associated with ongoing technology in the interest of customers and security of data. Market change and disruptive technology inevitably lead to new risks (Kovas, 2018). The following paragraphs explains the fundamental features of FinTech firms, the major drivers or enablers of FinTech start-ups and the advantages of these start-ups and innovative technologies in financial markets (Figure 1).

Features of FinTech Start-Ups Firms

In general, the main prominent features of FinTech innovations in financial market activities involves five different categories of innovations – payments, clearing & settlement; deposits, lending & capital raising; market provisioning; investment management; and data analytics & risk management (RBI, 2021c). One of the fundamental changes brought by new start-ups companies is the speed of coverage in the use and access to financial markets due to innovations in payments, clearing and settlement of services on the one hand and also reducing costs of operation on the other side. Major changes are seen through the use of mobile technology platforms in the form of new payment infrastructure like Google-Pay, Apple Pay and Android Pay, enabling easy access to financial services. Generally, the core features of FinTech firms possesses the qualities as:

Peer-to-Peer Lending: An alternative way in online platform that matches lenders with borrowers to provide unsecured loans, the interest rate may be fixed by mutual consent and agreement between the borrower and lender.

Crowdfunding: It refers to a method of funding a particular project by gathering funds raised through small amounts from a large group of population in site set up for specific purpose.

Smart Contracts: A contract or an agreement between borrower and lender is done through digital platform in terms of legal agreements, negotiations, verification, and protocols of complete contract.

Market Provisioning Services: A platform that facilitate efficient and cheaper provision of resources including information and relevant services to the market.

Online Purchase of Bancassurance Products: Banks in the new product model sell insurance products/third party products in the form of as a value addition product along with its conventional products or the insurance products/policies in online platform.

New Business Models Under Digitized Platform: Use of Big data, artificial intelligence, blockchain technology, distributed leger technology and digital platforms open to deliver financial products form the new features of business model in FinTech start-ups.

Use of Big Data and New Sources of Information in Digitised Way: Big data enables to gather data for heterogeneous group of individuals with accuracy in data analysis and handling it for varied purposes of the financial market study.

Drivers and Enablers of FinTech

FinTech has led the financial firms to re-design and re-shape the financial products, business models and the structure of market, provided strong regulatory and institutional framework for financial stability, integrity, financial inclusion and innovative platform of digital economy. We have experienced during Covid-19 pandemic, all financial transactions and payments system were performed under the digitized platform. There are various dimensions of enablers of FinTech start-ups. The financial institutions and technology companies are not competitors, they act as enabler in delivery of financial products and financial services in convenience, easy, faster and affordable way. The two fundamental drivers of FinTech are – mobile, internet connected devices and communication networks; and low-cost computing and data storage (World Bank, 2022a). We can describe the enablers of FinTech start-ups as under into four major perspectives:

- **Technology:** Technology accelerates the speed of payment and settlement processes that is leverage out through Artificial Intelligence and blockchain technology.
- **Regulatory Framework:** Regulatory Sandboxes for live testing of new products or services were set up with given timelines to foster responsible innovation in financial services and the interest of the customers' safety and security from ongoing technological risks.
- **Demands From Customers:** The experienced of the customers particularly during pandemic has accustomed customers experience with greater convenience, accessibility, faster deliveries of retail products.
- **Innovations and New Product Development:** Technological innovations in the form of digitized payments and transactions made easy scope for financial inclusion especially the underserved sections of the society with the help of mobile banking applications in an easier way.

Advantages of FinTech Start-Ups

The disruption of technology through innovative products and services has significant advantages to investors, bankers and customers at particular. Digital financial services, powered by FinTech, have the potential to lower costs by maximizing economies of scale, to increase the speed, security and transparency of transactions and to allow for more tailored financial services that serve the poor (World Bank, 2020a). To an investor or a banker, FinTech start-ups has combine benefits in terms of cutting costs and scalability of the businesses. Use of the artificial intelligence, block-chain technology and distributed ledger system enables banks to quickly furnish the delivery of financial products and services more efficiently. However, the availability of infrastructures differs across countries and may pose constraints or obstacles to potential competitors. This relates to the regulatory and supervisory framework to address for by the regulatory bodies and authorities in fulfilling the pre-requisites of FinTech start-ups and also successful

Figure 1. A framework of fintech start-up firms

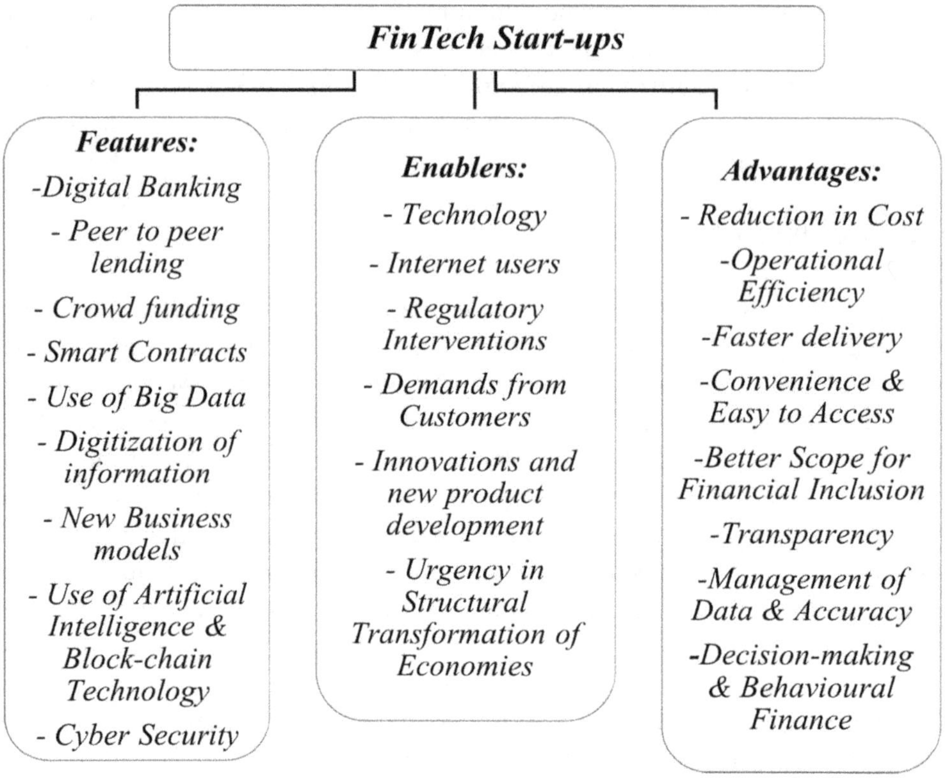

operation of the financial markets. The use of financial technology has significantly improved the working and functioning of the banks as against its traditional practices of operation in terms of settlement of payments, transparency, cost of transactions, accessibility benefits and inclusiveness. Firstly, digitization can reduce frictions in payment and settlement systems that increases the operational efficiency of the banks and financial institutions. Another significant advantage is the decline in marginal costs per account or transaction and scale efficiencies due to its scalability and inclusiveness under a given digital platform. Thirdly, since all the transactions are encrypted and stored, it enhances transparency and reduces the problem of information asymmetries. Fourthly, it has large potential to deliver range of benefits, specifically efficiency improvements and cost reductions as well as overall productivity of the banks and financial institutions. Further, the digitization platform has made easy to access and use financial services and products, even the marginalized sections of the society and illiterate persons can operate through mobile banking, mobile apps for transactions and payment services as well as opening of account, awareness of financial markets at large. The ongoing Covid-19 crisis has also led to the need for increased digital financial inclusion, particularly for those who are excluded financially and underserved sections of society with an array of financial products that suits their financial needs at affordable cost. Therefore, we can say that, technological developments led to access in financial services/ products and scope for digital financial inclusion.

FINANCIAL INNOVATIONS IN THE INDIAN BANKING SECTOR

With no exception, FinTech sector in India is also growing rapidly, backed up by mass market segment and government initiatives under innovative hubs centre and regulatory sandboxes. Significant impacts of FinTech in India is reflected in terms of increase in banking penetration, use of digitized modes of transactions and digital disruptions like adoption of mobile applications for payments services among others. This is regarded as a significant progress in the Indian banking sector as the problems of exclusion remained a major concern in the delivery of banking services through the traditional mode in a cash-driven economy. The use of Unified Payment Interface (UPI) has facilitated the use of digital financial products and services in the easiest way through the use of mobile applications to the masses including the illiterate people in rural areas. The FinTech products/services offered in Indian financial markets among others include payments system – payment banks, mobile wallets, payment gateway, payment infrastructure (ATMs & m POS); and online financial products- lending, insurance, e-NPS. Mutual Funds/Broking (RBI, 2018). Table 5 presents top Indian FinTech firms that raised funds during 2019-2020 which businesses are specialized in diverse fields including payment apps, payment gateways, lending platforms, retail products and bancassurance.

Table 5. Top Indian fintechs by fund raising in 2019-20

Rank	Company	Founded	Total Amount Raised ($Million)	Description
1	Paytm	2010	1000	App-based wallet for consumer payments
2	BharatPe	2017	154.3	QR code based payment app
3	Policybazaar	2008	150	Online insurance comparison platform
4	CRED	2018	145.6	Rewards-based platform for credit card bill payments
5	KhataBook	2016	140.6	Digital ledger account book
6	Acko	2017	101.6	Tech-enabled automotive insurance
7	ZestMoney	2015	30.47	Online platform for point-of-sale financing
8	Lendingkart	2014	87.87	Online platform providing working capital for SMEs
9	InCred	2016	85.9	Alternative lending platform focusing on SME, consumer & personal, home and education loans.
10	Pine Labs	1998	85	PoS software solutions for offline retailers
11	Billdesk	2000	84.8	Payment Gateway
12	Digit Insurance	2016	84.35	Insurance platform for individuals

Source: RBI (2020)

Digital innovations also re-shaped the lending platforms in India, driven by macroeconomic and institutional factors inherent to the region. The factors for rapid spur in digital lending in India are classified into two group – demand side factors and supply side factors (Box 1). Both the demand side factors and supply side determinants play a significant role in the successful planning and implementation of financial innovations and set up of FinTech start-ups effectively. For example, among the supply side factors, technology is one of the major ingredients that push the overall banking sector upgradation to new business models and strategies such as – use of Artificial intelligence, big data analytics, mobile internet facilities and so on. Above these, the government and regulatory bodies has constantly engaged towards digitization of financial sector and towards cashless economy. The Reserve Bank Innovation Hub, 2019; Regulatory Sandbox; Financial Inclusion Initiatives –PMJDY, JAM, Peer to Peer lending platforms, etc. cites the examples framing strong regulatory framework and good governance in the Indian financial system. The reason for increased in the speed of digitization process in India is backed up by the internet and mobile penetration such as use of smart phones, increase in mobile and broadband connections that led to demand for digitized products and services. Given these available factors from supply side by regulatory authorities, certain factors that lead to increase in FinTech start-up firms include changing dimensions of demography- composition of young population and demographic dividend, changing lifestyle with more digital friendly; macroeconomic factors like increase in GDP and per capita income; and the significant urgency for digital platform with the effect of recent pandemic to mention among others. These factors – demand and supply side together reinforced the development and upgradation of FinTech start-up firms in Indian banking sector.

Box 1: Factors for rapid spur in digital lending in India

Supply Side Drivers	Demand Side Drivers
Technological Advancements: - Mobile Internet facilities - Application Programming Interfaces (APIs) - Alternative Data - Artificial Intelligence - Big Data Analytics - Cloud Computing - Distributed Ledger System	*Demographics:* - Higher proportion of young population - Digital natives - Aspirational consumers (driven by life style needs
Government Initiatives: - Jan Dhan Yojana - Aadhaar Enrolment - Digital India - IndiaStack - Startup Ecosystem	*Economic Development:* - Increase in per capita GDP - Increase in per capita net national income
Regulatory Enablers: - Framework for Account Aggregators and Peer to Peer Lending Platforms - App based NBFCs - Regulatory Sandbox - Reserve Bank Innovation Hub - Financial Inclusion Initiatives	*Unmet Demand:* - Low credit penetration to informal economy/sub-prime or first time borrowers - Reluctance of traditional banks to lend to small borrowers with low or nil credit history
Internet/ Mobile Penetration: - Accessibility and Availability of Smart Phones - Increase in number of Internet Subscribers - Increase in Broadband Connections - Increase in Mobile Connections	*COVID 19 Pandemic:* - Pandemic induced financial stress - Reduced mobility and social distancing - Reduced employment and wages

Source: RBI (2021b)

Box 2: Number of complaints received under Digital Lending Applications (DLAs)	
February to July 2020	85
September to November 2020	133
December 2020	919
January 2021	661
February 2021	39
March 2021	250

Source: RBI (2021b)

The financial innovations also brought significant shift towards digital lending, though digital mode relative to the physical mode is at the nascent stage for scheduled commercial banks in India. Approximately, there were 1100 lending apps available for Indian android users regarding - loan, instant loan, quick loan, etc., and number of illegal loan apps found as approximately 600 as per the Working Group on Digital Lending (RBI, 2021b). Such types of risks are inherent in the technological innovations in finance, paving an undefined risk profile of the banks and space for security/safety of customers in particular. Further, the study also highlights the significantly increasing number of complaints across states in India so far as digital lending apps, say around 2562 complaints from January 2020 to March 2021 (Box 2).

Given the Supply side and Demand side factors for responsible growth in FinTech firms, the successful business of these start-up firms require proper funding in the early stages of operation, particularly expenses in research and development, establishment of Innovation Hubs to examine the live operations for validation of businesses, the regulatory sandboxes and its updates with live test of the firms in operations, among others in the very beginning of the operations. However, there is frequent quests for the inherent technological risks associated in FinTech firms and uncertainties from new entrants in the new business models, handling and management of data, privacy of information and risk mitigation mechanism employed to protect against fraudulent and illicit dealings of financial transactions like terrorist financing and parallel economy. A detailed analysis on the major constraints associated to FinTech firms is reported in the next section.

FINANCIAL TECHNOLOGIES: A CRITICAL REVIEW

Indeed, the technological innovations in financial sector has significant advantages and considerable experience is bestowed by countries in the delivery of financial products, regulatory compliance and protecting the interests of consumers at large. The Global Findex database of World Bank also highlighted a significant increase in the number of digital accounts opened by adults; and also use of digital products like digital payments, digital transactions, e-platform for selling and buying of agricultural products in many developing countries of the world. No doubt, digitization has brought significant opportunities in the mere delivery of the financial services and products digitally, however, digitization processes is prone to possible technological risks and uncertainties. According to the World Bank Survey on FinTech 2022, top six risks for which risk perception for the next five years was higher include – operational and cybersecurity, data protection, third-party services, illicit financial activities, legal and reputational, and consumer protection, which are inherent to technological foundation of FinTech and digital transformation (World Bank and CCAF, 2022; World Bank 2022b). Consumers of FinTech products are prone to receiving risks and less protection than consumers of traditional financial products due to coverage of their country's existing financial consumer protection regulation and so regulators need to supervise FinTech entrants in their markets (World Bank, 2021). We know that one of the major constraints of the FinTech products is the regulatory framework to counter the illicit financial dealings and also combat cybercrime specific to new business models under FinTech start-ups. Regulators followed three different measures while developing a dedicated regulatory framework for new start-up firms, new generation products and other technological innovations, namely – (a) wait & see (b) test & learn and (c) innovation facilitators, including regulatory sandboxes (World Bank, 2020b; World Bank and CCAF, 2022). The first measure opens the new entrant firms to innovate and grow till a time frame, say a period of six months in the first timeline introduced by the Reserve Bank of India Innovation Hub for FinTech start-ups, which is associated with high amount of risks as numerous deceitful mobile money players can handpicked the funds of customers; paved with unpredictable risk profiles of the banks since regulatory mechanism needs to coped up immediately with ongoing technology associated risks.

The second measure involves intense supervisory mechanism because the individual start-up firms are allowed to function it and supervise in a live environment to validate the framework of specialized businesses. Globally, the density of global FinTech related regulatory sandboxes has increased specifically from mid-2018 through 2020, depicting rapid growth around the globe to test FinTech innovations and regulations (World Bank, 2020b). Government and regulatory authorities support the operation of such start-up firms through regulatory sandboxes, tax facilitation, R & D financing, however, the survival of these firms is subject to the innovative capacity of such companies, considering institutional and regulatory environment of the regions (Baba, et al., 2020). The time frame given to approved the products may not be sufficient enough to understand the associated risks as the range of period for regulatory sandboxes is between 6-8 months in most of the countries of the world as a benchmark. The experience from regulatory sandboxes could be cited to structure the regulatory framework. However, the regulatory sandboxes do have common guidelines/ terms and conditions under a controlled virtual environment for live testing of functioning of firms on a small scale, which may not be found suitable and unfit in those countries determined by existing economic frameworks (Table 6).

Another dimensions central to FinTech firms is the management of data generated, compiled and exchanged in new platforms for protection of data and privacy issues. There is high probability of foul use of data through multiple channels. FinTech innovations pose specific challenges regarding privacy, cyber security and operational risk (Messy, 2017). Study by (Kaur et al., 2021) defined specific cybersecurity vulnerabilities in FinTech into three different categories - technology vulnerabilities that is susceptible to smart phones applications, websites, outdated security controls; second one being the human vulnerabilities that involves handling of passwords, extent of cyber awareness; and transaction vulnerabilities that is cloud-based transactions, exchange of virtual currencies and compliance. In lower income and developing countries with poor indices of governance mechanisms, legal and regulatory frameworks are weak, there are questions for safeguard of cybersecurity, privacy of data and cross-border transfer of data. FinTech works successfully in the simultaneous progress of digital technologies which calls for facilities of broadband internet, smartphones, data stations and advanced technologies. In remote areas of developing countries of the world, such facilities are not built up or at nascent stage of implementation, constrained by geographical factors with poor infrastructures; and still large segment of population in

Table 6. Individual features of sandbox by country, focused on financial inclusion

WBG Region	Type of Economy	Type of Sandbox	Testing Period	Legal System	Type of Regulator	Year
Africa	EMDE	Thematic, Product	(6-12) months	Civil Law & Common Law	Central Bank, Other Govt. Body	2018
East Asia & Pacific	EMDE & AE	Product, Policy, Thematic	(5-12) months	Common Law, Civil Law, Hybrid System	Central Bank, Financial Supervisor, Securities Regulator	2017 to 2020
Europe & Central Asia	AE	Product, Policy	(3-6) months	Common Law	Financial Supervisor	2016
Latin America & Caribbean	EMDE	Product, Policy	(3-24) months	Civil Law, Common Law	Central Bank, Financial Sector Regulator	2018to 2020
Middle East & North Africa	EMDE	Thematic, Cross-border, Product	(6-12) months	Civil Law, Hybrid System, Common Law	Central Bank, Other Govt. Body	2016 to 2018
South Asia	EMDE	Product, Policy	(6-9) months	Common Law, Civil Law, Hybrid System	Central Bank, Securities Regulator	2019 to 2020

Source: World Bank (2020b)

rural areas do not have access to internet facilities. Given these factors, the FinTech firms have to opt out of the profitable business that may harm its sustainable growth and efficiency. Studies by (Rau, 2018; Fuster et al., 2018) evidence that percentage of population using internet does not explain the volume of lending or nor significant development of FinTech lending activities. Further, a start-up firm with huge amount of investment for the successful working and functioning of the new business models and a shortage of funding may deteriorate the mere characteristics or discontinue business in the long-run. All these quests the risks for financial stability, integrity and consumer protectionism.

Some Critical Views on FinTech From Extant Literature

There is growing literature on modern technology and its impact on financial sector. The Bali FinTech Agenda (BFA) lays out key issues to consider in how technological innovation is changing the dimension of financial services in terms of - economic efficiency, growth, financial stability, inclusion and integrity (IMF, 2019). Most of the FinTech firms are at nascent stage of live testing cohort under the regulatory sandbox of regulatory compliance. Issues on regulatory compliance, understanding the business model adopted, safety and security of data, risk profile of banks, impact of technology on the financial lives of the underprivileged sections of society are major concerns of modern technology in the banking sector. One dimension of such innovative products of finance is its outcome towards financial inclusion and financial literacy as a major policy drive when the users are not sophisticated. Study by (Balasubramanian, et al., 2021) highlighted that modern technology has not received much attention to poor groups, rather it is confined to 'high end' finance where the users of technology are either firms or reasonably rich individuals; and the revealed that poor are not capable of learning but overtime through experience they stick with new technology, so it promises more scope of FinTech in such areas. No doubt, FinTech has improved the quantum of access to banking by reducing costs and resources (Bachas et al., 2018); still people specifically in developing counties with fragile infrastructure fail to support the FinTech operations, and even the poor may face the problems of technophobia (Kenny, 2002). In Europe, the reach and development of FinTech companies are relatively lower than other regions, partly explained by strong pre-existing banking and financial inclusion, stringent regulation and also supported by preference for cash-based transactions though FinTech lending and payment tools are growing rapidly (Baba, et al., 2020). FinTech solutions do not only come with opportunities but also introduce new and exacerbate existing risk such as cyber-attacks, money laundering, terrorist financing, threats to data privacy and consumer protection (Berg et al., 2020). This highlight the necessity of robust infrastructure for successful operation of FinTech firms and easy accessibility of financial products to extend the outreach at the bottom of pyramids. Study by (Branzoli and Supino, 2020) found that innovative business models is mainly driven by the degree of local economic development and the state of competition in the banking sector; however, FinTech borrowers generally lack access to finance and they tend to be riskier than the traditional bank borrowers. In other words, we can say that adaptation of modern technology may be found difficult or failed in the initial stage in the underprivileged sections of the society, but calls for mechanisms to captivate the people from convergence towards the traditional channels. Since, the FinTech firms are opened and kept for experimentation and examination stage, there are complex technological issues and handling of data, backed up by sufficient funding from Venture Capitalists for innovation, research and development processes.

At present, the working and functioning of banks and financial institutions are deliberated towards sustainable and green finance as a part and parcel of social responsibility goals defined under the SDGs. This reminds about the attention towards understanding the characteristics of the investors and their non-economic goals and attributes that affect ethical behaviour in their decision making process such as collectivism, environmentalism, materialism, religiosity, risk tolerance and social investing efficacy are collectively examined as investors' characteristics in the study and found significant too (Sharma et al, 2020; & Vyas et al. 2020). Thus we can say that technological revolution in the financial industry on the one side portrays the efficacy of the financial system in the delivery of products and services, but to make understand the underlying characteristics of the investors that directly or indirectly affect the financial system in the long-run is significant.

There is still ambiguity on the success and level of disruptions by FinTech players (Jinasena et al., 2020; Citigroup 2016) and how to understand the level of technology adoption across time and space (Fosso Wamba et al. 2019; Marikyan et al. 2020); as in many cases the new FinTech firms are complement in nature rather than as a substitute for traditional banking services, i.e., more of alternative sources to consumers like, online lending is an alternative for the type of borrower usually underserved by traditional banks in developing countries (Cortina and Schmukler, 2018). Thus, the optimality of FinTech firms is subject to value addition from the welfare aspects in products and services defined by the institutional, regulatory framework, stakeholders - both technology supplier as well as the start-up firms, individual customers and bankers in particular. Meanwhile, there are scanty literatures that focussed on the value assessment of FinTech firms (Chen et al. 2019); and more research are needed in this aspects from the sustainable business and societal value. These deliberations and discussions on the possible implications of adoption and use of FinTech firms form the major agenda and scope of research in the financial sector.

THE WAY FORWARD

The committees and working group forms in FinTech innovation hubs and regulatory sandboxes emphasized the relevant regulatory and legal framework necessitated to validate the products and services of

FinTech companies subject to the safety and security aspects of the customers. Some of the major policy directives generalized from various reports and publications of World Bank, Global FinTech Hubs, regulatory authorities cover the dimensions of regulatory and legal framework, mitigation of risks, consumer protection, safeguards of private data and handling of technologies among others.

Infrastructures for FinTech: A good infrastructure in the form of telecommunications, digital and financial infrastructure is prerequisite for the successful operation and working of the FinTech start-ups which are under the surveillance of regulatory sandboxes. A good infrastructure will enable the firms to perform efficiently and effectively in handling of data, processing and facilitation processes.

Enabling Legal and Regulatory Framework: We know that the FinTech firms are under the cohorts of regulatory sandboxes for the validation and maturity of the financial products with predefined objectives of each financial product designed. All these can be addressed through a strong regulatory and legal framework to protect against risks, safe entry of new entrants in the markets, new product generation processes, sustaining business and develop trust towards the customers in particular.

Robust Financial and Data Infrastructure to Sustain Business: Strong institutional framework to protect data, mitigate risks of any misuse of information, to understand new technologies to cope up with the ongoing state of technology is important to sustain the businesses. This is because the type of technological risks associated with FinTech start-up firms are undefinable and manifest towards high risk profile of the banks.

FinTech and Financial Inclusion: One of the policy directives of the digitization of economic activities is the inclusiveness by bringing the poor and underserved sections of the society under the single roof of formal financial system. Digitization of the financial products and financial services has led to faster, easier and convenience in the use and access of the excluded masses, specifically in developing countries of the world. The mere introduction of mobile apps for android users make it convenient to deal of financial transaction in a much easier way for borrowing, saving and micro-insurance in such countries of the world. Therefore, we can say that FinTech has large scope for financial inclusion and financial literacy in a very convenient way in remote and underserved regions of the world.

Consumer Protectionism: One perspective of the FinTech products is - customers' protectionism, i.e., threats to customer and investor protections, cyber risks, quality of financial services for households and firms. These need to be considered while implementing the innovations in financial products so far as to continue a framework with trust, confidence and integrity by consumers. Product suitability, product designs and distributions, product affordability, accessibility and accountability are some of the attributes to be designed for ensuring the demands/needs of the customers in the market segment.

Cross-Country Differences in Ecosystem and Performance: Each country is defined by unique ecosystem and the relative strength of market structure, competitive spirit, funding mechanism and banking regulations faced by new entrants in the market. Hence, there is no 'one size fits all' common strategy that can be implemented at the global level under the regulatory sandboxes of central banks, rather it is more determined by regional specific factors. According to McKinsey report (2022), there are six factors that can produce an impact on the ecosystem while examining cross country variations in market economy- the state of market structure and maturity; access to capital; regulatory and legal landscape; mobility of acquisition; need for scaling and internationalization; and customer openness.

These are the common factors that should be taken for consideration while dealing with the major issues arising out of the functioning and operation of FinTech hubs in its start-up stages. Hence, given the economic, institutional and regional ecosystem, each country is prevalent with its own unique structural characteristics and these factors need to be addressed while setting a common goal of innovation hubs at the global and regional levels. The future of financial system has to incorporate these dimensions of FinTech along with its introduction of financial products and new business model for the continuity of business and sustainable business model in the long run.

CONCLUSION

The present chapter gives an overview of FinTech firms and its dynamics in the global financial market. From the deliberations as experienced through various surveys and reports of World Bank and publications of regulatory bodies, the chapter highlights the major regulatory challenges and pre-requisites for successful operation of FinTech firms, particularly in the banking sector. Digitization of financial products has large scope for financial inclusion for underserved sections of the society through mobile banking and its applications as experienced in developing nations of the world. Further, it has significant advantages in use– convenience, faster, easier and cost effective. On the other side, threads like cyber security issues, fraudulent activities by incumbent firms like illicit money laundering, terrorism financing, risks profile of banks, cloning of data, etc. that asks for strong regulatory framework and mechanisms to overcome the undefined technological risks. The regulatory bodies have a significant role for optimization of the FinTech firms, hence not only adhering to good governance, regulatory compliance and risk mitigation framework; it needs continuous encouragement and support towards innovations given the regulatory sandboxes targets.

REFERENCES

Baba, C., Batog, C., Flores, E., Gracia, B., Karpowicz, I., Kopyrski, P., Roaf, J., Shagunina, A., Elkan, R. V., & Xu, X. C. (2020). *Fintech in Europe: Promises and Threats.* IMF Working Paper, WP/20/241.

Bachas, P., Gertler, P., Higgins, S., & Seira, E. (2018). Digital financial services go a long way: Transaction costs and financial inclusion. *AEA Papers and Proceedings. American Economic Association, 108*, 444–448. doi:10.1257/pandp.20181013

BalasubramanianP.ChandraS. V. R.MurlidharanA.PrasannaT. L. (2021). Fintech For The Poor: Do Technological Failures Deter Financial Inclusion? https://ssrn.com/abstract=3840021 doi:10.2139/ssrn.3840021

Berg, G., Guadamillas, M., Natarajan, H., & Sarkar, A. (2020). *Fintech in Europe and Central Asia: Maximizing Benefits and Managing Risks. Fintech Note, no. 4.* World Bank. doi:10.1596/33591

BranzoliN.SupinoI. (2020). *FinTech Credit: a critical review of the empirical literature.* Bank of Italy, Financial Stability Directorate, Directorate General for Economics, Statistics and Research, Occasional Paper. https://ssrn.com/abstract=3612726

CCAF. (2022). *FinTech regulation in Asia Pacific, Cambridge Centre for Alternative Finance at the University of Cambridge.* Cambridge Judge Business School. https://www.jbs.cam.ac.uk/insight/2022/fintech-regulation-in-apac/

Chen, M. A., Wu, Q., & Yang, B. (2019). How valuable is FinTech innovation? *Review of Financial Studies, 32*(5), 2062–2106. doi:10.1093/rfs/hhy130

Citigroup. (2016). Digital Disruption: How Fintech is Forcing Banking to a Tipping Point. *Citi GPS: Global Perspectives & Solutions.* https://www.citivelocity.com/citigps/digital-disruption/

Cortina, J. J., & Schmukler, S. L. (2018, April). The Fintech Revolution: A Threat to Global Banking? Research & Policy Briefs. *World Bank Group*, (14), 1–4.

Fosso Wamba, S., Kala Kamdjoug, J. R., Bawack, R., & Keogh, G. (2019). Bitcoin, Blockchain, and FinTech: A systematic review and case studies in the supply chain. *Production Planning and Control, 31*(2-3), 1–28. doi:10.1080/09537287.2019.1631460

Fuster, A., Goldsmith-Pinkham, P., Ramadorai, T., & Walther, A. (2018). Predictably unequal? The effects of machine learning on credit markets. *SSRN Working Paper*, 3072038.

Global FinTech Hub Report. (2018). *The Future of Finance is Emerging: New Hubs, New Landscapes.* University of Cambridge, Judge Business School. https://www.jbs.cam.ac.uk/wp-content/uploads/2020/08/2018-ccaf-global-fintech-hub-report-eng.pdf

International Monetary Fund. (2019). *Fintech: The Experience so far.* Policy Paper No. 2019/024.

Jinasena, D. N., Spanaki, K., Papadopoulos, T., & Balta, M. E. (2020). Success and Failure Retrospectives of FinTech Projects: A Case Study Approach. *Information Systems Frontiers.* Advance online publication. doi:10.100710796-020-10079-4

Kaur, G., Lashkari, Z. H., & Lashkari, A. H. (2021). *Understanding Cybersecurity Management in Fintech – Challenges, Strategies, and Trends.* Spinger Nature Switzerland. doi:10.1007/978-3-030-79915-1

Kenny, C. (2002). Information and communication technologies for direct poverty alleviation: Costs and benefits. *Development Policy Review, 20*(2), 141–157. doi:10.1111/1467-7679.00162

Khanna, V., & Sharma, R. (2017). Customer Switching Behavior in Retail Banking in India. *International Journal of Applied Business and Economic Research, 15*(9), 427–441.

Kovas, A. (2018). *Understanding the Risks of Fintech.* Expert Talk, Thomson Reuters.

Marikyan, D., Papagiannidis, S., & Alamanos, E. (2020). Cognitive dissonance in technology Adoption: A Study of Smart Home Users. *Information Systems Frontiers.* Advance online publication. doi:10.100710796-020-10042-3 PMID:32837263

McKinsey. (2022). *Europe's fintech opportunity.* McKinsey and Company Report. https://www.mckinsey.com/industries/financial-services/our-insights/europes-fintech-opportunity#/

Mehta, K., Sharma, R., & Khanna, V. (2023). Customer switching behaviour in Indian retail banking using logit regression. *International Journal of Business Excellence, 29*(4), 518–545. doi:10.1504/IJBEX.2023.130255

Messy, F.-A. (2017). FinTech Developments & Their Consequences for the Financial Industry & Regulators in Asia & Beyond. *Japan Spotlight*, 44-49.

Rau, R. (2018). Law, Trust, and the Development of Crowdfunding. *SSRN Working Paper*, 2989056.

RBI. (2018). *Report of the Working Group on Fin Tech and Digital Banking*. https://www.rbi.org.in/Scripts/PublicationReportDetails.aspx?UrlPage=&ID=892

RBI. (2020). FinTech: The Force of Creative Disruption. *RBI Bulletin*. https://www.rbi.org.in/Scripts/BS_ViewBulletin.aspx?Id=19899

RBI. (2021a). *Enabling Framework for Regulatory Sandbox*. RBI Report. https://www.rbi.org.in/Scripts/PublicationReportDetails.aspx?UrlPage=&ID=1187

RBI. (2021b). *Report of the Working Group on Digital Lending including Lending through Online Platforms and Mobile Apps*. RBI Press Release. https://www.rbi.org.in/Scripts/BS_PressReleaseDisplay.aspx?prid=52589

RBI. (2021c). *Statement on Developing and Regulatory Policies*. RBI Press Release. https://www.rbi.org.in/Scripts/BS_PressReleaseDisplay.aspx?prid=52368

Sharma, R., Mehta, K., & Vyas, V. (2020). Responsible Investing: A Study on Non-Economic Goals and Investors' Characteristics. *Applied Finance Letters*, *9*(SI), 63-78. doi:10.24135/afl.v9i2.245

Statista. (2022a). *Investments into fintech companies globally 2010-2022*. https://www.statista.com/statistics/719385/investments-into-fintech-companies-globally/

Statista. (2022b). *Largest fintech companies worldwide 2021, by market cap*. https://www.statista.com/statistics/1262288/largest-fintech-companies-by-market-cap/

Statista. (2022c). *Number of fintech start-ups worldwide 2018-2021, by region*. https://www.statista.com/statistics/893954/number-fintech-startups-by-region/

Trivedi, S., Mehta, K., & Sharma, R. (2021). Systematic Literature Review on Application of Blockchain Technology in E-Finance and Financial Services. *Journal of Technology Management & Innovation*, *16*(3), 90–102. doi:10.4067/S0718-27242021000300089

Vyas, V., Mehta, K., & Sharma, R. (2020). Investigating socially responsible investing behaviour of Indian investors using structural equation modelling. *Journal of Sustainable Finance & Investment*, 1–23. doi:10.1080/20430795.2020.1790958

World Bank. (2020a). *Digital Financial Services*. Author.

World Bank. (2020b). *Key Data from Regulatory Sandboxes across the Globe*. https://www.worldbank.org/en/topic/fintech/brief/key-data-from-regulatory-sandboxes-across-the-globe

World Bank. (2021). *Consumer Risks in Fintech: New Manifestations of Consumer Risks and Emerging Regulatory Approaches*. https://openknowledge.worldbank.org/handle/10986/35699

World Bank. (2022a). *Digital Development Overview*. https://www.worldbank.org/en/topic/digitaldevelopment/overview

World Bank. (2022b). *Fintech and the Future of Finance Overview Paper*. Author.

World Bank & CCAF. (2022). *The 3rd Global Fintech Regulator Survey*. World Bank Group and the University of Cambridge.

Chapter 12
Barriers and Potential of Blockchain Technology in FinTech

Bhanu Arora
https://orcid.org/0000-0001-9714-2168
Sushant University, India

Jagat Narayan Giri
Sushant University, India

Kanika Sachdeva
Sushant University, India

ABSTRACT

This chapter explores the barriers and potential of blockchain technology in the FinTech sector. It begins by highlighting the fundamental characteristics of blockchains, emphasizing their ability to securely store and transfer data without the involvement of intermediaries. The transparency provided by blockchain's transaction visibility is contrasted with traditional banking systems. The decentralized nature of blockchain is discussed, along with its applicability in various industries such as cryptocurrencies, financial services, risk management, IoT, and public and social services. The chapter acknowledges the extensive research conducted to analyze blockchain technology and its applications, leading to a need for a comprehensive examination. It addresses blockchain taxonomy, consensus techniques, applications, technological challenges, and recent developments, offering insights into the future possibilities of this technology. By identifying both the barriers and potential, this chapter aims to contribute to the understanding of blockchain technology's role in the FinTech industry.

DOI: 10.4018/978-1-6684-8624-5.ch012

INTRODUCTION

Industry and academics have recently focused on cryptocurrencies. In the year 2016, the market capitalization of bitcoin topped over $10 billion (Hileman, 2016). Bitcoin relies on blockchain. Blockchain was first suggested in the year of 2008 and its execution started in the year of 2009 (Nakamoto, 2008). In lay man terms blockchain is a type of public ledger that stores transactions in the form of blocks. New blocks add to this chain. Blockchain technology is decentralized, persistent, anonymous, and auditable. Blockchain allows decentralized transactions. Blockchain reduces costs and boosts efficiency.

Blockchain technology is not limited to the Bitcoin network. Peters et al. (2015) state that blockchain technology may find use in online payment systems and digital asset services (Foroglou and Tsilidou, 2015). Smart contracts, public services, the Internet of Things, reputation management systems, and security services are a few examples of the conceivable internet interactions that might be enabled by blockchain technology. The technology behind blockchain makes all of these things feasible (Noyes, 2016).

Despite the great promise it holds for the development of future internet services, the blockchain technology provides a number of critical problems that must be overcome. The capacity to scale is a big obstacle to overcome. At this time, a Bitcoin block is 1 megabyte in size and is mined every 10 minutes. Thus, high-frequency trading is impossible on the Bitcoin network, which can only process 7 transactions per second. However, bigger blocks need more storage and slower network propagation. Users will want to maintain such a massive blockchain, which will centralize it. As a result, striking a balance between the size of the blocks and their level of protection is challenging. Second, certain miners may earn much more their share if they are too greedy (Eyal and Sirer, 2018). Miners bury their blocks with the hopes of making more money in the future. As a result, the expansion of the blockchain is limited by the multiple branches. As a result of this, many solutions are required to address this problem. The true IP address of a user can be determined if one so chooses. Both Proof-of-Work (PoW) and Proof-of-Stake (PoS), two of the most used approaches for reaching agreement today, are riddled with severe faults. PoW consumes an excessive amount of power, but PoS consensus may lead to the wealthy becoming even wealthier. In order to further develop blockchain technology, these problems need to be overcome.

Blogs, wikis, forums, code, conference papers, and journal papers are all examples of different types of blockchain-related writing. In 2016, Tschorsch and Scheuermann carried out a comprehensive analysis of the technological aspects of decentralized digital currencies such as Bitcoin. Our study emphasises blockchain technology rather than digital currency (Tschorsch and Scheuermann, 2016). Blockchain technical paper from Nomura Research Institute (Zheng et al., 2017). Unlike the study which was carried out by Nomura Research Institute, our study covers current blockchain research and future prospects (Zheng et al., 2018). This study extends by covering blockchain technological specifics, consensus techniques, applications, research problems, and future prospects (Zheng et al., 2017).

BLOCKCHAIN ARCHITECTURE

Like a public ledger, blockchain blocks include all transaction records (Chuen, 2015). Figure 1 depicts a blockchain system. In most cases, a hash value is utilized in order to guarantee that each block precisely copies its parent block. The hashes of uncle blocks, which are blocks that are the offspring of the blocks that are ancestors of the current block, would likewise be preserved on the Ethereum blockchain (Buterin, 2014). Genesis blocks have no parents.

Figure 1. Example of a blockchain that consisting of an infinite chain of blockchains

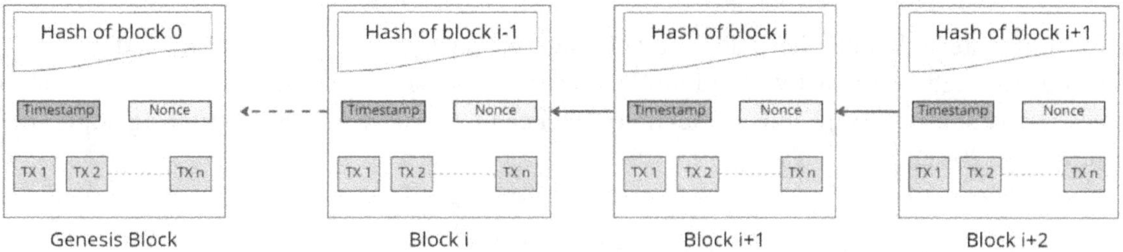

Block Architecture in a Blockchain Network

Figure 2 depicts an example of a block chain consisting of a block beginning and block body.

A block header includes the following:

- **Block version:** Specifies the rule set to use while validating blocks
- **Parent Block Hash:** An encoded 256-bit number that references the prior block
- **Merkle Tree Root Hash:** Hash value of the whole block of transactions
- **Timestamp:** Date and time now in seconds since 1970-01-01T00:00 UTC
- **nBits:** Existing hashing goal in a condensed version
- **Nonce:** A 4-byte value that begins at 0 and increments with each hash

The transaction counters and the actual transactions make up the block's body. The head of the block is called the header. In addition to the size of the transactions themselves, the block size also plays a role in determining the maximum number of transaction that may be included within a single block. Asymmetric cryptography is used to validate transactions inside the blockchain (Zheng et al., 2017). Untrustworthy environments utilize asymmetric cryptography digital signatures. After this comes the digital signature.

Figure 2. Block structure

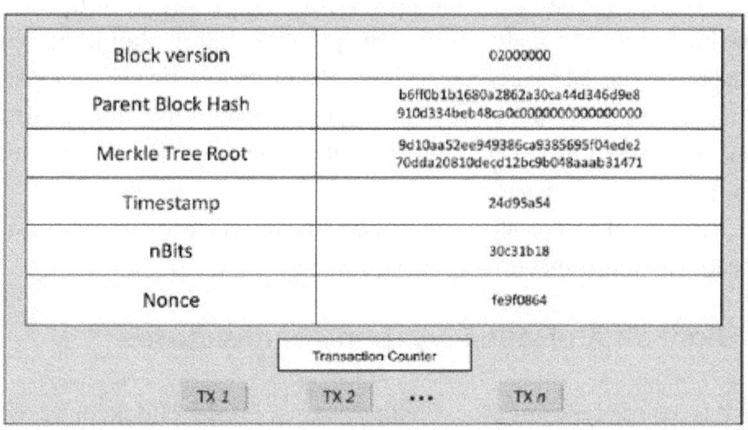

Digital Signature

Users have private and public keys. Private keys sign transactions. Public keys access digitally signed transactions throughout the network. Figure 3 illustrates blockchain digital signatures. Digital signatures have two phases: signing and verification. Blockchains employ ECDSA digital signature methods (Johnson et al., 2001).

Figure 3. The usage of a digital signature on a blockchain

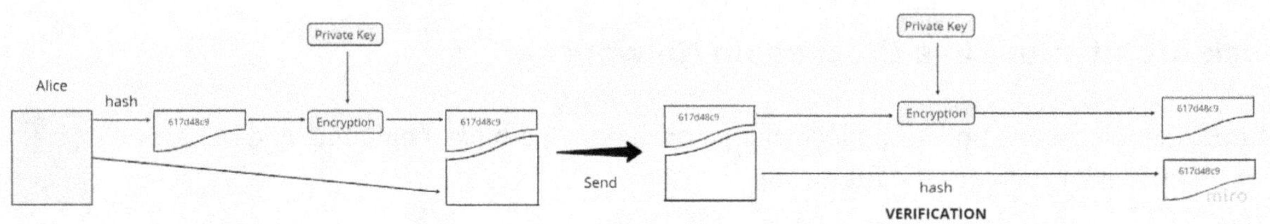

Blockchain's Essential Features

Here are some of blockchain's most distinguishing features.

- **Decentralization:** Each transaction in a typical centralized transaction system has to be certified by the centralized trustworthy organization (like the central bank), leading to in cost and performance constraints for the central server. Centralized transaction systems are often used in financial institutions. The blockchain network enables peer-to-peer transactions that do not need authentication from a central authority. Blockchain technology lowers server costs, including those associated with development and maintenance, as well as stumbling blocks in the performance of the central server.
- **Persistency:** Because each transaction that takes place anywhere on the network is required to be confirmed and documented in blocks located everywhere on the network, manipulation is extremely difficult to accomplish. Other nodes would check the validity of the transactions and blocks that have been published. Because of this, the deception should be obvious.
- **Anonymity:** Each user has a blockchain address. To protect their identity, users can create numerous addresses. User data is no longer centrally stored. This keeps blockchain transactions private. Blockchain's inherent restriction prevents absolute privacy preservation (details refer to Section v).
- **Auditability:** Each Bitcoin transaction might be tracked to prior transactions. It enhances blockchain data traceability and transparency.

A Taxonomy of Blockchain-Based System Architectures

In today's world, there are three types of blockchain systems: Public Blockchain systems, Private Blockchain systems, and Consortium Blockchain systems (Buterin, 2015). The distinctive characteristics of each of all three of these blockchains are dissected here. Table 1 compares.

Table 1. Examining the similarities and differences between public blockchains, consortium blockchains, and private blockchains

Type of Blockchain	Consensus Determination	Read Permission	Immutability	Efficiency	Centralized	Consensus Process
Public Blockchain	All of the Miners	Public	Almost hard to alter	Low	No	Permissions
Consortium Blockchain	Set of selected nodes	May be open or restricted	Can be altered	High	Partial	Permissioned
Private Blockchain	One institution	May be open or restricted	Can be altered	High	Yes	Permissioned

- **Consensus Determination:** If the blockchain in question is public, then every node on the network has the ability to take part in the process of arriving at a consensus. Further, a consortium blockchain restricts the nodes that are allowed to verify blocks to a limited group that has been picked in advance. This ensures that the integrity of the network is not compromised. A single entity is required to make all choices for a private blockchain, and this entity has the option of deciding who will form the ultimate consensus.
- **Read Permission:** Everyone is able to see public blockchain transactions, however in order to view private or consortium blockchain transactions, you will need to have appropriate authorization. The availability of the data to the general public may be decided either by the consortium or by the institution.
- **Immutability:** It is extremely difficult to manipulate the public blockchain since the network itself is dispersed in such a way that information is not centralised. However, this might take place if a majority of the consortium or the dominant corporation decides to reverse or tampering with the blockchain network or private blockchain.
- **Efficiency:** The public blockchain network is comprised of a large number of nodes; thus, the propagation of blocks and transactions is a slow process. The constraints of the public blockchain would be substantially more stringent if safety of the network were taken into consideration. As a direct consequence of this, transaction throughput is poor, and there is an excessive amount of delay. It's possible that private blockchains and consortium blockchains can function more efficiently with a smaller number of validators.
- **Centralized:** Private blockchains are highly concentrated since they are controlled by a single party, whereas consortium blockchains are mostly distributed. This is the fundamental contrast that can be made between the three different types of blockchains.
- **Consensus Process:** Any individual on the face of the globe is welcome to take part in the process of reaching agreement while it is being built on the public blockchain. Consortia blockchains and private blockchains, on the other hand, as well as public blockchains, do need to adhere to certain permission standards. In order for a consortium or private blockchain that has more than one node to take part in the process of reaching consensus, at least one of the nodes that make up the consortium or private blockchain must first be certified.

The public blockchain is able to attract many users because of their openness. Communities are also active. Daily public blockchain creation. Consortium blockchain has several business uses. Hyperledger builds business consortium blockchain frameworks (hyperledger, 2015). Ethereum provides consortium blockchain tools (ethereum, n.d.). Many companies employ private blockchain for efficiency and authenticity of data.

CONSENSUS ALGORITHMS

The Byzantine Generals (BG) Problem has been modified to address the issue of reaching agreement among blockchain's potentially untrustworthy nodes (Lamport et al., 1982). In this issue of BG, the city is surrounded by a group of Byzantine Generals responsible for a certain military unit. If just a subset of the generals attempted to storm the city, the assault would be unsuccessful. The generals are required to confer with one another before deciding whether or not to launch an assault. Nonetheless, there was a risk that certain generals might betray their side. It's possible that the traitor will provide each general with a unique choice. This environment cannot be relied upon in any way. In situations like these, it may be impossible to reach a consensus on anything. The blockchain system lacks a central node, therefore there is no way to ensure that the ledgers maintained by the various nodes are similar to one another. It is not necessary for nodes to have confidence in one another. As a consequence of this, a number of different approaches are necessary in order to ensure the ledgers' consistency over many nodes. Next, we outline a number of popular strategies for achieving blockchain consensus.

Approaches to Reach Consensus

Proof-of-Work, often known as PoW, is a method for reaching consensus that is utilised by the Bitcoin network (Nakamoto, 2008). In order to authenticate PoW, a challenging computational method is necessary. Proof-of-Work (PoW) requires each network node to continually alter a hash value based on the block header. This is done in order to validate transactions. According to the terms of the agreement, the value that was forecasted must be less than or on par with a particular amount that was provided. In order to accomplish what has to be done, the hash value needs to be continuously computed by every node in the dispersed network utilising one-of-a-kind nonces. Each of the other nodes is responsible for ensuring that the data obtained by one node is accurate. The fresh block will be checked for any potentially fraudulent transactions before it is used. Following the completion of the computation required to verify the outcome of the transactions, a new block is added to the blockchain to illustrate the result. The PoW mechanism is mining, and miners compute hashes. It is advised to utilise an incentive method, such as providing the miner a modest Bitcoin share, since authentication takes time (Nakamoto, 2008).

Since every node in the distributed network keeps its own copy of each transaction, it is very impossible to make any changes to the public blockchain. In spite of this, the blockchain network or a private blockchain may be altered or destroyed if the majority of the consortium or the organisation that has the most power chooses to do so. As a consequence, branches (or forks), as seen in Figure 4, may develop. It is improbable that the next block will be generated concurrently by two conflicting forks. The PoW protocol states that the link that becomes larger after is the actual one. Have a look at Figure 4 once again. Imagine that blocks A11 and C11 both create forks that are being verified simultaneously. When the miners are working on both of them, the newly produced block gets added to the respective forks. The miners working on the C11-C12 fork will switch to block A12 when a block (let's say A12) is added to block A11. Because it is no longer being incremented, C12 in the C11-C12 split is now an orphan

Figure 4. Branches in a blockchain scenario (the longer of the two branches would be accepted as the primary one, while the other would be deserted)

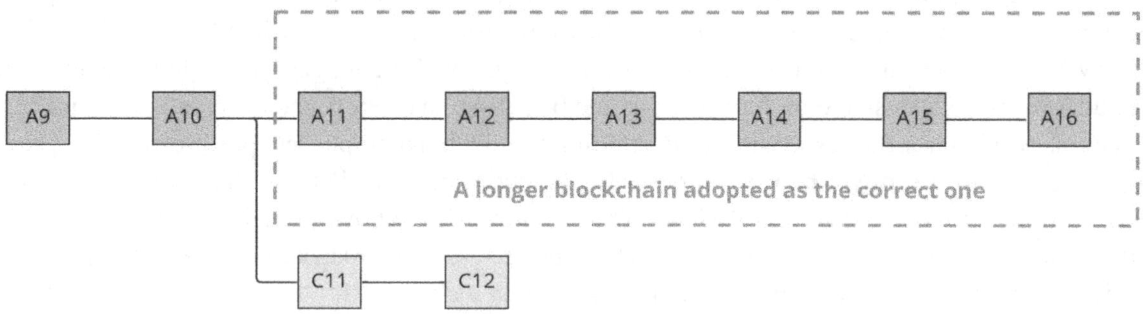

block. Once a sufficient number of blocks have been added to a blockchain, it becomes very impossible to undo those additions and change the transactions. The Bitcoin blockchain is considered authentic once around six blocks have been added to it (e.g., the chain of blocks A11, A12, A13, A14, A15 and A16 in Figure 4). Block interval is influenced by many parameter settings. Ethereum blocks are created every 17 seconds, whereas Bitcoin blocks are created every 10 minutes on average.

With PoW, miners are tasked with doing a number of computational tasks, but these operations are inefficient and drain the network's resources. As a means of mitigating this loss, certain PoW strategies have been devised that may also serve other purposes. For instance, the cryptocurrency Primecoin looks for distinctive patterns of prime numbers that could potentially be implemented in mathematical research (King, 2013). To mine the PoW block without using any energy, Proof of Burn recommends that miners transfer their money to addresses that cannot be redeemed (P4Titan, 2014). Miners may mine blocks by burning money without the requirement for strong gear like PoW.

Proof-of-Work is obsolete in favor of the more resource-friendly Proof-of-Stake (PoS). PoS asks customers to show their cash rather than looking for a nonce in an endless zone because it is believed that customers who have a greater amount of cash on hand are less likely to launch a hacking attempt on the network. As the individual with the greatest amount will automatically become the network's leader, the choosing mechanism based on account balances is fundamentally flawed. To choose the next block's forger, the stake amount and numerous possibilities are offered. In order to predict the next generator, Blackcoin makes use of randomness (Vasin, 2014). It uses a technique that accounts for the stake size while searching for the lowest possible hash value. Peercoin allows users to filter currencies by year. With Peercoin, the likelihood of having a coinage set mined for the next block increases with the age and size of the coinage in the set. When compared to PoW, PoS is superior in terms of energy efficiency and produces far less waste. Unfortunately, as a consequence of the low costs of mining, assaults can take place. Blockchains typically start off with PoW before they transition to PoS later on. Proof-of-Stake (PoS) is a type of cryptocurrency that will replace Proof-of-Work (PoW) coins like Ethash. Ethereum, for one, intends to make the switch from PoW coins like Ethash to PoS coins. (Wood, 2014) (Zamfir, 2015). No miners' signatures are required on a block after it has been mined for it to be valid. In this approach, not even a single coin holder with control over 50% of the total supply could prevent the creation of new blocks. Stake can occasionally take on other forms. For instance, when trying to mine the block, miners must prepare a significant amount of space on their hard drives due to the proof of capacity (burstcoin, 2014).

A replication strategy known as Practical Byzantine Fault Tolerance (PBFT) is one that is able to withstand byzantine defects (Miguel and Barbara, 1999). As PBFT can withstand up to a third of malicious byzantine copies, it is used as the consensus technique in Hyperledger Fabric (hyperledger, 2015). A round determines a fresh block. A primary would be chosen in every round in accordance with certain regulations. It also has the responsibility of guiding the deal. Three phases, pre-preparation, preparation, and commitment, might be used to describe the entire process. If more than 2/3 of nodes voted, a node advanced to the next level. PBFT requires the network to know all nodes. Similarly to how the Stellar Consensus Protocol (SCP) operates as a Byzantine agreement mechanism, the PBFT does as well (Mazieres, 2015). As a result, PBFT does not use a hashing technique. In PBFT, every node must poll its neighbours, but with SCP, users may pick and choose which users they trust. Antshares has developed and deployed dBFT, which is a byzantine fault tolerance protocol that is based on PBFT (antshares, 2016). dBFT only casts votes on nodes that are thought to be knowledgeable in the subject matter, as opposed to having each and every node vote and save transactions.

Delegation of Stake Proof (DPOS): As with POS systems, miners' stakes determine how often they get to build blocks. Whereas POS is a direct democracy, DPOS is a representative democracy. A block is created and validated by delegates chosen by stakeholders. Block validation would need a lot fewer nodes, which would speed up block confirmation and transaction confirmation. Alterations to the block size and time between blocks are possible. As consumers have the power to vote delegates out of office, dishonest ones are not a problem. DPOS is the cornerstone of Bitshares and has already been deployed (bitshares, n.d.).

Within a bigger network, a consensus process known as ripple making use of smaller networks that are individually trusted by the members of the larger network. On the network, the various sorts of nodes are responsible for the following distinct tasks: servers that take part in consensus and clients that just transfer payments. Every node in a PBFT network must make a query to every other node, while Ripple servers just have to make a query to their own Unique Node List (UNL). The server values UNL highly. While deciding whether or not to record a transaction, the server would poll the relevant UNL nodes. If 80% or more of the agreements were obtained, the deal would be entered into the books. UNL ledgers are considered trustworthy if the number of compromised nodes is fewer than 20%.

The Tendermint consensus algorithm is byzantine (Kwon, 2014). There is a round of voting to choose which block will be used next. A proposer will be chosen to declare a disputed block at this stage. As a result, selecting a proposer requires knowledge of all nodes. Others have suggested dividing it into three stages:

Prevote Step: To prevote a proposed block, validators must select whether or not to publish their vote.

Precommit Step: If the node has received over two-thirds of the necessary number of prevotes, it is going to transmit a precommit for the requested block. A node is considered to have entered the commit stage after it has obtained more than two-thirds of the precommits.

Commit Step: After the validity of that block has been established, the node will broadcast a commit for it. It is considered accepted by the node if it has gotten at least two-thirds of the necessary commits for the block.

Nodes in Tendermint still need to take precautions to protect their currencies even if the validating mechanism is quite similar to PBFT. A validator will be penalised if it is found to be unreliable.

Evaluating Consensus Algorithms

When selecting on a consensus method, it's vital to assess their benefits and drawbacks. We compare several consensus techniques in Table 2 using the characteristics provided by (Vukoli´c, 2015).

Table 2. Comparison of common consensus algorithms

Common Consensus Algorithms	Node Identity Management	Energy Saving	Accepted Power of Adversary	Example
Pow	Open	No	less than 25% computing power	Bitcoin
PoS	Open	Partial	less than 51% stake	Peercoin
PBFT	Permissioned	Yes	less than 33.3% faculty replicas	Hyperledger Fabric
DPOS	Open	Partial	less than 51% validators	Bitshares
Ripple	Open	Yes	less than 20% faculty nodes in UNL	Ripple
Tendermint	Permissioned	Yes	less than 33.3% byzantine voting power	Tendermint

Node Identity Management: During the process of selecting the starting point for every round, PBFT has to be aware of the identities of all miners, whereas Tendermint must remain aware of the identities of all validators. Nodes may simply join the network in order for them to take part in Proof-of-Work, Proof-of-Stake, Delegated Proof-of-Stake, or Ripple.

Energy Saving: The block header is hashed many times by miners so that they may obtain the required value in PoW. Because of this, a great deal of energy is required for the procedure. Miners in PoS and DPOS still hash the block header for the purpose to hunt for the target value, but given that the search area is narrower, they should spend a significantly smaller amount of time doing so. Mining is not required for the consensus process used by PBFT, Ripple, or Tendermint. As a result, its use of energy is significantly reduced.

Acceptance of the Opponent's Strength: It is generally agreed upon that one must possess 51% of the total hashing power of the network in order to assume control of it. In PoW systems, however, a mining strategy that is motivated only by financial gain may enable miners to increase their earnings while using only 25% of the available hashing power. With PBFT and Tendermint, you can fix as many as a third of the broken nodes. As long there are no more than 20% corrupt nodes in a UNL, Ripple is shown to keep its accuracy (Eyal and Sirer, 2014).

Advances on Consensus Algorithms

The best consensus algorithms balance usability, security, and productivity. Traditional consensus methods still have several problems despite recent improvements. In order to address some problems with existing blockchains, new consensus algorithms are now being created. By separating block creation from transaction confirmation, PeerCensus aims to dramatically increase the rate at which agreement is reached (Decker et al., 2016). To further guarantee a regular block generation rate, Kraft also suggested a new consensus technique (Kraft, 2016). It is well known that there is a risk involved for Bitcoin whenever there is a rise in the pace when new blocks are generated. To address this issue, researchers created the GHOST chain. This stands for "Greedy Heaviest-Observed Sub-Tree" (Sompolinsky and Zohar, 2013). Instead than just selecting the longest branch, GHOST assigns weights to each branch so that miners may choose the optimal one to follow. The consensus procedure of a peer-to-peer blockchain system says that anybody who offers non-interactive evidence of irretrievability of the previously captured snaps is agreed to create the block. This implies that the block may be constructed by anyone (Chepurnoy et al., 2016). Instead than storing whole blocks, miners simply need to save old block headers in such a system.

APPLICATIONS OF BLOCKCHAIN

Applications for blockchain technology are many and varied. We list numerous common blockchain uses in this section. We loosely group the blockchain's applications into five categories as shown in Figure 5:

- Finance
- Internet of Things
- Public and social services
- Reputation systems
- Confidentiality and safety

Figure 5. Industry segments where blockchain is most effective

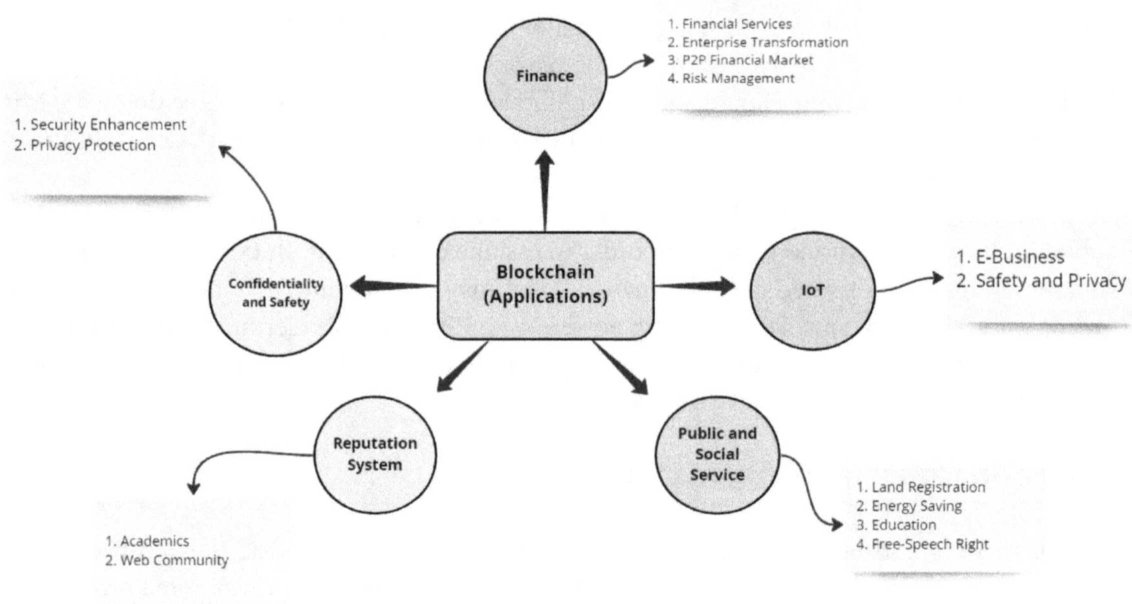

Finance

- **Financial Services:** Blockchain technologies like Bitcoin and Hyperledger have had a significant influence on conventional financial and commercial services (Nakamoto, 2008) and (hyperledger, 2015). As per a study done bt Peters, blockchain has the ability to upend the banking industry (Peters et al., 2015). Collateralization of financial derivatives is one example of a valid business application for blockchain that Morini highlighted, with the potential to reduce costs and risks (Morini, 2016). Microsoft Azure and IBM are just two examples of large software companies who are paying special attention to blockchain by providing hosted solutions like Blockchain-as-a-Service (azure, 2016) and (ibm, 2016).
- **Enterprise Transformation:** Blockchain technology, which has enabled the expansion of financial and commercial services, may be the key to a successful conclusion of the enterprise transformation for many established businesses. Think about a scenario involving postal workers (POs). By offering new financial and non-financial services, blockchain and cryptocurrency technologies can assist existing Postal Operators (POs), who now serve as a straightforward mediator between businesses and customers. Post Offices (POs) may each issue their own postcoin, a coloured version of Bitcoin, as suggested by the study of Jaag and Bach. Postcoin may gain popularity rapidly due to the public's trust in POs and the latter's huge retail network.
- **P2P Financial Market:** The development of a trustworthy P2P financial market might be facilitated by blockchain technology. Noyes investigated the possibility of developing a peer-to-peer (P2P) financial MPC (Multiparty Computing) marketplace by fusing together P2P practices with MPC protocols (Noyes, 2016b). Offloading computing chores to blockchain-based MPC marketplaces can be accomplished through the use of a web of anonymous peer processors.
- **Risk Management:** It is possible that efficiency in financial technology might be improved by coupling the framework of risk management with blockchain (FinTech). To assess the dangers of investments in the Luxembourgian market, Pilkington offered a novel risk management system that makes use of blockchain technology (Pilkington, 2016). Investors who now store their shares with a group of custodians face the chance of experiencing any of the aforementioned problems. Blockchain enables investments and collateral decisions to be made rapidly rather than after careful deliberation. Micheler and Heyde developed a way that would integrate a new system with blockchain in order to lower the degree of custody risk while maintaining an identical level of transactional security (Micheler and von derHeyde, 2016). Decentralized autonomous organizations (DAO) can collaborate on commercial projects thanks to blockchain-based smart contracts. A DAO-GaaS conflict model that is extremely trustworthy was made public in order to protect the consistency requirements that were produced as a consequence of business semantics (Norta et al., 2015).

Internet of Things (IoT)

The IoT is enabled and created by the combination of connected devices and services (Atzori et al., 2010). RFID-based logistics management, smart homes, e-health, smart grids, marine, and other use cases are all prime candidates for the next generation of Internet of Things innovation (Dixon et al., 2012) (Wang, et al., 2015). Blockchain, a distributed ledger technology, might be used to improve the IoT.

- **E-Business:** A novel IoT E-business model is put out by, who also implements the smart property transaction using a blockchain and smart contracts (Zhang and Wen, 2015). Distributed autonomous companies (DACs) are used as a decentralized transaction entity in this concept. To acquire currencies and exchange sensor data between themselves, people trade using DACs.
- **Safety and Privacy:** The sector around the web and the Internet of Things is characterized by a number of fundamental challenges, including security and privacy. The adoption of blockchain technology is another potential means of enhancing the privacy of Internet of Things applications. It was advised specifically that a unique design be used to aid the device in proving its production history independently of a third party and to allow for anonymous registration (Hardjono and Smith, 2016).

Public and Social Services

Public and social services are another area where blockchain technology may be put to good use.

- **Land Registration:** Land registration is a common use case for blockchain technology in government, since it allows for the secure and transparent recording of data regarding real estate ownership, including the location, size, and condition of individual plots, as well as the rights tied to them (NRI, 2015).
- **Education:** Blockchain was first designed to make it possible to conduct financial transactions in an environment without any trust. But, if we consider the time and effort put into both studying and teaching to be equivalent to currency, then blockchain technology may find use in the online education market. Devine advocated using blockchain technology to teach people how to code (Devine, 2015). For blockchain education, teachers might pack and insert blocks, and student achievements can be seen as currency.
- **Free-Speech Right:** Several have hypothesized that blockchain technology may be used to safeguard the core infrastructure of the internet, including things like user credentials and domain name systems. Namecoin is an open-source project that aims to increase decentralization of the Domain Name System (DNS), as well as security, resilience to censorship, privacy, and speed (namecoin, 2014). By strengthening the web's ability to withstand repression, it defends the right to free speech online.
- **Energy Saving:** Blockchain technology may find use in the renewable energy sector as well. To those who offer solar energy, there is a digital currency called solarcoin. This was introduced by Gogerty and Zitoli (Gogerty and Zitoli, 2011).

Mobile devices with digital signatures attached might take the role of seals on papers that are presented to administrative departments in the future public services connected with blockchains. Large amounts of paperwork can be considerably reduced in this way.

Reputation System

The degree to which the general public places their faith in you is directly related to your reputation. One's credibility increases as their reputation does. A person's standing in the community may be evaluated in light of their previous interactions with its members. The practise of altering one's public profile for malicious purposes is on the rise. As an example, many online service companies create a large number of fake accounts to boost their credibility.

- **Academics:** To kick things off, we'd give each institution and intellectual contribution a sum of money based on their perceived value to the field of education. A staff member may receive an award from an institution if some reputation records are transferred to them. All reputation changes might be easily tracked because transactions are kept on the blockchain.
- **Web Community:** Assessing a user's position inside a virtual group is essential. A blockchain-based reputation model was put out by Carboni, in which a client signs a voucher to indicate their satisfaction with the service and their desire to provide positive feedback (Barcelo, 2014). To deter the Sybil attack, a service provider must deduct an additional 3% of the network payment made after signing a voucher for the voting charge. The voting fee is used to determine a service provider's reputation.

Confidentiality and Safety

- **Strengthening Defenses:** Numerous mobile services and gadgets have proliferated recently, and they are showing signs of susceptibility to rogue nodes. In order to locate suspicious files using pattern matching methods, a number of anti-malware filters have been developed, and they all rely on a remote database to store and modify infection patterns. These centralized defences, nevertheless, are equally open to nefarious intruders. The security of decentralized networks may be improved by using blockchain technology. Charles in particular introduced BitAV, an unique anti-malware ecosystem that allows users to share infection patterns on a blockchain (Noyes, 2016a). BitAV can improve fault tolerance in this way. Noyes demonstrates how BitAV may increase scanning efficiency and fault dependability (Noyes, 2016a).
- **Privacy Protection:** Several mobile service and social network firms are gathering our sensitive data, which is already at danger from viruses and the increasing likelihood of private information exposure. Data collected is often stored on service providers' central servers, which are vulnerable to cyber-attacks. It's possible that data that's sensitive to privacy may be stored more securely with the use of blockchain technology.

BLOCKCHAIN TECHNOLOGY AND CHALLENGES FACED BY FINANCE INDUSTRY

There have been a lot of problems in the financial sector for a long time. Amazing technological progress has helped address several challenges, but certain innovations have also generated unanticipated difficulties. Because there is such a wide variety of available financial technology solutions today, it can be challenging for financial services firms to home in on the one that most closely satisfies their requirements. People seek a solution that would fix all of their problems at once because of this, and they are looking for a panacea.

Figure 6. Uses of blockchain in finance

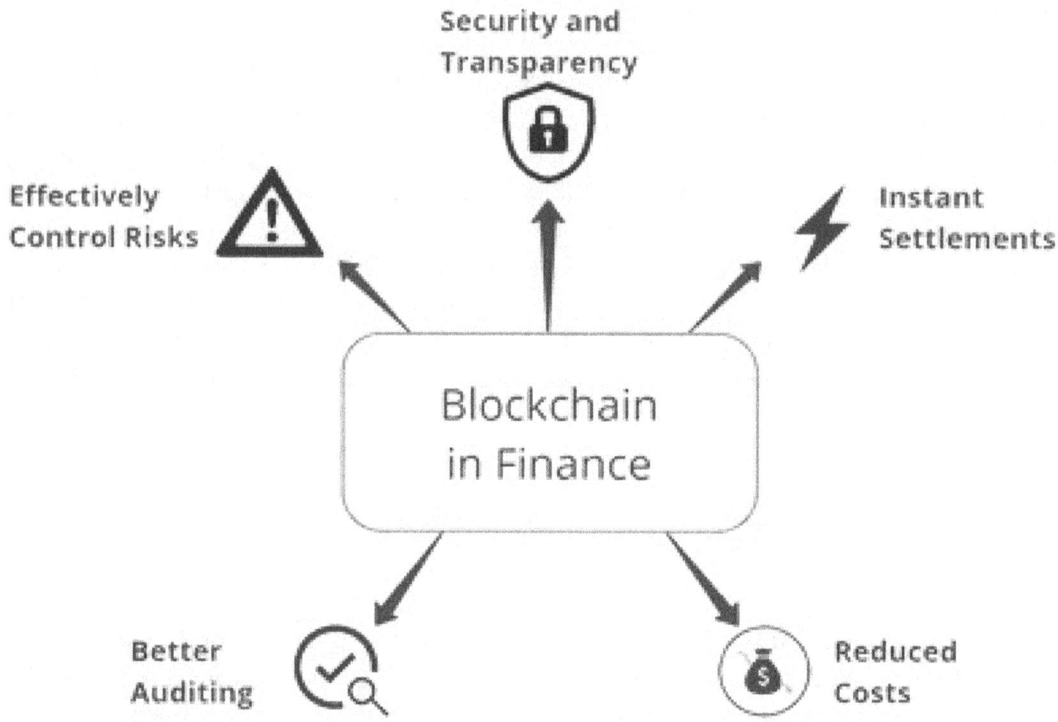

The use of blockchain systems in the banking and financial services industry has a great amount of untapped potential, and it also holds the key to the solution of a wide variety of urgent issues. Some of these technologies are discussed below:

Security and Transparency

The global economic and financial systems continue to be more centralized and convoluted. The vast majority of financial records are stored in centralized databases and are shared throughout a number of various divisions (front office, back office, etc.) before they can be accessed by anybody. There is a fundamental lack of openness in the system, making data security totally reliant on middlemen and database safeguards. Despite the fact that the database systems have the greatest degree of security, there is still a significant risk that data will be stolen or that servers will be hacked.

As no one is aware of the system's inner workings unless something goes wrong or data is hacked, this creates a fertile environment for security concerns. Even if some people do not want their financial details to be made public, it is still beneficial and essential for the system to have transparency since it benefits and aids both the customers and the suppliers of financial services.

Solution: Blockchain technology allows for simultaneous transparency and security in the financial services sector.

- **Immutability:** The data stored in a blockchain cannot be changed because of its immutable nature. It guarantees the safety, veracity, and accuracy of all information.
- **Privacy:** There are two different kinds of security keys that may be used: the public key and the private key. Everyone who participates in the system has a copy of the public key that is stored there. However, the private key is never revealed to anybody outside of individuals who are directly engaged in the transaction. As a result, the public key will let all users on the network to see the transaction, but the private key will restrict access to the stakeholders and transaction information. It protects the privacy of the system's participants' financial data while keeping it accessible for everybody.
- **Zero-Knowledge Proof Technology:** A variety of blockchain networks have used the zero-knowledge proof technology as a method for protecting users' privacy. The financial data may be checked without revealing any sensitive information.

Reduced Costs

Due to its concentration, the financial industry pours significant resources into:

- Acquiring central databases
- Bookkeeping
- Database maintenance
- Labour expenses
- Database security
- Middlemen' commissions
- Value transfer systems

These are periodic expenditures that need ongoing financial commitment. All these extra expenses raise the price of the system without providing any assurance that sensitive information would remain secure (Takyar, 2020).

Solution: Blockchain's potential to save expenses in the financial sector is immense. A research estimates that by 2022, DLT will have saved the financial services industry between $15 billion and $20 billion annually in infrastructure costs. Blockchain technology, a subset of DLT, has the potential to improve accountability, cut expenses, and fortify safety. Banks and other types of financial organizations may save costs by using smart contracts for the following reasons:

- Intermediaries
- Value transfers
- Bookkeeping

As a result, using blockchain technology in financial services may result in significant cost savings.

Effectively Control Risks

There is a great deal of danger involved for financial institutions when they provide loans, for example.

- The counterparty's inability to fulfil its commitments.
- Credit risk brought on by knowledge inequity.
- Believing in middlemen.

Commercial banks are no exception; placing trust in an intermediary makes it difficult to reliably and effectively monitor and manage loan utilisation. However, the risk is high, since the suppliers would incur huge costs in the event of a mishap (Metaverse in Financial Services Use Cases, n.d.).

Solution: When it comes to financial services, blockchain treats all participants as nodes. Hence:

- P2P transactions may be made possible, cutting out the middleman.
- Because all transactions are recorded on the network, concerns associated with money management and credit are mitigated.
- Smart contracts provide speedy payment of debts.
- Immutable data is more trustworthy.

The use of blockchain technology in the financial industry makes it simpler for suppliers of financial services to manage all risks.

Instant Settlements

Certain payments may take up to a week to clear under the present banking system. The widespread utilization of middlemen is largely to blame. Because the modern financial system is so complicated, each and every transaction has to entail the participation of several intermediaries until it can be completed. It's possible that these intermediaries be inside bank divisions like customer support or external companies like currency exchanges for overseas deals. In a centralized system, having several intermediates is one approach to guarantee security and authenticity, but it also causes many issues, such as slow settlement times and higher costs.

Solution: Financial P2P transactions are feasible using blockchain technology. This means that middlemen will be unnecessary, as transactions may be efficiently handled through smart contracts. Instantaneous monetary transactions will become possible once the system's "layers" are stripped away. With the assistance of blockchain-based payment systems, it is feasible to conduct instantaneous international transactions.

As an outcome of this, the blockchain technology may make it possible to conduct financial transactions very instantly.

Better Auditing

The auditing procedure takes a long time and costs a lot of money. There is no openness in the current controlled structure. Therefore, while audits, auditors and compliance professionals operating for creditors are not limited in any way in their ability to provide any specific material that they consider to be essential. It makes it easier for people to act in unethical ways, be dishonest, comply inconsistently, and prolong auditing processes.

Solution: Using blockchain technology makes it possible to streamline the auditing process for financial services, which is a significant time saver. It is possible for auditors to utilize the immutability of the data stored on a blockchain to check whether or not every one of the regulatory standards are being met and to get a more accurate picture of how a financial institution conducts its business.

Because of its record-keeping capabilities, blockchain technology will assist in ensuring that suppliers of financial services maintain their high standards of honesty and integrity. Any unexpected financial activity may be tracked down with relative ease. Due to the ease with which auditors may access data, auditing processes can be streamlined.

So, enhanced auditing is another another potential outcome of blockchain's application in the financial sector.

DIFFICULTIES AND RECENT PROGRESS

Since it is still a relatively young technology, blockchain is struggling to resolve some initial glitches. Section v.a. discusses scalability, Section v.b. privacy leakage, and Section v.c. selfish mining.

Scalability

The daily increase in transaction volume causes the blockchain to gain weight. At the moment, the blockchain that underpins Bitcoin can hold much more than 100GB worth of data. Every trade must be recorded so that it may be replicated later for auditing purposes. The Bitcoin blockchain fails to process transactions in the present moment because it is dependent on miners to generate new blocks and because it takes time to validate each block. Consequently, the network cannot process transactions. The number of transactions that may be processed by the network in a single second is around seven. Because the block capacity is so limited, miners tend to prioritise transactions that have a high transaction fee, which means that a significant number of relatively minor transactions might be delayed. Nevertheless, with larger block sizes, the pace of propagation would slow, leading to splits on the blockchain. Hence, scalability is a complex problem to solve.It's been suggested that there are two sorts of solutions to the blockchain's scalability issue:

- **Storage Optimisation of the Blockchain:** In order to address the intrinsic inefficiencies of the blockchain, a paradigm-shifting cryptocurrency strategy was developed (Carboni, 2015). All non-null balances are now recorded in an account tree database, and the network automatically deletes old transaction records. Hence, nodes are no longer required to store all transactions in order to verify their legitimacy. It's also possible that a lightweight client might help fix this problem. VerSum, a novel concept, was proposed as an additional means to enable the presence of lightweight clients (Bruce, 2014). It does this by comparing the result that was computed with results from a large number of servers. This ensures that the result is accurate.
- • **Redesigning the Blockchain:** When using Bitcoin-NG, the normal block is divided into two parts: a key block, which is used for determining who the next leader will be, and a microblock, which is used for capturing transactions. Competing for positions of authority among the miners. The existing leader would remain in control of the production of microblocks unless a new leader emerged to take their place. Bitcoin-NG added to and improved upon the most substantial (longest) chain methodology, according to which only significant blocks count and smaller ones have

no bearing on the process. The issue of increasing block size while maintaining network security has been addressed by the blockchain's new design.

Privacy Leakage

Transactions on the blockchain are considered very secure since users never reveal their true identities. Users may generate a huge number of addresses in case of a breach of sensitive data. Several research have shown that the Bitcoin transactions of a user may be linked together to reveal their identify (van den Hooff et al., 2014). A innovative approach was presented to connect users' pseudonyms to their actual IP addresses, even if they are behind a firewall or NAT (Eyal and Sirer, 2014). This collection, which may be taught, can be used to trace the origin of a transaction. There have been many different suggestions made for ways to improve the anonymity of blockchain transactions, but broadly speaking, they may be divided into two categories:

- **Mixing:** Blockchain employs pseudonymous user addresses. However, due to the fact that a large number of users often do business using the same address, it is still possible to track down actual people. For privacy reasons, a service known as mixing delivers funds to many recipients using different input addresses (Barcelo, 2014). With Mixcoin, there is an easy way to avoid scams and other fraudulent activities. The demands of the user, such as the amount of money being sent and the date of the transaction, are encrypted using the intermediary's private key (Möser, 2013). If the intermediary does not deliver the funds, it may be shown beyond a reasonable doubt that they deceived. Theft continues even after it's been uncovered. Coinjoin employs a mixing server to randomly switch the addresses of transaction outputs, hence reducing the likelihood of theft (Bonneau et al., 2014).
- **Anonymous:** According to Maxwell (2013), the Zerocoin system employs the usage of a zero-knowledge proof. When checking to see whether a currency is on a list of allowed coins, miners are not required to validate a transaction using a digital signature even when they are checking the list. Separating the payment source from the transaction data prevents transaction graph analysis. Yet, the destination and amount of payments remain transparent. According to Miers et al. (2013), one potential solution to this issue is called Zerocash. Zerocash makes use of a protocol known as Zero-Knowledge Succinct Non-interactive Arguments of Knowledge, or zk-SNARKs for short. It is not possible for users to see the entire value of their operations or the number of coins they presently own.

Selfish Mining

Yet, malicious actors targeting the blockchain might find complicity within miners. Most experts in the field believe that a transaction may be reversed and the blockchain altered if a majority of network nodes choose to do so.

In order to draw attention to the shortcomings of blockchain technology, a variety of alternative attacks, all based on selfish mining, have been created. According to Sasson et al. (2014), obstinate miners may sometimes resort to the trail strategy in order to continue mining blocks following the private chain gets abandoned. Nevertheless there are scenarios in which it may be 13% more productive than its equivalent without a stubborn path. Sapirshtein demonstrated that there are kinds of selfish mining therefore are more lucrative than basic forms of selfish mining, and that these forms of mining are lucrative for smaller miners as well (Nayak et al., 2016). The benefits, nevertheless, are quite minor. This demonstrates that malicious actors may profit from selfish mining with as little as 25% of the network's computational capability. During mining, honest miners would choose more blocks at random, using beacons and timestamps (Sapirshtein et al., 2015). To ensure that there are no hiccups in the operation of the network, it is essential that each block be generated and validated within a certain window of time. In point of fact, this is the basic idea that drives ZeroBlock. Nevertheless, in ZeroBlock (Billah, 2015), miners' greed is capped to the coin they may expect to mine.

DIRECTIONS THAT MAY BE TAKEN IN THE FUTURE

In both business and academia, the blockchain has already demonstrated its worth. We discuss probable future scenarios by referring to five different topics: experimentation with blockchain tech; counteracting centralization; using big data analytics; developing smart contracts; and deploying AI.

Blockchain Testing

There has been a proliferation of blockchain variants recently, with coindesk already listing over 700 different digital currencies. Yet, in order to attract investors attracted by the prospect of massive riches, some developers may overstate the performance of their blockchain. When deciding to use blockchain technology in their organizations, customers also need to know which blockchain would work best for them. Many blockchains need a framework for blockchain testing. There may be two distinct phases of blockchain testing: standardization and actual testing. The standardization procedure is when all criteria are developed and given final approval. When a blockchain is developed, it may be tested against these guidelines to see whether it lives up to its developers' claims about its capabilities. While evaluating a blockchain, it's important to keep a few things in mind.

Stop the Tendency to Centralization

Blockchain was conceived from the ground up to function as a decentralized network. Yet the mining pool is becoming more and more centralized. If it were to recruit respectable miners, the selfish pool may end up accumulating upwards of 51% of the overall power in the network over the long run. It is essential that solutions be given since the blockchain was not developed to satisfy the requirements of only a few enterprises.

Big Data Analytics

There's a possibility that big data and blockchain may complement one another. Because of this, we have separated the entire process into its individual phases: data management and data analytics. Blockchain is a good solution for keeping confidential information required for data management because of its decentralized and encrypted design. The data's validity may also be guaranteed by using blockchain technology, which has this capability as well. If, for example, medical records are maintained using blockchain technology, it will be exceedingly impossible to edit or steal such information. Blockchain technology also makes it incredibly tough to hack. It's possible that using blockchain transactions could prove helpful when it comes to analyzing enormous volumes of data. For example, information on the purchasing habits of individual users is retrievable. The research may help users foresee the buying and selling tendencies of prospective partners.

Smart Contract

In a digital setting, the conditions of a contract may be made legally binding by the implementation of an electronic transaction protocol, sometimes referred to in certain circles as a "smart contract" (Solat and Potop-Butucaru, 2016). Blockchain technology has now made it possible to implement this long-discussed concept. In blockchain technology, a "smart contract" is an item of code that may be automatically executed by miners when certain conditions are met. There are an increasing variety of smart contract development platforms available today, and the capabilities of individual smart contracts continue to expand. IoT and banking services are just two potential applications for blockchain technology (Solat and Potop-Butucaru, 2016) and (Peters et al., 2015).

The study of smart contracts is divided into two major fields of inquiry, namely development and assessment. A number of smart contracts have been deployed on the Ethereum network (Wood, 2014). There are now several platforms for the construction of smart contracts that are in varying levels of development. Some examples of these platforms are Hawk and Ethereum. An example of evaluation is the examination of code's performance. Problems with smart contracts might lead to devastating financial losses. For example, more than $60 million was taken from a smart contract belonging to the DAO because of a problem with recursive calls (Christidis and Devetsikiotis, 2016). As a result, it is essential to examine any threats posed by smart contract technology. The use of apps that are based on smart contracts is expected to increase in parallel with the fast development of blockchain technology. Organizations should think about how their applications run.

Artificial Intelligence

Artificial intelligence (AI) has the potential to solve several issues with blockchain. One area where an oracle is always needed is in determining whether or not a contract requirement has been satisfied. It's not uncommon for this oracle to be a trustworthy third party. Maybe one day we will be able to use AI to build a fully functional oracle. It has no human overlords and teaches itself from data it collects independently. No disagreements would arise, and the smart contract may even become smarter. But, AI is already having an impact on our daily lives. As of now, it's unclear whether or not blockchain technology and smart contracts can effectively regulate harmful AI features. Smart contract laws, for instance, may be used to restrict the ways in which autonomous vehicles can be exploited for evil.

CONCLUSION

The peer-to-peer architecture and decentralized characteristics associated with blockchain have garnered a lot of positive attention for the technology. Nonetheless, many blockchain studies are safe from censorship thanks to Bitcoin. Despite the fact that the usage of blockchain technology in Bitcoin might serve as the most well-known example, there are numerous more uses. Blockchain has shown that it has the potential to disrupt current markets due to the fact that it has four fundamental characteristics: decentralization, permanence, anonymity, and auditability. In this chapter, we are going to look at the blockchain in great depth. To begin, we will present a high-level review of the blockchain technology, during which we will touch on some of its core concepts and describe the architecture that lies behind it. Then, we'll talk about the most popular consensus algorithms used in blockchains today. In a number of ways, we compare and contrast these methods. Common uses for blockchain are also explored. Several future directions are discussed as well. The field of smart contracts is rapidly developing at the moment, and several potential uses have been proposed. However, at the time, it is difficult to implement many one-of-a-kind applications due to the numerous constraints and restrictions imposed by the languages used for smart contracts. We plan to analyze smart contracts in depth in the near future.

REFERENCES

Antshares. (2016). *Antshares Digital Assets for Everyone*. https://www.antshares.org

Atzori, L., Iera, A., & Morabito, G. (2010). The internet of things: A survey. *Computer Networks*, *54*(15), 2787–2805. doi:10.1016/j.comnet.2010.05.010

Azure. (2016). *Microsoft Azure: Blockchain as a Service*. https://azure.microsoft.com/enus/solutions/blockchain/

Barcelo, J. (2014). *User Privacy in the Public Bitcoin Blockchain*. Academic Press.

Billah, S. (2015). *One Weird Trick to Stop Selfish Miners: Fresh Bitcoins, A Solution for the Honest*. Miner.

Bitshares. (n.d.) *Bitshares – Your Share in the Decentralized Exchange*. https://bitshares.org/

Bonneau, J., Narayanan, A., Miller, A., Clark, J., Kroll, J. A., & Felten, E. W. (2014). Mixcoin: Anonymity for bitcoin with accountable mixes. *Proceedings of International Conference on Financial Cryptography and Data Security*, 486–504. 10.1007/978-3-662-45472-5_31

Bruce, J. (2014). *The Mini-Blockchain Scheme*. http://cryptonite.info/files/mbc-scheme-rev3.pdfburstcoin

Buterin, V. (2014) *A Next-Generation Smart Contract and Decentralized Application Platform*. White Paper.

Buterin, V. (2015). *On Public and Private Blockchains*. https://blog.ethereum.org/2015/08/07/onpublic-and-private-blockchains/

Carboni, D. (2015) *Feedback based Reputation on Top of the Bitcoin Blockchain*. arXiv *preprintarXiv*:1502.01504.

Chepurnoy, A., Larangeira, M., & Ojiganov, A. (2016) *A Prunable Blockchain Consensus Protocol based on Non-Interactive Proofs of Past States Retrievability*. arXiv preprint arXiv:1603.07926.

Christidis, K., & Devetsikiotis, M. (2016). Blockchains and smart contracts for the internet of things. *IEEE Access : Practical Innovations, Open Solutions*, *4*, 2292–2303. doi:10.1109/ACCESS.2016.2566339

Chuen, L. K. D. (Ed.). (2015) .Handbook of Digital Currency. Elsevier.

Coindesk. (2016) *State of Blockchain q1 2016: Blockchain Funding Overtakes Bitcoin*. https://www.coindesk.com/state-of-blockchain-q1-2016/

Decker, C., Seidel, J., & Wattenhofer, R. (2016). Bitcoin meets strong consistency. In *Proceedings of the 17th International Conference on Distributed Computing and Networking (ICDCN)*. ACM.

Devine, P. (2015). Blockchain learning: can crypto-currency methods be appropriated to enhance online learning? *ALT Online Winter Conference*.

Dixon, C., Mahajan, R., Agarwal, S., Brush, A., Saroiu, B. L. S., & Bahl, P. (2012). *An Operating System for the Home, NSDI*. USENIX.

Ethereum. (n.d.). *Consortium Chain Development*. https://github.com/ethereum/wiki/wiki/Consortium-Chain-Development

Eyal, I., & Sirer, E. G. (2014). Majority is not enough: Bitcoin mining is vulnerable. *Proceedings of International Conference on Financial Cryptography and Data Security*, 436–454. 10.1007/978-3-662-45472-5_28

Foroglou, G., & Tsilidou, A-L. (2015). *Further Applications of the Blockchain*. Academic Press.

Gogerty, N., & Zitoli, J. (2011). *Deko: An electricity-backed currency proposal. Social Science* Research Network.

Hardjono, T., & Smith, N. (2016). Cloud-based commissioning of constrained devices using permissioned blockchains. *Proceedings of the 2nd ACM International Workshop on IoT Privacy, Trust, and Security*, 29–36. 10.1145/2899007.2899012

Hyperledger. (2015) *Hyperledger Project*. https://www.hyperledger.org/ibm

Johnson, D., Menezes, A., & Vanstone, S. (2001). The elliptic curve digital signature algorithm (ECDSA). *International Journal of Information Security*, *1*(1), 36–63. doi:10.1007102070100002

King, S. (2013). *Primecoin: Cryptocurrency with Prime Number Proof-of-Work*. Academic Press.

King, S., & Nadal, S. (2012) *Ppcoin: Peer-to-Peer Crypto-Currency with Proof-of-Stake*. Self-Published Paper.

Kraft, D. (2016). Difficulty control for blockchain-based consensus systems. *Peer-to-Peer Networking and Applications*, *9*(2), 397–413. doi:10.100712083-015-0347-x

Kwon, J. (2014). *Tendermint: Consensus without mining*. Academic Press.

Lamport, L., Shostak, R., & Pease, M. (1982). The byzantine generals problem. *ACM Transactions on Programming Languages and Systems*, *4*(3), 382–401. doi:10.1145/357172.357176

Maxwell, G. (2013). *Coinjoin: Bitcoin Privacy for the Real World*. Post on Bitcoin Forum.

Mazieres, D. (2015). *The Stellar Consensus Protocol:AFederated Model for Internet-Level Consensus*. Stellar Development Foundation.

Metaverse in financial services use cases. (n.d.). Retrieved April 10, 2023, from https://buzzcrop.com/fixer-upper/metaverse-in-financial-services-use-cases

Micheler, E., & von derHeyde, L. (2016). *Holding, clearing and settling securities through blockchain technology creating an efficient system by empowering asset owners*. Social Science Research Network. doi:10.2139srn.2786972

Miers, I., Garman, C., Green, M., & Rubin, A. D. (2013). Zerocoin: Anonymous distributed e-cash from bitcoin. *Proceedings of IEEE Symposium Security and Privacy (SP)*, 397–411.

Miguel, C., & Barbara, L. (1999). Practical byzantine fault tolerance. *Proceedings of the Third.*

Morini, M. (2016). *From 'blockchain hype' to a real business case for financial markets*. Social Science Research Network. doi:10.2139srn.2760184

Möser, M. (2013). Anonymity of bitcoin transactions: An analysis of mixing services. *Proceedings of Münster Bitcoin Conference*, 17-18.

Nakamoto, S. (2008). *Bitcoin: A Peer-to-Peer Electronic Cash System*. https://bitcoin.org/bitcoin.pdf

Nayak, K., Kumar, S., Miller, A., & Shi, E. (2016). Stubborn mining: Generalizing selfish mining and combining with an eclipse attack. *Proceedings of 2016 IEEE European Symposium on Security and Privacy (EuroSandP)*, 305–320. 10.1109/EuroSP.2016.32

Norta, A., Othman, A. B., & Taveter, K. (2015). Conflict-resolution lifecycles for governed decentralized autonomous organization collaboration. *Proceedings of the 2015 2nd.* 10.1145/2846012.2846052

Noyes, C. (2016a). *Bitav: Fast Anti-Malware by Distributed Blockchain Consensus and Feedforward Scanning*. arXiv preprint arXiv:1601.01405.

Noyes, C. (2016b). *Efficient Blockchain-Driven Multiparty Computation Markets at Scale*. Technical Report.

NRI. (2015). *Survey on Blockchain Technologies and Related Services*. Technical Report.

Omohundro, S. (2014). Cryptocurrencies, smart contracts, and artificial intelligence. *AI Matters*, *1*(2), 19–21. doi:10.1145/2685328.2685334

P4Titan. (2014). *Slimcoin a Peer-to-Peer Crypto-Currency with Proof-of-Burn "Mining without Powerful Hardware*. Author.

Peters, G.W., Panayi, E., & Chapelle, A. (2015). *Trends in Crypto-Currencies and Blockchain Technologies: A Monetary Theory and Regulation Perspective*. Academic Press.

Pilkington, M. (2016). *Does the Fintech Industry need a New Risk Management Philosophy? A Blockchain Typology for Digital Currencies and e-money Services in Luxembourg*. Social Science Research Network.

Sapirshtein, A., Sompolinsky, Y., & Zohar, A. (2015). *Optimal Selfish Mining Strategies in Bitcoin*. arXiv preprint arXiv:1507.06183.

Sasson, E. B., Chiesa, A., Garman, C., Green, M., Miers, I., & Tromer, E. (2014). Zerocash: Decentralized anonymous payments from Bitcoin. *Proceedings of 2014 IEEE Symposium on Security and Privacy (SP)*, 459–474. 10.1109/SP.2014.36

Solat, S., & Potop-Butucaru, M. (2016). *ZeroBlock: Timestamp-Free Prevention of Block-Withholding Attack in Bitcoin*. Technical Report, Sorbonne Universites, UPMC University of Paris 6.

Sompolinsky, Y., & Zohar, A. (2013). *Accelerating Bitcoin's Transaction Processing. Fast Money Grows on Trees, not Chains*. IACR Cryptology ePrint Archive.

Takyar, A. (2020, December 28). *Blockchain in Finance: Blockchain Use Cases. LeewayHertz - Software Development Company*. https://www.leewayhertz.com/10-use-cases-of-blockchain-in-finance/

Tschorsch, F., & Scheuermann, B. (2016). Bitcoin and beyond: A technical survey on decentralized digital currencies. *IEEE Communications Surveys and Tutorials*, *18*(3), 2084–2123. doi:10.1109/COMST.2016.2535718

van den Hooff, J., Kaashoek, M. F., & Zeldovich, N. (2014). Versum: Verifiable computations over large public logs. *Proceedings of the 2014 ACM SIGSAC Conference on Computer and Communications Security*, 1304–1316. 10.1145/2660267.2660327

Vasin, P. (2014). *Blackcoin's Proof-of-Stake Protocol v2*. https://blackcoin.co/blackcoin-pos-protocolv2-whitepaper.pdf

Vukolić, M. (2016). The quest for scalable blockchain fabric: Proof-of-work vs. BFT replication. In *Open Problems in Network Security: IFIP WG 11.4 International Workshop, iNetSec 2015, Zurich, Switzerland, October 29, 2015, Revised Selected Papers* (pp. 112-125). Springer International Publishing.

Wang, H., Osen, O., Li, G., Li, W., Dai, H.-N., & Zeng, W. (2015). *Big data and industrial internet of things for the maritime industry in northwestern Norway. In IEEE Region 10 Conference*. TENCON.

Wood, G. (2014). *Ethereum: A Secure Decentralised Generalised Transaction Ledger*. Ethereum Project Yellow Paper.

Zamfir, V. (2015). *Introducing casper the friendly ghost*. Ethereum Blog.

Zhang, Y., & Wen, J. (2015). *An IoT electric business model based on the protocol of bitcoin*. Academic Press.

Zheng, Z., Xie, S., Dai, H., Chen, X., & Wang, H. (2017). An overview of blockchain technology: Architecture, consensus, and future trends. *Proceedings of the 2017 IEEE BigData Congress*, 557–564. 10.1109/BigDataCongress.2017.85

Chapter 13
Evolution of the P2P Lending System in FinTech:
A Systematic Review of Literature

Renuka Sharma
Chitkara Business School, Chitkara University, India

Kiran Mehta
Chitkara Business School, Chitkara University, India

Aditya Dhawan
Chitkara Business School, Chitkara University, India

ABSTRACT

With the aid of fintech, this study seeks to undertake a systematic review of peer-to-peer lending literature. In this chapter, the authors learn how fintech has aided peer-to-peer lending and how it has facilitated the provision of services like simple credit, the recording of borrower information, etc. Additionally, they examine the development of fintech, and the findings of this study demonstrate that COVID-19 has significantly altered the primary determinants of P2P lending. According to the findings, P2P fintech financing is now the most practical alternative credit option available to borrowers. Because they highlight the value of P2P lending platforms, their potential advantages, and the causes of defaults that do occur, the findings are significant and are likely to be of interest to investors, practitioners, academics, and legislators. The authors also learn about the evolution of the traditional lending system.

INTRODUCTION

The role of innovation in improving work processes cannot be overstated. While there have been numerous technological advancements lately, today focuses on "Fintech." This term, derived from the words "finance" and "technology," refers to using technology in financial services. The financial sector is crucial to society and has undergone significant changes, leading to the advent of the "fintech" era.

DOI: 10.4018/978-1-6684-8624-5.ch013

Despite its trendy nature, Fintech is vital in enhancing financial services, making previously exclusive services, such as loans, payments, and deposits, more widely available. As such, it is vital to understand Fintech as it will become increasingly pervasive, potentially replacing traditional banking methods. Many companies, including banks, have already incorporated Fintech into their systems, with chatbots being an excellent example of how it can provide customers with convenient problem-solving options at home.

Robot advisors are more cost-effective, transparent, and require less human interaction (Faloon & Scherer, 2017), making Fintech increasingly popular, particularly in the banking industry (Thakor, 2019). Fintech covers various financial services, including credit deposits, peer-to-peer lending, cryptocurrencies, and insurance. Fintech has made financial services more accessible to the public, with virtual wallets like Apple Pay allowing users to apply for loans and make payments without leaving their homes. Banks are concerned about the rise of Fintech, as services such as peer-to-peer lending may replace traditional banking methods. Similarly nature of investor has also changed over a period of time (Mehta & Sharma 2015). However, banks are more trusted than Fintech, especially for p2p lending, which usually deals with high-risk borrowers to whom banks are unwilling to lend money.

Cryptocurrency is another new term that has emerged with the rise of Fintech. It was created in 2009 and allowed anyone to buy cryptocurrencies like Bitcoin without the assistance of a bank. Blockchain technology stores the purchased cryptocurrency digitally, removing the need for banks. In addition, blockchain technology ensures that transactions are secure and verified. Although the cryptocurrency market has grown, it is run by a decentralized system, leading to risks (Catalini & Gans, 2016; Cong, 2019; Thakor, 2019; Trivedi et al., 2021). While Fintech and cryptocurrency are changing the payment system, digital currencies such as Bitcoin are unlikely to replace cash. Therefore, banks must focus on innovative technologies like p2p lending to keep up with the market and cover the services that Fintech provides.

With a growing understanding of Fintech, more people are downloading finance apps, mainly due to the COVID-19 pandemic, which has increased people's awareness of how they can stay financially healthy (Arora et al., 2022). Lockdowns and social distancing measures have forced people to stay home and made them wary of physical interaction, leading to a surge in finance apps like payment apps. Bank transactions have also been conducted online, and various Fintech technologies have been developed to support this shift (Fu & Mishra, 2022). People are moving towards Fintech due to the global financial crisis and a loss of trust in traditional banking methods (Goldstein et al., 2019; Fu & Mishra, 2022). The demand for lending apps is growing as people exhaust their savings and must borrow money to make ends meet.

It has been observed that lending apps are in high demand due to the depletion of people's reserves caused by the COVID pandemic. Research indicates that COVID has led to increased public acceptance of fintech, which has been instrumental in helping people survive during this crisis. The digital transformation brought about by the fourth industrial revolution has further spurred the use of fintech, disrupting traditional banking by providing digital services. As technology advances, the use and investment in fintech have also increased. The emergence of digital finance and the doubling of fintech investment, as reported by Accenture, demonstrate the significance of fintech in the current scenario. The initial stage of globalization allowed cross-border transactions, while the subsequent phases integrated finance with technology, and businesses began utilizing digital/advanced technology. "Big tech" is a term used to describe a group of technology companies that offer services like insurance, credit, and wealth management. Big tech and fintech are comparable, but big tech relies on data analytics to gain a competitive edge. Cooperation between fintech and banks can benefit both parties through digitalization, resulting in new research and development.

RESEARCH METHODOLOGY

For this work, we conducted a comprehensive literature review focusing on P2P lending and Fintech. We aimed to explain the operation of P2P lending and how it has evolved. Initially, we identified relevant publications and searched for peer-to-peer lending articles that examined monetary, demographic, and sociological factors that impact loan size and funding success in online P2P lending, considered an alternative finance option. Next, we used the ScienceDirect website to search for papers, using various related terms such as "online peer-to-peer lending," "online P2P lending," "Fintech revolution," "Impact of COVID-19 on Fintech lending," "Fintech," "P2P lending," "P2P lending risks and impacts," "early repayment risk," and "Defaults."

Our search yielded 40 papers, which we reviewed and found 25 relevant to our topic, while the remaining 15 were not. With these 25 papers, most of which focused on the P2P lending aspect of Fintech, we were able to move forward. After reviewing all the studies, we categorized our literature review into five topics: risks, impacts, advantages, defaults, and customer experience. By exploring these themes, we can better understand how P2P lending works and how to improve the user experience.

Figure 1. Selection process

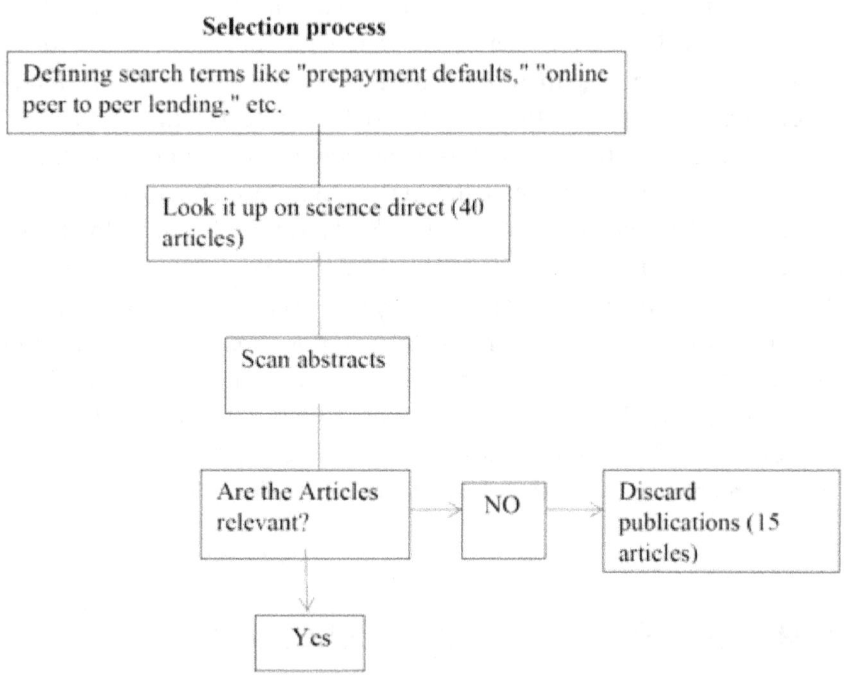

SYSTEMATIC REVIEW OF LITERATURE

In this literature review, we examined several variables related to peer-to-peer lending, including its origins and current expansion. Understanding the factors that contributed to the growth of P2P lending is critical before delving into its mechanics. One such factor is the rise of fintech and technology, which have transformed and expanded the lending system. In today's world, fintech lending (P2P lending) and ICOs operate more successfully due to technological advancements. Traditional financial intermediaries like banks use technology to provide better investment portfolios through rigorous screening. The fintech lending market has expanded significantly over the past 15 years, with its popularity growing due to the use of algorithms in evaluating loans and borrower ability. Customers are switching from one bank to another earlier now shifting to online platforms (Mehta et. al., 2023). Digital innovation is another critical aspect to consider in the rise of fintech lending. As an emerging trend, fintech leverages digital innovation and technology to provide more cost-effective and efficient financial services. Mobile payments and financing are innovations that have improved the user experience. Peer-to-peer lending is one of the areas in which fintech companies offer their services to enhance the customer experience.

One of the primary reasons why individuals prefer P2P lending platforms over traditional lending systems is that they offer better interest rates and rates of return. P2P lending also utilizes various factors, such as credit scores and other elements, to lower the cost of the lending process. In addition, P2P platforms give lenders access to a wealth of credit information about borrowers, allowing them to make informed decisions on their creditworthiness. Credit score and loan size are essential determinants of successful lending and default, with the social elements that lenders consider, including the borrower's gender, age, race, and other variables that may differ depending on location. While the popularity of P2P lending has increased in recent years, it is critical to determine the elements that influence borrower lending, especially during the COVID-19 pandemic. The pandemic has led to a total lockdown of nations, but the need for money remains, making loans necessary. As a result, P2P lending has increased throughout the pandemic, which was not the case before the outbreak. FinTech peer-to-peer lending has undergone significant changes due to the COVID-19 pandemic. According to Najaf, Subramaniam & F. Atayah (2021), borrowers are now more open to taking out long-term, high-interest loans that have yet to be thoroughly scrutinized. The emergence of peer-to-peer lending was fueled by the strict lending regulations imposed by traditional banks, which were further tightened during the pandemic. Consequently, accessing loans from banks became even more challenging, even with the availability of online lending platforms. Although banks have online lending platforms, borrowers often prefer peer-to-peer lending platforms because they offer a less stringent verification process. The beauty of FinTech technology is that it does not aim to replace traditional banks but rather targets a niche or untapped market that traditional banks have overlooked. Thus, individuals who cannot access bank loans due to strict regulations or lack of required documentation can obtain loans from peer-to-peer lending platforms (Thakor, 2020; Zhang et al., 2014).

RISKS ASSOCIATED WITH PEER-TO-PEER LENDING

The lending industry has undergone significant changes with the advent of peer-to-peer lending platforms, which require improvements in lending systems to ensure loan repayment. Historically, lenders relied on interviews to determine loan eligibility, resulting in mistakes such as inadequate information collection and loan defaults. However, using credit scoring models has proven effective in reducing loan default rates and increasing profitability. Introducing a minimum down payment rule based on creditworthiness has also helped mitigate risk. Fintech has caused some concern among banks, but it is unlikely to replace them since they are the backbone of the economy. Fintech companies mainly act as intermediaries, connecting borrowers and lenders. The fintech revolution has benefited areas with poor financial infrastructure. While technology offers many advantages, it poses risks such as discrimination, identity theft, and fraud. COVID-19 demonstrated the importance of digitalization, leading banks to embrace digital platforms to provide services to their customers. Lenders' perception of borrowers' trustworthiness, physical appearance, and similarity to themselves also play a role in lending decisions. Age is another factor, with people under 30 perceived as less qualified. Credit scoring models have been effective in reducing the risk of loan defaults. However, policies must be created to ensure borrower and user privacy and limit their participation in risky activities. The online lending system has increased investment risk, making it more challenging to predict default risk. An effective and efficient instance-based credit evaluation model has been developed to compare loans with similar ones to determine whether they are safe to give.

BENEFITS OF PEER-TO-PEER LENDING

Peer-to-peer lending has revolutionized the lending industry and is especially beneficial to small and medium-sized enterprises (SMEs) that contribute significantly to the economy but often need more collateral and financial documentation to secure loans through traditional lending systems. This can have profound economic implications since SMEs employ a significant portion of the population. However, P2P lending fintech has implemented new criteria, such as big data, to analyze credit risk more accurately and help SMEs qualify for loans. This has reduced interest rates, making loans more accessible to SMEs. Overall, P2P lending fintech positively influences SME finance and could help construct a legislative framework that eases access to finance for small enterprises. Previously, there was prejudice in the old lending system against lending to small companies. However, using credit scoring models in P2P lending has enabled lenders to assess a borrower's capacity and ability to repay loans without seeing the borrower. This has eliminated the prejudice and increased the number of SME loans in low- and middle-income areas. As P2P lending continues gaining popularity in the SME credit business, reducing credit rationing and ensuring that new loans are well-spent is essential. Additionally, when investors know the borrower personally, their investments increase by 20%. Overall, using P2P lending and credit scoring has greatly benefited SMEs in acquiring finance and expanding their businesses.

IMPROVEMENT IN CUSTOMER EXPERIENCE

The evaluation of fintech also involves examining the customer experience to gauge their satisfaction level. The customer experience is crucial, as highlighted by Barbu, Florea, Dabija, Constantin, and Barbu (2021). Thus, fintech companies offering services must analyze the experiences of their users. Research shows that organizations should focus on three factors - touchpoints, context, and quality - to enhance the customer experience. Fintech, a brilliant invention that improves customer experience by providing customized services, chat boxes for prompt communication during difficulties, and mobile payments for cross-border transactions, has been observed to provide a positive experience when the cost or perceived value is high. Fintech companies leverage technology to offer a platform that allows customers to conduct transactions from anywhere globally, resulting in higher perceived value. Hence, providing the same or additional services at a lower cost is essential to enhance perceived value, foster customer loyalty, and improve the customer experience. since we are talking about how experience of customer has changed and as we know that innovation in the financial services has changed the customer experience completely Weichert (2017). Fintech firms across the globe are playing major role in using new technology and new business models to provide customer a better experience with development of technology the customer expectation has also rise. and many businesses have shifted their focus to offering high-quality services.

P2P LENDING DEFAULT REASONS

Further research has been conducted to identify the causes of default and the variables that can be applied to reduce the default rate. In recent years, P2P lending platforms have emerged, and scholars have examined the factors contributing to loan failure. Loan ratings, interest rates, and other factors have been found to affect loan default rates (Li et al., 2020; Chen et al., 2016; Nigmonov, Shams and Alam, 2022). For example, when interest rates increase, borrowers' debt obligations become more burdensome, requiring them to pay more, which causes loan default (Bester, 1985; Stiglitz and Weiss, 1981, 1992). While borrower information obtained through P2P networks cannot eliminate the risk of default, more soft information must be gathered to predict the possibility of default. Social data has been shown to aid in forecasting loan defaults (Chen et al., 2016; Maa et al., 2018). However, it is essential to note that borrowers who default on a loan have typically missed many payments in the preceding year (Chen et al., 2019). As P2P lending systems continue to expand, cases of loan default are also increasing, as there is no intermediary to act as a buffer between investors and borrowers, and lenders bear sole responsibility for defaults. To reduce the risk of loan default, it is essential to utilize both hard and soft information to solve the issue of information asymmetry (Chen et al., 2016; Iyer et al., 2015; Lin et al., 2015). When issuing a loan, investors must consider additional vital criteria, such as the borrower's historical behaviour, age, loan amount, period, repayment history, and loan purpose. It has been found that borrowers with lengthier loan terms are more likely to default (Chen et al., 2019), and longer maturities result in longer exposure intervals, providing the borrower with an edge to default (Croux et al., 2020). Moreover, the purpose of the loan could also play a role in determining the likelihood of default. For example, the risk of default is higher when a person borrows money to support a small business, while the risk of default decreases when the loan is used to fund a wedding, home improvement, etc.

Housing conditions also play a role in loan defaults. For example, renters are likelier to fail on their mortgage than homeowners. Finally, research has been conducted on the contributing causes of default in the Chinese loan system (Gao et al., 2020). Overall, the findings suggest that to reduce loan default rates, investors should consider various variables and gather hard and soft information about borrowers. During the examination, it was discovered that several detrimental services, including the first zero-down mortgage in 2016, are the primary cause of defaults in China, resulting in significant losses for investors. Another contributing factor is insufficient information and expertise and the inefficient regulation of peer-to-peer systems. Assessing the borrower's DTI ratio is critical when granting loans, as it aids in determining their creditworthiness and repayment capacity. In response to the collapse of China's peer-to-peer lending network, the government has taken steps to criminalize illegal P2P transactions and recognize the dangers of zero-down payments. Furthermore, the lack of experience in online lending has resulted in the selection of untrustworthy borrowers. Unreasonable loan conditions, high-interest rates, and racial disparities in loan distribution are other causes of default. Publicly listed platforms, SOE-controlled, bank-controlled, or publicly traded corporations, are less likely to face defaults. Additionally, p2p lending organizations assign grades to borrowers based on their creditworthiness, repayment history, and other considerations, which aid the lender in determining whether or not to grant them a loan.

It is critical to consider prepayment risk, which is the risk associated with borrowers' desire to pay off their loans early. A susceptible subset tends to repay loans fully before the due date, especially when interest rates are low. Investors and lenders can use these default indicators to save money before granting loans to borrowers. As fintech peer-to-peer lending develops, the government must pay close attention to these indicators and establish specific laws and regulations to reduce loan default risk.

CONCLUSION

The paper posits that fintech represents the future of business, the economy, and information technology. It is anticipated that fintech will also contribute to worldwide environmental protection. Through research, several characteristics have impacted and influenced fintech literature over the last decade. First, the fintech research field has expanded significantly in recent years and is still evolving. Social factors, such as lenders' perceived borrowers, have impacted lending. Finally, while p2p lending is illegal in China, the government is implementing regulations to revitalize it. The influence of fintech on the financial industry is evident, but it will likely only partially replace traditional finance. Instead, the two are expected to collaborate to provide services more effectively. The fintech sector is still developing, and various challenges must be overcome to protect investors. In addition, the industry is expected to continue to evolve, with discoveries replacing or enhancing existing systems. It presents both an opportunity and a significant challenge for regulators, who must develop strict regulations to protect lenders and borrowers from risks such as default, low-interest rates, and illegal platforms. Traditional banks are also expanding into the fintech lending sector, indicating a trend towards fintech cooperation. However, fintech research is challenging due to the rapid rate of technological advancement in this new field. As such, it is critical to conduct further research focusing on the challenges presented by fintech, including protecting borrowers from falling prey to illegal platforms, preventing default risks, and eliminating loan system discrimination.

In conclusion, the study of fintech is critical due to its newness and the limited knowledge available. The government must take steps to educate people about fintech to safeguard them from potential harm. Lenders must also be protected from risks such as default, requiring accurate borrower information and records. Lastly, loan system discrimination has been a significant problem in the past but has been minimized by fintech advancements. Further study is needed to address these challenges as the fintech sector evolves, making this an important area of research for those interested in the fintech sector.

Figure 2. Fintech process

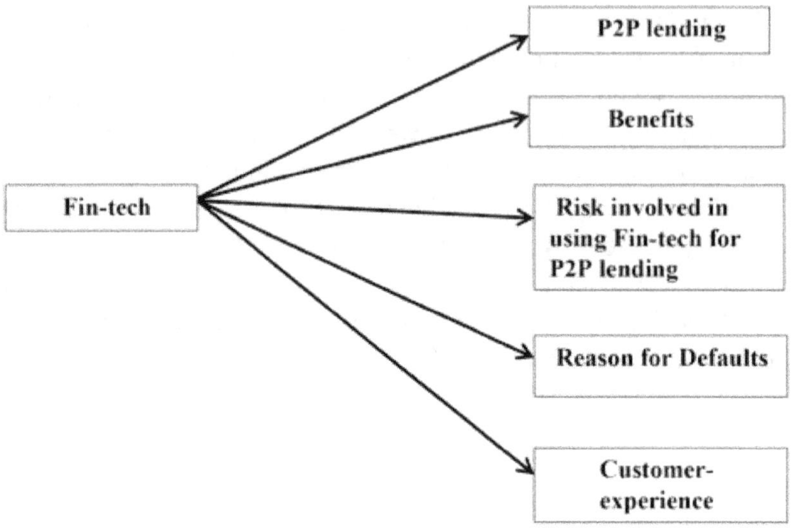

REFERENCES

Arora, M., Sharma, R., & Mehta, K. (2022). Personality Effects on Financial Responses Caused by the Perceived Financial Threat during the COVID-19 Pandemic. *The Journal of Wealth Management*, *25*(3), 72–89. doi:10.3905/jwm.2022.1.183

Barbu, C. M., Florea, D. L., Dabija, D. C., & Barbu, M. C. R. (2021). Customer experience in fintech. *Journal of Theoretical and Applied Electronic Commerce Research*, *16*(5), 1415–1433. doi:10.3390/jtaer16050080

Bester, H. (1985). Screening vs. rationing in credit markets with imperfect information. *The American Economic Review*, *75*(4), 850–855.

Catalini, C., & Gans, J. S. (2020). Some simple economics of the blockchain. *Communications of the ACM*, *63*(7), 80–90. doi:10.1145/3359552

Chen, E., & Zhang, H. (2017). P2P lending survey: Platforms, recent advances and prospects. *ACM Transactions on Intelligent Systems and Technology*, *8*(6), 72:1–72:28. doi:10.1145/3078848

Chen, L., Xie, Y., Li, P., & Li, Q. (2019). The signal of default risk from the description-text based on the empirical research of P2P lending. *Chinese Journal of Management Science*, *27*(4), 37–47.

Chen, X. H., Jin, F. J., Zhang, Q., & Yang, L. (2016). Are investors rational or perceptual in P2P lending? *Information Systems and e-Business Management*, *14*(4), 921–944. doi:10.100710257-016-0305-z

Cong, L. W., & He, Z. (2019). Blockchain disruption and smart contracts. *Review of Financial Studies*, *32*(5), 1754–1797. doi:10.1093/rfs/hhz007

Croux, C., Jagtiani, J., Korivi, T., & Vulanovic, M. (2020). Important factors determining Fintech loan default: Evidence from a lending club consumer platform. *Journal of Economic Behavior & Organization, 173*, 270–296. doi:10.1016/j.jebo.2020.03.016

Faloon, M., & Scherer, B. (2017). Individualization of Robo-Advice. *The Journal of Wealth Management, 20*(1), 30–36. doi:10.3905/jwm.2017.20.1.030

Fu, J., & Mishra, M. (2022). Fintech in the time of COVID– 19: Technological adoption during crises. *Journal of Financial Intermediation, 50*, 100945. doi:10.1016/j.jfi.2021.100945

Gao, M., Yen, J., & Liu, M. (2021). Determinants of defaults on P2P lending platforms in China. *International Review of Economics & Finance, 72*, 334–348. doi:10.1016/j.iref.2020.11.012

Goldstein, I., Jiang, W., & Karolyi, G. A. (2019). To FinTech and beyond. *Review of Financial Studies, 32*(5), 1647–1661. doi:10.1093/rfs/hhz025

Iyer, R., Khwaja, A. I., Luttmer, E. F., & Shue, K. (2016). Screening peers softly: Inferring the quality of small borrowers. *Management Science, 62*(6), 1554–1577. doi:10.1287/mnsc.2015.2181

Li, E., Liao, L., Wang, Z., & Xiang, H. (2020). Venture capital certification and customer response: Evidence from P2P lending platforms. *Journal of Corporate Finance, 60*, 101533. doi:10.1016/j.jcorpfin.2019.101533

Lin, M., Prabhala, N. R., & Viswanathan, S. (2013). Judging borrowers by the company they keep: Friendship networks and information asymmetry in online Peer-to-Peer lending. *Management Science, 59*(1), 17–35. doi:10.1287/mnsc.1120.1560

Ma, L., Zhao, X., Zhou, Z., & Liu, Y. (2018). A new aspect on P2P online lending default prediction using meta-level phone usage data in China. *Decision Support Systems, 111*, 60–71. doi:10.1016/j.dss.2018.05.001

Mehta, K., & Sharma, R. (2015). Individual Investors' Behavior: In Demographical Backdrop. SCMS Journal of Indian Management, 12(3), 25-36.

Mehta, K., Sharma, R., & Khanna, V. (2023). Customer switching behaviour in Indian retail banking using logit regression," *International Journal of Business Excellence, 29*(4), 518–545.

Najaf, K., Subramaniam, R. K., & Atayah, O. F. (2021). Understanding the implications of FinTech peer-to-peer (P2P) lending during the COVID-19 pandemic. *Journal of Sustainable Finance & Investment.*

Nigmonov, A., Shams, S., & Alam, K. (2022). Macroeconomic determinants of loan defaults: Evidence from the US peer-to-peer lending market. *Research in International Business and Finance, 59*, 101516. doi:10.1016/j.ribaf.2021.101516

Stiglitz, J. E., & Weiss, A. (1981). Credit rationing in markets with imperfect information. *The American Economic Review, 71*(3), 393–410.

Stiglitz, J. E., & Weiss, A. (1992). Asymmetric information in credit markets and its implications for macro-economics. *Oxford Economic Papers, 44*(4), 694–724. doi:10.1093/oxfordjournals.oep.a042071

Thakor, A. (2020). Corrigendum to: Fintech and Banking: What Do We Know? *Journal of Financial Intermediation*, *43*, 100858. Advance online publication. doi:10.1016/j.jfi.2020.100858

Thakor, A. V. (2019). Fintech and banking: What do we know? *Journal of Financial Intermediation*. https://doiorg.eres.qnl.qa/10.1016/j.jfi.2019.100833

Trivedi, S., Mehta, K., & Sharma, R. (2021). Systematic Literature Review on Application of Blockchain Technology in E-Finance and Financial Services. *Journal of Technology Management & Innovation*, *16*(3), 90–102. doi:10.4067/S0718-27242021000300089

Weichert, M. (2017). The future of payments: How FinTech players are accelerating customer-driven innovation in financial services. *Journal of Payments Strategy & Systems*, *11*(1), 23–33.

Zhang, Tang, Lu, & Dong. (2014). Trust Building in Online Peer-to-Peer Lending. *Journal of Global Information Technology Management, 17*(4), 250–266. doi:.2014.978624 doi:10.1080/1097198X

Chapter 14
Behavioral Finance and Cryptocurrency Market

Asheetu Bhatia Sarin
Vivekananda Institute of Professional Studies, Guru Gobind Singh Indraprastha University, India

ABSTRACT

With the unprecedented growth of technological development and digitalization across the globe, cryptocurrency has emerged to attract investors. It all started in the year 2013 when there were large fluctuations in the financial market. The novelty of this emerging asset class has led researchers to devise anomalous trade patterns and behavioral fallacies in the crypto market. This chapter will help researchers, academicians, and investors in understanding the importance of cognitive and emotional biases in the cryptocurrency market concerning investment decision-making. Moreover, the reader will be able to gain an understanding of the existing market and the challenges of cryptocurrency and financial technologies.

INTRODUCTION

The advances in the technological environment have led to the opening of the doors for creative new ideas and opportunities which led to changes in the economic environment. With this unprecedented growth of technological development and digitalization, Cryptocurrency has emerged to attract investors. It all started in the year 2013 when there were large fluctuations in the financial market. The newness of this emerging asset class has resulted in scholars, researchers, and investors devising abnormal investment patterns and behavioral anomalies in the cryptocurrency market (Shretryia & Kalra, 2021). Cryptocurrencies, Blockchain technology, and other potential applications are the relevant concept that has emerged in the "new economy". The instability in the stock market led to new prospects for investors. For this reason, a new asset class called cryptocurrency came into existence whereby individuals, as well as institutional investors, can invest. This led to the hype in the cryptocurrency market whereby Bitcoin was the most watched currency. Later on, other currencies came like Dogecoin, Ethereum, etc.

That is why it is important to understand Cryptocurrencies and blockchain technology and the impact of the investor's sentiment on Fintech markets.

DOI: 10.4018/978-1-6684-8624-5.ch014

A GENERAL PERSPECTIVE OF THE CRYPTOCURRENCY MARKET

According to the "European Central Bank" (2012), computer-generated money known as Cryptocurrencies is explained as "a type of digital money that is issued (released) by its developers and generally controlled by them, accepted and used among members of a particular virtual community" (p. 16). Due to dealing in encoded form and decentralized nature, it is known as Cryptocurrency.

Cryptocurrencies are electronic notes which use encoded techniques for the authentication and verification of a transaction (Khan et al. 2020). The cryptocurrency market is a rapidly evolving and highly volatile space that refers to "the decentralized digital currencies that use encryption techniques to regulate the generation of units and verify the transfer of funds" (Shretryia & Kalra, 2021). It is a relatively new market that has emerged over the past decade as a result of advances in computer technology and cryptography. Cryptocurrencies like Bitcoin, Litecoin, Dogecoin, Ripple, and Ethereum have received worldwide acceptance and have gained the attention of global players. This attention is due to the volatility of the exchange rates in terms of the distribution of world currency (Zhu et al, 2021). Therefore, cryptocurrencies are a kind of digital assets which are managed by a network. In general terms, these currencies utilize "distributed ledger technology" (DLT) to log, control, and for verifying a transaction they use encoded code which leads to the generation of new units of currency (Trivedi et al., 2021; Zhu et al, 2021). Like various physical currencies, these newly created currencies in the form of coins are used as a medium of exchange. The return yields from cryptocurrency investments are only generated via price rise. As a result, these assets are drawn from speculation which can be seen in the high capriciousness rate (Zhu et al, 2021).

The cryptocurrency market is characterized by various features:

1. **Decentralization:** Cryptocurrencies work on scattered networks. It is neither controlled by any central authority nor government authority.
2. **Volatility:** Cryptocurrency prices are known to be highly volatile and can experience significant fluctuations in a short period. This makes the market highly attractive to speculative investors.
3. **Lack of Regulation:** The cryptocurrency market is largely unregulated, which has led to concerns about market manipulation, fraud, and other illicit activities.
4. **Technological Advancements:** Cryptocurrencies are based on cutting-edge technology, including blockchain and distributed ledger systems. This has led to the development of new financial instruments and investment opportunities in the market.
5. **Limited Adoption:** Despite its growth, cryptocurrency usage is still relatively limited and has not yet achieved widespread adoption. This limits the market's liquidity and stability.

Despite its volatility, the cryptocurrency market has seen significant growth in recent years. The overall market capitalization of cryptocurrencies is currently valued at over USD 2 trillion as of April 2023, up from just a few hundred billion dollars in 2020. This growth has been fueled by increased adoption by businesses and individuals, as well as the development of new use cases for cryptocurrencies, like "decentralized finance" and "non-fungible tokens" (Trivedi et al., 2021).

However, the market is too subject to risks. One of the biggest risks is the potential for fraud and hacking. The decentralized nature of the market makes it difficult to regulate and secure, and there have been several high-profile incidents of exchanges being hacked and millions of dollars worth of cryptocurrencies being stolen. In addition, the regulatory environment for cryptocurrencies is still uncertain, with some governments cracking down on them while others embrace them.

Another risk is the potential for market crashes. The cryptocurrency market is highly speculative and can be influenced by hype and FOMO. This means that prices can rise rapidly but also fall just as quickly. In addition, there is no underlying asset backing most cryptocurrencies, which means that their value is based purely on supply and demand.

Despite these risks, many people are still investing in cryptocurrencies as a way to diversify their portfolios and potentially earn significant returns. However, it is important for investors to carefully research and understand the risks associated with investing in cryptocurrencies before making any decisions. At the same time, they should consider behavioral fallacies which affect their decisions.

ROLE OF BEHAVIORAL FINANCE

Investors believe that they have full information about the market. Then when it comes to decisions related to investment, they tend to be emotionally inclined. In any investment decision, the main point to consider is the investor's decision-making process (Sarin, 2019, pp. 1-3). Investment decisions are dependent on the proper evaluation of the alternatives available to investors. Hence, the process becomes difficult due to time as it considers the investors' behavioral impact (Sarin, 2019, pp. 1-3). The central aspect of behavioral finance is the consideration of the cognitive psychology aspects of an individual. Hence investors need to develop a positive vision, foresight, and perseverance to handle the same (Sarin and Chowdhury, 2018). Similarly, emotional decision-making is prevalent in the financial market. It shows the ups and downs of the investors and organization wherein cognitive and emotional aspects supersede logical aspects (Cristofaro, 2019, pp. 6-17).

In the current scenario, behavioral finance has become an essential component in the investment-decision-making process, because it greatly influences investors' performance and decision-making. One can increase their investment performance by identifying behavioral predispositions and judgment errors (Huang, 2022). So it becomes important to understand behavioral finance as it will help the investors to go for good investment opportunities and at the same time, they can avoid repeating expensive errors in the future (Sarin, 2019, pp. 1-3).

Daniel Kahneman and Amos Tversky came up with the concept of anomalies. According to them, the future is uncertain and decisions based on uncertainty cannot be aligned with the principles of the Efficient Market Hypothesis. The Efficient Market Hypothesis as given by Fama (1970) stated that any information or news should be available to all investors and these need to be reflected in the market prices fully and completely and prices must be equal to the securities' value (Collin, 2013; Kalsie and Kalra, 2015; Sarin, 2019, pp. 6-7). The EMF assumes that markets are rational and efficient, meaning that all relevant information is reflected in stock prices and that it is impossible to consistently outperform the market (Collin, 2013). However, behavioral finance takes into account the impact of cognitive and emotional bias on investor decision-making (Sarin, 2019, pp. 6-7). The intellectual thinker takes short routes that in reality distract from the concept of standard finance.

According to this Prospect theory proposed by Kahneman & Tversky in the year 1979, it stated that judgments are made on "perceived gains rather than losses", and "gains and losses" are evaluated in a different way differently (Kahneman and Tversky, 1979, pp. 16-20; Mehta & Sharma, 2015). Loss aver-

Figure 1. Prospect theory value function

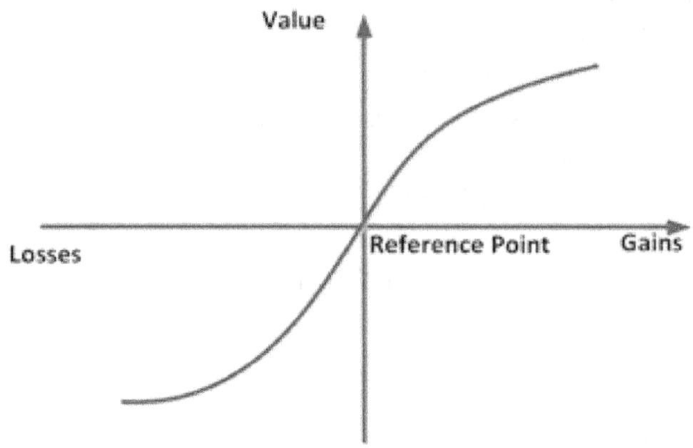

sion is when the same people choose the possible gains as their end economic result. The value function diagram shown in Figure 1 depicted more feelings of pain in comparison to gain (Chandra, 2016, p. 5).

Because Behavioral Finance taking the mainstream, Fama, the father of EMH felt that the markets were dominant and may deviate if the investors make stupid decisions based on their cognitive instincts (Fama, 1970). Different types of anomalies affect decision-making.

1. Market Anomalies

'Anomaly' in general is nothing but the deviation from what is set as a standard that is expected in normal parlances. Tversky & Kahneman (1986), explained market anomalies as "an anomaly is a deviation from the presently accepted paradigms that are too widespread to be ignored, too systematic to be terminated as random error, and too fundamental to be accommodated by relaxing the normative system".

Market inefficiency assumes just a logical and rational behavior that contradicts the Efficient Market Hypothesis. The variance in stock price and returns in financial markets paved the way for the field of 'Behavioral Finance'.

2. Fundamental Anomaly

Fundamental irregularities in stock performance contradict the Efficient Market Hypothesis and state that investors can earn abnormal returns. It folds in its layers in the form of value anomalies and small-cap effect, low price-to-book value, high-dividend yield, price-to-sales ratio, price-earnings, etc. (Iqbal et al., 2013).

3. Calendar Anomaly

This anomaly can be seen at a particular time. Some of the specific periods are the weekend effect, turn on the month effect, and turn on the year effect, January effect. The broadened framework also includes the announcements of information regarding stock splits, dividends, results, earnings, and mergers & acquisitions (Iqbal et al., 2013).

4. Technical Anomaly

Technical analysis includes the security's prices which need to anticipate based on historical prices. This anomaly depicts loopholes of EMH. Trend analysis, historical charts, moving averages techniques, relative strength, support, and resistance are some of the techniques used for Technical analysis. These anomalies questioned the existence of an efficient and stable market. The formation of behavioral finance discovers its roots here, which is the convention of psychology to finance. The irrational behavior of investors gave birth to the notion of biases which depicted how an investor reacts in certain circumstances.

The actual investors' behavior can be traced through realized time series data, as pointed out by the textbook written by Thaller (2005). Behavioral finance uses experimental facts, survey facts, as well as methods of psychology to find the appropriate solution about how certain events may alter an investor's decision and how the effects of these results on aggregate financial market behavior. Behavioral finance is a field of study that examines the psychological and emotional factors that influence financial decision-making. It aims to understand why people make certain financial decisions and how these decisions can deviate from rational expectations and standard financial models.

Understanding crashes in stock markets has been difficult for economists for several years. Theoretical foundations in financial economics rely ultimately on the assumption of the efficiency of markets (Kalsie and Kalra, 2015). Nonetheless, several studies have found empirical evidence that contrariwise is the cornerstone of efficient markets (Poyser, 2018). Behavioral economics uncover systematic deviations from rationality exposed by investors; instead, individuals are the victim of their cognitive biases leading to the existence of financial market inefficiencies, fragility, and anomalies. Particularly, cryptocurrency markets resemble in great fashion the criticisms of financial markets exposed by behavioral finance advocates. Studies of behavioral finance aim to explain why investors in stock market settings act as they do (Alsabban & Alarfaj, 2020). In this work, it is hypothesized that it is possible to explain the cryptocurrency market prices' puzzle from a behavioral finance perspective in which investors' cognitive biases and emotional biases play a major role to explain the volatility. According to the literature, herding can trigger the formation of a speculative bubble (Poyser, 2018).

Emotional biases indicated that investors' decisions are not easily predictable and subject to factors that vary among investors (Akinkoye and Bankole, 2020). Nigerian investors' emotional biases indicated that investment decisions are subject to various personal sentiments exhibited by them and are bound to make irrational decisions, resulting in market inefficiency (Akinkoye and Bankole, 2020).

BEHAVIORAL BIASES AFFECTING INVESTMENT DECISION-MAKING

During the 2017 Bitcoin hype, a lot of misconceptions about the whole industry started to circulate. The myths such as cryptocurrencies are good only for criminals, all blockchain activity is private, you can make anonymous transactions using all cryptocurrencies, etc. may have played a role in the cryptocurrency crash that followed the surge. As the market is still in the development stage, he legality factor associated is still widely focused on and is debatable. There are many deadlocks for Cryptocurrencies (Nadarajah & Chu, 2017), which are yet to be opened, but still, the crypto market is witnessing growth.

This growth may be due to behavioral biases, not the fundamentals as the fundamentalist approach denies cryptocurrencies are recording stable growth based on their recognition, different working pattern, and high volatility. In the behavioral finance spectrum, the growth and massive trading in cryptocurrencies may be due to the irrational behavior of investors. Also, scarce information and the sense of missing out on the opportunity for profit-making is pushing them to invest in massive proportions and causing herding as well as a market crash. The decision made by investors based on irrationality and the herding environment relies on market movement and behavior, not on rational trends. We observe herding behavior in these specific conditions (Jalal et al., 2020).

1. Herding

One of the most prevalent biases in the cryptocurrency market is the "herding" bias. This bias refers to the tendency of individuals to follow the actions and decisions of others, rather than making independent judgments. Herding is a kind of behavior wherein an individual follows another for doing any investment decisions. Experts and financial analysts usually considered judiciously the presence of herding, to element about the individual investors mostly depend on collective and set of people for information more than isolated evidence as a consequence leads to the price deviance of the securities from fundamental value; consequently, several good bet or chances for investment can be affected. It has been that academicians and experts paid attention to herding; as it impacted price change which in turn might influence the risk and return of asset pricing theories (Tan, Chiang, Mason & Nelling, 2008).

From the viewpoint of emotions, herding is related to emotional biases like home bias, gossip, taking out information about a particular stock, etc. Investors referred to herding when they believed that herding can help to get or remove useful and reliable information (Kallinterakis, Munir & Markovic, 2010).In the cryptocurrency market, this can manifest as investors buying or selling a particular cryptocurrency based on the actions of others, rather than analyzing the fundamentals of the asset. This result in market booms and busts as investors rush to buy or sell an asset based on the actions of others, rather than rational analysis.

Vidal-Tomas et al. (2019) witnessed that the small currency unit is also herding with the larger one leading to traders taking decisions on the main one. Moreover, this phenomenon of herding cannot be only attributed to Bitcoin as others are not herding with the main one. In the study by Ajaz & Kumar (2018), it was also proved that herding has an impact on the Fintech Market. In this CSAD method from the six major cryptocurrencies and CCI30 market indexes from August 2015 to January 2018 were used and market behavior was dependent on the price momentum.

Furthermore, investors turn out to the cryptocurrency market to increase its prices, when there is fear and the equity market is declining (Almeida & Gonçalves, 2023). Thereby it can be seen that most of the investors are keen on the cryptocurrency market during uncertain and ambiguous future times (Almeida & Gonçalves, 2023).

2. Overconfidence

Overconfidence is termed as an extra mile to self-confident behavior leading to extreme effects. As human beings, investors have the propensity to overrate their skills and forecasts for their achievement (Sarkar & Sahu, 2018). Overconfidence can be termed when people have unreasonable faith in their judgments. It usually overrates people's knowledge, amplifies their ability to control actions and at that juncture underrates possible risks. The actual performance of the asset is overrated because of this bias. Even though economic theories stated that investors act rationally and have full information when making any judgment or decision, however when it comes to real life, there is an abundance of information available in the market and all this information may not be considered for decision-making (Sarin & Chowdhury, 2018).

Overconfidence is related to the emotional state of how well a person comprehends their capabilities, skills, and the limits of their knowledge (Sarin and Chowdhury 2018). According to Sudzina et al. (2021), "Cryptocurrency early investors are more overconfident that is their agreeableness is less, extraversion is more and self-control is low, and they are mostly men which support overconfidence and are also low self-control". Precisely, it was concluded that women are less than 3 times as likely to use cryptocurrencies compared to men" (Sudzina et al., 2021; Sarin and Chowdhury, 2018).

3. Confirmation Bias

One more bias that affects investor decision-making in the cryptocurrency market is the "confirmation bias". This prejudice denotes the individual's propensity to explore options and comprehend information so as it takes into account existing notions (Sarin, 2019). Investors search for information and disregard that information that contradicts them that does not confirm these pre-notions (Sarin, 2019). This can lead to suboptimal investment decisions as investors ignore crucial information that could change their views. In the cryptocurrency market, this can lead to investors ignoring negative information about a particular cryptocurrency, and instead focusing on positive information that confirms their belief in the asset. This can lead to investors making poor investment decisions and losing money.

For example, Dogecoin investors can lead to overconfident and reluctant to consider alternative viewpoints, which can be dangerous in a rapidly changing market.

4. Self-Control Bias

It is another kind of Emotional Bias (EB) in which there is a propensity that bases individuals to consume the same at the cost of tomorrow's savings (Pompian 2006, p. 150). Self-Control Bias can be studied through the Life-cycle Hypothesis whereby an individual associates himself through the years of childhood to work to retirement whereby he balances his savings and consumption needs (Pompian 2006, p. 150). One of the studies investigated the existence of self-control bias among Indian investors based on investor type. It was found that poor self-control on their outflows can be seen in the new and untried individuals whereas good self-control was seen in the informed and alert investors (Sahi & Arora, 2012). Moreover, individuals having low confidence abilities are exposed to less risk and are more self-controlled and visa-versa (Sahi & Arora, 2012).

The main drawbacks of this bias are:

1. This bias causes investors to incur more spending today than savings. This is detrimental to the investment's nature, considering investors have lost time for future savings and go for short gains or sell off the good assets.
2. It causes people to plan less for retirement. Studies have shown that self-control people invest less in equity securities as they do not plan for their retirement

3. It can cause asset allocation imbalance problems. They do not take risks and have a portfolio to keep up with inflation.
4. They prefer short-term gains to long-term wealth ignoring the simple compounding values of investments.

Therefore, Self-Control bias is likely to influence investors in 4 ways: 1. control of spending, 2. planning less, 3. allocation of the portfolio, and 4. discipline welfare (Pompian, 2006, pp.153-162).

5. Optimism Bias

Optimism bias is a cognitive bias where an investor put more weight on positive performance than on negative one. In the context of behavioral finance, optimism bias can lead to unrealistic expectations about investment returns and a failure to adequately assess the risks involved (Parikh, 2017, p. 254). An example of optimism bias in financial decision-making could be an investor who overestimates the potential returns of a high-risk investment, such as a penny stock while underestimating the potential for losses. This bias can lead the investor to take on more risk than they should, leading to significant losses (Pompian, 2006, p. 163). Such Bias leads to holding onto loss, making stocks, and leading to losses in due time. Investors become emotionally biased toward a few stocks and thus leading to holding them for being optimistic.

The advisors often need to understand their own potential biases. The mistakes conducted by investors are:

1. It causes investors to overload themselves with company stocks. They feel there is less risk in holding these stocks.
2. It can cause investors to trust that they get returns irrespective of fees, inflation, and tax-adjusted. It eliminates the long-term benefits of compounding returns.
3. Investors prefer to get only good news about their investment and market and are optimum about it.
4. Investors think and believe they are above average in their ability and skills
5. Investors prefer geographical investments leading to home bias as they are optimistic about their local geographic areas (Pompian, 2006, p. 167).

Optimism bias can lead investors to overestimate the potential for positive outcomes in the cryptocurrency market and underestimate the risks involved. This can lead to a "bubble" mentality in which investors pile into cryptocurrencies in the hope of making quick profits, driving up prices even further. However, when sentiment turns negative, these investors may panic and sell off their holdings, causing a rapid drop in prices. When the sentiment of investors is "optimistic or bullish", there is herding in the cryptocurrency market, which leads to a price rise (Anamika & Subramaniam, 2022) However, when investor sentiment is "pessimistic", there is a decline in returns, and, investors tend to adopt risk-averse behavior when there is increased sentiment of investors (Burggraf et al., 2020, Almeida & Gonçalves, 2023). Conversely, it can be seen that "pessimistic" investors reduce their transactions when the Bitcoin price falls but "optimistic" investors continue their transactions (Almeida & Gonçalves, 2023). If the same trend continues in the long term, then "optimistic" investors are also forced to reduce their transactions (Almeida & Gonçalves, 2023). However, if Bitcoin prices surge in the short term, then both types of investors will increase their transactions (Almeida & Gonçalves, 2023).

The key to managing optimism bias in behavioral finance is to balance it with a realistic assessment of risks and potential outcomes. This can involve seeking out diverse perspectives and information sources, being aware of one's own biases, and taking a systematic approach to decision-making that takes into account all relevant information. By doing so, investors can make more informed and objective financial decisions that reflect both the potential for positive outcomes and the potential risks involved.

6. Loss Aversion Bias

Kahneman, as well as Tversky, established this concept along the lines that investors hold stocks to avoid losses instead of making gains from the same (Kahneman and Tversky, 1979, pp.16-20). Loss Aversion can be termed as a widespread occurrence in managerial under "risk and uncertainty", whereby the publics are extra profound to "losses than gains". Thus, according to Kahneman, investors are 'loss averse,' meaning that people are willing to take more risks to elude losses than to realize gains (Kahneman and Tversky, 1979, pp. 16-20). Loss aversion is when the same people choose the possible gains as their end economic result. The 'value function' is sharper for losses than gains meaning that the public is hurt more intensely by the decrease in the value than by the desire for an equal increase (Chandra, 2016, p. 5). Loss aversion means that the average investors carry an optimism bias towards their forecast; they are less willing to lose money than gain (Pompian 2006, p. 208).

So under these phenomena, it was seen that people will incline to losses and gamble, that is, venture capitalists will hold on to losing stock in anticipation of future recovery of its value. As per psychology, the possibility of loss revolves around twice being a more powerful motivator than making gains. Hence loss aversion tends to prevent people from unloading unprofitable investments. According to Godoi, et al. (2005), the emotional state connected with loss aversion can be linked to various factors like fear, risk, similar decision-making, investment patterns, guilt, greed, anger, and defense mechanisms.

The main implications of the same are:

1. This causes investors to hold loss-making investments for a longer duration.
2. The investors sell winners too early, in fear of evaporating profits.
3. They are unknowingly taking more risks in the portfolio.
4. They are holding unbalanced portfolios.

Hence loss aversion is a manifestation of the broad dominance of negativity. According to Thoma (2020), high prospect theory value cryptocurrencies tend to be overbought and overpriced earning low subsequent returns on average in the cross-section. Low prospect theory value cryptocurrencies tend to be underbought and underpriced earning high subsequent returns on average in the cross-section. All in all, the prospect theory value predicts future cryptocurrency returns with a negative sign in the cross-section.

Dogecoin's price fluctuations are also influenced by "loss aversion", whereby the investors are more inclined to harm than to the desire for happiness. This results to risk aversion and panic selling during periods of market volatility, as investors fear losing more money and try to cut their losses.

7. Recency Bias

Recency bias emphasized recent observations and events and is a cognitive bias. It causes people to take decisions on recent information (Pompian, 2006, p. 216). Recency bias is a psychological bias that can have an impact on investment decision-making, including in the cryptocurrency market. It refers to individuals' propensity to provide more importance to recent events or information when building judgments than seeing historical or long-term data (Zahera & Bansal, 2018).

The main implications of the same are:

1. Investors focus on forecasts made on past data that can be small for correct outcomes.
2. Investors tend to focus only on the upward trend and ignore the existing fundamental aspect (Pompian 2006, p. 221).
3. Ignoring proper allocation of assets (Pompian, 2006, p. 221).

In the context of the cryptocurrency market, recency bias can lead to investors focusing too much on short-term price movements or news events, without considering the underlying fundamentals or long-term trends of a particular cryptocurrency. This can result in impulsive and irrational investment decisions based on short-term price fluctuations or media hype, rather than a careful analysis of the asset's potential for long-term growth.

For example, during periods of high volatility in the cryptocurrency market, investors may be more likely to focus on recent price movements rather than considering the historical volatility of the asset. This can lead to panic selling or buying, as investors try to capitalize on short-term price fluctuations, rather than considering the underlying fundamentals of the asset.

Similarly, recency bias can influence investors' perceptions of the cryptocurrency market as a whole. If there has been a recent string of positive news or price movements, investors may become overly optimistic about the market's potential for growth, without considering the historical or long-term trends of the market.

To avoid the pitfalls of recency bias, investors need to take a long-term perspective and consider historical data and trends when making investment decisions. This can help investors avoid being influenced by short-term market movements or media hype, and make more rational investment decisions based on a careful analysis of the asset's potential for long-term growth.

8. "Gambler's Fallacy"

This is a "cognitive bias" that occurs when an individual believes that past events will influence future events, even when there is no evidence to support this belief. Specifically, the "gambler's fallacy" is the conviction that the likelihood of an event occurring increases if it has not occurred recently, or conversely, that the probability of an event occurring decreases if it has occurred frequently.

For example, if a person flips a coin and it lands on heads several times in a row, they may believe that the next flip is more likely to land on tails because "it's due" or "it's been a while since tails appeared." However, the outcome of each flip is independent of previous flips and the probability of the coin landing on heads or tails remains the same with each flip.

The gambler's fallacy can also occur in gambling situations. For example, a person may believe that a particular slot machine is more likely to pay out because it has not paid out recently, even though the odds of winning on a slot machine are determined by a random number generator and are not influenced by past events.

The gambler's fallacy can be costly in gambling and investment situations. It can lead individuals to make irrational decisions based on false beliefs about probability and increase their risk of losing money. It is important to recognize and avoid the gambler's fallacy by making decisions based on accurate information and a realistic understanding of probability.

The "gambler's fallacy" also affects investor decision-making in the cryptocurrency market. This bias refers to the belief that past events can influence future outcomes. In the cryptocurrency market, this can lead to investors believing that a cryptocurrency's price will change based on past price movements, rather than fundamentals. This can lead to investors buying or selling an asset based on past price movements, rather than prospects.

9. Status Quo Bias

In 1988, William Samuelson and Richard Zeckhauser gave this term as an EB that influences individuals facing an assortment of choices to select whatever option confirms the existing conditions instead of various options (Samuelson & Zeckhauser, 1988, pp. 7-59). Status Quo Bias is more predominant among investors with inherited, concentrated stock positions (Samuelson & Zeckhauser, 1988, pp. 7-59).

The main implications of the same are -

1. Status Quo causes investors not to take any action, hold investments, and take a high risk.
2. Investors are holding familiar and emotionally fond assets leading to a compromise on financial goals.
3. It is related to Loss aversion bias as an investor can modify their present position instead of remaining static in the long term (Pompian 2006, p. 251).

IMPACT OF BEHAVIORAL FINANCE ON THE CRYPTOCURRENCY MARKET

1. Bitcoin

The first blockchain product was "Bitcoin" which was developed by Santoshi Nakamoto. It came in the year 2008. Bitcoin transactions are processed on a 'distributed network of computers' using a technology called the "Blockchain". In this, each 'block' have certain data of several transactions, and once this 'block' is totaled up to make a chain, it cannot be changed, thereby making the Blockchain network highly resistant, safe, and secure to fraud or hacking.

Bitcoin is also unique in that there is a limited supply of bitcoins that can be created. The total supply is capped at 21 million bitcoins, and as of April 2023, over 18 million bitcoins have already been mined. This limited supply is one of the factors that contribute to the volatility of the Bitcoin market, as changes in demand can have a significant impact on the price. One of the key benefits of Bitcoin is that it allows for fast and cheap transactions, particularly for international payments. Bitcoin transactions can be processed in a matter of minutes, and fees are typically lower than those charged by traditional payment systems like credit cards or wire transfers. In addition, Bitcoin transactions can be made anonymously, making it a popular choice for those who value privacy.

Bitcoin is defined as "no particular person or entity owns the Bitcoin network much like no one owns the technology behind email" (Bitcoin.org). Bitcoin is ranked number one among all other cryptocurrencies. The reason for the same is that the general public has perceived and listened to it and not so much about other cryptocurrencies. The other reason for Bitcoin's huge market capitalization is its accessibility. Being the main currency of the digital world, it is one of the most strong market pullers in recent times. The entire Fintech sentiments follow the capriciousness of Bitcoin from a long and continuing perspective (Danial, 2022, p. 112).

The impact of optimism bias on the cryptocurrency market can be seen in the numerous boom and bust cycles that have occurred over the past decade. In 2017, for example, Bitcoin experienced a massive price surge, driven in part by optimism bias and the hype surrounding the technology. However, this was followed by a sharp correction in early 2018, as investors began to realize the risks and limitations of cryptocurrencies (Danial, 2022, p. 112).

Bitcoin, as a relatively new and highly volatile asset, is particularly interesting to study from a behavioral finance perspective. One of the key behavioral biases that can affect Bitcoin investors is the herd mentality. When the price of Bitcoin is rising, investors may feel a strong urge to join the herd and invest, fearing that they will miss out on potential gains. This can lead to a bubble-like environment where the price of Bitcoin becomes detached from its underlying value. Another behavioral bias is overconfidence. Investors may believe that they have a superior understanding of the market and can outperform other investors. This overconfidence can lead to excessive risk-taking and poor investment decisions.

Loss aversion is another behavioral bias that can influence Bitcoin investors. Thereby investors hold onto Bitcoin investments even when the price is falling, rather than selling and cutting their losses. Confirmation bias is also a common behavioral bias that can affect Bitcoin investors. Investors who are bullish on Bitcoin may seek out positive news and ignore negative news, leading to a distorted view of the market.

Finally, anchoring is a behavioral bias that can affect Bitcoin investors. It refers to "the concept of relying too much on first-hand information received when taking a decision." For example, an investor who bought Bitcoin at a high price may be anchored to that price and unwilling to sell at a lower price, even if the market has changed.

Understanding these behavioral biases can help investors make more informed decisions when investing in Bitcoin. It is important to avoid the herd mentality, stay grounded, and be aware of biases that can lead to poor investment decisions. By taking a rational and disciplined approach, investors can navigate the volatile Bitcoin market and potentially reap the benefits of this new and innovative asset class.

2. Ethereum

Ethereum is another major cryptocurrency. Ethereum is a "decentralized and open-source blockchain platform" that was launched in 2015. Like Bitcoin, Ethereum allows for "peer-to-peer transactions" without the need for intermediaries like banks. However, Ethereum's blockchain is designed to support the creation and deployment of "decentralized applications (dApps) and 'smart contracts'" (Deniz & Teker, 2020).

The native cryptocurrency used by the Ethereum platform is called "Ether" (ETH), which acts as transaction fees and computational services on the network. In addition, ETH can be traded on cryptocurrency exchanges like other digital assets (Danial, 2022, p. 109). One of the key benefits of Ethereum is its ability to support the development of decentralized applications. These applications can be used to build a wide range of use cases, from decentralized finance (DeFi) protocols to social media platforms to supply chain management systems. The decentralized nature of Ethereum also means that these applications can operate without the need for intermediaries or central authorities (Danial, 2022, p. 109).

Behavioral finance can help explain these price movements by highlighting the role of cognitive biases and herd behavior in driving market sentiment. For example, the bandwagon effect, where people tend to follow the crowd, can lead to herding behavior in the markets. Similarly, confirmation bias, where the public look for information that matches their philosophies thereby, can lead to irrational exuberance and inflated prices.

3. Ripple

Ripple is a digital payment protocol and cryptocurrency that was created in 2012 by Ripple Labs. The Ripple protocol allows for secure and instant peer-to-peer transactions, using a distributed ledger technology called the XRP Ledger. XRP is the native cryptocurrency of the Ripple protocol and is used to facilitate transactions and payment transfers on the network (Danial, 2022, p. 112). The token used for the cryptocurrency is premined (Danial, 2022, p. 112). XRP is also used as a bridge currency between different fiat currencies, which allows for faster and cheaper currency exchanges. This has led to the development of various XRP-based products and services, including remittance services and payment gateways.

One of the key biases that can affect Ripple investors is herding behavior. Herding behavior is where investors follow others, rather than making independent investment decisions. This can lead to momentum trading and speculative bubbles, as investors buy Ripple simply because others are doing so, without considering the underlying fundamentals of the asset.

Another bias that can influence Ripple investors is loss aversion resulting in risk aversion and panic selling during periods of market volatility, as investors fear losing more money and try to cut their losses.

Ripple's regulatory challenges can also be influenced by behavioral biases. For example, the SEC lawsuit against Ripple Labs may have caused some investors to engage in confirmation bias, seeking out information that supports their pre-existing beliefs about the asset and the company (Danial, 2022, p. 112). This can lead to overconfidence and reluctance to consider alternative viewpoints, which can be dangerous in a rapidly changing market. Overall, behavioral finance can help explain the investors' behavior in the Ripple crypto-market, and how psychological biases can influence investment decisions (Zahera & Bansal, 2018). Understanding these biases can help investors make more rational decisions and avoid common pitfalls in the cryptocurrency market.

4. Litecoin

In 2011 another cryptocurrency was created known as Litecoin It is a decentralized digital currency that operates on a peer-to-peer network, similar to Bitcoin. Like Bitcoin, Litecoin is based on blockchain technology. Litecoin differs from Bitcoin in several ways. First, it has a faster block generation time, whereby blocks being generated take only ¼ of the time taken by Bitcoin (Lewis, 2021, p. 194). This means that Litecoin transactions can be confirmed more quickly than Bitcoin transactions. Second, Litecoin uses a different hashing procedure, called 'Scrypt', which is memory-intensive and prevents mining centralization. Finally, Litecoin has a higher maximum supply than Bitcoin, with a total of 84 million Litecoins that can be mined, compared to Bitcoin's 21 million (Lewis, 2021, p. 194).

Litecoin has gained popularity as a cryptocurrency for fast and low-cost transactions. It is often used as a means of transferring value between individuals or businesses, and it has also been integrated into several payment systems and online merchants. Overall, Litecoin is a digital currency that offers some unique features compared to other cryptocurrencies, and it has gained a strong following among users and investors.

Litecoin, like other cryptocurrencies, can be influenced by the principles of behavioral finance. Behavioral finance studies how emotions and cognitive biases can affect investor behavior and ultimately impact financial markets.

One aspect of Litecoin's behavior that can be attributed to behavioral finance is its tendency to exhibit strong price movements. Litecoin's price can be influenced by investor sentiment, which can be affected by cognitive biases such as herd behavior and overconfidence. For example, if a large number of investors decide to buy Litecoin, this can lead to a surge in demand and a subsequent increase in its price. Another example of behavioral finance in Litecoin is the phenomenon of anchoring. Anchoring refers to the tendency of investors to fixate on a certain price point or value and use it as a reference point for making investment decisions. For example, if an investor bought Litecoin at a certain price and the price subsequently drops, they may hold onto their investment hoping to recoup their losses, rather than selling at a loss.

Additionally, availability bias can play a role in Litecoin's behavior. The availability bias is the tendency of investors to rely too heavily on information that is easily accessible, rather than seeking out a broader range of information. For example, investors may make decisions about Litecoin based on news headlines or social media buzz, rather than conducting a thorough analysis of the cryptocurrency's fundamentals and long-term prospects.

In conclusion, like any financial asset, Litecoin can be influenced by the principles of behavioral finance. Investors should be aware of these biases and strive to make informed investment decisions based on a thorough analysis of the cryptocurrency's fundamentals and long-term prospects, rather than relying solely on emotions and cognitive biases.

5. "Dogecoin"

In the year 2013, a 'decentralized and open-source cryptocurrency' was created known as Dogecoin. Dogecoin was created as a joke, slowly and gradually it increased momentum and has been used for various charitable causes and community-driven initiatives. Like other cryptocurrencies, Dogecoin also uses blockchain technology. One of the key features of Dogecoin is its fast transaction times and low transaction fees, which make it a popular choice for micro-transactions and small purchases. In addition, Dogecoin has a relatively large and active community, which has helped to drive its adoption and increase its value.

However, Dogecoin has also faced criticism and skepticism from some investors and analysts, who question its long-term viability and potential as a serious investment. Dogecoin has been subject to significant price volatility, and its value has been largely driven by social media hype and celebrity endorsements (Danial, 2022, p. 117).

Dogecoin's price fluctuations can be influenced by various behavioral finance biases, which can lead to irrational investment decisions and market volatility. One of the key biases that can affect Dogecoin investors is the bandwagon effect. This is the tendency of investors to buy an asset simply because others are doing so, without considering the underlying fundamentals of the asset. The social media hype and celebrity endorsements surrounding Dogecoin can contribute to this effect, leading to short-term spikes in demand and volatility. The hype and speculation surrounding Dogecoin can also be influenced by FOMO (fear of missing out), that is the investors' predisposition created by a fear of missing out on potential gains. This can lead to impulsive and irrational investment decisions, as investors try to enter the market at the last minute to capture gains (Deniz & Teker, 2020).

Overall, understanding these behavioral finance biases can help investors make more rational decisions and avoid common pitfalls in the Dogecoin market. It is important for investors to carefully consider the risks before investing in any cryptocurrency, and to maintain a long-term perspective to avoid being influenced by short-term hype and speculation.

CHALLENGES AND DEVELOPMENT OF FINTECH COMPANIES

The main nature of any cryptocurrency is that it's a digital form of currency in the form of coins which is built using blockchain technology (Lewis, 2021, p. 194). To avoid money laundering purposes and other illegal activities as well as to safeguard the interest of investors, cryptocurrencies are encoded to secure transactions (Huang, 2022). In comparison to the stock markets, the volatility and risk factor is more in cryptocurrency. According to De Bondt (2018), the premium generated from volatility in cryptocurrency can be elucidated partly by herding behavior and over-optimism. Moreover, Zhu et al (2021) in his study studied the relationship between the volatility of Bitcoin and investors' attention on a certain asset and it was concluded that behavioral finance plays an important role and investor attention has a granger cause on volatility changes in Bitcoin market (Deniz &Teker, 2020; Zhu et al., 2021).

There are several challenges associated with cryptocurrency and financial technologies, including:

1. **Security:** One of the main challenges facing cryptocurrency and financial technologies is security. As these technologies are digital, they are vulnerable to cyber-attacks and hacking attempts. Cryptocurrency exchanges and wallets have been targeted by hackers, resulting in the loss of millions of dollars' worth of cryptocurrencies.
2. **Regulation:** Another challenge is the lack of clear regulation in many countries. Governments and regulatory bodies are still grappling with how to classify and regulate cryptocurrencies and financial technologies. This uncertainty can create barriers to adoption and limit the potential of these technologies (Silva & Mira da Silva, 2022)
3. **Volatility:** Cryptocurrencies are notoriously volatile, with prices often fluctuating rapidly and unpredictably. This can make it difficult to use cryptocurrencies as a reliable store of value or means of exchange.
4. **Adoption:** Despite the growing popularity of cryptocurrencies and financial technologies, adoption is still relatively low compared to traditional financial systems. This can be attributed to a lack of understanding and awareness of these technologies among the general public.
5. **Scalability:** Cryptocurrencies and financial technologies are still in their early stages of development, and many systems are not yet capable of processing large volumes of transactions efficiently. This can lead to slow transaction times and high fees.

Overall, these challenges are not insurmountable, and progress is being made to address them. However, they do highlight the need for continued innovation and development in the cryptocurrency and financial technology space.

The impact of Fintech and blockchain technology on the cryptocurrency market has been significant. Some of the key ways in which Fintech and blockchain have influenced the cryptocurrency market:

1. **Increased Adoption:** FinTech has made it easier for people to access and use cryptocurrencies. With the rise of cryptocurrency wallets, exchanges, and payment systems, more people are using cryptocurrencies for everyday transactions. Blockchain technology has made it possible to create more secure and transparent systems for recording transactions, which has increased trust in cryptocurrencies.
2. **Improved Security:** Blockchain technology has significantly improved the security of cryptocurrency transactions. The use of decentralized ledgers makes it nearly impossible for hackers to manipulate data or steal funds. Fintech companies have also implemented robust security measures, such as two-factor authentication and biometric identification, to prevent fraud and unauthorized access.
3. **Increased Efficiency:** FinTech companies have developed platforms that allow for faster and more efficient cryptocurrency transactions. The use of blockchain technology has eliminated the need for intermediaries in some cases, which has reduced transaction fees and processing times.
4. **Innovation:** FinTech companies are constantly developing new products and services that utilize blockchain technology and cryptocurrencies. For example, some companies are using blockchain to create decentralized lending platforms, while others are using cryptocurrencies to facilitate cross-border payments.
5. **Regulatory Challenges:** The rise of fintech and blockchain technology has presented regulatory challenges for governments and financial institutions. Regulators are struggling to keep up with the rapidly evolving market, and there is a need for clear guidelines to ensure that cryptocurrencies are used safely and responsibly (Silva & Mira da Silva, 2022).

The development of Fintech companies has been quite significant in recent years. Fintech companies are disrupting traditional financial services by providing innovative and efficient solutions to financial problems.

Some key drivers of the development of Fintech companies include:

1. **Increased Access to Technology:** With the growth of the internet and mobile devices, more people have access to technology, making it easier to use digital financial services.
2. **Changing Consumer Preferences:** Consumers are demanding more personalized and convenient financial services. Fintech companies are using technology to create innovative solutions to meet these demands.
3. **Regulatory Changes:** Many countries are introducing regulatory changes that promote the growth of Fintech companies. For example, some countries have introduced sandbox environments where Fintech companies can test new products and services. Moreover, a Swiss financial company has opened a crypto bank where flat and digital currencies can be traded in the same online bank account (Silva & Mira da Silva, 2022).

4. **Collaborations Between FinTech and Traditional Financial Institutions:** Traditional financial institutions are partnering with Fintech companies to provide innovative services to customers.

Overall, Fintech companies are transforming the financial services industry and are likely to continue doing so in the future.

CONCLUSION AND RECOMMENDATIONS

The relevance of behavioral finance in the cryptocurrency market is growing, as the market is characterized by high volatility and complex decision-making environments. Cryptocurrency investors are often faced with unique challenges, such as the limited availability of reliable information and the absence of established norms and regulations. These factors can create fertile ground for cognitive biases and heuristics to impact investment decisions.

In the cryptocurrency market, investors are often exposed to new and untested investment opportunities, which can be tempting and lead to impulsive investment decisions. Additionally, the high volatility of the market and the rapid pace of innovation can lead to overconfidence in one's ability to predict future market movements.

By understanding the role of behavioral finance in the cryptocurrency market, investors can become better equipped to make informed investment decisions and reduce the risk of suboptimal investment outcomes. Behavioral finance can also provide policymakers with a framework to understand and address the unique challenges posed by the cryptocurrency market.

Moreover, the lack of regulation and the decentralized nature of the cryptocurrency market makes it more susceptible to the influence of biases. This can amplify the impact of biases on market volatility and efficiency. Lastly, the impact of biases in behavioral finance on the cryptocurrency market highlights the importance of considering psychological, social, and emotional factors in investment decision-making. A better understanding of these biases and their impact on the market can help investors make more informed investment decisions and contribute to a more stable and efficient cryptocurrency market. This chapter highlights the importance of being aware of the impact of biases in behavioral finance on investment decision-making. By understanding these biases and taking steps to mitigate their impact, investors can make more informed investment decisions and increase their chances of success. This can include developing a comprehensive investment strategy, seeking professional advice, and engaging in ongoing education and training.

In this chapter, I have sought to draw attention to understanding the relationship between behavioral finance and cryptocurrency. It will help financial advisors recognize behavioral biases while making the investment decision. Therefore, they can advise other investors properly to mitigate or manage such predispositions. This chapter tries to study research papers and studies across the various aspects of emotional and cognitive biases, which cannot be generalized. These biases can still occur despite having a realistic understanding of one's self-interest. The limitation of the study is other biases that can affect the investment decision in the cryptocurrency market; can be studied.

Future research could examine the impact of new technologies, such as blockchain and smart contracts, on investment decision-making and market efficiency. Moreover, the researcher can also study behavioral corporate finance and digitization for more insights. Individual investors can use the study for understanding in depth the impact of these behavioral factors on investment decisions and improving their investment performance and returns.

REFERENCES

Akinkoye, E. Y., & Bankole, O. E. (2020). Effect of Emotional Biases on Investor's Decision Making in Nigeria. *International Journal of Business and Management Future*, *1*(1), 33–39. doi:10.46281/ijbmf.v4i1.548

Almeida, J., & Gonçalves, T. C. (2023). A systematic literature review of investor behavior in the cryptocurrency markets. *Journal of Behavioral and Experimental Finance*, *37*, 100785. Advance online publication. doi:10.1016/j.jbef.2022.100785

Alsabban, S., & Alarfaj, O. (2020). An Empirical Analysis of Behavioral Finance in the Saudi Stock Market: Evidence of Overconfidence Behavior. *International Journal of Economics and Financial Issues*, *10*(1), 73–86. doi:10.32479/ijefi.8920

Anamika, A., & Subramaniam, S. (2022). Do news headlines matter in the cryptocurrency market? *Applied Economics*, *54*(54), 6322–6338. doi:10.1080/00036846.2022.2061904

Anamika, Chakraborty, M., & Subramaniam, S. (2021). Does sentiment impact cryptocurrency? *Journal of Behavioral Finance*, 1–17. doi:10.1080/15427560.2021.1950723

Burggraf, T., Huynh, T. L. D., Rudolf, M., & Wang, M. (2020). Do FEARS drive Bitcoin? *Review of Behavioral Finance*, *13*(3), 229–258. doi:10.1108/RBF-11-2019-0161

Chandra, P. (2016). *Behavioral Finance*. McGraw Hill Education.

Collin, R. (2013). *The Efficient Hypothesists: Bacheier, Samuelson, Fama, Ross, Tobin, and Shiller*. Palgave Macmillan.

Cristofaro, M. (2019). The role of affect in management decisions: A systematic review. *European Management Journal*, *1*(1), 6–17. doi:10.1016/j.emj.2018.12.002

Danial, K. (2022). Cryptocurrency Investing. John Wiley and Sons Inc. doi:10.1017/9781316676349.005

De Bondt., W. (2018). Speculative bubbles: Insights from behavioral finance. In The Cambridge Handbook of Psychology and Economic Behavior (pp. 101-166). Cambridge University Press. doi:10.1017/9781316676349.005

Deniz, A., & Teker, D. (2020). Determinants of Cryptocurrency Market: An Analysis for Bitcoin, Ethereum and Ripple. *International Journal of Business and Social Science*, *11*(11). Advance online publication. doi:10.30845/ijbss.v11n11p5

European Central Bank. (2012). *Virtual Currency Schemes*. Retrieved on February 11, 2023, from https://www.ecb.europa.eu/pub/pdf/other/virtualcurrencyschemes201210en.pdf

Fama, E. F. (1970). Efficient capital markets: A review of theory and empirical work. *The Journal of Finance, 25*(2), 383-417. doi:.1970.tb00518.x doi:10.1111/j.1540-6261

Godoi, K. C., Marcon, R., & da Silva, A. B. (2005). Loss aversion: A qualitative study in behavioral finance. *Managerial Finance*, *31*(4), 46–56. doi:10.1108/03074350510769613

Huang, H. (2022).An Investigation of Cryptocurrencies: Behavior Finance Perspective, In *Advances in Economics, Business and Management Research, vol. 652, 7th International Conference on Social Sciences and Economic Development (ICSSED 2022).* Atlantis Press International B.V.

Iqbal, S., Hussain, N., Latif, M., & Aslam, S. (2013). Investor Type and Financial Market Anomalies: A Comparison of Individual, Institutional and Foreign Investors and Role of Their Behaviors in Investing Decisions. *Middle East Journal of Scientific Research*, *17*, 1591–1596. doi:10.5829/idosi.mejsr.2013.17.11.11787

Jalal, R. N., Sargiacomo, M., Sahar, N. U., & Fayyaz, U. (2020). Herding Behavior and Cryptocurrency: Market Asymmetries, Inter-Dependency and Intra-Dependency. *Journal of Asian Finance Economics and Business.*, *7*(7), 27–34. doi:10.13106/jafeb.2020.vol7.no7.027

Kahneman, D., & Tversky, A. (1979). Prospect theory: An analysis of decision under risk. *Econometrica*, *2*(2), 263–291. doi:10.2307/1914185

Kallinterakis, V., Munir, N., & Radovic-Markovic, M. (2010). Herd Behaviour, Illiquidity and Extreme Market States: Evidence from Banja Luka. *Journal of Emerging Market Finance*, *9*(3), 305–324. doi:10.1177/097265271000900303

Kalsie, A., & Kalra, J. K. (2015). An empirical study on efficient market hypothesis of Indian capital markets. *Journal of Management Research and Analysis*, *2*(2), 108–114.

Khan, K., Zhao, H., Zhang, H., Yang, H., Shah, M. H., & Jahanger, A. (2020). The impact of COVID-19 pandemic on stock markets: An empirical analysis of world major stock indices. *Journal of Asian Finance, Economics and Business*, *7*(7), 463–474. doi:10.13106/jafeb.2020.vol7.no7.463

Lewis, A. (2021). *The basis of Bitcoins and Blockchains.* Mango Publishing Group.

Mehta, K., & Sharma, R. (2015). Individual Investors' Behavior: In Demographical Backdrop. SCMS Journal of Indian Management, 12(3), 25-36.

Nadarajah, S., & Chu, J. (2017). On the inefficiency of Bitcoin. *Economics Letters*, *150*(C), 6–9. doi:10.1016/j.econlet.2016.10.033

Pompian, M. M. (2006). *Behavioral Finance and Wealth Management – How to Build Optimal Portfolios That Account for Investor Biases.* John Wiley and Sons Inc. Retrieved from http://library.perbanas.ac.id/images/book/behavioralfinance.pdf

PoyserO. (2018). Herding behavior in cryptocurrency markets (Issue November). https://arxiv.org/abs/1806.11348

Sahi, S. K., & Arora, A. P. (2012). Individual investor biases: A segmentation analysis. *Qualitative Research in Financial Markets*, *4*(1), 6–25. doi:10.1108/17554171211213522

Sarin, A. B. (2019). *Behavioral Factors Affecting Investment Decisions and Performance: An Empirical Study of Investors in Delhi.* Ph.D., Lingayas Vidhyapeeth.

Sarin, A. B., & Chowdhury, J. K. (2018). Understanding behavioral biases influencing investment decisions An exploratory study. *International Research Journal of Management and Commerce, 1*, 584–596.

Sarkar, A. K., & Sahu, T. N. (2018). *Investment Behaviour: Towards an Individual-Centred Financial Policy in Developing Countries*. Emerald Publishing. doi:10.1108/9781787562790

Shrotryia, V. K., & Kalra, H. (2021). Herding in the crypto market: A diagnosis of heavy distribution tails. *Review of Behavioral Finance, 14*(5), 566–587. doi:10.1108/RBF-02-2021-0021

Silva, E. C., & Mira da Silva, M. (2022). Research contributions and challenges in DLT-based cryptocurrency regulation: A systematic mapping study. *Journal of Banking and Financial Technology, 6*(1), 63–82. doi:10.100742786-021-00037-2

Sudzina, F., Dobes, M., & Pavlicek, A. (2021). Towards the psychological profile of cryptocurrency early adopters: Overconfidence and self-control as predictors of cryptocurrency use. *Current Psychology*. Advance online publication. doi:10.100712144-021-02225-1

Thaler, R. (2005). Advances in Behavioral Finance II. Princeton University Press.

ThomaA. (2020).A Prospect Theory Model for Predicting Cryptocurrency Returns. doi:10.2139/ssrn.3753530

Trivedi, S., Mehta, K., & Sharma, R. (2021). Systematic Literature Review on Application of Blockchain Technology in E-Finance and Financial Services. *Journal of Technology Management & Innovation, 16*(3), 90–102. doi:10.4067/S0718-27242021000300089

Tversky A. & Kahneman D. (1986), Rational Choice and the Framing of Decisions. *The Journal of Business, 4*(2), S251-S278.

Vidal-Tomas, D., Ibanez, A. M., & Farinos, J. E. (2019). Herding in the cryptocurrency market: CSSD and CSAD approaches. *Finance Research Letters, 30*, 181-186. doi:10.1016/j.frl.2018.09.008

Zahera, S. A., & Bansal, R. (2018). Do investors exhibit behavioral biases in investment decision making? A systematic review. *Qualitative Research in Financial Markets, 2*(2), 210–251. doi:10.1108/QRFM-04-2017-0028

Zhu, P., Zhang, X., Wu, Y., Zheng, H., & Zhang, Y. (2021). Investor attention and cryptocurrency: Evidence from the Bitcoin market. *PLoS One, 16*(2), e0246331. doi:10.1371/journal.pone.0246331 PMID:33524059

Chapter 15
Convention of Blockchain in Financial Services:
A State-of-the-Art Literature Review

Sonal Trivedi
https://orcid.org/0000-0001-8711-2977
School of Management, Birla Global University, India

ABSTRACT

Literature reviews are used by practitioners and researchers to combine numerous bodies of knowledge. There are various SotA papers on blockchain applications. The authors looked at 100 articles about the use of blockchain in financial services that were published between 2013 and 2023. The data sources used for the same are Science Direct and Google Scholar. The three phases for conducting SotA reviews are provided in this chapter. In the 100 articles looked at for SotA in title, 69 were tagged as SotA reviews, and the rest were either tagged as 'literature review' or 'systematic literature review'. The summary of 69 articles is presented in the literature review section of the study. An interpretive synthesis of SotA reviews in the current study describes where we are presently in the field of application of blockchain in finance. The chapter also presents the changes brought by application of blockchain in the value chain of the banking sector and future scope of study in the field.

INTRODUCTION

The competitive business environment is being rapidly altered by blockchain technologies. Key stakeholders, on the other hand, remain sceptical about how, when, and what blockchain could do for their businesses. Through a Systematic Review of the Literature (SRL), the aim of the present study is to examine the economic & business implications of blockchain's potential reshaping of the financial services sector, as well as the obstacles and facilitators that specifically hinder blockchain adoption in this sector. The progressions brought by blockchain innovation in the monetary assistance industry are made sense in the view of 'Doormen Worth Chain Examination'. In addition, we offer the manager a number of suggestions for removing obstacles and easing the transition.

DOI: 10.4018/978-1-6684-8624-5.ch015

The usage of blockchain technology in various aspects of the "financial services industry" is referred to as "blockchain in finance."

There are numerous ways that blockchain technology can benefit financial services. Decentralised finance, or DeFi, has emerged as a result of the usage of blockchain in financial services.

Bitcoin, which was at first limited to use as a technique for cryptography for proliferating bitcoin and related digital currency exchanges (Tandon et al., 2021; Nakamoto, 2008), can be regarded as the world's introduction to blockchain technology. Tandon et al. 2020). However, over the past five years, supply chain management and IoT have both seen an increase in blockchain usage (Patil, Sangeetha, & Bhaskar, 2021).

In addition, as per the report of Statista (2020), the worldwide market for blockchain has expanded quickly as of late and is expected to reach a worth of 39 billion dollars by 2025. The features of blockchain, such as digital transactions, transparency, trust, a platform for multiple stakeholders, and so on, are the reason for its exponential growth (Dettling, 2018). According to Adams et al. (2017), researchers consider blockchain to be the foundational technology. As a result, a number of studies have been carried out to learn how blockchain technology is used. The purpose of this research is to determine the usefulness of blockchain technology in the financial services industry.

The Purpose of the Study

The present study determines the usefulness blockchain technology is in financial service industry.

The Research Question

Based on a primary literature review of the papers mentioned in the section 2 literature review, the issues which are the focus of the current study are as follows:

RQ 1: Describe the concept of blockchain technology.

RQ2: How has the financial service industry evolved over a decade?

RQ3: Describe the financial sector's use of blockchain technology.

Flow of Paper

This paper comprises of five sections – Introduction, Review of Literature, Research Methodology, Finding & Discussion, and Conclusion. The introduction section presents the concept of blockchain technology and its application in financial service industry. It also explains the concept of State-of-the-Art literature review. This section also presents the scope of study and research questions.

The next section presents the Review of Literature.

REVIEW OF LITERATURE

This section comprises of review of literature of previous study of last 10 years of research papers published in Scopus indexed journal. This section presents – Concept of Blockchain, Evolution of Financial Service Industry and Application of Blockchain in financial service industry.

Blockchain

Significance of Blockchain Innovation

The blockchain is a decentralised record which records exchanges on various PCs simultaneously (Walsh, 2021). The first blockchain was defined, created, and implemented by Satoshi Nakamoto, a pseudonym (The Economist, 2015).

Additionally, a blockchain is a network-based concept that is a peer-to-peer (P2P) distributed database. It consists of a number of blocks comprising transactions which are secured by PKI (public-key infrastructure) verified by the community, & timestamped by the network. Once an element of the blockchain has been added, it cannot be changed. Additionally, it maintains an ongoing record of previous actions (Zachariadis, Hileman, & Scott, 2019).

In addition, global economic reform and the industrial and commercial revolution are anticipated to be sparked by blockchain. Blockchain begins by using encryption to generate a digital security code. Users can then check their purchases without providing any personal information. The exchange will be finished naturally and scattered as the record saved on the blockchain is unalterable (Chang et al. 2020).

Because of its ability to change the economy, change how people interact with the economy, and restructure financial transactions, Blockchain is also referred to as the "next-generation Internet" and "a new foundational technology" (Zachariadis, Hileman & Scott, 2019). Additionally, blockchain is a decentralised transaction system powered by decentralised nodes and a secure database (Ertz & Boily, 2019). To put it another way, blockchain is a revolutionary technology which has caught the attention of businesses & governments all over the world. "Distributed ledger technology" basically refers to data & transactions gathered that are consecutively tracked & recorded over the distributed ledger network (Rashideh, 2020).

Additionally, Blockchain is the digital money's spine innovation, which might be considered a simple register where exchanges are recorded (Li et al. 2021). The entire data of the blockchain system is made available to the public, and a group of decentralised nodes that keep the system running check it for consistency.

Additionally, the term "block" refers to a continuously expanding list of records that are encrypted & linked to one another (Lin et al. 2020). Blockchains act as transaction ledgers in systems of cryptocurrency like Ethereum & Bitcoin, keeping a trace of past transactions & present state. According to Janssen et al., a group of blocks which are linked to each other like a chain & timestamp and have data stored in hash functions is also known as a blockchain.

As a database which is distributed, the blockchain permits only the addition of new data to existing data (Nofer et al. 2017). Blockchain is a chain of blocks where each block contains a hash pointer & the transaction list of the block before it in the chain. Consequently, if a new block is to be added, the only option is to add it at the end. A consensus procedure is used to decide what will be in the new block which will be added.

On the basis of the above definitions, a blockchain can be described as "based on a P-2-P network, a distributed database model, consisting of block series which contain verified and timestamped transactions approved by a network community, unalterable, and secured by public-key infrastructure (PKI).

The key aspects of blockchain are discussed in the following section.

According to Ali et al. 2020, trust and decentralisation are two of the key features of blockchain technology. The terms are described by Ali et al. 2020 in the following manner:

Trust: The decentralised method of the blockchain is what sets it apart. The association is shielded by the affirmation of work show, which disposes of the need to impart any centre individual to record and really take a look at trades; consequently, executives don't have to rely upon an untouchable to get their trades & assets.

Decentralisation: A programmer or administration cannot access the integrated record for individual growth due to the distributed and decentralised design of the blockchain. Thus, blockchain is a platform which makes it less necessary to use a centralised intermediary to protect one's assets.

Also, the blockchain can be categorised as execution, decentralisation, consensus mechanism, & client secrecy (Chang et al. 2020). The following is a description of these terms:

Execution: Rules and algorithms can be used to create interactions between nodes. Blockchain could likewise run programmes, assuming explicit circumstances are met. This novel technology is profitable due to the mixture of blockchain features like immutability, decentralisation, & anonymity.

Clients' secrecy: The blockchain reflects exchanges of addresses. On a blockchain, each operator has their own address, which can be kept secret or shared and includes numbers and letters. The generated address is used by individuals to interact with the blockchain network, and the private data of individuals is no longer held by a single entity. This means that some of the person's privacy is protected. Due to its limitations, blockchain, on the other hand, is unable to provide complete privacy protection.

Consensus mechanism: Since nobody believes in the substance of the ongoing framework, an agreement strategy is utilised. The group's goal is reaching a contract on the process of entire record must be verified. It is feasible to make a record which is absent by monitoring over fifty-one percent of the monetary hubs in the whole framework. Consequently, any damage is immediately apparent.

On the basis of the aforementioned features, it is likely to be drawn that blockchain eliminates the requirement for a third party or middleman, eradicates the risk posed by hackers, safeguards information and users' privacy, is easy to detect alteration, & appeals to users due to its ease of implementation. Subsequently, the qualities of blockchain innovation can be described as secure and simple for clients.

The Financial Services Industry

The financial services industry is made up of a wide range of businesses that provide economic services, such as insurance, banking, accounting, asset management, and so on. Despite the fact that the industry has evolved into a business sector over the past few decades, Nicholas Barbon officially established insurance in 1680. Over time, financial services evolved and reached institutions. In the nineteenth century, one of the sector's depressions resulted in bankruptcies with a quintile ratio, which served as a significant warning to lawmakers. After the crisis of 1929, people got worse off. According to Amidei & Giordano (2015), the Banking Act of 1933 (Glass-Steagall) constituted some rules for separation between certain financial industry sectors. This is stated in the article titled "Financial Services Modernization Act of 1999." This law placed severe restrictions on financial institutions and contributed to the gradual improvement of the economy. Services underwent significant change towards the end of the nineteenth century. The majority of banks, for instance, have been reorganised or merged. In response to changes in the financial markets, a new law is required. Some restrictions were invalidated when this law went into effect, and financial markets had more freedom. The banking industry has been consolidating for some time. While there were in excess of fourteen thousand business banks in 1984, the number diminished to less than nine thousand out of 1999, & usual size of banks increased. The financial services industry completed its transformation procedure following additional regulations.

Financial services are necessary for economic development & growth. Banking, savings, and investments, as well as debt and equity financing, benefit the public. They are shielded from uncertainty by these tools. These services can help you compete in markets both domestically and internationally. It is expressed in the book 'The Job of the Monetary Administrations Area in Extending Financial Opportunity that weakness can be diminished for needy individuals by administrations, and it gives opportunity to oversee resources for making gains with additional choices. (Martinez-Vergara & Valls-Pasola, 2021)

Transaction costs are fundamentally responsible for the existence of financial firms as well as other businesses (Baltensperger, 1980). In the absence of complete trust between the parties, market communications on the operations side and the customer side are characterised by risks such as difficulties between principals and agents and incomplete or asymmetric information. Costs, such as those associated with contracting, searching, and verifying information, are incurred when these issues are resolved in order to lower risk and build trust. According to Dewatripoint (2014), for example, lending is characterised by information asymmetries both ex ante, when creditors must determine a prospective debtor's risk profile, and ex post, when creditors must monitor debtors' capability to repay loans. A fundamental feature of payment markets is the need to keep track of payment obligations as well as the need to verify the authenticity of payment tokens or the identity of account holders (Kahn and Roberds, 2009). Customers need dependable counterparties with whom they can deposit funds and processes that are dependable for their delivery, and different actors in the process chain of payment need to have confidence that different connections won't open them to liability or fraud. Insurance & investments in the financial market are subject to moral hazard, adverse selection, and uncertainty regarding future outcomes. In order to provide their customers with a high-quality product, those who create investment products rely on reliable execution and underwriting services. Customers, on the other hand, need to be able to trust the operations & investments that help them purchase & sell. In order to align interests and monitor actions, internalisation of activities within a single financial services company overcomes principal-agent and asymmetric information obstacles. Trusted interactions between teams are guaranteed by this. Asset and liability management can be closely coordinated when deposit taking and lending are linked. The provider can verify the availability of funds prior to executing transfer instructions by combining payment execution with account management. Firms can tailor new investment products to market conditions and investor preferences by linking underwriting, trading, and sales. Further frictions arise when there is uncertainty regarding future outcomes, such as whether a borrower will go bankrupt. Rogers (2018) asserts that markets are incomplete due to the difficulty of defining a contract for all likely future world states and the solvency status of debtors. Resource allocations may therefore be ineffective.

Blockchain In Financial Service Industry

Effect of Blockchain on Financial Services

This portion discusses research that explains how blockchain technology affects the financial services industry. The majority of the papers discuss how blockchain can be used in the banking industry, but very few suggest how it could be used in the insurance sector.

The advantages of blockchain innovation are various in the financial area, for example, expanded straightforwardness, sped up exchange, expanded recognizability, decreased cost, the capacity to guard track of installment history, and diminished danger of extortion (Ali et al., 2020). Moreover, according to Garg et al., a number of Indian banks, including SBI, see blockchain as a means of improving the customer experience. The paper also talks about how back-end utilities, fund transfers, and registration use blockchain technology. This paper also explains, like the Ali et al. study, how blockchain technology will make banking operations more transparent, more traceable, less likely to be fraudulent, and less expensive.

In addition, according to Hassani, Huang, & Silva (2018), the implementation of smart contracts, speeding up transactions, reducing costs, and eliminating the need for KYC will all result from the usage of blockchain in the banking sector. Additionally, the study discusses the difficulties banks have encountered in implementing blockchain technology.

These studies are all focusing on the advantages of blockchain, such as its speed, transparency, low cost, lower risk of fraud, and increased banking system efficiency.

In addition, cryptocurrencies usage & the benefits of blockchain in banking can be elucidated by decreased costs, improved transparency, & quicker payments (Kimani et al., 2021). The application of blockchain technology in secondary markets, such as stock issuances and the payment ledger for bonds & notes, is also the subject of the article. The financial industry was the first to implement blockchain technology for managing back-office tasks (Fannings & Centres, 2016). Additionally, the article describes how Chain and NASDAQ are utilising blockchain technology to transfer and issue shares.

These two studies depicted the use of blockchain in banking & in the secondary market. Additionally, the transparent, secure, and quick nature of blockchain technology, which propelled its usage in the sector of finance, is the focus of these papers.

Moreover, blockchain usage in the business of insurance can be understood as the utilisation of blockchain in brilliant policies in protection, for forestalling extortion claims, smoothing out installments, taking out the prerequisite of middle people like specialists and dealers, & in advancing the practical field of the protection business (Kar and Navin, 2021). Furthermore, digital currencies, smart contracts, & digital record keeping are also potential applications of blockchain technology in financial services (Lewis, McPartland, and Ranjan, 2017).

Additionally, successful testing of the recordkeeping technology that underpins Bitcoin in relation to credit default swaps enables banks, which use blockchain technology in financial transactions, to gain a better understanding of significant financial movements (Nguyen, 2016).

As a result, these studies validate that blockchain technology has the power to revolutionise the finance industry by removing the necessity for intermediaries & foreign exchange, growing operational competence, & facilitating the functionality of financial services.

This study proposes a novel model in light of the technology's complexity: the features of blockchain adoption are determined by combining the Technology Acceptance Model (TAM) along with unknown external variables. Also, in his paper, Klarin (2020) did a SLR and talked about topics like blockchain, bitcoin, and cryptocurrencies. The paper gives directions to experts and academicians connected with the above-mentioned subject.

A progressive currency arrangement could be created utilising the Bitcoin blockchain. Consequently, Prybila et al. (2017) utilised a cycle runtime confirmation methodology to investigate different conceivable outcomes in their review. While Akcora et al. (2018) looked into the kinds of chainlets that indicate a loss risk and how they might affect the price and volatility of bitcoin, In addition, in preparation for additional legal and policy measures, the current policies of regulatory & fiscal approaches for digital currency are designed to reduce blockchain's energy consumption (Truby, 2018). The usage of blockchain can be seen in a variety of financial technologies, including the most well-known digital currency, Bitcoin.

As Bitcoin's value rises and mining motivation increases, new digital currencies based on carbonised concepts will emerge. Both of these factors will only exacerbate the situation.

In addition, the creation of Blockchain was intended to serve as the Bitcoin distributed ledger. According to Islam, Mäntymäki, and Turunen (2019), the development of new blockchains that make use of the Bitcoin source code has resulted from the growing interest in Bitcoin.

The significant roles that entities play in determining the bitcoin & cryptocurrency markets (Breidbach and Tana, 2021) "Fortune Hunter," "Trail Blazer," "Freshman," and "Idealist" are some of these names. The study classifies the general public as novices; those with little experience with cryptocurrency and who have invested are referred to as fortune hunters.

Moreover, the qualities of the cryptographic money market's swapping scale intricacy have started to look like those of customary and mature business sectors like monetary forms, securities, wares, and value (Watorek et al. 2020). The review makes sense of the fact that, in spite of its ongoing high unpredictability, the digital money market gives new speculation options, considering portfolio enhancement (Klarin, 2020).

Many cryptocurrencies have been created, but Bitcoin, which was developed using blockchain technology and is the most well-known and successful (Ghosh et al. 2020), Because it is secure, decentralised, and does not require a third party, blockchain technology was also used to build other cryptocurrencies.

The use of blockchain in the creation of cryptocurrencies, of which bitcoin is the most well-known, is explained in each of these papers. Additionally, the studies demonstrate that the capital market and trading will be transformed by these digital currencies.

RESEARCH METHODOLOGY

In systematic literature, there are generally 4 main phases: a) planning the review; b) finding and assessing articles; c) gathering and joining information; and d) offering the consequences of the survey. Using the approach developed by Durach et al. (2021), our SotA divides the 4 phases into 3 major phases with a number of steps to guarantee the method's precise execution. The three stages are: 1) the stage of planning; 2) the stage of execution; and 3) the results.

Phase 1: Stage of Planning

The planning to conduct SotA in the current study is explained below in four steps:

Step 1: Collect SotA articles. We searched ScienceDirect employing the strategy ("state of the art" "Blockchain "Finance') for research papers published from 2013 to 2023. The result was 1025 results. Then we filtered article type as review article, getting 179 results. Only 17 articles out of 179 were related to the subject area 'Business & Management, and 6 articles were from Economics, Econometrics, and Finance, resulting in a total of 21 articles. So we did manual screening of 179 results by reading the title and abstract to confirm the number of papers suitable for our study.

Step 2: Compiling all resources full-text articles was manually reviewed. For the purpose of analysis, we obtained articles that met our criteria. We also searched the references of the reviewed papers to guarantee comprehensive retrieval. Also, to find assets not ordered by these scholarly data sets, we looked through Google to identify research papers suitable for our study. We put the keywords state-of-the-art literature review, blockchain, and finance in Google Scholar, filtered for review articles, and found the results as 8290 research papers. Then we filtered the relevant papers by considering papers published in IEEE Explore, Wiley, Emerald, Elsevier, Springer, and Taylor & Francis. The final number of papers which we considered for our study was 100.

Step 3: The 100 reviewed papers identified in Step 2 were reviewed to identify information such as field and publication year. Then, excerpts from each article were collected regarding the use of the term "state-of-the-art review." At long last, we extracted portions portraying: the objectives or goals of the SotA review; the review's methodology-informed and method-based procedures; the results of investigations; and indicators of the SotA review's rigour.

A total of 69 articles were reviewed for the current study to provide discussion and results.

Step 4: The data extractions from Step 3 were further reviewed to answer the research question of the current study, and the information collected is presented in the literature review.

Phase 2: Stage of Execution

This stage is summarized in Table 1.

Table 1. Stage of execution

Research Question	RQ 1: Describe the concept of blockchain technology. RQ2: How financial service industry has evolved over a decade? RQ3: Describe the financial sector's use of blockchain technology.
Timeframe	2013-2023
Literature reviewed	Scopus Indexed Papers
Search Strategy	Keywords- State-of-the-Art; Blockchain; Finance Filter – Review Papers
Exclusion criteria	The papers which does not match with the objective of study were excluded by screening the abstract of papers.
Literature Analysis	Manual (Presented in section 2 of this study)

Phase 3: Results

Table 2 shows the number of times the term 'State of the Art' is used in Review-Based Papers since 2013 to 2023 under study.

Table 2. Results

Particular	Number of Times
Used in Title Only	69
Used in Abstract Only	11
Used in Problem statement Only	0
Used in Title and Abstract	67
Used in Title, Abstract and Problem statement	60
Adjective describing timeframe of a different review type e.g. systematic review	69
Used in Journal Manuscript Type and not used in article	0
Denoted as specific literature review methodology	15

FINDING AND DISCUSSION

Key Benefits of Blockchain in Financial Service Industry

Blockchain technology will streamline a number of processes that are currently distributed across numerous databases and systems by utilising smart contracts. Operations automation will deliver a long-term audit trajectory (Perera et al., 2020). The primary distinction between this software and existing software is that information is only dispersed in time rather than transferred or copied between parties. Multiple parties are the owners of the data. Blockchain works as a shared database & a secure, one-of-a-kind source of reliable data because the data is owned by the entire network. Significant industry concerns are addressed by diminishing covering exercises, taking out blunders, limiting interaction spillage, and giving admittance to a solitary confided-in source. This efficiency in the back office will result in a decrease in operational and administrative costs (Brophy, 2019). The consumer experience will also be significantly heightened by an upsurge in customer faith (Dal Mas et al., 2020), improved customer facilities (see Amponsah et al., 2021; Brophy 2019, Dal Mas et al., 2020; Gatteschi et al., 2018; Grima et al., 2020).

Porter's Value Chain Analysis

The cases that have been found can be divided into primary and support activities according to Porter's value chain.

Figure 1. Porter's value chain for banking
Source: Lamarque (2000)

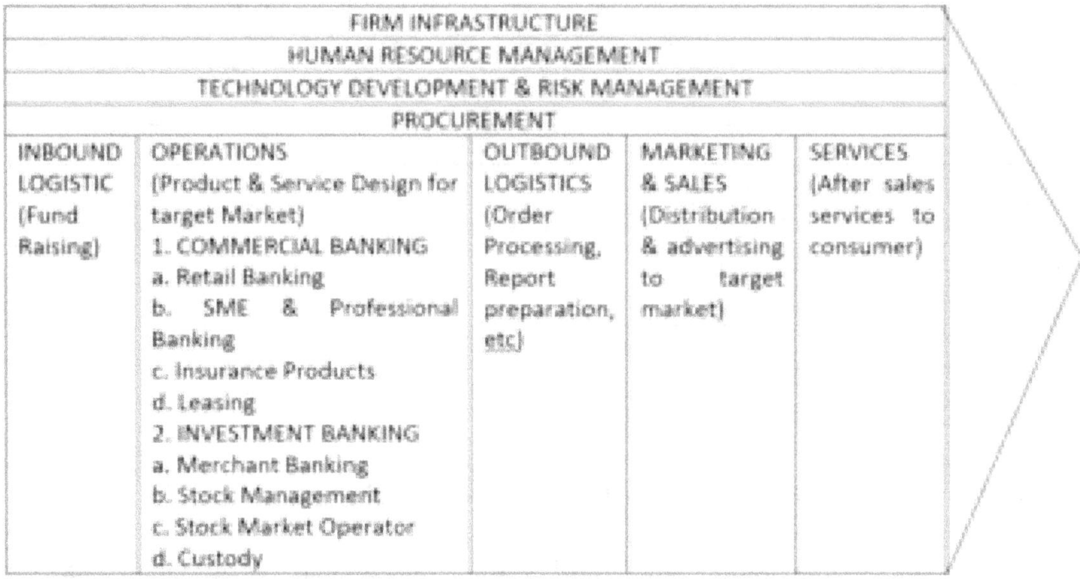

Claims the executives, extortion recognition, strategy organisation, and circulation are the essential exercises in Doorman's worth chain, which may be altogether influenced by blockchain. According to Amponsah et al., the execution of smart agreements for driving claims cycles would eliminate the ambiguity of the arrangement conditions and facilitate the mechanisation of dealing with and compensating executives with claims (Amponsah et al., 2021). The insurtech company Lemonade, which was established in 2015, is an example of the use of blockchain to achieve functional greatness. Using a combination of smart contracts and artificial intelligence, a claim is automatically approved and the applicant is paid in a fraction of the time (Grima et al. 2020). One more illustration on the procedure alteration is termed AXA Fizzy. Bubbly was presented by AXA in 2017, which is a parametric item for covering flight delays. By utilising blockchain technologies via smart contracts and linking to world data on air traffic, the procedure of a claim calculates reimbursements quickly and makes payments automatically if the terms of the policy are met (Kar and Navin, 2021).

By carrying out interaction's standards and promptly integrating information from different outer sources, savvy contracts lessen the probability of misrepresentation (Gatteschi, Lamberti, and Demartini, 2020). The twofold asserting was disposed of (Stojanovi et al., 2023) and additional evidence was provided. Since information should be visible and changed, extortion is easier to recognise (Dominguez Anguiano and Parte, 2023). Blockchain actually enhances the reliability of methods of financial reporting because the foundation of blockchain is the sharing of data by independent individuals with open access, transparency, and unchallengeable storage (McCallig et al. 2019).

Furthermore, entire cycles for overseeing strategies can be improved (Amponsah et al. 2022) by automatically verifying the policyholder at the moment of issuance to outsiders. In a business that requires extensive manual intervention and international participation, this reduces friction (Brophy, 2019).

Blockchain advancement is likewise subject to the capacity to sidestep mediators in computerised exchanges. The adoption of the blockchain, particularly smart contract applications, will result in the elimination of intermediaries in certain business sectors due to its automatic transaction management nature (Kar and Navin 2020; 2017; Spohrer and Risius).

Support activities must include third-party reconciliation and auditing. Accommodating information between the insurance agency and outsiders like specialists, claims help organisations, or reinsurers makes a great deal of administrative centre work, prompts blunders, and requires rehashing approval steps. Data mismatches will be eliminated, and the reconciliation process will be accelerated to the desired velocity when blockchain is implemented in these processes.

Figure 2. Impact of blockchain on value chain of banking
Source: Author Composition

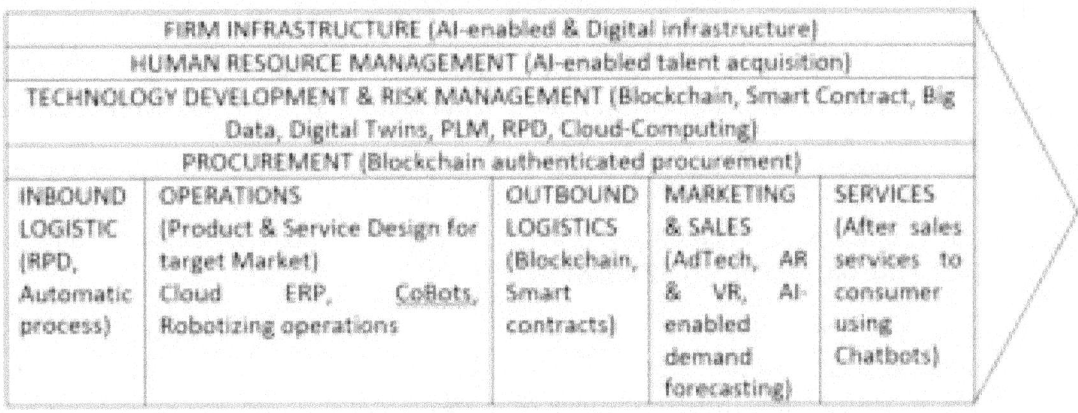

When it comes to auditing, blockchain can help supervisors work more efficiently. As a result, auditors can assist and offer their opinion thanks to the accurate representation of financial data (McCallig et al., 2019).

CONCLUSION

Blockchain-based solutions could significantly benefit the financial services industry. Blockchain was used in financial services to make decentralised finance possible. It is a method of financing that eliminates financial services industry middlemen by utilizing blockchain technology and smart contract. Blockchain is useful for a number of financial institutions and organisations to increase trust, increase transparency, and reduce costs. Businesses can utilise blockchain technology in numerous crucial fields, such as financial software. Blockchain applications ensure the integrity of data, making it possible for sellers to target the appropriate consumer segments. In banking payments, this technology is increasingly used. Most money is exchanged through bank accounts; consequently, payments are essential. Banks have long been at the forefront of the digital revolution. Banks can monitor each and every transaction quickly due to blockchain technology. Banks can settle transactions on a public blockchain with this technology. Banking chiefs need to satisfy a few prerequisites before a broadly involved innovation in the financial area can take place. By using intelligent contracts on the blockchain, it will be possible to pay directly for using a car, eliminating the need to find a solution for problems like electromobility. Businesses that use blockchain in finance can upload bills to the blockchain using smart contracts. Information like client information, due dates, and payment amounts can be saved on the blockchain. When the bill is paid by the customer, the smart contract makes changes to the status of the bill, & a notification is sent to the businesses for the same. Blockchain would be used to manage an extensive series of financial transactions in the future.

REFERENCES

Adams, R., Parry, G., Godsiff, P., & Ward, P. (2017). The future of money and further applications of the blockchain. *Strategic Change*, *26*(5), 417–422. doi:10.1002/jsc.2141

Ali, O., Ally, M., & Dwivedi, Y. (2020). The state of play of blockchain technology in the financial services sector: A systematic literature review. *International Journal of Information Management*, *54*, 102199. doi:10.1016/j.ijinfomgt.2020.102199

Amidei, F. B., & Giordano, C. (2015). The redesign of the bank-industry-financial market ties in the US Glass-Steagall and the 1936 Italian Banking Acts. In *Financial innovation, regulation and crises in history* (pp. 65–84). Routledge. doi:10.4324/9781315653969-6

Amponsah, A. A., Adekoya, A. F., & Weyori, B. A. (2022). A novel fraud detection and prevention method for healthcare claim processing using machine learning and blockchain technology. *Decision Analytics Journal*, *4*, 100122. doi:10.1016/j.dajour.2022.100122

Baltensperger, E. (1980). Alternative approaches to the theory of the banking firm. *Journal of Monetary Economics*, *6*(1), 1–37. doi:10.1016/0304-3932(80)90016-1

Chang, Y., Iakovou, E., & Shi, W. (2020). Blockchain in global supply chains and cross border trade: A critical synthesis of the state-of-the-art, challenges and opportunities. *International Journal of Production Research*, *58*(7), 2082–2099. doi:10.1080/00207543.2019.1651946

Dettling, W. (2018). How to teach blockchain in a business school. *Business Information Systems and Technology 4.0: New Trends in the Age of Digital Change*, 213-225.

Dewatripont, M. (2014). European banking: Bailout, bail-in and state aid control. *International Journal of Industrial Organization*, *34*, 37–43. doi:10.1016/j.ijindorg.2014.03.003

Dominguez Anguiano, T., & Parte, L. (2023). The state of art, opportunities and challenges of blockchain in the insurance industry: a systematic literature review. *Management Review Quarterly*, 1-22.

Dominguez Anguiano, T., & Parte, L. (2023). *The state of art, opportunities and challenges of blockchain in the insurance industry: A systematic literature review*. Manag Rev Q. doi:10.100711301-023-00328-6

Durach, C. F., Kembro, J. H., & Wieland, A. (2021). How to advance theory through literature reviews in logistics and supply chain management. *International Journal of Physical Distribution & Logistics Management*, *51*(10), 1090–1107. doi:10.1108/IJPDLM-11-2020-0381

Ertz, M., & Boily, É. (2019). The rise of the digital economy: Thoughts on blockchain technology and cryptocurrencies for the collaborative economy. *International Journal of Innovation Studies*, *3*(4), 84–93. doi:10.1016/j.ijis.2019.12.002

Fanning, K., & Centers, D. P. (2016). Blockchain and its coming impact on financial services. *Journal of Corporate Accounting & Finance*, *27*(5), 53–57. doi:10.1002/jcaf.22179

Feyen, E., Frost, J., Gambacorta, L., Natarajan, H., & Saal, M. (2021). *Fintech and the digital transformation of financial services: implications for market structure and public policy*. BIS Papers.

Gatteschi, V., Lamberti, F., & Demartini, C. (2020). Blockchain technology use cases. *Advanced applications of blockchain technology*, 91-114.

Hassani, H., Huang, X., & Silva, E. (2018). Banking with blockchain-ed big data. *Journal of Management Analytics*, *5*(4), 256–275. doi:10.1080/23270012.2018.1528900

Javaid, M., Haleem, A., Singh, R. P., Suman, R., & Khan, S. (2022). A review of Blockchain Technology applications for financial services. *BenchCouncil Transactions on Benchmarks, Standards and Evaluations*, 100073.

Kar, A. K., & Navin, L. (2021). Diffusion of blockchain in insurance industry: An analysis through the review of academic and trade literature. *Telematics and Informatics*, *58*, 101532. doi:10.1016/j.tele.2020.101532

Kimani, D., Adams, K., Attah-Boakye, R., Ullah, S., Frecknall-Hughes, J., & Kim, J. (2020). Blockchain, business and the fourth industrial revolution: Whence, whither, wherefore and how? *Technological Forecasting and Social Change*, *161*, 120254. doi:10.1016/j.techfore.2020.120254

LamarqueE. (2000). Key Activities in the Banking Industry: An Analysis by the Value Chain. SSRN.

Li, Z., Zhong, R. Y., Tian, Z. G., Dai, H. N., Barenji, A. V., & Huang, G. Q. (2021). Industrial Blockchain: A state-of-the-art Survey. *Robotics and Computer-integrated Manufacturing*, *70*, 102124. doi:10.1016/j.rcim.2021.102124

Martínez-Vergara, S. J., & Valls-Pasola, J. (2021). Clarifying the disruptive innovation puzzle: A critical review. *European Journal of Innovation Management*, *24*(3), 893–918. doi:10.1108/EJIM-07-2019-0198

McCallig, J., Robb, A., & Rohde, F. (2019). Establishing the representational faithfulness of financial accounting information using multiparty security, network analysis and a blockchain. *International Journal of Accounting Information Systems*, *33*, 47–58. doi:10.1016/j.accinf.2019.03.004

Nofer, M., Gomber, P., Hinz, O., & Schiereck, D. (2017). Blockchain. *Business & Information Systems Engineering*, *59*(3), 183–187. doi:10.100712599-017-0467-3

Patil, P., Sangeetha, M., & Bhaskar, V. (2021). Blockchain for IoT access control, security and privacy: A review. *Wireless Personal Communications*, *117*(3), 1815–1834. doi:10.100711277-020-07947-2

Rashideh, W. (2020). Blockchain technology framework: Current and future perspectives for the tourism industry. *Tourism Management*, *80*, 104125. doi:10.1016/j.tourman.2020.104125

Rogers, C. (2018). The conceptual flaw in the microeconomic foundations of dynamic stochastic general equilibrium models. *Review of Political Economy, 30*(1), 72–83. doi:10.1080/09538259.2018.1442894

Stojanović, M., Radenković, M., Popović, S., Mitrović, S., & Bogdanović, Z. (2023). A readiness assessment framework for the adoption of 5G based smart-living services. *Information Systems and e-Business Management, 21*(2), 1–25. doi:10.100710257-023-00625-3

Tandon, A., Dhir, A., Islam, A. N., & Mäntymäki, M. (2020). Blockchain in healthcare: A systematic literature review, synthesizing framework and future research agenda. *Computers in Industry, 122*, 103290. doi:10.1016/j.compind.2020.103290

Tandon, A., Kaur, P., Mäntymäki, M., & Dhir, A. (2021). Blockchain applications in management: A bibliometric analysis and literature review. *Technological Forecasting and Social Change, 166*, 120649. doi:10.1016/j.techfore.2021.120649

Van Maanen, H., & Berghout, E. (2002). Cost management of IT beyond cost of ownership models: A state of the art overview of the Dutch financial services industry. *Evaluation and Program Planning, 25*(2), 167–173. doi:10.1016/S0149-7189(02)00010-1

Walsh, C., O'Reilly, P., Gleasure, R., McAvoy, J., & O'Leary, K. (2021). Understanding manager resistance to blockchain systems. *European Management Journal, 39*(3), 353–365. doi:10.1016/j.emj.2020.10.001

Zachariadis, M., Hileman, G., & Scott, S. V. (2019). Governance and control in distributed ledgers: Understanding the challenges facing blockchain technology in financial services. *Information and Organization, 29*(2), 105–117. doi:10.1016/j.infoandorg.2019.03.001

Chapter 16
A Study on the Application of Blockchain Technology in the Banking and Financial Sector in India

Rajat
G.L. Bajaj Institute of Management, India

Monica Nirolia
Baba Mastnath University, India

ABSTRACT

Modern technology is influencing our daily lives, from using a remote to control equipment to utilizing voice notes to give orders. Because of its properties of decentralization, enforceability, and sharing, blockchain technology is frequently used in banking, digital asset trade, and other sectors. Blockchain has emerged as a popular issue in fintech research, influencing the evolution of traditional financial forms. It is regarded as the foundation of the digital economy. Blockchain technology may be defined as a data structure that keeps transactional records and, by ensuring security, transparency, and decentralization, eliminates the possibility of fraudulent behaviour or transaction repetition without the use of a third party. This study examines the characteristics and challenges of blockchain technology, the impact of blockchain technology on the operation and administration of the banking and financial sector and the possibilities for blockchain technology implementation in banking and financial sector in India.

INTRODUCTION

Blockchain technology is now widely employed in digital asset trade, finance, banking, and other industries. Blockchain has emerged as a hot topic in fintech research, with implications for the future of outdated monetary forms. It is identified as the digital financial system's foundation. The once-common paper money transaction is on the wane as electronic payments take over the mainstream. Central bank

DOI: 10.4018/978-1-6684-8624-5.ch016

digital currency application scenarios will be "practiced" for future official issue by the end of April 2020. Satoshi Nakamoto, an unidentified entity, formed the idea of "Bitcoin". He also issued a white paper on Bitcoin in May 2008. He didn't say anything about himself. He explained how the money would function. "Bitcoin", a virtual cash test, turned into the first large blockchain breakthrough. The second one invention became known as "Blockchain", and it turned into created with the idea that the technology that powered "Bitcoin" should be eliminated from the cash and applied for a variety of different inter-organizational collaboration. Since, its introduction in 2008, blockchain era has been one of the hottest problems in fintech studies, infiltrating all factors of the conventional economic market, altering the operation mode of the economic industry's operation gadget and even the complete social and commercial gadget.

REVIEW OF LITERATURE

The relevant literature review for the study is as follows:

- Ramchandra et al. (2022) aimed to evaluate the influence of blockchain technology on the banking sector. Blockchain technology is considered one of the most promising technologies for the banking industry. Infrastructure, channels, platforms and scenarios are considered to be the four years that Internet finance has been successful. Blockchain is known as a growing technology that attracts energy service providers, startups and tech developers. Technology provides many benefits for creating new processes by reducing financial constraints. Blockchain technology confirms the transparency & security of business solutions. It also works for the energy sector and the state of the energy sector by analyzing current market conditions and information. However, when it comes to blockchain scalability, the system is essential to update and improve the process. Also, cryptocurrencies like Bitcoin have become an important concept in the current business world. These issues include the time it takes to put a transaction on a block and the time it takes to get approval.
- Jena (2022) in this research paper researcher examine the "Factors Affecting the Adoption of Blockchain Technology in the Banking Sector: An Extended UTAUT Model". Over time, technological innovation has significantly revolutionized banking. In the financial industry, digital innovation began with the introduction of money to replace barter systems, and subsequently eventually replaced wax seals with digital signatures. As a result, this study extended "the unified theory of acceptance and use of technology" (UTAUT) in order to identify the major determinants of bankers' desire to employ blockchain technology. The findings of this study will assist government officials, decision-makers, and economists in improving banking instructions for the rapid and easy deployment of blockchain technology.
- Kumari and Devi (2022) in this research researcher examined the "Impact of FinTech and Blockchain Technologies on Banking and Financial Services". Banks and financial institutions around the world are taking advantage of the introduction of new technology. This article undertook a survey of the literature on FinTech and blockchain in the banking and financial sector. It discovered that banks and financial institutions are going through major transformations in order to stay up with digital technology revolution. The research proposed that FinTech will bring about extensive improvements in making an investment standard that provide advanced customer

records and are supported through blockchain technology. Blockchain in FinTech can give a lot more effective financial alternative than we presently have based on equity and decentralization.

- Patki and Sople (2020) aimed to shed light on the utility, benefits and Challenges of Blockchain Technology (BCT) in the banking industry in India. The whitepaper shows how BCT can solve key issues, including the speed and security of data transfer, the cost of different partners, the processing of payments, and the creation of new products and services. The whitepaper also mentions the many benefits offered by BCT, such as automating the verification process and eliminating the need for multiple states to manually verify the validity of the transaction. With the advent of BCT, India's finance and financial institutions are poised to take the economy to a new level. This research includes a research study on how existing BCTs help banks visualize and manage their banking processes effectively and efficiently. The respondents were commercial companies and fintech companies in the country. Looking at the final result, it shows that some Indian banks have started walking with BCT and are receiving blessings. However, they face extreme conditions in new generation models and applications. Terrorism and structural issues should be addressed, taking into account cross-border trade and joint operations between BCT members. Due to data protection, banks now use BCT authorization response for very good (small) ecosystems. It's like the "WhatsApp" group type that admins decide to organize organizations, but not quite. However, the decision will be different for each bank, depending on the environment required to upload BCT Responses. The test is limited to US banks and fintech groups, as well as smaller players in the banking industry. Financial institutions in India have adopted BCT to varying degrees. With full implementation over time, BCT will change the image of Indian companies. With BCT, banking processes can be more transparent, faster, more efficient and intermediaries can be eliminated. Perhaps the most important blessings are distribution, approval and job stability.
- Sankaranarayanan and Rajagopalan (2020) stated that blockchain is a new technology based on methods/algorithms, cryptography and business models to manage data between different participants without third party intervention or central authority. It is essentially a distributed file or public record of all changes or digital events completed and shared with participants. All changes in the public register are confirmed by the agreement of the majority of the participants in the system. This is also called a three-entry bookkeeping system (double entry + cryptography). This process is like a jigsaw puzzle, because each personal data is stored as a "block", in this block there are no errors other than relationships, and the data is not deleted. It's actually time to work. By 2020, fundamental changes will transform India's entire economy. With the development of blockchain technology, bitcoin, cryptocurrency, artificial intelligence, robotics and cybersecurity. In recent years, banks have introduced internet banking, mobile banking, debit card, credit card, BHIM, UPI, NNFT, NPCL etc. to meet customer demand from better services, i.e., digitalization.
- Albeshr and Nobanee (2020) defined that blockchain technology is a technology that stores digital information in a shared public database. The technology became famous mainly after the launch of the first cryptocurrency, Bitcoin. Bitcoin uses this technique to securely track data. First, this article will briefly introduce the general concept of block chain and how it works. Next, it will discuss some general applications of blockchain. Also a little review on technology in general and banking in particular. Like other services and products, completely changing due to "digitalization and technology"; shopping, food ordering and delivery, movie and TV marketing, navigation services ... and more. Blockchain can and will revolutionize banking services as it offers high security, high flexibility, distribution and better transactions. In addition, the relationship between

blockchain technology, fintech and sustainability will be discussed. Finally, the future prospects and challenges of the adoption and use of blockchain technology in the financial industry and services will be discussed.

- Prakash et al. (2020) have focused on analyzing the Blockchain implementations in India done thus far for accepting the technology, both within and beyond the financial sphere, as well as issues in the adoption of blockchain technology in India. Blockchain technology has the potential to transform how businesses, financial institutions, and governments conduct business and to spark a global fourth industrial revolution. This study is an attempt to examine key blockchain implementations in India completed thus far for adopting the technology, both inside and beyond the financial arena, as well as issues in the adoption of blockchain technology in India.
- Mallesha and Haripriya (2019) was an attempt to examine the blockchain technology in banking sector. People are more willing to adopt new technology as the necessity for modernity in our daily life grows. Blockchain is a bank program that is highly important and runs well. It is a large subject with many facets that are difficult to explore in a short amount of time. "Banks in India have undergone a dramatic shift from "regular banking" to "accommodation banking." The conclusion of this research was done to determine the transparency of money without the involvement of a third party. It is an investigation into the blockchain technology framework and the banking industry. The financial industry plays a significant role, and critical issues are included. Blockchain technology is transforming the banking industry's future.
- In Singh et al. (2018), the researchers study a blockchain technology in changing the world. Now a day we are moving towards digitalization, so that we have 'Bitcoins' to back this up. Bitcoin is a sort of digital currency that can be exchanged on the blockchain, the shared ledger technology. Bitcoins are essentially electricity transformed into lengthy strings of code with monetary value. We are all aware that each creation must overcome several obstacles; the same is true for blockchains. After reviewing the functioning mechanism and features of blockchains, it can be concluded that this technology would undoubtedly benefit society.
- Knezevic (2018) focused to analyze the impact of blockchain technology platforms on financial transactions through cryptocurrencies and other transactions. The subject of research is not only the use of technology, but also its commercialization. To understand the platform, the starting point of this study is to analyze how the technology works, then analyze the advantages of business and marketing business and finally the article discusses the impact of new technology on business and most importantly financial business. The main point is that the blockchain has a huge impact on the financial market, it can also change the financial market and the way we trade, our interaction with the police is the method of researching members. Copyright and organic food. Using a combination of available data and information from technology, business, finance and politics, 4 scenarios for the future of technology are created. The approach is combined with analysis to confidently prove the first hypothesis. The findings show that research technology is already having a significant impact on the financial industry, is in the early stages of transforming many industries, and has the potential to impact these businesses over the next five to ten years. Businesses are discovering the power of these technologies to take advantage of the fourth revolution.
- Zheng et al. (2017) defined that Blockchain, the basis of Bitcoin, has attracted attention recently. Blockchain acts as an immutable database that allows transactions to be executed in a distributed manner. Blockchain-based applications are popping up in endless forms, including in areas such as financial services, reputation, and the Internet of Things. However, there are many challenges

to overcome in blockchain technology, such as scalability and security issues. In this article, the overview of blockchain technology is given. We first deliver a summary of the blockchain design and relate some consent procedures used in different blockchains. In addition, the challenges and recent developments are briefly summarized. We also recorded the future of blockchain.

- Parekh et al. (2017) discussed that a blockchain is an electronic record of digital data, events, or transactions that are cryptographically hashed, verified, stored via and the "distribution" or "collaboration" of participants using group consensus as the most relevant to eliminate the need for a third party. The technological process created by blockchain technology is going away before it can solve big problems and be brought into the mainstream.

OBJECTIVES OF THE STUDY

1. To study the various characteristics and challenges faced in the application of blockchain technology in India.
2. To examine the implementation of blockchain technology in banking sector & financial sector in India.

RESEARCH METHODOLOGY

This study is conceptual and descriptive in nature. The data is collected from various sources, i.e., the official websites, research papers, articles, and newspapers.

RESULT ANALYSIS AND DISCUSSION

Blockchain Technology

A blockchain is defined as a chain of blocks, each containing transaction data. "A blockchain consists of as many blocks as transactions, and each block references to the preceding block, they are referred to as blockchains". Because several copies of a blockchain are distributed across many computers over the Internet, it is impossible to modify the blockchain.

Characteristics/Features of Blockchain Technology

The features of blockchain technology are as follows:

- **Increased Capacity:** The initial and most significant characteristic of blockchain is to increase capacity. The most impressive aspect of this blockchain technology is that it boosts the overall network capacity. Because there are many computers working together, the total power is greater than that of a few machines when things are centralized.

- **Increased Security:** Blockchain technology is regarded more secure than its competitors because there is no single point of failure. Because blockchain functions on a well-distributed network of nodes, data is always circulated via numerous nodes, ensuring that even if one node is hacked or broken in any way, the integrity of the original data is not affected.
- **Consistency:** The creation of permanent ledgers is one of the key characteristics of blockchain. Any centrally located database is vulnerable to fraud and hacking since it relies on a third party middleman for security. Another reality is that once blocks of transactions are put to the ledger, they cannot be changed by anybody afterwards. As a result, it will be protected from editing, deleting, or updating by any network user.
- **Faster Settlement:** The traditional banking systems are extremely sluggish, most likely because they require extensive settlement time and typically take days to complete. This is one of the primary reasons that these financial institutions must modernize their banking systems. We can overcome this problem by using blockchain, which can settle money transfers at extremely quick rates. This eventually saves time and money for these organizations while also providing convenience to the client.
- **Decentralised System:** Now, people can retain the assets on a network via decentralised technology without being subject to the supervision and control of a single person, business, or other body. Through this, the owner has direct control over their account via a key connected to the account, giving them the ability to transfer their assets to anyone they like. The decentralization of the web made possible by blockchain technology is nothing short of a revolution in the online world.
- **Distributed Ledger Technology:** Public ledgers make transaction statistics and participants to be had to the general public. Such ledgers lack protection or authority, which isn't always the case with personal or federated ledgers, which can also be related right into a blockchain device. That is because the community ledger is maintained by all other users on the machine. The dispensed ledger makes the process visible & reliable with the aid of permitting everyone with the essential gets right of entry to look at the ledger.
- **Consensus:** Blockchain technologies are mainly powerful due to the consensus algorithm. It is a critical component of any blockchain and a distinguishing function. Simply defined, consensus is a decision-making mechanism for the network's energetic nodes. Right here, the nodes can reach a consensus quite rapidly.

Working of Blockchain Technology

There are five key steps to processing and verifying transactions and information on the blockchain. The transaction process in the blockchain can be done as follows:

Figure 1 shows the step to step process of blockchain technology. The process can also understand by taking an example. Suppose, there are two parties A & B. Firstly, both the parties decide to exchange a unit of value such as digital currency or a digital representation of some other asset (title of land, birth certificate or educational degree) and initiate the transaction. Secondly, transactions are packed with other pending transactions to form a block. Blocks are sent to the blockchain system's network of participating computers. Thirdly, participating computers evaluate transactions and through mathematical calculations determine whether they are valid, based on agreed upon rules. When consensus is reached, usually between 51% of the participating computers, the transaction is considered verified. Fourthly, each tested block of transactions is time-stamped with a cryptographic hash. Each block also contains

Figure 1. Process of blockchain technology

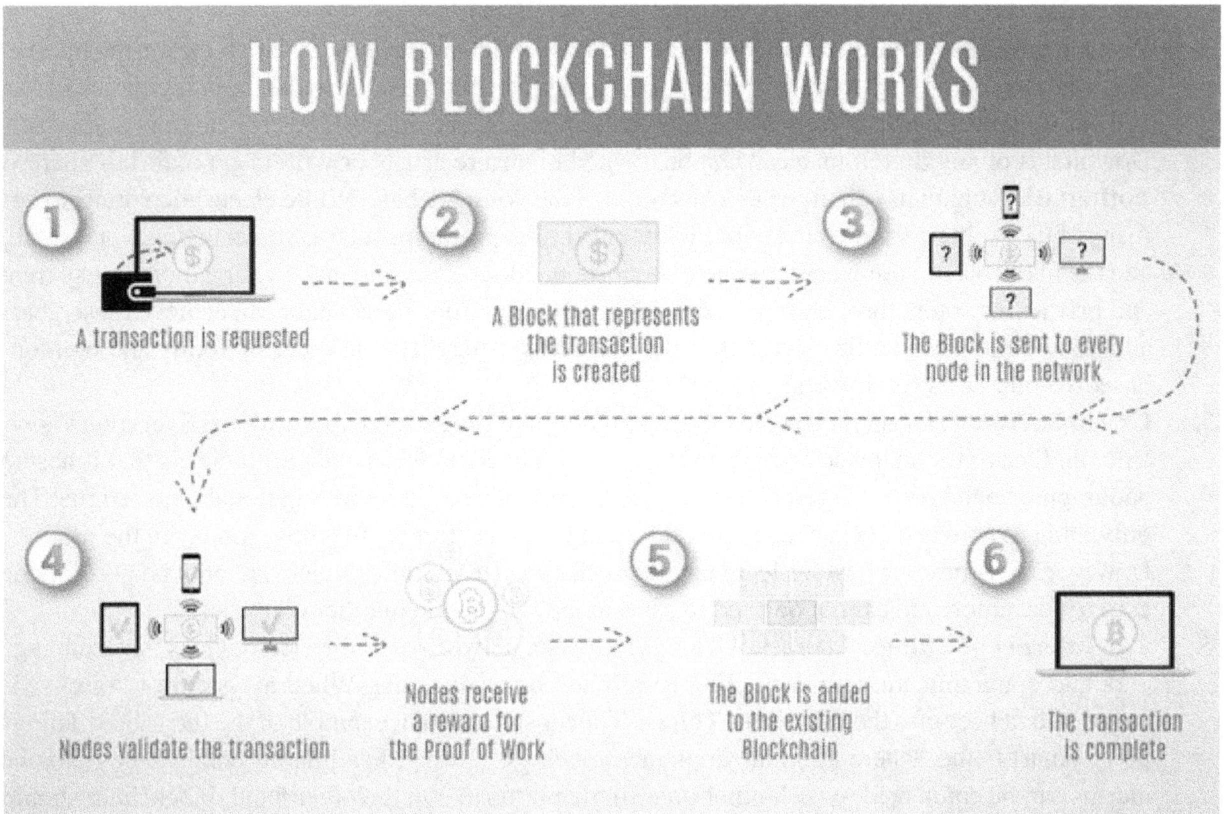

a reference to the hash of the previous block, resulting in a sequence of records that cannot be falsified, except by assuring the participating computers that the single block and all previous blocks are identical. The manipulated figures are authentic. Such a feat is considered impossible. Fifthly, the unit of value moves from Party A's account to Party B's account.

Application Areas of Blockchain Technology in India

There are many areas in which blockchain technology is used. The areas in which it is used are as follows:

1. **Healthcare:** Blockchain technology is used to track and trace medical supplies across the network. By using these tools, the circulation of counterfeit drugs can be prevented and controlled, and invalid and defective drugs can be recovered easily and quickly. The security of user information is an important goal of healthcare, as is information exchange and reporting that helps improve the health of hospitals, governments, and research centers.
2. **Transfer Contracts and Wills:** We are moving from the days when a contract involving many intermarries and an opinion on paper was signed. Thanks to blockchain technology, wills, contracts and properties will now be replaced by digital thoughts. Smart contracts are another name for them. Legal smart contracts bind all parties on paper. This information is stored on the blockchain

network and can be retrieved as needed, thus linking all participants to the terms set in the smart contracts.

3. **Protection of Copyrights and Royalties:** In today's world, music, movies, blogs, etc. on the Internet requires a lot of copyright and ownership. Blockchain technology can make these regulations safer and easier to use. It also provides real-time and accurate financial analysis for creators and artists. Downloads of any digital material can be tracked to ensure artists or writers get their fair share.
4. **Voting:** Blockchain has emerged as a key topic in the voting debate. While electronic voting solves many of the problems associated with traditional voting, problems such as secret voting, voter fraud, and the high cost of voting equipment are important. Blockchain can make voting more transparent and private for voters through smart contracts and encryption. Blockchain can achieve these goals and allow for the modernization of the voting process using different types of voting and opinion-based voting. Used for university elections.
5. **Cryptocurrency:** Cryptocurrencies is the most popular blockchain applications. Everyone knows Bitcoin. One of the many advantages of adopting blockchain for cryptocurrencies is that it has no geographic boundaries. Therefore, cryptocurrencies can be used for international transactions. The only thing to note is that exchange rates can change and customers may lose money in the process. However, this option is best for local payments like Paytm in India, which can only be used in one country or region and cannot be used to send money to people in other countries.
6. **The Internet of Things:** Internet of Things (IoT) is a network of connected devices that exchange data and communicate with each other to provide better insights. When a system of "things" is connected, it becomes the Internet of Things. The most important example of the Internet of Things is the smart home, where all home appliances such as lighting, heating, air conditioning, smoke alarms can be connected to each other on a single platform. On the other hand, blockchain should provide security for a highly decentralized system. System security in IoT depends on the least secure device having weak links. In this case, blockchain can ensure that data received from IoT devices is secure and only visible to trusted parties.
7. **Asset Administration:** Blockchain is becoming more and more important in the financial industry, and asset management is no exception. Wealth management generally refers to the management and marketing of various assets such as fixed income, real estate, stocks, funds, mutual funds, commodities and other investments that an individual may own. The traditional way of managing business assets can be very costly, especially if the business involves multinational and cross-border payments. Blockchain Broker, Auditor, Settlement Manager etc. This can be very helpful in such cases as it eliminates the need for intermediaries, as blockchain technology provides an open and transparent way to eliminate abuse.
8. **Blockchain Application for Anti Money Laundering:** Blockchain AML applications have valuable features that can prevent money laundering. Each blockchain transaction creates a permanent path of immutable data. So it is easy for the authorities to trace the source of the money. A blockchain ledger can perform tasks such as tracking, verifying, and recording a complete history of all transactions. Wallet, Currency, Outgoing Wallet, Money etc. If all trade levels are not confirmed, the trade will be canceled immediately. Blockchain also allows for risk assessment and reporting tools for money laundering. This allows for system-wide analysis rather than monitoring entry and exit points.
9. **Blockchain for Advertising:** AD Blockchain implementation is a decentralized information technology that provides the highest level of security, traceability and transparency while supporting

distribution. Once digital information is recorded on a blockchain, it is immutable, meaning that anyone can read it, but cannot change it. Advertisers can use blockchain to track spend as it stores data and transactions in real time. Ultimately, this could provide a level of transparency that current systems cannot. Transparency just isn't good. Speed is important in advertising. It is difficult to keep track of inventory and ensure product quality. Blockchain technology can be stored.

Blockchain Technology in Banking Sector

Business finance always requires a lot of manual work. The mediator should play an appropriate role. This affects the system and increases costs. It leads to errors and fraud. But blockchain technology transforms all subtractions into additions in the traditional way. It helps increase productivity by allowing faster processing of digital data and making data faster, while increasing security and transparency. Because blockchain uses distributed information, it records all business transactions in a stable, unbreakable chain. This helps identify and prevent unwanted interference. It also reduces the possibility of data errors. Blockchain technology is not just good for banks. However, it is still beneficial for customers to use banking services. It provides excellent privacy and data management. It also ensures consistency of printed customer documents. It also keeps them up to date and allows them to interact with customers.

Why Are Banks Adopting Blockchain Technology?

For a long time, the banking industry has faced operational and functional issues. Blockchain technology is viewed as a viable solution to these problems. Banks have already begun to experiment with blockchain technology in order to enhance their operations. Several institutions have begun to use blockchain for payments and other financial activities. The following are some reasons behind blockchain technology adoption in banking sector:

1. **Authenticity:** Blockchain ensures data integrity and accurate authenticity.
2. **Simplified Process:** Blockchain improves the effectiveness and efficiency of all banking activities.
3. **Economic Advantages:** It includes lower operational expenses, less infrastructure, and lower transaction costs.

List of Banks Using Blockchain Technology in India

There are various banks which started using blockchain technology for its operation. Figure 3 shows the names of some banks which are using blockchain technology in India.

Figure 2. List of Indian banks using blockchain technology

Private banks	Public Banks
• IndusInd Bank • Yes Bank • RBL Bank • IDFC Bank • South Indian Bank • Federal Bank • HDFC Bank • ICICI Bank • Kotak Mahindra Bank • Axis Bank	• Bank of Baroda • SBI • Canara Bank • Indian Bank

Uses of Blockchain Technology by the Listed Banks in Their Operations

The list of the operations in which blockchain technology is used by the banks are as follows:

Faster Payments: Sending money from one bank to another or from one country to another is not easy. Banks can use technology to make payments faster by creating a distribution system (cryptocurrency). Blockchain technology has the potential to speed up the payment process while reducing costs. Banks can use blockchain to reduce the need for third-party verification. In 2016, 90% of the members of the European Payments Council said that blockchain technology could change the banking industry in the next decade.

Clearance and Settlements Systems: Banks can use the blockchain to settle transactions and track them better than existing systems like SWIFT. Even the largest banks in the world have too many money transfer problems. Even something as simple as a bank transfer must go through many intermediaries and comply with regulatory requirements before it can be sent. Payment orders can only be processed with the payment system "SWIFT" technology. Many intermediaries are used for money transfer. These processes are expensive and time consuming. Thanks to blockchain technology, banks will be able to track all transactions worldwide. Banks can work without intermediaries and regulators to process and resolve changes in a timely manner.

Buying and Selling Assets: Blockchain technology reduces asset transaction costs by eliminating middlemen and transferring assets. According to research and analysis, adopting blockchain for security transactions could save the world more than $20 million a year in operating costs. Buying and selling digital assets like stocks is difficult because it requires a lot of tracking which organization owns what. Asset trading previously involved a network of clearinghouses and brokers. These changes are based on recorded data. Accomplishing the same task in electronics is not easy. Therefore, often buyers and sellers have to rely on third parties to manage their information. Blockchain technology has the potential to revolutionize finance by keeping a decentralized record of digital assets.

Blockchain for Accounting and Auditing: Accounting is one of the slowest areas to digitize in online banking. To digitize the financial process, many regulatory standards regarding data availability and integrity must be addressed. Financial transactions and analytics will change drastically due to blockchain technology. Blockchain technology has the potential to increase compliance and improve record keeping, according to experts in the field. Instead of posting separate receipts, businesses can add the information to a ledger. All entries will be classified and open to all participants. Thus, the data will be more secure and accessible. Blockchain technology will act as a virtual protector verifying all transactions.

Digital Identity Verification: Many businesses, banks and financial institutions still use digital authentication techniques to identify their customers. Customers are forced to move to other companies through a slow and complex process. Consumers and businesses will benefit from a faster, safer and more efficient customer verification process through blockchain integration. Blockchain technology will make it possible for other companies to use customer data to identify customers on other services.

Trade Finance: Another area where blockchain development is poised to revolutionize is the financial market. Business finance includes international trade and all financial activities related to trade. Did you know that many financial transactions today still rely on documents such as invoices, credit cards or promissory notes? Many order management systems allow you to do this online and this can take a long time. Blockchain-based financial transactions will improve the economy by eliminating time-consuming processes, documents and bureaucracy. Consider the following example: In a traditional financial transaction, each participant is responsible for keeping records of their own business information. All these documents should be constantly checked against each other. An error in one document can be repeated in other copies of the document. How can Blockchain help? No need to use blockchain to store multiple copies of the same document. This is because data can be compiled into a digital copy that is updated in real time and accessible to all network partners.

Peer-to-Peer Transfer: Customers can use P2P transfers to transfer money online from bank accounts or credit cards to another. There are many P2P exchange apps on the market today. However, they all have their limitations. For example, some only allow you to transfer funds in certain areas. Others prohibit money transfers if both parties live in the same country. In addition, P2P services may require high fees and may not have sufficient security to store important customer information. Blockchain development can solve all these problems. This tool will help in classifying joint to joint. More importantly, the blockchain has no geographic restrictions and allows for worldwide peer-to-peer transfers.

Hedge Funds: Hedge fund is a joint venture consisting of a fund manager and several business partners. However, these participants are usually traders rather than ordinary investors. Hedge funds seek to maximize investor returns while minimizing risk. Decentralized crypto hedge funds provide an open platform for many investors and participatory strategies. Funding is usually provided by financial managers working for a company. This decentralization shows the promise of blockchain in the financial services industry.

Share Trading and Stock Exchange: Trading goods and commodities always requires a large number of intermediaries, including traders and retailers. The traditional product buying and selling process consists of many stages and bureaucracy and can take up to three days. However, because blockchain technology is decentralized, it can remove all back-and-forth barriers and allow transactions from computers anywhere in the world. There will no longer be specific servers connected to each other on the network. Transactions on the blockchain increase efficiency by eliminating duplicate data. Thus, small transactions between merchants can be processed quickly outside of the blockchain, and only the last transaction is recorded on the blockchain, without intermediate steps.

Borrowing and Lending: One of the biggest concepts in blockchain and banking in recent years, DeFi (Decentralized Finance) wants to change many aspects of traditional finance, including lending. DeFi's goal is not to improve the banking industry, but to increase the accessibility of financial services to individual customers. However, in banking, blockchain technology can also be used to improve bank loans. The ability to demonstrate the capability provided by technology can reduce the risk of the loan failing. Blockchain can also identify potentially honest or fraudulent customers, strengthen banks' know-your-customer (KYC) system, and prevent financial fraud (AML).

Figure 3. Summary of functions with the impact of the blockchain

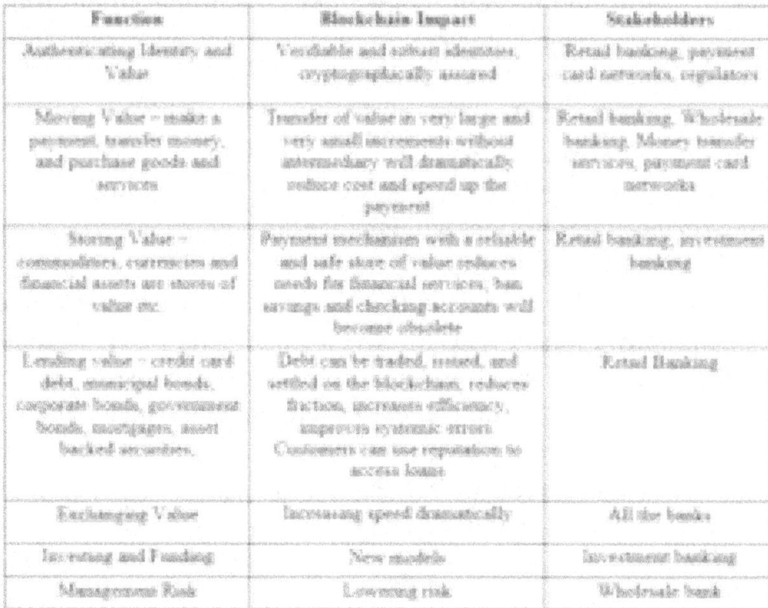

Function	Blockchain Impact	Stakeholders
Authenticating Identity and Value	Verifiable and robust identities, cryptographically assured	Retail banking, payment card networks, regulators
Moving Value – make a payment, transfer money, and purchase goods and services	Transfer of value in very large and very small increments without intermediary will dramatically reduce cost and speed up the payment	Retail banking, Wholesale banking, Money transfer services, payment card networks
Storing Value – commodities, currencies and financial assets are stores of value etc.	Payment mechanism with a reliable and safe store of value reduces needs for financial services; ban savings and checking accounts will become obsolete	Retail banking, investment banking
Lending value – credit card debt, municipal bonds, corporate bonds, government bonds, mortgages, asset backed securities.	Debt can be traded, issued, and settled on the blockchain, reduces friction, increases efficiency, improves systemic errors. Customers can use reputation to access loans	Retail Banking
Exchanging Value	Increasing speed dramatically	All the banks
Investing and Funding	New models	Investment banking
Management Risk	Lowering risk	Wholesale bank

Benefits of Blockchain Technology in the Banking Sector

The following is a full description of blockchain technology's implementation in the banking sector and its benefits:

1. **Less Fraudulent Activities and Improved Security:** Security is most important principle of banking sector. So that banking sector is always try to fight with fraudulent activities. But banks have failed to tackle these fraudulent activities. Now, blockchain technology is introduced to tackle these problems.
2. **International Transactions Are Becoming Less Expensive and Faster:** Currently, money transfers between countries takes a lot of time and requires involvement of many third parties. This implies that when the money reaches at its destination, the sender has lost a substantial sum of money. Blockchain finance is an innovative method that has the ability to change the way money is handled and used. Blockchain technology has the ability to accelerate & reduce the cost of cross-border payments.
3. **Reduced Human Error and Less Operational Costs:** According to various data, human error in keeping records and accounting is one of the leading sources of fraudulent activity. Blockchain technology efficiently prevents such mistakes by recording transactions in an automatic method that cannot be modified afterwards.

Future of Blockchain in Banking

According to banking experts, for blockchain to become a widely used technology in the business world, it must meet several requirements. Banks must first develop the necessary infrastructure to run the global network with solutions that will take full advantage of the blockchain. Businesses will only be affected if blockchain is widely used. However, the investment will be worth it. Blockchain is expected to help banking institutions make payments faster and more accurately while reducing one-time transaction costs. Blockchain-enabled banking apps will provide a better customer experience and help modern banks compete with fintech companies.

Blockchain Technology in the Indian Financial Services Sector

For years, blockchain technology has been defined inside the monetary offerings enterprise for its unrivalled potential to reinforce productiveness, time performance, and transparency in the atmosphere. We can say that blockchain reduces the possibility of operating risks & data breaches. It is easy to identify how the capabilities of blockchain make it the best for monetary programs. Blockchain enables comfortable, simple transactions and promotes them between industrial peers. It can also be used to allow humans to rapidly understand the use of Virtual IDs. Banks and other financial corporations are already adopting blockchain to improve their services, do away with fraud and lower out-of-pocket costs. Here are five blockchain monetary offering use cases that are gaining prominence in the enterprise:

- Clearing and Settlements
- Cross-Border Transaction
- Trade Finance Platforms
- Credit Reporting
- Digital Identity Verification

Figure 4. List of financial services using blockchain technology

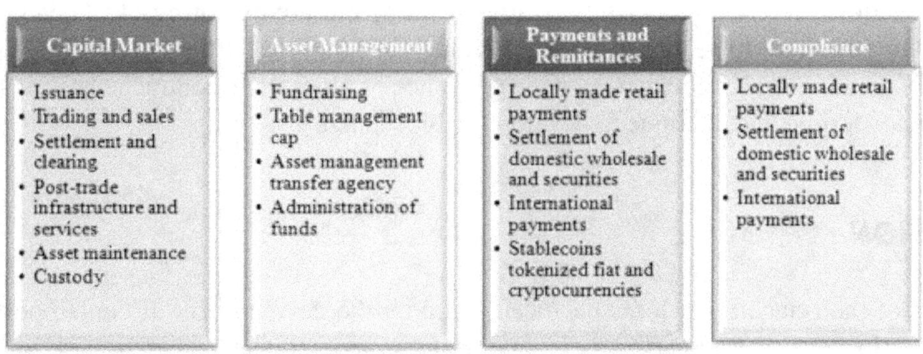

Challenges: Blockchain Technology in Banking and Financial Services

Despite the great potential of blockchain technology, it also faces some issues that can slow its use. Problems include:

1. **Interoperability:** Competitive blockchain systems do not have worldwide principles. More interoperability is required for blockchains to be compatible with larger networks and integrate into existing operations and operations. If all parties are connected to the same blockchain network, they can complete the transaction efficiently. As more and more blockchain networks compete with each other, interoperability issues are becoming more and more serious.
2. **Privacy:** The nature of blockchain technology requires all users of the system to share information openly. Because information is accessible to everyone, there are many problems with private transactions on the blockchain. Private blockchains are more secure, but have problems interacting with other blockchains.
3. **Security:** Because blockchains use complex cryptocurrencies, attacks must be very difficult. Cybersecurity attackers must have critical computing power to exploit security breaches. Multiple security protections are required, including infrastructure security, insider threat protection, cyber-attack protection, and authorization of both parties to access the blockchain. Depending on the type of transaction, the blockchain system can be permissioned or unauthorized.
4. **Scalability:** As blockchain applications grow in space, larger blockchain files and high-speed data access are required. Fast and accurate trading is very important for profitability. Blockchain technology must process data quickly to manage the large amount of data existing systems have.
5. **Encryption:** Encrypting blockchain data is fraught with challenges. If the key is public, anyone can access the encrypted data and it is very difficult to recover the blockchain unlock key if lost. Blockchain technology uses encryption, but if people find new ways to manage or misuse data, it can be cracked by criminals.
6. **Electricity Use:** Using blockchain technology needs a lot of energy. The technology produces large amounts of carbon monoxide. It requires more processing than the world's fastest supercomputer.
7. **Legal Framework:** There is no national or international law governing blockchain technology or its applications. While many countries around the world are exploring blockchain applications, more attention needs to be paid to the legal implications of blockchain technology. The limitations or issues mentioned above may reduce the relevance of blockchain contracts; however, they can be resolved over time and continue to develop the blockchain.

CONCLUSION

The progress of the financial business has been aided by the development of contemporary financial technologies. Blockchain has emerged as an important topic in fintech research, with implications for the future of old monetary forms. It is identified as the digital financial system's foundation. The use of the blockchain era in the banking quarter has not only changed the employer control paradigm, but also inspired banking business such as payment systems, intermediation ventures, loans and asset introductions. There are also major hurdles to implementation in the blockchain era. The substantial deployment of economic technology, especially blockchain technology, is the destined reform trend of the banking industry. Banks have to actively study the functions of the present day financial generation as well as the impact of technological advancements on banking operations. To increase efficiency and lower risks, they ought to utilize the most recent technology to create a variety of banking-specific apps. By doing this, they will grab the chance to use and develop financial technology in the future. This paper provides an in-depth examination of the blockchain revolution in the banking industry. Blockchain is the finest innovation since the internet. As a result, in my opinion, blockchain is a brilliant disruptive technology that will revolutionize the banking sector in a positive way in the near future.

REFERENCES

Agarwal, A., Parihar, M., & Shah, T. (2020). *Feasibility of Adoption of Blockchain Technology in Banking and Financial Sector of India*. Innovations in Computational Intelligence and Computer Vision.

AlbeshrA.NobaneeH. (2020). Blockchain Applications in Banking Industry: A Mini-Review. SSRN. doi:10.2139/ssrn.3539152

Analytics Vidhya. (2022, October 20). *Complete Guide on Getting started with Blockchain Technology*. https://www.analyticsvidhya.com/blog/2022/10/complete-guide-on-getting-started-with-blockchain-technology/

Arjun, R., & Suprabha, K. (2020). Innovation and Challenges of Blockchain in Banking: A Scientometric view. *International Journal of Interactive Multimedia and Artificial Intelligence.*

Bagrecha, N., Polishwala, I., Mehrotra, P., Sharma, R., & Thakare, B. S. (2020). Decentralized Blockchain Technology: Application in Banking Sector. *International Conference for Emerging Technology*.

Bhargava, D., Sandeep, C., Gopal, M., & Sahil, M. (2023). A Review of Blockchain Technology in Different Sectors: Challenges and Solutions. *4th International Conference on Signal Processing and Communication.* 10.1109/ICSPC57692.2023.10125283

Chowdhury, M., Suchana, K., Alam, S., & Khan, M. (2021). Blockchain Application in Banking System. *Journal of Software Engineering and Applications*, *14*(7), 298–311. doi:10.4236/jsea.2021.147018

Dora, S., & Srinivasan, V. (n.d.). Investigating the use of Blockchain technology in facilitating international fund transfer with respect to banking sector of Sultanate of Oman. *Journal of Student Research*.

Garg, P., Gupta, B., Chauhan, A., Sivarajah, U., Gupta, S., & Modgil, S. (2021). Measuring the perceived benefits of implementing blockchain technology in banking sector. *Technological Forecasting and Social Change*, *163*, 163. doi:10.1016/j.techfore.2020.120407

Gupta, A., & Gupta, S. (2018). Blockchain Technology application in Indian Banking Sector. *Delhi Business Review*, *19*(2), 75–84. doi:10.51768/dbr.v19i2.192201807

Hydrogen. (2019, December 12). *5 Common Blockchain Applications in Financial Services*. https://www.hydrogenplatform.com/blog/5-common-blockchain-applications-in-financial-services

Intellipaat. (2023, May 9). *Application of Blockchain in the Banking Sector*. https://intellipaat.com/blog/blockchain-in-banking/

Javaid, M., Haleem, A., Singh, R., Suman, R., & Khan, S. (2022). A review of Blockchain Technology applications for financial services. *BenchCouncil Transactions on Benchmarks, Standards and Evaluations, 2*(3).

Jena, R. K. (2022). Examining the Factors Affecting the Adoption of Blockchain Technology in the Banking Sector: An Extended UTAUT Model. *International Journal of Financial Studies, 10*(90), 1–20. doi:10.3390/ijfs10040090

Khadka, R. (2020). *The impact of Blockchain Technology in Banking. Business Management.* Centria University of Applied Sciences.

Khanna, P., & Haldar, A. (2023). Will adoption of blockchain technology be challenging: Evidence from Indian banking industry. *Qualitative Research in Financial Markets, 15*(2), 361–384. doi:10.1108/QRFM-01-2022-0003

Kitsantas, T., Vazakidis, A., & Chytis, E. (2019). A Review of Blockchain Technology and Its Applications in the Business Environment. *International Conference on Enterprise, Systems, Accounting, Logistics & Management.*

Knezevic, D. (2018). Impact of Blockchain Technology Platform in Changing the Financial Sector and Other Industries. *Montenegrin Journal of Economics, 14*(1), 109–120. doi:10.14254/1800-5845/2018.14-1.8

Kumari, A., & Devi, C. N. (2022). The Impact of FinTech and Blockchain Technologies on Banking and Financial Services. *Technology Innovation Management Review, 12*(1/2). Advance online publication. doi:10.22215/timreview/1481

Laura, J. (2017). *The blockchain technology and its applications in the financial sector.* School of Business, Aalto University.

Mallesha, C., & Haripriya, S. (2019). A Study on Blockchain Technology in Banking Sector. *International Journal of Advanced Research in Commerce, Management & Social Science, 2*(3), 123–132.

Medium. (2019, October 15). *How Blockchain technology works.* https://medium.com/@ipspecialist/how-blockchain-technology-works

Pal, A., Tiwari, C. K., & Behl, A. (2021). Blockchain technology in financial services: A comprehensive review of the literature. *Journal of Global Operations and Strategic Sourcing, 14*(1), 61–80. doi:10.1108/JGOSS-07-2020-0039

Palihapitiya, T. (2020). Blockchain Revolution in Banking Industry. *Conference on Blockchain in Banking Industry.*

Parekh, N., Sadanand, P., & Jain, S. (2017). Blockchain Technology. *Journal of Emerging Technologies and Innovative Research, 4*(6), 177–179.

Patki, A., & Sople, V. (2020). Indian Banking Sector: Blockchain Implementation, Challenges and way forward. *Journal of Banking & Financial Technology, 4*(1), 65–73. doi:10.100742786-020-00019-w

Prakash, N., Solanki, S., Gabriel, E.E., & Bangari, M. (2020). Blockchain Technology–Revamping the Indian Financial Sector Landscape and Roadblocks Ahead. *Palarch's Journal of Archaeology of Egypt/Egyptology, 17*(6), 1084-1092.

Qingquan, HE. (2021). Application of Blockchain Technology in Commercial Banks. *E3S Web of Conferences.*

Ramchandra, M., Kumar, K., Sarkar, A., Mukherjee, S., & Agarwal, K. (2022). Assessment of the impact of blockchain technology in the banking industry. *Materials Today: Proceedings, 56*(4), 2221–2226. doi:10.1016/j.matpr.2021.11.554

Ravi, S. (2023). *Block Chain Technology & Its Use in Banking Sector.* Business World.

Rjoub, H., Adebayo, T., & Kirikkaleli, D. (2023). Blockchain technology-based Fintech banking sector involvement using adaptive neuro-fuzzy-based K-nearest neighbor's algorithm. *Financial Innovation, 9*(1), 65. doi:10.118640854-023-00469-3 PMID:36919101

Saidat, Z., Silva, M., Daboubi, D., Naimi, A., & Aldomy, R. (2022). How can Blockchain Revolutionize the Jordanian Banking Sector. *Journal of Southwest Jiaotong University, 57*(3), 311–325. doi:10.35741/issn.0258-2724.57.3.25

Sankaranarayanan, G., & Rajagopalan, K. (2020). Usages of blockchain technology in banking sector and its implication on Indian economy. *Alochana Chakra Journal, IX*(V), 7383–7389.

Shaik, G., & Kumar, S. (2021). A study on the blockchain technology and its awareness on business and industry. *Natural Volatiles & Essential Oils, 8*(4), 330–341.

Sharma, D. (2020). Application of Block Chain in an Indian Banking Sector. *Global Scientific Journals, 8*(5), 526–530.

Singh, A., Shahare, P., Vikram, P., Srivastava, V., & Maan, M. (2023). Financial Sector and Blockchain Technology: Challenges and Applications. *Journal of Pharmaceutical Negative Results, 14*(2), 1566–1575.

Singh, S., Sharma, A., & Jain, P. (2018). A Detailed Study of Blockchain: Changing the World. *International Journal of Applied Engineering Research, 13*(14), 11532–11539.

Toubal, M. (2021). *Blockchain Technology in the Banking Sector: Application and Challenges.* Department of Informatics and Media, Uppsala University.

Trivedi, S., Mehta, K., & Sharma, R. (2021). Systematic Literature Review on Application of Blockchain Technology in E-Finance and Financial Services. *Journal of Technology Management & Innovation, 16*(3), 89–102. doi:10.4067/S0718-27242021000300089

Upgrade. (2023, January 24). *Application of Blockchain Technology in Banking and Financial Sector in India.* Knowledge Hut. https://www.knowledgehut.com/blog/blockchain/applications-of-blockchain-technology-in-india

W3Schools. (n.d.). *Blockchain- Introduction.* https://www.w3schools.in/blockchain/introduction-to-blockchain-technology

Weerawarna, R., Miah, S., & Shao, X. (2023). Emerging advances of blockchain technology in finance: a content analysis. *Pers Ubiquit Comput*.

Wikipedia. (n.d.). *Blockchain*. https://en.wikipedia.org/wiki/Blockchain

Zheng, Z., Xie, S., Dai, H., Chen, X., & Wang, H. (2017). An overview of Blockchain Technology: Architecture, Consensus, and Future Trends. *IEEE 6th International Congress on Big Data,* 557-564.

Chapter 17
Blockchain Adoption in the Financial Sector:
Challenges, Solutions, and Implementation Framework

Kumar Shalender
Chitkara University, India

Babita Singla
Chitkara University, India

Sandhir Sharma
Chitkara University, India

ABSTRACT

Blockchain technology can be easily considered one of the most revolutionary innovations of our times. The open ledger has proved enormously beneficial for the financial sector, and thanks to its characteristics like decentralized structure, high safety, and immutable traceability, its adoption has witnessed unprecedented growth in the financial sector. That said, there are many challenges that blockchain adoption in the financial domain faces, and this research takes a close look at all these issues that can potentially hamper its adoption in the sector. The research found that primary inhibitors in the growth of blockchain include cost factors, lack of regulations, rigid work culture, and inadequate infrastructure and offer solutions to tackle these issues. Further, the study also develops a conceptual model involving important stakeholders and interaction variables between them to facilitate the adoption of an open ledger in the sector.

DOI: 10.4018/978-1-6684-8624-5.ch017

INTRODUCTION

There is no doubt about the revolutionary potential of blockchain technology that it brings to the table across product categories and service domains. In the last half a decade, the open ledger has made significant progress in the financial sector and its wide range of applications in overseas remittances, fund transfers, maintaining records, and processing transactions have made the technology favourite among finance professionals. The origin of blockchain technology can be traced back to the launch of Bitcoin in the year 2008 following which the open ledger became synonymous with digital currencies. The majority of its applications remain restricted to the field of cryptocurrency although post-2015, other business verticals also start using the blockchain in a big manner (Accenture 2017). The decentralized structure of the blockchain coupled with its immutable characteristics has today opened new avenues of growth in the financial sector. Some of the most prominent applications of blockchain in the financial sector include transaction management, decentralized finance, non-fungible tokens, and customer dealing among others. The technology is also extensively used in back-end processing, handling intermediaries, and managing insurance claims in the allied sectors of finance. Further, blockchain use cases is growing in finance category which testifies to the relevance and importance of the technology and assures stakeholders that the technology is going to stay here for years to come. That said, the growing use of technology has also met with many challenges which, if left unaddressed, might hamper the blockchain adoption in the long run among financial professionals. There are many key challenges that industry professionals are facing and prominent among these are issues related to the cost of adoption of the technology, lack of standards and regulations, and rigid work culture (Andreas 2015). In addition, the issues related to the lack of knowledge, skills, and infrastructure to support the implementation of an open ledger are also acting as an impediment. All these challenges are very critical and in order to support the widespread adoption of blockchain in the financial sector, it is absolutely mandatory for the players in the financial ecosystem to come together and put collaborative effort into creating a win-win situation that will bring holistic benefits and advantages for the entire sector. It is only by creating an inclusive system for both companies and consumers, benefits of adopting blockchain in financial field can be realized fully.

KEY CHALLENGES AND SOLUTIONS

Combining the literature review (Chesbrough 2003; Chesbrough 2010; Cai 2018; Biswas and Gupta 2019) and real-world case studies of blockchain adoption, the study has been able to finalise the following key challenges that are inhibiting the growth of open ledger and its applications among the financial sector players. These challenges have been discussed below one by one and the study also offers detailed insights into the possible solutions that might help in solving these issues in a comprehensive manner:

High Cost: Both literature and our in-depth discussion with the industry experts and analysts point to the high cost that is keeping blockchain technology from realising its full potential in the financial sector (Accenture 2017). There is no doubt about the multiple benefits that the use of open ledger offers but it is equally important to understand that in today's business environment where all the financial resources are intensely contested, making a huge investment in blockchain could prove to be a tricky task. The gloomy outlook on global growth is weighing on prospects of blockchain adoption with the majority of shareholders not being very inclined to make new investments in the field of technology. The relatively unknown nature of blockchain technology is also creating confusion among financial institutions as professionals are not fully aware of the exact amount that needs to be invested for the integration of the technology into their business practices. This unsurety and uncertainty about the investment coupled with rather weak economic cues are keeping the financial sector from taking the fresh initiative in this regard. The lack of clarity also stems from the reason that leaders in finance are unclear about the objective of blockchain integration in business processes (Antioco et al. 2008). For example, there can be a number of reasons behind the adoption of blockchain in the financial sector. It could be used for sorting internal processes, speeding up overseas remittances, or managing claims among others. In the absence of clarity on where exactly the blockchain will be utilised, managers are unable to make a call and proceed ahead with the integration of the technology.

Solution: It is very important to understand that before implementing the blockchain solution in the financial sector, the top leadership of the organisation must have clarity about the implementation process and the goals they want to achieve with this technology integration. First and foremost, it is important for the top management to decide which particular area they want to go ahead with the integration of blockchain technology. Once clarity on this particular aspect is achieved, the next step is to list down all the processes and procedures that will use the open ledger for realizing better efficiency and effectiveness. Another important parameter here to consider is to make sure that the organisation must also take into account the running cost of implementing the blockchain solutions as both initial investment and the operational cost once the solution is integrated is important for determining the long-term prospect of the technology adoption in the company and the sector. The example of India's biggest bank, i.e., State Bank of India (SBI) can guide organizations to adopt blockchain technology by carefully considering the cost implications related to the open ledger technology. Before implementing blockchain solutions, SBI clearly identified the application area of the technology, allocated a specific budget for it, constituted a team for accomplishing the task, and then finally went ahead with the implementation of the technology that is now proving significantly beneficial for the organization.

Lack of Regulations: One of the primary advantages associated with the use of the blockchain is its completely decentralized structure. The technology is not bound by any regulatory mechanism and this complete absence of a controlling authority is like a double-edged sword. The absence of the controlling authority offers relief from regulatory interventions and complete control in the hands of transacting parties. However, this decentralization also comes with its own share of disadvantages and the primary among these demerits is the absence of a redressal mechanism that a person or an organisation can resort to in case of any illegal transactions or activities come to the notice (Buitenhek 2016). This lack of regulations is particularly problematic in the financial sector as the segment has to maintain strict compliance with the rules and regulations to avert any kind of undesirable situation resulting from the infringement of laws in place. Especially when it comes to financial menaces such as text evasion, racketeering, money laundering, and terror financing, the use of the blockchain can offer safe havens to unscrupulous elements and sabotage the economy to the great extent possible. The pseudonymous nature of blockchain transactions makes it very easy for persons to stay anonymous and carry out illegal transactions without getting caught up in the net of legal agencies. The lack of regulations is one of the most critical hurdles that is keeping the financial sector from adopting blockchain technology in full force. The problem is really very critical and with no information disseminated to the regulatory authorities, central banks, or other statutory organisations, it becomes absolutely impossible for the functionaries, administrators, and regulators to keep track of the transactions and trace them in case of any suspicious activity is found. In the case of the financial sector, there is strict control in terms of the overall administration of the banking practices, financial activities, possible frauds, and potential risks the various functional procedures and operations could possibly lead to. In such a heavily regulated environment, the use of blockchain might cause friction among the functional departments as making the switch from a heavily regulated environment to a completely decentralized atmosphere is not a very smooth affair. As financial transactions have to be processed in a manner that they can be tracked if the need arises, the use of blockchain might not allow banks and financial institutions to use public blockchain networks.

Solution: It is absolutely mandatory that in order to realise the full potential of blockchain technology, a general consensus in terms of a common policy framework must be evolved among the participating stakeholders. The middle path should be adopted so that while the benefits of the decentralized technology will remain on offer, the overall regulatory framework will keep a strict vigil on unauthorised transactions and block potential illegal activities that could be done through the use of an open ledger in the financial domain. The role of policymakers becomes very crucial as they need to sit down with organisations and come up with an evolved consensus for framing regulations and compliance related to the open ledger. This will make the entire blockchain domain more useful not only for the financial sector but for all the firms and organisations operating across industries. The use of private blockchain networks and permissioned blockchain networks are rising as both these forms offer safer and more secure transaction experiences to stakeholders across the globe. Players in the blockchain industry also need to reach a consensus as integrating a user-friendly regulatory framework for propagating the technology will help in broadening the field of the open ledger among the wider range of prospective users cutting across product categories and service domains. The use of blockchain networks that comes with strict user controls should be prioritized and by closely collaborating with the other stakeholders in the blockchain ecosystem, the adoption scope of the blockchain networks can be taken to a different level altogether. Many firms today including the likes of IBM and AWS offer private blockchain networks which are very helpful and can solve the issue by offering a middle path between the decentralized structure of the blockchain and the maintenance of necessary controls (Scott et al. 2017). This explains the high demand for these private blockchains in the financial sector with more and more organisations finding these networks a perfect fit for both enhancing their operational efficiency and maintaining regulations to deal with any unwanted situation.

Rigid Work Culture: One of the subtler aspects that often go unnoticed in the integration of blockchain is the rigid work culture of the banks, financial institutions, and non-banking financial corporations (NBFCs). In order to fully embrace the open ledger, organisations need to move away from their conventional legacy systems and adapt to new practices based on higher levels of decentralization, fewer regulations, and a low amount of overall control (Jospeh et al. 2017). Meeting all these requirements will help in integration of the blockchain technology in the organisation. One of the primary challenges with the current work culture of financial institutions is the centralised authority that these firms usually operate and this rigidness has come on account of the fact that this culture has been in existence for a very long time. There is a definitive hierarchy under which the employees work and accordingly, there is a change of command that is enforced to make sure that the operational processes and functional procedures are run without any kind of disruption. This entire work philosophy changes when the introduction of blockchain comes into the picture. The primary characteristic of the open ledger is decentralization which means that the conventional, typical system through which things move in the organisation will no longer remain operational (Kulshrestha et al. 2022). This, in turn, poses a great challenge to the bureaucratic structure of the banks and might not go down well with the officials who are at the helm of the power and continue to retain their dominance even at the expense of organisations' efficiency and profitability. Another important challenge that financial institutions face is their difficulty in collaborating with completely autonomous organisations that are operating the blockchain networks that the company has opted to use. Collaborating with such organisations also brings a new set of work cultures to the table which means the organisation has to further make adjustments to accomplish the integration of the open ledger in the organisation.

Solution: It is essential for companies in financial sector to take their employees into confidence before implementing blockchain technology in the financial sector. The top management and leaders of the company must explain the benefits of the open ledger and how its incorporation will lead to more beneficial results for the organisation. Especially the focus of the efforts of the top management must be on boosting the business profitability and achieving the long-term goals of the organisation (Larios-Hernández 2017). It is also important that organisations should integrate the blockchain technology statement into the functional objectives of the organisation so that each and every department must realise how this technology integration will ultimately enhance the quality of their day-to-day work. This kind of focus is also essential to bring all the stakeholders on board and convince them that the adoption of blockchain technology will definitely lead to a profitable scenario with all-encompassing benefits to them (Omohundro 2014). A more effective way of implementing the blockchain is to get its benefits and merits listed, printed, and then distributed among employees with a focus on real-world examples of how this integration has enhanced the profitability potential of firms. The focus and support of the top management are critical here as without their consent, it'll become very will become very difficult for the people at the business level to assimilate the efforts and convince people at the operational level to go ahead and adopt the technology wholeheartedly.

Inadequate Infrastructure: Blockchain technology has been around for a while now. To be precise, the open ledger has been a business since 2009 although the majority of its use cases have popped up in the last couple of years only. Professionals across the business verticals in the financial domain have now started to realise the immense potential that blockchain can offer but in order to implement the technology, there is a requirement of both human resources and technology infrastructure. Both these operant (soft) and operand (hard) resources are in scarcity as the financial sector is struggling to get its hands on the capable manpower and IT infrastructure that will fulfil the need of the domain (Shalender and Sharma 2022). Even more crucial part of this issue is the scalability challenge as after the incorporation of the technology at the primary level, the financial sector has to make sure that it has the capability to scale up operations with the help of the open ledger. In case blockchain technology is not able to operate at the desired levels of scalability then it will create a bigger problem in the future as operations won't be able to support allied operations with the desired level of effectiveness and efficiency. It is, therefore, required that before implementing the blockchain, financial institutions must make sure that they arrange for all necessary resources that will help in blockchain integration - not only in the present context but also in future scenarios (Tempini 2017). Further, the focus of the sector must be to train human resources and deploy sufficient resources for infrastructure development so that not only the integration of blockchain becomes possible for firms but the challenge related to its scalability can also be addressed in both medium and long terms.

Solution: In order to find a credible solution to the problem of inadequate infrastructure (both hard and soft), it is absolutely mandatory that all the stakeholders in the blockchain ecosystem come together and collaborate to generate new opportunities in the sector. The focus of these efforts must be to build the infrastructure in order to make sure that technology adoption and its scalability can be achieved in a desirable manner. The primary responsibility of the industry is to focus on the development of human resources and training the manpower to make them competent enough so that the adoption, implementation, and integration can be done without causing any major disruption to the existing conventional system of a company. Policymakers also need to play their part and must focus on framing constructive policies that will help in filling the wild gulf that exists between the current scenario and desired scenario related to the technology infrastructure of blockchain networks (Tschorsch and Scheuermann 2016). Emphasis must be placed on training enough human resources on new-age technologies so that the overall shortage of both human and non-human resources can be addressed in a satisfactory manner. Easing the policies related to blockchain integration in financial domain, encouraging the participating stakeholders in further research and development, and inspiring shareholders to invest money in the anticipation of attractive future rewards help in addressing the issue of shortages related to the infrastructure. It is also important to note that bringing the shareholders and investors on board is one of the prerequisites for addressing this issue of the infrastructure gap. While shareholders can be convinced through the high profitability associated with the integration of blockchain, entrepreneurs, investors, venture capitalists, and communities can be brought in by highlighting the capability of the technology to offer holistic benefits for all the stakeholders including the society at large. Such an approach will definitely encourage all the stakeholders to work with a single-point agenda of adopting blockchain and put concerted efforts to achieve the desired levels of blockchain integration.

BLOCKCHAIN ADOPTION FRAMEWORK

Based on the specific challenges and their solution proposed in the section above, the study come up with a conceptual model that can facilitate the integration of blockchain in the financial domain. As illustrated in Figure 1, there are three important stakeholders that have been identified by the study: a) organisations, b) users, and c) policymakers. We have also conceptualized that interaction between these three stakeholders is determined by a) Easy and user-friendly interface (between organisation and users), b) Awareness and Safety (between policymakers and users), and c) Open and Constructive Plans (between organizations and policymakers). At the centre of this conceptual framework is infrastructure support which comes in terms of both human and non-human resources that are essential for the adoption of blockchain technology in the financial sector. It is very important for organisations in the financial factor to embrace blockchain technology to leverage benefits associated with the open ledger. Not only does this technology helps in enhancing the profitability of the company but also helps organisations to operate efficiently in their business processes. In order to make sure that the integration will result in the achievement of objectives, firms must offer an interface that is easy and user-friendly in its operating characteristics.

The important role of the policymakers in this conceptual framework is to make sure that they offer open and constructive plans that can be easily adopted by organisations in the financial domain. Without unnecessarily complicating the situation and coming up with stringent measures to comply with, the officials and statutory organisations should offer guidelines and codes that will help in the evolution of blockchain integration in the financial domain. The policy should be encouraging and inspiring so that new businesses and entrepreneurs can embrace the technology, come up with new inventions, and feel motivated to incorporate an open ledger in their functional procedures and operational mechanisms. The interaction between policymakers and users is also very important and the role of the officials here is to disseminate the information about the adoption of blockchain so that users can rest assured with their migration from conventional financial practices to open-ledger-based functions. Statutory organisations

Figure 1.

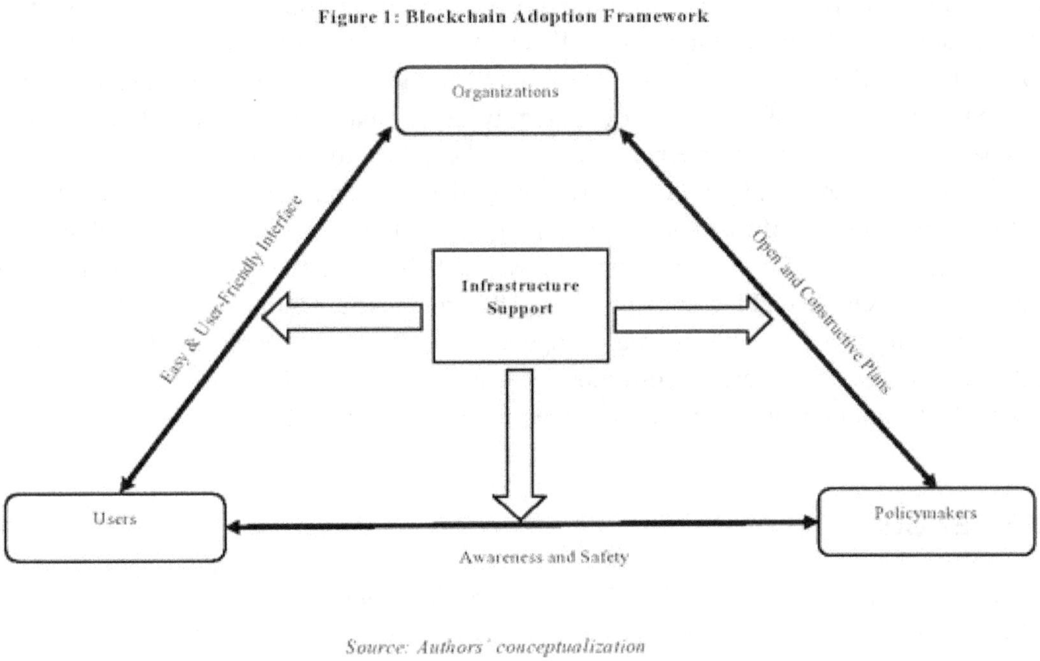

and regulators must also focus on the safety and security aspects so that users feel safe while making a switch to blockchain technology. It is only when the integration of these three stakeholders happens in an effective and efficient manner, the adoption of the open ledger in the financial domain can happen in a meaningful manner.

CONCLUSION AND DISCUSSION

There is no doubt about the enormous potential of blockchain technology for different product categories and service domains. Especially when it comes to the financial sector, an open ledger can open up new possibilities for growth and profitability for the companies operating in the world of monetary transactions. From entrepreneurs and businesses to established banks and NBFCs, each participant in value chain of the financial sector can tremendously benefit from the integration of blockchain technology. However, it is equally important to emphasize that the realisation of the full potential of blockchain technology is still struggling with a number of issues. The challenges faced by the adoption of blockchain technology discussed above in the chapter are the primary reasons why the open ledger is not able to demonstrate its significance for the financial sector to its fullest. The cost factor is one of the primary issues as organisations require a hefty amount of money to integrate the blockchain into their operational procedures. The lack of regulations and standardised practices that can offer a security net to users is also hampering the adoption potential of blockchain technology. Another important impediment to the growth of blockchain in the financial factor is the rigid work culture with many employees preferring to work with legacy systems while refusing to make their move towards the open ledger technology. Lack of a trained workforce and IT infrastructure is also coming in the blockchain technology to find a prominent place in the financial sector. All these issues are really challenging and in order to overcome the obstacles, it is important that participants in ecosystem come together and strive for a comprehensive solution that will facilitate the integration of open ledger technology in the financial domain. All stakeholders including researchers, innovators, practitioners and policymakers have to join forces and work towards innovating novel solutions that will help in incorporating the blockchain into the functional procedures and operational mechanisms of financial firms. The participation of the private blockchain networks must be encouraged as these offer the most optimum way to help widen the possibility of blockchain adoption in the financial sector and allied domains. Given the immense potential of the blockchain in terms of its all-encompassing benefits, offering higher operational efficiency, increasing functional effectiveness, and delivering elevated levels of customer service at a considerably low-cost is among the primary merits of the technology and help it to become the mainstay of the financial sector in the coming years.

REFERENCES

Accenture. (2017). *Banking on blockchain. A value analysis for investment banks.* https://www.accenture.com/_acnmedia/Accenture/Conversion-Assets/DotCom/Documents/Global/PDF/Consulting/Accenture-Banking-on-Blockchain.pdf

Andreas, M. (2015). *Masteing Bitcoin: Unlocking Digital Cryptocurrencies.* O'Reilly.

Antioco, M., Moenaert, R. K., & Lindgreen, A. (2008). Reducing ongoing product design decision-making bias. *Journal of Product Innovation Management, 25*(6), 528–545. doi:10.1111/j.1540-5885.2008.00320.x

Biswas, B., & Gupta, R. (2019). Analysis of barriers to implement blockchain in industry and service sectors. *Computers & Industrial Engineering, 136*, 225–241. doi:10.1016/j.cie.2019.07.005

Buitenhek, M. (2016). Understanding and Applying Blockchain Technology in Banking: Evolution or Revolution? *Journal of Digital Banking, 1*(2), 111–119.

Cai, W. C. (2018). Disruptions of Financial Intermediation by Fin Tech: A Review on Crowdfunding and Blockchain. *Accounting and Finance, 58*(4), 965–992. doi:10.1111/acfi.12405

Chesbrough, H. W. (2003). *Open innovation: The new imperative for creating and profiting from technology.* Harvard Business School Press.

Chesbrough, H. W. (2010). Business model innovation: Opportunities and barriers. *Long Range Planning, 43*(2/3), 354–363. doi:10.1016/j.lrp.2009.07.010

Joseph, N., Kar, A. K., Ilavarasan, P. V., & Ganesh, S. (2017). Review of discussions on internet of things (IoT): Insights from twitter analytics. *Journal of Global Information Management, 25*(2), 38–51. doi:10.4018/JGIM.2017040103

Kulshrestha, D., Tiwari, M. K., Shalender, K., & Sharma, S. (2022). Consumer Acatalepsy Towards Buying Behaviour for Need-Based Goods for Sustainability During the COVID-19 Pandemic. *Indian Journal of Marketing*, *52*(10), 50–63. doi:10.17010/ijom/2022/v52/i10/172347

Larios-Hernández, G. J. (2017). Blockchain entrepreneurship opportunity in the practices of the unbanked. *Business Horizons*, *60*(6), 865–874. doi:10.1016/j.bushor.2017.07.012

Omohundro, S. (2014). Cryptocurrencies, smart contracts, and artificial intelligence. *AI Matters*, *1*(2), 19–21. doi:10.1145/2685328.2685334

Scott, B., Loonam, J., & Kumar, V. (2017). Exploring the rise of blockchain technology: Towards distributed collaborative organizations. *Strategic Change*, *26*(5), 423–428. doi:10.1002/jsc.2142

Shalender, K., & Sharma, N. (2022). Integrating strategic flexibility and marketing system to achieve sustainable competitive advantage: Conceptual refinement and framework. *World Review of Entrepreneurship, Management and Sustainable Development*, *18*(1-2), 175–194. doi:10.1504/WREMSD.2022.120794

Tempini, N. (2017). Till data do us part: Understanding data-based value creation in data-intensive infrastructures. *Information and Organization*, *27*(4), 191–210. doi:10.1016/j.infoandorg.2017.08.001

Tschorsch, F., & Scheuermann, B. (2016). Bitcoin and beyond: A technical survey on decentralized digital currencies. *IEEE Communications Surveys and Tutorials*, *18*(3), 2084–2123. doi:10.1109/COMST.2016.2535718

Chapter 18
Blockchain Technology:
Perspective From the Banking Sector

Gurpreet Kaur
Chitkara Business School, Chitkara University, India

ABSTRACT

Blockchain is one of the revolutionary tools that has proven to be effective in resolving various problems in the banking industry. Blockchain technology has diversified applications over varied sectors as it facilitates the systematic recording of transactions in an effective, cheap, and safe manner. Blockchain technology offers various services to the banking industry which have improved the scalability and security of the banks. Thus in order to captivate the interest of researchers, academicians and bankers, the chapter presents a comprehensive review of the impact of blockchain on the banking industry. Moreover there is an urgent need to conduct extensive research into several aspects of banking with blockchain so as to overcome hindrances in the adoption of blockchain. The study provides a holistic framework highlighting the present status and future prospects of the adoption of blockchain technology in banks. Further, it describes how the adoption of blockchain can make the banking industry more secure and facilitate faster transaction recording.

INTRODUCTION

Block chain is form of database which help to record or distribute the information but not to edit the data. It is a technology that helps in sharing information securely. Data and transactions can be recorded on a block chain permanently, transparently, and immutably. As a result, this makes it possible to exchange anything valuable, whether it be a tangible item or something less tangible. Three main features define a block chain that is it must, first and foremost, be cryptographically secure secondly, should have the ability to update and transform banks' credit information and payment clearing systems by changing the technology that supports them and thirdly, block chain applications should improve the efficiency of the financial sector (Guo & Liang, 2016). A decentralized market where users can exchange and trade crypto currencies were made possible by Bitcoin (Huumo et al., 2016). Distributed ledger operators can boost the accuracy of trade data and lower settlement risk by programming clearing and settlement to be

DOI: 10.4018/978-1-6684-8624-5.ch018

almost instantaneous and making transactions irrevocable (Rega et al., 2018). Documents and ownership of money can be easily held publicly and decentralized on the blockchain in a financial context. Parties to routine banking transactions no longer have to rely on tedious manual verification procedures carried out by imperfect people, but rather on a peer-to-peer network governed by inflexible mathematical principles that are hard-coded into the system. Further, block chain enables the implementation of "smart contracts, "Self-executing contracts created using blockchain technology have the ability to automate a variety of human tasks, from claim processing and compliance to will distribution. Thus blockchain has a vital role to play in the banking sector as it improvise the banks by enhancing the security, transparency. This paper is an attempt to get better insights about block chain applications in banks. The chapter is segregated into different sections. Section 2 relates to review of literature. Section 3 presents the analysis of literature review and Section 4 deals with discussion and conclusion Section 5 describes the suggestions and future scope of study. Section 6 contains references.

REVIEW OF LITERATURE

A review of literature is conducted for which papers /articles were obtained from databases such as Science Direct, Sage, Emerald, Google Scholar etc.N umerous academics have previously performed study on the use of blockchain technology in banking Zhang et al. (2021) studies a hybrid blockchain system with a modularity network for central bank digital currency. The results of three simulation studies on scheme, network, and opinion show how this system may greatly speed up consensus and transaction processing. Hsani and Sherimon (2021) studied how blockchain technology help the banking industry in providing consumers with the simplest services possible and explore the applications that go along with it. Pal (2021) attempted to study using quantitative or qualitative methods, explore the use of blockchain technology in the financial services sector. Chowdhury et al. (2021) provided an overview of the possibilities for using the Blockchain in a safe financial system. Similar studies were conducted by Rajnak and Puschmann (2021), Gan et al. (2021), Awotunde et al. (2021), for having better insights relating to blockchain framework. Ji and Tia (2021) in a study, the impact of security, fraud prevention, and privacy of blockchain on business intelligence efficiency is examined in order to ascertain whether blockchain can affect the business intelligence efficiency of banks. Sethapat and Innet (2021) examines problems, points out difficulties, and addresses upcoming projects in this quickly developing area.An analysis of CBDC projects by central banks was done and examines the use of blockchain for CBDC. Dashkevich et al. (2020) identified the advantages and disadvantages that central banks face as a result of the implementation of blockchain. Palihapitiya (2020) conducted research into the potential impact of the Blockchain platform on the banking industry. In-depth analysis of the blockchain revolution in banking is provided in this article. Laroiya and Komalvalli (2020) analyzed the real - time applications used by various organizations throughout the world, as well as prospective use cases that are currently being developed. Gupta and Gupta (2018) In a study, it was shown how important filtering and removal would become for the banking industry in the future and how big data from blockchain will affect banking data analytics. Ozturan et al, (2018) focused on evaluating the banking sector's capability for blockchain technology. Turkish banking as a user of blockchain technology is being reviewed as a case study. Knezevic (2018) carried out study into the impact that crypto currencies will have on the financial sector and other firms using the blockchain technology platform. Taufiq et al. (2018) the goal of this study was to pinpoint the factors that influenced the Indonesian banking industry's decision to embrace the blockchain payment system. Malhotra et al. (2022) undertook a PRISMA-guided thorough review of how Blockchain technology has been used for KYC and other application areas between 2014 to come.

The research studies in the past have proved that the implementation of blockchain will revolutionize the banking sector by bringing accessibility, efficiency, and transparency. It would help in bringing ease in banks and improving efficiency in the banking sector. Rodeck and Curry (2022) analysed implementation & operation of block chain in depth. It was concluded that Hashing-based blockchain technology serves as the backbone of the platforms used to trade crypto currencies and carry out smart contracts. Karim et al. (2022) offered specific examples of how blockchain technology is used in many industries. The study's authors come to the conclusion that the use of blockchain technology, which enables decentralized, secure, transparent, and temper-proof financial transactions, has the potential to revolutionize the financial services industry. Cucari et al. (2022) blockchain would improve data openness and visibility, speed up execution, and enable the transmission of checks and money directly within the application, according to research on its usage in interbank processes. In order to increase data openness and visibility, speed up execution, and make it possible to transfer checks and money directly inside the application, using blockchain in interbank processes is recommended in the study. Garg et al. (2021) By applying blockchain, researchers assessed the financial benefits of adopting blockchain technology in the banking sector. Khan et al. (2021) in his research study discussed as to how blockchain can resolve the issues of banking sector such as storage of data, confidentiality, scalability, and transparency. Rahmayati (2021) investigated on how to strengthen Islamic banking's financial services through the use of blockchain applications that improve Islamic financial technology (fintech) in terms of features like security, transparency, efficiency, and permanence (STEP). The paper concluded that STEP, which is a crucial component of simplifying the process, facilitating access, and showing the role of blockchain in Islamic banking business products, can strengthen financial services by using the blockchain technology adopted by Islamic banking in Indonesia. Albeshr and Nobanee (2020) examined how blockchain technology is used in the financial industry. It was determined that due to its high levels of security, transaction transparency, and decentralization, blockchain technology has the potential to profoundly alter and reinvent banking services. In another similar study Khadka (2020) examined the challenges and limitations of blockchain technology, as well as its possible effects on the financial industry. The study concluded that the efficiency of numerous banking industry sectors may be improved by blockchain technology. It has the ability to improve and transform capital markets, financial reporting, cross-border payments, trade finance, and compliance. In other study conducted by Rega et al. (2018), a review of block chain applications in the banking industry (namely, the active initiatives and consortiums) as well as some crucial considerations for the banking industry were conducted. According to the report, Blockchain technology has the potential to boost international trade and ensure the accessibility of the financial system.

In order to address the issues limiting the acceptance of such technologies into banking systems Khanna and Haldar (2022), undertook a study to comprehend the challenges the Indian banking industry faced in using this technology. Zhang and Huang (2022), This study analysed the functional and non-functional requirements for CBDC design in addition to reviewing the literature on blockchain-based CBDC schemes already in existence. The paper concludes that the Blockchain's characteristics are appropriate for CBDC design requirements. Sazu and Jahan (2022) conducted a study to conduct deep inspection into aspects of banking with blockchain technology and concluded that Implementation of big data with blockchain technology has the potential to significantly affect transaction prices, speed, and security for banks. The researchers have found many obstacles in its implementation in banking because of the resistance from banking authorities. Jayasuriya and Sims (2021) a study that examined adoption issues and common misconceptions about blockchain technology's current and future use cases in banking. In this study, the consequences of blockchain-based banking on behaviour, society, the economy, regulations, and management are identified. Baiod et al. (2021) intended to investigate the major problems, blockchain-based solutions, and application cases in the respective industries. Scalability, security, and regulation are the three main barriers to blockchain adoption that the study highlights. It also shows how these barriers may affect their utilisation. Kabir and Islam (2021) in a study attempted to explain the elements influencing the banking industry's desire to use blockchain. The effects of big data from blockchain on banking analytics in the future will show how signal extraction and filtering are becoming more and more important in the banking industry. Saheb and Mamaghani (2021) aimed to advance the body of knowledge on the business value of IT by identifying the cultural barriers and organisational principles that prevent blockchain adoption in the banking industry. The poll indicates that those organisational values that are related to business operations are the most crucial for blockchain in the banking sector. It will increase the corporate processes' transparency, dependability, and traceability. Cocco et al. (2017) examined the difficulties and possibilities of adopting blockchain technology into the banking industry. Guo and Liang (2016) in a study attempted to provide a solution to the issues raised by the self-governing character of blockchain technology, as well as by regulations and actual decentralization system implementation. Current obstacles cannot stop history since technical, legal, and other issues with blockchain technology will finally be resolved.

Few researchers have pinpointed certain actions that might aid in the efficient implementation of blockchain technology in banking. Kemyani et al. (2022) examine the progress in blockchain technology for major accounting and financial operations in the banking industry. The study placed a strong emphasis on the government's responsibility for regulating the application of this technology in sectors related to finance and for organising seminars and workshops for people in the financial industry. Younus et al. (2022) in a study investigated as to how blockchain technology be integrated into the current financial and banking systems, with an emphasis on the most crucial conditions for such systems, such as safe and open banking and financial systems. The article introduces the smart contract for blockchain-based financial and banking systems, which is crucial for forming pre-defined agreements among many customers. Shah and Jani (2018) in a paper seeks to describe both the structure and operation of the blockchain technology. The paper concludes that regulators should be involved and help influence innovation. They will be able to do this in order to comprehend the technology, evaluate the risk, and enable the development of solutions to their particular challenges.

The above review presents a detailed information regarding the implementation of the blockchain and how its adoption will be helpful for banking sector. Further the obstacles in implementation of blockchain is highlighted & probable measure for ensuring the safe application of blockchain in the banking is stated.

It is observed that there is paucity of study on the applied issues of blockchain technology in banking. Therefore the present paper is insightful in highlighting the problem areas of blockchain and enumerate such measures if applied appropriately will ensure safety, security, transparency within the banking sector.

ANALYSIS OF LITERATURE

The literature study being conducted by the author states that most of the studies on the application of block-chain in banking were done in 2021.

Figure 1. Chart
Source: Author's Compilation

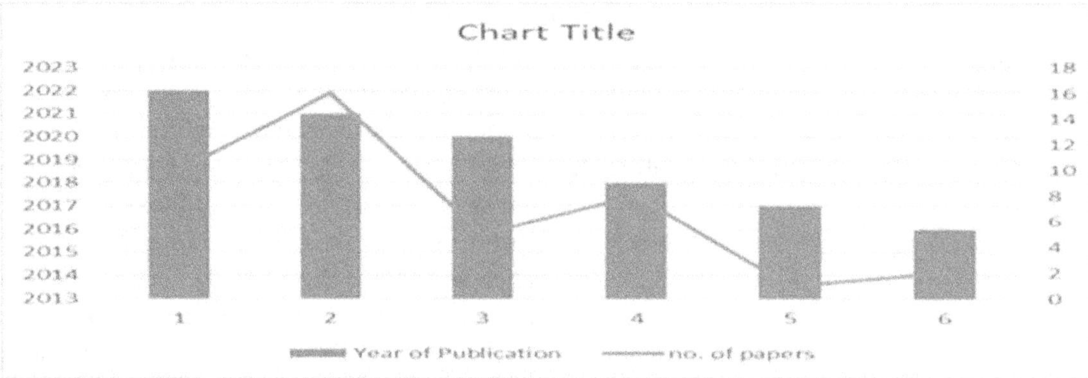

Table 1. Authors and journals

Authors & Year of publication	Name of the Journal
Sazu & Jahan(2022)	Data science in Finance and Economics
Zhang & Huang(2022)	ICT Express
Kemyani, et.al(2022)	Journal of Research in Business and Management
Karim, et.al(2022)	Block chain technology and computational Excellence for soceity
Khanna & Haldar(2022)	Qualitative Research in Financial Markets
Cucari, et.al(2022)	Technology Analysis & Strategic Management
Malhotra, et.al(2022)	Wireless personal communications
Dhanda(2022)	Regulatory Aspects Of Artificial Intelligence on Block chain
Garg, et.al(2021)	Technological forecasting and social change
Rahmayati(2021)	Jurnal Ilmu Manajemen dan Bisnis Islam
Jayasuriya & Sims(2021)	Journal of Risk and financial Management
Zhang, et.al(2021)	IEEE
Hsani & Sherimon(2021)	International Journal of Technology
Baiod, et.al(2021)	Journal of International Technology and Information management
Saheb & Mamaghani(2021)	The Journal of High Technology Management Research
Pal(2021)	Journal of Global Operations and strategic Sourcing
Chowdhury, et.al(2021)	Journal of software Engineering and Applications
Rajnak & Puschmann(2021)	Information Systems and e-business models in banking
Gan, at.al(2021)	Technology Analysis & Strategic Management
Awotunde, et.al(2021)	International conference on Hybrid Intelligent systems
Kabir & Islam(2021)	AIP conference Proceeding
Fen Ji &Ai Tia(2021)	Kybernetes
Sethapat & Innet(2021)	Third International Conference on Block chain computing and Application
Dashkevich, et.el(2020)	IEEE acess
Laroiya& Komalvalli(2020)	Handbook of Research on Block Chain Technology
Gupta & Gupta(2018)	Delhi Business Review
Ozturan, et.al(2018)	International journal of Business Marketing and Management
Knezevic(2018)	Montenegrin Journal of Economics
Taufiq, et.al(2018)	International conference on information management and technology
Chen, et.al(2018)	International conference on information management and technology and application
Cocco, et.al(2017)	Future internet
Guo&Liang(2016)	Financial Innovation

Source:Author's Compilation.

Table 1 depicts the Journal description wherein these papers are published.
Table 2 mentioned table depicts the highest number of citations paper-wise.

Table 2. Title of papers

Title of paper	Citations
Where is current research on block chain technology?	2128
Block chain apllication and outlook in the banking sector	863
Banking on blockchain: Costs savings thanks to Block Chain Technology	282
Banking with blockchain-ed big data	183
A survey of Block chain application in differrent domain	100
Measuring the perceived benefits of implementing blockchain technology in the banking sector	96
Impact of block chain technology platform in changing the financial sector and other industries	58
Strengthening Islamic Banking service In Indonesia Through Block chain Technology: The Anp-Step Approach	38
Block chain application on central bank: A systematic mapping study	38
The impact of block chain on business models in banking	35
Application of Block chain Technology	33
Application of block chain technology in Banking and Finance	31
Exploring the barriers and organizational Exploring the barriers and organizational values of blockchain adoption in the banking industry	26
The affecting factors of blockchain technology adoption of payments system in Indonesia banking Industry.	24
Block Chain technology: application in Indian banking sector	23
Block chain and central bank digital currency	22
Block chain technology in financial services: A comprehensive review of the Literature	22
The impact of Block chain in Banking Processes: the Interbank spunta case study	21
Block chain technology and its application across multiple domains: a survey	19
Application of block chain technology in Banking and Finance beyond digital currencies	17
A Hybrid Model for Central Bank Digital Currency Based on Blockchain	17

Source:Author's Compilation

DISCUSSION AND CONCLUSION

Each business has advantages and disadvantages of its own, but only the banking or finance industry helps the other industries grow and enables them to maximise their significant investments (Dhanda, 2022).

Banking sector is one of the crucial sector is the economy as it channelizes the funds. It is important for upgrade the working of banking from time to time so as to enable to meet global standards. After the internet, blockchain is the second best innovation ever. Blockchain technology provides a banking sector with a number of exciting opportunities (Chowdhury, 2021). It can offer faster payments, lower fees than banks, a higher volume of financial transactions, and greater performance and security. Block chain technology has huge potential to transform India's current financial industry applications (Gupta & Gupta, 2018). By making banking transactions extremely secure, swift, transparent, and affordable, it has developed into a disruptive force that is revolutionizing the Indian banking industry. But while integrating this technology, the banking industry is dealing with a number of difficulties. In order to overcome the obstacles preventing blockchain from being adopted in banking globally and to maximize its potential to revolutionize the economy, there is a need for substantial research and development into a number of aspects of banking with blockchain (Knezevic, 2018).

As a result of Analysis of cutting-edge blockchain research and technology in the banking and financial industry, it was discovered that although a lot of studies in other domains, no systematic review has yet summarized the research on blockchain application in this sector (Gan et al., 2021). A systematic orderly and timely record is very important for the users of blockchain (Chen et al., 2018). A planned mapping study with the goal of collecting a database Information on blockchain technology will be helpful for regulators ensuring smooth functioning of the banking sector.

RECOMMENDATIONS AND FUTURE SCOPE OF STUDY

Blockchain technology is one of the best innovation for the banking as it will bring ease in the working together with ensuring safely, security, transparency in the banking system. For proper systematic implementation of this technology in banking, it is important that government intervention is much needed as it can play key role in providing sufficient, timely guidance on the usage of such technology. The regulators should lay down such policies so as ensure smooth and efficient usage (Arora et al., 2022).

Future researchers should work on emphasizing, creating more awareness on effectively utilizing the blockchain technology in banking industry. The study will pave a way for regulators in forming suitable policies/ developing framework which helps in removing the obstacles in implementing blockchain and will further ensure optimum utilization of such technology for enhancing banking services.

REFERENCES

Al Hsani, A. K., & Sherimon, V. (2021). An examination of the utilization of blockchain innovation in banking sector. *ARIV-International Journal of Technology*, 1-9.

Al Kemyani, M. K., Al Raisi, J., Al Kindi, A. R. T., Al Mughairi, I. Y., & Tiwari, C. K. (2022). Blockchain applications in accounting and finance: Qualitative Evidence from the banking sector. *Journal of Research in Business and Management*, *10*(4), 28–39.

AlbeshrS.NobaneeH. (2020). *Blockchain Applications in Banking Industry: A Mini-Review*. Available at SSRN 3539152. doi:10.2139/ssrn.3539152

Arora, M., Sharma, R., & Mehta, K. (2022). Personality Effects on Financial Responses Caused by the Perceived Financial Threat during the COVID-19 Pandemic. *The Journal of Wealth Management*, *25*(3), 72–89. doi:10.3905/jwm.2022.1.183

Awotunde, J. B., Ogundokun, R. O., Misra, S., Adeniyi, E. A., & Sharma, M. M. (2021). Blockchain-based framework for secure transaction in mobile banking platform. In *International Conference on Hybrid Intelligent Systems* (pp. 525-534). Springer. 10.1007/978-3-030-73050-5_53

Baiod, W., Light, J., & Mahanti, A. (2021). Blockchain technology and its applications across multiple domains: A survey. *Journal of International Technology and Information Management*, *29*(4), 78–119. doi:10.58729/1941-6679.1482

Chen, W., Xu, Z., Shi, S., Zhao, Y., & Zhao, J. (2018, December). A survey of blockchain applications in different domains. In *Proceedings of the 2018 International Conference on Blockchain Technology and Application* (pp. 17-21). 10.1145/3301403.3301407

Chowdhury, M. U., Suchana, K., Alam, S. M. E., & Khan, M. M. (2021). Blockchain application in banking system. *Journal of Software Engineering and Applications*, *14*(7), 298–311. doi:10.4236/jsea.2021.147018

Cocco, L., Pinna, A., & Marchesi, M. (2017). Banking on blockchain: Costs savings thanks to the blockchain technology. *Future Internet*, *9*(3), 25. doi:10.3390/fi9030025

Cucari, N., Lagasio, V., Lia, G., & Torriero, C. (2022). The impact of blockchain in banking processes: The Interbank Spunta case study. *Technology Analysis and Strategic Management*, *34*(2), 138–150. do i:10.1080/09537325.2021.1891217

Daluwathumullagamage, D. J., & Sims, A. (2021). Fantastic beasts: Blockchain based banking. *Journal of Risk and Financial Management, 14*(4), 1-43.

Dashkevich, N., Counsell, S., & Destefanis, G. (2020). Blockchain application for central banks: A systematic mapping study. *IEEE Access : Practical Innovations, Open Solutions*, *8*, 139918–139952. doi:10.1109/ACCESS.2020.3012295

Dhanda, N. (2022). Cryptocurrency and Blockchain: The Future of a Global Banking System. In Regulatory Aspects of Artificial Intelligence on Blockchain (pp. 181-204). IGI Global.

Gan, Q., Lau, R. Y. K., & Hong, J. (2021). A critical review of blockchain applications to banking and finance: A qualitative thematic analysis approach. *Technology Analysis and Strategic Management*, 1–17. doi:10.1080/09537325.2021.1979509

Garg, P., Gupta, B., Chauhan, A. K., Sivarajah, U., Gupta, S., & Modgil, S. (2021). Measuring the perceived benefits of implementing blockchain technology in the banking sector. *Technological Forecasting and Social Change*, *163*, 120407. doi:10.1016/j.techfore.2020.120407

Guo, Y., & Liang, C. (2016). Blockchain application and outlook in the banking industry. *Financial Innovation*, *2*(1), 1–12. doi:10.118640854-016-0034-9

Gupta, A., & Gupta, S. (2018). Blockchain technology: Application in Indian banking sector. *Delhi Business Review*, *19*(2), 75–84. doi:10.51768/dbr.v19i2.192201807

Hassani, H., Huang, X., & Silva, E. (2018). Banking with blockchain-ed big data. *Journal of Management Analytics*, *5*(4), 256–275. doi:10.1080/23270012.2018.1528900

Ji, F., & Tia, A. (2021). The effect of blockchain on business intelligence efficiency of banks. *Kybernetes*.

Kabir, M. R., & Islam, M. A. (2021, July). Behavioural intention to adopt blockchain technology in Bangladeshi banking companies. In AIP Conference Proceedings (Vol. 2347, No. 1, p. 020025). AIP Publishing LLC. doi:10.1063/5.0051654

Karim, S., Rabbani, M. R., & Bawazir, H. (2022). Applications of blockchain technology in the finance and banking industry beyond digital currencies. In *Blockchain Technology and Computational Excellence for Society 5.0* (pp. 216–238). IGI Global. doi:10.4018/978-1-7998-8382-1.ch011

Khadka, R. (2020). *The impact of blockchain technology in banking: How can blockchain revolutionize the banking industry?* Academic Press.

Khan, M. K., Nisar, K., Farooq, Y., Habib, S., Danish, M., & Hyder, I. (2021). *An Improved Banking Application Model Using Blockchain.* Academic Press.

Khanna, P., & Haldar, A. (2022). Will adoption of blockchain technology be challenging: evidence from Indian banking industry. *Qualitative Research in Financial Markets.*

Knezevic, D. (2018). Impact of blockchain technology platform in changing the financial sector and other industries. *Montenegrin Journal of Economics, 14*(1), 109–120. doi:10.14254/1800-5845/2018.14-1.8

Laroiya, C., Saxena, D., & Komalavalli, C. (2020). Applications of blockchain technology. In *Handbook of research on blockchain technology* (pp. 213–243). Academic Press. doi:10.1016/B978-0-12-819816-2.00009-5

Malhotra, D., Saini, P., & Singh, A. K. (2022). How blockchain can automate KYC: Systematic review. *Wireless Personal Communications, 122*(2), 1987–2021. doi:10.100711277-021-08977-0

Ozturan, M., Atasu, I., & Soydan, H. (2019). Assessment of blockchain technology readiness level of banking industry: Case of Turkey. *International Journal of Business Marketing and Management (IJBMM), 4*(12), 1-13.

Pal, A., Tiwari, C. K., & Behl, A. (2021). Blockchain technology in financial services: a comprehensive review of the literature. *Journal of Global Operations and Strategic Sourcing.*

Palihapitiya, T. (2020). *Blockchain Revolution in Banking Industry.* University of Moratuwa.

Rahmayati, R. (2021). Strengthening Islamic Banking Services In Indonesia Through Blockchain Technology: The Anp-Step Approach. At-Tijaroh. *Jurnal Ilmu Manajemen Dan Bisnis Islam, 7*(2), 259–272. doi:10.24952/tijaroh.v7i2.4368

Rajnak, V., & Puschmann, T. (2021). The impact of blockchain on business models in banking. *Information Systems and e-Business Management, 19*(3), 809–861. doi:10.100710257-020-00468-2

Rega, F. G., Riccardi, N., Li, J., & di Carlo, F. (2018). *Blockchain in the banking industry: an Overview.* Research Gate.

Rodeck, D., & Curry, B. (2022). What is blockchain. *Forbes.* www. forbes. com/advisor/investing/cryptocurrency/what-is-blockchain/

Saheb, T., & Mamaghani, F. H. (2021). Exploring the barriers and organizational values of blockchain adoption in the banking industry. *The Journal of High Technology Management Research, 32*(2), 100417. doi:10.1016/j.hitech.2021.100417

Sazu, M. H., & Jahan, S. A. (2022). Impact of blockchain-enabled analytics as a tool to revolutionize the banking industry. *Data Science in Finance and Economics, 2*(3), 275–293. doi:10.3934/DSFE.2022014

Sethaput, V., & Innet, S. (2021, November). Blockchain Application for Central Bank Digital Currencies (CBDC). In *2021 Third International Conference on Blockchain Computing and Applications (BCCA)* (pp. 3-10). IEEE. 10.1109/BCCA53669.2021.9657012

Shah, T., & Jani, S. (2018). Applications of blockchain technology in banking & finance. Parul CUniversity.

Sharma, A., & Sharma, R. (2022). Exploring Tax Decision Factors: A Perspective from North Indian Tax Practitioners. *Journal of Tax Reform*, *8*(3), 285–297. doi:10.15826/jtr.2022.8.3.122

Taufiq, R., Hidayanto, A. N., & Prabowo, H. (2018, September). The affecting factors of blockchain technology adoption of payments systems in Indonesia banking industry. In *2018 International Conference on Information Management and Technology (ICIMTech)* (pp. 506-510). IEEE. 10.1109/ICIMTech.2018.8528104

Trivedi, S., Mehta, K., & Sharma, R. (2021). Systematic literature review on application of blockchain technology in E-finance and financial services. *Journal of Technology Management & Innovation*, *16*(3), 89–102. doi:10.4067/S0718-27242021000300089

Yli-Huumo, J., Ko, D., Choi, S., Park, S., & Smolander, K. (2016). Where is current research on blockchain technology? A systematic review. *PLoS One*, *11*(10), e0163477. doi:10.1371/journal.pone.0163477 PMID:27695049

Younus, D., Muayad, A., & Abumandil, M. (2022). *Role of smart contract technology blockchain services in finance and banking systems: Concept and core values*. Academic Press.

Zhang, J., Tian, R., Cao, Y., Yuan, X., Yu, Z., Yan, X., & Zhang, X. (2021). A hybrid model for central bank digital currency based on blockchain. *IEEE Access : Practical Innovations, Open Solutions*, *9*, 53589–53601. doi:10.1109/ACCESS.2021.3071033

Zhang, T., & Huang, Z. (2022). Blockchain and central bank digital currency. *ICT Express*, *8*(2), 264–270. doi:10.1016/j.icte.2021.09.014

Chapter 19
Consumers' Preferences Towards Digital Payments While Online and Offline Shopping Post COVID-19

Babita Singla
Chitkara University, India

Kumar Shalender
Chitkara University, India

Sandhir Sharma
Chitkara University, India

ABSTRACT

The purpose of this study is to assess customer preferences in the digital era from online payments while shopping from omni channel retail. This study used demographic and descriptive research approach for the investigation to examine customer preferences towards digital payment. Furthermore, based on the topics discussed, personally administered survey was carried out by the researcher with the consent of the retail mall and shop managers in terms of positive or negative omni-channel sentiments application users. It has broken down numerous barriers, including political, physical, and climate barriers.

INTRODUCTION

Shopping is one of the oldest words, dating back to the prehistoric era. Merchants in ancient Greece used to set up stalls or shops in a marketplace known as an agora to sell their wares. In ancient Rome, the Forum served as a marketplace. To exchange goods and services, fairs and markets were created. People went to weekly markets in nearby towns to shop. The rise of consumer society in the 18th century is closely related to the current phenomenon of shopping. Shopping has been done for centuries under the

DOI: 10.4018/978-1-6684-8624-5.ch019

names of "trading," "bartering," and even "marketing." Shopping is described as an operation in which a consumer selects from a variety of products. Because of factors such as how the consumer is handled, comfort, mood, and the type of products purchased, the shopping experience can vary from friendly to negative. As the number of people with disposable income grew as a result of increasing prosperity and social mobility, the growth of consumption contributed to the rise of "shopping" – retail stores selling unique items and the acceptance of shopping.

ONLINE SHOPPING

Online shopping is known as electronic commerce, or e-Commerce. It began to transition from a real-time market to an online market. Today, the internet is used to conduct all of these companies. E-commerce, or online shopping, provides everyone with an equal opportunity to sell their goods through e-stores (website dedicated to selling of product, a virtual store). It has broken down numerous barriers, including political, physical, and climate barriers. We've seen a massive increase in online shopping over the last decade. It was created by computer scientists who were involved in online shopping at the time. Then it spread to the general public and eventually replaced the real market place. E-commerce did not originate with "The Internet," but it did begin to evolve with it. The internet is open to all in the world, and online marketing is approaching its pinnacle in terms of gaining a larger share of the market.

HISTORY OF ONLINE SHOPPING

Consumers want convenience and for products to be delivered to their door in a timely manner without having to go into a store, and they want to shop on the go. Evolution of technology and the services offered by online marketing have become a part of our daily lives. Instead of driving to a high-end bookstore to purchase a book, we can now search the internet for the best prices and reviews at our leisure.

LITERATURE REVIEW

Earlier the word "Retail" has been related with the "Brick and Mortar store" (Harris, 2012). With the help of the digitalization, e-commerce was emerged as a new channel and customers have multiple option of shopping which is also called as multichannel retailing (Verhoef et al., 2015). However, due to the division between online and offline channels, they had bad experiences while interacting with this multichannel concept during their shopping journey (Beck and Rygl, 2015).

According to Aubrey and Judge (2012), Omni-channel retail blurs the gap between the online and offline channel by working together side by side and supporting each other. Omnichannel retailing merges the services of offline and online channels. With the help of this new phase of retailing, customer can easily start their shopping journey from one channel and can end it on another channel (Mosquera et al., 2017). This will provide a seamless experience during customers shopping journey and improves convenience and engagement (Alexander and Alvarado, 2017).

Aubrey and Judge (2012) found that technologies enable retailers to upgrade product availability, improve customer engagement, increase more interaction with the brand instead of channel, develop brand image and increase customer experience. Integration of interactive technologies in the offline space can improve the experience of customers during their shopping journey (Pantano & Di Pietro, 2012). Retailers are replacing their staff members and sales associates with the technology (Colby and Parasuraman, 2003).

PROBLEM STATEMENT

Consumers have opted for e-commerce and Omni channel platforms in reaction to the changed circumstances following the COVID-19 outbreak. Consumer behavior has shifted in favor of digital, influencing tastes and purchasing decisions. Retailers are preparing for the changes as well, using QR codes, offering more digital information in shops, and investing in digital resources. The scale of change in the last six months has been tectonic, and the lockdown has had an effect on human and consumer behavior. Because of re-prioritization in transactions, there has been a major revival in the exchange in goods directly relevant to essential human needs, and customers have turned away from some luxury items like make-up. People are adopting digital in fields such as entertainment, fitness, education, medicine, and distribution. The most significant shift in customer behavior that we have seen is that consumers are still hesitant to switch to brick-and-mortar stores. People come in, but they spend less time in the shop. Furthermore, consumers' window shopping has decreased, and only those with a "clear motive" are coming in.

While several states are starting to reopen, there is still a lot of concern about the retail industry's health. Can capacity be limited to 20%, 50%, or 75% of total capacity? Will people feel comfortable going into shops, trying on goods, and exchanging money with employees if stores are allowed to open? According to a new survey, 90 percent of shoppers are reluctant to shop in stores due to COVID-19 issues. What if, after a few months, all of the stores are forced to close due to a new outbreak of the virus?

Whether the transition results in something entirely new, such as a subscription service or an app, or something morphed, such as establishing a social presence to connect with consumers, the COVID-19 age has presented an opportunity. Small and medium businesses around the world should feel inspired and motivated to reconsider and reshape how their businesses go forward, as difficult as it is for us to use that word to describe the current situation.

It analyze factors involved both in online and offline shopping in India. So far, this type of attempt is not made in this field and it is necessary to do research in this area. This helps the public and online/offline traders to take necessary steps to improve the customer related factors in buying with the development strategies. The results of the study would suggest the factors that are essential for both online and offline customer satisfaction. It also highlights the present condition of online customer satisfaction, various factors of services, customer loyalty, patronage, recommendation and price sensitivity in India. The study's findings will aid the general public in making wiser decisions about whether to buy goods and services in person or online.

OBJECTIVES OF THE STUDY

- To identify the factors of customer satisfaction between online customer and offline customer.
- To analyze the customer loyalty and recommendations made by the online customers and offline customer.

- To calculate the impact of digital payment and price sensitivity of online and off-line customers.

RESEARCH METHODOLOGY

Both analytical and descriptive types of methodology are used to conduct the investigation. The key sources for the study are primary and secondary data. The data were collected from the customer in India. The basic data are gathered using the survey approach. A carefully constructed questionnaire is used to perform the survey. To produce data, random sampling is used. The study's samples are chosen in a methodical manner. 120 of the 150 questionnaires that were distributed and collected were deemed to be appropriate for the study. The basic data is gathered using a random sample technique. To get responses from both online and offline clients, the random sampling approach is used. The researcher used a convenience sampling technique to collect 30 samples from chosen taluks, totaling 120.

ANALYSIS AND INTERPRETATION

Table 1. Demographic of online shopping customers

Gender	Online Shopping	Off-Line Shopping	Total
Male	38 31.7%	22 18.3%	60 50.0%
Female	47 39.1%	13 10.8%	60 50%
Total	**85** **70.8%**	**35** **29.2%**	**120** **100.0%**

Source: Primary data

From Table 1, online customers are 31.7% and 39.1% for male and female respectively. Overall 70.8% people uses online shopping and 20.2% people uses Off-line shopping. Among female 39.1% go for online shopping and 10.8% Off-line shopping. Table 2 clearly shows that online shopping habitual is found more in both men and women as they are tend to do that for best products without taking much risk.

Distribution of age groups online shopping is done by majority of the respondents with 65.0% than offline shopping. To precise, age group between 31 to 40 years are much involving in online shopping with 25.8% and 13.3% respectively followed by the age group between 21 to 30. The percentages for them are 19.2% and 11.7% respectively.

It is found that 7.5% of Online shopping customers and 5.0% of Off-line shopping customers are with the educational qualification up to SSLC, 15.0% of Online shopping customers and 7.5% of Off-line shopping customers are with the educational qualification up to HSC, 17.5% of Online shopping customers and 13.3% of Off-line shopping customers are graduate and 23.3% of Online shopping customers and 10.8% % of Off-line shopping customers are with professional qualification. The maximum numbers of customers preferring online shopping are with professional qualification with 23.3% and the minimum

Table 2. Demographic factor age wise (in years)

Age Wise	Online Shopping	Off-Line Shopping	Total
Up to 20	07 5.8%	04 3.3%	11 9.2%
21 to 30	23 19.2%	14 11.7%	37 30.8%
31 to 40	31 25.8%	16 13.3%	47 39.2%
Above 40	17 14.2%	08 6.7%	25 20.8%
Total	**78** **65.0%**	**42** **35%**	**120** **100%**

Source: Primary data

Table 3. Frequency distribution of educational qualification

Educational Qualification	Online Shopping	Off-Line Shopping	Total
Up to SSLC	09 7.5%	06 5.0%	15 12.5%
Up to HSC	18 15.0%	09 7.5%	27 22.5%
Graduate	21 17.5%	16 13.3%	37 30.8%
Professional	28 23.3%	13 10.8%	41 34.2
Total	**76** **63.3%**	**44** **36.7%**	**120** **100.0%**

numbers of customers are with SSLC qualification with 7.5%. The customers who are graduate tend to buy more in offline because with 13.3%

Table 4. Demographic factor Income wise

Monthly Income	Online Shopping	Off-Line Shopping	Total
Less than Rs.10,000	08 6.7%	12 10.0%	20 16.7%
Rs. 10,001 to 20,000	14 11.7%	11 9.2%	25 20.8%
Rs. 20,001 to 30,000	18 15.0%	13 10.8%	31 25.8%
Above Rs.40,000	27 22.5%	17 14.2%	44 36.7
Total	**67** **55.8%**	**53** **44.7%**	**120** **100.0%**

Source: Primary data

Table 5. Frequency distribution of marital status

Monthly Income	Online Shopping	Off-Line Shopping	Total
Single	43 35.8%	23 19.2%	54 45.0%
Married	36 30.0%	18 15.0%	66 55.0%
Total	**79** **65.8%**	**41** **34.2%**	**120** **100.0%**

It is found that among the earning group of < Rs.10,000, 6.7% belong to Online shopping customers and 10.0% to Off-line shopping customers. 11.7% of Online shopping customers and 9.2% of Off-line shopping customers are with the earning group of Rs.10,000 to Rs.20, 000. The monthly income group of Rs.20,000 to 30,000 consists of 15.0% of Online shopping customers and 10.8% of Off-line shopping customers. 22.5% of Online shopping customers and 14.2% of Off-line shopping customers are with the range of above Rs.40, 000. The maximum numbers of customers with monthly income of above Rs.40, 000 go for online purchase with 22.5% and for offline purchase with 14.2%. Because of the reason that more income more purchase and less income less purchase.

It if found that 30.0% of Online shopping customers and 15.0% of Off-line shopping customers are married and 35.3% of Online shopping customers and 19.2% of Off-line shopping customers are single. The maximum number of customers who go for online shopping are single with 35.8% and the minimum numbers of customer selecting offline purchase are married with 15.0%. The married customers tend to buy many products for their families by using the offline marketing.

Table 6. Mean of customer satisfaction of online and offline shopping

Customer Satisfaction	Online Shopping	Offline Shopping
The after-sale service was satisfactory	4.143	3.754
I am pleased with the cost of your product	3.781	3.693
The discounts given were satisfactory	3.875	3.511
The ads have satisfied me	3.783	3.366
You're satisfied with the rest of your favorite brand's products	3.838	3.402
I'm pleased with the delivery process	3.891	3.330
I am satisfied with the delivery timeliness	3.833	3.765

Source: Primary data

Based on mean score, 'The after-sale service was satisfactory.' is the most important factor in the factors of customer satisfaction of online customers with 4.143 followed by 'I'm pleased with the delivery processes with 3.891. The least factor in customer satisfaction is 'I am pleased with the cost of your product' with 3.781.

Table 7. Mean of customer loyalty of online shopping customers

Customer Loyalty	Online Shopping	Offline Shopping
Will continue to invest in it	3.994	3.594
You will continue to use even though others offered lower rates	3.754	3.237
You will purchase it even though other brands offered exclusive discounts or enticing prizes	3.509	3.306
Your devotion is always going high	3.657	3.254
Overall, you have a good attitude about it	3.629	3.146

Source: Primary data

In the offline shopping, 'I am satisfied with the delivery timeliness' is the most important factor with 3.765 followed by 'The after-sale service was satisfactory' with 3.754. The least factor in this section is 'I'm pleased with the delivery processes with 3.330.

Based on mean score, 'Will continue to invest in it' is the most important factor on customer loyalty of online customers with 3.994 by Online shopping customers and 3.594 by Off-line shopping customers, followed by 'You will continue to use even though others offered lower rates' with 3.754 by Online shopping users and 'You will purchase it even though other brands offered exclusive discounts or enticing prizes' with 3.306 by Off-line shopping customers. The least factor is "You will purchase it even though other brands offered exclusive discounts or enticing prizes' with 3.509 by Online shopping customers and 'Overall, you have a good attitude about it' with 3.146 by Off-line shopping customers.

Table 8. Mean of price sensitivity

Price Sensitivity	Online Shopping	Offline Shopping
If competitors provide services at a lower cost, switch to them	3.863	3.657
Charge a higher price to your preferred institution than to competitors	3.449	3.237
The prices of services have a huge effect on consumer loyalty	3.663	3.443
The price of an institution dictates whether or not to continue patronizing it	3.640	3.420

Source: Primary data

Based on mean score, 'If competitors provide services at a lower cost, switch to them' is the most important factor in price sensitivity of online customers with 3.863 by Online shopping customers and 3.657 by Offline shopping customers, followed by 'The prices of services have a huge effect on consumer loyalty' with 3.663 by Online shopping customers and 3.443 by Offline shopping customers, 'The price of an institution dictates whether or not to continue patronizing it' with 3.640 by Online shopping customers and 3.420 by Offline shopping customers. The least factor is 'Charge a higher price to your preferred institution than to competitors' with 3.449 by online shopping customers and 3.237 by Offline shopping customers.

Based on mean score, 'Recommend to other' is the most important factor on recommendation with 4.169 by Online shopping customers and 3.757 by Off-line shopping customers, followed by 'Encour-

Table 9. Mean of recommendation

Recommendation	Online Shopping	Offline Shopping
Recommend it to others	4.169	3.757
Encourage your friends and family to come	3.949	3.614
Good things should be said about it	3.903	3.580
Convey the discounts that are present in it	3.823	3.520
Convey the value of receiving goods and services on time	3.751	3.380

Source: Primary data

age your friends and family to come' with 3.949 by Online shopping customers and 3.614 by Off-line shopping customers, 'Good things should be said about it' with 3.903 by Online shopping customers and 3.580 by Off-line shopping customers. The least factor is 'Convey the value of receiving goods and services on time' with 3.751 by online shopping customers and 3.380 by Off-line shopping customers.

HYPOTHESIS

Null Hypothesis: There is no significant difference between Online and Offline shoppers with respect to Factors of Customer Satisfaction.

Table 10. 'T' test for significant difference between online and offline shopping with respect to factors of customer satisfaction

Factors of Customer Satisfaction	Types of Shopping				t Value	P Value
	Online		Off-Line			
	Mean	SD	Mean	SD		
Tangibility	18.99	3.61	19.66	3.58	2.436	0.015*
Reliability	18.28	4.28	18.28	3.88	0.025	0.980
Responsiveness	18.05	4.01	18.39	4.00	1.113	0.266
Credibility	17.96	4.30	17.93	4.01	0.099	0.921
Security	28.27	5.97	28.04	6.01	0.503	0.651

Source: Computed from Primary data

Since P value is less than 0.05, the null hypothesis rejected at 5% level, with regard to tangibility factor. Hence, there is a significant difference between Online and Offline shopping with regards to tangibility. Based on mean score, Offline shopping is much satisfied with the tangibility factors of customer satisfaction. There is no significant difference between Online and Offline shopping with regard to reliability, responsiveness, credibility, security and overall factors of customer satisfaction, since P value is greater than 0.05. Hence, the null hypothesis is accepted with regard to reliability, responsiveness, credibility, security and overall factors of customer satisfaction.

FINDINGS

- Both men and women are more likely to shop online on a regular basis.
- Among the various age groups, online shopping is preferred by the majority of respondents (65.0%) over offline shopping.
- Customers with technical qualifications prefer online shopping the most (23.3 percent), while customers with SSLC qualifications prefer online shopping the least (7.5 percent).
- Consumers with a monthly income of more than Rs.40, 000 go online 22.5 percent of the time and offline 14.2 percent of the time.
- The majority of consumers who shop online are single, accounting for 35.8% of the total.
- The most important factor in consumer loyalty of online consumers is 'satisfied with the after-sale service,' with a score of 4.143, and the least important factor is 'price of the purchase,' with a score of 3.781.
- With a score of 3.994 for online shoppers and 3.594 for offline shoppers, the most significant element in customer loyalty for online shoppers is "will continue to purchase in it."
- The most significant factor in price sensitivity of online consumers is 'Shift to rivals if they sell services at more competitive rates,' with 3.863 for online shoppers and 3.657 for offline shoppers.
- The most relevant element in recommendation is 'recommend to other citizens,' which received 4.169 votes from online shoppers and 3.757 votes from offline shoppers.

When it comes to 'Customer Satisfaction,' there is a substantial difference between online and offline shopping when it comes to the factor 'Tangibility,' but no significant difference when it comes to 'Reliability,' 'Responsiveness, Reputation, and Protection.'

CONCLUSION

From the analysis, it is clear that Gender, age, educational income and marital status wise people are interested in both Online and offline shopping but few percentage of people changes their practice of buying in online because of the pandemic Covid-19. The offline (in-store) mode of shopping is still preferred by consumers when purchasing pricey goods. According to the reply, internet shopping offers a choice of goods, saves time, and gives customers a fresh shopping experience.

Even though customers still prefer the traditional method of purchasing, the survey's findings demonstrate the importance of businesses taking the online market seriously. They also show that consumers have a good attitude and behavior towards online shopping. In the country, online purchasing has increased since COVID-19, and respondents have a favorable perception of it.

REFERENCES

Aubrey, C., & Judge, D. (2012). Re-imagine retail: Why store innovation is key to a brand's growth in the 'new normal', digitally-connected and transparent world. *Journal of Brand Strategy*, *1*(1), 31–39.

Azam, A., Qiang, F., & Abdullah, M. I. (2012). *E-satisfaction in Business-to-Consumer Electronic Commerce.* Paper presented at the International Trade & Academic Research Conference (ITARC), London, UK.

Baker, M., & Hart, S. (2008). *The Marketing Book.* Buttersworth-Heinmann. doi:10.4324/9780080942544

Baldwin, C. (2013). High Street stores embrace digital to entice customers. *Computer Weekly*, 23–25.

Bartlett, M. S. (1954). A note on the multiplying factors for various chi square approximations. *Journal of the Royal Statistical Society. Series A (General)*, *16*, 296–298.

Bentler, P. M. (1989). EQS, Structural equations, Program manual (version 3.0). BMDP Statistical Software, Inc.

Lee, M. S., Hsiao, H. D., & Yang, M. F. (2011). The study of the relationships among experiential marketing, service quality, customer satisfaction and customer loyalty. *The International Journal of Organizational Innovation*, *3*(2), 352–378.

Levitt, K. (2013). *The multi-screen path to purchasing 2013.* https://www.comscore.com/Insights/Presentations_and_Whitepapers

McNealy, R. M. (1998). *Making Customer Satisfaction Happen* (1st ed.). Kluwer Academic.

Mehta, K., Sharma, R., & Khanna, V. (2023). Customer switching behaviour in Indian retail banking using logit regression. *Int. J. Bus. Excell.*, *29*(4), 518–545. doi:10.1504/IJBEX.2023.130255

Payne, M., Peltier, J. W., & Barger, V. A. (2017). Omni-channel marketing, integrated marketing communications and consumer engagement. *Journal of Research in Interactive Marketing*, *11*(2), 185–197. doi:10.1108/JRIM-08-2016-0091

Shalender, K., Singla, B., Sharma, S., & Oberemok, M. (2023). COVID-19 and Its Impact on Construction and Transport Construction Economy: An Integrated Framework. *Lecture Notes in Networks and Systems*, *510*, 747–753. doi:10.1007/978-3-031-11051-1_76

Singla, B. (2022). Impact of institute closures and learning practices on education in COVID-19 Pandemic: Omnichannel in education. *Proc. – International Conference Advancement in Data Science, E-Learning and Information Systems, ICADEIS 2022.* 10.1109/ICADEIS56544.2022.10037467

Weinberg, B. D., Parise, S., & Guinan, P. J. (2007). Multi-channel marketing: Mindset and program development. *Business Horizons*, *50*(5), 385–394. doi:10.1016/j.bushor.2007.04.002

Wolfinbarger, M., & Gilly, M. C. (2003). eTailQ: Dimensionalizing, measuring and predicting retail quality. *Journal of Retailing*, *79*(3), 183–198. doi:10.1016/S0022-4359(03)00034-4

Compilation of References

Abberger, K., & Nierhaus, W. (2008). How to define a recession*? CESifo Forum*, *9*(4), 74–76.

Accenture. (2017). *Banking on blockchain. A value analysis for investment banks*. https://www.accenture.com/_acnmedia/Accenture/Conversion-Assets/DotCom/Documents/Global/PDF/Consulting/Accenture-Banking-on-Blockchain.pdf

Adalid, R., Álvarez-Blázquez, Á., Assenmacher, K., Burlon, L., Dimou, M., López-Quiles, C., Fuentes, N. M., Meller, B., Muñoz, M., Radulova, P., & d'Acri, C. R. (2022). *Central bank digital currency and bank intermediation.* ECB Occasional Paper, No. 293.

Adams, R., Parry, G., Godsiff, P., & Ward, P. (2017). The future of money and further applications of the blockchain. *Strategic Change*, *26*(5), 417–422. doi:10.1002/jsc.2141

Africa C. E. O. Forum. (2021). *How Digitalization is strengthening Financial services post – COVID.* Retrieved from https://www.theafricaceoforum.com/en/ressources/how-digitization-is-strengthening-financial-services-post-covid/

Agarwal, A., Parihar, M., & Shah, T. (2020). *Feasibility of Adoption of Blockchain Technology in Banking and Financial Sector of India*. Innovations in Computational Intelligence and Computer Vision.

Agur, I., Ari, A., & Dell'Ariccia, G. (2022). Designing central bank digital currencies. *Journal of Monetary Economics*, *125*, 62–79. doi:10.1016/j.jmoneco.2021.05.002

Ahmed, S., & Broek, N. (2017). Food supply: Blockchain could boost food security. *Nature*, *550*(7674), 43. doi:10.1038/550043e PMID:28980633

Ahram, T., Sargolzaei, A., Sargolzaei, S., Daniels, J., & Amaba, B. (2017). Blockchain technology innovations. *Proc. IEEE Technol. Eng. Manage. Conf. (TEMSCON),* 137-141.

Akinkoye, E. Y., & Bankole, O. E. (2020). Effect of Emotional Biases on Investor's Decision Making in Nigeria. *International Journal of Business and Management Future*, *1*(1), 33–39. doi:10.46281/ijbmf.v4i1.548

Akomea-Frimpong, I., Adeabah, D., Ofosu, D., & Tenakwah, E. J. (2021). A review of studies on green finance of banks, research gaps and future directions. *Journal of Sustainable Finance & Investment*, 1–24.

Al Hsani, A. K., & Sherimon, V. (2021). An examination of the utilization of blockchain innovation in banking sector. *ARIV-International Journal of Technology*, 1-9.

Al Kemyani, M. K., Al Raisi, J., Al Kindi, A. R. T., Al Mughairi, I. Y., & Tiwari, C. K. (2022). Blockchain applications in accounting and finance: Qualitative Evidence from the banking sector. *Journal of Research in Business and Management*, *10*(4), 28–39.

Al, A., & Ahmed, A. (2021). Cryptography in financial markets: Potential channels for future financial stability. *Academy of Accounting and Financial Studies Journal*, *25*(4), 1528–2635.

Alalwan, A. A., Dwivedi, Y. K., & Rana, N. P. (2017). Factors influencing adoption of mobile banking by Jordanian bank customers: Extending UTAUT2 with trust. *International Journal of Information Management*, *37*(3), 99–110. doi:10.1016/j.ijinfomgt.2017.01.002

AlbeshrA.NobaneeH. (2020). Blockchain Applications in Banking Industry: A Mini-Review. SSRN. doi:10.2139/ssrn.3539152

Ali, O., Ally, M., & Dwivedi, Y. (2020). The state of play of blockchain technology in the financial services sector: A systematic literature review. *International Journal of Information Management*, *54*, 102199. doi:10.1016/j.ijinfomgt.2020.102199

Aljadani, A. (2022). DLCP2F: A DL-based cryptocurrency price prediction framework. *Discover Artificial Intelligence*, *2*(1), 1–19. doi:10.100744163-022-00036-2

Alkhowaiter, W. A. (2020). Digital payment and banking adoption research in Gulf countries: A systematic literature review. *International Journal of Information Management*, *53*, 102102. doi:10.1016/j.ijinfomgt.2020.102102

Allen, F., & Carletti, E. (2019). The Global Financial Crisis: Lessons and Opportunities. *Journal of Financial Stability*, *42*, 1–6. doi:10.1016/j.jfs.2019.05.005

Allen, F., Demirguc-Kunt, A., Klapper, L., & Martinez Peria, M. S. (2016). The foundations of financial inclusion: Understanding ownership and use of formal accounts. *Journal of Financial Intermediation*, *27*, 1–30. doi:10.1016/j.jfi.2015.12.003

Almeida, J., & Gonçalves, T. C. (2023). A systematic literature review of investor behavior in the cryptocurrency markets. *Journal of Behavioral and Experimental Finance*, *37*, 100785. Advance online publication. doi:10.1016/j.jbef.2022.100785

Alsabban, S., & Alarfaj, O. (2020). An Empirical Analysis of Behavioral Finance in the Saudi Stock Market: Evidence of Overconfidence Behavior. *International Journal of Economics and Financial Issues*, *10*(1), 73–86. doi:10.32479/ijefi.8920

Al-SheryaniK.NobaneeH. (2020). Green Finance: A Mini-Review. Available at SSRN 3538696.

Amidei, F. B., & Giordano, C. (2015). The redesign of the bank-industry-financial market ties in the US Glass-Steagall and the 1936 Italian Banking Acts. In *Financial innovation, regulation and crises in history* (pp. 65–84). Routledge. doi:10.4324/9781315653969-6

Ammer, M. A., & Aldhyani, T. H. (2022). Deep Learning Algorithm to Predict Cryptocurrency Fluctuation Prices: Increasing Investment Awareness. *Electronics (Basel)*, *11*(15), 2349. doi:10.3390/electronics11152349

Amponsah, A. A., Adekoya, A. F., & Weyori, B. A. (2022). A novel fraud detection and prevention method for healthcare claim processing using machine learning and blockchain technology. *Decision Analytics Journal*, *4*, 100122. doi:10.1016/j.dajour.2022.100122

Analytics Vidhya. (2022, October 20). *Complete Guide on Getting started with Blockchain Technology*. https://www.analyticsvidhya.com/blog/2022/10/complete-guide-on-getting-started-with-blockchain-technology/

Anamika, A., & Subramaniam, S. (2022). Do news headlines matter in the cryptocurrency market? *Applied Economics*, *54*(54), 6322–6338. doi:10.1080/00036846.2022.2061904

Anamika, Chakraborty, M., & Subramaniam, S. (2021). Does sentiment impact cryptocurrency*? Journal of Behavioral Finance*, 1–17. doi:10.1080/15427560.2021.1950723

Anandkumar, R. (2021). A Hybrid Deep Learning-based Chaos Dynamic System for CryptoCurrency Prediction. *Melange, 7*(2).

Andreas, M. (2015). *Masteing Bitcoin: Unlocking Digital Cryptocurrencies*. O'Reilly.

Anginer, D., Demirguc-Kunt, A., Huizinga, H., & Ma, K. (2018). Corporate governance of banks and financial stability. *Journal of Financial Economics*, *130*(2), 327–346. doi:10.1016/j.jfineco.2018.06.011

Ansari, Z. N., & Kant, R. (2017). Exploring the framework development status for sustainability in supply chain management: A systematic literature synthesis and future research directions. *Business Strategy and the Environment*, *26*(7), 873–892. Advance online publication. doi:10.1002/bse.1945

Ansari, Z., & Kant, R. (2016). A state-of-art literature review reflecting 15 years of focus on sustainable supply chain management. *Journal of Cleaner Production*, *142*, 2524–2543. Advance online publication. doi:10.1016/j.jclepro.2016.11.023

Antioco, M., Moenaert, R. K., & Lindgreen, A. (2008). Reducing ongoing product design decision-making bias. *Journal of Product Innovation Management*, *25*(6), 528–545. doi:10.1111/j.1540-5885.2008.00320.x

Antshares. (2016). *Antshares Digital Assets for Everyone*. https://www.antshares.org

Anvarovich, N. E. (2022a). Transformation of the Banking Sector in Uzbekistan in the Context of Covid-19 Coronavirus Pandemia. *Academic Journal of Digital Economics and Stability*, *13*, 76–85.

Arjun, R., & Suprabha, K. (2020). Innovation and Challenges of Blockchain in Banking: A Scientometric view. *International Journal of Interactive Multimedia and Artificial Intelligence.*

Arjun, R., Kuanr, A., & Suprabha, K. R. (2021). Developing banking intelligence in emerging markets: Systematic review and agenda. *International Journal of Information Management Data Insights*, *1*(2), 100026.

Arner, D. W., Barberis, J. N., & Buckley, R. P. (2015). The Evolution of Fintech: A New Post-Crisis Paradigm? SSRN *Electronic Journal*. https://doi.org/ doi:10.2139/SSRN.2676553

Arora, M., Sharma, R., & Mehta, K. (2022). Personality Effects on Financial Responses Caused by the Perceived Financial Threat during the COVID-19 Pandemic. *The Journal of Wealth Management*, *25*(3), 72–89. doi:10.3905/jwm.2022.1.183

Arun, T., & Kamath, R. (2015). Financial inclusion: Policies and practices. *IIMB Management Review*, *27*(4), 267–287. doi:10.1016/j.iimb.2015.09.004

Attaran, M. (2022). Blockchain technology in healthcare: Challenges and opportunities. *International Journal of Healthcare Management*, *15*(1), 70–83. doi:10.1080/20479700.2020.1843887

Atzei, N., Bartoletti, M., & Cimoli, T. (2017). A survey of attacks on Ethereum smart contracts. *Lecture Notes in Computer Science*, *7*(2), 109–123. doi:10.1007/978-3-662-54455-6_8

Atzori, L., Iera, A., & Morabito, G. (2010). The internet of things: A survey. *Computer Networks*, *54*(15), 2787–2805. doi:10.1016/j.comnet.2010.05.010

Aubrey, C., & Judge, D. (2012). Re-imagine retail: Why store innovation is key to a brand's growth in the 'new normal', digitally-connected and transparent world. *Journal of Brand Strategy*, *1*(1), 31–39.

Auer, R., Frost, J., Gambacorta, L., Monnet, C., Rice, T., & Shin, H. S. (2022). Central bank digital currencies: Motives, economic implications, and the research frontier. *Annual Review of Economics*, *14*(1), 697–721. doi:10.1146/annurev-economics-051420-020324

Awang Abu Bakar, N. S., Yahya, N., Khairuddin, I. E., Zainal Abidin, A. F., Mohamad Zain, J., Idris, N. B., & Engku Ali, E. R. A. (2023). The Central Bank Digital Currency in Malaysia: A Literature Review. In *International Conference on Business and Technology* (pp. 307-317). Springer. 10.1007/978-3-031-08090-6_18

Awotunde, J. B., Ogundokun, R. O., Misra, S., Adeniyi, E. A., & Sharma, M. M. (2021). Blockchain-based framework for secure transaction in mobile banking platform. In *International Conference on Hybrid Intelligent Systems* (pp. 525-534). Springer. 10.1007/978-3-030-73050-5_53

Azam, A., Qiang, F., & Abdullah, M. I. (2012). *E-satisfaction in Business-to-Consumer Electronic Commerce.* Paper presented at the International Trade & Academic Research Conference (ITARC), London, UK.

Azure. (2016). *Microsoft Azure: Blockchain as a Service.* https://azure.microsoft.com/enus/solutions/blockchain/

Baabdullah, A. M., Alalwan, A. A., Rana, N. P., Kizgin, H., & Patil, P. (2019). Consumer use of mobile banking (M-Banking) in Saudi Arabia: Towards an integrated model. *International Journal of Information Management*, *44*, 38–52. doi:10.1016/j.ijinfomgt.2018.09.002

Baabdullah, A. M., Alalwan, A. A., Rana, N. P., Patil, P., & Dwivedi, Y. K. (2019). An integrated model for m-banking adoption in Saudi Arabia. *International Journal of Bank Marketing*, *37*(2), 452–478. doi:10.1108/IJBM-07-2018-0183

Baabdullah, A. M., Rana, N. P., Alalwan, A. A., Islam, R., Patil, P., & Dwivedi, Y. K. (2019). Consumer adoption of self-service technologies in the context of the Jordanian banking industry: Examining the moderating role of channel types. *Information Systems Management*, *36*(4), 286–305. doi:10.1080/10580530.2019.1651107

Baba, C., Batog, C., Flores, E., Gracia, B., Karpowicz, I., Kopyrski, P., Roaf, J., Shagunina, A., Elkan, R. V., & Xu, X. C. (2020). *Fintech in Europe: Promises and Threats.* IMF Working Paper, WP/20/241.

Bačanin Džakula, N. 2021. Cryptocurrency Forecasting Using Optimized Support Vector Machine with Sine Cosine Metaheuristics Algorithm. In *Sinteza 2021-International Scientific Conference on Information Technology and Data Related Research* (pp. 315-321). Singidunum University.

Bachas, P., Gertler, P., Higgins, S., & Seira, E. (2018). Digital financial services go a long way: Transaction costs and financial inclusion. *AEA Papers and Proceedings. American Economic Association*, *108*, 444–448. doi:10.1257/pandp.20181013

Bagrecha, N., Polishwala, I., Mehrotra, P., Sharma, R., & Thakare, B. S. (2020). Decentralized Blockchain Technology: Application in Banking Sector. *International Conference for Emerging Technology.*

Bai, C., Dallasega, P., Orzes, G., & Sarkis, J. (2020). Industry 4.0 technologies assessment: A sustainability perspective. *International Journal of Production Economics*, *229*, 107776. doi:10.1016/j.ijpe.2020.107776

Baiod, W., Light, J., & Mahanti, A. (2021). Blockchain technology and its applications across multiple domains: A survey. *Journal of International Technology and Information Management*, *29*(4), 78–119. doi:10.58729/1941-6679.1482

Baker, M., & Hart, S. (2008). *The Marketing Book.* Buttersworth-Heinmann. doi:10.4324/9780080942544

BalasubramanianP.ChandraS. V. R.MurlidharanA.PrasannaT. L. (2021). Fintech For The Poor: Do Technological Failures Deter Financial Inclusion? https://ssrn.com/abstract=3840021 doi:10.2139/ssrn.3840021

Balasubramanian, S., Shukla, V., Sethi, J. S., Islam, N., & Saloum, R. (2021). A readiness assessment framework for Blockchain adoption: A healthcare case study. *Technological Forecasting and Social Change*, *165*, 120536. doi:10.1016/j.techfore.2020.120536

Baldwin, C. (2013). High Street stores embrace digital to entice customers. *Computer Weekly*, 23–25.

Baltensperger, E. (1980). Alternative approaches to the theory of the banking firm. *Journal of Monetary Economics*, *6*(1), 1–37. doi:10.1016/0304-3932(80)90016-1

Banca D'Italia. (n.d.). *TARGET2*. Retrieved from https://www.bancaditalia.it/compiti/sistemi-pagamenti/target2/index.html?com.dotmarketing.htmlpage.language=1

Bank for International Settlements. (2016). *Committee on Payment and Market Infrastructures. Fast payments–Enhancing the speed and availability of retail payments*. Bank for International Settlements.

Barbesino, P., Camerani, R., & Gaudino, A. (2005). Digital finance in Europe: Competitive dynamics and online behavior. *Journal of Financial Services Marketing*, *9*(4), 329–343. doi:10.1057/palgrave.fsm.4770164

Barbu, C. M., Florea, D. L., Dabija, D. C., & Barbu, M. C. R. (2021). Customer experience in fintech. *Journal of Theoretical and Applied Electronic Commerce Research*, *16*(5), 1415–1433. doi:10.3390/jtaer16050080

Barcelo, J. (2014). *User Privacy in the Public Bitcoin Blockchain*. Academic Press.

Barde, S. (2022). Blockchain and Cryptocurrencies. *Emerging Computing Paradigms*, 235-246. doi:10.1002/9781119813439.ch13

Barontini, C., & Holden, H. (2019). *Proceeding with caution-a survey on central bank digital currency. Proceeding with Caution-A Survey on Central Bank Digital Currency.* BIS Paper, No. 101.

Bartlett, M. S. (1954). A note on the multiplying factors for various chi square approximations. *Journal of the Royal Statistical Society. Series A (General)*, *16*, 296–298.

Bech, M. L., & Hancock, D. (2020). *The evolution of payment systems: an overview*. BIS Quarterly Review.

Bech, M. L., & Hancock, D. (2020). The evolution of payment systems: Lessons learned from the crisis and beyond. *Journal of Financial Market Infrastructures*, *8*(3), 1–26.

Bengio, Y., Courville, A., & Vincent, P. (2013). Representation learning: A review and new perspectives. *IEEE Transactions on Pattern Analysis and Machine Intelligence*, *35*(8), 1798–1828. doi:10.1109/TPAMI.2013.50 PMID:23787338

Bengio, Y., Lamblin, P., Popovici, D., & Larochelle, H. (2007). Greedy layer-wise training of deep networks. *Advances in Neural Information Processing Systems*, *19*, 153.

Bentler, P. M. (1989). EQS, Structural equations, Program manual (version 3.0). BMDP Statistical Software, Inc.

Berg, G., Guadamillas, M., Natarajan, H., & Sarkar, A. (2020). *Fintech in Europe and Central Asia: Maximizing Benefits and Managing Risks. Fintech Note, no. 4*. World Bank. doi:10.1596/33591

Bernards, N., & Campbell-Verduyn, M. (2019). Understanding technological change in global finance through infrastructures: Introduction to Review of International Political Economy Special Issue 'The Changing Technological Infrastructures of Global Finance'. *Review of International Political Economy*, *26*(5), 773–789. doi:10.1080/09692290.2019.1625420

Bernstein, D. J., & Lange, T. (2016). *SafeCurves: Choosing safe curves for elliptic-curve cryptography*. https://safecurves.cr.yp.to/

Bester, H. (1985). Screening vs. rationing in credit markets with imperfect information. *The American Economic Review*, *75*(4), 850–855.

Bhandarkar, V. V., Bhandarkar, A. A., & Shiva, A. (2019). Digital stocks using Blockchain technology the possible future of stocks? *International Journal of Management*, *10*(3), 44–49. doi:10.34218/IJM.10.3.2019/005

Bhargava, D., Sandeep, C., Gopal, M., & Sahil, M. (2023). A Review of Blockchain Technology in Different Sectors: Challenges and Solutions. *4th International Conference on Signal Processing and Communication.* 10.1109/ICSPC57692.2023.10125283

Bhatnagar, S., Sharma, D., & Agrawal, S. (2021). Can Industry 4.0 revolutionize the Wave of green finance adoption: A bibliometric analysis. In *Recent Advances in Smart Manufacturing and Materials: Select Proceedings of ICEM 2020* (pp. 515-525). Springer Singapore.

Bhowmik, D. (2022). Monetary policy implications of central bank digital currency with special reference to india. *Asia-Pacific Journal of Management and Technology*, *2*(3), 1–8.

Bhowmik, D. (2022). Monetary policy implications of central bank digital currency with special reference to India. *Asia-Pacific Journal of Management and Technology*, *2*(3), 1–8.

Billah, S. (2015). *One Weird Trick to Stop Selfish Miners: Fresh Bitcoins, A Solution for the Honest.* Miner.

Bindseil, U. (2019). Central bank digital currency: Financial system implications and control. *International Journal of Political Economy*, *48*(4), 303–335. doi:10.1080/08911916.2019.1693160

Biswas, B., & Gupta, R. (2019). Analysis of barriers to implement blockchain in industry and service sectors. *Computers & Industrial Engineering*, *136*, 225–241. doi:10.1016/j.cie.2019.07.005

Bitshares. (n.d.) *Bitshares – Your Share in the Decentralized Exchange.* https://bitshares.org/

Boel, M. (2019). Payment systems. In The Oxford Handbook of Banking and Financial History. OUP.

Bolt, W., Lubbersen, V., & Wierts, P. (2022). Getting the balance right: Crypto, stablecoin and central bank digital currency. *Journal of Payments Strategy & Systems*, *16*(1), 39–50.

Bonilla, C. A., Merigó, J. M., & Torres-Abad, C. (2015). Economics in Latin America: A bibliometric analysis. *Scientometrics*, *105*(2), 1239–1252. doi:10.100711192-015-1747-7

Bonneau, J., Clark, J., & Goldfeder, S. (2015). On bitcoin as a public randomness source. IACR Cryptol. ePrint Archive, p. 1015.

Bonneau, J., Narayanan, A., Miller, A., Clark, J., Kroll, J. A., & Felten, E. W. (2014). Mixcoin: Anonymity for bitcoin with accountable mixes. *Proceedings of International Conference on Financial Cryptography and Data Security*, 486–504. 10.1007/978-3-662-45472-5_31

Boot, A., Hoffmann, P., Laeven, L., & Ratnov, L. (2021). Fintech: What's old, what's new? *Journal of Financial Stability*, 1–13.

Bordo, M. D. (2021). Central Bank Digital Currency in Historical Perspective: Another Crossroad in Monetary History (No. w29171). National Bureau of Economic Research.

Bordo, M. D., & Levin, A. T. (2017). *Central bank digital currency and the future of monetary policy (No. w23711).* National Bureau of Economic Research. doi:10.3386/w23711

Boukhatem, J., Ftiti, Z., & Sahut, J.-M. (2021). Bond market and macroeconomic stability in East Asia: A nonlinear causality analysis. *Annals of Operations Research*, *297*(1-2), 53–76. Advance online publication. doi:10.100710479-020-03519-6

Boyack, K. W., & Klavans, R. (2010). Co-Citation Analysis, Bibliographic Coupling, and Direct Citation: Which Citation Approach Represents the Research Front Most Accurately? *Journal of the American Society for Information Science and Technology*, *12*(61), 2389–2404. doi:10.1002/asi.21419

BranzoliN.SupinoI. (2020). *FinTech Credit: a critical review of the empirical literature.* Bank of Italy, Financial Stability Directorate, Directorate General for Economics, Statistics and Research, Occasional Paper. https://ssrn.com/abstract=3612726

Braun, V., & Clarke, V. (2006). Using thematic analysis in psychology. *Qualitative Research in Psychology*, *3*(2), 77–101. doi:10.1191/1478088706qp063oa

Bruce, J. (2014). *The Mini-Blockchain Scheme*. http://cryptonite.info/files/mbc-scheme-rev3.pdfburstcoin

Buitenhek, M. (2016). Understanding and Applying Blockchain Technology in Banking: Evolution or Revolution? *Journal of Digital Banking*, *1*(2), 111–119.

Burggraf, T., Huynh, T. L. D., Rudolf, M., & Wang, M. (2020). Do FEARS drive Bitcoin? *Review of Behavioral Finance*, *13*(3), 229–258. doi:10.1108/RBF-11-2019-0161

Buterin, V. (2014) *A Next-Generation Smart Contract and Decentralized Application Platform*. White Paper.

Buterin, V. (2015). *On Public and Private Blockchains*. https://blog.ethereum.org/2015/08/07/onpublic-and-private-blockchains/

Cai, R., & Guo, J. (2021). Finance for the environment: A scientometrics analysis of green finance. *Mathematics*, *9*(13), 1537. doi:10.3390/math9131537

Cai, W. C. (2018). Disruptions of Financial Intermediation by Fin Tech: A Review on Crowdfunding and Blockchain. *Accounting and Finance*, *58*(4), 965–992. doi:10.1111/acfi.12405

Cancino, C. A., Merigó, J. M., Torres, J. P., & Diaz, D. (2018). A bibliometric analysis of venture capital research. *Journal of Economics, Finance and Administrative Science*, *23*(45), 182–195. doi:10.1108/JEFAS-01-2018-0016

Capobianco-Uriarte, M. de las M., Casado-Belmonte, M. del P., Marín-Carrillo, G. M., & Terán-Yépez, E. (2019). A Bibliometric Analysis of International Competitiveness (1983–2017). *Sustainability (Basel)*, *11*(7), 1877. doi:10.3390u11071877

Carboni, D. (2015) *Feedback based Reputation on Top of the Bitcoin Blockchain*. arXiv *preprintarXiv*:1502.01504.

Carstens, A. (2019). *The future of money and the payment system: what role for central banks?* Bank for International Settlements.

Castillo-Vergara, M., Alvarez-Marin, A., & Placencio-Hidalgo, D. (2018). A bibliometric analysis of creativity in the field of business economics. *Journal of Business Research*, *85*, 1–9. doi:10.1016/j.jbusres.2017.12.011

Catalini, C., & Gans, J. S. (2020). Some simple economics of the blockchain. *Communications of the ACM*, *63*(7), 80–90. doi:10.1145/3359552

CCAF. (2022). *FinTech regulation in Asia Pacific, Cambridge Centre for Alternative Finance at the University of Cambridge*. Cambridge Judge Business School. https://www.jbs.cam.ac.uk/insight/2022/fintech-regulation-in-apac/

Cetorelli, N., & Goldberg, L. (2012). Banking Globalization and Monetary Transmission. *The Journal of Finance*, *67*(5), 1811–1843. doi:10.1111/j.1540-6261.2012.01773.x

Chakraborty, S., & Sural, S. (2018). Smart Contract Architecture for IoT Applications. In *Proceedings of the 2nd International Conference on Inventive Communication and Computational Technologies* (pp. 295-299). ACM. https://doi.org/10.1145/3157967.3157980

Chandra, P. (2016). *Behavioral Finance*. McGraw Hill Education.

Chang, S. E., & Chen, Y. (2020). When Blockchain meets supply chain: A systematic literature review on current development and potential applications. *IEEE Access : Practical Innovations, Open Solutions*, *8*, 62478–62494. doi:10.1109/ACCESS.2020.2983601

Chang, V., Baudier, P., Zhang, H., Xu, Q., Zhang, J., & Arami, M. (2020). How Blockchain can impact financial services–The overview, challenges and recommendations from expert interviewees. *Technological Forecasting and Social Change*, *158*, 120166. doi:10.1016/j.techfore.2020.120166 PMID:32834134

Chang, Y., Iakovou, E., & Shi, W. (2020). Blockchain in global supply chains and cross border trade: A critical synthesis of the state-of-the-art, challenges and opportunities. *International Journal of Production Research*, *58*(7), 2082–2099. doi:10.1080/00207543.2019.1651946

Chan, H. F., Dulleck, U., Fooken, J., Moy, N., & Torgler, B. (2022). Cash and the hidden economy: Experimental evidence on fighting tax evasion in small business transactions. *Journal of Business Ethics*, 1–26.

Chapron, G. (2017). The environment needs cryptogovernance. *Nature*, *545*(7655), 403–405. doi:10.1038/545403a PMID:28541332

Chaturvedula, C., Bang, N. P., Rastogi, N., & Kumar, S. (2015, June). Price manipulation front running and bulk trades: Evidence from India. *Emerging Markets Review*, *23*, 26–45. doi:10.1016/j.ememar.2015.04.001

Chaum, D., Grothoff, C., & Moser, T. (2021). *How to issue a central bank digital currency.* arXiv preprint arXiv:2103.00254.

Chen, E., & Zhang, H. (2017). P2P lending survey: Platforms, recent advances and prospects. *ACM Transactions on Intelligent Systems and Technology, 8*(6), 72:1–72:28. doi:10.1145/3078848

Chen, T., Li, X., Luo, X., & Zhang, X. (2017), Under-optimized smart contracts devour your money. *Proceedings of 24th International Conference on Software Analysis, Evolution and Reengineering, SANER,* 442–446. 10.1109/SANER.2017.7884650

Chen, Y.-H., Chen, S.-H., & Lin, I.-C. (2018). Blockchain based smart contract for bidding system. *Proc. IEEE Int. Conf. Appl. Syst. Invention (ICASI),* 208-211. 10.1109/ICASI.2018.8394569

Chen, H., & Siklos, P. L. (2022). Central bank digital currency: A review and some macro-financial implications. *Journal of Financial Stability*, *60*, 100985. doi:10.1016/j.jfs.2022.100985

Chen, L., Xie, Y., Li, P., & Li, Q. (2019). The signal of default risk from the description-text based on the empirical research of P2P lending. *Chinese Journal of Management Science*, *27*(4), 37–47.

Chen, M. A., Wu, Q., & Yang, B. (2019). How valuable is FinTech innovation? *Review of Financial Studies*, *32*(5), 2062–2106. doi:10.1093/rfs/hhy130

Chen, W., Xu, Z., Shi, S., Zhao, Y., & Zhao, J. (2018, December). A survey of blockchain applications in different domains. In *Proceedings of the 2018 International Conference on Blockchain Technology and Application* (pp. 17-21). 10.1145/3301403.3301407

Chen, X. H., Jin, F. J., Zhang, Q., & Yang, L. (2016). Are investors rational or perceptual in P2P lending? *Information Systems and e-Business Management*, *14*(4), 921–944. doi:10.100710257-016-0305-z

Chen, Y., & Wang, Q. (2019). A smart contract-based incentive mechanism for crowd sensing. *IEEE Transactions on Mobile Computing*, *18*(11), 2548–2561. doi:10.1109/TMC.2019.2909559

Chepurnoy, A., Larangeira, M., & Ojiganov, A. (2016) *A Prunable Blockchain Consensus Protocol based on Non-Interactive Proofs of Past States Retrievability*. arXiv preprint arXiv:1603.07926.

Chesbrough, H. W. (2003). *Open innovation: The new imperative for creating and profiting from technology*. Harvard Business School Press.

Chesbrough, H. W. (2010). Business model innovation: Opportunities and barriers. *Long Range Planning*, *43*(2/3), 354–363. doi:10.1016/j.lrp.2009.07.010

Cho, D. H., Moon, S. H., & Kim, Y. H. (2021). Genetic feature selection applied to KOSPI and cryptocurrency price prediction. *Mathematics*, *9*(20), 2574. doi:10.3390/math9202574

Chodorow-Reich, G., Gopinath, G., Mishra, P., & Narayanan, A. (2020). Cash and the economy: Evidence from India's demonetization. *The Quarterly Journal of Economics*, *135*(1), 57–103. doi:10.1093/qje/qjz027

Chong, W. K., & Ng, K. K. (2019). Time series forecasting for stock prices using deep learning. *Journal of Computational Science*, *30*, 110–119.

Chorzempa, M. (2021). China, the United States, and central bank digital currencies: How important is it to be first? *China Economic Journal*, *14*(1), 102–115. doi:10.1080/17538963.2020.1870278

Chowdhury, M., Suchana, K., Alam, S., & Khan, M. (2021). Blockchain Application in Banking System. *Journal of Software Engineering and Applications*, *14*(7), 298–311. doi:10.4236/jsea.2021.147018

Christiaens, T. (2016). *Digital subjectivation and financial markets: Criticizing Social Studies of Finance with Lazzarato.* https://doi.org/ doi:10.1177/2053951716662897

Christidis, K., & Devetsikiotis, M. (2016). Blockchains and smart contracts for the internet of things. *IEEE Access : Practical Innovations, Open Solutions*, *4*, 2292–2303. doi:10.1109/ACCESS.2016.2566339

Chuen, L. K. D. (Ed.). (2015) .Handbook of Digital Currency. Elsevier.

Citigroup. (2016). Digital Disruption: How Fintech is Forcing Banking to a Tipping Point. *Citi GPS: Global Perspectives & Solutions.* https://www.citivelocity.com/citigps/digital-disruption/

Cobo, M. J., López-Herrera, A. G., Herrera-Viedma, E., & Herrera, F. (2011). Science mapping software tools: Review, analysis, and cooperative study among tools. *Journal of the American Society for Information Science and Technology*, *62*(7), 1382–1402. doi:10.1002/asi.21525

Cocco, L., Pinna, A., & Marchesi, M. (2017). Banking on Blockchain: Costs savings thanks to the Blockchain technology. *Future Internet*, *9*(3), 25. doi:10.3390/fi9030025

Coindesk. (2016) *State of Blockchain q1 2016: Blockchain Funding Overtakes Bitcoin.* https://www.coindesk.com/state-of-blockchain-q1-2016/

Collin, R. (2013). *The Efficient Hypothesists: Bacheier, Samuelson, Fama, Ross, Tobin, and Shiller.* Palgave Macmillan.

Cong, L. W., & He, Z. (2019). Blockchain disruption and smart contracts. *Review of Financial Studies*, *32*(5), 1754–1797. doi:10.1093/rfs/hhz007

Corbet, S., Larkin, C., & Lucey, B. (2020). The contagion effects of the COVID-19 pandemic: Evidence from gold and cryptocurrencies. *Finance Research Letters*, *35*, 101554. Advance online publication. doi:10.1016/j.frl.2020.101554

Cortina, J. J., & Schmukler, S. L. (2018, April). The Fintech Revolution: A Threat to Global Banking? Research & Policy Briefs. *World Bank Group*, (14), 1–4.

Coulter, K. A. (2022). *'Stop Creating Private Money!': Should the Bank of England Introduce a Central Bank Digital Currency to Compete with Cryptocurrency? A Review of the UK Bank of England's Proposed Retail CBDC.* A Review of the UK Bank of England's Proposed Retail CBDC.

Cova, P., Notarpietro, A., Pagano, P., & Pisani, M. (2022). *Monetary policy in the open economy with digital currencies.* Bank of Italy Temi di Discussione (Working Paper) No, 1366.

Cristofaro, M. (2019). The role of affect in management decisions: A systematic review. *European Management Journal, 1*(1), 6–17. doi:10.1016/j.emj.2018.12.002

Crosby, M., Pattanayak, P., Verma, S., & Kalyanaraman, V. (2016). Blockchain Technology: Beyond Bitcoin. *Applied Innovation, 2*(6-10), 71–81. doi:10.1016/j.apin.2016.01.001

Croux, C., Jagtiani, J., Korivi, T., & Vulanovic, M. (2020). Important factors determining Fintech loan default: Evidence from a lending club consumer platform. *Journal of Economic Behavior & Organization, 173*, 270–296. doi:10.1016/j.jebo.2020.03.016

Cryer, J. D., & Chan, K. S. (2008). *Time series analysis: with applications in R.* Springer Science & Business Media.

Cucari, N., Lagasio, V., Lia, G., & Torriero, C. (2022). The impact of blockchain in banking processes: The Interbank Spunta case study. *Technology Analysis and Strategic Management, 34*(2), 138–150. doi:10.1080/09537325.2021.1891217

Daluwathumullagamage, D. J., & Sims, A. (2021). Fantastic beasts: Blockchain based banking. *Journal of Risk and Financial Management, 14*(4), 1-43.

Danial, K. (2022). Cryptocurrency Investing. John Wiley and Sons Inc. doi:10.1017/9781316676349.005

Daniel, R. L. B. (2016). *SECG SEC 1: Elliptic Curve Cryptography* (Version 2.0). https://www.secg.org/sec1-v2.pdf

Dashkevich, N., Counsell, S., & Destefanis, G. (2020). Blockchain application for central banks: A systematic mapping study. *IEEE Access : Practical Innovations, Open Solutions, 8*, 139918–139952. doi:10.1109/ACCESS.2020.3012295

Daulton, S., Eriksson, D., Balandat, M., & Bakshy, E. (2022, August). Multi-objective bayesian optimization over high-dimensional search spaces. In *Uncertainty in Artificial Intelligence* (pp. 507–517). PMLR.

Davoodalhosseini, S. M. (2022). Central bank digital currency and monetary policy. *Journal of Economic Dynamics & Control, 142*, 104150. doi:10.1016/j.jedc.2021.104150

Decker, C., Seidel, J., & Wattenhofer, R. (2016). Bitcoin meets strong consistency. In *Proceedings of the 17th International Conference on Distributed Computing and Networking (ICDCN).* ACM.

Delmolino, K., Arnett, M., Kosba, A., Miller, A., & Shi, E. (2016). Step by step towards creating a safe smart contract: Lessons and insights from a cryptocurrency lab. *Proceedings of the 22nd ACM SIGSAC Conference on Computer and Communications Security,* 79-91. 10.1007/978-3-662-53357-4_6

Deloitte Tax & Consulting. (2022). *Digital Finance: European Parliament adopts MiCA Regulation, paving the way for innovation-friendly crypto regulation.* Retrieved from:https://www2.deloitte.com/content/dam/Deloitte/lu/Documents/financial-services/lu-rna-digital-finance-mica-regulation.pdf

Demirgüç-Kunt, A., & Klapper, L. (2013). Measuring financial inclusion: Explaining variation in the use of financial services across and within countries. *Brookings Papers on Economic Activity*, 279-321. doi:10.1353/eca.2013.0002

Deniz, A., & Teker, D. (2020). Determinants of Cryptocurrency Market: An Analysis for Bitcoin, Ethereum and Ripple. *International Journal of Business and Social Science, 11*(11). Advance online publication. doi:10.30845/ijbss.v11n11p5

Desalegn, G., & Tangl, A. (2022). Enhancing green finance for inclusive green growth: A systematic approach. *Sustainability (Basel), 14*(12), 7416. doi:10.3390u14127416

Dettling, W. (2018). How to teach blockchain in a business school. *Business Information Systems and Technology 4.0: New Trends in the Age of Digital Change*, 213-225.

Devine, P. (2015). Blockchain learning: can crypto-currency methods be appropriated to enhance online learning? *ALT Online Winter Conference.*

Dewatripont, M. (2014). European banking: Bailout, bail-in and state aid control. *International Journal of Industrial Organization*, *34*, 37–43. doi:10.1016/j.ijindorg.2014.03.003

Dhanda, N. (2022). Cryptocurrency and Blockchain: The Future of a Global Banking System. In Regulatory Aspects of Artificial Intelligence on Blockchain (pp. 181-204). IGI Global.

Dinh, H. T. L., & Dinh, T. C. (2022, August). Verification of the Impact of Central Bank Digital Currency (CBDC) Issuance on Net Interest Income of Vietnamese Commercial Banks. In *2022 IEEE/ACIS 7th International Conference on Big Data, Cloud Computing, and Data Science (BCD)* (pp. 301-305). IEEE.

Dixon, C., Mahajan, R., Agarwal, S., Brush, A., Saroiu, B. L. S., & Bahl, P. (2012). *An Operating System for the Home, NSDI.* USENIX.

Dominguez Anguiano, T., & Parte, L. (2023). The state of art, opportunities and challenges of blockchain in the insurance industry: a systematic literature review. *Management Review Quarterly*, 1-22.

Dominguez Anguiano, T., & Parte, L. (2023). *The state of art, opportunities and challenges of blockchain in the insurance industry: A systematic literature review.* Manag Rev Q. doi:10.100711301-023-00328-6

Dora, S., & Srinivasan, V. (n.d.). Investigating the use of Blockchain technology in facilitating international fund transfer with respect to banking sector of Sultanate of Oman. *Journal of Student Research.*

Durach, C. F., Kembro, J. H., & Wieland, A. (2021). How to advance theory through literature reviews in logistics and supply chain management. *International Journal of Physical Distribution & Logistics Management*, *51*(10), 1090–1107. doi:10.1108/IJPDLM-11-2020-0381

Dwivedi, Y. K., Hughes, L., Ismagilova, E., Aarts, G., Coombs, C., Crick, T., Duan, Y., Dwivedi, R., Edwards, J., Eirug, A., Galanos, V., Ilavarasan, P. V., Janssen, M., Jones, P., Kar, A. K., Kizgin, H., Kronemann, B., Lal, B., Lucini, B., ... Williams, M. D. (2021). Artificial Intelligence (AI): Multidisciplinary perspectives on emerging challenges, opportunities, and agenda for research, practice and policy. *International Journal of Information Management*, *57*, 101994. doi:10.1016/j.ijinfomgt.2019.08.002

Elangovan, D., Long, C. S., Bakrin, F. S., Tan, C. S., Goh, K. W., Yeoh, S. F., Loy, M. J., Hussain, Z., Lee, K. S., Idris, A. C., & Ming, L. C. (2022). The use of blockchain technology in the health care sector: Systematic review. *JMIR Medical Informatics*, *10*(1), e17278. doi:10.2196/17278 PMID:35049516

Engert, W., & Fung, B. S. C. (2017). *Central bank digital currency: Motivations and implications* (No. 2017-16). Bank of Canada Staff Discussion Paper.

Erol, S., Jäger, A., Hold, P., Ott, K., & Sihn, W. (2016). Tangible Industry 4.0: A scenario-based approach to learning for the future of production. *Procedia CIRP*, *54*, 13–18. doi:10.1016/j.procir.2016.03.162

Erro-Garcés, A. (2019). Industry 4.0: Defining the research agenda. *Benchmarking*, *28*(5), 1858–1882. doi:10.1108/BIJ-12-2018-0444

Ertz, M., & Boily, É. (2019). The rise of the digital economy: Thoughts on blockchain technology and cryptocurrencies for the collaborative economy. *International Journal of Innovation Studies*, *3*(4), 84–93. doi:10.1016/j.ijis.2019.12.002

Ethereum. (n.d.). *Consortium Chain Development*. https://github.com/ethereum/wiki/wiki/Consortium-Chain-Development

European Central Bank. (2012). *Virtual Currency Schemes*. Retrieved on February 11, 2023, from https://www.ecb.europa.eu/pub/pdf/other/virtualcurrencyschemes201210en.pdf

European Central Bank. (2019). *TARGET2 - Frequently Asked Questions*. Retrieved from https://www.ecb.europa.eu/paym/target/target2/html/index.en.html

Eyal, I., & Sirer, E. G. (2014). Majority is not enough: Bitcoin mining is vulnerable. *Proceedings of International Conference on Financial Cryptography and Data Security*, 436–454. 10.1007/978-3-662-45472-5_28

Falcone, P. M. (2020). Environmental regulation and green investments: The role of green finance. *International Journal of Green Economics*, *14*(2), 159–173. doi:10.1504/IJGE.2020.109735

Faloon, M., & Scherer, B. (2017). Individualization of Robo-Advice. *The Journal of Wealth Management*, *20*(1), 30–36. doi:10.3905/jwm.2017.20.1.030

Fama, E. F. (1970). Efficient capital markets: A review of theory and empirical work. *The Journal of Finance, 25*(2), 383-417. doi:.1970.tb00518.x doi:10.1111/j.1540-6261

Fanning, K., & Centers, D. P. (2016). Blockchain and its coming impact on financial services. *Journal of Corporate Accounting & Finance*, *27*(5), 53–57. doi:10.1002/jcaf.22179

Farrell, L., Fry, T. R., & Risse, L. (2016). The significance of financial self-efficacy in explaining women's personal finance behaviour. *Journal of Economic Psychology*, *54*, 85–99. doi:10.1016/j.joep.2015.07.001

Farza, K., Ftiti, Z., Hlioui, Z., Louhichi, W., & Omri, A. (2021). Does it pay to go green? The environmental innovation effect on corporate financial performance. *Journal of Environmental Management*, *300*, 113695. doi:10.1016/j.jenvman.2021.113695 PMID:34649325

Farza, K., Ftiti, Z., Hlioui, Z., Louhichi, W., & Omri, A. (2022). The Effect of Corporate Board Characteristics on Environmental Innovation. *Environmental Modeling and Assessment*, *27*(6), 1021–1042. doi:10.100710666-022-09836-3

Fegatelli, P. (2022). A central bank digital currency in a heterogeneous monetary union: Managing the effects on the bank lending channel. *Journal of Macroeconomics*, *71*, 103392. doi:10.1016/j.jmacro.2021.103392

Fernández-Villaverde, J., Sanches, D., Schilling, L., & Uhlig, H. (2020). *Central bank digital currency: central banking for all?* NBER Working Paper Series, No 26753.

Ferrari, A. (2016). Mobile payments: The Kenyan experience. *Journal of Payments Strategy & Systems*, *10*(1), 59–71.

Feurer, M., Klein, A., Eggensperger, K., Springenberg, J. T., Blum, M., & Hutter, F. (2015). Efficient and robust automated machine learning. *Advances in Neural Information Processing Systems*, 2962–2970.

Feyen, E., Frost, J., Gambacorta, L., Natarajan, H., & Saal, M. (2021). *Fintech and the digital transformation of financial services: implications for market structure and public policy*. BIS Papers.

Flyvbjerg, B. (2006). Five misunderstandings about case-study research. *Qualitative Inquiry*, *12*(2), 219–245. doi:10.1177/1077800405284363

Fonchamnyo, D. C. (2013). Customers' perception of e-banking adoption in Cameroon: An empirical assessment of an extended TAM. *International Journal of Economics and Finance*, *5*(1), 166–176.

Foroglou, G., & Tsilidou, A-L. (2015). *Further Applications of the Blockchain*. Academic Press.

Fosso Wamba, S., Kala Kamdjoug, J. R., Bawack, R., & Keogh, G. (2019). Bitcoin, Blockchain, and FinTech: A systematic review and case studies in the supply chain. *Production Planning and Control*, *31*(2-3), 1–28. doi:10.1080/09537287.2019.1631460

Foster, S., & Gupta, A. (2020). Fintech and digital payments: A global review of trends and challenges. *International Journal of Advanced Research in Engineering and Technology*, *11*(4), 1–18.

Frank, A. G., Dalenogare, L. S., & Ayala, N. F. (2019). Industry 4.0 technologies: Implementation patterns in manufacturing companies. *International Journal of Production Economics*, *210*, 15–26. doi:10.1016/j.ijpe.2019.01.004

Frankó, A., Oláh, B., Sass, Z., Hegedüs, C., & Varga, P. (2022, May). Towards CBDC-supported Smart Contracts for Industrial Stakeholders. In *2022 IEEE 5th International Conference on Industrial Cyber-Physical Systems (ICPS)* (pp. 1-6). IEEE. 10.1109/ICPS51978.2022.9816857

Fratini Passi, L. (2022). Open banking and digital transformation in Italy: The current situation and the challenges ahead. *Journal of Payments Strategy & Systems*, *16*(4), 358–368.

Fu, J., & Mishra, M. (2022). Fintech in the time of COVID– 19: Technological adoption during crises. *Journal of Financial Intermediation*, *50*, 100945. doi:10.1016/j.jfi.2021.100945

Fuster, A., Goldsmith-Pinkham, P., Ramadorai, T., & Walther, A. (2018). Predictably unequal? The effects of machine learning on credit markets. *SSRN Working Paper*, 3072038.

Galiautdinov R., (2020a). Brain machine interface: the accurate interpretation of neurotransmitters' signals targeting the muscles. *International Journal of Applied Research in Bioinformatics*. Doi:10.4018/IJARB.20200102

Galiautdinov, R., (2020b). MicroService Oriented Architecture in distributed Artificial Intelligence systems and the language of AI in bio-neural systems. *International Journal of Applied Research in Bioinformatics*. doi:10.4018/IJARB.2020070103

Galiautdinov, R. (2023). Nonlinear Filtering Methods in Conditions of Uncertainty. In E. Oyekanlu (Ed.), *Applied AI and Multimedia Technologies for Smart Manufacturing and CPS Applications*. doi:10.4018/978-1-7998-7852-0.ch010

Galiautdinov, R., & Mkrttchian, V. (2019a). Math model of neuron and nervous system research, based on AI constructor creating virtual neural circuits: Theoretical and Methodological Aspects. In V. Mkrttchian, E. Aleshina, & L. Gamidullaeva (Eds.), *Avatar-Based Control, Estimation, Communications, and Development of Neuron Multi-Functional Technology Platforms* (pp. 320–344). IGI Global. doi:10.4018/978-1-7998-1581-5.ch015

Galiautdinov, R., & Mkrttchian, V. (2019b). Brain machine interface – for Avatar Control & Estimation in Educational purposes Based on Neural AI plugs: Theoretical and Methodological Aspects. In V. Mkrttchian, E. Aleshina, & L. Gamidullaeva (Eds.), *Avatar-Based Control, Estimation, Communications, and Development of Neuron Multi-Functional Technology Platforms* (pp. 345–360). IGI Global. doi:10.4018/978-1-7998-1581-5.ch016

Gan, Q., Lau, R. Y. K., & Hong, J. (2021). A critical review of blockchain applications to banking and finance: A qualitative thematic analysis approach. *Technology Analysis and Strategic Management*, 1–17. doi:10.1080/09537325.2021.1979509

Gao, M., Yen, J., & Liu, M. (2021). Determinants of defaults on P2P lending platforms in China. *International Review of Economics & Finance*, *72*, 334–348. doi:10.1016/j.iref.2020.11.012

García, A., Lands, B., Liu, X., & Slive, J. (2020). *The potential effect of a central bank digital currency on deposit funding in Canada (No. 15)*. Bank of Canada.

Garg, P., Gupta, B., Chauhan, A. K., Sivarajah, U., Gupta, S., & Modgil, S. (2021). Measuring the perceived benefits of implementing blockchain technology in the banking sector. *Technological Forecasting and Social Change*, *163*, 120407. doi:10.1016/j.techfore.2020.120407

Gatteschi, V., Lamberti, F., & Demartini, C. (2020). Blockchain technology use cases. *Advanced applications of blockchain technology*, 91-114.

Gervais, A., Karame, G. O., Wüst, K., Glykantzis, V., Ritzdorf, H., & Capkun, S. (2016). On the security and performance of proof of work blockchains. *Proceedings of the 2016 ACM SIGSAC Conference on Computer and Communications Security*, 3-16. 10.1145/2976749.2978341

Ghobakhloo, M. (2020). Industry 4.0, digitization, and opportunities for sustainability. *Journal of Cleaner Production*, *252*, 119869. doi:10.1016/j.jclepro.2019.119869

Gkillas, K., & Longin, F. (2019a). Is Bitcoin the New Digital Gold? Evidence From Extreme Price Movements in Financial Markets. SSRN *Electronic Journal*. https://doi.org/ doi:10.2139/SSRN.3245571

Global FinTech Hub Report. (2018). *The Future of Finance is Emerging: New Hubs, New Landscapes*. University of Cambridge, Judge Business School. https://www.jbs.cam.ac.uk/wp-content/uploads/2020/08/2018-ccaf-global-fintech-hub-report-eng.pdf

Godoi, K. C., Marcon, R., & da Silva, A. B. (2005). Loss aversion: A qualitative study in behavioral finance. *Managerial Finance*, *31*(4), 46–56. doi:10.1108/03074350510769613

Gogerty, N., & Zitoli, J. (2011). *Deko: An electricity-backed currency proposal. Social Science* Research Network.

Goldstein, I., Jiang, W., & Karolyi, G. A. (2019). To FinTech and beyond. *Review of Financial Studies*, *32*(5), 1647–1661. doi:10.1093/rfs/hhz025

Golosova, J., & Romanovs, A. (2018, October). Overview of the blockchain technology cases. In *2018 59th International Scientific Conference on Information Technology and Management Science of Riga Technical University (ITMS)* (pp. 1-6). IEEE. 10.1109/ITMS.2018.8552978

Gomber, P., Koch, J. A., & Siering, M. (2017). Digital Finance and FinTech: Current research and future research directions. *Journal of Business Economics*, *87*(5), 537–580. doi:10.100711573-017-0852-x

Gomez, J. C., Paniagua, J., & Santos, L. (2019). Fintech and financial inclusion: A review. *Sustainability*, *11*(1), 1–20.

Goodfellow, I., Bengio, Y., & Courville, A. (2016). *Deep learning*. MIT Press.

Gourisaria, M. K., Agrawal, R., Singh, V., Rautaray, S. S., & Pandey, M. (2022). AI and IoT Enabled Smart Hospital Management Systems. In *Data Science in Societal Applications* (pp. 77–106). Springer. doi:10.1007/978-981-19-5154-1_6

Guo, Y., & Liang, C. (2016). Blockchain application and outlook in the banking industry. *Financial Innovation*, *2*(1), 1–12. doi:10.118640854-016-0034-9

Gupta, A., & Gupta, S. (2018). blockchain technology application in Indian banking sector. *Delhi Business Review*, *19*(2), 75-84. https://www.sciencedirect.com/science/article/abs/pii/S0959652619347390

Gupta, A., & Gupta, S. (2018). Blockchain Technology application in Indian Banking Sector. *Delhi Business Review*, *19*(2), 75–84. doi:10.51768/dbr.v19i2.192201807

Gupta, R., & Nalavade, J. E. (2022). Metaheuristic Assisted Hybrid Classifier for Bitcoin Price Prediction. *Cybernetics and Systems*, 1–25. doi:10.1080/01969722.2022.2129376

Gurama, Z. U., Mansor, M., & Pantamee, A. A. (2015). Tax evasion and Nigeria tax system: An overview. *Research Journal of Finance and Accounting*, *6*(8), 202–211.

Hair, J. F., Anderson, R. E., Tatham, R. L., & William, C. (1998). *Multivariate data analysis*. Academic Press.

Hair, J., Black, W., Babin, B., & Anderson, R. (2010). Multivariate data analysis (7th ed.). Prentice Hall Inc.

Hamza, H., & Jedidia, K. B. (2020). Central Bank Digital Currency and Financial Stability in a Dual Banking System. In Impact of Financial Technology (FinTech) on Islamic Finance and Financial Stability (pp. 233-252). IGI Global. doi:10.4018/978-1-7998-0039-2.ch012

Hardjono, T., & Smith, N. (2016). Cloud-based commissioning of constrained devices using permissioned blockchains. *Proceedings of the 2nd ACM International Workshop on IoT Privacy, Trust, and Security*, 29–36. 10.1145/2899007.2899012

Hasan, M. M., Yajuan, L., & Khan, S. (2020). *Promoting China's Inclusive Finance Through Digital Financial Services.* https://doi.org/ doi:10.1177/0972150919895348

Hassani, H., Huang, X., & Silva, E. (2018). Banking with blockchain-ed big data. *Journal of Management Analytics*, *5*(4), 256–275. doi:10.1080/23270012.2018.1528900

Hayashi, F., & Toh, Y. L. (2022). *Assessing the Case for Retail CBDCs: Central Banks' Considerations.* Payments System Research Briefing.

Heuvel, S. (2014). *The demand for short-term, safe assets and financial stability: Some evidence and implications for central bank policies.* Academic Press.

Hitam, N. A., Ismail, A. R., Samsudin, R., & Alkhammash, E. H. (2022). The Effect of Kernel Functions on Cryptocurrency Prediction Using Support Vector Machines. In *International Conference of Reliable Information and Communication Technology* (pp. 319-332). Springer. 10.1007/978-3-030-98741-1_27

Hu, A. S., Parlour, C. A., & Rajan, U. (2019). Cryptocurrencies: Stylized facts on a new investible instrument. *Financial Management*, *48*(4), 1049–1068. doi:10.1111/fima.12300

Huang, H. (2022).An Investigation of Cryptocurrencies: Behavior Finance Perspective, In *Advances in Economics, Business and Management Research, vol. 652, 7th International Conference on Social Sciences and Economic Development (ICSSED 2022).* Atlantis Press International B.V.

Huang, J., Kong, L., Chen, G., Wu, M.-Y., Liu, X., & Zeng, P. (2019). Towards Secure Industrial IoT: Blockchain System with Credit-Based Consensus Mechanism. *IEEE Transactions on Industrial Informatics*, *15*(6), 1–1. doi:10.1109/TII.2019.2903342

Huang, Y. (2022). Virtual Currencies, ICOs and Central Bank Digital Currencies in China. In *Law and Practice of Crowdfunding and Peer-to-Peer Lending in Australia, China and Japan* (pp. 125–141). Springer. doi:10.1007/978-981-19-3834-4_7

Hydrogen. (2019, December 12). *5 Common Blockchain Applications in Financial Services.* https://www.hydrogenplatform.com/blog/5-common-blockchain-applications-in-financial-services

Hyperledger. (2015) *Hyperledger Project*. https://www.hyperledger.org/ibm

Iman, R. (2018A). Digital remittances: An examination of the impact of fintech on remittances. *Journal of Money Laundering Control*, *21*(3), 369–378. doi:10.1108/JMLC-10-2017-0066

Iman, S. (2018B). A Review on E-wallets: A Payment Instrument in Digital World. *International Journal of Advanced Science and Technology*, *117*, 29–38.

Inozemtsev, M. I., & Nektov, A. V. (2022). Digital Platforms for Cross-Border Settlement of CBDC. In The Platform Economy (pp. 131-145). Palgrave Macmillan. doi:10.1007/978-981-19-3242-7_9

Insights, C. B. (2021). *Fintech 250: The Top Fintech Companies Of 2021*. Retrieved from https://www.cbinsights.com/research/fintech-250-startups-companies-to-watch/

Intellipaat. (2023, May 9). *Application of Blockchain in the Banking Sector*. https://intellipaat.com/blog/blockchain-in-banking/

International Monetary Fund. (2019). *Fintech: The Experience so far.* Policy Paper No. 2019/024.

Iqbal, S., Hussain, N., Latif, M., & Aslam, S. (2013). Investor Type and Financial Market Anomalies: A Comparison of Individual, Institutional and Foreign Investors and Role of Their Behaviors in Investing Decisions. *Middle East Journal of Scientific Research*, *17*, 1591–1596. doi:10.5829/idosi.mejsr.2013.17.11.11787

Iyer, R., Khwaja, A. I., Luttmer, E. F., & Shue, K. (2016). Screening peers softly: Inferring the quality of small borrowers. *Management Science*, *62*(6), 1554–1577. doi:10.1287/mnsc.2015.2181

Jack, W., & Suri, T. (2011). Mobile money: The economics of M-PESA. National Bureau of Economic Research.

Jalal, R. N., Sargiacomo, M., Sahar, N. U., & Fayyaz, U. (2020). Herding Behavior and Cryptocurrency: Market Asymmetries, Inter-Dependency and Intra-Dependency. *Journal of Asian Finance Economics and Business.*, *7*(7), 27–34. doi:10.13106/jafeb.2020.vol7.no7.027

Javaid, M., Haleem, A., Singh, R. P., Suman, R., & Khan, S. (2022). A review of Blockchain Technology applications for financial services. *BenchCouncil Transactions on Benchmarks, Standards and Evaluations*, 100073.

Javaid, M., Haleem, A., Singh, R., Suman, R., & Khan, S. (2022). A review of Blockchain Technology applications for financial services. *BenchCouncil Transactions on Benchmarks, Standards and Evaluations, 2*(3).

Javaid, M., Haleem, A., Singh, R. P., Khan, S., & Suman, R. (2021). Blockchain technology applications for Industry 4.0: A literature-based review. *Blockchain: Research and Applications*, *2*(4), 100027.

Jebarajakirthy, C., & Shankar, A. (2021). Impact of online convenience on mobile banking adoption intention: A moderated mediation approach. *Journal of Retailing and Consumer Services*, *58*, 102323. doi:10.1016/j.jretconser.2020.102323

Jena, R. K. (2022). Examining the factors affecting the adoption of blockchain technology in the banking sector: An extended UTAUT model. *International Journal of Financial Studies*, *10*(4), 90. doi:10.3390/ijfs10040090

Jiang, X., Li, X., Yang, J., & Li, J. (2020). Feature selection and engineering for time series forecasting: A review. *Expert Systems with Applications*, *144*, 113–138.

Ji, F., & Tia, A. (2021). The effect of blockchain on business intelligence efficiency of banks. *Kybernetes*.

Jinasena, D. N., Spanaki, K., Papadopoulos, T., & Balta, M. E. (2020). Success and Failure Retrospectives of FinTech Projects: A Case Study Approach. *Information Systems Frontiers*. Advance online publication. doi:10.100710796-020-10079-4

Johansson, M., & Hellström, D. (2021). The impact of fintech on traditional banking services. *Journal of Financial Services Marketing*, *26*(3), 136–148.

Johnson, D., Menezes, A., & Vanstone, S. (2001). The elliptic curve digital signature algorithm (ECDSA). *International Journal of Information Security*, *1*(1), 36–63. doi:10.1007102070100002

Jonker, N., Van der Cuijsen, C., Bijlsma, M., & Bolt, W. (2020). *Pandemic payment patterns*. DeNederlandscheBank.

Joseph, N., Kar, A. K., Ilavarasan, P. V., & Ganesh, S. (2017). Review of discussions on internet of things (IoT): Insights from twitter analytics. *Journal of Global Information Management, 25*(2), 38–51. doi:10.4018/JGIM.2017040103

Kabir, M. R., & Islam, M. A. (2021, July). Behavioural intention to adopt blockchain technology in Bangladeshi banking companies. In AIP Conference Proceedings (Vol. 2347, No. 1, p. 020025). AIP Publishing LLC. doi:10.1063/5.0051654

Kagermann, H., Wahlster, W., & Helbig, J. (2013). *Recommendations for Implementing the Strategic Initiative Industrie 4.0: Securing the Future of German Manufacturing Industry. Final Report of the Industrie 4.0 Working Group*. Acatech, Forschungsunion.

Kahneman, D., & Tversky, A. (1979). Prospect theory: An analysis of decision under risk. *Econometrica, 2*(2), 263–291. doi:10.2307/1914185

Kahn, M. C. M., Singh, M. M., & Alwazir, J. (2022). *Digital money and central bank operations*. International Monetary Fund. doi:10.5089/9798400206955.001

Kallinterakis, V., Munir, N., & Radovic-Markovic, M. (2010). Herd Behaviour, Illiquidity and Extreme Market States: Evidence from Banja Luka. *Journal of Emerging Market Finance, 9*(3), 305–324. doi:10.1177/097265271000900303

Kalsie, A., & Kalra, J. K. (2015). An empirical study on efficient market hypothesis of Indian capital markets. *Journal of Management Research and Analysis, 2*(2), 108–114.

Kambil, A. (2008). What is your recession playbook? *The Journal of Business Strategy, 29*(5), 50–52. doi:10.1108/02756660810902341

Kamdjoug, J. R. K., Wamba-Taguimdje, S. L., Wamba, S. F., & Kake, I. B. E. (2021). Determining factors and impacts of the intention to adopt mobile banking app in Cameroon: Case of SARA by afriland First Bank. *Journal of Retailing and Consumer Services, 61*, 102509. doi:10.1016/j.jretconser.2021.102509

Kar, A. K., & Navin, L. (2021). Diffusion of blockchain in insurance industry: An analysis through the review of academic and trade literature. *Telematics and Informatics, 58*, 101532. doi:10.1016/j.tele.2020.101532

Karim, S., Rabbani, M. R., & Bawazir, H. (2022). Applications of blockchain technology in the finance and banking industry beyond digital currencies. In *Blockchain Technology and Computational Excellence for Society 5.0* (pp. 216–238). IGI Global. doi:10.4018/978-1-7998-8382-1.ch011

Katsiampa, P. (2019a). An empirical investigation of volatility dynamics in the cryptocurrency market. *Research in International Business and Finance, 50*, 322–335. doi:10.1016/j.ribaf.2019.06.004

Kaur, G., Lashkari, Z. H., & Lashkari, A. H. (2021). *Understanding Cybersecurity Management in Fintech – Challenges, Strategies, and Trends*. Spinger Nature Switzerland. doi:10.1007/978-3-030-79915-1

Keister, T., & Sanches, D. (2019). *Should Central Banks Issue Digital Currency?* Federal Reserve Bank of Philadelphia Working Paper.

Keister, T., & Monnet, C. (2022). Central bank digital currency: Stability and information. *Journal of Economic Dynamics & Control, 142*, 104501. doi:10.1016/j.jedc.2022.104501

Kenny, C. (2002). Information and communication technologies for direct poverty alleviation: Costs and benefits. *Development Policy Review, 20*(2), 141–157. doi:10.1111/1467-7679.00162

Kessler, M. M. (1963). Bibliographic coupling between scientific articles. *American Documentation, 24*, 123–131.

Khadka, R. (2020). *The impact of blockchain technology in banking: How can blockchain revolutionize the banking industry?* Academic Press.

Khadka, R. (2020). *The impact of Blockchain Technology in Banking. Business Management*. Centria University of Applied Sciences.

Khalil, M., Khawaja, K. F., & Sarfraz, M. (2021). The adoption of blockchain technology in the financial sector during the era of fourth industrial revolution: A moderated mediated model. *Quality & Quantity*, 1–18.

Khan, M. K., Nisar, K., Farooq, Y., Habib, S., Danish, M., & Hyder, I. (2021). *An Improved Banking Application Model Using Blockchain*. Academic Press.

Khan, Singh, & Kirti. (2021). Critical factors for Blockchain technology implementation: A supply chain perspective. *Journal of Industrial Integration and Management*.

Khan, K., Zhao, H., Zhang, H., Yang, H., Shah, M. H., & Jahanger, A. (2020). The impact of COVID-19 pandemic on stock markets: An empirical analysis of world major stock indices. *Journal of Asian Finance, Economics and Business*, *7*(7), 463–474. doi:10.13106/jafeb.2020.vol7.no7.463

Khanna, P., & Haldar, A. (2022). Will adoption of blockchain technology be challenging: evidence from Indian banking industry. *Qualitative Research in Financial Markets*.

Khanna, P., & Haldar, A. (2023). Will adoption of blockchain technology be challenging: Evidence from Indian banking industry. *Qualitative Research in Financial Markets*, *15*(2), 361–384. doi:10.1108/QRFM-01-2022-0003

Khanna, V., & Sharma, R. (2017). Customer Switching Behavior in Retail Banking in India. *International Journal of Applied Business and Economic Research*, *15*(9), 427–441.

Kher, V., Terjesen, S., & Liu, C. (2019). The cryptocurrency revolution: The rise of bitcoin. *Journal of International Management*, *25*(2), 107–118.

Kim, Y. S., & Kwon, O. (2019). *Central bank digital currency and financial stability*. Bank of Korea Working Paper, No. 6.

Kimani, D., Adams, K., Attah-Boakye, R., Ullah, S., Frecknall-Hughes, J., & Kim, J. (2020). Blockchain, business and the fourth industrial revolution: Whence, whither, wherefore and how? *Technological Forecasting and Social Change*, *161*, 120254. doi:10.1016/j.techfore.2020.120254

Kim, Y. S., & Kwon, O. (2022a). Central Bank Digital Currency, Credit Supply, and Financial Stability. *Journal of Money, Credit and Banking*. Advance online publication. doi:10.1111/jmcb.12913

King, S. (2013). *Primecoin: Cryptocurrency with Prime Number Proof-of-Work*. Academic Press.

King, S., & Nadal, S. (2012) *Ppcoin: Peer-to-Peer Crypto-Currency with Proof-of-Stake*. Self-Published Paper.

Kirkby, R. (2018a). Cryptocurrencies and Digital Fiat Currencies. *The Australian Economic Review*, *51*(4), 527–539. doi:10.1111/1467-8462.12307

Kitsantas, T., Vazakidis, A., & Chytis, E. (2019). A Review of Blockchain Technology and Its Applications in the Business Environment. *International Conference on Enterprise, Systems, Accounting, Logistics & Management*.

Knezevic, D. (2018). Impact of Blockchain Technology Platform in Changing the Financial Sector and Other Industries. *Montenegrin Journal of Economics*, *14*(1), 109–120. doi:10.14254/1800-5845/2018.14-1.8

Kolozsi, P. P., Lehmann, K., & Szalai, Z. (2022). Is CBDC strengthening the monetary transmission mechanism? In Central Banking, Monetary Policy and the Future of Money (pp. 94-119). Edward Elgar Publishing. doi:10.4337/9781800376403.00011

Kovas, A. (2018). *Understanding the Risks of Fintech*. Expert Talk, Thomson Reuters.

Kraft, D. (2016). Difficulty control for blockchain-based consensus systems. *Peer-to-Peer Networking and Applications*, *9*(2), 397–413. doi:10.100712083-015-0347-x

Kshetri, N. (2018). Blockchain's roles in meeting key supply chain management objectives. *International Journal of Information Management*, *39*, 80–89. doi:10.1016/j.ijinfomgt.2017.12.005

Kulshrestha, D., Tiwari, M. K., Shalender, K., & Sharma, S. (2022). Consumer Acatalepsy Towards Buying Behaviour for Need-Based Goods for Sustainability During the COVID-19 Pandemic. *Indian Journal of Marketing*, *52*(10), 50–63. doi:10.17010/ijom/2022/v52/i10/172347

Kumari, A., & Devi, C. N. (2022). The Impact of FinTech and Blockchain Technologies on Banking and Financial Services. *Technology Innovation Management Review*, *12*(1/2). Advance online publication. doi:10.22215/timreview/1481

Kumhof, M., & Noone, C. (2021). Central bank digital currencies—Design principles for financial stability. *Economic Analysis and Policy*, *71*, 553–572. doi:10.1016/j.eap.2021.06.012

Kwon, J. (2014). *Tendermint: Consensus without mining*. Academic Press.

Kwon, O., Lee, S., & Park, J. (2022). Central bank digital currency, tax evasion, and inflation tax. *Economic Inquiry*, *60*(4), 1497–1519. doi:10.1111/ecin.13091

LamarqueE. (2000). Key Activities in the Banking Industry: An Analysis by the Value Chain. SSRN.

Lamport, L., Shostak, R., & Pease, M. (1982). The byzantine generals problem. *ACM Transactions on Programming Languages and Systems*, *4*(3), 382–401. doi:10.1145/357172.357176

Larios-Hernández, G. J. (2017). Blockchain entrepreneurship opportunity in the practices of the unbanked. *Business Horizons*, *60*(6), 865–874. doi:10.1016/j.bushor.2017.07.012

Laroiya, C., Saxena, D., & Komalavalli, C. (2020). Applications of blockchain technology. In *Handbook of research on blockchain technology* (pp. 213–243). Academic Press. doi:10.1016/B978-0-12-819816-2.00009-5

Laura, J. (2017). *The blockchain technology and its applications in the financial sector*. School of Business, Aalto University.

Lee, J. W. (2020). Green finance and sustainable development goals: The case of China. *Journal of Asian Finance Economics and Business*, *7*(7), 577–586. doi:10.13106/jafeb.2020.vol7.no7.577

Lee, J., Kao, H. A., & Yang, S. (2014). Service innovation and smart analytics for industry 4.0 and big data environment. *Procedia CIRP*, *16*, 3–8. doi:10.1016/j.procir.2014.02.001

Lee, M. S., Hsiao, H. D., & Yang, M. F. (2011). The study of the relationships among experiential marketing, service quality, customer satisfaction and customer loyalty. *The International Journal of Organizational Innovation*, *3*(2), 352–378.

Lei, A., Cruickshank, H., Cao, Y., Asuquo, P., Ogah, C. P. A., & Sun, Z. (2017, December). Blockchain-based dynamic key management for heterogeneous intelligent transportation systems. *IEEE Internet of Things Journal*, *4*(6), 1832–1843. doi:10.1109/JIOT.2017.2740569

Levitt, K. (2013). *The multi-screen path to purchasing 2013*. https://www.comscore.com/Insights/Presentations_and_Whitepapers

Lewis, A. (2021). *The basis of Bitcoins and Blockchains*. Mango Publishing Group.

Li, B., & Wang, Y. (2018). RZKPB: A privacy-preserving Blockchain-based fair transaction method for sharing economy. *Proc. 17th IEEE Int. Conf. Trust Secur. Privacy Comput. Commun./12th IEEE Int. Conf. Big Data Sci. Eng. (TrustCom/BigDataSE),* 1164-1169. 10.1109/TrustCom/BigDataSE.2018.00161

Liao, H., Tang, M., Luo, L., Li, C., Chiclana, F., & Zeng, X. J. (2018). A bibliometric analysis and visualization of medical big data research. *Sustainability (Basel)*, *10*(1), 1–18. doi:10.3390u10010166

Liao, W., Zheng, Y., Xu, Q., & Zhang, Y. (2019). Deep learning models for stock price prediction: A survey. *Frontiers in Neuroinformatics*, *13*, 23.

Li, E., Liao, L., Wang, Z., & Xiang, H. (2020). Venture capital certification and customer response: Evidence from P2P lending platforms. *Journal of Corporate Finance*, *60*, 101533. doi:10.1016/j.jcorpfin.2019.101533

Li, L., Yu, Y., Li, Z., & Li, X. (2019). Smart contract-based secure data sharing scheme for cloud storage. *Future Generation Computer Systems*, *100*, 968–980. doi:10.1016/j.future.2019.05.003

Lin, M., Prabhala, N. R., & Viswanathan, S. (2013). Judging borrowers by the company they keep: Friendship networks and information asymmetry in online Peer-to-Peer lending. *Management Science*, *59*(1), 17–35. doi:10.1287/mnsc.1120.1560

Liu, G., Huang, Y., & Huang, Z. (2021). Determinants and mechanisms of digital financial inclusion development: Based on urban-rural differences. *Agronomy (Basel)*, *11*(9), 1833. Advance online publication. doi:10.3390/agronomy11091833

Liu, X., Wang, Q., Wu, G., & Zhang, C. (2022). Determinants of individuals' intentions to use central bank digital currency: Evidence from China. *Technology Analysis and Strategic Management*, 1–15. doi:10.1080/09537325.2022.2131517

Liu, X., Zhan, F. B., Hong, S., Niu, B., & Liu, Y. (2012). A bibliometric study of earthquake research: 1900–2010. *Scientometrics*, *92*(3), 747–765. doi:10.100711192-011-0599-z

Liu, Y., Zhang, Y., Yang, X., Wang, J., & Zhang, L. (2019). A smart contract-based approach to secure data storage in cloud computing. *IEEE Transactions on Cloud Computing*, *7*(3), 759–770. doi:10.1109/TCC.2018.2847744

Li, W., Andreina, S., Bohli, J.-M., & Karame, G. (2017). Securing Proof-of-Stake Blockchain Protocols. In J. Garcia-Alfaro, G. Navarro-Arribas, H. Hartenstein, & J. Herrera-Joancomartí (Eds.), *Data Privacy Management, Cryptocurrencies and Blockchain Technology* (pp. 297–315). Lecture Notes in Computer Science. Springer International Publishing. doi:10.1007/978-3-319-67816-0_17

Li, X., Jiang, P., Chen, T., Luo, X., & Wen, Q. (2017). A survey on the security of blockchain systems. *Future Generation Computer Systems.*

Li, Y., Du, X., Liu, J., & Qiao, C. (2019). Blockchain and Internet of Things-based credit scoring system for P2P lending. *Computer Networks*, *149*, 90–99. doi:10.1016/j.comnet.2018.11.036

Li, Z., Zhong, R. Y., Tian, Z. G., Dai, H. N., Barenji, A. V., & Huang, G. Q. (2021). Industrial Blockchain: A state-of-the-art Survey. *Robotics and Computer-integrated Manufacturing*, *70*, 102124. doi:10.1016/j.rcim.2021.102124

Lorenzo, L., & Arroyo, J. (2022). Analysis of the cryptocurrency market using different prototype-based clustering techniques. *Financial Innovation*, *8*(1), 1–46. doi:10.118640854-021-00310-9

Lundqvist, T., de Blanche, A., & Andersson, H. R. H. (2017). Thing-to-thing electricity micropayments using Blockchain technology. *Proc. Global Internet Things Summit*, (Jun), 1–6.

Luo, C., Pan, L., Chen, B., & Xu, H. (2022). Bitcoin Price Forecasting: An Integrated Approach Using Hybrid LSTM-ELM Models. *Mathematical Problems in Engineering*. doi:10.1155/2022/2126518

Ma, L., Zhao, X., Zhou, Z., & Liu, Y. (2018). A new aspect on P2P online lending default prediction using meta-level phone usage data in China. *Decision Support Systems*, *111*, 60–71. doi:10.1016/j.dss.2018.05.001

Malaquias, R. F., & Hwang, Y. (2019). Mobile banking use: A comparative study with Brazilian and US participants. *International Journal of Information Management*, *44*, 132–140. doi:10.1016/j.ijinfomgt.2018.10.004

Maleki, N., Nikoubin, A., Rabbani, M., & Zeinali, Y. (2020). Bitcoin price prediction based on other cryptocurrencies using machine learning and time series analysis. *Scientia Iranica*, *0*(0), 0. doi:10.24200ci.2020.55034.4040

Malhotra, D., Saini, P., & Singh, A. K. (2022). How blockchain can automate KYC: Systematic review. *Wireless Personal Communications*, *122*(2), 1987–2021. doi:10.100711277-021-08977-0

Mallesha, C., & Haripriya, S. (2019). A Study on Blockchain Technology in Banking Sector. *International Journal of Advanced Research in Commerce, Management & Social Science*, *2*(3), 123–132.

Marikyan, D., Papagiannidis, S., & Alamanos, E. (2020). Cognitive dissonance in technology Adoption: A Study of Smart Home Users. *Information Systems Frontiers*. Advance online publication. doi:10.100710796-020-10042-3 PMID:32837263

Martínez-Vergara, S. J., & Valls-Pasola, J. (2021). Clarifying the disruptive innovation puzzle: A critical review. *European Journal of Innovation Management*, *24*(3), 893–918. doi:10.1108/EJIM-07-2019-0198

Maxwell, G. (2013). *Coinjoin: Bitcoin Privacy for the Real World.* Post on Bitcoin Forum.

Mazieres, D. (2015). *The Stellar Consensus Protocol:AFederated Model for Internet-Level Consensus*. Stellar Development Foundation.

McCallig, J., Robb, A., & Rohde, F. (2019). Establishing the representational faithfulness of financial accounting information using multiparty security, network analysis and a blockchain. *International Journal of Accounting Information Systems*, *33*, 47–58. doi:10.1016/j.accinf.2019.03.004

McKinsey & Company. (2020). *Buy now, pay later: A fresh approach to lending*. Retrieved from https://www.mckinsey.com/business-functions/risk/our-insights/buy-now-pay-later-a-fresh-approach-to-lending

McKinsey. (2022). *Europe's fintech opportunity*. McKinsey and Company Report. https://www.mckinsey.com/industries/financial-services/our-insights/europes-fintech-opportunity#/

McNealy, R. M. (1998). *Making Customer Satisfaction Happen* (1st ed.). Kluwer Academic.

Medium. (2019, October 15). *How Blockchain technology works*. https://medium.com/@ipspecialist/how-blockchain-technology-works

Mehta, K., & Sharma, R. (2015). Individual Investors' Behavior: In Demographical Backdrop. SCMS Journal of Indian Management, 12(3), 25-36.

Mehta, K., Sharma, R., & Khanna, V. (2023). Customer switching behaviour in Indian retail banking using logit regression," *International Journal of Business Excellence*, *29*(4), 518–545.

Mehta, K., Sharma, R., & Khanna, V. (2023). Customer switching behaviour in Indian retail banking using logit regression. *International Journal of Business Excellence*, *29*(4), 518–545. doi:10.1504/IJBEX.2023.130255

Mehta, K., Sharma, R., & Vyas, V. (2019, June 17). Efficiency and ranking of sustainability index of India using DEA-TOPSIS. *Journal of Indian Business Research*, *11*(2), 179–199. doi:10.1108/JIBR-02-2018-0057

Mehta, K., Sharma, R., Vyas, V., & Kuckreja, J. S. (2022). Exit strategy decision by venture capital firms in India using fuzzy AHP. *Journal of Entrepreneurship in Emerging Economies*, *14*(4), 643–669. doi:10.1108/JEEE-05-2020-0146

Merigó, J. M., Pedrycz, W., Weber, R., & de la Sotta, C. (2018). Fifty years of Information Sciences: A bibliometric overview. *Information Sciences*, *432*, 245–268. doi:10.1016/j.ins.2017.11.054

Messy, F.-A. (2017). FinTech Developments & Their Consequences for the Financial Industry & Regulators in Asia & Beyond. *Japan Spotlight*, 44-49.

Metaverse in financial services use cases. (n.d.). Retrieved April 10, 2023, from https://buzzcrop.com/fixer-upper/metaverse-in-financial-services-use-cases

Micheler, E., & von derHeyde, L. (2016). *Holding, clearing and settling securities through blockchain technology creating an efficient system by empowering asset owners*. Social Science Research Network. doi:10.2139srn.2786972

Michel, N. (2022). *Central Bank Digital Currencies Are about Control—They Should Be Stopped. Center for Monetary and Financial Alternatives*. Cato Institute.

Miers, I., Garman, C., Green, M., & Rubin, A. D. (2013). Zerocoin: Anonymous distributed e-cash from bitcoin. *Proceedings of IEEE Symposium Security and Privacy (SP)*, 397–411.

Miguel, C., & Barbara, L. (1999). Practical byzantine fault tolerance. *Proceedings of the Third.*

Minesso, M. F., Mehl, A., & Stracca, L. (2022). Central bank digital currency in an open economy. *Journal of Monetary Economics*, *127*, 54–68. doi:10.1016/j.jmoneco.2022.02.001

Mkrttchian, V., Gamidullaeva, L., & Galiautdinov, R. (2019). *Design of Nano-scale Electrodes and Development of Avatar-Based Control System for Energy-Efficient Power Engineering: Application of an Internet of Things and People (IOTAP) Research Center. International Journal of Applied Nanotechnology Research*. doi:10.4018/IJANR.2019010104

Mohamed, M. (2018). Challenges and benefits of industry 4.0: An overview. *International Journal of Supply and Operations Management*, *5*(3), 256–265.

Mohanta, B. K., Jena, D., Panda, S. S., & Sobhanayak, S. (2019). Blockchain technology: A survey on applications and security privacy challenges. *Internet of Things*, *8*, 100107. doi:10.1016/j.iot.2019.100107

Mohanty, S., & Dash, R. (2022). Neural Network-Based Bitcoin Pricing Using a New Mutated Climb Monkey Algorithm with TOPSIS Analysis for Sustainable Development. *Mathematics*, *10*(22), 4370. doi:10.3390/math10224370

Morini, M. (2016). *From 'blockchain hype' to a real business case for financial markets*. Social Science Research Network. doi:10.2139srn.2760184

Möser, M. (2013). Anonymity of bitcoin transactions: An analysis of mixing services. *Proceedings of Münster Bitcoin Conference*, 17-18.

Moulin, F., Tomasini, M., & Zanetti, M. (2018). Bayesian optimization for financial risk management. *Journal of Risk and Financial Management*, *11*(2), 22.

Nadarajah, S., & Chu, J. (2017). On the inefficiency of Bitcoin. *Economics Letters*, *150*(C), 6–9. doi:10.1016/j.econlet.2016.10.033

Najaf, K., Subramaniam, R. K., & Atayah, O. F. (2021). Understanding the implications of FinTech peer-to-peer (P2P) lending during the COVID-19 pandemic. *Journal of Sustainable Finance & Investment*.

Nakamoto, S. (2008). *Bitcoin: A Peer-to-Peer Electronic Cash System*. Available online: http://www.Bitcoin.org/bitcoin.pdf

Nakamoto, S. (2008). Bitcoin: A peer-to-peer electronic cash system. *Decentralized Business Review*, 21260.

Nakamoto, S. (2008). *Bitcoin: A Peer-to-Peer Electronic Cash System*. https://bitcoin.org/bitcoin.pdf

Narayanan, A., Bonneau, J., Felten, E., Miller, A., & Goldfeder, S. (2016). *Bitcoin and Cryptocurrency Technologies: A Comprehensive Introduction*. Princeton University Press.

Nayak, K., Kumar, S., Miller, A., & Shi, E. (2016). Stubborn mining: Generalizing selfish mining and combining with an eclipse attack. *Proceedings of 2016 IEEE European Symposium on Security and Privacy (EuroSandP)*, 305–320. 10.1109/EuroSP.2016.32

Nazaritehrani, A., & Mashali, B. (2020). Development of E-banking channels and market share in developing countries. *Financial Innovation*, *6*(1), 1–19. doi:10.118640854-020-0171-z

Neugebauer, R., Hippmann, S., Leis, M., & Landherr, M. (2016). Industrie 4.0-From the perspective of applied research. *Procedia CIRP*, *57*, 2–7. doi:10.1016/j.procir.2016.11.002

Nguyen, C. T., Hoang, D. T., Nguyen, D. N., Niyato, D., Nguyen, H. T., & Dutkiewicz, E. (2019). Proof-of-Stake Consensus Mechanisms for Future Blockchain Networks: Fundamentals, Applications and Opportunities. *IEEE Access : Practical Innovations, Open Solutions*, *7*, 85727–85745. doi:10.1109/ACCESS.2019.2925010

Niemand, T., Rigtering, J. P. C., Kallmünzer, A., Kraus, S., & Maalaoui, A. (2021). Digitalization in the financial industry: A contingency approach of entrepreneurial orientation and strategic vision on digitalization. *European Management Journal*, *39*(3), 317–326. doi:10.1016/j.emj.2020.04.008

Nigmonov, A., Shams, S., & Alam, K. (2022). Macroeconomic determinants of loan defaults: Evidence from the US peer-to-peer lending market. *Research in International Business and Finance*, *59*, 101516. doi:10.1016/j.ribaf.2021.101516

Nikolic, I., Kolluri, A., Sergey, I., Saxena, P., & Hobor, A. (2018). Finding the greedy, prodigal, and suicidal contracts at scale. *Proceedings of the 27th USENIX Security Symposium*, 811-828. https://www.usenix.org/system/files/conference/usenixsecurity18/sec18-nikolic.pdf

Nofer, M., Gomber, P., Hinz, O., & Schiereck, D. (2017). Blockchain. *Business & Information Systems Engineering*, *59*(3), 183–187. doi:10.100712599-017-0467-3

Norta, A., Othman, A. B., & Taveter, K. (2015). Conflict-resolution lifecycles for governed decentralized autonomous organization collaboration. *Proceedings of the 2015 2nd.* 10.1145/2846012.2846052

Noyes, C. (2016a). *Bitav: Fast Anti-Malware by Distributed Blockchain Consensus and Feedforward Scanning*. arXiv preprint arXiv:1601.01405.

Noyes, C. (2016b). *Efficient Blockchain-Driven Multiparty Computation Markets at Scale*. Technical Report.

NRI. (2015). *Survey on Blockchain Technologies and Related Services*. Technical Report.

Nso, M. A. (2018). The role of e-banking as a marketing tool. *Innovative Marketing*, *14*(4), 56–65. doi:10.21511/im.14(4).2018.05

Oberoi, S., & Kansra, P. (2022). Blockchain Technology in the Insurance Industry. In Applications, Challenges, and Opportunities of Blockchain Technology in Banking and Insurance (pp. 160-172). IGI Global. doi:10.4018/978-1-6684-4133-6.ch009

Obiora, K.I. (2022). *Special Remarks at the IMF CBDC Seminar in Frankfurt Germany, June*. Academic Press.

Odeh, A., Keshta, I., & Al-Haija, Q. A. (2022). Analysis of Blockchain in the Healthcare Sector: Application and Issues. *Symmetry*, *14*(9), 1760. doi:10.3390ym14091760

Omohundro, S. (2014). Cryptocurrencies, smart contracts, and artificial intelligence. *AI Matters*, *1*(2), 19–21. doi:10.1145/2685328.2685334

Onyeka, V. N., & Nwankwo, C. (2016). The effect of tax evasion and avoidance on Nigeria's economic growth. *European Journal of Business and Management*, *8*(24), 158–166.

Otusanya, O. J. (2011). The role of multinational companies in tax evasion and tax avoidance: The case of Nigeria. *Critical Perspectives on Accounting*, *22*(3), 316–332. doi:10.1016/j.cpa.2010.10.005

Ozili, P. K. (2022b). Central bank digital currency in Nigeria: opportunities and risks. In The New Digital Era: Digitalisation, Emerging Risks and Opportunities (Vol. 109, pp. 125-133). Emerald Publishing Limited. doi:10.1108/S1569-37592022000109A008

Ozili, P. K. (2023a). eNaira central bank digital currency (CBDC) for financial inclusion in Nigeria. In Digital Economy, Energy and Sustainability: Opportunities and Challenges (pp. 41-54). Cham: Springer International Publishing.

Ozili, P. K. (2018). Impact of digital finance on financial inclusion and stability. *Borsa Istanbul Review*, *18*(4), 329–340. doi:10.1016/j.bir.2017.12.003

Ozili, P. K. (2022a). Can central bank digital currency increase financial inclusion? Arguments for and against. In *Big Data Analytics in the Insurance Market* (pp. 241–249). Emerald Publishing Limited. doi:10.1108/978-1-80262-637-720221013

Ozili, P. K. (2022c). Global Central Bank Digital Currency Research and Developments: Implication for Cryptocurrency. Cryptocurrency. *Concepts, Technology, and Issues.*

Ozili, P. K. (2023). Central bank digital currency research around the World: A review of literature. *Journal of Money Laundering Control*, *26*(2), 215–226. doi:10.1108/JMLC-11-2021-0126

Ozili, P. K. (2023b). CBDC, Fintech and cryptocurrency for financial Inclusion and financial stability. *Digital Policy. Regulation & Governance*, *25*(1), 40–57. doi:10.1108/DPRG-04-2022-0033

Ozturan, M., Atasu, I., & Soydan, H. (2019). Assessment of blockchain technology readiness level of banking industry: Case of Turkey. *International Journal of Business Marketing and Management (IJBMM)*, *4*(12), 1-13.

Ozturk, A. B., Bilgihan, A., Salehi-Esfahani, S., & Hua, N. (2017). Understanding the mobile payment technology acceptance based on valence theory: A case of restaurant transactions. *International Journal of Contemporary Hospitality Management*, *29*(8), 2027–2049. doi:10.1108/IJCHM-04-2016-0192

P4Titan. (2014). *Slimcoin a Peer-to-Peer Crypto-Currency with Proof-of-Burn "Mining without Powerful Hardware.* Author.

Pal, A., Tiwari, C. K., & Behl, A. (2021). Blockchain technology in financial services: a comprehensive review of the literature. *Journal of Global Operations and Strategic Sourcing.*

Pal, A., Tiwari, C. K., & Behl, A. (2021). Blockchain technology in financial services: A comprehensive review of the literature. *Journal of Global Operations and Strategic Sourcing*, *14*(1), 61–80. doi:10.1108/JGOSS-07-2020-0039

Palihapitiya, T. (2020). Blockchain Revolution in Banking Industry. *Conference on Blockchain in Banking Industry.*

Palihapitiya, T. (2020). *Blockchain Revolution in Banking Industry*. University of Moratuwa.

Parekh, N., Sadanand, P., & Jain, S. (2017). Blockchain Technology. *Journal of Emerging Technologies and Innovative Research*, *4*(6), 177–179.

Patil, P., Sangeetha, M., & Bhaskar, V. (2021). Blockchain for IoT access control, security and privacy: A review. *Wireless Personal Communications*, *117*(3), 1815–1834. doi:10.100711277-020-07947-2

Patki, A., & Sople, V. (2020). Indian Banking Sector: Blockchain Implementation, Challenges and way forward. *Journal of Banking & Financial Technology*, *4*(1), 65–73. doi:10.100742786-020-00019-w

Payne, M., Peltier, J. W., & Barger, V. A. (2017). Omni-channel marketing, integrated marketing communications and consumer engagement. *Journal of Research in Interactive Marketing, 11*(2), 185–197. doi:10.1108/JRIM-08-2016-0091

PayPal. (2021). *PayPal Holdings, Inc. Reports Fourth Quarter and Full Year 2020 Results.* https://investor.paypal-corp.com/news-releases/news-release-details/paypal-holdings-inc-reports-fourth-quarter-and-full-year-2020/

Pazarbasioglu, C., Mora, A. G., Uttamchandani, M., Natarajan, H., Feyen, E., & Saal, M. (2020). *Digital Financial Services.* Academic Press.

Pearce, S. (2021). *Smart contracts: The good, the bad and the ugly.* TechRadar. https://www.techradar.com/news/smart-contracts-the-good-the-bad-and-the-ugly

Peters, G.W., Panayi, E., & Chapelle, A. (2015). *Trends in Crypto-Currencies and Blockchain Technologies: A Monetary Theory and Regulation Perspective.* Academic Press.

Petrovic, A., Strumberger, I., Bezdan, T., Jassim, H. S., & Nassor, S. S. (2021, November). Cryptocurrency Price Prediction by Using Hybrid Machine Learning and Beetle Antennae Search Approach. In *2021 29th Telecommunications Forum (TELFOR)* (pp. 1-4). IEEE. 10.1109/TELFOR52709.2021.9653305

Piazzesi, M., & Schneider, M. (2020). *Credit lines, bank deposits or CBDC? competition and efficiency in modern payment systems.* Unpublished, Stanford University.

Pilkington, M. (2016). *Does the Fintech Industry need a New Risk Management Philosophy? A Blockchain Typology for Digital Currencies and e-money Services in Luxembourg.* Social Science Research Network.

Pompian, M. M. (2006). *Behavioral Finance and Wealth Management – How to Build Optimal Portfolios That Account for Investor Biases.* John Wiley and Sons Inc. Retrieved from http://library.perbanas.ac.id/images/book/behavioralfinance.pdf

Pop, C., Pop, C., Marcel, A., Vesa, A., Petrican, T., & Cioara, T. (2018). Decentralizing the stock exchange using Blockchain an ethereum-based implementation of the bucharest stock exchange. *Proc. IEEE 14th Int. Conf. Intell. Comput. Commun. Process. (ICCP),* 459-466. 10.1109/ICCP.2018.8516610

PoyserO. (2018). Herding behavior in cryptocurrency markets (Issue November). https://arxiv.org/abs/1806.11348

Prakash, N., Solanki, S., Gabriel, E.E., & Bangari, M. (2020). Blockchain Technology–Revamping the Indian Financial Sector Landscape and Roadblocks Ahead. *Palarch's Journal of Archaeology of Egypt/ Egyptology, 17*(6), 1084-1092.

Pritchard, A. (1969). Statistical Bibliography or Bibliometrics? *The Journal of Documentation, 25*, 348–349.

Qingquan, HE. (2021). Application of Blockchain Technology in Commercial Banks. *E3S Web of Conferences.*

Rahmayati, R. (2021). Strengthening Islamic Banking Services In Indonesia Through Blockchain Technology: The Anp-Step Approach. At-Tijaroh. *Jurnal Ilmu Manajemen Dan Bisnis Islam, 7*(2), 259–272. doi:10.24952/tijaroh.v7i2.4368

Rajnak, V., & Puschmann, T. (2021). The impact of blockchain on business models in banking. *Information Systems and e-Business Management, 19*(3), 809–861. doi:10.100710257-020-00468-2

Ramchandra, M., Kumar, K., Sarkar, A., Mukherjee, S., & Agarwal, K. (2022). Assessment of the impact of blockchain technology in the banking industry. *Materials Today: Proceedings, 56*(4), 2221–2226. doi:10.1016/j.matpr.2021.11.554

Ramírez-Correa, P., Rondán-Cataluña, F. J., Arenas-Gaitán, J., & Martín-Velicia, F. (2019). Analysing the acceptation of online games in mobile devices: An application of UTAUT2. *Journal of Retailing and Consumer Services, 50*, 85–93. doi:10.1016/j.jretconser.2019.04.018

Ramos de Lunaa, I., Liébana-Cabanillas, F., Sánchez-Fernández, J., & Muñoz-Leiva, F. (2019). Mobile payment is not all the same: The adoption of mobile payment systems depending on the technology applied. *Technological Forecasting and Social Change*, *146*, 931–944. doi:10.1016/j.techfore.2018.09.018

Ramos de Luna, I., Liébana-Cabanillas, F., Sánchez-Fernández, J., & Muñoz-Leiva, F. (2019). What drives mobile payment adoption? A meta-analysis. *Computers in Human Behavior*, *99*, 182–198. doi:10.1016/j.chb.2019.04.008

Rashideh, W. (2020). Blockchain technology framework: Current and future perspectives for the tourism industry. *Tourism Management*, *80*, 104125. doi:10.1016/j.tourman.2020.104125

Rau, R. (2018). Law, Trust, and the Development of Crowdfunding. *SSRN Working Paper*, 2989056.

Ravi, S. (2023). *Block Chain Technology & Its Use in Banking Sector*. Business World.

RBI. (2018). *Report of the Working Group on Fin Tech and Digital Banking*. https://www.rbi.org.in/Scripts/PublicationReportDetails.aspx?UrlPage=&ID=892

RBI. (2020). FinTech: The Force of Creative Disruption. *RBI Bulletin*. https://www.rbi.org.in/Scripts/BS_ViewBulletin.aspx?Id=19899

RBI. (2021a). *Enabling Framework for Regulatory Sandbox*. RBI Report. https://www.rbi.org.in/Scripts/PublicationReportDetails.aspx?UrlPage=&ID=1187

RBI. (2021b). *Report of the Working Group on Digital Lending including Lending through Online Platforms and Mobile Apps*. RBI Press Release. https://www.rbi.org.in/Scripts/BS_PressReleaseDisplay.aspx?prid=52589

RBI. (2021c). *Statement on Developing and Regulatory Policies*. RBI Press Release. https://www.rbi.org.in/Scripts/BS_PressReleaseDisplay.aspx?prid=52368

Rega, F. G., Riccardi, N., Li, J., & di Carlo, F. (2018). *Blockchain in the banking industry: an Overview*. Research Gate.

Reuters. (2021). *Google Pay under scrutiny in Italy over alleged privacy abuse*. Reuters. https://www.reuters.com/article/us-alphabet-italy-google-pay-idUSKBN29I2SO

Ricks, M., Crawford, J., & Menand, L. (2020). *FedAccounts: digital dollars*. Vanderbilt Law Research Paper, 18-33.

Rjoub, H., Adebayo, T., & Kirikkaleli, D. (2023). Blockchain technology-based Fintech banking sector involvement using adaptive neuro-fuzzy-based K-nearest neighbor's algorithm. *Financial Innovation*, *9*(1), 65. doi:10.118640854-023-00469-3 PMID:36919101

Rodeck, D., & Curry, B. (2022). What is blockchain. *Forbes*. www. forbes. com/advisor/investing/cryptocurrency/what-is-blockchain/

Rogers, C. (2018). The conceptual flaw in the microeconomic foundations of dynamic stochastic general equilibrium models. *Review of Political Economy*, *30*(1), 72–83. doi:10.1080/09538259.2018.1442894

Roxana, N., Aue, M., Uae, R., & Moşteanu, N. R. (2019). International Financial Markets face to face with Artificial Intelligence and Digital Era. *Theoretical and Applied Economics*, *26*(3), 123–134.

Rubmann, M., Lorenz, M., Gerbert, P., Waldner, M., Justus, J., Engel, P., & Harnisch, M. (2015). Industry 4.0: The future of productivity and growth in manufacturing industries. *Boston Consulting Group, 9*(1), 54-89.

Sachs, J. D., Woo, W. T., Yoshino, N., & Taghizadeh-Hesary, F. (2019). Importance of green finance for achieving sustainable development goals and energy security. In *Handbook of Green Finance* (pp. 3–12). Springer. doi:10.1007/978-981-13-0227-5_13

Saheb, T., & Mamaghani, F. H. (2021). Exploring the barriers and organizational values of blockchain adoption in the banking industry. *The Journal of High Technology Management Research, 32*(2), 100417. doi:10.1016/j.hitech.2021.100417

Sahi, S. K., & Arora, A. P. (2012). Individual investor biases: A segmentation analysis. *Qualitative Research in Financial Markets, 4*(1), 6–25. doi:10.1108/17554171211213522

Sai, B. D. S., Nikhil, R., Prasad, S., & Naik, N. S. (2023). A decentralised KYC based approach for microfinance using blockchain technology. *Cyber Security and Applications, 1*, 100009. doi:10.1016/j.csa.2022.100009

Saidat, Z., Silva, M., Daboubi, D., Naimi, A., & Aldomy, R. (2022). How can Blockchain Revolutionize the Jordanian Banking Sector. *Journal of Southwest Jiaotong University, 57*(3), 311–325. doi:10.35741/issn.0258-2724.57.3.25

Salb, M., Zivkovic, M., Bacanin, N., Chhabra, A., & Suresh, M. (2022). Support vector machine performance improvements for cryptocurrency value forecasting by enhanced sine cosine algorithm. In *Computer Vision and Robotics* (pp. 527–536). Springer. doi:10.1007/978-981-16-8225-4_40

Saleh, F. (2021). Blockchain without Waste: Proof-of-Stake. *The Review of Financial Studies, 34*(3), 1156–1190. doi:10.1093/rfs/hhaa075

Samaniego, M., Jamsrandorj, U., & Deters, R. (2016). Blockchain as a service for IoT. *Proc. IEEE Int. Conf. Internet Things (iThings) IEEE Green Comput. Commun. (GreenCom) IEEE Cyber Phys. Social Comput. (CPSCom) IEEE Smart Data (SmartData),* 433-436. 10.1109/iThings-GreenCom-CPSCom-SmartData.2016.102

Sankaranarayanan, G., & Rajagopalan, K. (2020). Usages of blockchain technology in banking sector and its implication on Indian economy. *Alochana Chakra Journal, IX*(V), 7383–7389.

Sapirshtein, A., Sompolinsky, Y., & Zohar, A. (2015). *Optimal Selfish Mining Strategies in Bitcoin*. arXiv preprint arXiv:1507.06183.

Sarin, A. B. (2019). *Behavioral Factors Affecting Investment Decisions and Performance: An Empirical Study of Investors in Delhi*. Ph.D., Lingayas Vidhyapeeth.

Sarin, A. B., & Chowdhury, J. K. (2018). Understanding behavioral biases influencing investment decisions An exploratory study. *International Research Journal of Management and Commerce, 1*, 584–596.

Sarkar, A. K., & Sahu, T. N. (2018). *Investment Behaviour: Towards an Individual-Centred Financial Policy in Developing Countries*. Emerald Publishing. doi:10.1108/9781787562790

Sasson, E. B., Chiesa, A., Garman, C., Green, M., Miers, I., & Tromer, E. (2014). Zerocash: Decentralized anonymous payments from Bitcoin. *Proceedings of 2014 IEEE Symposium on Security and Privacy (SP)*, 459–474. 10.1109/SP.2014.36

Sazu, M. H., & Jahan, S. A. (2022). Impact of blockchain-enabled analytics as a tool to revolutionize the banking industry. *Data Science in Finance and Economics, 2*(3), 275–293. doi:10.3934/DSFE.2022014

Scott, B., Loonam, J., & Kumar, V. (2017). Exploring the rise of blockchain technology: Towards distributed collaborative organizations. *Strategic Change, 26*(5), 423–428. doi:10.1002/jsc.2142

Sethaput, V., & Innet, S. (2021, November). Blockchain Application for Central Bank Digital Currencies (CBDC). In *2021 Third International Conference on Blockchain Computing and Applications (BCCA)* (pp. 3-10). IEEE. 10.1109/BCCA53669.2021.9657012

Shah, T., & Jani, S. (2018). Applications of blockchain technology in banking & finance. Parul CUniversity.

Shahriari, B., Swersky, K., Wang, Z., Adams, R. P., & De Freitas, N. (2016). Taking the human out of the loop: A review of Bayesian optimization. *Proceedings of the IEEE, 104*(1), 148–175. doi:10.1109/JPROC.2015.2494218

Shahvaroughi Farahani, M., & Farrokhi-Asl, H. (2022). Improved market prediction using meta-heuristic algorithms and time series model and testing market efficiency. *Iran Journal of Computer Science*, 1–33.

Shahvaroughi Farahani, M., & Razavi Hajiagha, S. H. (2021). Forecasting stock price using integrated artificial neural network and metaheuristic algorithms compared to time series models. *Soft Computing*, *25*(13), 8483–8513. doi:10.100700500-021-05775-5 PMID:33935586

Shaik, G., & Kumar, S. (2021). A study on the blockchain technology and its awareness on business and industry. *Natural Volatiles & Essential Oils*, *8*(4), 330–341.

Shalender, K., & Sharma, N. (2022). Integrating strategic flexibility and marketing system to achieve sustainable competitive advantage: Conceptual refinement and framework. *World Review of Entrepreneurship, Management and Sustainable Development*, *18*(1-2), 175–194. doi:10.1504/WREMSD.2022.120794

Shalender, K., Singla, B., Sharma, S., & Oberemok, M. (2023). COVID-19 and Its Impact on Construction and Transport Construction Economy: An Integrated Framework. *Lecture Notes in Networks and Systems*, *510*, 747–753. doi:10.1007/978-3-031-11051-1_76

Shankar, A., & Jebarajakirthy, C. (2019). The influence of e-banking service quality on customer loyalty: A moderated mediation approach. *International Journal of Bank Marketing*, *37*(5), 1119–1142. doi:10.1108/IJBM-03-2018-0063

Sharifi, A.M., Khalili Damghani, K., Abdi, F., & Sardar, S. (2022). A hybrid model for predicting bitcoin price using machine learning and metaheuristic algorithms. *Journal of Applied Research on Industrial Engineering, 9*(1), 134-150.

Sharma, R., Mehta, K., & Vyas, V. (2020). Responsible Investing: A Study on Non-Economic Goals and Investors' Characteristics. *Applied Finance Letters, 9*(SI), 63-78. doi:10.24135/afl.v9i2.245

Sharma, R., Mehta, K., & Vyas, V. (2020). Responsible Investing: A Study on Non-Economic Goals and Investors' Characteristics. Applied Finance Letters, 9(SI), 63-78. https://doi.org/ doi:10.24135/afl.v9i2

Sharma, A., & Sharma, R. (2022). Exploring Tax Decision Factors: A Perspective from North Indian Tax Practitioners. *Journal of Tax Reform*, *8*(3), 285–297. doi:10.15826/jtr.2022.8.3.122

Sharma, D. (2020). Application of Block Chain in an Indian Banking Sector. *Global Scientific Journals*, *8*(5), 526–530.

Sharma, R., Mehta, K., & Goel, A. (2022). Non-linear relationship between board size and performance of Indian companies. *The Journal of Management and Governance*. Advance online publication. doi:10.100710997-022-09651-8

Sharma, R., Mehta, K., & Sharma, O. (2021). Exploring Deep Learning to Determine the Optimal Environment for Stock Prediction Analysis. *International Conference on Computational Performance Evaluation,* ComPE 2021, 148–152. 10.1109/ComPE53109.2021.9752138

Shen, W., & Hou, L. (2021). China's central bank digital currency and its impacts on monetary policy and payment competition: Game changer or regulatory toolkit? *Computer Law & Security Report*, *41*, 105577. doi:10.1016/j.clsr.2021.105577

Sheth, H., & Dattani, J. (2019). Overview of blockchain technology. *Asian Journal for Convergence in Technology.*

Shrotryia, V. K., & Kalra, H. (2021). Herding in the crypto market: A diagnosis of heavy distribution tails. *Review of Behavioral Finance*, *14*(5), 566–587. doi:10.1108/RBF-02-2021-0021

Silva, E. C., & Mira da Silva, M. (2022). Research contributions and challenges in DLT-based cryptocurrency regulation: A systematic mapping study. *Journal of Banking and Financial Technology*, *6*(1), 63–82. doi:10.100742786-021-00037-2

Singh, A., Shahare, P., Vikram, P., Srivastava, V., & Maan, M. (2023). Financial Sector and Blockchain Technology: Challenges and Applications. *Journal of Pharmaceutical Negative Results*, *14*(2), 1566–1575.

Singh, N., Sinha, N., & Liébana-Cabanillas, F. J. (2020). Determining factors in the adoption and recommendation of mobile wallet services in India: Analysis of the effect of innovativeness, stress to use and social influence. *International Journal of Information Management*, *50*, 191–205. doi:10.1016/j.ijinfomgt.2019.05.022

Singh, S., Sharma, A., & Jain, P. (2018). A Detailed Study of Blockchain: Changing the World. *International Journal of Applied Engineering Research*, *13*(14), 11532–11539.

Singla, B. (2022). Impact of institute closures and learning practices on education in COVID-19 Pandemic: Omnichannel in education. *Proc. – International Conference Advancement in Data Science, E-Learning and Information Systems, ICADEIS 2022*. 10.1109/ICADEIS56544.2022.10037467

Slawotsky, J. (2022). Digital currencies and great power rivalry: China as a disseminator in the digital age. *Asia Pacific Law Review*, *30*(2), 242–264. doi:10.1080/10192557.2022.2085412

Small, H. (1973). Co-citation in the scientific literature: A new measure of the relationship between two documents. *Journal of the American Society for Information Science*, *24*(4), 265–269. doi:10.1002/asi.4630240406

Solat, S., & Potop-Butucaru, M. (2016). *ZeroBlock: Timestamp-Free Prevention of Block-Withholding Attack in Bitcoin*. Technical Report, Sorbonne Universites, UPMC University of Paris 6.

Sompolinsky, Y., & Zohar, A. (2013). *Accelerating Bitcoin's Transaction Processing. Fast Money Grows on Trees, not Chains*. IACR Cryptology ePrint Archive.

Sony, M., & Naik, S. (2020). Key ingredients for evaluating Industry 4.0 readiness for organizations: A literature review. *Benchmarking*, *27*(7), 2213–2232. doi:10.1108/BIJ-09-2018-0284

Staff, H. B. R. (2021). Smart Contracts: Hype vs. Reality. *Harvard Business Review*. https://hbr.org/2021/07/smart-contracts-hype-vs-reality

Stamoulis, D., Kanellis, P., & Martakos, D. (2002). An approach and model for assessing the business value of e-banking distribution channels: Evaluation as communication. *International Journal of Information Management*, *22*(4), 247–261. doi:10.1016/S0268-4012(02)00011-7

Statista. (2020). *Mobile payment transaction value worldwide from 2015 to 2019 and forecasted till 2024*. Retrieved from https://www.statista.com/statistics/226530/mobile-payment-transaction-value-worldwide/

Statista. (2022a). *Investments into fintech companies globally 2010-2022*. https://www.statista.com/statistics/719385/investments-into-fintech-companies-globally/

Statista. (2022b). *Largest fintech companies worldwide 2021, by market cap*. https://www.statista.com/statistics/1262288/largest-fintech-companies-by-market-cap/

Statista. (2022c). *Number of fintech start-ups worldwide 2018-2021, by region*. https://www.statista.com/statistics/893954/number-fintech-startups-by-region/

Stiglitz, J. E., & Weiss, A. (1981). Credit rationing in markets with imperfect information. *The American Economic Review*, *71*(3), 393–410.

Stiglitz, J. E., & Weiss, A. (1992). Asymmetric information in credit markets and its implications for macro-economics. *Oxford Economic Papers*, *44*(4), 694–724. doi:10.1093/oxfordjournals.oep.a042071

Stock, T., Obenaus, M., Kunz, S., & Kohl, H. (2018). Industry 4.0 as enabler for a sustainable development: A qualitative assessment of its ecological and social potential. *Process Safety and Environmental Protection*, *118*, 254–267. doi:10.1016/j.psep.2018.06.026

Stojanović, M., Radenković, M., Popović, S., Mitrović, S., & Bogdanović, Z. (2023). A readiness assessment framework for the adoption of 5G based smart-living services. *Information Systems and e-Business Management, 21*(2), 1–25. doi:10.100710257-023-00625-3

Sudzina, F., Dobes, M., & Pavlicek, A. (2021). Towards the psychological profile of cryptocurrency early adopters: Overconfidence and self-control as predictors of cryptocurrency use. *Current Psychology*. Advance online publication. doi:10.100712144-021-02225-1

Suen, R. (2019). Jack Dorsey's Square transformed the payment industry by making it cheap and easy for small businesses to accept credit cards. *Business Insider.* https://www.businessinsider.com/how-square-transformed-the-payment-industry-2019-8

Suresh Babu, C. V. (2023). *Introduction to Data Science* (1st ed.). Anniyappa Publications.

Swan, M. (2015). *Blockchain: blueprint for a new economy*. O'Reilly Media, Inc.

Szabo, N. (1997). *The idea of smart contracts*. Nick Szabo's Papers and Concise Tutorials.

Taghizadeh-Hesary, F., & Yoshino, N. (2019). The way to induce private participation in green finance and investment. *Finance Research Letters, 31*, 98–103. doi:10.1016/j.frl.2019.04.016

Takyar, A. (2020, December 28). *Blockchain in Finance: Blockchain Use Cases. LeewayHertz - Software Development Company*. https://www.leewayhertz.com/10-use-cases-of-blockchain-in-finance/

Tamilmani, K., Rana, N. P., Wamba, S. F., & Dwivedi, R. (2021). The extended Unified Theory of Acceptance and Use of Technology (UTAUT2): A systematic literature review and theory evaluation. *International Journal of Information Management, 57*, 102269. doi:10.1016/j.ijinfomgt.2020.102269

Tandon, A., Dhir, A., Islam, A. N., & Mäntymäki, M. (2020). Blockchain in healthcare: A systematic literature review, synthesizing framework and future research agenda. *Computers in Industry, 122*, 103290. doi:10.1016/j.compind.2020.103290

Tandon, A., Kaur, P., Mäntymäki, M., & Dhir, A. (2021). Blockchain applications in management: A bibliometric analysis and literature review. *Technological Forecasting and Social Change, 166*, 120649. doi:10.1016/j.techfore.2021.120649

Tapscott, A., & Tapscott, D. (2017). How blockchain is changing finance. *Harvard Business Review, 1*(9), 2–5.

Tapscott, D., & Tapscott, A. (2016). *Blockchain revolution: how the technology behind bitcoin is changing money, business, and the world.* Portfolio / Penguin.

Tasca, P., & Tessone, C. J. (2019). A Taxonomy of Blockchain Technologies: Principles of Identification and Classification. *Ledger, 4*. doi:10.5195/ledger.2019.140

Taufiq, R., Hidayanto, A. N., & Prabowo, H. (2018, September). The affecting factors of blockchain technology adoption of payments systems in Indonesia banking industry. In *2018 International Conference on Information Management and Technology (ICIMTech)* (pp. 506-510). IEEE. 10.1109/ICIMTech.2018.8528104

Tempini, N. (2017). Till data do us part: Understanding data-based value creation in data-intensive infrastructures. *Information and Organization, 27*(4), 191–210. doi:10.1016/j.infoandorg.2017.08.001

Tessaro, S. (2016). Sloth: A Lightweight Delay Function for ASIC-Resistant Proof-of-Work Based on Nakamoto's Consensus Algorithm. *Journal of Cryptology, 29*(2), 613–638.

Thakor, A. V. (2019). Fintech and banking: What do we know? *Journal of Financial Intermediation*. https://doiorg.eres.qnl.qa/10.1016/j.jfi.2019.100833

Thakor, A. (2020). Corrigendum to: Fintech and Banking: What Do We Know? *Journal of Financial Intermediation, 43*, 100858. Advance online publication. doi:10.1016/j.jfi.2020.100858

Thakor, A. V. (2020). Fintech and banking: What do we know? *Journal of Financial Intermediation.*

Thaler, R. (2005). Advances in Behavioral Finance II. Princeton University Press.

ThomaA. (2020).A Prospect Theory Model for Predicting Cryptocurrency Returns. doi:10.2139/ssrn.3753530

Tikhomirov, S., & Yakovlev, A. (2019). Formal verification of smart contracts: Short survey. *Proceedings of the 3rd International Conference on Cryptography, Security and Privacy*, 278-283. https://doi.org/10.1145/3312446.3312456

Toubal, M. (2021). *Blockchain Technology in the Banking Sector: Application and Challenges*. Department of Informatics and Media, Uppsala University.

Toufaily, E., Zalan, T., & Dhaou, S. B. (2021). A framework of blockchain technology adoption: An investigation of challenges and expected value. *Information & Management*, *58*(3), 103444. doi:10.1016/j.im.2021.103444

Trivedi, S., Mehta, K., & Sharma, R. (2021). Systematic Literature Review on Application of Blockchain Technology in E-Finance and Financial Services. *Journal of Technology Management & Innovation*, *16*(3), 90–102. doi:10.4067/S0718-27242021000300089

Truby, J. (2018). Decarbonizing Bitcoin: Law and policy choices for reducing the energy consumption of Blockchain technologies and digital currencies. *Energy Research & Social Science*, *44*, 399–410. doi:10.1016/j.erss.2018.06.009

Tschorsch, F., & Scheuermann, B. (2016). Bitcoin and beyond: A technical survey on decentralized digital currencies. *IEEE Communications Surveys and Tutorials*, *18*(3), 2084–2123. doi:10.1109/COMST.2016.2535718

Tversky A. & Kahneman D. (1986), Rational Choice and the Framing of Decisions. *The Journal of Business*, *4*(2), S251-S278.

Upgrade. (2023, January 24). *Application of Blockchain Technology in Banking and Financial Sector in India*. Knowledge Hut. https://www.knowledgehut.com/blog/blockchain/applications-of-blockchain-technology-in-india

Vaidya, S., Ambad, P., & Bhosle, S. (2018). Industry 4.0–a glimpse. *Procedia Manufacturing*, *20*, 233–238. doi:10.1016/j.promfg.2018.02.034

Vallet, G., Kappes, S., & Rochon, L. P. (Eds.). (2022). *Central Banking, Monetary Policy and the Future of Money*. Edward Elgar Publishing. doi:10.4337/9781800376403

van den Hooff, J., Kaashoek, M. F., & Zeldovich, N. (2014). Versum: Verifiable computations over large public logs. *Proceedings of the 2014 ACM SIGSAC Conference on Computer and Communications Security*, 1304–1316. 10.1145/2660267.2660327

Van Eck, N. J., & Waltman, L. (2010). Software survey: VOSviewer, a computer program for bibliometric mapping. *Scientometrics*, *84*(2), 523–538. doi:10.100711192-009-0146-3 PMID:20585380

van Eck, N. J., & Waltman, L. (2017). Citation-based clustering of publications using CitNetExplorer and VOSviewer. *Scientometrics*, *111*(2), 1053–1070. doi:10.100711192-017-2300-7 PMID:28490825

Van Maanen, H., & Berghout, E. (2002). Cost management of IT beyond cost of ownership models: A state of the art overview of the Dutch financial services industry. *Evaluation and Program Planning*, *25*(2), 167–173. doi:10.1016/S0149-7189(02)00010-1

Vasileiou, E., Georgantzis, N., Attanasi, G., & Llerena, P. (2022). Green innovation and financial performance: A study on Italian firms. *Research Policy, 51*(6), 104530. doi:10.1016/j.respol.2022.104530

Vasin, P. (2014). *Blackcoin's Proof-of-Stake Protocol v2*. https://blackcoin.co/blackcoin-pos-protocolv2-whitepaper.pdf

Venkatesh, V., Thong, J. Y., & Xu, X. (2012). Consumer acceptance and use of information technology: Extending the unified theory of acceptance and use of technology. *Management Information Systems Quarterly, 36*(1), 157–178. doi:10.2307/41410412

Vidal-Tomas, D., Ibanez, A. M., & Farinos, J. E. (2019). Herding in the cryptocurrency market: CSSD and CSAD approaches. *Finance Research Letters, 30*, 181-186. doi:10.1016/j.frl.2018.09.008

Vives, X. (2017). The impact of FinTech on banking. *European Economy*, (2), 97–105.

Vlcek, B. (2011). Mobile payments and anti-money laundering regulations. *Journal of Money Laundering Control, 14*(4), 352–361. doi:10.1108/13685201111170839

Vodrážka, M., Bízek, T., & Vojta, M. (2022). Are there relevant reasons to introduce a retail CBDC in the Czech Republic from the perspective of the payment system? *BIS Papers*, 65.

Vogel, P. S. (2021, May). *Why smart contracts may not be smart after all*. CIO Dive. https://www.ciodive.com/news/smart-contracts-limitations/599279/

Vukolić, M. (2016). The quest for scalable blockchain fabric: Proof-of-work vs. BFT replication. In *Open Problems in Network Security: IFIP WG 11.4 International Workshop, iNetSec 2015, Zurich, Switzerland, October 29, 2015, Revised Selected Papers* (pp. 112-125). Springer International Publishing.

Vyas, V., Mehta, K., & Sharma, R. (2020). Investigating socially responsible investing behaviour of Indian investors using structural equation modelling. *Journal of Sustainable Finance & Investment*, 1–23. doi:10.1080/20430795.2020.1790958

Vyas, V., Mehta, K., & Sharma, R. (2023). The nexus between toxic-air pollution, health expenditure, and economic growth: An empirical study using ARDL. *International Review of Economics & Finance, 2023*(84), 154–166. doi:10.1016/j.iref.2022.11.017

W3Schools. (n.d.). *Blockchain- Introduction*. https://www.w3schools.in/blockchain/introduction-to-blockchain-technology

Walsh, C., O'Reilly, P., Gleasure, R., McAvoy, J., & O'Leary, K. (2021). Understanding manager resistance to blockchain systems. *European Management Journal, 39*(3), 353–365. doi:10.1016/j.emj.2020.10.001

Wamba-Taguimdje, S. L., Wamba, S. F., Kamdjoug, J. R. K., & Wanko, C. E. T. (2020). Impact of Artificial Intelligence on Firm Performance: Exploring the Mediating Effect of Process-Oriented Dynamic Capabilities. In *Digital Business Transformation* (pp. 3–18). Springer. doi:10.1007/978-3-030-47355-6_1

Wamba-Taguimdje, S. L., Wamba, S. F., Kamdjoug, J. R. K., & Wanko, C. E. T. (2020). Influence of artificial intelligence (AI) on firm performance: The business value of AI-based transformation projects. *Business Process Management Journal, 26*(7), 1893–1924. doi:10.1108/BPMJ-10-2019-0411

Wang, G., & Hausken, K. (2022). A game between central banks and households involving central bank digital currencies, other digital currencies and negative interest rates. *Cogent Economics & Finance, 10*(1), 2114178. doi:10.1080/23322039.2022.2114178

Wang, H., Osen, O., Li, G., Li, W., Dai, H.-N., & Zeng, W. (2015). *Big data and industrial internet of things for the maritime industry in northwestern Norway. In IEEE Region 10 Conference*. TENCON.

Wang, M., Li, X., & Wang, S. (2021). Discovering research trends and opportunities of green finance and energy policy: A data-driven scientometric analysis. *Energy Policy*, *154*, 112295. doi:10.1016/j.enpol.2021.112295

Wang, S. H., Zhang, X., & Zhang, Y. D. (2021). DSSAE: Deep stacked sparse autoencoder analytical model for COVID-19 diagnosis by fractional Fourier entropy. *ACM Transactions on Management Information Systems*, *13*(1), 1–20. doi:10.1145/3451357

Wang, T., & Ji, C. (2022). How Does Digital Finance Affect People's Income: Evidence from China. *Security and Communication Networks*, *2022*, 1–15. doi:10.1155/2022/8288855

Wang, Y., Lucey, B. M., Vigne, S. A., & Yarovaya, L. (2022a). The Effects of Central Bank Digital Currencies News on Financial Markets. *Technological Forecasting and Social Change*, *180*, 121715. Advance online publication. doi:10.1016/j.techfore.2022.121715

Wang, Y., & Zhi, Q. (2016). The role of green finance in environmental protection: Two aspects of market mechanism and policies. *Energy Procedia*, *104*, 311–316. doi:10.1016/j.egypro.2016.12.053

Weerawarna, R., Miah, S., & Shao, X. (2023). Emerging advances of blockchain technology in finance: a content analysis. *Pers Ubiquit Comput.*

Weichert, M. (2017). The future of payments: How FinTech players are accelerating customer-driven innovation in financial services. *Journal of Payments Strategy & Systems*, *11*(1), 23–33.

Weinberg, B. D., Parise, S., & Guinan, P. J. (2007). Multi-channel marketing: Mindset and program development. *Business Horizons*, *50*(5), 385–394. doi:10.1016/j.bushor.2007.04.002

Whisker, R., & Eshwar Lokanan, M. (2019). Cryptocurrencies and anti-money laundering regulations: The need for KYC. *International Journal of Financial Research*, *10*(4), 45–57. doi:10.5430/ijfr.v10n4p45

WhitedT. M.WuY.XiaoK. (2022). Central Bank Digital Currency and Banks. Available at SSRN 4112644.

Widayani, A., Fiernaningsih, N., & Herijanto, P. (2022). Barriers to digital payment adoption: Micro, small and medium enterprises. *Management & Marketing*, *17*(4), 528–542. doi:10.2478/mmcks-2022-0029

Wikipedia. (n.d.). *Blockchain.* https://en.wikipedia.org/wiki/Blockchain

Wolfinbarger, M., & Gilly, M. C. (2003). eTailQ: Dimensionalizing, measuring and predicting retail quality. *Journal of Retailing*, *79*(3), 183–198. doi:10.1016/S0022-4359(03)00034-4

Wood, G. (2014). *Ethereum: A Secure Decentralised Generalised Transaction Ledger.* Ethereum Project Yellow Paper.

World Bank & CCAF. (2022). *The 3rd Global Fintech Regulator Survey.* World Bank Group and the University of Cambridge.

World Bank. (2016). *The Global Findex Database 2014: Measuring financial inclusion around the world.* World Bank.

World Bank. (2020a). *Digital Financial Services.* Author.

World Bank. (2020b). *Key Data from Regulatory Sandboxes across the Globe.* https://www.worldbank.org/en/topic/fintech/brief/key-data-from-regulatory-sandboxes-across-the-globe

World Bank. (2021). *Consumer Risks in Fintech: New Manifestations of Consumer Risks and Emerging Regulatory Approaches.* https://openknowledge.worldbank.org/handle/10986/35699

World Bank. (2022a). *Digital Development Overview.* https://www.worldbank.org/en/topic/digitaldevelopment/overview

World Bank. (2022b). *Fintech and the Future of Finance Overview Paper*. Author.

Xu, J. (2022). Developments and implications of central bank digital currency: The case of China e-CNY. *Asian Economic Policy Review, 17*(2), 235–250. doi:10.1111/aepr.12396

Xu, L. D., Xu, E. L., & Li, L. (2018). Industry 4.0: State of the art and future trends. *International Journal of Production Research, 56*(8), 2941–2962. doi:10.1080/00207543.2018.1444806

Yang, Y., Yao, D., Liu, S., & Wang, X. (2019). A smart contract-based access control model for secure data sharing in cloud storage. *Journal of Network and Computer Applications, 140*, 34–44. doi:10.1016/j.jnca.2019.03.013

Yao, D., Liu, S., Yang, Y., & Wang, X. (2019). A smart contract-based approach for secure data sharing in cloud storage. *Future Generation Computer Systems, 97*, 736–745. doi:10.1016/j.future.2019.02.018

Ye Id, Y., Pu, Y., & Xiong, A. (2022). *The impact of digital finance on household participation in risky financial markets: Evidence-based study from China*. Academic Press.

Yin, R. K. (2017). *Case study research and applications: Design and methods*. Sage publications.

Yli-Huumo, J., Ko, D., Choi, S., Park, S., & Smolander, K. (2016). Where is current research on Blockchain technology systematic review. *PLoS One, 11*(10), e0163477. doi:10.1371/journal.pone.0163477 PMID:27695049

Younus, D., Muayad, A., & Abumandil, M. (2022). *Role of smart contract technology blockchain services in finance and banking systems: Concept and core values*. Academic Press.

Yu, C. H., Wu, X., Zhang, D., Chen, S., & Zhao, J. (2021). Demand for green finance: Resolving financing constraints on green innovation in China. *Energy Policy, 153*, 112255. doi:10.1016/j.enpol.2021.112255

Zachariadis, M., Hileman, G., & Scott, S. V. (2019). Governance and control in distributed ledgers: Understanding the challenges facing blockchain technology in financial services. *Information and Organization, 29*(2), 105–117. doi:10.1016/j.infoandorg.2019.03.001

Zahera, S. A., & Bansal, R. (2018). Do investors exhibit behavioral biases in investment decision making? A systematic review. *Qualitative Research in Financial Markets, 2*(2), 210–251. doi:10.1108/QRFM-04-2017-0028

Zamfir, V. (2015). *Introducing casper the friendly ghost*. Ethereum Blog.

Zanero, S. (2017). Cyber-physical systems. *Computer, 50*(4), 14–16. doi:10.1109/MC.2017.105

Zhang, R., & Chan, W. K. (2020). Evaluation of Energy Consumption in Block-Chains with Proof of Work and Proof of Stake. *Journal of Physics: Conference Series, 1584*(1), 012023. doi:10.1088/1742-6596/1584/1/012023

Zhang, Tang, Lu, & Dong. (2014). Trust Building in Online Peer-to-Peer Lending. *Journal of Global Information Technology Management, 17*(4), 250–266. doi:.2014.978624 doi:10.1080/1097198X

Zhang, Y., & Wen, J. (2015). *An IoT electric business model based on the protocol of bitcoin*. Academic Press.

Zhang, D., Zhang, Z., & Managi, S. (2019). A bibliometric analysis on green finance: Current status, development, and future directions. *Finance Research Letters, 29*, 425–430. doi:10.1016/j.frl.2019.02.003

Zhang, J., Tian, R., Cao, Y., Yuan, X., Yu, Z., Yan, X., & Zhang, X. (2021). A hybrid model for central bank digital currency based on blockchain. *IEEE Access : Practical Innovations, Open Solutions, 9*, 53589–53601. doi:10.1109/ACCESS.2021.3071033

Zhang, T., & Huang, Z. (2022). Blockchain and central bank digital currency. *ICT Express, 8*(2), 264–270. doi:10.1016/j.icte.2021.09.014

Zhang, Y., Sun, Y., Chen, J., & Liu, J. (2019). GasReducer: Detecting and Mitigating Gas-Costly Patterns in Ethereum Smart Contracts. *IEEE Transactions on Dependable and Secure Computing*, *17*(2), 405–419. doi:10.1109/TDSC.2018.2863135

Zhang, Z., & He, W. (2020). Disruptive innovation and firm value: The impact of fintech on the payment industry. *Technological Forecasting and Social Change*, *160*, 120237. doi:10.1016/j.techfore.2020.120237

Zheng, Z., Xie, S., Dai, H., Chen, X., & Wang, H. (2017). An overview of Blockchain Technology: Architecture, Consensus, and Future Trends. *IEEE 6th International Congress on Big Data,* 557-564.

Zheng, Z., Xie, S., Dai, H. N., Chen, X., & Wang, H. (2018). Blockchain challenges and opportunities: A survey. *International Journal of Web and Grid Services*, *14*(4), 352–375. doi:10.1504/IJWGS.2018.095647

Zheng, Z., Xie, S., Dai, H., Chen, X., & Wang, H. (2017). An overview of blockchain technology: Architecture, consensus, and future trends. *Proceedings of the 2017 IEEE BigData Congress*, 557–564. 10.1109/BigDataCongress.2017.85

Zheng, Z., Xie, S., Dai, H., Chen, X., & Wang, H. (2017, June). *An overview of blockchain technology: Architecture, consensus, and future trends. In 2017 IEEE international congress on big data (BigData congress)*. IEEE.

Zhong, P., Zhong, Q., Mi, H., Zhang, S., & Xiang, Y. (2019). Privacy-protected Blockchain system. *Proc. 20th IEEE Int. Conf. Mobile Data Manage. (MDM),* 457-461. 10.1109/MDM.2019.000-2

Zhou, X., Tang, X., & Zhang, R. (2020). Impact of green finance on economic development and environmental quality: A study based on provincial panel data from China. *Environmental Science and Pollution Research International*, *27*(16), 19915–19932. doi:10.100711356-020-08383-2 PMID:32232752

Zhu, P., Zhang, X., Wu, Y., Zheng, H., & Zhang, Y. (2021). Investor attention and cryptocurrency: Evidence from the Bitcoin market. *PLoS One*, *16*(2), e0246331. doi:10.1371/journal.pone.0246331 PMID:33524059

Zupic, I., & Čater, T. (2015). Bibliometric methods in management and organization. *Organizational Research Methods*, *18*(3), 429–472. doi:10.1177/1094428114562629

About the Contributors

Kiran Mehta (Ph.D.) is an educator, trainer, consultant, and researcher. She has almost twenty years of experience. She has published several research articles in a variety of international publications, including Emerald, Taylor & Francis, and Sage. She is the author of "Financial Services," a text book published by CENGAGE. She has created study materials for a number of Indian institutes. Her areas of interest include climate finance, sustainable business, portfolio management, stock market efficiency, technology and education, entrepreneurship, and venture capital.

Renuka Sharma is a Professor (Finance) at Chitkara Business School at Chitkara University in Punjab. She has over 20 years of teaching and research experience (more than twelve years post-doctoral and eight years before to obtaining her PhD). She has authored numerous research papers, a few of which have been published in international/national journals (Taylor & Francis, Emerald, Sage, Inderscience, etc.) and the rest have been presented at international/national conferences (IIM Bangalore, Shillong, Calcutta, Indore, and Kozhikode, among others), with numerous papers selected for Best Paper Awards. She also serves as a reviewer for numerous prestigious journals published by Emerald, Elsevier, and Inderscience, among others. Currently, she is guiding two PhD scholars and has successfully defended five others. She has worked as a consultant for numerous start-ups and MSMEs. In addition, she has authored two textbooks published by Cengage and Vikas Publications. Furthermore, she has created study materials for various business-related courses offered by esteemed Indian universities and institutions. Her expertise has been sought after as a resource person for multiple MDPs and FDPs focusing on research and finance. Moreover, she is also an entrepreneur.

Poshan (Sam) Yu is a Lecturer in Accounting and Finance in the International Cooperative Education Program of Soochow University (China). He is also an External Professor of FinTech and Finance at SKEMA Business School (China), a Visiting Professor at Krirk University (Thailand) and a Visiting Researcher at the Australian Studies Centre of Shanghai University (China). Sam leads FasterCapital (Dubai, UAE) as a Regional Partner (China) and serves as a Startup Mentor for AIC RAISE (Coimbatore, India). His research interests include financial technology, regulatory technology, public-private partnerships, mergers and acquisitions, private equity, venture capital, start-ups, intellectual property, art finance, and China's "One Belt One Road" policy.

* * *

C. V. Suresh Babu is a pioneer in Content Development. A true entrepreneur, He floated Anniyappa Publications, a company which is very active in bringing out books related to Computer Science and Management. Dr. C. V. Suresh Babu has also ventured into SB Institute, a centre for knowledge transfer. He holds Ph.D in Engineering Education from National Institute of Technical Teachers Training & Research, Chennai along with seven Master degrees in various disciplines such as Engineering, Computer Applications, Management, Commerce, Economics, Psychology, Law and Education. He also has the UGC-NET/SET qualifications in the disciplines of Computer Science, Management, Commerce and Education to his credit. Currently, Professor, Department of Information Technology, School of Computing Science, Hindustan Institute of Technology and Science, (Hindustan University), Padur, Chennai, Tamil Nadu, India Personal blog: .

Asheetu Bhatia Sarin is an Assistant Professor (Management) at Vivekananda Institute of Professional Studies affiliated to GGSIPU, Delhi. She is having around 9+ years of teaching experience in the field of Commerce and Management. She has done Ph.D. in Behavioral Finance, did her post-graduation (MBA) from ICFAI Business School in Finance and Marketing, and earned her graduate degree in B.Com (H) from Delhi University. She is a lifetime member of the Indian Commerce Association and has to her credit many national and International publications.

Nicola Del Sarto is assistant professor at University of Florence. He received a Ph.D in Management of Innovation, sustainability and healthcare from Scuola Superiore Sant'Anna in 2019. Nicola's research interests focus on small businesses and start-ups and support mechanisms such as incubators, accelerators, corporate accelerator programs and finance for innovation. Moreover, he investigated the processes of business creation under the Open Innovation paradigm. Nicola holds a Master degree in economics from University of Pisa and a post graduate master in Management, innovation and engineering of services from Scuola Superiore Sant'Anna. Nicola's work has been published in high-quality peer reviewed journals and presented at international conferences.

Rinat Galiautdinov is a Principal Software Developer and Software Architect having the expertise in Information Technology and Computer Science. Mr. Galiautdinov is also an expert in Banking/Financial industry as well as in Neurobiological sphere. Mr. Rinat Galiautdinov works on the number of highly important researches (including such the spheres as: Drones, Financial Systems and Private Money, Brain interface and neuro-biology) as an independent researcher and projects holder and developer.

Raja Narayanan is an Associate Professor at the School of Commerce and Management (SCMS), Dayananda Sagar University Bangalore. He holds more than two decades of teaching experience, out of which, twelve years are from Institutions in South Africa. He has two times been recognised and honored with the best lecturer award in South Africa. He has published 26 articles in peer-reviewed journals and 12 articles in the Scopus Indexed Journals. He also participated and presented 38 research papers in national and international level Conferences. He is a member and reviewer of an International Magazine-International Journal of E-Business Research (IJEBR) published by Elsevier. He has guided 4 Ph.D. Scholars. He also evaluated and adjudicated twenty-five Ph.D. thesis in the field of Management and Commerce as the panel of External examiners in Various Universities such as Annamalai, Barathiyar, Bharathidasan, Madras and Manonmaniyam sundarnar University. He is a lifetime member of the Association of Accounting Technician (AAT). He handled various courses like Financial Management,

Research Methodology, Corporate Finance, Security Analysis and Portfolio Management, and Project Finance.

Monica Nirolia (Ph.D, M.Phil, M.Com (Hons.), B.Com (Hons.)) is doing her doctoral research work in the field of banking sector. She has done M.Phil, M.Com (Hons.), B.Com (Hons.) from Maharshi Dayanand University, Rohtak (Haryana). She has published research papers in various National & International journals. She has participated and presented papers in several National & International conferences and seminars. She has participated in the workshops also. Her area of interest includes Accounting & Finance, Business Economics, Securities & Portfolio Management, Human Resource Management, etc.

Rajat [Ph.D, M.Com (Hons.), B.Com (Hons.), UGC NET] is working as an Assistant Professor in GL Bajaj Institute of Management, Greater Noida (U.P). Prior to this, he has worked as Assistant Professor at Chaudhary Ranbir Singh University, Jind (Haryana). He has a teaching experience of over 3 years. He has done M.Com (Hons.) from Maharshi Dayanand University, Rohtak (Haryana). He has published 9 research papers in National & International journals of repute and also, contributed 5 chapters in the edited books. He has participated in many conferences, seminars, workshops & FDP's and presented more than 10 papers. His area of interest includes Financial Management, Financial Institutions & Markets, Managerial Economics & Research Methodology, etc.

Kumar Shalender is a Post-Doctoral Fellow of the Global Institute of Flexible Systems Management and a Doctor of Philosophy in Strategic Management. He has more than 14-year experience in the domain of Business Policy, Strategic Management, and Business Model Development and a total of 70 Publications including presentations at international/national conferences and book chapters to his credit. His current research areas include the field of Metaverse, Blockchain Technology, and Sustainable Development with a special focus on sustainable cities and mobility ecosystems in India.

Sofia Devi Shamurailatpam has a Ph.D. in Economics with specialization in the area of Banking and Financial Economics. Currently she is serving as an Assistant Professor in the Department of Banking and Insurance, Faculty of Commerce, The Maharaja Sayajirao University of Baroda. She has published several research papers in her credit and authored a book entitled "Banking Reforms in India: Consolidation, Restructuring and Performance, published by Palgrave Macmillan, UK (2017). Her major research area of interests includes Economics of Banking, Financial Economics, Agricultural Economics and Development Economics particularly Contemporary issues on Sustainability.

Jeevesh Sharma is currently working as assistant professor in Manipal University Jaipur. Her research is published in various Scopus, Wos, ABDC and other journals indexed journals. He has also written number of book chapters under the publication house Taylor and Francis, IGI Global, and Springer. FinTech, CSR are the researcher area.

Babita Singla is an Associate Professor at Chitkara Business School, Chitkara University, Punjab, India. She spent a decade pursuing a career in academics, teaching, and research with passion and diligence. She worked as an Assistant Professor at the institute of national repute NIT Jalandhar. She completed an MBA program from RIMT-Mandi Gobindgarh, Punjab, India (2008-2010) in Finance & Marketing, and subsequently earned a doctoral degree from IKGPTU, Jalandhar, India. Her undergraduate studies in Mathematics and Economics from Government Rajindra College, Bathinda. She has cleared the National Eligibility Test (UGC NET) in 2011. She has over twenty research publications in international and national journals, over 11 publications/ presentations in international and national conferences, including 8 Keynote lectures/Invited Talks and ten books to her credit. Her current research interests are in business management, omnichannel retail, marketing management, and managerial economics. She loves to generate new ideas and devise feasible solutions to broadly relevant problems. She enjoys embracing the lessons learned from failure, stands up, and continues to grow.

Sonal Trivedi has more than 10 years of experience in academics. She has authored two national books and published 8 Scopus indexed papers. She has chaired 5 conferences and granted 6 Patents. She has attended and presented papers in various international and national conference. She is also reviewer of various Scopus indexed journals.

Index

D

E

F

G

H

I

L

M

N

O

P

R

S

T

U

www.ingramcontent.com/pod-product-compliance
Lightning Source LLC
LaVergne TN
LVHW060416300926
849162LV00006B/1437